Visualization and Virtual Reality

3D Programming with Visual Basic for Windows

Lee Adams

Windcrest®/McGraw-Hill

New York San Francisco Washington, D.C. Auckland Bogotá
Caracas Lisbon London Madrid Mexico City Milan
Montreal New Delhi San Juan Singapore
Sydney Tokyo Toronto

NOTICES

Microsoft®   Microsoft Corp.
MS®
MS-DOS®
Visual Basic™
Windows™

Intel®   Intel Corp.

Lee Adams™   Lee Adams

Windcrest™   McGraw-Hill, Inc.

Paintbrush™   Zsoft Corporation

Pizazz™   Application Techniques, Incorporated

Other brand names or product names capitalized throughout this book are trademarks or registered trademarks of their respective holders.

FIRST EDITION
FIRST PRINTING

©1994 by **Lee Adams**.
Published by Windcrest Books, an imprint of McGraw-Hill, Inc.
The name "Windcrest" is a registered trademark of McGraw-Hill, Inc.

Library of Congress Cataloging-in-Publication Data

Adams, Lee.
   Visualization and virtual reality : 3D programming with Visual
Basic for Windows / by Lee Adams.
     p. cm.
   Includes index.
   ISBN 0-8306-4121-1 ISBN 0-8306-4124-6 (pbk.)
   1. Windows (Computer programs) 2. Microsoft Visual Basic for
Windows. 3. Virtual reality. I. Title.
QA76.76.W56A33 1993
006.6'762-dc20   93-30586
                                       CIP

Acquisitions editor: Jennifer DiGiovanna
Editorial team: Joanne Slike, Executive Editor
                 Lori Flaherty, Managing Editor
                 Mark Vanderslice, Editor
Production team: Katherine G. Brown, Director
                  Susan E. Hansford, Typesetting
                  Rose McFarland, Layout
                  Cindi Bell, Proofreading
Design team: Jaclyn J. Boone, Designer
              Brian Allison, Associate Designer   WP1
Cover design and illustration: Sandra Blair, Harrisburg, Pa.   4225

Contents

_____ **PART ONE** _____

GRAPHICS PROGRAMMING

APPENDICES

Introduction

Welcome to the exhilarating world of computer graphics programming. It's a field rich with challenge and reward, and it's waiting for you to explore. Graphics is an important trend in software applications, especially Windows applications. But, more important, graphics is a trend that is here to stay. Industry analysts are predicting that the computer graphics market will swell by 10% each year leading to the turn of the century. The worldwide market surpassed $40 billion early in the 1990s. These are impressive figures and they affect you directly, whether your project is software, shareware, or freeware. The importance of graphics in the marketplace could be your bellweather to success.

Opportunities for success in today's global arena are found in biotechnology, design, computers, entertainment, information technology, communication, and other emerging fields. Computer programming and application development play central roles in these areas of opportunity, which can germinate in traditional corporations, in entrepreneur-based startup companies, in home-based businesses, in individual consulting, and in virtual corporations.

This book can help you acquire the skills you need to participate in today's software opportunities. It can also help hone skills you might already have. You'll learn how to put 3D animation to work for you in simulations, visualizations, and virtual reality. You'll discover practical ways to increase your prowess as a programmer and as a developer. You'll be better poised to take timely advantage of today's exciting opportunities in software, shareware, and freeware. Whether you program for a living, or live for programming, this book is for you.

Getting the most from this book

You'll want to get the most from this book. Why? Because competitiveness is more than a buzzword in today's world, it's a fact—and it's right here, right now. Being competitive puts you on the fast-track to success.

As a developer, you can position your application to appeal to more users if you add images to your product, especially animated images. By supercharging your application with graphics, you can transform it into a more productive tool for your user. Remember, the competition is brisk. Anything you do to make your software more appealing, more effective, more entertaining, or more productive will assure your application its rightful place in the existing base of 6,000 Windows products.

Using applied animation in your applications is an effective way to broaden your software's appeal. More than 90% of what we experience is visual. More than 90% of what we learn is through sight. More than 90% of our interaction with the world is through our eyes. A Windows application that uses imagery to reinforce its functionality enjoys more powerful interaction with the user. If the imagery is moving, even better. Those moving images are called *animation*. Applied animation can push your application out ahead of the competition. Way out ahead.

Tomorrow's applications will take advantage of the computer's ability to provide different forms of output. Images, especially animated 3D images, can exploit the capabilities of the graphics engine that is built into each copy of Windows, using 16 or 256 colors and more, in resolutions ranging from 640 × 480 to 1024 × 768 and higher.

You can put all this potential to work for you in your own applications. Animation can be used for its own sake to clarify, to entertain, to teach. Applied animation can be used to simulate anything the human mind can conceive, or to visualize anything the human mind can imagine. Even the emerging field of virtual reality relies in large part upon animated imagery.

If you are a graphics programmer or an aspiring graphics programmer, then you likely already realize that empowering your software with animation, simulation, visualization, or virtual reality is more than just important, it's imperative. Your users expect it. Your clients demand it. Your supervisor counts on it. Your success depends on it.

Where to start

This book is a good starting point, because it offers practical solutions that can help you build graphics-based Windows applications. If you want to build Windows applications that use graphics, or if you are already involved in building Windows applications, then you will want to read this book. The sample applications and the text discussion are aimed at you, whether you're a casual programmer, and corporate programmer, or an independent developer. You will benefit from reading the book if one of the following categories describes you:

- You're a programmer or developer new to Windows graphics.
- You're an experienced programmer or developer of Windows graphics applications.
- You're the technical manager of a Windows programming environment.
- You're a project manager or a team leader.
- You're a programmer, developer, or technical manager who is selecting software tools for Windows application development.
- You're a software developer who plans to use animation or 3D images in your Windows applications.
- You're a contract programmer who needs a competitive edge to help you attract new clients and better serve your existing clients in the marketplace.
- You're a corporate programmer who wants to broaden the graphics features your applications offer to in-house clients and branch office locations.
- You're an independent developer who wants to maintain a competitive edge in Windows programming techniques.
- You're a part-time programmer, amateur coder, casual programmer, or graphics afficionado who wants to broaden your Windows programming skills.
- You're a manager, consultant, or researcher who needs to track current trends in Windows graphics applications.
- You're an entrepreneurial-minded programmer considering establishing your own home-based business as a contract programmer, systems consultant, or independent developer.

What you need

To get the most from the book, you'll need four things:

- A computer.
- An operating system.
- A development system.
- A desire to learn more about graphics programming.

The computer is the hardware. The operating system is DOS and Windows. The development system is the Visual Basic compiler you're using. The final requirement, your desire to learn more about graphics programming, is why you're already reading these lines.

You'll need a computer system capable of running Microsoft Windows and Visual Basic if you want to build and run the sample applications presented in the book. Some pundits say the best choice is a personal computer with at least 4MB of memory, using a fast 386, 486, 586, or newer Intel processor. It's important to realize, however, that even a 386sx with 2MB of memory is suitable for learning about graphics programming. You'll also want an industry-standard VGA or SVGA display adapter (graphics card) in your computer, along with a compatible display. A mouse is recommended.

At the time this is being written, you need MS-DOS version 3.1 or higher in order to run Windows. The sample applications in the book are designed to work with Windows versions 3.0 and 3.1, and higher.

You can build and test the sample applications with almost any version of Visual Basic. At the time this is being written, compatible compilers includes versions 1.0, 2.0, and 3.0.

The sample applications

The sample applications in the book were first prototyped and tested using Microsoft Visual Basic Development System for Windows, Professional Edition, version 2.0, on a 33 MHz 80386DX with 4MB of memory, equipped with an SVGA running Windows in $640 \times 480 \times 16$-color mode. During the development cycle, each application was also compiled using Microsoft Visual Basic for Windows, Standard Edition, version 2.0 in order to ensure cross-compiler compatibility.

The sample applications were validated and verified by compiling them with both the Professional and Standard editions of Visual Basic versions 3.0, 2.0, and 1.0. The demos were tested on machines with numeric coprocessors and without. The sample applications have been rigorously put through their paces in 2-color, 16-color, and 256-color modes in resolutions of 640×480, 800×600, and 1024×768. This exhaustive testing is your assurance of good quality, prototype code that is compatible with a variety of versions of Visual Basic.

What this book provides

The book provides solutions. The book is crafted to promote your programming creativity, and it does so by delivering a series of easy-to-follow tutorials and hands-on, here's-how, sample applications. The book is chock-full of programming solutions, including:

- A 3D toolkit for Windows (a $199 value).
- An animation toolkit (a $149 value).
- A kinematics simulation toolkit for Windows (a $295 value).
- A virtual reality toolkit (a $195 value).

The book is really three books in one. First, it is an introduction to graphics programming for the Windows operating system running on today's and tomorrow's personal computers. Second, it is an ambitious tutorial guide to applied animation, knowledge-based simulation, 3D visualization, and virtual reality. Third, it is an annotated collection of sample applications that you can learn from, tinker with, and use as inspired building blocks for your own projects.

Source code

Full source code for the sample applications is provided in the book and on the companion disk. The rigorously tested source code includes a set of toolkit modules that you can paste into your own applications. Included in the book is full source code for a 3D toolkit featuring:

- Z-buffer hidden-surface removal.
- Facet shading.
- Movable light source.
- Library of prebuilt 3D solid parts.
- Support for assemblies, moving parts, and hierarchical modeling.
- Animation drivers.
- Support for VGA and SVGA graphics.
- Support for 16-color and 256-color modes.
- Open architecture and extensible design.

Also included in the book is full source code for three additional tool kits, including:

- An animation toolkit including a fully interactive playback engine with forward, reverse, freeze-frame, and single-step capabilities.
- A kinematics simulation toolkit with script-driven animation building and playback capabilities
- A virtual reality toolkit.

The full-featured functionality of these toolkits is demonstrated throughout the book by six ready-to-build sample applications. The sample apps cover graphics topics like 3D modeling and shading, animation engines and editors, kinematics physically-based animation, and virtual reality. The sample applications and their foundation toolkits are provided as 12,000 lines of program listings in the book—and as nearly 700K of source code on the companion disk.

3D toolkit for Windows The 3D toolkit provides you with the ability to build 3D entities like boxes, spheres, cylinders, cones, wedges, and curved surfaces. The toolkit uses the Z-buffer method of hidden-surface management, ensuring that no matter how many entities you place in your 3D scene, each item will be correctly drawn. The toolkit uses backface-culling routines to ensure that only the visible portions of each 3D entity are rendered. A special module of light-source functions gives you the power to reposition the light-source almost anywhere in your 3D scene.

Animation toolkit for Windows The animation toolkit gives you the ability to design, build, store, retrieve, and play animated sequences in the Windows environment. The toolkit implements the powerful and versatile frame-animation paradigm. Each image (frame) from the animation sequence is stored on disk during the build process. For playback, the software loads the entire animation sequence into memory, from where it can deliver animation at rates up to 18 frames per second. The software is smart enough to be able to detect low memory conditions and to reconfigure itself to run the animation from disk, if need be. Of course, the animation playback routines provide you with full interactive control, including forward, reverse, freeze-frame, single-step, and more.

Kinematics simulation toolkit for Windows The kinematics toolkit gives you the ability to automate the build process by specifying position, velocity, acceleration, and other constraints for the entities in your 3D scene. This powerful simulation paradigm gets you started in the thrilling field of physically-based animation and the promise it holds for modeling the real world.

Virtual reality toolkit for Windows The virtual reality toolkit uses an innovative algorithm that gives you the ability to manage an exploration-based virtual reality (VR) session on a standard personal computer. The toolkit's functionality is demonstrated by sample program that presents a 3D maze for you to explore during your VR session.

The book's solution-centered approach rests solidly on a foundation of sample source code. You'll find 12,000 lines of program listings. The disk contains nearly 700K of source files, all royalty-free, ready for you to paste into your own applications.

How to adapt the code for your own use If you intend to use the source code in your own work, be sure to read the provisions of the License, which is presented in the book as FIG. 7 and which is provided on the companion disk as license.doc. Remember, however, that the license is nonexclusive. This means that every purchaser of the book enjoys the same options as you do. Also remember that the source code is not production code (what developers call *beta*), but rather it is advanced prototype code (or *alpha code*). Most of the wrinkles have been ironed out of the sample applications, but the demos have not been optimized for either speed or size. They have instead been optimized for their role in the teaching toolset.

Special features

You can use this book and your favorite copy of Visual Basic to create 3D and animation software that takes full advantage of personal computers running in the cooperative, multitasking operating environment of Windows. The book helps you master the skills you need to get things done in Windows.

A learning tool The book is first and foremost a learning toolset. More important, it is a learning kit that is backed by the combined experience and reputation of the author and the publisher. Graphics programming is a diverse, complex field, and no single book or expert has all the answers, but more than 150,000 readers worldwide are your assurance that this book can help you upgrade your competitive skills. The track record speaks for itself. Many successful retail software products contain graphics features inspired by previous books in the Windcrest graphics series from Windcrest/McGraw-Hill. So you're in good company. If you receive just one workable new idea from the book, or if you use just a single block of code from the book in your own application, then you'll have received full value.

Marketwise tutorials The discussion in the book and the sample applications follow a theme best described as *marketwise*. This street-savvy approach means you benefit from text and tutorials that focus on graphics topics relevant in today's world. You'll find no toy programs here, but instead real code for real coders. You get hard-working, no-nonsense code permeated with the potential to supercharge your own graphics apps. Whether you're interested in entertainment programming, physically-based simulation, knowledge-based simulation, visualization, or virtual reality, you'll find ready-to-use coding ideas that can help you get your next prototype up and running before your competition, or before your supervisor's deadline.

Hands-on learning The sample applications and toolkits in the book are designed for hands-on learning. Experienced teachers know that you learn by doing; any other approach is frivolous by comparison. The program listings in the book and the source files on the disk provide you with a set of here-is-how-it's-done demos. You can build and run these samples on your own personal computer and see for yourself how the code works in the real world.

Commitment to graphics The book practices what it preaches. As they say on the street, it talks the talk and it walks the walk. Inside the book you'll find plenty of screen prints that show how the sample applications perform their magic. You'll also find many hand-drawn line illustrations that help clarify topics being discussed in the text. All these images throughout the book's pages reflect an unshakeable belief in the power of graphics to communicate. If you've struggled through graphics-impaired books from other sources, you already realize that trying to master graphics from a text-only discussion is like a fly mastering flypaper.

Complete and unabridged The book is complete and unabridged. Nothing is missing. There are no loose ends that will torpedo your own development project. Each sample application is ready to build and test on your own personal computer. In addition, the text discussion gives you enough background information so you'll seldom need to go hunting elsewhere for answers to help you understand either the topics or their sample apps.

Document conventions The layout and typography of the book adhere to conventions that promote ease of understanding. Headings and subheadings are organized in a manner that allows you to grasp the essence of the text when you are skimming. Whenever a new word or phrase is intro-duced in the text, it is often displayed in italics. This indicates that a defi-nition can be found in the glossary at the back of the book. All the program listings are grouped in the appendices so that the readability and flow of the text is not interrupted.

Device-independent philosophy The book endorses a programming philoso-phy of *device independence*. This means that the graphics perform equally well on different display adapters and displays.

Device-independent graphics The sample applications throughout the book provide device-independent graphics by sensing and supporting different display resolutions and different color modes.

Display resolutions The sample applications support display resolutions of 640×480, 800×600, and 1024×768 pixels. At program startup the code senses the display resolution and resizes the application's window to pro-vide a standard-size viewport.

Color The sample applications support 1-bit 2-color modes, 4-bit 16-color modes, and 8-bit 256-color modes.

Device-independent animation The sample applications throughout the book support *device-independent animation*. This means that the appli-cations are flexible enough to operate on personal computers with differ-ent amounts of memory, running at different speeds, and using different graphics adapters.

Memory-based and disk-based The sample applications can play animation sequence directly from memory or directly from disk. This means that your own applications can provide frame-based animation playback from disk on any personal computer that lacks enough memory to load the entire animation sequence into RAM.

16 MHz to 100 MHz The sample applications use a timer-based animation paradigm that ensures pleasing playback on personal computers running at clock speeds from 16 MHz to 100 MHz.

VGA and SVGA Full support for VGA and SVGA display adapters is pro-vided. The animation sequences in the sample applications play back cor-rectly in 2-color, 16-color, and 256-color modes using dithered palettes. The sample application in chapter 4 shows you how to use 256-color palettes of custom colors.

Images of program output The book is generously appointed with a rich se-lection of screen images that illustrate the graphics produced by the sam-ple applications. These images make it possible for you to use the book when you are not at your computer—when you're commuting, for exam-ple. They also provide a benchmark that shows how the graphics should appear on your own personal computer system.

Illustrations, charts, and tables A substantial collection of illustrations, charts, and tables appears throughout the main body of the book. The hand-drawn illustrations have been especially crafted to support the discussion in the text. The numerous tables in the book have been assembled to help you make sense of data relationships.

Ready-to-build Visual Basic source listings The book contains a sizable assortment of ready-to-build sample applications. These demos introduce important features such as:

- Multicompiler, cross-platform support.
- Open architecture.
- Extensible design.
- Royalty-free, merge-ready resources.

Multicompiler, cross-platform support Each sample application offers multicompiler, cross-platform support. Multicompiler support means that you can build the sample applications using almost any version of Visual Basic that supports Windows application development. Cross-platform support means that the finished executables can run on personal computers with a variety of different memory, display adapter, and processor configurations.

Open architecture The sample applications and the toolkit modules feature an open architecture that encourages understanding, modification, and maintainability. The program listings are seeded with plenty of remarks and comments. Whenever practical, the functions are implemented in a manner that encourages recycling in your own applications. The six sample applications that you'll find in the book are compelling examples of how easily the toolkit modules can be seamlessly integrated into powerful, full-featured applications for Windows.

Extensible design The sample applications feature *extensible design*. This means it is easy to extend the code by adding new features. The 3D toolkit, for example, can be expanded to support additional 3D entities and additional color rendering paradigms. The kinematics toolkit, which presently supports forward kinematics, can be extended to support inverse kinematics, forward dynamics, and inverse dynamics. The animation engine can be adapted to support animation sequences of varying lengths.

The sample applications and what they do There are six sample applications in the book. Each application exercises the programming toolkits already described. In order of appearance in the book, the six sample applications are:

- startup
- objects

- animate
- assembly
- kinematx
- maze

The first sample application, *startup*, is a template for graphics application development. You can use it as a starting point for your own applications. It provides a nested menu system with accelerator keys. The code demonstrates color, palettes, font, and viewport programming.

The next demo, *objects*, is a 3D geometry sampler that can generate solid, fully shaded entities like boxes, spheres, half-spheres, cylinders, half-cylinders, cones, wedges, and more.

The application named *animate* is a generic animation engine that you can use as a template to develop your own applications. In its current implementation, animate supports interactive animation of a rotating 3D entity.

The sample application *assembly* demonstrates how to animate articulated solids that have joints. The robotic arm is created by using hierarchical modeling techniques.

The next sample application, *kinematx*, is an animated forward kinematics editor that uses script files to define constraints like velocity, duration, acceleration, and so on. The tutorials include orbiting spheres and a moving camshaft simulation.

The final sample application, *maze*, is an interactive, animated, virtual reality sampler. After using the editor to build and save a series of viewpoint frames to disk, you can start a virtual reality session and immerse yourself in a 3D maze. The virtual reality manager provides an environment where you can explore the maze, but prevents any attempt to walk through the maze's walls.

How the book is organized

The book is organized into four sections that take you on a tour of applied animation, simulation, visualization, and virtual reality programming. The four parts are concerned with:

- Graphics programming skills.
- 3D programming skills.
- Animation programming skills.
- Simulation programming skills.

Graphics programming skills

Part One, "Graphics programming," gets you started with Windows programming in general and with Windows graphics programming in particular. A hands-on tutorial in chapter 4 provides a sample application. The background skills that you'll learn in part one can be applied to almost every graphics project you'll ever encounter.

3D programming skills

Part Two, "3D programming," provides you with a solid understanding of view geometry, rendering, and modeling. A hands-on tutorial in chapter 9 provides a sample application. The 3D programming skills that you'll learn in part two can be applied to a wide range of Windows applications, including animation, simulation, visualization, and virtual reality.

Animation programming skills

Part Three, "Animation programming," provides you with a working knowledge of the animation capabilities of the GDI, which is the graphics engine that is built into every copy of Windows. A hands-on tutorial in chapter 12 provides you with a powerful and versatile animation engine that you can use as a cornerstone for your own animated applications. Another animation tutorial in chapter 13 provides here-is-how-it's-done instruction in 3D motion-control programming.

Simulation programming skills

Part Four, "Simulation programming," provides you with an understanding of knowledge-based simulation, physically-based animation, and virtual reality programming. A hands-on tutorial in chapter 17 illustrates the break-free potential of kinematics programming, where parameters like velocity, acceleration, and duration can be used to build animation scripts for automated simulations of 3D entities. Another tutorial in chapter 19 provides a virtual reality prototype that lets you explore the twisting and turning passageways of a 3D maze in real-time on your own personal computer.

How to build the sample applications

Appendix A provides you with the information you need to build each sample application with your own copy of Visual Basic. A troubleshooting guide and a tour of the companion disk ensure minimum fuss as you explore the exhilarating world of applied animation in Windows.

Visual Basic source listings

The source listings for the toolkits are provided in Appendix B. The program listings for the sample applications are presented in Appendix C. As a convenience to you, all the source code is also provided on the companion disk that comes bundled with the book. A directory listing of the source files on the companion disk is presented in Appendix A.

Glossary and Index

An extensive, up-to-date glossary gives you a handy way to find out the meaning of any graphics terms you find puzzling. The index is a quick and efficient way to locate sections of the book that discuss topics of interest to you.

1 You can paste the source code from the book into your own applications as described in the License. Toolkits for animation, simulation, visualization, and virtual reality are provided, as well as six hands-on tutorial demonstration programs.

Where do you go from here?

Where you go next depends on your needs. The structure of the book does not force upon you any particular dogma for learning. You can read the book from start to finish or you can skip randomly from topic to topic. Either approach is the right approach if it produces results for you. Here are a few suggestions.

If you are a beginner to Windows programming or to graphics programming, you should proceed to Part 1, Graphics programming. This will give you the background you need to tackle the more advanced projects that appear later in the book.

If you are an experienced programmer, you can use the table of contents or the index to direct you to the section of the book that can help you most. For a discussion of 3D programming paradigms, be sure to check chapters 6, 7, and 8. You might wish to read chapter 11 for a good overview of animation programming. Chapter 15 contains an introduction of knowledge-based simulation, including reasoning, probability, game-theory, and physics-based simulation. You'll find a practical introduction to virtual reality in chapters 18 and 19.

If you have specific programming needs, check the table of contents. The index can also help you narrow your search. You might also refer to the quick reference table provided inside the front cover of the book.

Discussion about how the source code works appears in each of the tutorial chapters. This includes chapters 4, 9, 12, 13, 17, and 19. These code-centered discussions appear under headings like "Programmer's guide to the sample application." By skimming these sections of the book, you can quickly identify chunks of code that you can paste directly into the application you're developing. This approach can save you many hours of programming time.

If you want a quick overview of the book, you can either skim or read chapters 6, 7, 8, 11, 15, and 18. These chapters provide the thematic kernel of the book. They cover topics ranging from 3D modeling to animation to simulation to virtual reality.

Where can you find more information?

No single book has all the answers. The discipline of computer graphics programming is too diverse, too complex, too evolving for a single text to monopolize the field. Here are a few additional sources of information that you might find of use to you.

For a well-rounded guide to animation programming for Windows, you may wish to consider Visual Basic Animation Programming, published in 1993 as Windcrest book 4224.

For an informative introduction to graphics programming skills for Windows, you might enjoy *High-Performance C Graphics Programming for Windows*, published in 1992 by Windcrest/McGraw-Hill (book no. 4103). For an authoritative guide to animation programming for Windows, you might wish to consider *C for Windows Animation Programming*, published in 1993 by Windcrest/McGraw-Hill (book no. 4114). And for the C/C++ version of the book you are reading now, you might wish to consider *Windows Visualization Programming with C/C++: 3D Visualization, Simulation, and Virtual Reality*, published in 1993 by Windcrest/McGraw-Hill (book no. 4115).

Windcrest is an imprint of TAB Books, a division of McGraw-Hill. You can often find these books in bookstores that have computer book sections. If not, ask your bookseller to order them for you, or else write the publisher and ask for the current Windcrest/McGraw-Hill catalog.

Part One

Graphics
programming

Your task in Part One is to prepare yourself for graphics programming in Windows. You want to achieve a degree of proficiency in the fundamental skills of developing for Windows in general, and developing graphics applications for Windows in particular. You want to build a level of confidence in your fundamental programming skills that will carry you through the advanced tutorials later in the book.

In Part One of the book you'll learn about the parts of a typical application for Windows, including the global module, the startup module, and the form module. In chapter 2, "Getting started with Windows programming," you'll learn about persistent graphics, dialog boxes, and well-behaved applications.

In chapter 3, "Getting started with graphics programming," you'll master the GDI—the graphics engine that is built into every retail copy of Windows. You'll use devices and contexts to produce images on any drawing surface. You'll see how to create and select drawing tools like pens, brushes, and color. You'll learn how to work with shapes, bitmaps, regions, and text.

In chapter 4, a hands-on tutorial shows you how to put your new skills to work. A sample application demonstrates features like display-independence, various auto-detect functions, nested menus, and a dazzling demonstration of color using palette manipulation techniques that work in both 16-color and 256-color modes.

Before you begin to delve into the fundamental skills of graphics programming for Windows, you'll need to acquaint yourself with some of the words and phrases that are used by experienced Windows developers. The first chapter, "Concepts and terms," provides you with the background knowledge you need to get started.

1
Concepts and terms

This chapter introduces some of the basic concepts and terms that you'll be using as you explore Part One, "Graphics programming." You want to be able to understand the technical words that are used in the next few chapters, because this background knowledge will make it easier for you to firmly grasp the fundamental skills required for Windows application development.

Defining concepts and terms

This chapter is about the concepts and terms that make up the world of Windows application programming in general, and graphics programming in particular. You'll become familiar with what each concept means and, more important, the role it plays in the overall system of application development for Windows.

Launching an application

When a user selects your application icon, Windows launches the application. This is just another way of saying Windows starts the application running. Windows first sets aside some memory for the application, then it loads the executable code from disk into memory and sets up a local stack (working space) for the application. Windows then loads in the application's data and resources.

Application resources

Application resources include the menu system, accelerator keys, dialog boxes, message boxes, icons, and bitmaps used by the application at runtime. Windows will sometimes load these resources into memory at the

3

same time it launches an application; other times Windows waits until the application actually needs a resource before loading it into memory from disk. You'll need to be careful to distinguish between system resources and application resources to avoid confusion.

System resources

System resources are system-wide input/output services like memory, disk access, keyboard input, mouse input, and access to the display. Windows acts like a referee in a game with many players to ensure that system resources are available to all. Your application is one of the players. If more than one Windows application is running, for example, system memory might be limited. Windows uses a built-in memory manager that acts in the background to ensure that each application has the memory it requires. Sometimes this means swapping code, data, and resources out of physical memory to make room for another application.

Messages

A *message* is how Windows passes input to your application. Windows continually polls the keyboard, the mouse, and the timer. When an event occurs on one of these devices, Windows builds an appropriate message and posts it in the system queue. The *system queue* is a first-in-first-out list of messages. Windows is smart enough to know if a message is intended for only your application. If so, the message is posted in a separate queue that Windows maintains explicitly for your application.

The message loop

The *message loop* is a block of code that is built into your application by Visual Basic. This block keeps looping while your application is running. The message loop asks Windows to check if any messages have arrived for your application.

The message handler

After a message loop fetches an incoming message from the system queue, it passes the message to another block of code in your application called the *message handler*. The message handler inspects the parameters of the message. It can do so because each message is a uniform kernel of data. The message handler then calls the custom functions that you've specified in your menu design. Another name for message handler is window procedure.

The viewport

The *viewport* is what graphics programmers call the client area of the application's window. It is the blank space inside the window that your application uses to display images and text.

The GDI

The GDI is the *graphics device interface*. It is a part of the Windows application programming interface (the API). The GDI provides access to the high-performance graphics engine that is built into every retail copy of Windows. By calling the functions of the GDI, your application can tap directly into the full power of Windows' graphics capabilities. The executable code for the graphics engine is in a DLL file called gdi.exe.

The DLL

The DLL is a *dynamic link library*. Dynamic because the functions in the library are not logically linked to your application until run-time. The callable functions of the Windows API are provided in three run-time libraries. These three DLLs are kernel.exe, user.exe, and gdi.exe. The kernel.exe DLL provides functions for managing application windows and for supporting the entire Windows environment. The user.exe DLL provides system services like memory management and multitasking. The gdi.exe DLL provides a set of graphics functions that are especially well-suited for color manipulation, 3D rendering, and animation.

Devices

Devices are focal points of input and output. The keyboard, the mouse, and the timer are examples of input devices. The display, the printer, and the disk drive are examples of output devices. Your application can also use simulated devices. Bitmaps and metafiles are simulated devices in memory. A bitmap is an array of bytes that can be used as a drawing surface. A bitmap stores an image. A metafile, on the other hand, is a list of GDI function calls that can be used to store the means for recreating an image, rather than storing the image itself.

Device-contexts

A *device-context* is a description of a particular device.

Display-contexts

A *display-context* is one type of device-context. A display-context describes a window on the display. It specifies how graphics output is to be written to the viewport of the window by the GDI. Before your application calls a GDI graphics function, it must provide device-context information to the GDI. You do so by creating a display-context, which automatically specifies parameters such as the:

- Background color—the default is white.
- Background mode—opaque or transparent.

- Brush color—white by default.
- Pen color—the default is black.
- Text color—black by default.
- Font.
- Edges of the clipping region.
- Location of the 0,0 origin in the viewport.
- Location of the pen—0,0 is the default.
- Location of the brush.

Compatible display-contexts

A *compatible display-context* is a device-context that refers to a simulated display. This virtual display is located in memory and possesses attributes similar to the genuine display-context of the display window. Compatible display-contexts are handy for animation, where the next image is built on a hidden page before being copied to the display window. A compatible display-context also provides a convenient method for maintaining persistent graphics. A compatible display-context is implemented as a bitmap in memory.

Persistent graphics

Persistent graphics are images that are refreshed whenever they are inadvertently damaged (corrupted). If another application's window covers part of your application's window, then part of your app's viewport is corrupted. When the other application is eventually moved away, you want to quickly refresh the affected portion of the viewport so the image looks complete again. By using a compatible display-context to maintain a backup copy of the viewport image in memory, you can copy a clean image to the display whenever it's needed. The need for refreshing can also occur when the user moves your application's window past the edge of the display.

Drawing tools

Drawing tools provided in gdi.exe include pens, brushes, bitmaps, and fonts to perform output operations. Pens draw lines and shapes. Brushes fill areas with color. Bitmaps provide images. Fonts provide text, captions, and titles. Before you can use a drawing tool, you must create it and select it into the display-context or compatible display-context. When you are finished using a drawing tool, you must delete it.

Output operations

Drawing tools perform output operations like lines, polygons, rectangles, ellipses, text, bitblts, metafiles, and others.

Drawing tool functions

You use *drawing tool functions* to create, select, and delete drawing tools.

Drawing attribute functions

Drawing attribute functions are specialized GDI routines that modify the way drawing tools operate. You can change the background color and the background mode (opaque or transparent). You can also change the drawing mode of a drawing tool. The default drawing mode is overwrite, but you can use OR, XOR, AND, NOT, and other modes to combine the color of the drawing tool with the existing color of the pixel. You can also use drawing attribute functions to change the text color and to stretch a bitmap image.

RGB color

Color is an attribute of pens, brushes, and fonts. You must specify a color whenever you create a pen or a brush. A color is usually described by specifying the intensities of the red, green, and blue guns of the cathode ray tube (the display). Such a description is called RGB color. An intensity value of 0 turns off a gun. A value of 255 sets it to brightest intensity. A GDI call of RGB(0,0,0) produces black; RGB(255,255,255) produces bright white. If the color you have requested is supported by the display adapter, the GDI provides the color as a pure hue, otherwise the GDI simulates the requested color by dithering.

Dithering

Dithering is the mixing of pixels of available colors to create an approximation of a color not supported by the display adapter. For example, a palette of 16 pure hues can be simultaneously displayed by an industry-standard VGA display adapter. If you request a 17th color when Windows is running on a VGA, the GDI attempts to fulfill your request by dithering. However, if you request a 17th color when Windows is running in a 256-color mode on an SVGA, the GDI satisfies your request by providing a pure hue that conforms exactly to the RGB specifications you have provided.

Palettes

A *palette* is a collection of colors. The default palette is the system palette. Another name for system palette is hardware palette. When Windows starts, it resets the display adapter in order to obtain a palette of colors suitable for general windowing operations. Your application can use the system palette, but it can also use logical palettes. A logical palette is a palette that is defined by your application. Depending on whether Windows is running in 16-color or 256-color mode, the colors you request for your logical palette are provided as dithered patterns or as pure hues.

Regions

Two categories of *regions* are supported by the GDI. They are fill-regions and clipping-regions. A fill-region is a polygon-shaped area that can be filled with color by using a brush. A clipping-region is an invisible rectangular area that is used to clip graphics output which falls outside the rectangle.

Where do you go from here?

Now that you've familiarized yourself with some of the basic concepts and terms used in Windows application development, you're ready to start learning the fundamental skills. The next chapter, "Getting started with Windows programming," teaches you how to build a typical graphics application.

2
Getting started with
Windows programming

This chapter introduces you to the fundamental techniques you'll need for developing Windows applications. It describes the parts of a typical Windows application and discusses how to create a typical Windows application. Your task in this chapter is to prepare yourself for graphics programming. You want to achieve a degree of proficiency in the fundamental skills of developing for Windows in general. You want to know about menu systems with accelerator keys, nested menus, and more. You want to know how to associate your own code with the menu items in your application. This background knowledge will make it easier for you to understand upcoming chapters concerning graphics programming. You'll learn about the parts of a typical application for Windows, including the global module, the startup module, and the form module. You'll also delve into persistent graphics and multiple instances.

Application parts

A typical Windows application consists of a collection of source files such as a:

- project file
- global module file
- startup module file
- form module file

Project file

The project file uses a .mak extension. When Visual Basic builds your program, it inspects the project file to determine which source modules must be combined to produce the executable.

Global module file

The global module file uses a .bas extension. The global module contains declarations of constants and variables that are used throughout the entire program. Any function in any module has access to a constant or variable that has been declared in the global module. Any external functions that your application calls (such as the functions that are built into the graphics device interface of Windows) must be declared in the global module.

Startup module file

The startup module uses a .bas extension. If your application needs to initialize any variables at program startup, you can place the appropriate statements in a function named Main() in the startup module.

Form module file

The form module uses a .frm extension. The form module contains the specifications for the menu system that your application will use at runtime. The form module also contains the code that you've written to support the menu items. Visual Basic inserts a message loop into your finished application that provides input to your menu system.

The *message loop* is a block of code in a function called WinMain(), which is the execution starting-point for your application. As a Visual Basic programmer, you never need to concern yourself with WinMain() because Visual Basic handles all this low-level "grunt work" for you by automatically building a WinMain() function into every executable you develop. When Windows first launches your application it calls WinMain(), which often contains code to create and show the application's window.

The message loop is a block of code within WinMain() that is executed repeatedly while your application is running. The message loop asks Windows to check for messages waiting in the system queue. If Windows informs the message loop that there are messages waiting for your application, the message loop asks Windows to fetch a message. Windows delivers the message to a separate part of your application called the message handler.

The *message handler* is a function in your application that makes branching decisions based on the attributes of the incoming message. Simply put, the message handler is a switcher for incoming messages. The message handler can make decisions based on:

- A menu item selected by the user.
- A timer event.

- A need to refresh the client area.
- A request to resize or move the window.
- Various other events.

Visual Basic takes care of all the detail involved in connecting the code you've written to the incoming messages, especially those messages that result from the user making a menu selection.

How to create an application

Whether you're a professional developer or a casual programmer, the most efficient way to build a Windows application is to take existing source code and adapt it. Many experienced programmers use a standardized simple application as a template, which becomes a starting point for a more complex application. It serves as a framework to support the features and functions of the new application. This concept of reusing existing code has a number of important advantages.

A benefit of using a template is knowing that you're building on a solid foundation. As the sample applications in this book demonstrate, starting with a reusable template makes it easy to develop high-performance, reliable, full-featured graphics applications. After you've developed a simple application to provide basic functions like menuing, display autodetect, and other housekeeping operations, you can thereafter use the code as a starting point for advanced applications development, secure in the knowledge that you've debugged and validated the original code.

Common window and viewport

An important ingredient of a device-independent graphics program is the size and location of its window and viewport (client area). A Windows graphics application that claims to be device-independent must be able to position and display its window equally well in 2-color, 16-color, and 256-color modes, and in screen resolutions ranging from 640 × 480 to 1024 × 768 pixels. The code to enforce this protocol must detect the color mode and screen resolution at startup. The code must also be smart enough to resize the window to provide a consistent viewport across all supported resolutions. Prototyping, debugging, and testing the code on all supported displays is a nit-picking exercise in programming savvy. It makes sense to save the code as a reusable template that you can use over and over again. The tutorial in chapter 4 provides exactly this capability, and the sample application is in fact used as a template for the sophisticated graphics demos that appear later in the book.

Common user interface

Building a menu system for your application involves carefully cross-referencing the contents of your form module and the menu items. If you add accelerator keys it complicates the exercise even further. Features like nested menus and message boxes can be tricky to code, too. Don't reinvent the wheel—reuse the code. Adding and deleting menu elements from an existing menu system is simple and straightforward as opposed to building a new menu system from the ground up. In addition, if you use the same prototype as a template for all of your projects, you're likely to produce applications with similar user interfaces. The concept of a common user interface is one of the philosophical underpinnings of the Windows operating system.

Practical design tips

The following are some principles you should keep in mind when creating a menu system for your application. A good menu system possesses attributes like:

- consistency
- clarity
- forgivability
- ergonomic design
- proven in use
- standardization

Consistency

Your application is *consistent* when it uses familiar concepts, keystrokes, and mouse movements to implement similar functions. The user must be able to rely on common sense to find items in your application's menu system. For example, suppose your graphics application offers menu items named sphere, cylinder, and wedge. Suppose that when the user selects sphere or cylinder, a nested menu appears which allows the user to specify color. On the other hand, if the user selects wedge and your application uses instead a dialog box to prompt for color, then the application would be violating the principle of consistency.

Clarity

Clarity means that your menu system is labelled in a manner that avoids ambiguity and redundancy. The user must be able to use context and intuition to make sense of a menu item. For example, you would want to avoid using Do, Run, and Go interchangeably as menu items indicating action. It is better to decide on one of the verbs and use it consistently throughout your menu system. Clarity also means that your application should adopt nested menus rather than a single menu stuffed with a lengthy list of menu items. Hierarchies of menus provide clarity.

Forgivability

Your application possesses *forgivability* when it is ready to forgive errors the user makes. Most users learn an application by trial and error. Using this approach, it is easy to select a menu item that is inappropriate for the current context of the program. Your application should restrict the opportunities for such innocent mistakes while the user is exploring, and when an inappropriate menu item is selected your application should be smart enough to handle the situation gracefully. In other words, forgivability means that your application protects the user from the user.

Ergonomic design

Ergonomic design means that your application is aware of the user's limitations. For example, your application should not use a message box to inform the user of a complicated series of commands and then expect the user to remember the commands after closing the message box. Your application should instead lead the user through the required actions step by step.

Proven in use

The most important attribute of a good menu system is that it is proven in actual use. It means that your menu design has been tested by sample users. Professional developers know the insidious trap of familiarity. Idiosyncrasies and peculiarities of a menu system are quickly overlooked as they become familiar to the programmers. The sooner a new menu design is tested on real users the better.

Standardization

An application that adheres to industry standards includes certain standard features and functions. It provides commonly used and expected menus like File, Edit, and Help. It displays unavailable menu items as grayed text. It indicates toggled menu items by a check-mark. Adherence to industry standards means that familiar menu items are provided, such as the File menu's New, Open..., Save, Save As..., and Exit menu items.

By following these design tips when you build a menu system for your application, you ensure that your program is easy to learn and easy to use. As the sample applications in this book demonstrate, designing and implementing practical menu systems can be quick and easy, even for advanced graphics applications.

Persistent graphics

Persistent graphics are images that are immune to unwanted side effects. Suppose, for example, that the user moves another application's window, covering part of your application's window. When the offending window is moved away, part of your application's window will be uncovered and Windows paints (refresh) this rectangle with the default background color, usually white, unless you specify otherwise.

All of the sample applications throughout this book keep a duplicate copy of the viewport image in a hidden bitmap in memory. Whenever a portion of the application's window needs to be refreshed, the code copies the hidden image to the display window. As you'll soon learn, persistent graphics are an essential ingredient of a Windows graphics application, especially an animated application.

Where do you go from here?

Now that you've familiarized yourself with the parts that make up a typical Windows application and learned some fundamental concepts of Windows programming, you're ready to take a look at graphics programming. The next chapter, "Getting started with graphics programming," teaches you how to tap directly into the power of Windows' built-in graphics engine, the GDI.

3
Getting started with graphics programming

This chapter introduces you to some concepts and skills for developing graphics applications for Windows. It discusses how to choose a drawing surface, how to select drawing tools, and how to tell the graphics engine what to do. You'll learn all about display-contexts and how to use them and gain a thorough understanding of some of the drawing tools provided by the GDI graphics engine and how to use them. Along the way, you'll learn about RGB color and palettes. You'll also become familiar with drawing functions—bitblts, regions, and shapes. The background knowledge you acquire in this chapter gives you the skills you need to work with the advanced graphics examples later in the book.

The GDI

The *GDI* is the graphics device interface. Stated more precisely, it is the device-independent graphics interface that is built into every retail copy of Windows. You can think of it as a Windows-hosted graphics engine. Some programmers like to think of the GDI as a graphics programming language.

The functions provided in the GDI can be called by any Visual Basic application running in the Windows environment. The GDI can be instructed to direct its graphics output to the display, to memory, to the printer, to a disk file, and to other devices. The tutorials in this book focus mainly on using the GDI with the display and with memory.

Although Windows is a graphical interface, your application never directly manipulates the graphics hardware (the display adapter). Instead, your code issues instructions to the GDI, which is responsible for getting the desired results from the graphics hardware. This arrangement relieves you of much of the tedium of hardware compatibility. Windows provides a significant degree of device-independence although, as you'll see later in the book, advanced graphics application development sometimes means you need an understanding of color modes, display resolutions, memory availability, and other hardware specifics.

Choosing your drawing surface

Because the GDI is capable of doing so many different things, you must ensure that it assumes the same context you are assuming whenever you call one of its functions. A *context* is a set of attributes (assumptions) that describe the current output device.

Devices

You'll remember from previous chapters that *devices* are focal points of input and output. The keyboard, mouse, and timer are examples of input devices. The display, printer, disk drive, and modem are examples of output devices. Output devices can also mean simulated devices in memory such as bitmaps and metafiles. Before your application calls a graphics function, you must provide device-context information to the GDI.

Device-contexts A *device-context* represents an output device and its device driver. The display adapter is an example of an output device. The Windows-supplied file, vga.drv, is an example of a device-driver. Device-contexts can describe a variety of output devices. A display-context is just one type of device-context.

Display-contexts A *display-context* represents a window on the display. The display-context describes how graphics output is to be written to the viewport (client area) of a particular window. Some programmers use the acronym *DC* to mean display-context.

Using a display-context

You can either use the display-context that Visual Basic has reserved for your application's window or you can call the GDI to create your own display-contexts. While a display-context is active, you can modify its default attributes if you wish, and you can use drawing tools to perform output operations. When you're finished drawing, it is good programming practice to release any display-context that you've created.

Creating a display-context To create a display-context, your application calls GetDC(). You pass to the GDI the handle of the window on which you intend to draw. The handle is the window's identification number.

Default attributes When the GDI creates a display-context for you, it assumes a drawing surface with:

- A white background color.
- An opaque background mode.
- A white brush.
- A black pen.
- Black text.
- The default proportional font.
- A clipping region that equals the client area.
- Coordinates 0,0 at the upper-left corner.
- The pen located at 0,0.
- The brush located at 0,0.

The meaning of these attributes will become more apparent as you delve into the tutorial in the next chapter. Your application can, of course, alter any of these default attributes to suit its own requirements.

Using drawing tools with a display-context The drawing tools provided by the GDI include pens, brushes, bitmaps, and fonts. *Pens* draw lines and shapes. *Brushes* fill areas with color. *Bitmaps* provide rectangular images and drawing surfaces. *Fonts* provide text, captions, and titles. After you've created a display-context, you can use drawing tools to perform output operations on the device described by the display-context. Output includes effects such as shape operations (lines, rectangles, polygons, and ellipses), bitmap operations like bitblts, region operations, and text operations. You'll learn more about drawing tools and output operations later in the chapter.

Releasing a display-context After you've finished drawing, your application can release the display-context by calling the GDI's ReleaseDC(). Because Windows maintains a finite number of display-contexts, you should always take care to release a display-context after you are finished with it. You can always create another one later if you again need to draw in your application's window. All Visual Basic applications reserve a display-context called Form1.hDC at program startup for the display window and keep it available until the application terminates. If you want to work with graphics on hidden surfaces, however, you'll want to create your own display-contexts.

Selecting your drawing tools

After you've chosen your drawing surface by obtaining a display-context, you'll want to select your drawing tools. It's important to realize that drawing tools are not the same as drawing functions, which is another name for output operations.

Drawing tools vs. output operations

Drawing tools are pens, brushes, bitmaps, and fonts. Pens draw lines and shapes. Brushes fill areas with color. Bitmaps provide rectangular images and drawing surfaces. Fonts provide text, captions, and titles.

Output operations include shape functions (lines, rectangles, polygons, and ellipses), bitmap functions (bitblts), region functions, and text functions.

Drawing tools provided by the GDI

The GDI provides four primary drawing tools: a pen, brush, bitmap, and font. Each of these tools can be used alone or in conjunction with other tools. The tools can be modified by your application in order to produce different types of graphic output. Each tool can create graphics on the display or in memory. If you are drawing on the display, you are usually creating images in the application's window. If you are drawing in memory, you are usually creating images on a hidden bitmap.

In order to use a tool, you must create it and select it for either the display-context of the application's window or for the compatible display-context of a hidden surface in memory. The GDI also provides a set of default tools that you do not need to create—you simply select them into the context you are using.

Creating and selecting a pen

To create a pen, your application makes a call to CreatePen(). This function takes three arguments—pen style, pen width, and pen color. The style can be solid, dash, dot, or a combination of dash and dot. The default pen width is one pixel, but you can set it wider. The pen color is always a solid color if pen width is one pixel. On a 16-color VGA, this means the GDI sets the pen color to one of the available solid colors if you request a color which would otherwise require dithering. If the pen width is greater than one pixel, the GDI uses dithering if the color you request is not a solid hue. Before you can use the pen you've created, your application must call SelectObject() to select the pen into the display-context. You'll see plenty of examples of CreatePen() and SelectObject() in the sample applications later in the book.

The appearance of any line is affected by two factors. These are the background attribute and the drawing mode.

Background attribute

The *background attribute* governs how the GDI handles the empty spaces of dashed lines and dotted lines. It does not affect solid lines. If your application sets the background attribute to transparent, the GDI will not modify any pixels that fall in the empty spaces of a dashed or dotted line. If you set the background attribute to opaque, the GDI draws the empty spaces in a color equal to the current background of the drawing surface. This means that any pixels that fall in the empty spaces of a dashed or dotted line will be overwritten. To set the background attribute you call SetBkMode(). The default is opaque. As you'll see later, SetBkMode() also affects any text that your application uses.

Drawing modes

The *default drawing mode* is overwrite. The drawing mode governs how the GDI applies new imagery over existing imagery. Your application can use the SetROP2() function to change the drawing mode that the GDI uses for pens and for filled objects like polygons. Supported drawing modes include OR, XOR, AND, NOT, and others. These Boolean operators are called *raster-operation codes*.

Creating and selecting a brush

To create a brush, your application usually calls CreateSolidBrush(). Before you can use the brush to fill areas of color you must select it into the display-context by calling SelectObject().

The call to CreateSolidBrush() takes one argument, the color. You indicate a color by using the GDI's RGB() macro to specify the intensities of the red, green, and blue guns. Pure medium blue, for example, is RGB(0,0,127). If the color you request is available as a solid hue, the GDI provides it exactly as you requested it. RGB(0,0,127) is an example of a solid hue that is available on a VGA. On the other hand, RGB(0,0,143) is a slightly brighter blue that is not available as one of the 16 pure hues on a VGA running Windows. If the color you request is not one of the solid colors available on the display adapter, then the GDI uses dithering to simulate the color. This dithering occurs on both a 16-color VGA and on a 256-color SVGA, even though the SVGA is capable of providing additional pure hues. Later in this chapter you'll learn how to create customized pure hues for your brushes when your application is running in 8-bit 256-color mode.

Specifying RGB color

As you learned in chapter 1, color is an attribute of pens, brushes, and fonts. You must specify a color whenever you create a pen or a brush. A color is usually described by specifying the intensities of the red, green, and blue guns of the display hardware. Such a description is called *RGB color*. An intensity value of 0 turns off a gun. A value of 255 sets it to brightest intensity. A GDI call of RGB(0,0,0) produces black. RGB(255,255,255) produces bright white. Because each gun provides a range of 64 different levels of intensity, the RGB() macro can describe $64 \times 64 \times 64 = 262,144$ different colors. Because of hardware limitations, a VGA can display only 16 of these colors at the same time. An SVGA can display any 256 of these 262,144 colors at the same time. An accelerator-based display adapter (such as the Mach 32 series from ATI Technologies, Inc.) can display up to 65,536 colors from the list of 262,144 possible colors that can be described by the RGB() macro.

Dithering is the mixing of pixels of available colors to create an approximation of a color not supported by the display adapter. If you request a 17th color when Windows is running on a 16-color VGA, the GDI attempts to fulfill your request by dithering. However, if you request a 17th color when Windows is running in a 256-color mode on an SVGA, the GDI can satisfy your request by providing a pure hue that conforms exactly to the RGB specifications you have provided. To obtain access to these extra hues, you usually must create your own palette.

As you learned in chapter 1, a *palette* is simply a collection of colors. The default palette is called the system palette. Another name for system palette is hardware palette. When Windows starts, it resets the display adapter in order to obtain a palette of colors suitable for general windowing operations. Your application can use the system palette, but it can also use logical palettes. A *logical palette* is a palette that is defined by your application. Depending on whether Windows is running in 16-color or 256-color mode, the colors you request for your logical palette will be provided as dithered patterns or as pure hues.

Creating and using a logical palette

To create a logical palette you follow four steps. First, your application sets up a data structure that contains a description of the various hues that will be contained in the palette. Second, you call the GDI's CreatePalette() function to create the logical palette. Third, your application calls the GDI's SetClipboardData() function to copy the new palette into the Windows clipboard. Finally, you use Visual Basic's GetData method to copy the palette from the clipboard into your application. The sample application in the next chapter provides working source code to show exactly how this is done.

How to tell the GDI what to do

After you've chosen a drawing surface and selected your drawing tool, you'll want to be able to tell the GDI what to do. You can use your tools to draw shapes, fill areas with color, move bitmaps, manipulate regions, display text, and more.

Shapes

Your application can use pens and brushes to create a variety of shapes. The LineTo() function draws a line from the current pen position to a point you specify as an argument when you call LineTo(). The current pen position can be moved by calling MoveTo(). Your application can use Polyline() to draw a set of connected line segments. You can call Polygon() to draw a closed, multisided polygon which the GDI automatically fills with the current brush color. Similarly, your application can create a rectangle by calling Rectangle(), which the GDI fills with the current brush color. To draw an ellipse or circle, you call Ellipse(). Again, the outline of the shape is drawn using the color, style, and thickness of the current pen, and the interior is filled by the GDI using the current brush.

Bitmaps

A *bitmap* is an array of bits in memory that represents a drawing surface or a rectangular image. Your application can draw on a bitmap in memory just like it can draw in the viewport of the application's window on the display. You can also copy bitmaps from display to memory, from memory to display, and from one location on the display to another location on the display.

Creating a bitmap Before you can use a bitmap you must create it. Before you can create it you usually create a compatible display-context in memory. As you learned in chapter 1, a *compatible display-context* is simply a device-context that refers to a simulated display located in memory. The compatible display-context possesses attributes similar to the display-context of your application's display window. Another name for compatible display-context is memory display-context.

Your application can create a compatible display-context by calling the GDI's CreateCompatibleDC() function. To create a bitmap for this DC you call CreateCompatibleBitmap(). To select the newly created bitmap into the compatible display-context, your application calls SelectObject(). The bitmap is now ready to use as a drawing surface or as a vehicle for moving an image. You'll see plenty of hands-on examples of both later in the book.

Moving a bitmap Your application can move a bitmap (and the image it contains) from one location to another by calling the GDI's BitBlt() function. Other names for moving a bitmap are *blitting* and *bit-blitting*. Blitting is useful for certain types of animation where individual 2D rectangles (so-called actors) are moved.

Using a hidden frame If a bitmap's dimensions are equal to the window's viewport dimensions, the bitmap can be used as a hidden frame. Hidden frames are used for many types of animation. They are also handy for maintaining persistent graphics.

Software-controlled refresh operations As you've already seen in chapter 1, *persistent graphics* are images that are refreshed whenever they are inadvertently damaged or corrupted. For example, when another application's window is moved away and uncovers part of your application's window, you'll want to quickly refresh the affected portion of the viewport so the image looks complete again. By using a compatible display-context to maintain a backup copy of the viewport image in memory, you can use BitBlt() to copy a clean image to the display whenever it's needed.

BitBlt() raster operators The GDI provides a masterful selection of raster operators that you can use with the BitBlt() function. For a thorough discussion, including hands-on examples showing how to implement a transparent bitblt function capable of pasting odd-shaped, multicolored images onto multicolored backgrounds, see the author's other books on animation programming:

- *Visual Basic Animation Programming*, published in 1993 by Windcrest/McGraw-Hill (book no. 4224)
- *C for Windows Animation Programming*, published in 1993 by Windcrest/McGraw-Hill (book no. 4114)

Both books are available through your favorite bookstore, or you can write to the publisher and request the current catalog.

Regions

Regions are rectangular and polygonal areas that have special meaning to the GDI. Two categories of regions are provided by the GDI. They are fill-regions and clipping-regions.

Using a fill-region A *fill-region* is a polygonal, elliptical, or rectangular area that can be filled with a brush. Your application can create a rectangular fill-region by calling CreateRectRgn(). To create a round-cornered rectangular region, call CreateRoundRect(). To create an ellipse-shaped region, your application can call CreateEllipticRgn(). To fill a region, you use the FillRgn() function. The 3D modeling and shading toolkit that is demonstrated later in the book uses CreatePolygonRgn() and FillRgn() to shade each facet that makes up a 3D solid. A region must be selected into the appropriate context by using SelectObject() before it can be used.

Using a clipping-region A *clipping-region* is a rectangular region that is used to clip graphics output. To use a clipping-region, your application first calls CreateRectRgn() to create a region, then SelectClipRgn() to select it as the current clipping-region. Any subsequent graphics output will be clipped at the edges of the region.

Where do you go from here?

Now that you've familiarized yourself with how to choose your drawing surface, how to select your drawing tools, and how to tell the graphics engine what to draw, you're ready to delve into a hands-on session. The next chapter presents a ready-to-build sample application that demonstrates device-independent graphics, autodetect of display resolution and available colors, manipulation of palettes, a nested menu system, and titling.

4
Tutorial:
Windows graphics
programming

This chapter provides a hands-on tutorial that demonstrates all the fundamental skills you learned in the previous three chapters, all of which are needed to develop Windows graphics applications. A User's Guide shows you how to operate the sample application named startup, and Programmer's Guide with detailed explanations to guide you through the source code.

You'll learn how persistent graphics are maintained, how palettes are used, and how the sample application is able to automatically support 2-color, 16-color, and 256-color modes in resolutions from 640 × 480 to 1024 × 768. More important, you'll discover how you can use the program listing as a template for your own graphics applications.

Finally, you'll see how to use a bitmap in a compatible display-context to provide bungle-proof persistent images while your graphics application is running, how to use RGB color to create a dazzling range of dithered color on a VGA running in 16-color mode, and how to display both text and titles.

A user's guide to the sample application

In this section, you'll learn how to use the sample application. However, before you can run the demo you must build it. The program listings for the sample application are presented as FIG. C-1 in Appendix C. The source files are also provided on the companion disk. See Appendix A if you need assistance compiling the program.

Starting the sample application

There are two quick ways to start the sample application. You can start it directly from the Visual Basic editor or you can start it from Windows' Program Manager.

Startup from Visual Basic If you're using Visual Basic to prototype and experiment with the source code, you can run the sample application directly from your editor.

Startup from Windows' Program Manager If you've previously compiled the sample application into an executable, you can start it from Windows' Program Manager. From the Windows desktop, pull down the File menu and select Run. When the dialog box appears, type the full pathname of the program. The full pathname includes the drive letter, directories, subdirectories, filename, and extension of the program you want Program Manager to run. Here is a generic example.

        c:\directory\subdirectory\startup.exe

You should substitute, insert, or delete the directory names shown in the example to accurately reflect your own system, of course. When you select the OK button of the dialog box, the sample application will be launched.

Using the sample application

When the sample application starts up, a splash sign-on notice appears. Choose the OK button to continue.

Four menus are listed on the menu bar of the demo. They are File, Edit, Go, and Use. You can use the File menu to quit the program. The Edit menu contains no active features. You can use the Go menu to explore nested menus, titles and captions, and color palettes. If you select the Use menu, you can investigate the run-time conditions of your system, including display resolution, available colors, memory mode, and Windows version.

You can use either a mouse or the keyboard to operate the sample application. If you're using a mouse, simply point and click. If you're using the keyboard, press Alt to move the focus to the menu bar, then press the appropriate underscored mnemonic key to pull down a menu. Strike U to pull down the Use menu, for example. Then press an item's mnemonic key to select that item from the menu. Striking R, for example, will select the Resolution of display item from the Use menu. Alternatively, you can use the up and down arrow keys to move the highlight bar to the menu item you want, then press Enter to select it.

The Use menu The features that are provided by the Use menu are shown in FIG. 4-1. You'll want to verify the demo's mastery of its environment. You can do this by choosing any of the menu items named Resolution of display, Available colors, Memory mode, or Windows version. The message box shown in FIG. 4-2 appears when you select Resolution of display. The sample application

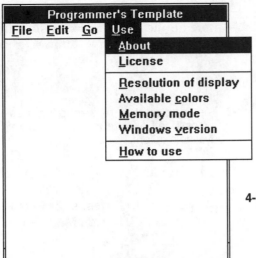

4-1 The sample application startup.frm provides information about the run-time environment.

4-2 The sample application startup.frm displays a message box to report the graphics mode being used by Windows.

supports resolutions ranging from 640 × 480 to 1024 × 768. The message box shown in FIG. 4-3 appears when you select Available colors. The sample application supports 2-color, 16-color, 256-color, and 65,000-color modes.

If you select Memory mode from the Use menu, a message box will appear advising you whether Windows is running in real, standard, or enhanced mode. If you select Windows version from the Use menu, a message box appears indicating the version of Windows that is running. The sample application explicitly supports existing versions 3.0 and 3.1. It also anticipates the so-called vaporware versions of 3.2, 3.3, and 4.0. (That code may never have an opportunity to execute, of course.)

4-3 The demo application startup.frm uses a message box to report the number of available colors.

The Go **menu** The features that are provided by the Go menu are shown in FIG. 4-4. If you choose either of the first two menu items, you'll be able to explore nested menuing, as shown in FIG. 4-5.

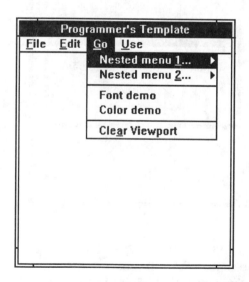

4-4 The sample app startup.frm demonstrates a menu system suitable for graphics applications.

If you select Color demo from the Go menu, you'll delve into the color capabilities of your display adapter, as shown in FIG. 4-6. Two sets of swatches are shown. The top set is the system palette. If your system is running Windows on a VGA in 16-color mode, the system palette shows all 16 hardware colors that are available. The bottom set of swatches shows a range of red shades, which the GDI simulates by dithering. Remember, as you learned in chapter 3, the GDI uses dithering to satisfy your applica-

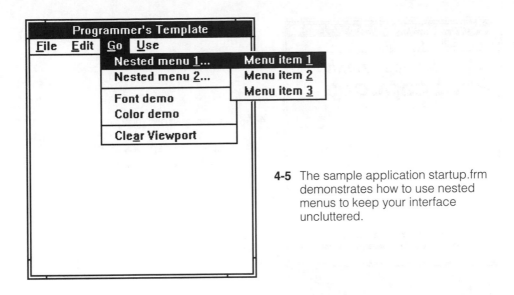

4-5 The sample application startup.frm demonstrates how to use nested menus to keep your interface uncluttered.

4-6 The demo application startup.frm shows you how to use color-palettes. Shown here is a print from a VGA's standard 4-bit 16-color mode using dither patterns. When Windows is running in SVGA 8-bit 256-color mode the custom-color palette is displayed using pure hues instead of dithered colors.

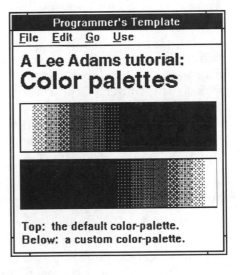

tion's requests for colors not available on the display adapter. On the other hand, if your system is running Windows on an SVGA in 256-color mode, the top set of swatches in FIG. 4-6 shows only the first 16 colors of the 20 that are being used by Windows for general windowing operations. The bottom set of swatches shows a range of red shades, which the GDI provides as custom-defined pure hues from 0% brightness to 100% brightness.

If you select Font demo from the Go menu, you'll be presented with the image shown in FIG. 4-7. If you're using Windows 3.1 or higher, the title might be displayed using the Arial font. If you're still using Windows 3.0, the Helv font may be used.

Programmer's template

File Edit Go Use

A Lee Adams tutorial:

Font captions

The titles use sizes 16 and 24.
The captions use the default system font.

4-7 The demo application startup.frm
shows you how to select and use fonts
for titles and captions in your
applications.

Persistent graphics You'll want to satisfy yourself that the sample application supports persistent graphics. First, choose Color demo from the Go menu. Then place the mouse cursor on the menu bar and drag the window until part of it is past the edge of the screen. When you move the window back to the center of the screen, you'll see how the demo refreshes the viewport image. You'll also want to start another application and use it to partially cover the window of the sample application. When you uncover the sample application, you'll see how the demo quickly refreshes the corrupted portion of its viewport.

Quitting the sample application

To quit the sample application, choose Exit from the File menu. A message box will appear, as shown in FIG. 4-8, providing you with an opportunity to confirm or cancel your request. (You'll remember from chapter 2 how important it is to protect the user from inadvertent actions.)

A programmer's guide to the sample application

This section provides a description of how the source code works. The discussion occasionally refers to line numbers. These line numbers correspond to source code in the program listings presented in FIG. C-1 in Appendix C. For guidance on building the sample application, see the notes in Appendix A.

The source files for the sample application are also provided as st*.* on the companion disk.

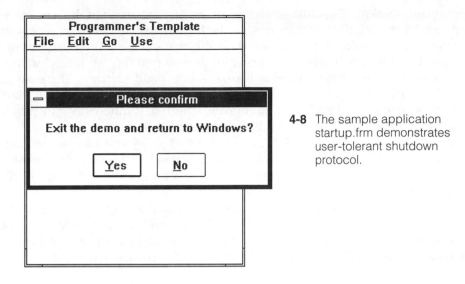

4-8 The sample application startup.frm demonstrates user-tolerant shutdown protocol.

How the global module works

The global module, stglobal.bas, declares a set of constants and variables that are visible throughout the project. This module also declares Windows API functions that might be called at run-time. This source listing is generously commented to make it easy for you to understand the purpose of each line of code. The code at lines 0075 through 0081, for example, declares variables that are used to support the hidden backup bitmap that is used to refresh the display window, thereby providing persistent graphics. The code at lines 0083 through 0099 declares structures and variables that are used to support 256-color palette operations in the sample application. The constants that are defined at lines 0101 through 0127 are convenient symbols for values that are needed to call functions resident in the Windows API. The declarations for these external functions are provided at lines 0129 through 0203.

How the startup module works

The startup module, stmain.bas, contains a function named Main() that is called when the application starts running. You'll want to note how the code at lines 0035 through 0038 initializes some run-time tokens to either True or False. Next, the code at 0039 through 0046 examines the graphics adapter capabilities. It stores these technical specifications for later use. Then the code at lines 0047 through 0050 determines the run-time memory mode (enhanced or standard) and the version of Windows.

The block of code at lines 0051 through 0091 plays an important role in ensuring device-independent graphics. Notice how the code adjusts the size of the application's window by a few pixels, depending on the resolution of the display. This adjustment is necessary because of differences in font height in different screen modes. If the font in the window's caption bar is one pixel taller, for example, then Windows makes the application's caption bar one pixel higher in order to accommodate the font, but this means that the application's client area is one pixel shorter. The code at lines 0051 through 0091 ensures that the sample application uses a standard-size viewport (client area), no matter whether Windows is running in 640 × 480, 800 × 600, or 1024 × 768 resolution.

Next, the code at lines 0092 through 0096 displays an interactive message box. The MB_OKCANCEL token produces two buttons on the message box: OK and Cancel. Line 0094 inspects the user's selection and line 0095 terminates the application if the user chose Cancel.

You should pay careful attention to the code at lines 0097 through 0113, where the application's window is initialized. The code is generously sprinkled with comments so you can understand the purpose of each statement. Finally, the code at lines 0115 through 0119 checks for the presence of a mouse.

How the form module works

The form module, startup.frm, contains the script for the application's menu system, the functions that are called for various menu item selections, and a set of core functions that provide housekeeping functions and graphics output. You want to firmly grasp how this file works so you'll be prepared for the advanced sample applications later in the book.

The script for the menu system is located at lines 0001 through 0139. This script is embedded in every .frm listing by Visual Basic versions 2.0 and newer. If you're using Visual Basic version 1.0, you can refer to the script as you use Visual Basic's menu design window to specify the menu system for the sample application. The attributes of the application's window (or form) are specified at lines 0003 through 0014. If you're using version 2.0 or 3.0 of Visual Basic, then you can simply load and run the source files on the companion disk (or else key-enter the listings exactly as presented in FIG. C-1 in Appendix C).

The functions that are named with the IDM_ prefix are activated whenever the user makes a selection from the application's menu system. You'll want to note how the IDM menu ID constants are used here. If you activate the Visual Basic menu design window, you'll see how the menu ID constants are attached to the application's menu system. Visual Basic appends the _Click() suffix to create a name for the function that it will call whenever the menu item is selected. For example, note the code at lines 0212 through 0214. This Sub function is called whenever the user selects About from the Using menu.

The Sub function at line 0308 performs some general housekeeping chores and then displays the font titling example. You should walk through the code at lines 0308 through 0339. It shows how to properly set up before using text and how to tidy up afterwards.

Also of interest is the code at line 0338, which copies the new viewport image to the hidden bitmap. The hidden bitmap now contains a pristine image ready to refresh the viewport if the application's window is moved or uncovered.

The Sub function at line 0344 provides a demonstration of palette manipulation. This block adheres to the same general coding style just described. You'll want to note in particular the block of code at lines 0371 through 0408, which creates and displays a palette of pure hues if Windows is running in 256-color mode. Remember, the structure named palette was created at lines 0086 through 0097 in the global module, stglobal.bas. The For...Next loop at lines 0378 through 0384 initializes the structure with values corresponding to the RGB components of the palette colors. Line 0385 calls the GDI's CreatePalette() function to create the palette. Line 0390 uses Visual Basic's Clipboard.Clear method to clear the Clipboard, then line 0391 calls the GDI's OpenClipboard() function. The newly created palette is copied into the Clipboard by the call to the GDI's SetClipboardData() function at line 0396. Line 0397 closes the Clipboard. The palette becomes active when line 0402 uses Visual Basic's GetData method to copy the palette from the Clipboard into the application.

The Sub function at line 0252 fires whenever the user wants to ascertain the display resolution. You can see how the code uses nested If...End If blocks to enforce a system of machine reasoning that will deduce the correct resolution.

The function at line 0227 fires whenever the user wants to discover the number of available colors. Note again how machine reasoning using nested If...End If blocks ensure that the software arrives at the correct answer.

The Sub function at line 0551 fires when the user wants to know the run-time memory mode. As you'll remember from earlier in this chapter, the startup code fetches a value by calling GetWinFlags() at line 0048 in stmain.bas. The If...End If statements at lines 0554 and 0559 use the And operator to isolate bits, thereby detecting the memory mode that Windows is using.

The function at line 0586 fires when the user wants to know what version of Windows is running. By carefully manipulating and inspecting the value of a variable named WindowsVersion, the code can discern the version. An earlier call to GetVersion() at line 0050 in stmain.bas loaded WindowsVersion with a value to be inspected.

Persistent graphics The Sub function at line 0182 is activated whenever Windows advises the application that the client area must be refreshed. This function must be named Form_Paint() in order to ensure it is automatically called at run-time. The call to zCopyToDisplay at line 0183 simply copies the contents of the backup page to the display window. This event will occur if the window is uncovered or moved. Code inside zCopyToDisplay checks to ensure that a hidden bitmap was successfully created at startup before attempting to copy a clean image to the viewport.

Graceful shutdown The function at line 0285 fires if the application is about to be shut down. The If...End If block at lines 0290 through 0294 ensures that the hidden bitmap is deselected from the memory display-context and deleted from memory. The call to DeleteDC() at line 0293 releases the memory display-context.

Resizing The Sub function at line 0189 fires whenever the user attempts to resize, minimize, or maximize the application's window. This block of code is provided as an example. It is not necessary for the successful operation of this particular application, but the animation samples later in the book rely on a standard-size window.

The core functions Many of the remaining functions the .frm module listing provide the core functions of the application. The zInitFrame() function at line 0656 creates the hidden frame that is used to refresh the display window whenever the viewport becomes corrupted. The functions at lines 0619 and 0626 clear the display window and the hidden frame (the hidden bitmap used for persistent graphics). In both functions, a call to the GDI's PatBlt() function is the simplest and fastest way to set the viewport to white.

The two functions at lines 0636 and 0646 copy the bitmap from the hidden frame to the display window and vice versa. In each case, a call to BitBlt() copies the image. The memory display-context, hFrameDC, that is used by the hidden bitmap is already in effect. It was created at startup by the statement at line 0661.

Customizing the demo

The sample demo application can serve as a prototype for more advanced graphics software you might want to build. Here are a few tips on adapting the code for your own use. (Remember to read the License, provided in FIG. 7 in the introduction, "Getting the most from this book.")

To change the application's title as it appears on the caption bar of the window, change line 0102 in the stmain.bas startup module.

To add or delete menu items, make the appropriate changes using Visual Basic's menu design window. You'll need to define additional menu ID constants if you're adding new menu items, of course. You'll then have to add code to the appropriate _Click() functions that Visual Basic associates with the menu selections.

Sample applications elsewhere in the book support VGA, SVGA, accelerator-based, and coprocessor-based display adapters running in resolutions from 640 × 480 to 1024 × 768 and using 2-color and 16-color. To upgrade these applications to explicitly support 256-colors modes, simply paste in the palette-ready code found at lines 0370 through 0408 in the startup.frm module. Don't forget the structure definition at lines 0083 through 0099 in the stglobal.bas global module. For additional general programming guidance, you might want to consider some of the author's other books:

- *Visual Basic Animation Programming*, Windcrest/McGraw-Hill, 1993 (4224)
- *C for Windows Animation Programming*, Windcrest/McGraw-Hill, 1993 (4114)
- *High-Performance C Graphics Programming for Windows*, Windcrest /McGraw-Hill (4103)

All three books are available through your favorite bookstore, or you can write to the publisher and request the current catalog.

Where do you go from here?

Now that you've practiced some of the fundamental programming skills required for developing graphics applications for Windows, you're ready to explore more advanced techniques. Where you go from here depends on your needs. The next section in the book is Part Two, "3D programming." It teaches you how to display a 3D scene, how to illuminate and shade surfaces, and how to create 3D entities like boxes, spheres, cylinders, wedges, cones, and others. If you prefer instead to use the book's 3D toolset as a black box, you can go right ahead and jump forward to Part Three "Animation programming." You're the one in the driver's seat. The book is designed to accommodate whatever learning style you choose to use.

Part Two

3D programming

Your task in Part Two is to prepare yourself for 3D programming in Windows. You want to acquire the fundamental skills required for 3D modeling and rendering. You want to become confident that your knowledge and understanding of 3D scenes and the entities they contain will carry you through the advanced animation and simulation tutorials later in the book.

In Part Two of the book you'll learn about view geometry, rendering, modeling, hidden-surface removal, and more. Chapter 5, "Concepts and terms," is your introduction to the buzzwords used by 3D programmers. In chapter 6, "Getting started with view geometry," you'll learn how to display a 3D scene in the viewport of your application's window. In chapter 7, "Getting started with rendering," you'll see how to illuminate and shade surfaces. In chapter 8, "Getting started with modeling," you'll discover how to create various 3D entities, including boxes, spheres, cylinders, cones, wedges, and others. You'll also learn how hierarchical modeling can build complex assemblies from groups of entities. In chapter 9, a hands-on tutorial shows you how to put your new 3D skills to work. A sample application demonstrates 3D entities in wire-frame and fully-shaded modes. You can use this 3D sampler to experiment with camera position, lighting, and other attributes of the modeling environment.

Before you begin to delve into the fundamental skills of 3D programming for Windows, you want to acquaint yourself with some of the words and phrases that are used by experienced 3D programmers. The next chapter, "Concepts and terms," provides you with the background knowledge you need to get started.

5
Concepts and terms

This chapter introduces some basic concepts and terms you'll be using while you explore Part Two, "3D programming." You'll want to know the technical words used in the next four chapters, in order to use 3D graphics in your Windows applications. In this chapter, you'll read about the concepts and terms that describe 3D programming for Windows. You'll become familiar with what each concept means, and you'll learn about the role each concept plays in the overall paradigm of 3D programming.

Defining concepts and terms

3D The term *3D* is an acronym for three-dimensional. A 3D entity possesses the three dimensions of width, height, and depth.

3D modeling *3D modeling* refers to the creation of computer images that accurately represent the shapes of three-dimensional objects.

Rendering *Rendering* refers to the methods used to add color, shading, brightness, texture, and other surface attributes to the entities produced by the 3D modeling process.

View geometry *View geometry* refers to the calculations, the mathematics, and the conceptual model that are used to manipulate and display a 3D scene. View geometry is concerned with the volume of 3D space that is visible to the camera. It also pertains to the location and orientation of the camera. View geometry is distinct from modeling geometry.

Modeling geometry *Modeling geometry* refers to the calculations and mathematics that are used to create individual 3D entities such as boxes, spheres, cylinders, cones, wedges, curved surfaces, and others. Modeling geometry is distinct from rendering geometry.

Rendering geometry *Rendering geometry* refers to the calculations and mathematics that are used to calculate illumination values for the 3D entities in a 3D scene. Rendering geometry is also used to determine if some entities obscure other entities from view.

3D entities A *3D entity* is a simple solid like a box (called a *parallelepiped* by 3D programmers), a sphere, a cylinder, a cone, and others. 3D entities are also called *primitives* and *subobjects*. 3D primitives are built from facets, half-edges, and vertices.

Facets, half-edges, and vertices *Facets* are flat polygons that are used to model the exterior surface of a 3D primitive. This paradigm is called *boundary representation (b-rep) modeling.* A box, for example, can be built from six facets. Each edge of a facet is called a *half-edge.* When the half-edges of two facets abut one another, the common border that results is called an *edge. Vertices* are corners. A four-sided facet possesses four vertices. A 3D primitive like a box possesses eight vertices.

3D transformations *3D transformations* are manipulations in 3D space. A 3D primitive is subjected to various transformations before it is displayed as part of a 3D scene. The aggregate of these transformations is called the *3D transformation sequence.* Some 3D programmers call it the *visualization pipeline.*

3D space *3D space* refers to a volume of space. Any unique location (point) in 3D space can be described by its XYZ coordinates. The center of the space volume is called the *origin.* It is usually described as 0,0,0. The 3D transformation sequence contains different types of 3D space (and 2D space as well), known as *coordinate systems.* In a coordinate system, the X-coordinate refers to the left-right location of a point. The Y-coordinate refers to the up-down location. The Z-coordinate refers to the near-far location.

3D transformation sequence The *3D transformation sequence* consists of object coordinates, structure coordinates, world coordinates, camera coordinates, image-plane coordinates, and raster coordinates. Each 3D entity must be transformed through each of these coordinate systems before it is displayed in the application's window.

Object coordinates *Object coordinates* are 3D XYZ coordinates that define the fundamental shape and size of a 3D primitive.

Structure coordinates *Structure coordinates* are 3D XYZ coordinates that describe a 3D primitive as part of a group of primitives that together form an assembly (a structure). A 3D representation of a robotic arm, for example, is a 3D structure that might be assembled by using primitives such as cylinders, wedges, and cones. A structure is subsequently treated as if it were a single 3D primitive during further transformations.

World coordinates   *World coordinates* are 3D XYZ coordinates that describe a 3D primitive (or structure) at a specific location and orientation in the 3D world being used by the application. When a 3D primitive is moved to a specific location, it is called *translation*. When a 3D primitive is twisted to a specific orientation, it is called *rotation*.

Camera coordinates   *Camera coordinates* are 3D XYZ coordinates that describe the location and orientation of a 3D entity relative to the camera's viewpoint. Camera coordinates describe how the entity appears to the camera.

Image-plane coordinates   *Image-plane coordinates* are 2D XY coordinates that represent how a 3D entity would appear to the camera if a two-dimensional *image-plane* (a flat viewing surface) were inserted between the camera and the entity. Image-plane coordinates are device-independent because they can fall within any range of values. Moving the image-plane farther from the camera makes the image occupy a larger area on the image-plane, and vice versa.

Raster coordinates   *Raster coordinates* are 2D XY coordinates that result when image-plane coordinates are scaled to fit the application's viewport. Some 3D programmers refer to raster coordinates as *display coordinates*. Raster coordinates are device-dependent because they fit a specific viewport.

View-volume   The *view-volume* usually means the 3D perspective view-volume. This is the volume of space that is visible to the camera. Other types of view-volumes are the canonical view-volume and the rectangular view-volume. Another name for canonical view-volume is *normalized 3D perspective view-volume*, which results when the view-volume is scaled down to the –1 to +1 range. The rectangular view-volume is a view-volume that has been especially distorted in order to simplify the calculations for hidden-surface removal in 3D scenes.

Hidden-surface removal   3D programmers often use *hidden-surface removal* as a generic concept to refer both to individual 3D primitives and to complex 3D scenes. Two types of hidden-surface removal are demonstrated by the sample applications in this book. They are back-face culling and Z-buffer depth-sorting.

Back-face culling   *Back-face culling* is a method of hidden-surface removal that is used to process individual 3D entities. Back-face culling refers to algorithms that detect and discard facets that face away from the camera. Remember, each 3D solid in a scene is built from a set of facets. Any facet that is facing backward cannot be seen from the camera's viewpoint. Image a sphere, for example. Backward-facing facets on the sphere's surface are located on the portion of the sphere facing away from the camera. These facets cannot be seen.

Z-buffer depth-sorting *Z-buffer depth-sorting* is a method of hidden-surface removal that is used to process complex 3D scenes containing a number of individual 3D primitives. The Z-coordinates of each facet indicate its distance (depth) from the camera. By carefully sorting all the Z-values in a scene, the software can ensure that only the nearest facets are drawn. Because the nearest facets will obscure any facets farther from the camera, the Z-buffer method is a satisfactory approximation of how human vision works in the real world.

Shading *Shading* refers to color that is applied to a facet as a result of the facet's *brightness* (the level of illumination exhibited by the facet). Some 3D programmers use the word *rendering* to mean shading. The location of the light-source directly affects the shading of each entity in a 3D scene.

Virtual luminance *Virtual luminance* describes how bright a facet would appear in the real world. Virtual luminance is expressed as a percentage from 0% (cloaked in complete darkness) to 100% (the brightest possible). After a 3D rendering function has calculated the virtual luminance of a facet, the resulting value must be converted to an intensity suitable for RGB display. This conversion is necessary for most display hardware because RGB displays do not begin to produce a visible pixel until a gun's intensity reaches 35. Remember, you learned in chapter 3 that the Windows API specifies an intensity range of 0 to 255 for RGB displays. This means that the serviceable range of the guns is actually 35 to 255, and the guns are more sensitive at the higher ranges.

Hierarchical modeling *Hierarchical modeling* refers to 3D modeling algorithms that build complex 3D objects by combining primitives. These complex objects are called *structures, assemblies, subassemblies,* or *hierarchies.* A structure can contain flexible joints and pivot-points if the XYZ coordinates of some primitives (the progeny) are described as offsets from other primitives (the parents) in the same structure. Such a pivoting structure is called an *articulated entity.*

Where do you go from here?

Now that you've familiarized yourself with some of the basic concepts and terms used in 3D programming for Windows, you're ready to start learning the fundamental skills. The next chapter, "Getting started with view geometry," teaches you how to display a 3D scene in the viewport of your application's window.

6

Getting started
with view geometry

This chapter teaches you how to use view geometry to display a 3D scene in the viewport of your application's window. It discusses concepts such as transformations, view-volumes, rendering methods, and hidden-surface removal. You'll learn about the various coordinate systems that make up the 3D visualization pipeline, as well as understanding 3D view-volumes and their importance to clipping operations and hidden-surface removal. You'll also become aware of the different rendering methods available to 3D programmers.

B-rep modeling is covered, and you'll find out about primitives, facets, half-edges, and Euler operations. You'll see how the 3D visualization pipeline is built from a series of coordinate systems, including object, structure, world, camera, image-plane, and raster coordinates. You'll learn about yaw, roll, and pitch—and you'll discover translation, rotation, and extrusion. You'll find out how to normalize and manipulate your camera's view-volume in order to simplify the task of hidden-surface removal in 3D scenes.

Different shading methods like flat shading, color interpolation shading, and normal-vector interpolation shading are discussed. You'll investigate two methods for hidden-surface removal, back-face culling and z-buffer depth-sorting. The 3D knowledge you'll acquire in this chapter will provide you with the background you need to proceed to the more advanced 3D material in the book.

A 3D primer

3D images can supercharge your Windows application development. Effective use of 3D modeling and rendering techniques can add realism and excitement to your software, especially if it's an application that supports animation, visualization, or simulation. An understanding of 3D geometry and the ability to use a 3D library are assets for any aspiring Windows programmer.

This book provides a 3D tool set that you can use with your own application development. More important, however, the 3D functions provided in Appendix B are extensible. This means you can readily adapt them to meet your own specialized requirements—and you can add more features to the existing source code. In its current implementation, the book's 3D toolkit provides you with a versatile environment for b-rep modeling. It offers advanced features such as back-face culling, z-buffer depth-sorting, a moveable light-source, and a ready-to-use library of pre-built solids like boxes, spheres, half-spheres, cylinders, half-cylinders, cones, wedges, and curved surfaces. It is a powerful b-rep modeling tool.

B-rep modeling

B-rep is an acronym for *boundary representation*. A b-rep model portrays a 3D entity by rendering its outer surface. You can think of this outer surface as the exterior boundaries of the entity—hence the phrase *boundary representation*. Although other methods of 3D modeling are available, b-rep modeling is fast, accurate, and versatile. It's the most popular 3D paradigm in use today, and it's especially well-suited to the graphics capabilities of the Windows Graphics Device Interface (GDI). The GDI offers four tools particularly useful for 3D programming. These tools are:

- The RGB() macro.
- Dithering.
- The CreateSolidBrush() function.
- The CreatePolygonRgn() function.

The RGB() macro provides precise, individual control over the RGB guns found in most display hardware. This makes it easy to specify color during the 3D illumination and rendering processes. The GDI's built-in dithering capabilities mean that almost any shade of any color can be simulated, even when Windows is running in a 16-color VGA mode. As you learned in chapter 3, the CreateSolidBrush() function provides an efficient way to apply areas of color to an image. The CreatePolygonRgn() function is especially useful for defining a region (the facet) to be filled with color by the brush.

In order to display a 3D scene using b-rep modeling, you need to become familiar with three types of calculations:

- view geometry
- modeling geometry
- rendering geometry

View geometry deals with an entire 3D scene. Modeling geometry deals with individual 3D entities. Rendering geometry deals with subjective appearance.

View geometry

As mentioned in chapter 6, view geometry refers to the calculations used to manipulate and display an entire 3D scene. View geometry is concerned with the volume of 3D space that is visible to the camera. It deals with the location and orientation of the camera.

Modeling geometry

As you learned in chapter 5, modeling geometry is used to create individual 3D primitives.

Primitives A *3D primitive* is a simple solid—like a parallelepiped, a sphere, a cylinder, a cone, a wedge, and others. 3D primitives are also called entities and subobjects. 3D primitives are built from facets, half-edges, and vertices.

Facets, half-edges, and vertices *Facets* are flat polygons. They are two-dimensional surfaces. Facets are used to model the exterior surface of a 3D primitive. As you've already learned, this paradigm is called boundary representation (b-rep) modeling. A box, for example, can be built from six facets. Each edge of a facet is called a *half-edge*. Half-edges, like facets, cannot exist in the real world, of course, because facets have no thickness. When the half-edges of two facets abut one another on a 3D model, the common border that results is called an *edge*. Unlike half-edges, edges do exist in the real world. Vertices are corners. A four-sided facet possesses four vertices. A 3D primitive like a box possesses eight vertices. In addition to facets, half-edges, and vertices, a 3D primitive can be further defined by Euler operations.

Euler operations Euler operations simulate the way things work in the real world. A Euler operator transforms a 3D entity by adding or deleting facets, edges, half-edges, and vertices. Joining, intersection, and subtraction are examples of Euler operators. Joining means attaching two 3D primitives to each other. Think of it as gluing together two entities. Intersection refers to a common volume of space occupied by two primitives. Think of it as pouring two entities into a mold. Subtraction means the void occupying a common volume of space occupied by two primitives. Think of it as drilling a hole in an entity. Euler operations are named after the 18th-century mathematician Leonard Euler, who is credited with originating a formula useful for describing surfaces.

Rendering geometry

As you discovered in the previous chapter, rendering geometry manipulates the subjective appearance of a 3D scene. Rendering geometry also concerns the calculations used to infer an illumination value for each facet in a scene. Rendering geometry usually relies upon an illumination model, which provides a paradigm to explain how light and surfaces act in their 3D environment. As you'll discover later in this chapter, different illumination models (and rendering geometry) are preferred by different programmers. The choices include flat shading, color interpolation shading, normal-vector interpolation shading, ray-tracing, and others.

3D transformations

Before a primitive can be displayed as part of a 3D scene in the viewport of your application's window, it must be transformed. 3D transformations are manipulations in 3D space. The sum of the transformations is the 3D transformation sequence. Another name for 3D transformation sequence is the visualization pipeline.

3D space is a specific volume of space. Any location in 3D space can be described by its XYZ coordinates relative to the origin. The origin is the center of the volume, usually defined as XYZ coordinates 0,0,0. The 3D transformation sequence contains different types of 3D space. Each type of 3D space possesses its own coordinate system. In a three-dimensional coordinate system, the X-coordinate refers to left-right location. The Y-coordinate refers to up-down location. The Z-coordinate refers to near-far location. In a two-dimensional coordinate system, the X-coordinate refers to left-right location and the Y-coordinate refers to up-down location.

3D transformation sequence

As shown in FIG. 6-1, a typical 3D transformation sequence consists of six coordinates:

- object
- structure
- world
- camera
- image-plane
- raster

A 3D primitive must be transformed through each of these coordinate systems before it can be displayed in your application's window. Each coordinate system represents a different form of 3D space. Object coordinates, for example, represent object-space.

Object coordinates Object coordinates are XYZ coordinates that define the fundamental shape and size of a 3D primitive such as a box, sphere, cylinder, cone, wedge, and others. Object coordinates describe object-space.

Structure coordinates Structure coordinates are XYZ coordinates that describe a primitive in its role as part of a group of primitives that form a

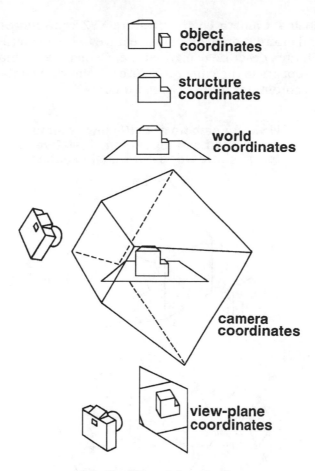

6-1 The 3D modeling pipeline.

larger structure. Structure coordinates describe structure-space. As you learned in the previous chapter, structure coordinates are used in hierarchical operations. A structure is treated as a single 3D primitive during subsequent transformations. Hierarchical modeling can build complex 3D solids by attaching primitives to each other. These complex solids are called structures, assemblies, subassemblies, or hierarchies. A hierarchical structure can contain flexible joints. This is possible because the XYZ coordinates of some primitives (progeny) are defined as offsets relative to other primitives (parents) residing in the same structure. Structures with pivoting or jointed sections are called *articulated entities*.

World coordinates World coordinates are XYZ coordinates that describe a primitive (or a structure) at a specific location and orientation in the 3D world being used by the application. World coordinates describe world-space. When a 3D entity is moved to a specific location in world-space, it is called translation. When a primitive is twisted to a specific orientation in world-space, it is called rotation.

Camera coordinates Camera coordinates are XYZ coordinates that define the location and orientation of an entity relative to the camera's viewpoint. Camera coordinates describe camera-space. Camera coordinates indicate how an entity appears to the camera. Figure 6-2 shows the relationship between camera coordinates and world coordinates.

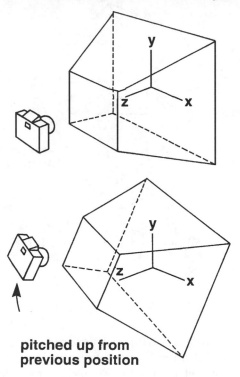

How the camera and 3D view-volume are rotated and repositioned relative to the static world-coordinate system

pitched up from previous position

6-2 The relationship between the XYZ world coordinate system and the 3D view-volume.

Image-plane coordinates Image-plane coordinates are XY coordinates that represent how a 3D entity would appear to the camera if a two-dimensional image-plane were inserted between the camera and the entity. Image-plane coordinates describe image-space. Image-plane coordinates are device-independent because they can fall within any range of values. Moving the image-plane farther from the camera makes the image occupy a larger area on the image-plane, and vice versa. As shown in FIG. 6-1, another way of saying image-plane coordinates is view-plane coordinates.

Raster coordinates Raster coordinates are XY coordinates that result when image-plane coordinates are scaled to fit the application's viewport. Raster

coordinates describe display-space. Some programmers refer to raster coordinates as display coordinates. Raster coordinates are device-dependent
because they fit a specific viewport. Raster coordinates are also called
screen coordinates.

Right-hand coordinate system

In most 3D modeling systems, every set of XYZ coordinates for object-
space, structure-space, world-space, and camera-space is expressed using the right-hand coordinate system, which is the most widely used 3D
coordinate system. It specifies +Z as nearer to the camera and –Z as farther from the camera, relative to the 0,0,0 origin. The right-hand coordinate system specifies +X as right and –X as left. It specifies +Y as up and
–Y as down.

Why is it called the right-hand coordinate system? Hold your right
hand up, with your flattened palm towards your face and your fingers
pointing upward. Extend your thumb out to the right. Your index finger
should be pointing up. Bend your middle finger so it points directly at your
face. Curl the remaining two fingers in towards your palm. You've just created your own personal right-hand coordinate system. Your thumb indicates +X; your index finger indicates +Y; and your middle finger indicates
+Z. The center of your palm is the 0,0,0 origin, of course.

Yaw, roll, and pitch

You can think of each coordinate system in the 3D visualization pipeline
as coexisting with a spherical coordinate system. An XYZ coordinate system and its companion spherical coordinate system share the same 3D
space. Whereas an XYZ coordinate system uses distance to describe a 3D
entity, a spherical coordinate system uses angles. These angles are yaw,
roll, and pitch. Yaw refers to compass headings. Roll means tilting left or
right. Pitch means tilting forward or back. Together, an XYZ coordinate
system and a spherical coordinate system can define a 3D entity's location
and orientation in 3D space. The XYZ coordinate system can be used to
translate (move) the entity to a particular location. The spherical coordinate system can then be used to rotate (spin) the entity into a particular
orientation.

3D view-volumes

A 3D view-volume is the volume of 3D space that is visible to the camera.
Three types of view-volumes are used by the 3D functions in this book:

- 3D perspective view-volume
- normalized 3D perspective view-volume
- rectangular view-volume

3D perspective view-volume

A 3D perspective view-volume is shown in FIG. 6-3. It is simply a truncated right-angle pyramid whose vertex is located at the camera lens. Any 3D entities located outside the view-volume cannot be seen by the camera. The conceptual representation in FIG. 6-3 also shows the near and far clipping-planes.

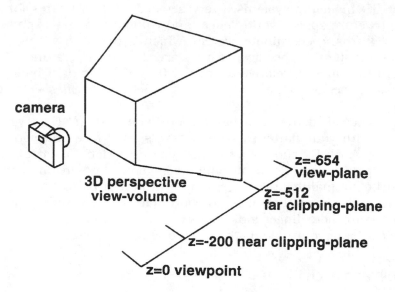

6-3 The 3D perspective view-volume.

Near and far clipping-planes The near and far clipping-planes are optionally set by the programmer in order to discard 3D entities located too far from or too near to the camera. The far clipping-plane ensures that the 3D formulas do not waste time rendering entities so distant they will not occupy more than a single pixel. The near clipping-plane ensures that entities located too near the camera will be discarded. Such entities would appear distorted if rendered.

Normalized 3D perspective view-volume

A normalized 3D perspective view-volume is simply a 3D perspective view-volume that has been scaled to fit within a range of –1 to +1. A simplified conceptual representation is shown in FIG. 6-4.

Canonical view-volume Another name for normalized 3D perspective view-volume is *canonical view-volume*. In a canonical view-volume, Z-values range from 0 to –1, X-values range from –1 to +1, and Y-values range from –1 to +1. Using a canonical view-volume simplifies some of the mathematics required to clip 3D facets that intersect the top, bottom, right, or left sides of the view-volume.

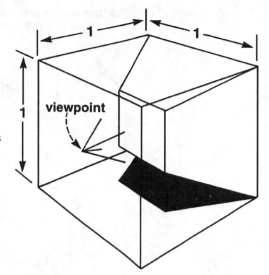

6-4 How the normalized 3D perspective view-volume is derived.

How to scale down to fit a normalized view-volume The illustration in FIG. 6-5 depicts a normalized 3D perspective view-volume. Compare this with the standard 3D perspective view-volume in FIG. 6-3. You'll notice, for example, how the far clipping-plane has been scaled down from –512 to –1. The distance of the near clipping-plane from the camera has been scaled from –200 to –0.390625. The original scale of the 3D perspective view-volume in FIG. 6-3 was selected because it produces a 3D world convenient for the sample applications presented later in the book. As FIG. 6-6 shows, the image-plane possesses the same dimensions as the viewport used by the

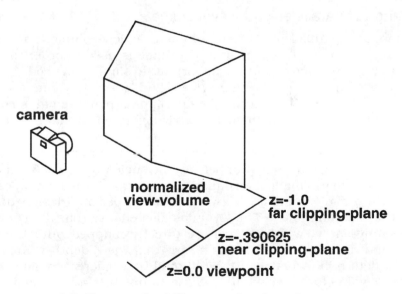

6-5 The normalized 3D perspective view volume.

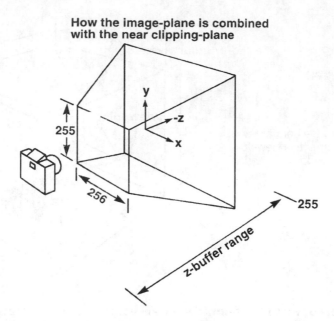

**How the image-plane is combined
with the near clipping-plane**

6-6 A 3D perspective view-volume suitable for use with Z-buffer hidden-surface removal.

sample applications. This convenient side-effect simplifies the toolkit's display functions. The mathematical formulas that scale the 3D perspective view-volume down to a canonical view-volume are discussed in chapter 9 when the 3D source code is analyzed.

Rectangular parallelepiped view-volume

A rectangular parallelepiped view-volume is a view-volume that has been especially distorted. This type of view-volume is used in order to simplify the clipping functions and, more important, to simplify the code needed to operate a Z-buffer depth-sorting system (hidden-surface removal for the entire scene). As FIG. 6-7 shows, the far clipping-plane remains constant, but the near clipping-plane is deliberately deformed so that a rectangular box is created.

Why use a rectangular parallelepiped view-volume? A rectangular view-volume introduces a number of efficiencies into the 3D modeling pipeline. The mathematical formulas used to transform a canonical view-volume into a rectangular view-volume are especially designed to preserve the Z depth-values. The formulas also ensure that the contents of the rectangular view-volume can be directly mapped onto the image-plane (and the 2D viewport). This means that the Z depth-values can be used to determine whether a facet should be rendered or not. Only the nearest Z-value for any particular XY location should be drawn because it will necessarily obscure the entities located behind it.

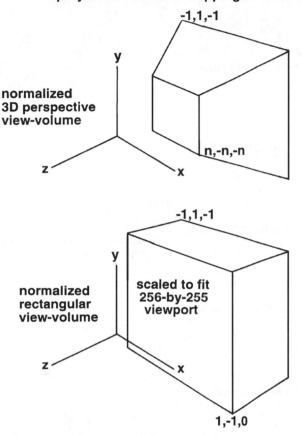

How a perspective view-volume is transformed into a rectangular view-volume in order to simplify calculations for clipping of 3D entities

-1,1,-1

y

normalized 3D perspective view-volume

z   x

n,-n,-n

-1,1,-1

y

normalized rectangular view-volume

scaled to fit 256-by-255 viewport

z   x

1,-1,0

6-7 Conceptual representation of the transformation from normalized 3D perspective view-volume to a normalized rectangular view-volume that uses parallel projection.

Because the top, bottom, left, and right sides of the view-volume are right angle planes, clipping is simplified. If the X-coordinate of a facet's vertex is greater than +1, for example, then it must be clipped. The value of +1 is a constant that always indicates the right side of the view-volume. Compare this situation with the 3D perspective view-volume shown in the top part of FIG. 6-7. Complex and onerous calculations are required to compute the clipping values at various points along the right side of a 3D perspective view-volume. Clipping solids is an exercise already fraught with intricacies, as FIG. 6-8 shows. Using a canonical view-volume keeps the math simple and reduces the time required to model and render a scene.

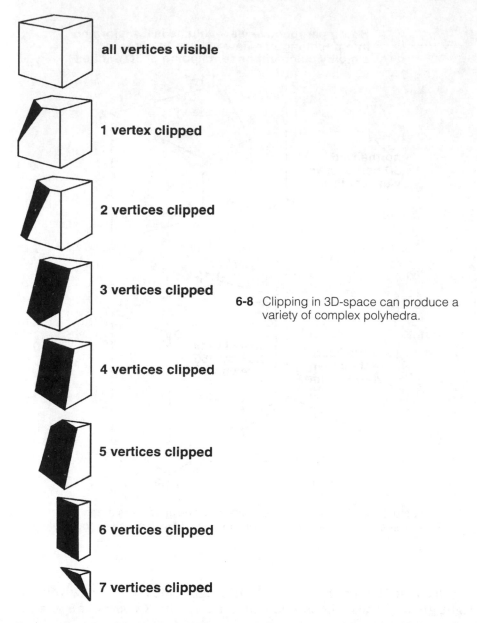

all vertices visible

1 vertex clipped

2 vertices clipped

3 vertices clipped

6-8 Clipping in 3D-space can produce a variety of complex polyhedra.

4 vertices clipped

5 vertices clipped

6 vertices clipped

7 vertices clipped

Rendering methods

The three methods of rendering are wire-frame, solid, and shaded.

Wire-frame mode

Wire-frame models are built using only edges. The software does not attempt to detect or remove hidden surfaces. If a wire-frame model is built using facets, the facets are not shaded but are transparent.

Solid modeling mode

Solid models are built using opaque facets. Hidden surfaces are detected and removed, usually by back-face culling. A solid model appears like it would appear in the real world, except that no attempt is made to shade the model to satisfy existing lighting conditions.

Shaded solids

Shaded models are built using facets that have been shaded according to the intensity of light striking each facet. As mentioned in chapter 5, rendering geometry manipulates the subjective appearance of entities in a 3D scene. It does this by calculating an illumination value for each facet or pixel in a scene. Rendering geometry usually relies upon an illumination model, which is a paradigm explaining how surfaces and illumination are expected to act. Different illumination models are available, including flat shading, color interpolation shading, normal-vector interpolation shading, ray-tracing, and others.

Lambert shading Lambert shading is named after 18th-century mathematician Johann Heinrich Lambert. It is also called constant shading, facet shading, and flat shading. The relationship between the incoming light ray and the surface normal of the facet is used to calculate the brightness of a facet. In mathematical terms, it is called the specific surface normal method.

Gouraud shading Gouraud shading is named after motorcar designer Henri Gouraud. It is also called *smooth shading, color interpolation shading*, and *intensity interpolation shading*. Gouraud shading uses color interpolation (averaging) along scan-lines to smooth the harsh edges between facets. In mathematical terms, it is called the average surface normal method.

Phong shading Phong shading is named after computer science researcher Bui Phong. It is also called *normal-vector interpolation shading*. Phong shading uses the relationships between surface normals, incoming light rays, and lines of sight to produce smooth-shaded surfaces with highlights (specular reflections). In mathematical terms, it is called the individual normal interpolation method.

Ray tracing Ray-tracing algorithms work by following individual paths of reflected light and refracted light through the 3D scene. It is a very time-consuming method, but ray-tracing makes it possible to produce subtle effects like reflections and shadows. In mathematical terms, it is called the *cosine power specular reflection method.*

Hidden-surface removal

As you learned in the previous chapter, hidden-surface removal is essential if you're trying to create 3D images that faithfully represent the real world. Two types of hidden-surface removal are demonstrated by the sample applications in this book. They are back-face culling and Z-buffer depth-sorting. Back-face culling is applied to individual 3D primitives. The Z-buffer depth-sorting method is applied to an entire 3D scene.

Between them, these two types of hidden-surface removal ensure a coherent 3D image. Here's why: first, the Z-buffer depth-sorting method guarantees that entities nearer the camera will obscure entities farther from the camera—just like your visual experiences in the real world. Second, the back-face culling method ensures that portions of an entity whose facets face away from the camera are not seen by the camera—just like your visual experiences in the real world.

Back-face culling

Back-face culling is used to process individual 3D primitives like boxes, spheres, cylinders, cones, wedges, and others. Back-face culling detects and discards facets that face away from the camera (facets that face away from you, the viewer). Because each 3D solid in a scene is built using facets, any facet facing backward cannot be seen from the camera's viewpoint.

The back-face culling algorithm is founded on the standard equation for a plane. The equation is used to test the camera's XYZ location in order to determine on which side of the plane the camera is located. Remember, each facet is a plane. The test is reliable because a 3D programmer using b-rep modeling always describes a facet by the XYZ coordinates of its vertices in counterclockwise order as viewed from outside the solid on whose surface the facet resides. If the standard equation for a plane indicates that the camera is located on the inside of the plane, then the facet is facing away from the camera and is not visible. If the equation indicates that the camera is located on the outside of the plane, then the facet is facing towards the camera and is visible. The mathematical calculations for back-face culling will be discussed in more detail when the 3D source code for the sample application in chapter 9 is analyzed.

Z-buffer depth-sorting

As you learned in the previous chapter, Z-buffer depth-sorting is used to process complex scenes containing numerous 3D primitives. The Z-coordinates of each facet indicate its distance from the camera. This distance is called depth. By sorting the Z-values in a scene, the Z-buffer algorithm can ensure that only the nearest facets are drawn. Because the nearest facets will obscure any facets farther from the camera in a rectangular view-volume as shown in FIG. 6-9, the Z-buffer method is a trustworthy approximation of how human vision works in the real world.

What is a Z-buffer? A Z-buffer is an array of bytes in memory. Each byte corresponds to a pixel on the viewport of your application's window. Each byte in the Z-buffer contains the depth-value (the Z-value of the XYZ

How facets are clipped for display in the 3D viewing-pipeline

discard facet if nearer than near clipping-plane

discard facet if wholly or partially beyond far clipping-plane

discard facet if behind the camera

6-9 Conceptual representation of how the 3D routines clip and cull facets depending on their relationship to the 3D perspective view-volume. As shown here, only portions of facets depicted as solid color will be displayed by the modeling pipeline.

triplet) of the corresponding point in the nearest facet. As each facet is processed by the Z-buffer algorithm, the value of a particular byte is changed if a smaller value (indicating a nearer facet) is discovered. When every point on every facet has been processed, as shown in FIG. 6-10, the Z-buffer will contain the depth-values for only the nearest (visible) points in the scene.

At the same time the algorithm is calculating the depth-values, it is managing a frame-buffer. Like the Z-buffer, the frame-buffer is an array of bytes. Each byte corresponds to a pixel on the viewport of your application's window. Whenever the algorithm writes a depth value to a byte in the Z-buffer, it also writes a color value to the corresponding byte in the frame-buffer. When every point on every facet has been processed by the Z-buffer algorithm, the frame-buffer will contain color values for each pixel on the viewport of your application's window.

Why use a z-buffer? The Z-buffer depth-sorting algorithm is used by most b-rep modeling systems because it is foolproof. No matter how complicated the scene, the Z-buffer depth-sorting method never fails to produce a visually correct image. This is because a Z-buffer uses a pixel-based algorithm where each point being processed corresponds to exactly one pixel on the display. Other hidden-surface methods sometimes use facet-based algorithms. These methods can easily become hamstrung by complicated scenes when they attempt to divide facets into ever-smaller rectangles in a bid to make sense of the scene.

Limitations of a byte-resolution z-buffer As you'll soon learn, the 3D functions provided by the source code in the book use a z-buffer composed of bytes (expressed in Visual Basic as a string that is one character in

A particular scan-line can be located in six different configurations. The software must be smart enough to know which line segments to use when interpolating a point along the scan-line.

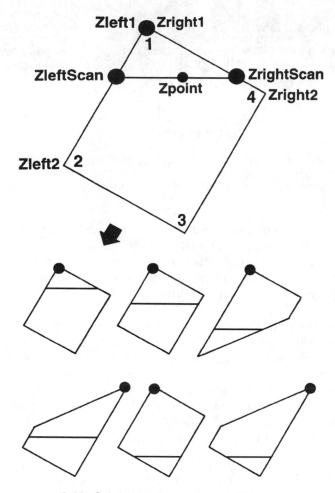

6-10 Subtleties of scan-line analysis.

length). One byte in the Z-buffer corresponds to one pixel on the viewport of the application's window. This arrangement keeps memory requirements small. Because each sample application uses a viewport 256 pixels across by 255 pixels high, a Z-buffer of 65,280 bytes can store the depth-values for all the pixels in the scene. However, a byte can store only 256 different values. This means the resolution of the Z-buffer is limited to a range of 0 to 255. If the 3D world were 512 units deep, for example, the Z-buffer could not differentiate between points differing by only one or two units of depth. In your own application development, you can overcome this limitation by using a Z-buffer composed of integers or floating-point values.

Where do you go from here?

Now that you've learned how view geometry displays a 3D scene in the viewport of your application's window, you're ready to move ahead in 3D programming. The next few chapters teach you how to illuminate and shade surfaces, and how to create 3D primitives like boxes, spheres, cylinders, cones, wedges, and others.

7
*Getting started
with rendering*

This chapter covers using rendering geometry to illuminate and shade the facets in a 3D scene. It discusses concepts like color, the light-source, and shadow maps so you can become familiar with rendering geometry. You'll learn about RGB color and its cousin, descriptive color. You'll also gain an understanding of light sources and shadows and become aware of concepts like surface realism and transparency.

We'll also delve into RGB color and 8-bit, 256-color rendering, as well as descriptive color and the special RGB codes for producing it. You'll also find out how to calculate the brightness of a facet in a 3D scene. You'll see how to position the light source, and how to change its location. You'll also find out how to render transparent surfaces using a looping algorithm. The rendering knowledge you'll acquire in this chapter will equip you to learn about 3D modeling in subsequent chapters.

Using RGB color

As you've already learned in the two previous chapters, *3D modeling* refers to functions that represent the shapes of three-dimensional objects. *Rendering* refers to methods that add color, shading, brightness, texture, and other surface attributes to 3D entities. Modeling and rendering rely upon three types of geometry:

- view geometry
- modeling geometry
- rendering geometry

View geometry manipulates and displays a 3D scene. *Modeling geometry* creates 3D primitives such as boxes, spheres, cylinders, cones, wedges, curved surfaces, and others. *Rendering geometry* calculates illumination values for the entities in a 3D scene. It then shades the facets of the entities, often supplementing the shading with texture, reflections, shadows, and detailing.

The b-rep modeling paradigm is the most popular 3D system used on personal computers today. That's because it is well-suited to the graphics capabilities of the Windows Graphics Device Interface (GDI). The GDI provides many functions useful for 3D programming, including:

- RGB()
- dithering
- CreateSolidBrush()
- CreatePolygonRgn()

Together, these four tools provide the following capabilities. The RGB() macro provides individual control over the RGB guns found in most VGA-compatible and SVGA-compatible display hardware. This makes it easy to specify pure hues in 256-color SVGA modes and 65,000-color accelerator-based modes, but even when Windows is running in a 16-color VGA mode the GDI's dithering engine can simulate almost any shade of any color. The CreateSolidBrush() function provides an efficient way to apply color to a region, and the CreatePolygonRgn() function can be used to define the facet-shaped region that is to be filled by the brush.

The call to CreateSolidBrush() takes one argument, the color. You indicate a color by using the GDI's RGB() macro to specify the intensities of the red, green, and blue guns. If the requested color is supported by the display adapter as a solid hue, the GDI provides it exactly as requested. RGB(0,0,127) is an example of a pure blue hue that is available on a VGA, but RGB(0,0,143) is a slightly brighter blue that is not one of 16 pure hues available on a VGA. If the requested color is not available on the display adapter, then the GDI uses dithering to simulate the color. As shown in FIG. 7-1, the 0-to-255 range of the RGB() macro is mapped by the GDI to the 0-to-63 range available in the display hardware. This means that your application can call either RGB(127,127,127) or RGB(130,130,130) and the same medium gray will result. However, a call of RGB(131,131,131) produces a slightly brighter gray.

You must specify a color whenever you create a brush. You usually do this by specifying the intensities of the red, green, and blue guns. Because each gun provides a range of 64 different levels of intensity, the RGB() macro can describe 262,144 different colors ($64 \times 64 \times 64 = 262,144$). Because of hardware limitations, a VGA can simultaneously display only 16 of these colors as pure hues. The GDI can use dithering to approximate most of the remaining colors. Dithering is the mixing of pixels of available colors to create an approximate visual simulation of a color. If you request

Dithering thresholds for 4-bit 16-color modes				
255	203	151	99	47
251	199	147	95	43
247	195	143	91	39
243	191	139	87	35
239	187	135	83	31
235	183	131	79	27
231	179	127	75	23
227	175	123	71	19
223	171	119	67	15
219	167	115	63	11
215	163	111	59	7
211	159	107	55	3
207	155	103	51	0

127 produces solid normal intensity blue, green, cyan, red, magenta, brown, and gray. 191 produces solid light gray.

7-1 GDI dithering thresholds for specifying RGB colors in 4-bit 16-color modes.

a 17th color on a 16-color VGA, the GDI attempts to fulfill your request by dithering. If you request a 17th color when Windows is running in a 256-color mode on an SVGA, the GDI can satisfy your request by providing a pure hue if you create your own palette.

8-bit, 256-color rendering

As you've already learned in previous chapters, a *palette* is a collection of colors. When Windows starts, it resets the display adapter in order to obtain a palette of colors suitable for general windowing operations. Your application can use this so-called *system palette*, but it can also use logical palettes defined by your application. If Windows is running in a 256-color mode, the colors you request for your logical palette will be provided as pure hues by the GDI. This is because an SVGA can simultaneously display any 256 of the 262,144 possible colors at the same time. Windows sets aside the first 20 hues for its own use, so your application define another 236 custom colors if it wants.

To create a logical palette your application must follow four steps. The sample application in chapter 4 showed how this is done:

1. Set up a data structure containing a description of the hues that will be contained in the palette.
2. Call CreatePalette() to create the logical palette.

3. Use the GDI's SetClipboardData() function to copy the newly created palette into the Windows Clipboard.

4. Use Visual Basic's GetData method to copy the palette from the Clipboard into your application.

Using 256 colors for rendering introduces two new factors which must be considered. These new factors are gamma correction and the human visual system.

As you've learned in previous chapters, *shading* means applying color to a facet corresponding to the brightness of the facet. *Brightness* is the level of illumination exhibited by the facet. The brightness of the facet is also called *virtual luminance*. Virtual luminance is expressed as a percentage from 0% (darkest) to 100% (brightest).

After a 3D rendering function has calculated the virtual luminance of a facet, the resulting value must be converted before being displayed. This conversion is necessary because most RGB displays do not produce noticeable pixel brightness until a gun's intensity reaches a level of 35. You've already learned that the Windows API specifies an intensity range of 0 to 255 for RGB displays. This means that the serviceable range of the guns is actually 35 to 255. The process that converts the virtual luminance value in order to compensate for this nonlinearity of the display hardware is called *gamma correction*. (By convention, early researchers used the gamma symbol in their mathematical equations for color correction, so the process has come to be known as gamma correction.)

The table in FIG. 7-2 shows a set of gamma-corrected intensity settings suitable for SVGA 256-color modes. You'll want to note, for example, that if the human eye is to perceive an intensity of 50%, your application must call RGB() with a value of 135, not 127, even though 127 is 50% of 255. The discrepancy is more dramatic at lower intensities. In order for the human eye to perceive 10% brightness, the RGB gun must be set to a value of 51, which is actually 21% of 255, as FIG. 7-2 illustrates. This is a significant margin of error which your application cannot afford to overlook when using a 256-color mode for 3D modeling and rendering.

Color shift is also a problem. Suppose, for example, you wish to display a virtual luminance value of (0,63,255), which is another way of saying 0% red, 25% green, and 100% blue. If you don't convert the values before you call RGB(), then the green component appears too low. The displayed color appears too blue. Without gamma correction, the displayed hue will be 0% red, 18% green, and 100% blue, as shown in FIG. 7-2. What was wanted was a green component of 25%, not 18%. If your application does not consider gamma correction, then not only is the contrast distorted, but even the hue itself might shift—introducing a reddish, greenish, or bluish tinge to your 3D entity.

The situation is further complicated by the idiosyncrasies of the human eye. It is more sensitive to comparative ratios than absolute values. Here is

Virtual luminance conversions

Virtual	RGB	Virtual	RGB	Virtual	RGB	Virtual	RGB	Virtual	RGB
100%	255	80%	207	60%	159	40%	107	20%	67
99%	251	79%	203	59%	155	39%	103	19%	67
98%	251	78%	203	58%	155	38%	103	18%	63
97%	247	77%	199	57%	151	37%	99	17%	63
96%	247	76%	199	56%	151	36%	99	16%	63
95%	243	75%	195	55%	147	35%	95	15%	59
94%	239	74%	191	54%	143	34%	91	14%	59
93%	239	73%	191	53%	143	33%	91	13%	55
92%	235	72%	187	52%	139	32%	87	12%	55
91%	235	71%	187	51%	139	31%	87	11%	55
90%	231	70%	183	50%	135	30%	83	10%	51
89%	227	69%	179	49%	131	29%	83	9%	51
88%	227	68%	179	48%	131	28%	79	8%	47
87%	223	67%	175	47%	127	27%	79	7%	47
86%	223	66%	175	46%	123	26%	79	6%	47
85%	219	65%	171	45%	119	25%	75	5%	43
84%	215	64%	167	44%	115	24%	75	4%	43
83%	215	63%	167	43%	115	23%	71	3%	39
82%	211	62%	163	42%	111	22%	71	2%	39
81%	211	61%	163	41%	111	21%	71	1%	35

Valid for 8-bit, 16-bit, and 24-bit color modes
(including 256-color and 65536-color Windows modes)

7-2 Virtual luminance conversions for 8-bit 256-color modes. The luminance produced by the RGB guns is not a linear relationship and requires compensation at lower intensities.

an example. Your eye perceives the difference between medium gray (127,127,127) and light gray (191,191,191) as much greater than the difference between light gray (191,191,191) and bright white (255,255,255), even though both use an intensity difference of 64 units (191–127=64 and 255–191=64). Medium gray is two-thirds of light gray, so your eye reacts more acutely because, in the second example, light gray is only three-quarters of bright white (127/191=.67 and 191/255=.75).

Many of these difficulties are avoided if your application is running in the 16-color VGA mode because when Windows dithers the colors it provides a coarse implementation of gamma correction.

Using descriptive color

When most people think of color, they don't visualize it as the red, green, blue, cyan, magenta, brown, and yellow of the RGB color system. Most individuals are more comfortable with descriptions like sky blue, cadmium yellow, lime green, and antique white. This is called *subjective color* or *descriptive color*.

Nominal descriptive color for 3D entities

Your application can use nominal descriptive color to render 3D primitives in a wider variety of hues. As you'll soon see, the 3D functions provided in this book can render 3D solids in shades of red, green, blue, cyan, magenta, brown, and gray. However, you can easily adapt the source code to offer hues such as navy blue, gold, olive green, and others.

RGB codes for subjective color

The table in FIG. 7-3 provides RGB intensity settings for different flavors of white, gray, and black. Note, for example, how shifting the values of the red and blue settings can produce the perception of a warm gray or a cold gray. As FIG. 7-3 shows, the same subtle manipulations can be used to produce white, ivory, titanium white, and antique white.

Subjective color			
Color	**Red**	**Green**	**Blue**
White	255	255	255
Ivory	255	255	243
Titanium White	255	255	247
Antique White	251	235	215
Light Gray	191	191	191
Dark Gray	127	127	127
Cold Gray	115	127	127
Warm Gray	127	127	107
Black	0	0	0
Ivory Black	23	23	15
Lamp Black	15	23	19

7-3 RGB intensity values for subjective colors in the white, gray, and black spectrum.

The table in FIG. 7-4 provides RGB intensity settings for different blends of blue, including sky blue and navy blue. The table in FIG. 7-5 shows how to produce light yellow, cadmium yellow, and gold for your 3D primitives. The table in FIG. 7-6 provides RGB intensity settings for green, dark green, olive green, and lime green.

Subjective color			
Color	**Red**	**Green**	**Blue**
Blue	0	0	255
Navy Blue	0	0	127
Sky Blue	127	191	235
Sky Blue (light)	127	191	255
Sky Blue (dark)	63	127	235

7-4 RGB intensity values for subjective colors in the blue spectrum.

In order to use descriptive color in your 3D modeling and rendering application, you must take into account the relative strengths of the RGB settings, not the absolute values. Suppose, for example, that your application is rendering a 3D primitive using the color orange. The conversion

7-5 RGB intensity values for subjective colors in the yellow spectrum.

Subjective color			
Color	Red	Green	Blue
Yellow	255	255	0
Light Yellow	255	255	191
Gold	255	215	11
Cadmium Yellow	255	191	15

7-6 RGB intensity values for subjective colors in the green spectrum.

Subjective color			
Color	Red	Green	Blue
Green	0	255	0
Dark Green	0	127	0
Olive Green	79	127	63
Lime Green	63	207	63

table in FIG. 7-7 shows the correct intensity settings for different illumination levels. If 100% orange is defined as 255,127,0, then 50% orange will be 127,63,0. You'll want to note how the ratio between the red and green guns has been preserved. In this simplified example the blue gun has no effect because it is off.

Subjective color shading algorithm			
Facet shading	Red	Green	Blue
100% (ie Orange)	255	127	0
90%	227	111	0
80%	203	99	0
70%	175	87	0
60%	151	75	0
50%	127	63	0
40%	99	47	0
30%	75	35	0
20%	51	23	0
10%	23	11	0
0% (ie Black)	0	0	0

7-7 RGB intensity values for subjective orange at different levels of illumination.

The table in FIG. 7-8 uses a more complicated example. The color salmon is described in RGB terms as 255,127,115. Notice the subtle difference between the green and blue guns. As FIG. 7-8 shows, it becomes difficult to preserve this subtlety at a brightness of 10% or 20%.

Setting the light source location

The light source plays a critical role in shading calculations. Its location relative to a facet determines the level of illumination falling on the facet.

Subjective color shading algorithm			
Facet shading	Red	Green	Blue
100% (ie Salmon)	255	127	115
90%	227	111	103
80%	203	99	91
70%	175	87	79
60%	151	75	67
50%	127	63	55
40%	99	47	43
30%	75	35	31
20%	51	23	23
10%	23	11	11
0% (ie Black)	0	0	0

7-8 RGB intensity values for subjective Salmon orange at different levels of illumination.

This influences the brightness of the facet, which can range from 0% to 100%.

Calculating illumination intensity

Shaded models are built using facets. Each facet is shaded according to the intensity of light striking each facet. As you discovered in previous chapters, rendering geometry calculates an illumination value for each facet or pixel in a scene. Rendering geometry relies upon an illumination model, which is a paradigm explaining how surfaces and illumination are expected to act. Different illumination models are used, including facet shading, color interpolation shading, normal-vector interpolation shading, and others. The 3D functions in this book use facet shading.

Facet shading is also called *constant shading, flat shading,* and *Lambert shading.* The relationship between the incoming light ray and the surface normal of the facet determines the brightness of a facet. This relationship is called Lambert's cosine law.

This law specifies that the cosine of the angle between an incoming light ray vector and the surface normal vector of a facet is equal to the dot product of these two vectors divided by the product of the length of these two vectors. (For a lightning course in rendering math, refer to Appendix D, Math primer for graphics programming. The *surface normal* is a line that is perpendicular to the surface of the facet plane. A *vector* describes both magnitude and direction.)

What all this convoluted mathematical terminology means is that it's relatively straightforward for the software to calculate the angle at which light rays are striking the surface of the facet. If the angle between the light ray and the facet's surface normal is 0°, this means the light ray is perpendicular to the facet. It is producing maximum brilliance. If the angle between the light ray and the facet's surface normal is 90° or greater, this means no light is striking the facet. It is cloaked in shadow. The brightness of the facet can be altered only if your application repositions either the facet or the light source.

Moving the light source

Moving the light source can be accomplished by redefining the vector that describes the incoming light ray. Because most b-rep modeling systems define the light ray as a unit vector, this redefinition is not difficult.

A *unit vector* is a vector with a magnitude (length) of one unit. In 3D geometry, a vector is comprised of X, Y, and Z components. The square of the vector's length is equal to the sum of the squares of its three components. Because the magnitude of a unit vector is always one unit, this means that the sum of the squares of the vector's components always equals one. If your application specifies a heading and an altitude for the light source, the three components of the unit vector can be calculated by four short lines of code using trigonometry. The appropriate code is analyzed when the sample 3D application in chapter 9 is discussed.

Rendering shadows

Many b-rep modeling systems can render shadows using an algorithm derived from the Z-buffer depth-sort algorithm. As you learned in previous chapters, *Z-buffer depth-sorting* is a method of hidden-surface removal that is used to process complex 3D scenes containing a number of individual 3D primitives. The Z-coordinates of each facet indicate its distance or depth from the camera. By sorting the Z-values in a scene, the software can identify the nearest facets. Because the nearest facets obscure any facets farther from the camera, the Z-buffer method is a foolproof system for hidden-surface removal.

Moving the camera to the light source location

If the camera position is temporarily moved to the location of the light source, a special type of Z-buffer is produced called a *shadow-map*. As FIG. 7-9 shows, a shadow-map can be used to discover the shape of shadows in a 3D scene. If the camera (repositioned at the light source) cannot see a facet, it is because a nearer facet is obscuring the facet. The nearer facet receives the light and the farther facet falls within the shadow cast by the nearer facet.

The shadow-map

A shadow-map is, in effect, a light source Z-buffer. Or, stated more precisely, it corresponds to the frame-buffer used by the Z-buffer depth-sort functions. The shadow-map is an array of bytes representing the pixels of an imaginary viewport that represents the scene the light source sees.

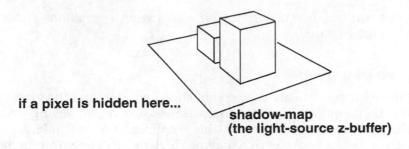

if a pixel is hidden here...

**shadow-map
(the light-source z-buffer)**

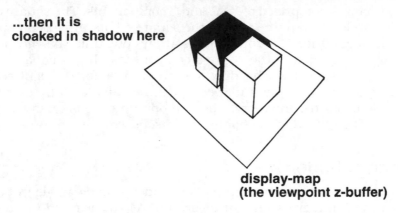

**...then it is
cloaked in shadow here**

**display-map
(the viewpoint z-buffer)**

7-9 Conceptual representation of the relationship between shadow-map and display-map when rendering shadows in a Z-buffer 3D modeling pipeline.

Using the shadow-map modeling pipeline

In order to derive and display the shadows in a 3D scene, an application uses a shadow-map modeling pipeline. The steps involved are:

1. Move the camera to the light source position.
2. Store depth-values in the shadow map.
3. For each facet being rendered . . .
   ~ if the facet faces away from the light source set a shadow-indicator to True;
   ~ else if the facet is partly or wholly obscured by another facet, set the shadow-indicator to True;
   ~ else set the shadow-token to False.
   ~ Move the camera back to the observer's viewpoint.
   ~ If the shadow-indicator is False, then render the facet, loop back to Step 3, and continue with the next facet;
   ~ else if the shadow-indicator is True, then for each pixel in the facet . . .
     • Use reverse-modeling and calculate world coordinates.
     • Move the camera to the light source position, determine if the pixel is obscured, and set a pixelshadow-indicator to True or False.

- Move the camera back to the observer's viewpoint.
- If the pixelshadow-indicator is True, then render the pixel in shadow.
- Otherwise render the pixel in illumination.

Ray-tracing a 3D scene

Rendering geometry can also be used to ray-trace a 3D scene. As FIG. 7-10 shows, the 3D perspective view-volume can be pierced by vectors emanating from the camera position. These vectors, which correspond to lines-of-sight, can be projected onto a view-plane window. If the view-plane window is partitioned into a grid corresponding to the dimensions of the viewport of the application's window, then the first point struck by the line-of-sight will be rendered.

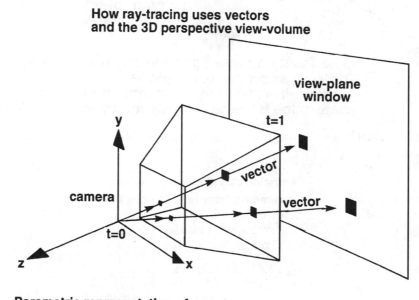

How ray-tracing uses vectors and the 3D perspective view-volume

Parametric representation of a vector

$$x = x_{start} + t(x_{change})$$
$$y = y_{start} + t(y_{change})$$
$$z = z_{start} + t(z_{change})$$

7-10 Conceptual representation of ray-tracing geometry.

In order to calculate the intersection of a vector with a facet in 3D space, as shown in FIG. 7-11, the standard equation for a plane is used, as shown in FIG. 7-12. A typical ray-tracing algorithm follows four steps.

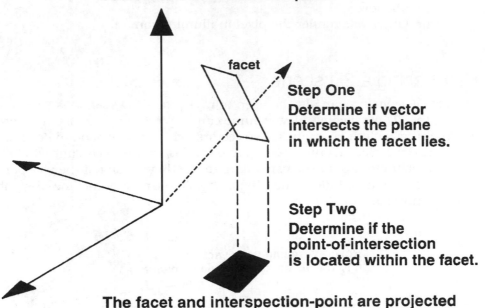

How to calculate the intersection of a vector with a facet in 3D space

facet

Step One

Determine if vector intersects the plane in which the facet lies.

Step Two

Determine if the point-of-intersection is located within the facet.

The facet and interspection-point are projected onto an appropriate 2D plane.
A point-in-rectangle algorithm test is then used to determine if the vector has intersected the facet.

7-11 Conceptual representation of intersection geometry used in ray-tracing calculations.

equation of a plane: ax + by + cz = 0

parametric representaton of a vector:

$$x = x_{start} + t(x_{change})$$
$$y = y_{start} + t(y_{change})$$
$$z = z_{start} + t(z_{change})$$

$$t = -\frac{(ax + by + cz + d)}{(ax + by + cz)}$$

if the denominator is 0, then the vector and plane do not intersect

7-12 The standard equation for a plane can be used to determine if a light-ray intersects the plane in which a facet lies.

1. Partition the view-plane window with a grid that matches the resolution of the display viewport.
2. Select a point on the view-plane window that corresponds to the pixel being tested, as shown in FIG. 7-10.

3. Establish the vector from the camera position at 0,0,0 to the selected point on the view-plane window.

4. Use the vector to find the appropriate intersections with 3D entities inside the 3D perspective view-volume, as shown in FIG. 7-11 and FIG. 7-12.

For a refresher course in vector mathematics, refer to Appendix D, Math primer for graphics programming.

Surface realism

Your application can enhance the realism of 3D entities by using three additional techniques of rendering geometry. These techniques are:

- texture mapping
- reflection mapping
- detail polygons

Texture mapping

Texture mapping uses bitmap images of textures and patterns. Texture mapping is also called *pattern mapping*. Each pixel (also called a *texel*) of the two-dimensional bitmap is transformed through the various coordinate systems of the 3D transformation sequence. It can thus be mapped onto the surface of the corresponding facets of the 3D entity.

Reflection mapping

Reflection mapping is a technique for adding reflections to a facet. These reflections correspond to other facets that are present in the 3D scene. The reflection mapping algorithm works in a manner similar to the shadow-map algorithm already described in this chapter. If the camera is temporarily moved to the location of the facet, then the image the camera sees will be the image that should be applied to the facet. The pattern mapping technique described in the previous paragraph can be used to map the reflected image (seen by the camera) to the facet.

Detail polygons

Detail polygons are two-dimensional polygons containing extra detail for an otherwise solid facet in a 3D scene. A 3D architectural image, for example, might make use of detail polygons for doors. The detail polygon would be a line drawing of the trim, moldings, and hardware that are found on the door. After the 3D scene has been modeled, the various line endpoints in the detail polygon are transformed through the 3D visualization pipeline and mapped onto the 3D facet that represents the door. This technique works well with the b-rep modeling system.

Rendering transparent surfaces

Even transparent surfaces can be rendered using the Z-buffer depth-sort algorithm, especially if the surfaces do not refract (bend) the light waves that pass through them.

Z-buffer-based non-refractive transparency

By using four buffers, a system can be implemented for Z-buffer-based nonrefractive transparency. One buffer each is used to store the transparency values, tokens, colors, and Z-depths for each pixel in the 3D scene. These buffers are called *transparent buffers*.

The transparency-rendering loop

A looping algorithm can be used to build the 3D scene. This is called a *transparency-rendering loop*. It operates by rendering transparent facets from farthest to nearest, gradually modifying the hue of the affected pixel.

1. Render all opaque facets using the conventional Z-buffer depth-sort method.
2. Process all transparent facets into the transparent buffers, storing a transparency value, a token, the color, and the depth-value.
3. For each pixel in the scene, if the transparent Z-buffer value is nearer than the opaque Z-buffer depth-value, then calculate and reset the transparency value, token, color, and depth-value for the various transparent buffers.
4. If the pixel's token is on, interpolate the transparent buffers with the opaque Z-buffer and frame-buffer by using the transparency value. The transparent depth-value of a pixel replaces the depth-value in the opaque Z-buffer and the token is reset to off.
5. Return to Step 3 and repeat the process to render progressively nearer transparent points at each pixel location.

Where do you go from here?

Now that you've learned how rendering geometry can display the entities in a 3D scene, you're ready to move on to modeling. The next chapter teaches you how to create 3D primitives like boxes, spheres, cylinders, cones, wedges, and others.

8
Getting started with modeling

This chapter teaches you how to use modeling geometry to create 3D entities. It describes the fundamental concepts of 3D primitive modeling and then goes on to discuss hierarchical modeling techniques. The modeling knowledge you're about to acquire in this chapter will provide you with the background you need to master more advanced material later in the book.

You'll learn how to manipulate the XYZ object coordinates of 3D object-space in order to construct primitives such as boxes, deformed boxes, spheres, half-spheres, cylinders, half-cylinders, cones, wedges, curved surfaces, bulged surfaces, and others. You'll see how to use sweeps, extrusions, and meshes to extend your modeling prowess. You'll become familiar with hierarchical modeling, and you'll discover how parents and progeny can be used to build complex 3D solids with moving parts. You'll learn about different types of 3D editors, including primitive modelers, hierarchical modelers, staging editors, and articulated motion editors. Finally, we'll cover advanced concepts like elision, pruning, and culling.

Modeling geometry

As you learned in previous chapters, modeling geometry creates individual *3D primitives*. A 3D primitive is a simple solid like a parallelepiped, a sphere, a cylinder, a cone, a wedge, and others. 3D primitives are also called *entities* and *subobjects*.

3D primitives are built from *facets*. Facets are flat polygons used to model the exterior surface of a 3D primitive. As you've already learned, this paradigm is called *boundary representation (b-rep) modeling*. A box, for example, consists of six facets.

Before a primitive can be displayed as part of a 3D scene, it must be *transformed*. 3D transformations are manipulations in 3D space. The sum of the transformations is the *3D transformation sequence* (also called the *3D visualization pipeline*).

As you've already learned, any location in 3D space can be described by its XYZ coordinates, relative to the *origin*. The origin is the center of the 3D space, specified as XYZ coordinates 0,0,0. The 3D transformation sequence contains different types of 3D space, each with its own coordinate system. In 3D space, X refers to left or right, Y refers to up or down, and Z refers to near or far. A typical 3D transformation sequence consists of six coordinates:

- object
- structure
- world
- camera
- image-plane
- raster

A 3D primitive must be transformed through each of these coordinate systems before it can be displayed. Each coordinate system represents a different form of 3D space. *Object coordinates*, the primary topic of this chapter, represent object-space. Object coordinates are XYZ coordinates that define the fundamental shape and size of a 3D primitive such as a box, sphere, cylinder, cone, wedge, and others. By manipulating the size, shape, and location of the facets that make up a primitive in 3D object-space, you can construct different types of primitive solids. By combining primitive solids in 3D structure-space, you can construct different types of complex solids.

As you've already learned in previous chapters, each coordinate system in the 3D visualization pipeline coexists with a spherical coordinate system, sharing the same 3D space. The XYZ coordinate system uses X, Y, and Z distances to describe a 3D entity. The *spherical coordinate system* uses yaw, roll, and pitch angles to describe the 3D entity. Yaw refers to compass headings, roll means tilting left or right, and pitch means tilting forward or back.

These two coordinate systems provide the tools for modeling different 3D primitives like boxes, spheres, cylinders, cones, wedges, and others. You can use the XYZ coordinate system to move (translate) a facet to a particular location. Then you can use the spherical coordinate system to spin (rotate) the facet into a particular orientation. You can thus build any primitive solid you want at any size and orientation in 3D object-space.

Parallelepipeds

A parallelepiped is a box-like primitive. Six facets are all that's needed to construct a parallelepiped, as shown in FIG. 8-1. The resulting box possesses eight vertices. The XYZ coordinates of these vertices can be inspected by different functions when the primitive is modeled, when back-face culling is implemented, and when the facets are shaded (see FIGS. 8-2, 8-3, and 8-4).

How the vertices of a parallelepiped are ordered as 3D object-coordinates

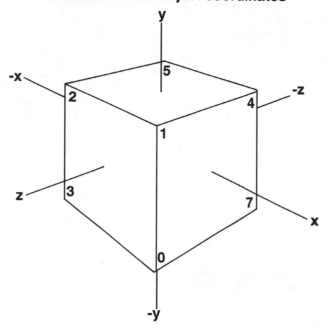

8-1 Object coordinates for a parallelepiped.

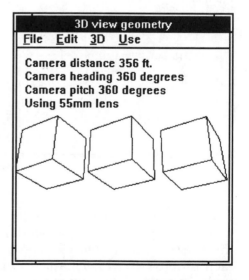

8-2 The sample application objects.frm is a 3D sampler capable of producing a variety of subobjects, including boxes (parallelepipeds), shown here running in wire-frame mode.

Consider, for example, the facet that is bounded by vertices 0, 1, 2, and 3 in FIG. 8-1. As you learned in previous chapters, programmers using the b-rep modeling paradigm always describe a facet using vertices ordered in a counterclockwise direction when the facet is viewed from out-

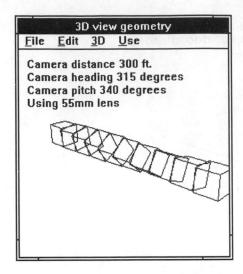

8-3 The 3D sampler can orient a subobject to any yaw, roll, or pitch angle. The sample application objects.frm is shown here running in wire-frame mode.

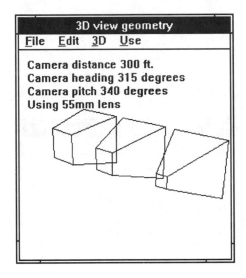

8-4 The demo application startup.frm can create new subobjects by deforming existing primitives.

side the solid. The 0-1-2-3 facet lies in the XY plane of the 3D object-space coordinate system. This means that the Z-value for each vertex is identical. The 0-7-4-1 facet lies in the YZ plane. This means that the X-value for each of its vertices is identical. Only the Y and Z coordinates vary. You could, of course, define a box not positioned at right angles in the 3D coordinate system, but it would add an unnecessary extra amount of work. (Because the box passes through the 3D transformation sequence, it can always be rotated during later stages.) The main objective of object-space, after all, is to define the fundamental shape of the primitive.

Spheres and half-spheres

A typical sphere produced by the sample application in the next chapter is shown in FIG. 8-5. Here is how it is built. First, a function calculates 36 vertices evenly spaced around the girth of the sphere. Next, the same function uses sine and cosine to compute another set of corresponding vertices for a line 20° south of the first line. Together, these two sets of vertices can provide four corners for each of 36 facets forming a belt around the girth of the sphere. By using a loop, the program can read the appropriate vertices in counterclockwise order and use back-face culling as each facet is rendered. After the belt is finished, the software begins work on the next belt.

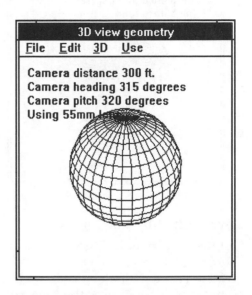

8-5 The 3D sampler can generate spheres of various sizes at different locations and orientations in 3D-space. The demo application objects.frm is shown here running in wire-frame mode. See 8-6 for fully-shaded mode. See 8-7 for a half-sphere.

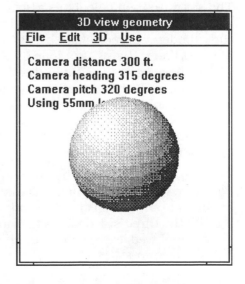

8-6 A sphere rendered in shaded mode. The sample application objects.frm can generate a variety of primitives, including spheres, cylinders, cones, wedges, curved surfaces, complex assemblies, and others. See 8-5 for wire-frame mode.

To build a half-sphere, the software uses the origin (0,0,0) as a vertex and then uses sine and cosine to calculate a set of 36 vertices around the equator of the sphere, as shown in FIG. 8-7. A series of three-sided facets are rendered in order to construct the flat surface of the halved sphere.

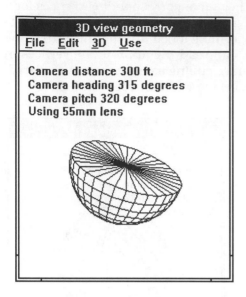

8-7 A half-sphere rendered in wire-frame mode by the sample application objects.frm. See 8-5 for a full sphere.

Cylinders and half-cylinders

A typical cylinder produced by the sample application in the next chapter is shown in FIG. 8-8. You can think of this cylinder as a disk that has been extruded (stretched) along the Z-axis. A modeling function sets the XY coordinates to 0 and moves the Z-coordinate to the nearest end of the cylinder. The software then calculates a set of 36 vertices around the circumference of the cylinder. The code then moves the Z-coordinate to the farthest end of the cylinder and recalculates a set of 36 vertices around the circumference of the cylinder. By using a loop to select from these two sets of XYZ coordinates, the program can build the facets that make up the curved surface of the cylinder. To build the half-cylinder shown in FIG. 8-9, a single facet is used and only half of the curved surface is rendered.

Cones and wedges

A typical cone produced by the sample application in the next chapter is illustrated in FIG. 8-10. After calculating the vertices that make up the disk at the bottom of the cone, the software simply uses a single point to help it build the three-sided facets that make up the curved surface of the cone.

A set of wedges produced by the sample application in the next chapter is shown in FIG. 8-11. The program uses a simple variation of the technique for parallelepipeds, described previously.

8-8 A cylinder rendered in wire-frame mode by the sample application objects.frm. See 8-9 for a half-cylinder.

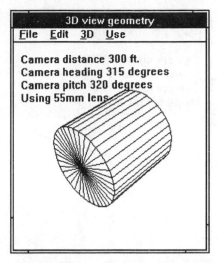

8-9 A half-cylinder rendered in wire-frame mode by the sample application objects.frm. See 8-8 for a full cylinder.

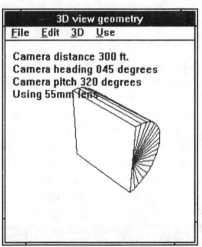

8-10 A 3D cone rendered in wire-frame mode by the sample application objects.frm.

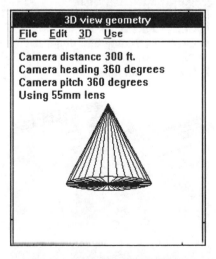

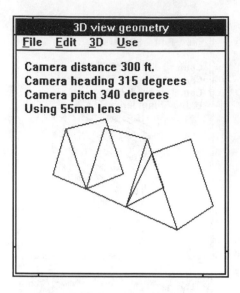

8-11 A selection of 3D wedges rendered in wire-frame mode by the sample application objects.frm.

Curved surfaces

A typical curved surface produced by the sample application in the next chapter is shown in FIG. 8-12. Here is how it's done: first, a parametric equation for a 2D curved line is used to generate a set of XY coordinates for a curve. Next, the 3D functions set the Z-value to an appropriate depth and calculate the XYZ object-coordinates for the near edge of the curved surface. The program then resets the Z-value to an appropriate depth for the far edge of the curved surface and calculates another set of XYZ object coordinates. The vertices along the two curves can then be used to model the facets that make up the surface. By modifying the parametric equation

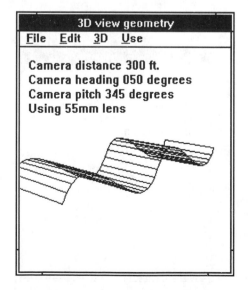

8-12 A curved surface rendered in wire-frame mode by the sample application objects.frm. See 8-13 for shaded mode.

for a 2D curved line, the sample application can generate a bulged surface like the one shown in FIG. 8-14.

Extensible techniques

Many of the modeling techniques you've just learned are really just simplifications of advanced techniques like sweeps, extrusions, and meshes. By carefully manipulating the XYZ coordinates of the vertices that make up a facet, you can position the facet anywhere in 3D object-space. By combining facets you can construct 3D solids of different shapes. You're usually either *extruding* or *sweeping*.

Sweeps Sweeps add a third dimension to a 2D shape. As you've already learned, you can sweep a facet around successive belts to build a 3D sphere. Another way of constructing the curved surface shown in FIG. 8-13 is to build a facet and sweep it along a parametric curve. A sweep is really just a curved extrusion.

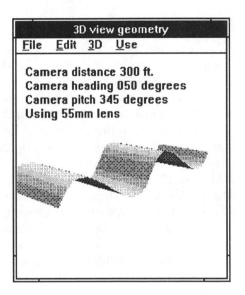

8-13 A curved surface rendered in shaded mode by the sample application objects.frm. See 8-12 for wire-frame mode.

Extrusions Extrusions also add a third dimension to a 2D shape. When you extrude a shape, you pull it out from the 2D plane on which it's drawn. Consider a drawing of a 2D disk, for example. If you extrude a disk by pulling it up from its 2D plane, you can create a cylinder.

Meshes The curved surface shown in FIG. 8-13 and the bulged surface shown in FIG. 8-14 are *simplified meshes*. Only two sides of each primitive are curved. The other two sides are straight lines. If the program is retooled to produced a primitive possessing four curved sides, then the resulting mesh of facets can be used to model free-form curves.

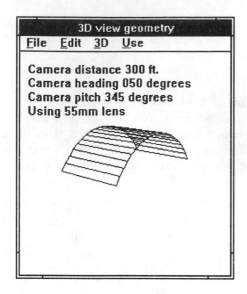

8-14 A bulged surface rendered in wire-frame mode by the sample application objects.frm.

Hierarchical modeling

As you know, *structure coordinates* are part of the 3D transformation sequence. They are XYZ coordinates that describe a 3D primitive as part of a group of primitives forming a more complex structure.

Structure coordinates describe structure-space and they are used in so-called *hierarchical operations*. Hierarchical modeling can build complex 3D solids by attaching primitives to each other. These complex solids are called *structures, assemblies, subassemblies,* or *hierarchies.* A hierarchical structure can contain flexible joints, moving parts, rotating elements, and so on. This is possible because the XYZ coordinates of some primitives (the progeny) are defined as offsets which are relative to other primitives (their parents). Parents and progeny together form the complex 3D structure. Structures with moving parts are called *articulated entities.* B-rep modeling systems that offer hierarchical modeling capabilities must often provide a suite of different 3D editors.

Types of 3D editors

A hierarchical modeling environment typically provides a *primitives modeler*, a *hierarchical modeler*, a *staging editor*, and an *articulated motion editor*.

Primitives modeler A primitives modeler provides interactive tools that allow the user to build 3D primitives such as boxes, spheres, cylinders, cones, wedges, and others.

Hierarchical modeler A hierarchical modeler provides interactive tools that allow the user to combine together primitives in order to construct complex 3D solids. As you'll soon see, the sample application in the next chapter demonstrates functions suitable for both a primitives modeler and a hierarchical modeler.

Staging editor A staging editor provides interactive tools that allow the user to specify the location (in world-space) of a stand-alone primitive or a structure. You can think of this as choreographing an animation sequence. As you'll discover, all of the animation demos in the book provide functions typically found in a staging editor. The 3D kinematics sampler described in chapter 17, "Kinematics programming," provides source code that uses physically-based animation to automate the staging process.

Articulated motion editor An articulated motion editor provides interactive tools that allow the user to indicate the movement of a limb or component of a complex 3D solid. Such movement is called *articulated motion*. Think of it this way: the staging editor is used to specify the locations of a 3D robotic structure as it moves through the 3D world. The articulated motion editor is used to describe the sway of the robot's arms and the sweep of the robot's legs as the android (the structure) travels across the 3D world. The staging editor defines global movement while the articulated motion editor defines local movement. The animated sample application described in chapter 13, "3D motion-control programming," provides source code to implement articulated motion in hierarchical models.

Using subassemblies

A typical structure or *subassembly* produced by the sample application in the next chapter is shown in FIG. 8-15. A fully-shaded version is depicted in FIG. 8-16. A *subassembly modeling pipeline* makes it easy to construct complex 3D solids.

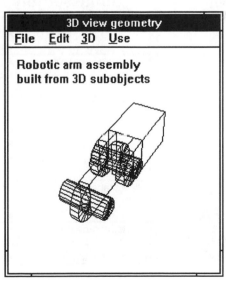

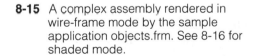
8-15 A complex assembly rendered in wire-frame mode by the sample application objects.frm. See 8-16 for shaded mode.

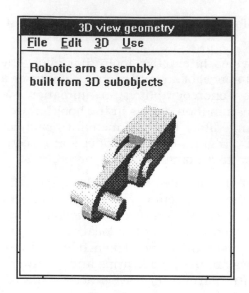

8-16 A complex assembly rendered in shaded mode by the sample application objects.frm. See 8-15 for wire-frame mode.

The subassembly modeling pipeline The table in FIG. 8-17 describes the purposes of various stages in the subassembly modeling pipeline. Structure coordinates are used in order to define the 3D subassembly by translating (moving), extruding (resizing), and rotating (spinning) the 3D primitives comprising the assembly. If a primitive (the progeny) is defined in XYZ coordinates expressed relative to another primitive (the parent), then the position of the progeny can be articulated, especially if the parent and progeny share a common interface. That interface can be a joint, an axle,

Subassembly modeling pipeline	
Object coordinates	The 3D definition of a subobject like a box, sphere, cylinder, wedge, cone, etc.
Structure coordinates	A 3D assembly defined as the rotation, translation, and extrusion of objects comprising the assembly.
World coordinates	The rotation and translation of the structure coordinates to position the assembly in the 3D world.
Camera coordinates	How the 3D world and its contents appears to a camera at a particular viewpoint and orientation.
View-plane coordinates	How the 3D image appears on a two-dimensional viewport placed in front of the camera.
Raster coordinates	How the image appears after being reduced or enlarged to fit the raster viewport (the display).

8-17 The subassembly hierarchical modeling pipeline.

a fulcrum, a hinge, and so on. Both parent and progeny abut the common interface.

Complicated 3D structures often require a formal database in order to simplify the storage, manipulation, and retrieval of XYZ structure coordinates. When the 3D modeler works its way through the database, it often uses specialized operations like *elision*, *pruning*, and *culling*.

Elision Elision refers to decisions by a 3D modeler to refrain from rendering primitives or structures when the entity is distant or when only a simplified image is needed.

Pruning Pruning refers to decisions by a 3D modeler to discard an entire structure if it lies outside the 3D view-volume. As you learned in previous chapters, the 3D view-volume is the volume of 3D space that is visible to the camera.

Culling Culling refers to decisions by a 3D modeler to discard a primitive or a structure if rendering it would involve only a few pixels.

Where do you go from here?

Now that you've familiarized yourself with view geometry, rendering geometry, and modeling geometry, you're ready to delve into a hands-on tutorial. In the next chapter you'll have an opportunity to inspect working source code for a sample 3D application that provides features such as:

- Built-in 3D primitives, including user-selectable boxes, spheres, half-spheres, cylinders, half-cylinders, cones, wedges, deformable parallelepipeds, curved surfaces, bulged surfaces, and others.
- Automatic back-face culling of 3D solids.
- Z-buffer depth-sort removal of hidden-surfaces in scenes with numerous 3D entities.
- A user-selectable, movable light-source.
- User-selectable rendering modes, including wire-frame and fully-shaded.
- User-selectable shading colors, including blue, green, red, cyan, magenta, brown, and gray.
- Hierarchical modeling capabilities, including a complex solid with a flexible joint.
- An adjustable camera focal-length.
- A movable near clipping-plane.
- A camera mode that is compatible with virtual reality application development.

The knowledge you've acquired in this and the two previous chapters provides you with the savvy you need to understand how the sample application works—and you'll have the ability to paste its functions into your own projects if you want.

9
Tutorial:
3D programming

This chapter provides a hands-on tutorial to exercise the 3D skills you learned in the previous four chapters. These programming skills are necessary to developing animation, simulation, visualization, and virtual reality applications. A Programmer's Guide provides detailed explanations of the source code for both the sample application and the underlying 3D toolkits.

You'll see how 3D primitives like boxes, spheres, cylinders, cones, wedges, and others are constructed and displayed. You want to understand how to toggle between wire-frame and fully shaded displays. You'll want to see how to manipulate the camera. Your most important task, however, is to learn how to use the functions of the 3D toolset in your own graphics applications.

This chapter will also show you how to use XYZ object coordinates to build 3D primitives like boxes, deformed boxes, clipped boxes, spheres, half-spheres, cylinders, half-cylinders, cones, wedges, curved surfaces, bulged surfaces, and others. You'll find out how to move the near clipping-plane in order to clip primitives that are too near to the camera. You'll discover how to build complex structures using the techniques of hierarchical modeling. You'll learn how to adjust the camera's focal length and how to disable the camera's fixed-target mode in order to facilitate virtual reality programming. You'll become familiar with how the various parts of a 3D application are put together.

A user's guide to the sample application

In this section, you'll learn how to use the sample application named OBJECTS. Before you can run it, however, you must build it. The source listings for the sample application are presented as FIG. C-2 in Appendix C. Source listings for the 3D toolkits that must be linked-in to build the finished application are presented in Appendix B. All source files are also provided on the companion disk. See Appendix A if you need assistance compiling the program.

Starting the sample application

There are two ways to start the sample application. You can start it directly from the Visual Basic editor or you can start it from Windows' Program Manager.

Startup from Visual Basic If you're using Visual Basic to prototype and experiment with the sample application, you can run the demo directly from Visual Basic.

Startup from Windows' Program Manager If you've already compiled the sample application, you can start it from Windows' Program Manager. From the Windows desktop, pull down the File menu and select Run. When the dialog box appears, type the full pathname of the program. The full pathname includes the drive letter, directories, subdirectories, filename, and extension of the program you want Program Manager to run. Here's an example.

c:*directory**subdirectory*\objects.exe

You'll want to substitute directory names that reflect your own system. When you select the OK button of the dialog box the sample application will be launched.

Using the sample application

When the sample application starts up, a splash sign-on notice appears. Choose OK to continue. Four menus are listed on the demo's menu bar. They are File, Edit, 3D, and Use. You can use the File menu to quit the program. The Edit menu contains no active features. You can use the 3D menu to explore 3D primitives, hierarchical modeling, light-source shading, toggling the rendering mode, adjusting the camera focal length, and more. Select the Use menu to explore the run-time system, including display resolution, available colors, memory mode, and Windows version.

You can use either a mouse or the keyboard to operate this sample application. If you're using a mouse, simply point and click. If you're using the keyboard, press Alt to move the focus to the menu bar, then press the appropriate underscored mnemonic key to pull down a menu, then press a mnemonic key to select an item from the menu. You can also use the up and down arrow keys to move the highlight bar to the menu item you want. Then press Enter to select it.

The Use menu The features provided by the Use menu are cloned from the sample application in chapter 4. You can choose from menu items that report the resolution of the display, the number of available colors, the runtime memory mode, and the Windows version. The sample application supports screen resolutions from 640 × 480 to 1024 × 768. Provided the required hardware and software is available, the sample application supports standard and enhanced mode.

The 3D **menu** The 3D menu provides a suite of choices that you can use to exercise the modules of the 3D toolkit, as shown in FIG. 9-1. To get started, you might first wish to select the wire-frame rendering mode, as depicted by FIG. 9-2. Using this mode results in quicker rendering, which you may find convenient while you investigate the various 3D primitives which the sample application can draw. It's recommended that you stick with the default 55mm camera lens, as shown in FIG. 9-3.

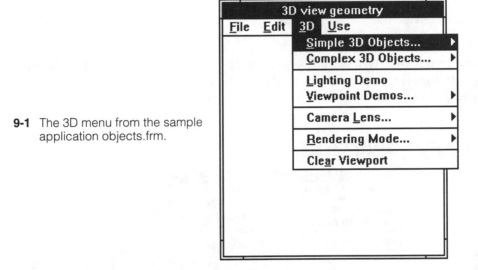

9-1 The 3D menu from the sample application objects.frm.

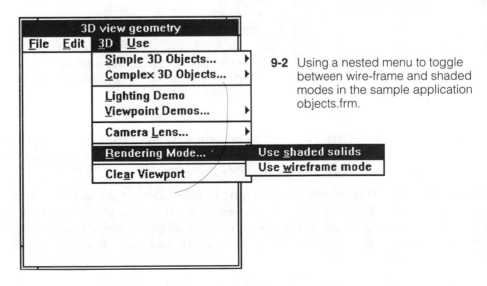

9-2 Using a nested menu to toggle between wire-frame and shaded modes in the sample application objects.frm.

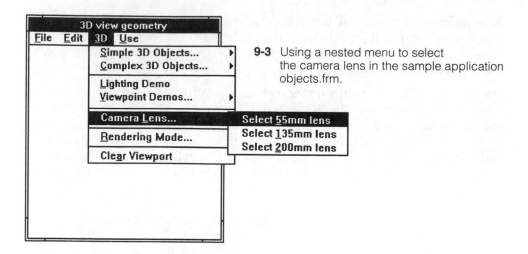

9-3 Using a nested menu to select the camera lens in the sample application objects.frm.

The primitives When you select Simple 3D Objects from the 3D menu, a nested menu appears, listing the 3D primitives supported by the sample application. This menu structure is shown in FIG. 9-4.

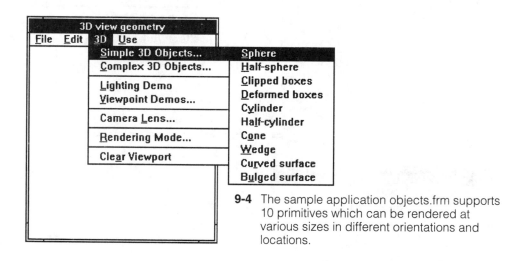

9-4 The sample application objects.frm supports 10 primitives which can be rendered at various sizes in different orientations and locations.

The complex solids When you select Complex 3D Objects from the 3D menu a nested menu appears, as shown in FIG. 9-5. You can choose from two different implementations of complex solids modeling.

Investigating the 3D primitives A sampling of fully shaded primitives is provided in FIG. 9-6. The shading colors used in each primitive is hard-coded into the sample application, but you can easily alter the color schemes, as you'll find out in the programmer's guide section of this chapter, coming up. The 3D solids are rendered using dithered facets.

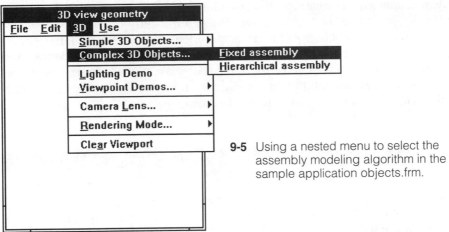

9-5 Using a nested menu to select the assembly modeling algorithm in the sample application objects.frm.

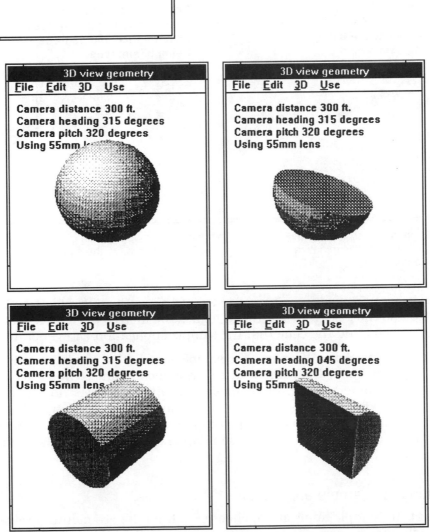

9-6 Samples of shaded primitives produced by the sample application objects.frm.

Other demonstrations The window images shown in FIG. 9-7 illustrate the output of the Lighting Demo and the Clipped Boxes. The lighting demonstration shows how the brightness of a facet changes as the facet's orientation is changed, thereby altering its relationship to the position of the light-source. The clipped boxes show how the near clipping-plane can be moved in order to clip nearer portions of a 3D primitive. In this implementation of the sample application, clipping occurs only when the boxes are rendered in fully-shaded mode.

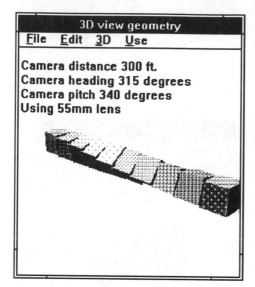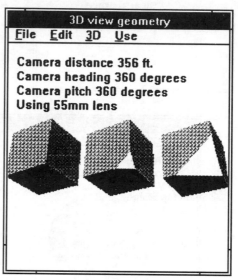

9-7 Samples of shaded demonstrations from the sample application objects.frm. Shown at left is the illumination demonstration. Shown at right is the front clipping-plane demonstration.

Other images The window images in FIG. 9-8 show the output of the Curved Surface and the Bulged Surface menu items. The images in FIG. 9-9 show the complex solid and the cone that the sample application can generate.

Camera manipulation Whenever the sample application renders a primitive or a complex solid, the camera direction is locked on to the entity being drawn. The camera's fixed-target mode is disabled, however, for the virtual reality viewpoint demos shown in FIG. 9-10 and FIG. 9-11. This built-in capability of the 3D toolkits makes point-of-view simulation possible, including virtual reality sessions, flight simulation, architectural walkthroughs, and so on.

Quitting the sample application

To quit the sample application, choose Exit from the File menu. A message box will appear, providing you with an opportunity to confirm or cancel your request.

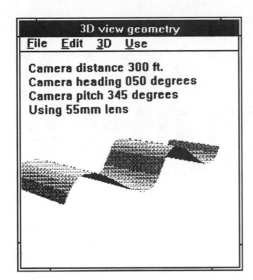
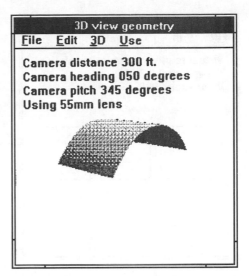

9-8 Samples of shaded surfaces from the sample application objects.frm. Shown at left is a curved surface. Shown at right is a bulged surface.

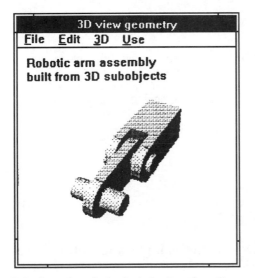
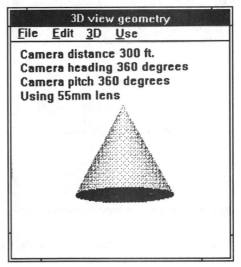

9-9 Samples of shaded displays from the sample application objects.frm. Shown at left is a complex assembly of subobjects. Shown at right is a cone.

A programmer's guide to the sample application

This section provides a description of how the source code works. The text offers significant detail when discussing the code because many of the 3D toolkit functions that are found in this sample application are also used in more advanced demos you'll encounter later in the book. You can refer back to this chapter for an analysis of the source code when you're investigating how the 3D toolkit drives the various visualization, simulation,

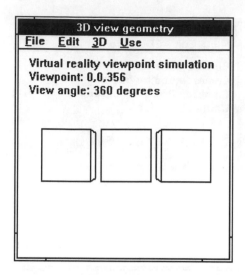

9-10 By disabling the fixed-target camera mode of the 3D toolkit, the sample application objects.frm can provide a testing environment for virtual reality scenarios.

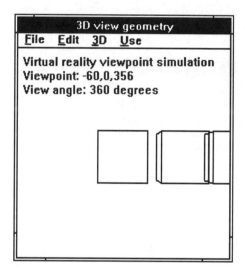

9-11 The sample application objects.frm can provide prototyping capabilities for virtual reality environments. Shown here is a viewpoint located west of the origin. See 9-10 for the startup position.

animation, and virtual reality features of the sample applications presented in later parts of the book.

The source listings for the sample application are presented as FIG. C-2 in Appendix C. Source listings for the linked-in 3D toolkits are provided in Appendix B. For tips on building the sample application, see Appendix A. The source files for the sample application are also provided on the companion disk as objects.mak, obglobal.bas, obmain.bas, objects.frm, engine3d.bas, shapes3d.bas, deform3d.bas, lights3d.bas, and assemb3d.bas.

How the global module works

The global module, obglobal.bas, declares constants and variables that are visible throughout the entire project. This module also declares the Windows

API functions that may be called by the application at run-time. You'll want to note lines 0092 through 0138, where Visual Basic's Type statement is used to create a structure that defines 3D entities used in hierarchical modeling.

How the startup module works

The startup module, obmain.bas, is cloned from the startup module described in chapter 4. The only difference is at line 0116, where a call to aazInitialize3D initializes the 3D engine in engine3d.bas. (The aa prefix scheme is used throughout all of the toolkits to ensure that Visual Basic sorts the functions into an order that makes it easier for you to understand how the source code works.)

How the form module works

The form module contains code that manages the 3D toolkits in order to create boxes, spheres, cylinders, cones, and complex models. You want to understand how this code works so you'll be prepared for the animated 3D applications later in the book.

Calling the 3D toolkit The Sub function IDM_DrawSphere_Click() at lines 0890 through 0942 is a good example of how the application calls graphics functions in the 3D toolkit. This function is activated when the user asks the application to render a 3D sphere. The other IDM_ functions in the .frm module use a similar approach. Here's how it works.

The SetCapture() call at line 0894 locks the mouse so it can't be pilfered by other applications while the sphere is being rendered by the sample application. The code at lines 0895 through 0905 clears the viewport, clears the hidden page, and resets the Z-buffer of the 3D toolkit. These are general housekeeping chores.

Next, the code at lines 0907 through 0921 displays a set of captions on the viewport. Note the If...End If statements at lines 0915 through 0921 and how they test the camera's focal length before writing a string of text to the display.

Before drawing the sphere, the code at lines 0923 through 0926 configures the camera and the light-source. A camera heading of 315 degrees is similar to facing north-northeast. A camera pitch of 320 degrees is the same as tilting 40 degrees down from the horizontal. A light source position of 60 degrees elevation and 180 degrees heading puts the light-source directly behind you, the viewer.

The application is now ready to draw the sphere. The call to zSetHierarchyMode() at line 0928 tells the 3D toolkit that only stand-alone 3D primitives are about to be rendered, not parts of a hierarchical entity. The next three statements at lines 0929 through 0931 set the size, orientation, and location of the sphere. The call to zSetShadingColor() at line 0932 asks the 3D toolkit to use green shades for the facets of the sphere. Finally, line 0936 instructs the 3D toolkit to model and render the sphere.

After the sphere is drawn, the statement at line 0941 copies the viewport image to the hidden bitmap. The call to the GDI's ReleaseCapture() function at line 0938 unlocks the mouse.

Most of the other Sub functions that render 3D images operate in a similar manner. The comment line that appears just before each function tells you the purpose of the code. After you've learned how the 3D toolkit operates, you'll be able to return to this section of code and see how each IDM_ function gets its job done.

The function at line 1103 is responsible for rendering a series of rotating boxes in order to demonstrate different shades of brightness on facets.

Hierarchical modeling The IDM_ Sub function at line 0853 renders a complex 3D entity made up of primitives whose location and orientation is hard-coded. It calls another function located at line 1449 to help it get the job done. The IDM_ Sub function at line 0291 uses hierarchical modeling to render a complex 3D entity with a moveable joint. This block of code calls a function located at line 1499. By comparing these two functions you can see the difference between hard-coding and variable-coding. In the zDrawRoboticArm() function at line 1449, each primitive's size, orientation, and location is specified by numeric constants. This means if one primitive's location is changed, for example, it is unable to affect any other primitives that may be attached to it. However, the zBuildAssembly() function at line 1499 uses variables to specify the size, orientation, and location of each primitive in the complex solid. Note lines 1536 and 1537, for example, which use variables initialized earlier at lines 1505 and 1512. This means if the parent is changed (at line 1505, for example), then the progeny is automatically affected (line 1536). The struct variable used in this section of code was declared and initialized at lines 0095 through 0122 in the obglobal.bas global module.

Although the zBuildAssembly() function is 295 lines in length, most of those statements involve specifying the primitives that make up the hierarchical solid. The complex entity is drawn by a loop at lines 1757 through 1794. The loop occupies only 37 lines of source code, and many of those lines are Select Case statements. You should note how the Select Case block at lines 1770 through 1793 determines which 3D primitive to draw on each iteration of the loop.

The animated sample application in chapter 13, "3D motion-control programming," shows how you can animate the moving joint of this hierarchical structure.

Persistent graphics The Form_Paint function at line 0254 is activated whenever the client area must be refreshed. This will occur if the window is uncovered or moved.

Graceful shutdown The function at line 1009 is activated when the application is about to shut down. The If...End If block at lines 1014 through 1018 ensures that the hidden bitmap is deselected from the memory display-context and deleted from memory.

Core functions Core housekeeping functions for the application are found at lines 1797 through 1852. These functions are discussed in more detail in chapter 4. They are cloned from the graphics template described there.

3D functions The 3D functions that are called by the application are provided by five additional modules. These modules are named engine3d.bas, shapes3d.bas, deform3d.bas, lights3d.bas, and assemb3d.bas. By using the sample application as a guide, you can use the 3D modeling and shading capabilities of the 3D toolkits in your own application development.

How the engine3d toolkit works

The source listing for the engine3d toolkit is presented in FIG. B-1 in Appendix B. This module provides control over camera pitch, camera heading, and camera-to-target distance. The engine3d toolkit also provides control over the size, location, orientation, and color of each 3D primitive. It provides automatic back-face culling for all solids, and it shades each facet according to the angle between the facet and the light-source. By default, engine3d provides a light-source located above, behind, and slightly to the left of the camera position. The toolkit also provides a Z-buffer depth-sort system for ensuring the proper detection and handling of visible-surfaces and hidden-surfaces in scenes composed of multiple solids. The Z-buffer is hard-coded to a size of 256×255 pixels, which corresponds to the viewport dimensions of each sample application in the book. The modeling and shading functions of the engine3d toolkit will run in 2-color, 16-color, and 256-color modes using dithered shades. See the palette-sensitive code described in chapter 4 if you want to alter the 3D engine to use a 256-color palette.

The basic functions and capabilities provided by the engine3d toolkit are extended by the other components of the toolset. These other components are shapes3d, deform3d, lights3d, and assemb3d. Code in each of these modules calls functions in engine3d in order to provide advanced 3D features like built-in primitives, deformed entities, a moveable light-source, and hierarchical modeling.

Constants The code at lines 0040 through 0064 defines a set of convenience values that will be used throughout the module. Each of these constants is prefaced with a z and is otherwise spelled using uppercase characters.

Variable declarations Variables that are used for 3D modeling are declared at lines 0068 through 0110. Variables for shading and back-face culling are declared at lines 0114 through 0129. Variables that are needed for viewport management and palette manipulation are declared at lines 0133 through 0138. Variables for view-volumes are declared at lines 0142 through 0151. Variables that are used for Z-buffer operations are declared at lines 0155 through 0180. Variables for a hidden-bitmap that is used as a temporary image-workspace are declared at lines 0184 through 0187.

Initialization The zInitialize3D() function at lines 0194 through 0296 prepares the 3D environment. Note line 0195, for example, which ensures that this function is called only once. The code in this function is generously commented so you'll be able to work out how it operates. The function displays a startup notice, checks the dimensions of the viewport to ensure they match the 256×255 Z-buffer, sets the location of the light-source, and initializes the camera. The code then defines a default 3D primitive, sets the near and far clipping-planes, initializes the hidden workspace, and sets up the Z-buffer.

You'll want to carefully note how the MsgBox statement is used to alert the user if the application encounters any problems when it initializes the 3D toolkit. The code at line 0214 becomes active if an unexpected viewport dimension is encountered. The code at line 0273 guards against inadvertent division-by-zero conditions.

Rendering mode The zUseWireframeMode() function at line 0301 sets a run-time token that indicates whether wire-frame or fully shaded rendering is wanted. The shading functions later in the module check this token before they render each facet.

Fixed-target camera functions The functions at lines 0315 through 0440 adjust the camera when it is in fixed-target mode. A camera using this mode always points at the center of the world-space, no matter where you position the camera. The functions in this section set the camera heading, camera pitch, and camera-to-target distance. The heading and pitch automatically infer and set the location of the camera, of course, because it always points at the target. What you're really describing is the view angle.

Virtual reality camera functions The functions at lines 0447 through 0557 adjust the camera when it is in virtual reality mode. A camera using this mode can be pointed in any direction. The functions in this section toggle between fixed-target and virtual reality mode, set the camera heading, the camera pitch, and the camera location.

Instancing The functions at lines 0564 through 0670 are used to manipulate the translation (location), orientation (attitude), size (extrusion), and shading color of 3D primitives.

Clipping-planes The functions at lines 0677 through 0706 set the near and far clipping-planes (see FIG. 6-3 in chapter 6). Review the code in objects.c to see how these functions are used to clip the 3D boxes at various distances from the camera.

3D view geometry The functions at lines 0713 through 0850 provide the view geometry for this 3D toolkit. This section of code is the foundation of the 3D transformation sequence (see FIG. 6-1 in chapter 6). The zSetObjAngle() function at line 0721 sets the orientation of the 3D primitive in world-space. The zSetCamAngle() function at line 0736 sets the orientation of the 3D world in camera-space (see FIG. 6-2). The zGetworldCoords() function at line 0751 transforms object coordinates to world coordinates. The zGet CameraCoords() function at line 0769 transforms world coordinates to camera coordinates. As you've already learned in previous chapters, camera coordinates make up the view seen by the camera. This is the 3D perspective view-volume (see FIG. 6-3). The zNormalizeView() function at line 0789 scales this 3D perspective view-volume to a normalized view-volume (see FIG. 6-5). Then the zRectangularView() function at line 0804 deforms the normalized view-volume into a rectangular view-volume suitable for Z-buffer depth-sorting. Finally, the zScaleToRaster() function at line 0820 scales the rectangular view-volume to match the dimensions of the application's viewport (see FIG. 6-7).

Facet functions The zDrawFacet() function at lines 0857 through 1033 draws a generic 3D facet. This function is called whenever a 3D primitive or a 3D complex solid is rendered. The code calls the functions described in the previous paragraph to transform each vertex of the facet through the 3D transformation sequence. This is done at lines 0862 through 0918. Then the code at lines 0920 through 0955 identifies the topmost vertex and sorts the remaining vertices into counterclockwise rotation so they can be processed later by the Z-buffer functions (see FIG. 6-10). Next, the code at lines 0957 through 0963 calls another function in order to clip the facet to the view-volume (see FIG. 6-9).

If the facet is being rendered in wire-frame mode, the code at lines 0965 through 0991 is processed. Otherwise, the facet is being rendered in fully-shaded mode and the section at lines 0993 through 1031 is processed. As you can see, a series of calls to the GDI's LineTo() function are used in order to draw a wire-frame facet. The GDI's CreateSolidBrush(), CreatePolygonRgn(), and PaintRgn() functions are used in order to render a fully shaded facet.

All graphics output is sent to the hidden workspace. Line 1029 calls the Z-buffer depth-sorting function, which decides whether to copy some of the pixels from the hidden workspace to the display viewport. This approach makes it possible to take advantage of the GDI's dithering capabilities, yet still use a Z-buffer to calculate depths on a pixel-by-pixel basis.

View-volume clipping The zClipToViewVolume() function at lines 1040 through 1082 clips facets to the normalized 3D perspective view-volume. This function is called by line 0957 in zDrawFacet() for each facet that is rendered. The zClipToViewVolume() implements the clipping regimen illustrated in FIG. 6-9 in chapter 6. Facets behind the camera are discarded. Facets entirely between the camera and the near clipping-plane are discarded. The offending portion of a facet is clipped (by the Z-buffer functions) if the facet intersects the near clipping-plane. Facets that intersect the far clipping-plane are discarded. Finally, any facet wholly beyond the far clipping-plane is discarded.

Back-face culling The zVisibilityTest() function at line 1089 uses the standard equation for a plane to determine on which side of the facet the camera viewpoint is located. It sets a variable to denote whether the facet is visible (facing towards the camera) or hidden (facing away from the camera). The variable is checked by functions in the shapes3d and deform3d modules when they create 3D primitives.

Facet shading The zGetBrightness() function at line 1101 calculates the brightness level of a facet. It works by comparing the facet's surface normal with the incoming light-ray. Maximum intensity is achieved with there is no difference between the two vectors.

Hidden workspace The functions at lines 1151 through 1211 manage the hidden bitmap that provides a temporary workspace for the images produced by the 3D toolkit. Functions are provided to create the hidden bitmap, clear it, delete it, and copy a pixel from the hidden bitmap to the viewport. The zCopyPixelToViewPort() function at line 1194 is called by the Z-buffer routines whenever they determine that a facet's pixel is nearer to the camera than the existing entry in the Z-buffer.

The Z-buffer The functions at lines 1218 through 1410 manage the Z-buffer depth-sorting operations. The zFindDepth() function at line 1218 calculates the Z-depth of a specified pixel inside a facet. This function is called repeatedly by the zDoZBufferTest() function located at line 1327, which processes the entire facet. The loop in zDoZBufferTest() tests each pixel in each scan-line in the facet. You'll want to carefully note line 1343, which will render a pixel only if it falls between the near clipping-plane and the far clipping-plane. If a facet intersects the near clipping-plane, for example, only the portion of the facet beyond the near clipping-plane will be drawn.

The zWriteZBuffer() function at line 1357 writes a Z-value to the Z-buffer. The zReadZBuffer() function at line 1374 reads a Z-value from the Z-buffer. The zResetZBuffer() at line 1396 resets every entry in the Z-buffer to the maximum distance. This function should always be called before a new scene is rendered.

How the shapes3d toolkit works

The source listing for the shapes3d toolkit is provided in FIG. B-2 in Appendix B. This module provides additional drivers for the engine3d toolkit. The code in the shapes3d module makes calls to engine3d functions in order to draw boxes, spheres, half-spheres, cylinders, cones, wedges, and curved surfaces. The functions in shapes3d have access to some of the variables used by engine3d. This means the shapes3d functions can determine if a facet is backward-facing, and whether it has been clipped or discarded by the view-volume clipping function in engine3d. Each function in shapes3d can also make a call to a function named zGetAssembly Coords() in the assemb3d module. If the primitive being rendered is part of a hierarchical solid, then the code in assemb3d will ensure that the proper set of XYZ coordinates are used. If the primitive being rendered is a stand-alone solid, then the code in assemb3d is not called.

Boxes The zDrawCube() function at line 0085 models and renders a box. You can see how the code manipulates the eight facets that comprise the box. The code from lines 0093 through 0273 is actually executed twice. During the first pass, no facets are drawn, but they are checked to determine if they are discarded or clipped by the view-volume clipping function. If so, the entire box is discarded. If not, then the second pass renders the facets. You might want to refer again to the zDrawFacet() function in the engine3d module to see how these two functions work together. The zDrawCube() function repeatedly calls the zGetCubeCoords() function located at line 0284 to calculate and store the various XYZ coordinates used during modeling.

Spheres The zDrawSphere() function at line 0335 renders a 3D sphere. You'll want to note lines 0346 through 0362, which makes the function smart enough to vary the size of the facets, depending on the size of the sphere and whether the program is executing in 16-color mode or 256-color mode. (See the code discussed in chapter 4 if you want to add 256-color mode capabilities.) The function repeatedly calls the zGetSphereShape() function located at line 0608 to compute the location of vertices around the surface of the sphere.

Cylinders The zDrawCylinder() function at line 0622 renders a 3D cylinder. The comments beside the code show how the body and ends of the cylinder are calculated and modeled. The code repeatedly calls the zGetCylinder Shape() function located at line 0860 to compute the location of XYZ coordinates on the surface of the cylinder.

Curved surfaces The zDrawCurve() function at line 0875 renders a 3D curved surface. The parametric curve calculations are at lines 0901 through 0903. You'll want to pay particular attention to the code at lines 0968 through 0990, which draws the obverse side of the facet if the facet faces away from the camera. As FIG. 8-12 and FIG. 8-13 show in chapter 8, this produces a more informative image. The zDrawCurve() function repeatedly calls the zGetCurveShape() function located at line 0999, which calculates the XY coordinates of a parametric curve in 2D space.

Cones and wedges The zDrawCone() function at line 1015 renders a 3D cone. It calls the zGetConeShape() function at line 1185 to compute the XYZ coordinates of points on the surface of the cone. The zDrawWedge() function at line 1198 renders a 3D wedge. This code is an adaptation of the code in zDrawCube() that renders a 3D box. The code repeatedly calls the zGetWedgeCoords() function located at line 1367 to calculate XYZ coordinates for the vertices of the wedge.

Half-spheres The zDrawHemisphere() function at line 1412 renders a 3D half-sphere. This code is cloned from the sphere code and the cylinder code. Half a sphere is rendered using technology from zDrawSphere(), then the flat surface at the equator is rendered using technology from zDraw Cylindor().

How the deform3d toolkit works

The source listing for the deform3d toolkit is provided in FIG. B-4 in Appendix B. This module provides additional drivers for the engine3d toolkit. The code in the deform3d module makes calls to engine3d functions in order to draw deformed boxes, bulged surfaces, and half-cylinders. This module is similar in form and functionality to the shapes3d module. The zDrawDeformBox() function at line 0071 deforms the south-facing facet of a box, making the end of the box either smaller or larger, as shown by FIG. 8-4 in chapter 8. Compare the code in this function with the code in zDrawCube() in shapes3d. The zDrawHalfCylinder() function at line 0344 renders a half-cylinder, using code cloned from zDrawCylinder() in shapes3d. The zDrawBulge() function at line 0663 is a modification of zDrawCurve() in engine3d.

How the lights3d toolkit works

The source listing for the lights3d toolkit is provided in FIG. B-3 in Appendix B. This module provides code that can reposition the light-source used by the engine3d toolkit. The zSetLightPosition() function at line 0035 resets the elevation angle and heading angle of the light-source. Note how lines 0046 and 0049 limit the possible positions. The heading can be set to any value from 0 degrees to 360 degrees, but the elevation can only range from horizontal (0 degrees) to vertical (90 degrees).

How the assemb3d toolkit works

The source listing for the assemb3d toolkit is provided in FIG. B-5 in Appendix B. This module provides hierarchical modeling drivers for the engine3d toolkit. The code in the assemb3d module configures 3D primitives to be part of a complex 3D solid. Unless a 3D primitive is processed by assemb3d, the primitive will be rendered as a stand-alone entity.

Parents and progeny This hierarchical modeling module works by inserting another set of 3D coordinates into the 3D transformation sequence. The XYZ coordinates of the structure-space it creates (see FIG. 8-17 in chapter 8) are used to reposition and reorient primitives in their role as part of a larger complex 3D solid (see FIG. 8-16). The zGetAssemblyCoords() function at line 0059 calculates these structure coordinates. Note how lines 0070 through 0078 calculate the rotation and translation for a parent in structure-space. Line 0080 calls another function named zGetSubAssyCoords() to calculate a nested set of coordinates if the primitive is a progeny. Remember, as you've already learned in previous chapters, progeny can be positioned and moved relative to their parents in order to produce articulated motion.

Hierarchical mode The zSetHierarchyMode() function at line 0087 toggles the hierarchical modeling mode. It sets a variable in the engine3d module. Neither shapes3d nor deform3d will call assemb3d if hierarchical modeling is toggled off. The zSetHierarchyLevel() function at line 0120 specifies whether a primitive is a parent or a progeny. Note how enough levels are provided so that the progeny can be the parent of another set of progeny.

Instancing The functions at lines 0141 through 0209 set the orientation and position of the entire assembly in 3D structure-space. The functions at lines 0216 through 0315 set the orientation and position of progeny relative to the position of the parent, which is itself relative to structure-space, of course.

Customizing the demo

This sample application can serve as a prototype for more advanced 3D software you might want to build. Here are a few tips on adapting the code for your own use. Before you begin, though, remember to read the License, provided as FIG. 7 in the introduction to the book.

To change the application's title as it appears on the caption bar of the window, change line 0103 in the obmain.bas startup module. To add or delete menu items, make changes in Visual Basic's menu design window. You'll also need to add code to support the menu items you've added. To upgrade the sample application to explicitly support custom colors in 256-color modes, see the discussion concerning palettes in chapter 4.

Where do you go from here?

Now that you've practiced some of the fundamental skills required for developing 3D applications for Windows, you're ready to explore the techniques of animation. However, you're the best judge of where you go from here. The next section in the book is Part Three, "Animation programming." It teaches you how to implement a frame-based, interactive animation system on a personal computer running Windows. If you choose instead to use the animation toolset as a black box, you can jump forward to Part Four, "Simulation programming." Whichever approach you take, the decision is yours. As you've already learned, the book is organized to be helpful to you no matter what learning style you use.

Part Three

Animation programming

Your task in Part Three is to prepare yourself for animation programming in Windows. You want to familiarize yourself with the fundamental skills required for 3D animation authoring, building, and playback. You also want the self-assurance that your understanding of PC-based animation will carry you through the advanced simulation and virtual reality tutorials that appear later in the book.

In Part Three of the book you'll learn about animation engines, animation control paradigms, 4D space-time, and more. Chapter 10, "Concepts and terms," is your introduction to the specialized language used by 3D animation programmers. In chapter 11, "Getting started with animation," you'll learn how to implement high-performance, frame-based animation sequences on personal computers running Windows. You'll discover the various paradigms that are used to control an animation sequence. In chapter 12 a hands-on tutorial shows you how to put your new animation knowledge to work. A sample application demonstrates 3D animation functions that can be used to prototype your own application development. You'll see how to rotate and move the 3D entities in a scene, and how to reposition the camera. In chapter 13 another hands-on tutorial demonstrates 3D motion-control programming. As you explore the sample application, you'll find out about articulated motion when you animate a complex 3D solid with independent moving parts.

Before you begin to delve into the fundamental skills of 3D animation programming for Windows, you'll want to acquaint yourself with some of the words phrases used by experienced animators. The next chapter, "Concepts and terms," provides tou with the background knowledge you need to get started.

10
Concepts and terms

This chapter introduces some basic concepts and terms that you'll be using while you explore Part Three, "Animation programming." You'll need to understand the technical language used in the next three chapters. This background knowledge will make it easier for you to grasp the fundamental skills required for using animated 3D graphics in your own Windows applications. Not only will you become familiar with what each term means, you'll also learn how each concept fits into the broader practice of 3D animation programming as a whole.

Defining concepts and terms

Authoring platform

An *authoring platform* is the development system used by a programmer to develop animated applications. It includes the software (the so-called *authoring tools*) that the programmer uses to design, build, and store an animation sequence. At a broader level, an authoring platform also includes the computer hardware configuration used by the programmer—processor type and speed, amount of memory, hard disk size and access time, display adapter, and monitor.

Delivery platform

A *delivery platform* is the software that is used to play the animation sequence on the user's computer. Delivery platforms are also called *playback engines*, *animation engines*, and *players*. Again, at a broader level, a delivery platform also includes the computer hardware configuration of the user.

Implementation and control

Together, *implementation* and *control* provide the means for producing animation sequences on personal computers under Windows. Implementation refers to the mechanics of creating the illusion of movement on the display. You can think of implementation as the interface between the software and the hardware. Control is concerned with managing the entities and events that are being animated. You can think of control as the interface between the subject matter and the software.

Animation engine

An *animation engine* is the software that manages the playback of an animation sequence. Animation engines are also called *playback engines* and *players*. Some engines are interactive, allowing the user to adjust the direction and rate of playback at run-time.

Computer-assisted traditional animation

Computer-assisted traditional animation (*CATA*) refers to the use of computers to automate the process of traditional animation, which includes techniques like cell animation and film animation. An example of traditional animation is the typical Saturday morning TV cartoon program. Computer-assisted traditional animation is 2D animation.

Procedural animation

Procedural animation is object-oriented animation. It can be 2D or 3D. Each entity in the scene is treated as an object. The software uses programmer-defined rules to calculate the next position of each *entity* (actor) during playback. The rules can describe not only the actor's behavior in the scene (*staging*), but also the actor's behavior in relation to other actors present in the scene (*procedural interaction*).

Physically based animation

Physically based animation is 3D animation that uses the laws of physics to regulate the motion of entities during playback. Physically based animation is also called *constraint-based animation* because the motion is governed by so-called *constraints*. Four types of physically based animation are available:

- forward kinematics
- forward dynamics
- inverse kinematics
- inverse dynamics

Forward kinematics concerns the process of calculating the result of the application of velocity or acceleration to an entity. *Forward dynamics* concerns the process of calculating the result of the application of force, loads, and constraints to an entity. *Inverse kinematics* is the process of calculating the velocity or acceleration required to move an entity from one position to another during a specified period of time. *Inverse dynamics* is the process of calculating the forces, loads, or constraints required to move an entity from one position to another during a proscribed period of time.

Interactive animation

Interactive animation refers to any animation playback that provides a means for the user to control the animation. Interactive animation can be 2D or 3D. A typical interactive animation engine provides forward/reverse, start/stop, single-step, and freeze-frame capabilities.

Virtual reality-based animation

Virtual reality-based animation is interactive 3D animation that is used to *model* (simulate) a 3D environment which the user can explore.

4D space-time

Computer animation is the visual display of *4D space-time*. The 4D paradigm is derived from the concept of 3D. Entities in the real-world possess the three dimensions of width, height, and depth. This is 3D, or three-dimensional modeling. When such an entity is displayed by a computer, the image is presented in 3D-space using XYZ coordinates. When the image is animated the fourth dimension of time is added. Animation is, after all, movement across space over time. An animated 3D entity is a representation of 4D space-time using XYZT coordinates.

How is animation implemented under Windows?

As you've already learned, *implementation* refers to the mechanics of creating the illusion of movement on the display. It is the interface between the software and the hardware. Four types of implementation are available under Windows:

- fixed-loop animation
- idle-loop animation
- timer-based message-handler animation
- timer-based direct-call animation

Each of these four types of implementation can be effected as either *real-time animation* or as *frame animation*.

Real-time animation

Real-time animation refers to animated sequences where each image element is drawn by the software at the same time the animation is being presented. Real-time animation is called *cast-based animation* by multimedia programmers.

Frame animation

Frame animation refers to animated sequences that fetch and display previously drawn images (*frames*). Frame animation uses static images, whereas real-time animation uses dynamic images. The frames used by a frame-based animation sequence can be stored in memory or on hard disk.

Staging

Staging refers to the process of choreographing an animation sequence. Staging means specifying the location of entities (actors) as they move about the scene.

Articulated motion

Articulated motion refers to the process of animating hierarchical entities. Articulated motion specifies things like rotating joints, swinging arms, moving parts, and so on. Consider, for example, the animation of a 3D android. Staging would be used to specify the location of the android as it walks across the scene; articulated motion would be used to specify how its arms swing while it walks.

Where do you go from here?

Now that you've familiarized yourself with some of the basic concepts and terms used in animation programming, you're ready to start learning the fundamental skills. The next chapter, "Getting started with animation," teaches you about animation authoring, building, and playback on personal computers running Windows.

11
Getting started with animation

This chapter teaches you how to use Windows-compliant animation to display moving 3D scenes in the viewport of your application's window. It discusses the concepts of implementation, control, 4D space-time, frame animation, physically based animation, and others. You'll learn about implementation and control and how these two concepts provide the underpinnings for animation programming. You'll also grasp the various low-level tools at your disposal, including blitting and page copying.

Also covered is how animation can be implemented in a Windows application using different types of animation engines and paradigms. You'll discover why timer-based message-handler animation is the best medium for producing Windows-compliant animation sequences. You'll see why the process of control is so important, and you'll investigate different forms of control, including computer-assisted traditional animation, procedural animation, and physically based animation. You'll also delve into interactive animation and virtual reality-based animation.

Implementation vs. control

Animation programming is founded on the concepts of *implementation* and *control.* Implementation involves the mechanics of creating the illusion of movement on the display. Control is concerned with managing the image-content of the animation itself.

Implementation

Implementation is the interface between the software and the hardware. Implementation refers to the hardware-dependent algorithms and the code that produce the illusion of movement on the display. Implementation is facilitated through two different types of animation engines. Either form of engine can use any one of four different types of animation paradigms.

Animation engines As an application developer, you can create, build, and store your animation sequences using two types of animation engines: *real-time animation* and *frame animation*.

Real-time animation Real-time animation refers to animated sequences in which each image element is drawn by the software while the animation is being presented. Each frame is usually built on a hidden bitmap and copied to the display when it has been completed. Real-time animation is called *cast-based animation* by multimedia programmers.

Frame animation Frame animation refers to animated sequences that fetch and display previously drawn frames. The frames used by a frame-based animation sequence can be stored in memory or on hard disk.

Animation paradigms Whether you're using a real-time animation engine or a frame-based animation engine, you can implement it using any one of four different paradigms, including

- fixed-loop
- idle-loop
- timer-based message-handler
- timer-based direct-call

Fixed-loop animation A *fixed loop* is a block of code that executes repeatedly for a preset number of iterations. While the loop is executing, other applications in the Windows environment are prevented from running. The fixed loop monopolizes all the system resources. Fixed-loop code is useful for brief splashes of animation (so-called *spot animation*), provided that the animation sequence is brief enough to avoid adversely affecting other applications that might be running.

Idle-loop animation If you're a responsible application developer you'll modify your fixed loop and make it an idle loop. Instead of monopolizing the entire computer system, your application makes calls to the GDI's GetMessage() and DispatchMessage() functions in order to check for user input while the loop is executing. This provides Windows with opportunities to service other applications. This paradigm is called *idle-loop animation* because your animation sequence runs only if the rest of the system is idle—that is, if no other application needs processor time.

Timer-based message-handler animation Timer-based algorithms offer the most effective means of controlling animation playback under Windows. It meshes seamlessly with Visual Basic's way of doing things. After you have activated a Timer tool, Windows sends regular timer events to your application. You can use each event as a cue to display the next frame in an animation sequence.

This approach is noteworthy for its versatility. It provides two different ways to display the next frame. First, whenever a timer message is received, your application can call the function you provide to display the next frame. Second, routines anywhere in your application can directly call the function you provide to display the next frame. This makes it easy to implement freeze-frame and single-step features for the user of your application.

Control

As you've just learned, implementation is the interface between the software and the hardware. Control, on the other hand, is the interface between the subject matter and the software. Three types of control are available for your real-time and frame-based animation sequences:

- Computer-assisted traditional animation.
- Procedural animation.
- Physically based animation.

Computer-assisted traditional animation Traditional animation is a mature technology that evolved from the so-called "magic lantern" parlor games of the 1820s. Traditional animation uses single-frame photography of individual celluloid sheets stacked on top of each other and illuminated from below. On each cel is a hand-drawn image of a cartoon character, a prop, or a background. Saturday-morning TV cartoon programs are examples of traditional film animation. When computers are recruited to assist in the production of traditional animation, the process is called *computer-assisted traditional animation* (*CATA*). It is sometimes called *scripted animation* by computer programmers.

Scripted animation is managed by a script. Individual *entities* (actors) move in front of a background. Actors can include characters, props, and scenery elements. Multimedia developers refer to these entities as *cast-members*. The paradigm is called *cast-based animation* (especially if it is being produced using real-time animation). This type of animation control is called *explicit control.*

Scripted animation goes by many names. It is also called *character animation, cel animation, conventional animation, traditional animation,* and *film animation.* You're entering a milieu where the tricks of the trade are already well-documented and well-established. Probably the most productive trick used by traditional animators is *inbetweening* (or *tweening*).

Tweening means creating intermediate drawings from a set of key drawings prepared by a senior animator. Each key drawing represents an important moment in the animation sequence. Junior animators draw all the intermediate frames that must appear between two *key drawings* (or *key frames*). Tweening is time-consuming, laborious work. It is the type of chore for which computers are well-suited. When a personal computer is used to generate intermediate images from two key frames, the process is called *interpolation*. The interpolations can follow a straight line (*linear interpolation*) or a curve (*spline interpolation* or *curved interpolation*).

A number of "rules of animation" have been discovered (or invented) during the 70-year history of film animation. The three most important rules are *deformation*, *camera mechanics*, and *staging*.

Deformation refers to the squashing and stretching of an entity. A bouncing ball should be squashed (compressed) each time it strikes the floor. It should be stretched (extended) when it bounces away. Subtle deformations like these add a lifelike quality to an animation sequence.

Camera mechanics are concerned with camera movement. The slow-in/slow-out principle states that any camera movement must start very slowly. It should build up gradually to full speed. It should then reduce speed gradually before stopping gently. This carefully choreographed slow-in/slow-out camera movement is the only way to avoid jerky camera pans and zooms.

Staging is concerned with directing the animation. Choreography, timing, plot development, dramatic lighting, actor entrances and exits, props, scenery, costume, and other elements fall under the purview of staging.

Procedural animation *Procedural animation* is object-oriented animation. During animation playback, the software prepares the next frame by calculating the next position for each entity in the scene. These calculations are based on programmer-defined rules of behavior. The rules describe an entity's behavior in the scene itself and its behavior relative to other entities in the scene. In the latter case, the process is called *procedural interaction*. The actors, props, and scenery elements that make up a scene are the cast of players for the animation sequence. Procedural animation is similar to cast-based animation, a technique used by multimedia programmers.

Physically based animation *Physically based animation* uses the laws of physics to manage the motion of 3D entities during animation playback. Physically based animation is also called *constraint-based animation*. Motion in a constraint-based system is modeled using *constraints*, which are limiting conditions or forces.

Consider the animation of a bouncing baseball, for example. Gravity is one force among many acting on the ball. The baseball is not being pushed up by gravity, it is being pushed down. The force of gravity is called a constraint. The motion of the baseball is being constrained (limited) by the force of gravity. When the ball hits the rolled surface of the infield, it does not penetrate the surface, but instead bounces back. The baseball cannot pass through the surface. It is constrained to one side of the surface.

Physically based animation is concerned with positions, velocities, forces, mass, and constraints. This method of animation control embodies:

- forward kinematics
- forward dynamics
- inverse kinematics
- inverse dynamics

Kinematics means the positions and velocities of 3D entities. *Dynamics* means laws of physics such as force, mass, and others that govern those positions and velocities.

Forward kinematics *Forward kinematics* is the process of calculating what happens when velocity or acceleration is applied to an entity. Forward kinematics does not concern itself with forces or mass, but considers only the motion itself. Your application can use forward kinematics to check if two entities collide during an animation sequence.

Forward dynamics *Forward dynamics* is the process of calculating what happens when force, loads, or constraints are applied to an entity. In general, dynamics concerns itself with the laws of physics that govern kinematics. Your application can use dynamics to calculate the motion (the kinematics) of an entity that results from forces acting on the entity. You can also use dynamics to calculate forces resulting from the motion of the entity. Like its cousin, forward kinematics, forward dynamics can check if two entities collide, but it can also calculate the forces resulting from the impact.

Inverse kinematics *Inverse kinematics* is the process of calculating the velocity or acceleration required to move an entity from one location to another location during a specified period of time. Inverse kinematics uses a programmer-supplied target location and calculates the amount of velocity or acceleration required to move the entity to that location.

Inverse dynamics *Inverse dynamics* is the process of calculating the forces or constraints required to move an entity of specified mass from one location to another location during a specified period of time. Inverse dynamics uses a programmer-supplied target location and calculates the forces required to move the entity to that location.

Interactive animation As you learned in the previous chapter, *interactive animation* refers to an animation playback environment that provides a means for the user to influence the animation. Typical interactive controls include forward/reverse, start/stop, single-step, and freeze-frame capabilities. Interactive animation can be implemented using either a real-time engine or a frame-based engine. Interactive animation can provide the functionality of computer-assisted traditional animation, procedural animation, and physically based animation.

Virtual reality-based animation As you've already learned, *virtual reality-based animation* is interactive 3D animation that is used to simulate a 3D environment, which the user can explore. Virtual reality can be designed to operate in three modes:

- passive
- exploratory
- interactive

A *passive virtual reality* session is not interactive. An automated tour through the 3D environment is provided while the user simply observes. Architectural walkthroughs and flypasts are examples of passive virtual reality.

An *exploratory virtual reality* session allows the user to roam through the 3D environment. The user interacts with the virtual reality engine, but cannot interact with any entities residing inside the virtual space. A simulated museum exhibit is an example of exploratory virtual reality.

An *interactive virtual reality* session allows the user to interact with entities within the virtual environment. The user can push, pull, grab, throw, and influence entities residing in virtual space. A motor vehicle training simulator is an example of interactive virtual reality.

4D space-time

Computer animation is the visual display of 4D space-time. The 4D paradigm is derived from the concept of 3D. Entities in the real world possess the three dimensions of width, height, and depth. This is 3D (three-dimensional) modeling. When a 3D entity is portrayed by a computer, the image is presented in 3D-space using XYZ coordinates. When the entity is animated, the fourth dimension of time is added. Animation is movement across space over time. An animated 3D entity is a display of 4D space-time using XYZT coordinates.

In order to manage 4D space-time, your application must monitor and update three sets of animation dynamics at run-time:

- motion
- update
- viewing

Taken together, these dynamic attributes describe all aspects of an animation sequence.

Motion dynamics

Motion dynamics refers to the location, orientation, and juxtaposition of individual entities. Motion dynamics is also called *time-varying position.* If the scene is rendered in 3D, motion dynamics are described by the rotation and translation of an entity.

Update dynamics

Update dynamics is concerned with changes in shape, color, and texture. During a bouncing ball sequence, for example, update dynamics ensures that the ball is suitably deformed (squashed) each time it strikes the floor.

Viewing dynamics

Viewing dynamics is concerned with changes in lighting, camera, and viewpoint. During an animation sequence the camera can zoom in or zoom out, pan left or right, tilt up or down, truck in or truck out, or track alongside a moving object. Viewing dynamics manages these camera movements, as well as changes in lighting and illumination.

Animation implementation

The Windows GDI provides a set of low-level tools useful for animation. The most effective of these tools are *graphic arrays* and the GDI functions that manipulate them. A graphic array is a block of memory containing a rectangular image. This image is called a *bitmap* (or a *bitblt*, pronounced *bit-blit*). Larger images (full-screen or full-window) are usually called *bitmaps*. Smaller images are called either bitmaps or bitblts.

Blitting

Pasting a bitblt at a new location is called *blitting*. Your application can call the GDI's BitBlt() function to copy a bitmap from a source location and paste it at a target location. You can copy from:

- A memory location to the screen.
- The screen to a memory location.
- One memory location to another.
- One screen position to another screen position.

Page copying

Copying a window-sized bitmap is called *page copying*. A *page* is a buffer in memory. Animators call it a *hidden frame*. Your application can call Bit Blt() to copy the contents of the display window to a hidden frame. BitBlt() can also copy the contents of the hidden frame (the bitmap) back to the screen (the viewport of your application's window). This is the basis of frame animation.

Mattes and friskets

In addition to simply pasting bitmaps, the GDI provides *raster operators* that can produce different visual effects when writing the bitmap at the new location. Raster operators use boolean logic. A transparent put can be implemented by combining the XOR and OR operators. This makes it possible to cleanly paste odd-shaped, multicolored images onto multicolored backgrounds. The transparent put operation uses a white matte to prepare the area where the image will be pasted. The code uses a frisket metaphor to protect the existing scene from being overwritten by the background portion of the bitmap rectangle. Because the background portion of the rectangle does not show, it is called transparent. Mattes and friskets mean you can animate multicolored objects against a multicolored background.

For hands-on examples showing how to implement a transparent put function see the author's other books on animation programming: *C for Windows Animation Programming*, published in 1993 by Windcrest/McGraw-Hill (book no. 4114); and *Visual Basic Animation Programming*, published in 1993 by Windcrest/McGraw-Hill (book no. 4224). Both books are available through your favorite bookstore, or you can write to the publisher and request the current catalog.

Frame animation

As you've already learned, frame animation uses static images. During a frame animation sequence, the animation engine fetches and displays previously completed full-window images that have been stored on disk. A typical engine is smart enough to load the entire animation sequence into memory, if space permits, for better playback performance.

During development, many programmers paste small bitmap images onto the viewport of the application's window in order to assemble each completed frame. The software then saves the image from the display to the hard disk. If your application must build frames at run-time, you can make the entire process invisible to the user by building each completed image on a hidden page and saving each frame to the hard disk. If bitmap images are impractical, some programmers draw each frame from scratch. The software then saves each completed frame to the hard disk. Again, if your application needs to build new frames at run-time, the entire process can be concealed from the user by building each frame on a hidden page and saving to hard disk.

Playback of a frame animation sequence is usually disk-to-display or memory-to-display. The frames of the animation sequence are usually stored on hard disk. If memory permits, a typical playback engine attempts to load all necessary frames into memory, from where they can be quickly displayed by copying them in sequence to the viewport of the application's window. If insufficient memory is available, the engine loads individual frames from disk during playback. In such cases, animation performance is directly related to hard disk performance. In all cases, animation performance is affected by viewport size.

Figure 11-1 lists arguments for the SetTimer() function, and shows the resulting frames per second. Figure 11-2 shows the elapsed time for individual frames for SetTimer(1) (18.2 fps).

11-1 Arguments for the GDI's SetTimer() function.

SetTimer( ) arguments		
Clock ticks	ms	Events per second
1	55	1000/55 = 18.2 fps
2	110	1000/110 = 9.1 fps
3	165	1000/165 = 6.1 fps
4	220	1000/220 = 4.5 fps
5	275	1000/275 = 3.6 fps
6	330	1000/330 = 3.0 fps

11-2 Time cues for animation running at 18 fps.

Animation Timing	
Frame Number	Elapsed time
1	.0555
2	.1111
3	.1667
4	.2222
5	.2778
6	.3333
7	.3889
8	.4444
9	.5000
10	.5555
11	.6111
12	.6667
13	.7222
14	.7778
15	.8333
16	.8889
17	.9444
18	1.0000

Frame storage of 256 × 255 viewport As you've already learned, the sample applications in the book use a viewport whose dimensions are 256 pixels across and 255 pixels high. If Windows is running in a two-color mode, each frame requires 8,160 bytes of storage space:

$(256 \times 255 \times 1bpp) / 8bpb = 8,160$

where *bpp* is bits-per-pixel and *bpb* is bits-per-byte. If the animation is running in a VGA 16-color mode, then 32,640 bytes are needed for each frame:

$(256 \times 255 \times 4bpp) / 8bpb = 32,640$

If Windows is using an SVGA 256-color mode, then 65,280 bytes are needed to store each frame:

$(256 \times 255 \times 8bpp) / 8bpb = 65,280$

If the application is running on a system using an accelerator-based 65,000-color mode, then 130,560 bytes are required for each frame:

$(256 \times 255 \times 16bpp) / 8bpb = 130,560$

These file storage requirements are summarized in FIG. 11-3.

Uncompressed file storage		
256-by-255 viewport		
Bits per pixel	Color	Storage required
1	2	8160 bytes
4	16	32,640 bytes
8	256	65,280 bytes
16	65536	130,560 bytes

11-3 Storage requirements for uncompressed images.

Where do you go from here?

Now that you've familiarized yourself with the implementation and control of frame-based animation sequences on personal computers running Windows, you're ready to delve into a hands-on tutorial. In the next chapter you'll be invited to inspect the source code for a sample application that provides 3D animation features such as:

- Interactive control over playback, including forward/reverse, start/stop, freeze-frame, and single-step modes.
- Explicit animation support for 2-color and 16-color modes, and nominal support for 256-color mode.
- Playback in VGA and SVGA display resolutions, including 640 × 480, 800 × 600, and 1024 × 768.
- Well-behaved animation algorithms that permit other applications to continue running in the Windows environment.
- Windows-compliant code that ensures the sample application continues animating even when its window is partially covered.

The knowledge you've acquired in this chapter provides you with the background you need to grasp how the animated sample application works. You'll have the ability to merge its functions into your own applications.

12
Tutorial:
3D animation programming

This chapter provides a hands-on tutorial that demonstrates the animation fundamentals you learned in the previous two chapters. You'll delve into important programming skills for developing animation, simulation, visualization, and virtual reality applications. A User's Guide shows you how to run the sample application and a Programmer's Guide provides explanations of how the source code for the animation engine works.

You'll learn how the source code works in the sample application and how the animation engine builds the animation sequence and saves each frame to disk. You want to know how the code can switch to disk-based animation playback if it can't find enough memory to store the entire animation sequence. You want to learn how the keyboard is used to provide interactive controls like start/stop, forward/reverse, freeze-frame, and single-step. Finally, you'll learn how to use the functions of the animation engine in your own graphics applications.

You'll see how to use an array of pointers to filenames to manage animation sequences, including pointers to select sequential filenames while the code saves each frame to disk during the build process. Later, during playback, you'll discover how to allocate memory when the animation engine attempts to load the entire animation sequence into RAM—and you'll discover how to cancel the load if memory is insufficient—and run the animation directly from disk instead. Overall, you'll become familiar with how to put together the various parts of an animated application for Windows.

A user's guide to the sample application

In this section, you'll learn how to use the sample application named *animate*. Before you can run this application, you must build it. The source listings for the sample application are presented as FIG. C-3 in Appendix C. Source listings for toolkits that must be linked in to build the finished application are presented in Appendix B. All source files are also provided on the companion disk. See Appendix A if you need assistance compiling the program.

Starting the sample application

There are two ways to start the sample application. You can start it directly from the Visual Basic editor or you can start it from Windows' Program Manager.

Startup from Visual Basic If you're using Visual Basic to prototype and experiment with the sample application, you can run the sample application directly from your editor.

Startup from Windows' Program Manager If you've already compiled the sample application, you can start it from Windows' Program Manager. From the Windows desktop, pull down the File menu and select Run. When the dialog box appears, type the full pathname of the program. Here's an example:

    c:\directory\subdirectory\animate.exe

You should substitute directory names that reflect your own system. When you select the OK button of the dialog box, the sample application will start.

Using the sample application

When the sample application starts up, a splash sign-on notice appears. Choose OK to continue.

Four menu names are displayed on the menu bar. They are File, Edit, Run, and Using. You can use the File menu to quit the program. The Edit menu contains no active features. You can use the Run menu to explore the animation build process, saving to disk, loading from disk, and animation playback. The Using menu contains a brief run-time help message.

You can use either a mouse or the keyboard to operate this sample application. If you're using a mouse, simply point and click. If you're using the keyboard, press Alt to move the focus to the menu bar, then press the appropriate underscored mnemonic key to pull down a menu and select a mnemonic key to choose an item from the menu. Alternatively, you can use the up and down arrow keys to move the highlight bar to the menu item you want and then press Enter.

The Run menu The Run menu controls the animation engine. The features provided in the menu are shown in FIG. 12-1. If you select the Production menu item, the nested menu depicted in FIG. 12-2 appears. If you're experimenting with the sample application for the first time, you may wish to se-

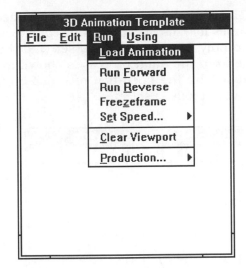

12-1 The Run menu from the sample application animate.frm.

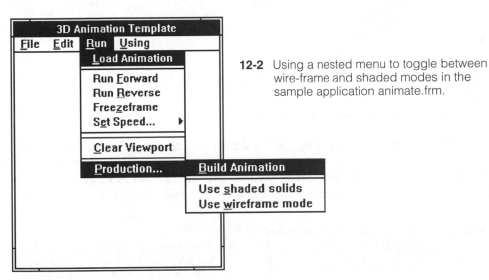

12-2 Using a nested menu to toggle between wire-frame and shaded modes in the sample application animate.frm.

lect wire-frame mode. This will speed up the animation-building process, allowing you to play the finished animation sequence sooner than if you had selected the fully shaded mode.

Building an animation When you select Build Animation from the Production menu, it is important to realize that a build process can be interrupted at any time by pressing Ctrl-Break if you're running the demo program from the Visual Basic editor. This trapdoor allows you to cancel a build that is in progress if it is consuming more time than you can accommodate. Some animation sequences presented later in the book require 3 hours to build in fully shaded mode. However, the sample application that you're investigating here requires less time. For example, an 80386DX running at 33

MHz without a numeric coprocessor needs only 35 seconds to build all 36 frames for this 3D animation sequence if you've selected wire-frame mode, and only 21 minutes if you selected the fully shaded mode. A sample image from the build process is shown in FIG. 12-3. The difference in time is caused by the operation of the Z-buffer depth-sort routines when fully shaded mode is selected.

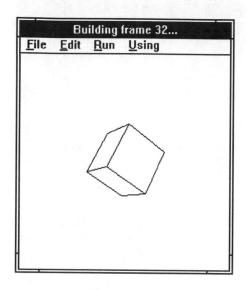

12-3 A sample image from the sample application animate.frm during an animation build session.

Loading an animation To load an animation sequence from disk, select Load Animation from the Run menu, as shown in FIG. 12-1. If enough extended memory is available, the animation engine will load all 36 frames into memory. When it's finished, the message box shown in FIG. 12-4 will

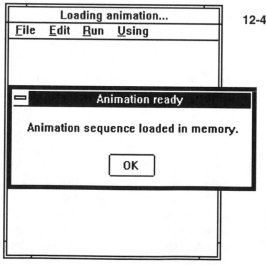

12-4 The sample application animate.frm uses a message box to advise the user when the animation sequence has been loaded into memory from disk.

be displayed. If insufficient physical memory is available and Windows memory manager cannot use virtual memory, then the sample application will advise you that it intends to load each frame from disk as needed during playback of the animation sequence.

The default playback speed is 18 frames per second. Personal computers running at 25 MHz or faster (and using the VGA's 640 × 480 × 16-color mode) can sustain this rate. You can reset the animation playback rate to any of the settings in the Set Speed menu as shown in FIG. 12-5. The rate can be set either before, during, or after playback.

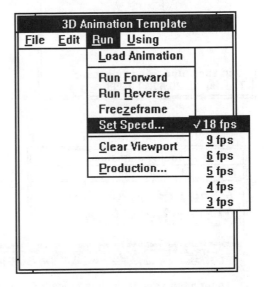

12-5 Using a nested menu to select the animation playback speed in the sample application animate.frm.

Windows-compliant A typical frame from a playback session provided by the sample application is shown in FIG. 12-6. During playback, you can use the mouse to drag the application's window partially off-screen—and the animation will continue to run. If you start another program and it partially covers the sample application's window, the animation will still continue to run.

Robust menuing If you attempt to load an animation sequence from disk after it has already been loaded, the software is robust enough to recognize the redundancy and to gracefully avoid the duplication of work, as shown in FIG. 12-7. Likewise, if you attempt to build an animation sequence that already exists on disk, the software is intelligent enough to realize that the added work is not necessary, as shown in FIG. 12-8.

Running an animation To start an animation sequence that you've loaded in from disk, simply select Run Forward from the Run menu, as shown in FIG. 12-1. The playback will begin. You can then pull down the Run menu and select Run Reverse to run the animation sequence backwards. To explore single-step control, select Freezeframe from the Run menu while the anima-

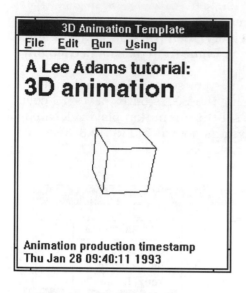

12-6 A typical image generated during animation playback by the sample application animate.frm.

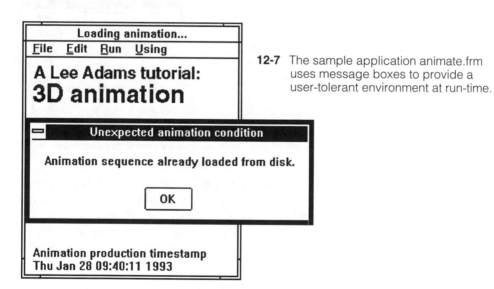

12-7 The sample application animate.frm uses message boxes to provide a user-tolerant environment at run-time.

tion is running. Then press the right arrow key to advance to the next frame. Strike the left arrow key to back up to the previous frame. Pressing and holding down the right arrow key will cause the animation sequence to play at the fastest rate supported by your hardware.

Quitting the sample application

To quit the sample application, choose Exit from the File menu. A message box will appear, allowing you to confirm or cancel your request.

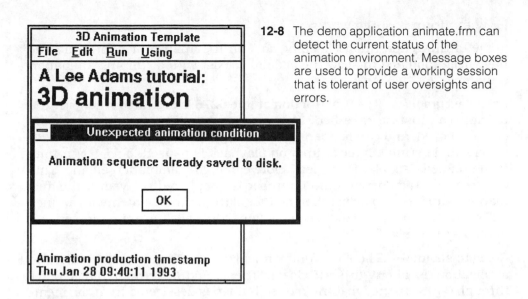

12-8 The demo application animate.frm can detect the current status of the animation environment. Message boxes are used to provide a working session that is tolerant of user oversights and errors.

A programmer's guide to the sample application

This section describes how the source code works. The discussion emphasizes the .frm module because many of the 3D toolkit functions that are found in this sample application have already been discussed in chapter 9.

The source listings for the sample application are presented as FIG. C-3 in Appendix C. Source listings for the linked-in toolkits are provided in Appendix B. For tips on building the sample application, see Appendix A. The source files for the sample application are also provided on the companion disk as anglobal.bas, anmain.bas, animate.frm, anplay.bas, engine3d.bas, shapes3d.bas, deform3d.bas, assemb3d.bas, and lights3d.bas.

How the global module works

The global module, anglobal.bas, is cloned from global modules described earlier in the book. You'll want to note the code at lines 0100 through 0117, which declares constants and variables that support the animation authoring and playback functions. The code at lines 0119 through 0167 provides animation scripting capabilities that manage the movement of the camera, light-source, and actors. You'll also want to familiarize yourself with the code at lines 0169 through 0181, which help manage disk-related operations.

How the startup module works

The startup module, anmain.bas, is responsible for initializing a set of variables when the application is launched. You'll want to note lines 0058 through 0093, where an array of filenames is initialized. Each file will store one frame from the animation sequence.

How the form module works

Some of the general housekeeping code in the animate.frm form module have been modified to allow the code to coexist with a running animation sequence.

Persistent graphics The Sub function at line 0276 is activated whenever the client area must be refreshed. This event occurs if the window is uncovered or moved, and can happen when the animation is running. Line 0280 checks to determine if the animation playback is paused. If so, a run-time token named Redisplay is toggled before calling the animation engine. This ensures that the current frame number is simply redisplayed. If the animation sequence is playing, then neither of the If...End If statements at lines 0277 or 0280 will fire and the code at line 0286 calls the animation engine to display the next frame.

Graceful shutdown The IDM_ function at line 0388 is activated when the application is about to shut down. The If...End If block at lines 0401 through 0405 ensures that the hidden bitmap is deselected from the memory display-context and deleted from memory. Line 0400 releases the timer resource that was used to manage the animation playback. The If...End If block at lines 0393 through 0399 checks to see if an animation sequence was loaded into RAM. If so, the loop at lines 0395 through 0397 deletes the 36 bitmaps from memory. Finally, line 0406 shuts down the 3D toolkit and line 0407 shuts down the application itself.

Managing the timer The Sub function at line 0811 is activated when an incoming timer event is detected. Because the Windows operating system gives a higher priority to timer events than to menuing functions, it is necessary to insert special code here to accommodate slower processors. If a 16MHz 80386SX is attempting to run the animation sequence at 18 frames per second, for example, the user will not be able to pull down any menus from the menu bar. The selected menu will simply never appear because the next timer event occurs before Windows has an opportunity to display the requested menu. Line 0813 decrements a variable named TimerCounter and the following line tests its value. Its normal state is zero, but if a menu has been selected then the code at line 0777, for example, will set it to a higher value, thereby allowing the If...End If statement at line 0814 to fire. This causes a delay of enough duration to give Windows time to display the menu on slower processors. If no menu has been chosen by the user, then line 0818 executes whenever an incoming timer event occurs, and a function named zShowNextFrame() is called to display the next frame in the animation sequence.

Managing the animation engine The function named zSaveAnimation() at line 0620 builds the images and saves each frame to disk. The function at line 0607 fires whenever the user selects Forward Playback from the Run menu. The If...End If statement at line 0608 checks to ensure that the animation is in fact ready for playback. After setting a few run-time tokens, the code at line 0614 calls a function named zShowNextFrame() to display the next frame.

The function at line 0784 is activated whenever the user selects Reverse Playback from the Run menu. The code in this block is similar to the code described in the previous paragraph.

The Sub function at line 0698 fires whenever the user pauses the playback. Line 0707 sets a run-time token named Pause to True. Subsequent calls to zShowNextFrame(), which checks the value of Pause, will merely redisplay the current frame. When the animation is paused, the Sub function at line 0247 allows the arrow keys to control the display of frames. If the user presses the right arrow key, for example, then line 0265 carefully ensures that the animation direction is correctly set and calls zShowNextFrame(). Note how the code at lines 0259 through 0261 masterfully toggles and juggles some run-time values before and after calling the animation engine.

How the core functions work

The core functions in the remainder of the .c source file fall into two categories. The first category of routines provides animation authoring functions that create the frames and save them to disk. The second category consists of routines that provide animation playback functions to display the next frame, to reset the animation rate, and to load the animation sequence from disk into memory.

Animation authoring functions Three authoring functions are provided. The first authoring function, at line 0620, looks after creating all 36 frames and saving them to disk. It does so by calling the second authoring function, at line 0824, which creates one frame and saves it to disk. This second function works by calling a third authoring function, at line 0895, which draws the appropriate image on the frame being built.

The zSaveAnimation() function at line 0620 supervises the animation-building process. Lines 0633 through 0644 initializes the camera starting position and path it will follow during the animation. The struct that holds these parameters was declared in the anglobal.bas global module. Next, lines 0646 through 0653 initialize the light-source starting position and the path it will follow during the animation. Then, lines 0655 through 0671 initialize the actor (in this instance, a box), its starting position, and the path it will follow during the animation. Finally, the loop at lines 0673 through 0682 repeatedly calls zBuildFrame() to build each frame in the animation sequence.

The zBuildFrame() function at line 0824 builds one frame and saves it to disk. You'll want to carefully note the code at line 0828, which produces an ongoing progress report message on the application's caption bar during the build process. The code calls zDrawCel() to draw the image and then displays the titles and time stamp (lines 0831 through 0850). It then calls zSaveFrame() in the anplay.bas module to save the bitmap to disk.

The zDrawCel() function at line 0895 draws the appropriate image on the frame currently being assembled by zBuildFrame(). Note how the variable FrameNum is used to update the camera, light-source, and actor before the code at lines 0966 through 0971 draws the box being animated.

How the animation module works

Three functions are provided as core routines in the anplay.bas source file. The zShowNextFrame() function, at line 0094, is the animation engine itself. It displays the next frame in the animation sequence. It is intelligent enough to understand if the animation is running in forward or reverse mode. If the animation is paused, the animation engine merely redisplays the current frame. The zLoadFrame() function, at line 0029, is called repeatedly in order to load the entire animation sequence from disk into memory. If insufficient memory is available (in real mode), the calling function is smart enough to cancel the load and set a token that advises the animation engine to load each frame as needed from disk during playback. The zSaveFrame() function, at line 0058, is called repeatedly in order to save the animation sequence to disk.

You'll want to pay careful attention to zShowNextFrame(). If all frames have been loaded into memory, the code at lines 0100 through 0127 executes. Lines 0100 through 0111 check various run-time tokens. The If...End If statements at lines 0112 and 0118 adjust the frame ID number, depending on whether the animation is running in forward or reverse mode. The call to the GDI's BitBlt() function at line 0126 copies the appropriate frame bitmap to the display. If the animation is running from disk, then the code at lines 0129 through 0161 executes. This block of code is structured similar to the code just described, except for the file-loading statements at lines 0152 through 0159.

The zLoadAnimation() function at line 0493 in the animate.frm form module loads the entire animation sequence from disk. First, it creates the bitmaps that will store the frames. The For...Next loop at lines 0511 through 0516 increments an index that points to elements in an array of bitmap handles in order to create and store all bitmaps. The For...Next loop at lines 0530 through 0539 increments an index that points to elements in an array of filenames while it is loading the animation sequence. These two arrays were declared in the anglobal.bas global module and initialized in the anmain.bas startup module.

If an error occurs during the bitmap-loading process, the block of code at lines 0543 through 0545 uses another For...Next statement to delete all the bitmap objects that were created before the error occurred.

Where do you go from here?

Now that you've practiced some of the fundamental skills required for developing 3D animation software for Windows, you're ready to explore more advanced techniques. The next chapter, "3D motion-control programming," provides a hands-on tutorial that demonstrates articulated motion. You'll see how to use hierarchical modeling to create animated displays of complex 3D solids with moving parts.

13
Tutorial:
3D motion-control
programming

This chapter provides a hands-on tutorial that demonstrates the motion-control fundamentals presented in previous chapters. A User's Guide shows you how to run the sample application, and a Programmer's Guide provides explanations of how hierarchical modeling techniques are integrated with the animation engine. You'll learn how the animation engine uses hierarchical modeling to build each frame in the animation sequence and then save it to disk. You'll also learn how to use hierarchical modeling functions in your own animated graphics applications.

This chapter will show you how to use a hierarchical structure to create a complex 3D solid that can be animated using articulated motion. You'll see how to position the progeny relative to the parent and how to adapt the animation engine discussed in chapter 12 to support complex 3D entities with moving parts.

A user's guide to the sample application

In this section you'll learn how to use the sample application named assembly. Before you can run the application, you must build the executable. The program listings for the sample application are presented as FIG. C-4 in Appendix C. Source listings for toolkits that must be linked in to build the finished executable are presented in Appendix B. All source files are also provided on the companion disk. See Appendix A for tips on compiling the program.

Starting the sample application

There are two ways you can start the sample application. You can start it directly from Visual Basic or you can launch it from Windows' Program Manager.

Startup from Visual Basic You can run the sample application directly from Visual Basic if you've loaded the assembly.mak project file.

Startup from Windows' Program Manager From the Windows desktop, pull down the File menu and select Run. When the dialog box appears, type the full pathname of the program, as in this example:

c:*directory**subdirectory*\\assembly.exe

You should substitute directory names that reflect your own system, of course. When you select the OK button of the dialog box the sample application will start.

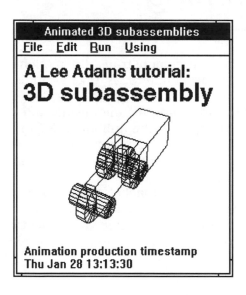

13-1 The first frame from the animation sequence generated by the sample application assembly.frm. See 13-2 for the final frame of the sequence.

Using the sample application

When the sample application starts up, the sign-on notice appears. Choose OK to continue.

Four menu names are displayed on the menu bar. They are File, Edit, Run, and Using. You can use the File menu to quit the program. You can use the Run menu to build the animation, save it to disk, load it from disk, and play the animation sequence.

You can use a mouse or the keyboard to operate this sample application. If you're using a mouse, just point and click. If you're using the keyboard, press Alt to move the focus to the menu bar, then press the appropriate mnemonic key to pull down a menu and select an item from the menu.

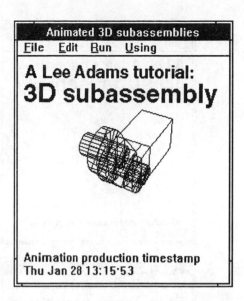

13-2 The final frame of the animation sequence produced by the sample application assembly.frm. See 13-1 for the first frame of the sequence.

The Run **menu** The Run menu controls the animation engine. Refer back to the previous chapter for a detailed discussion of how to build an animation and save it to disk. Be sure to select wire-frame mode before starting the build process for the first time.

Loading an animation To load an animation sequence from disk, select Load Animation from the Run menu. The animation engine will load all 36 frames into memory.

Running an animation To start an animation sequence that you've loaded in from disk, select Run Forward from the Run menu. The animation will begin to play. You can select Run Reverse from the Run menu to play the animation sequence backwards. To use single-step control, select Freezeframe from the Run menu while the animation is running. The keyboard controls become active. Press the right arrow key to advance to the next frame. Press the left arrow key to back up to the previous frame. Press and hold the right arrow key to play the animation sequence at the fastest rate possible on your hardware.

Quitting the sample application

To quit the sample application, choose Exit from the File menu. A message box will appear, allowing you to confirm or cancel your request.

A programmer's guide to the sample application

This section describes how the source code works. The source listings for the sample application are presented as FIG. C-4 in Appendix C. Source listings for the linked-in toolkits are provided in Appendix B. For tips on building the

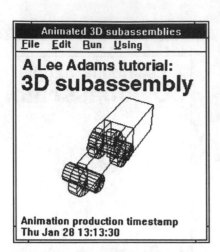

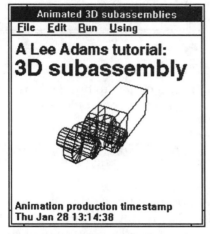

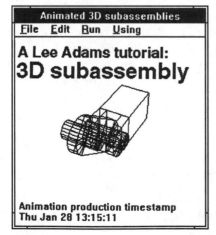
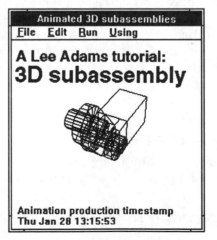

13-3 A sampling of frames from the animation sequence produced by the sample application assembly.frm.

sample application, see Appendix A. The source files for the sample application are also provided on the companion disk as asglobal.bas, asmain.bas, assembly.frm, asplay.bas, engine3d.bas, shapes3d.bas, deform3d.bas, assemb3d.bas, and lights3d.bas.

How the global module works

The asglobal.bas global module declares constants, variables, and external functions visible throughout the entire project. This listing is similar to the global module described in the previous chapter. Refer to chapter 12 if you require further discussion. You'll want to take note of the expanded animation script section at lines 0119 through 0222.

How the startup module works

The asmain.bas startup module is called when the application is launched. It is used to initialize variables. Again, refer to chapter 12 for a more detailed discussion.

How the form module works

You should understand how the hierarchical modeling component of this code works so you can add articulated motion to your own applications. The discussion in this chapter focuses on hierarchical modeling for animation. Other sections of the source code were discussed in chapter 12; refer to that chapter for a more detailed analysis of those sections.

Data types Declaration of data types for the hierarchical modeling features of this application were provided at lines 00123 through 0196 in the global module. First, a set of struct types are declared that define paths and movement. Lines 0123 through 0129 declare a struct type that specifies camera movement during the animation sequence. Lines 0130 through 0135 declare a struct type that specifies movement of the light-source during the animation. Lines 0136 through 0145 declare a struct type that specifies movement of an entity (actor) during the animation sequence. Lines 0146 through 0152 declare a struct type that specifies movement of an entire 3D complex solid during the animation.

Next, a set of struct types are declared that specify starting parameters. The code at lines 0153 through 0157 declares a struct type that specifies the starting location of the camera. The code at lines 0158 through 0161 declares a struct type that specifies the starting location of the light-source. The code at lines 0162 through 0169 declares a struct type that specifies the location and orientation of a 3D primitive in world-space. This primitive will represent the entire 3D complex solid. The code at lines 0170 through 0196 declares a struct type that specifies a 3D primitive in its role as a part of the complex 3D solid.

Finally, the code at lines 0198 through 0205 in the global module declares variables of the struct types declared at lines 0123 through 0196.

Initializing the hierarchy The source code at lines 0620 through 0928 in the form module initializes the variables that comprise the hierarchical solid. The camera's startup position and path is initialized at lines 0633 through 0644. You'll want to experiment with lines 0642 and 0643, as the comments alongside suggest, in order to get a feel for how the camera's path can be manipulated during the animation. The light-source's starting position and path is initialized at lines 0646 through 0653.

The starting position and path of the complex 3D solid is initialized at lines 0655 through 0662. The location, orientation, and dimensions of the various primitives that comprise the complex 3D solid are initialized at lines 0663 through 0928. The articulated motion of the level 2 progeny (the moving part) is initialized at lines 0798 through 0928. After you've built and tested the sample application successfully, you'll want to tinker with line 0928 in order to adjust the motion of the moving part.

Note in particular how some primitives are initialized relative to other primitives in the complex 3D solid. Lines 0882 through 0884 are a good example. Line 0884 shows a backward-referencing formula in action.

Building the hierarchy The code that builds the complex 3D solid is located at lines 1152 through 1219. This section of code is an enhancement of the corresponding code from the previous chapter's animation engine—and it is cloned from the sample application discussed in chapter 9. You'll want to pay special attention to lines 1174 and 1176, which differentiate between parent and progeny (called level 1 and level 2 components in the source listing).

Where do you go from here?

Now that you've practiced hierarchical modeling for 3D animation software, you're ready to explore simulation, visualization, and virtual reality techniques. Part Four, "Simulation programming," gives you the background knowledge you need to delve into the physically based kinematics animation demo and the virtual reality sampler later in the book.

Part Four

Simulation programming

Your task in Part Four is to prepare yourself for knowledge-based 3D simulation programming for Windows. You want to familiarize yourself with the fundamental skills required for physically based animation and virtual reality. You also want to be confident that your understanding of 3D simulation will prepare you for the advanced kinematics demo and the virtual reality sampler that appear later in this part of the book.

In Part Four of the book you'll learn how to apply what you've already learned about 3D functions and animation engines to the diverse field of knowledge-based simulation. Chapter 14, "Concepts and terms," is your introduction to the words and phrases used by simulation programmers. In chapter 15, "Getting started with knowledge-based simulation," you'll learn about game-theory-based simulation, reasoning-based simulation, and physics-based simulation. When you explore game theory, you'll delve into zero-sum and nonzero-sum games, decision tables, max-min strategies, evolutionary stable strategies, and unwinnable games. When you investigate machine reasoning, you'll find out about Boolean logic, Bayesian logic, heuristic logic, fuzzy logic, connectionism, and genetic algorithms. You'll also learn about probability calculations. When you investigate physics-based simulation, you'll review fundamental principles of physics like velocity, speed, mass, elastic collisions, and others.

In chapter 16, "Getting started with kinematics and dynamics," you'll see how constraint-based animation can produce a realistic model of movement in the real-world. In chapter 17 a hands-on tutorial shows you how to put your new kinematics knowledge to work. A sample application demonstrates functions that use velocity and time to automatically manage the movement of entities in a computer-controlled animation sequence. In chapter 18, "Getting started with virtual reality," you'll learn about universes, entities, degrees-of-freedom, viewpoint nodes, and more. In chapter 19 a hands-on tutorial gives you an opportunity to experiment with a virtual reality sampler. The sample application provides a 3D maze from which there is only one exit.

Before you begin to investigate knowledge-based simulation for Windows, you want to familiarize yourself with some of the words and phrases used by experienced developers. The next chapter, "Concepts and terms," provides you with the background information you need to get started.

14
Concepts and terms

This chapter introduces some basic concepts and terms that you'll be using while you explore Part Four, "Simulation programming." You'll want to be able to understand the technical language used in the next five chapters. This background knowledge will make it easier for you to learn the fundamental skills required for using knowledge-based 3D simulations in your own animated Windows applications. You'll also learn how each term and each concept fits into the diverse field of knowledge-based simulation programming.

Defining concepts and terms

Simulation

Simulation is the use of computer software to model and analyze the behavior of systems occurring in the real world. The systems being modeled can be natural systems or they can be manufactured systems. A flight simulator, for example, models and simulates a manufactured system (an aircraft). A biotech simulator, on the other hand, models and simulates a natural system (a chromosome string). Here's a good way to think of it: a computer model describes what the thing is, a computer simulation shows what the thing does. In other words, the model describes the system's appearance, the simulation shows the system's behavior.

Knowledge-based simulation

Knowledge-based simulation uses knowledge-based methods of science to enhance the accuracy and usefulness of the simulation. Knowledge-based methods can include game theory and decision tables, reasoning and logic, probability and certainty, the laws of physics and chemistry, and others.

The simulation pipeline

The *simulation pipeline* is the chain of software functions that produces the run-time simulation. A simulation pipeline relies mainly on 3D functions and animation engines. These capabilities can be enhanced with methods of visualization, simulation, and virtual reality. Visualization adds measurements, color, quantification, and attributes to the 3D pipeline that you learned about in part two of the book. Simulation adds spatial and temporal controls to the animation pipeline that you explored in part three of the book. Virtual reality adds interactive controls to the software chain.

Game-theory-based simulation

Game-theory-based simulation relies on the science of game theory. A game is any activity, enterprise, situation, or endeavor between or amongst humans. The game can be serious or it can be trivial, it can be competitive or it can be cooperative, it can be a single occurrence or a repeated event, but the strategy adopted by each player determines the player's gain or loss each time the game is played. Game-theory-based simulations often use matrices called *decision tables* to compute the best strategy for zero-sum and nonzero-sum games. Game theory can be used to develop efficient strategies for single games and for iterated games—against the same opponent and against random opponents.

Zero-sum and nonzero-sum games

In a *zero-sum game*, a gain for one player is always a loss for the other player. In a *nonzero-sum game*, a gain for one player is not necessarily at the expense of the other player. Both players can win.

Prisoner's dilemma

A *prisoner's dilemma* is a special type of game in which a player has only two options—either cooperate or cheat. Cooperating usually means acting in the interest of the common good. Cheating usually means acting in self-ish interest. A cheater grabs, whereas a cooperator shares. The outcome of a prisoner's dilemma game depends not just on what the player does, but on what the opponent does. The player has no way of knowing the opponent's strategy beforehand.

Here's the crux of the dilemma. If player A cheats (grabs) and player B cooperates (shares), then player A grabs the maximum gain at B's expense. Player B is awarded a so-called *sucker's payoff* in this case. However, if player B cheats too, then neither wins. In fact, both players experience a loss when both cheat. If they both cooperate (share), they are rewarded with a moderate gain (that is not nearly as large as the gain they could achieve by cheating, of course).

So what strategy should player A adopt? Thinking it through, player A realizes that player B will also want the maximum gain and will likely cheat. But if they both cheat they both lose. So it makes sense for both to cooperate and settle for a less-than-optimum gain, but a gain nonetheless. But if player B is likely to act rationally and cooperate, isn't this a good opportunity for player A to take advantage of B by cheating and grabbing the maximum gain? So there's the dilemma. Should player A cooperate or cheat?

Max-min strategy

A *max-min strategy* is a strategy that attempts to maximize the potential for gain while minimizing the potential for loss.

Evolutionary-stable strategy

An *evolutionary-stable strategy* (*ESS*) is one that makes sense over a large number of games. It ensures the survival of the player in the long run.

Unwinnable game

An *unwinnable game* is a special type of game in which the best outcome a player can hope for is to minimize the loss. The player can never win (gain). Consider, for example, that you've placed a long-distance telephone call to a software support facility. You are greeted by an automated answering device that informs you your call is being queued until a technical support person becomes available. Then the elevator music begins.

How long should you wait before hanging up? It might take two minutes or it might take twenty minutes before your call is handled—and every minute is costing you long-distance charges. If you hang up after two minutes, then you'll have to call back another day and perhaps wait another two or three minutes anyway before being connected. In that case, you would have wasted two minutes in toll charges on today's call. But if you keep hanging on for two, three, five, ten minutes, there's still no guarantee your call will ever be answered before the end of the business day. You're playing an unwinnable game. The best you can hope for is to keep your long-distance costs as low as possible.

Reasoning

Reasoning is the thinking process that draws conclusions or makes inferences. Reasoning is problem-solving thinking. *Machine reasoning* is the process of using computer software to model and simulate a thinking process or a problem-solving process. It often relies upon different forms of logic, including Boolean logic, Bayesian logic, heuristic logic, fuzzy logic, connectionism, genetic algorithms, and others.

Boolean logic *Boolean logic* uses if/then reasoning. It is based upon predicate calculus (calculations using special symbols). Boolean logic is suited for cognitive simulation software.

Bayesian logic *Bayesian logic* uses permutations and combinations. It is based upon probability calculus. Bayesian logic is suited for cognitive simulation software.

Heuristic logic *Heuristic logic* uses best-guess reasoning. It is based upon common-sense. Heuristic logic is suited for expert-system software.

Fuzzy logic *Fuzzy logic* uses approximate reasoning or best-fit reasoning. It is based upon possibility calculus. Fuzzy logic is suited for process control.

Connectionism

Connectionism uses connection-based algorithms. It is based upon the physical brain. Neural networks are a form of connectionism. Connectionism is suited for pattern matching.

Genetic algorithms

Genetic algorithms use processes of selection and mutation. Genetic programming is based upon the evolution of organisms. Genetic algorithms are suited for exploration control.

Deductive reasoning

Deductive reasoning uses a knowledge base to infer an effect from observed causes. Here's an example of deductive reasoning using the typical given-if-then paradigm. *Given* that squirrels are usually quicker than cats, *if* you see a cat chasing a squirrel, *then* the squirrel is likely to get away safely.

Inductive reasoning

Inductive reasoning uses empirical observations. For example, suppose you've just moved to a new part of the country and you observe the neighbor's cat chasing a squirrel who seems to always elude the cat. If you see this happening time and time again, you might infer that squirrels are generally quicker than cats. You've just used inductive reasoning.

What you've really done, of course, is add to your mind's knowledge base the fact that squirrels are usually quicker than cats. That information is now available for deductive reasoning in future situations. Suppose, for example, you see the other neighbor's cat chasing a different squirrel. Using deductive reasoning (and the new information you've just acquired through inductive reasoning) your thinking might run like this.

Given that squirrels are usually quicker than cats, *if* you see a cat chasing a squirrel, *then* the squirrel is likely to get away safely.

Abductive reasoning

Abductive reasoning infers a probable cause from observed effects. It is the reverse of deductive reasoning, which infers an effect from observed causes. Here's how abductive reasoning works. Suppose, for example, you glance out the window and spot a squirrel frantically scrambling up your oak tree. Using abductive reasoning, you might infer that the probable cause of the squirrel's behavior is the neighbor's cat in hot pursuit of the squirrel. Of course, the cat might not have been involved, but in the absence of contradictory observations or knowledge, it's reasonable for you to draw that conclusion. You might, for example, say that you're 90% certain that the cat was involved. Abductive reasoning is useful even if you've never seen your neighbor's cat chasing a squirrel. You might observe the squirrel's frenetic behavior and use abductive reasoning to infer that it was being pursued by another animal of unknown type. You've perhaps seen dogs, cats, and raccoons in the neighborhood, so you might be only 25% certain your neighbor's cat was involved.

Cognitive computing

Cognitive computing means using software to simulate the thinking process of the human mind.

Probability

Probability is a branch of mathematics concerned with the likelihood of events happening. The probability of an event occurring is obtained by dividing the number of favorable events by the number of possible results. For example, the probability of drawing a deuce from a deck of 52 randomly shuffled cards is 4 divided by 52, or .076923. Probability calculations use permutations, combinations, and binomial coefficients.

Permutations *Permutations* are lineups of members selected from a general population. For example, the total number of lineups of 4 colors chosen from a palette of 10 colors is 5,040. The permutation calculation is $10 \times 9 \times 8 \times 7 = 5,040$. It is the order of the members in the lineup that matters, not the content. That's why the number 5,040 seems so high. When you're using permutations, you consider a lineup of red-green-blue-cyan to be different from a lineup of red-green-cyan-blue, even though the same four colors are involved.

Combinations *Combinations* are committees of members chosen from a general population. For example, the total number of committees of 4 persons chosen from a group of 10 people is 210. (The binomial calculations that produce this result are discussed in the next chapter.) It is the content of the committee that matters, not the order of the members. When you're using combinations, you consider a committee of Kim, Ken, Karen, and Kevin to be the same as a committee of Kevin, Karen, Ken, and Kim, because the same four people are involved, only in different order.

Conditional probability

Conditional probability can be used to calculate the likelihood of an event occurring after a prerequisite event has occurred. For example, suppose that two cards are drawn from a randomly shuffled deck of cards. The probability of drawing a spade on the second draw after a spade was drawn on the first draw is .2353. To arrive at this figure, the number of spades remaining after the first draw is divided by the number of cards remaining after the first draw. If a spade was drawn first, this formula is 12 divided by 51. Remember, as you've already learned, the probability of an event occurring is the number of favorable events divided by the number of possible events.

Physics-based simulation

Physics-based simulation uses principles of physics to manage the events being modeled and simulated. The software considers factors such as velocity, speed, displacement, acceleration, deceleration, mass, density, linear momentum, kinetic energy, inelastic collisions, elastic collisions, and others.

Velocity *Velocity* is the rate of change of displacement over time. It is speed in a specified direction. Velocity is a vector quantity.

Speed *Speed* is displacement over time. It is a scalar quantity, such as 65 mph or 100 kph. No direction is provided.

Displacement *Displacement* is distance measured from a fixed reference point. It is a vector quantity that uses a specified direction.

Acceleration *Acceleration* is the rate of increase of velocity over time. It is a vector quantity, such as 12 meters per second per second.

Deceleration *Deceleration* is the rate of decrease of velocity over time.

Mass *Mass* is the quantity of matter in an entity. It is an indication of the entity's inertia.

Density *Density* is mass per unit of volume. It reflects how much matter is present per unit of volume.

Linear momentum *Linear momentum* is the product of mass and velocity.

Kinetic energy *Kinetic energy* is the energy possessed by an entity because of its motion. It is the potential to do work.

Inelastic collision In an *inelastic collision*, linear momentum is conserved but kinetic energy is not conserved. Some kinetic energy is lost as heat, work done, or physical damage. The entities involved in an inelastic collision are rigid or semi-rigid bodies.

Elastic collision In an *elastic collision*, linear momentum and kinetic energy are conserved.

Physically based animation

Physically based animation is 3D animation that uses physics to manage an entity's motion. Because the motion is regulated by constraints, physically based animation is also called *constraint-based animation*.

Constraints

Constraints are forces, loads, and matter that affect the motion of an entity in a physically based animation sequence.

How physically based animation is implemented

Physically based animation can be implemented as forward kinematics, forward dynamics, inverse kinematics, and inverse dynamics. *Forward kinematics* concerns what happens when velocity or acceleration is applied to an entity. *Forward dynamics* concerns what happens when force, loads, and other constraints are applied to an entity. *Inverse kinematics* calculates the velocity or acceleration that is required to move an entity from one location to another location during a specified period of time. *Inverse dynamics* calculates the forces, loads, or other constraints required to move an entity from one location to another location during a specified period of time.

Virtual reality

Virtual reality is a real-time simulation of 4D space-time. It provides a means for humans to interact with a simulated 3D environment. Simply put, virtual reality is a human-computer interface. It is a way for a user to visualize, manipulate, and interact with a database. The database is the virtual environment, the virtual entities it contains, and the script that defines how the environment and the entities interact with the user. *VR* is an acronym for virtual reality.

Universe A *universe* is a particular 3D environment, including the entities it contains and the script for managing the simulation. Some VR software can load different universes from disk in order to provide different virtual experiences.

Entity An *entity* is an actor, entity, prop, or scenery element that exists in the virtual environment.

Sensor From the user's point of view, a *sensor* is a point in 3D space in the virtual environment that responds to certain actions by the user. From the programmer's point of view, a sensor is a section of code that polls the input devices to determine if the user has triggered an event. For example, a 3D box (an entity) in the virtual environment might be scripted to change color from blue to red if the box is touched by the VR user (or by the software's representation of the user in virtual space).

The simulation manager A simulation manager is an enhanced animation engine that manages a virtual reality session. It performs four functions:

- update
- enforce
- sense
- move

First, the simulation manager updates the display image each time the user changes location or shifts the direction of gaze. For example, it generates an appropriate 3D image if the user turns to observe a doorway leading to a virtual room. Second, the simulation manager enforces the VR rules. For example, it prevents the user from walking through a closed door. Third, the simulation manager's sensors detect when portions of the virtual environment must respond to actions of the user. For example, it might illuminate the virtual room when the user enters. Fourth, the simulation manager implements the scripted motion of moving entities in the virtual environment. For example, it might automatically update the face of a clock in the virtual room.

VR rules *VR rules* are the laws that govern a virtual reality session. A VR rule, for example, might dictate that a user cannot pass through a closed door. However, another VR rule might allow a user to pass through a window, even if it's closed. Different universes can possess different sets of VR rules.

Degrees-of-freedom *Degrees-of-freedom* refers to the axis of rotation and translation provided by an input device. A mouse, for example, provides two degrees-of-freedom.

Bat A *bat* is a floating, mouselike input device that provides three degrees-of-freedom. The user can usually select from XYZ translation or yaw-roll-pitch rotation, but cannot use both simultaneously.

Bird A *bird* is a floating, mouselike input device that provides six degrees-of-freedom. The user can simultaneously select from XYZ translation and yaw-roll-pitch rotation.

Where do you go from here?

Now that you've familiarized yourself with some of the basic concepts and terms used in simulation programming, you're ready to start learning the fundamental skills. The next chapter, "Getting started with knowledge-based simulation," teaches you about game theory, machine reasoning, probability, and physics.

15
Getting started with knowledge-based simulation

This chapter shows you how to use knowledge-based simulation to manage and display moving 3D scenes in the viewport of your application's window. Knowledge-based simulation can be implemented in a Windows' application using different disciplines and paradigms. Concepts such as game theory, logic, reasoning, probability, and physics and the underlying principles of knowledge-based simulation are discussed. Game theory, including zero-sum and nonzero-sum games, max-min strategies, and unwinnable games will help you to understand machine reasoning, including the six different forms of logic and the three different types of reasoning. The concept of probability is discussed as well as simulations based on the laws of physics.

You'll delve into machine reasoning and the six forms of logic it can use, including Boolean logic, Bayesian logic, heuristic logic, fuzzy logic, connectionism, and genetic algorithms. The science of formal reasoning is important to cognitive computing, and you'll investigate deductive reasoning, inductive reasoning, and abductive reasoning. You'll discover how to calculate probability by using permutations and combinations as you delve into sampling, complementary events, biased probability space, and conditional probability. Finally, you'll explore physics-based simulation, including velocity, acceleration, collisions, and more. The information you'll learn in this chapter will prepare you for the high-performance tutorials coming up.

The simulation pipeline

As you've already learned in the previous chapter, *simulation* means using computer software to model and analyze the behavior of real systems.

The systems being simulated can be natural systems or they can be manufactured systems. For example, a spaceflight simulation might model and simulate a manufactured system (the NASA space shuttle). A wildlife management simulation might model and simulate a natural system (an ecosystem embodying the interplay between predators, food supply, weather patterns, and species populations).

These two examples highlight the differences between modeling and simulation. Modeling can describe what the system is, but only simulation can show what the system does. Modeling describes the system's appearance and technical specifications. Simulation demonstrates (or predicts) the system's behavior and performance characteristics. Knowledge-based simulations are implemented using a *simulation pipeline.*

A simulation pipeline is any collection of software algorithms and functions that can produce an animated simulation sequence in the viewport of your application's window. A minimum configuration is an animation engine and a 3D toolkit. The animation engine is for motion. The 3D toolkit is for modeling and rendering. These minimal components can be upgraded by using additional programming techniques such as visualization, simulation, and virtual reality. Each adds something new to the pipeline:

- Visualization adds quantification.
- Simulation adds spatial and temporal controls.
- Virtual reality adds interactive controls.

Visualization *Visualization* adds measurement, color, quantification, qualification, and other attributes to the 3D functions that you studied in Part Two of the book. Visualization provides a sense of purpose. Fidelity is the goal. Visualization makes concrete what otherwise exists only in our imaginations. Visualization is the process that transforms the contents of the human imagination to the computer display. Whatever can be imagined by the mind can be modeled, rendered, and displayed by the computer—and the process is called visualization. All that's needed are parameters—the programmer's decision about which variables, measurements, and other parameters will be used by the 3D functions. Think of it this way: a 3D entity's XYZ dimensions are usually provided as units of displacement (distance, length, and so on). But it need not be that way. Visualization means unshackling our minds and using other measurements as input for the XYZ components. For example, X might be speed, Y might be temperature, and Z might be time. Even complex mathematical theories can be visualized using this approach.

Visualization is a thinking tool. It extends the breadth and power of human imagination. It amplifies and multiplies our intelligence and our creativity. It is an important element in the knowledge-based simulation pipeline, because only after you've visualized something can you can use simulation to investigate its behavior.

Simulation *Simulation* adds spatial and temporal controls to the animation functions that you explored in Part Three of the book. *Spatial* refers to space; *temporal* refers to time. Simulation is 4D space-time, expressed as XYZT coordinates. It is animation with a sense of purpose. Simulation is animation that purports to represent a system (a thing or a process) from the real world. If the system has been modeled accurately and with fidelity, then the simulation will be able to visually demonstrate the performance of the system over time. It might even be able to predict the behavior of the system. When special knowledge is used to manage a simulation, the result is knowledge-based simulation. The consummate knowledge-based simulation is virtual reality.

Virtual reality *Virtual reality* is a simulation of 4D space-time presented in an interactive, real-time context. VR provides a means for interacting with a simulated 3D environment. In its role as a human-computer interface, virtual reality provides a way for the user to manipulate and interact with a database. The database is visual. It is comprised of the 4D space-time (the artificial reality) and the entities (artificial objects) it contains, as well as a script specifying how the system and its universe interacts with the user.

A *universe* is a particular configuration of a virtual reality. The universe includes the virtual environment, the entities it contains, and a script for managing the simulation, as well as its sensors and entities. *Entities* are actors, props, or scenery elements in the virtual environment. *Sensors* are objects in the virtual environment that can interact with the user by responding to the user's actions or location. As you've already learned, a programmer considers a sensor as any block of code that polls the input devices to determine if the user has done something to trigger an event in the virtual environment. Sensors are integrated into the simulation manager of the virtual reality engine.

The *simulation manager* is an animation engine that has been modified to manage a virtual reality session. It performs various functions, including updating the display image, enforcing the VR rules, sensing when interaction occurs, and moving virtual entities.

Together and individually, the programming techniques of visualization, simulation, and virtual reality can be used to enhance a minimal configuration of animation engine and 3D toolkit in order to create an infrastructure for knowledge-based simulation.

Knowledge-based simulation

Knowledge-based simulation is simulation that uses special knowledge to boost the run-time performance and fidelity of a simulation. Knowledge-based simulations often rely upon disciplines like game theory, logic, reasoning, probability theory, and physics.

Each of these disciplines brings a different perspective to the simulation. *Game theory* is the science of calculating appropriate strategies for dealing with competitive or adversarial situations, events, and endeavors. *Logic* is the science that provides the formal principles for reasoning. *Reasoning* is the thinking process that draws conclusions and makes inferences. It is problem-solving thinking. Probability theory provides a mechanism for predicting the likelihood of an event's occurrence. The laws of physics describe behavior in the real world.

As you learned in the previous chapter, knowledge-based simulation often relies upon different forms of logic, including Boolean logic, Bayesian logic, heuristic logic, as well as different forms of cognitive computing, including fuzzy logic, connectionism, and genetic algorithms, as shown in FIG. 15-1.

Knowledge-based simulation	
Boolean logic	Based upon predicate calculus. Uses *if...then* reasoning. Suited for cognitive simulation.
Bayesian logic	Based upon probability calculus. Uses permutations, combinations. Suited for cognitive simulation.
Heuristic logic	Based upon common-sense. Uses best-guess reasoning. Suited for expert-systems.
Fuzzy logic	Based upon possibility calculus. Uses approximate reasoning. Suited for process-control.
Neural networks	Based upon the physical brain. Uses connection-based algorithms. Suited for pattern-matching.
Genetic algorithms	Based upon evolution of organisms. Uses selection/mutation algorithms. Suited for exploration-control.

15-1 Programming algorithms for knowledge-based simulation.

Boolean logic uses if/then reasoning based upon *predicate calculus*. (A calculus is simply a set of calculations that uses operators and operands especially suited to the subject matter.) Boolean logic is used in cognitive simulation software that imitates the thinking process of the human mind. A related form of logic called *Bayesian logic* uses permutations and combinations. It is based upon probability calculus. Bayesian logic is also often used in cognitive simulation software.

Heuristic logic is best described as best-guess reasoning based upon common sense. Heuristic logic is used in expert-system software. Its cousin, *fuzzy logic,* on the other hand, uses approximate reasoning or best-fit reasoning. It is based upon possibility calculus. Fuzzy logic is used in process-control applications.

Connectionism uses connection-based algorithms based upon the physical brain. Neural networks are an implementation of connectionism. Connectionism is used for pattern detection, pattern recognition, and pattern matching. Another nature-based discipline, *genetic programming,* uses selection and mutation based upon the principles of evolution. Genetic algorithms are suited for exploration, discovery, and search applications.

Whether Boolean, Bayesian, heuristic, fuzzy, connectionist, or genetic, the science of logic casts its influence over most simulation software. However, only game-theory-based simulation has the ability to make logic sometimes seem illogical.

Game-theory-based simulation

Game-theory-based simulation is named for the science of game theory. A *game* is any activity, enterprise, situation, or endeavor between or amongst humans. A so-called game can be serious or trivial. It can be competitive, adversarial, or cooperative. It can be a single occurrence or repeated many times. It can be played against the same opponent or against randomly selected opponents.

The strategy used by each player determines the player's *payoff,* which is the gain or loss experienced by the player each time the game is played. As shown in FIG. 15-2, game theory-based simulations often use a matrix called a decision-table to analyze the available strategies for a particular game.

Game-theory decision-table

	Player X COOPERATE	Player X CHEAT
Player Y COOPERATE	X+3, Y+3 Moderate GAIN for X Moderate GAIN for Y	X+5, Y+0 Maximum GAIN for X Maximum LOSS for Y
Player Y CHEAT	X+0, Y+5 Maximum LOSS for X Maximum GAIN for Y	X+1, Y+1 Moderate LOSS for X Moderate LOSS for Y

Prisoner's dilemma game-tables

The ranking of the rewards always adheres to two preconditions if the game is a so-called prisoner's dilemma.

Precondition 1 $A > B > C > D$ where A represents Maximum GAIN for the player, B represents Moderate GAIN, C represents Moderate LOSS, and D represents Maximum LOSS.

Precondition 2 $\dfrac{A+D}{2} \leq B$

Zero-sum and nonzero-sum games

Any game-theory decision-table can be considered as either a Zero-sum game or a Nonzero-sum game. In a zero-sum game, a win for one player is always a loss for the other player (ie X+5, Y-5). In a nonzero-sum game, both players can win (ie X+3, Y+3). Each player's perception of the game is influenced by personality type, access to outside information affecting the size of the rewards, communication with the other player, and so on.

15-2 Fundamentals of game-theory.

Zero-sum and nonzero-sum games

Games can be categorized as either *zero-sum* or *nonzero-sum*. In a zero-sum game a gain for one player is always a loss for the other player. In a nonzero-sum game, a gain for one player is not necessarily at the expense of the other player. Both players can win.

Here's an example of a nonzero-sum game. Suppose two retailers are competing in the same neighborhood. Each retailer could aggressively reduce prices in order to compete, and one of them will eventually dominate the market, perhaps driving the other out of business. This strategy offers maximum gain but threatens maximum loss. However, if both retailers are willing to settle for less than total market domination, each might decide to refrain from competing on the basis of price. Retailer A, who normally charges $1, might observe that Retailer B is charging $1.25. Rather than use this price advantage to attract new customers and extra profit, Retailer A instead simply raises the price from $1 to $1.25 and pockets the extra profit from existing customers. The retailers are discreetly engaging in what amounts to informal price-fixing. Both retailers survive in the marketplace. Both players win in this nonzero-sum game, because the loser is a third party. In this instance the losers are the consumers, who must pay the artificially inflated prices of the conniving retailers (at least until a nationwide chain notices the profit potential and decides to establish a retail outlet in the neighborhood). Notice that game theory does not consider morals, ethics, or laws—only strategies and their results.

On the other hand, here's an example of a zero-sum game. Suppose two competing antique dealers have decided to submit written bids for an antique being offered at private auction. A floor bid has been established by the auction house, so each dealer knows the minimum price the seller will accept. The dealers also know the maximum price each can expect to receive when they resell the antique in their retail shop. Each dealer could adopt either a cautious strategy or a bold strategy. A cautious strategy means bidding low. This is less likely to be the winning bid but offers larger profit in the end. A bold strategy means bidding high, near the maximum retail price. This is much more likely to be the winning bid but offers smaller profit potential. No matter which strategy prevails, though, only one of the dealers is going to win—and it's going to be at the expense of the other dealer. Only one of the dealers will enjoy the privilege of buying the antique at auction, marking up the wholesale price, and making a profit at retail. The other dealer will not have an antique to sell. This is a zero-sum game.

Decision tables Both of the examples just mentioned can be simplified through the use of *decision-tables*. The example in FIG. 15-2 provides a decision-table suitable for zero-sum games. If each gain and loss is assigned a numeric value, then algorithmic formulas can be developed. This means that software functions can be used to calculate the advantages and disadvantages of each strategy. This type of analysis is particularly important in *prisoner's dilemma* games.

Prisoner's dilemma A prisoner's dilemma is a special type of game in which each player possesses only two options: either cooperate or cheat. Cooperating is usually deemed to mean acting in the interest of the common good. Cheating is usually deemed to mean acting in the player's selfish interest. A cheater grabs and a cooperator shares; it's as simple as that. The outcome of a prisoner's dilemma game depends not only on the player's behavior, but also on the opponent's behavior. A player has no advance knowledge of the opponent's strategy.

Suppose, for example, that player A and player B are environmentalists who protest by throwing a cream pie in the face of a pro-development local politician during a news conference. The two players are arrested and detained in separate cels, unable to communicate with each other. The authorities don't know who actually threw the pie (in fact both players simultaneously tossed the ballistic), so the most serious indictment that can be registered against both players is mischief. But if one of the players were to testify against the other, then the thrower could be charged with assault, a more serious offense. So each player is presented with an ultimatum by the investigating officer: "Testify against your partner and we'll drop the charges against you."

So far so good. Player A begins to consider the situation. The prisoner's dilemma rapidly becomes evident. Suppose that player A cooperates (with fellow-environmentalist player B) and says nothing. Provided that player B also cooperates and keeps mum, then player A will be charged with the lesser offense of mischief. The result is likely to be a $250 fine for each player. But what's stopping player B from squealing on player A? Player A would be charged with assault while player B goes free. Player A might end up with the humiliation of a suspended sentence, mandatory probation, plus a heftier $1000 fine.

It gets worse, though. Player A speculates that if player B is thinking this situation through the same way player A is thinking it through, then B will realize A is likely to cooperate, so B will be tempted to cheat and take advantage of A's naive and trusting nature. So perhaps player A should cheat. But if both cheat, then both face the risk of the more serious assault charge.

As the decision-table in FIG. 15-2 shows, if player A cheats and player B cooperates, then player A grabs the maximum gain at player B's expense. However, if player B cheats too, then neither player wins. Both players experience a loss when both cheat. If both players cooperate they are rewarded with a moderate gain. In order for a game to be a prisoner's dilemma, the moderate gain must be a value not nearly as large as the maximum gain achieved by cheating.

What strategy does player A use? Thinking it through, player A realizes that player B also wants the maximum gain and is likely to cheat. But there's the dilemma. If they both cheat they both lose. So it makes sense for both to cooperate and settle for only a moderate gain, rather than the maximum gain. But that raises yet another dilemma. If player B is likely to act rationally and cooperate, this presents a tempting opportunity for player A to take advantage of B by cheating and grabbing the maximum gain. So, should player A cooperate or cheat?

Single-game vs. iterative games

A player can perceive a game as a single event or as a series of repeated games. This perception has a significant effect on the strategy that a clear-headed, rational player is likely to adopt.

Max-min strategy for single-game In a game played once only, a rational player can minimize potential loss by playing cheat. This is because there is simply no way to predict or to enforce the cooperation of the other player. That doesn't necessarily mean that a player will always play cheat. The player's perception of the opponent's personality, playing style, past performance, and even the availability of outside information might influence the player to adopt a different strategy. No matter what the outcome of the game, each player might have no regrets, feeling that their strategy was the best choice at the time. This situation is called an *equilibrium* by game theorists. Equilibriums are often cited as proof of rational strategies by the players, because (even with the benefit of hindsight) the players would not change their strategies.

Max-min strategies for iterative games When developing a strategy for repeated games, two types of scenarios need to be considered. First, the repeated games might be played against the same opponent. Second, the repeated games might be played against different opponents randomly selected from a large population of strangers.

Against the same opponent In repeated games against the same opponent, a rational player can maximize gain by playing cooperate on the first move, and thereafter only playing cheat in direct retaliation to cheating by the opponent.

Against random opponents In repeated games against random opponents from a large population, a rational player will play cooperate against an unfamiliar opponent, and against familiar opponents who have cooperated in previous games. The rational player will play cheat against a familiar player who cheated in previous games.

What constitutes a good strategy sometimes depends on your point of view. What is beneficial for an individual player might not be good for the whole population of players, as FIG. 15-3 shows. What if everyone cheated? Or what if no one cheated?

Evolutionary-stable strategies

An *evolutionary-stable strategy* (*ESS*) is a strategy that ensures survival over the long term if most players in the population are using it.

Game-theory strategies

Type of game	Best strategy	Reasoning
Single game against unfamiliar opponent	ALWAYS CHEAT	In a single game, logic dictates that a rational player can minimize potential loss by always playing CHEAT, because there is simply no way to predict or to enforce cooperation of the other player.
Many games against the same opponent	FORGIVING GRUDGE (TIT-FOR-TAT)	In repeated games against the same opponent, a rational player can maximize gain by playing COOPERATE on the first move, and only playing CHEAT in direct retaliation to cheating by the opponent.
Many games against random opponents	UNFORGIVING GRUDGE	In repeated games against random opponents from a large population, a rational player will play COOPERATE against an unfamiliar opponent and familiar opponents who cooperated in previous games. A rational player plays CHEAT against a familiar player who cheated in previous games.

ESS strategies

Evolutionary-stable strategies (ESS) guarantee survival in a large population. Many strategies are available. Three are described here. The size of rewards is a critical factor in determing which strategies are stable over the long-term.

ALWAYS COOPERATE -- This strategy is stable in a Cooperator population. The Cooperators will be driven to extinction if the population contains significant numbers of Cheaters. Cooperators can coexist with Grudges.

ALWAYS CHEAT -- This strategy can be stable in a population comprised mainly of Cooperators or comprised mainly of other Cheaters. Cheaters will be driven to extinction if the population contains a significant number of Grudges. In a population comprised mainly of Cooperators, Cheaters may initially thrive but will sometimes drive themselves to extinction after victimizing and eliminating all the Cooperators.

UNFORGIVING GRUDGE -- This stragegy is stable and will survive in a population comprised mainly of Cooperators. Grudges will survive and will drive Cheaters to extinction in a population of Cheaters containing a significant minority of Grudges.

15-3 Fundamentals of game-theory strategies.

Consider, for example, a population of players who trade pieces of food amongst each other in order to ensure a balanced diet. Players who attempt to exist only on foodstuffs that they've gathered or grown will suffer from malnutrition and disease. Each player specializes in producing just one type of food.

A cooperator accepts a morsel of food from another player and in exchange gives a piece of food to the other player. This strategy is called *always cooperate*. Players using this strategy are called *traders*.

A cheater takes a morsel of food from the other player and then simply runs away. Clearly, the temptation to cheat is significant because a cheater gets twice the amount of food. This strategy is called *always cheat*. Players using this strategy are called *raiders*.

A grudge will cooperate in new encounters and in encounters with known cooperators, but will always cheat against players who have previously cheated. This strategy is called *unforgiving grudge*. Players using this strategy are called *unforgiving retaliators*.

But what are the long-term consequences of these various strategies for the population as a whole? Will the population thrive or will it become extinct?

Always cooperate This strategy is stable over the long term in a population consisting mainly of other cooperators. However, if the population contains significant numbers of cheaters the cooperators will eventually be driven to extinction. Cooperators can coexist with grudges, however, because the grudges will never be provoked into cheating.

Always cheat This strategy can be stable in a population consisting mainly of cooperators. In some ratios, however, the cheaters might initially thrive by taking advantage of the cooperators, but will often drive themselves to extinction after victimizing and eliminating all of the cooperators. The cheaters will also be driven to extinction if the population contains a significant number of grudges.

Unforgiving grudge Players using this strategy will survive in a population consisting mainly of cooperators, provided not too many grudges are present. In a population consisting mainly of cheaters, grudges will eventually drive the cheaters to extinction if there is a significant minority of grudges (so they can enjoy the advantages of occasionally bumping into each other).

Other strategies Other strategies are available, of course. Grudges can be flexible, forgiving past transgressions of their opponents. A grudge, for example, might punish a former cheater by cheating during the next confrontation, but thereafter might cooperate. Players using this strategy are called *forgiving retaliators.* It is also feasible that some players will use arbitrarily shifting strategies.

Unwinnable games

An *unwinnable game* is a special type of game in which the best outcome a player can hope for is to minimize the potential loss. The player cannot win. You've already encountered an example of an unwinnable game in the previous chapter. Suppose that you've placed a long-distance telephone call to a software support facility. An automated answering device informs you that your call is being put on hold until a technical support person becomes available. It might be fifteen minutes before your call is answered. Every minute means long-distance toll charges, but if you hang up after two minutes, then you'll just have to call back another day, and perhaps be confronted by the same problem. In that case, you'll have wasted two minutes worth of toll charges on today's futile call. But no matter how long you keep hanging on, there's no guarantee your call will ever be answered. You are a player in an unwinnable game. The best you can hope for is to keep your long-distance costs to a minimum.

Dollar auction The *dollar auction* is another example of an unwinnable game. Consider the following situation. You and a group of acquaintances are gathered at a reception. In order to liven up the affair, someone stands up and offers to sell a $100 bill to the highest bidder, no matter how low the bid is. The rules are simple for this dollar auction. The player making the highest bid earns the right to buy the $100 bill from the auctioneer for the amount of the bid. Here's the catch, though. The player making the second-highest bid must pay that amount to the auctioneer, and receives nothing in return.

Sooner or later someone will bid $1. After all, that means a $99 profit. Of course, someone else will bid $2, and so on. But what happens when the bid is $99? Suppose the previous bid was $98. The second-place player stands to lose a whopping $98, while the player with the winning $99 bid makes a $1 dollar profit.

The game has become unwinnable. After thinking it through, the second-place player decides to bid $100. This is a break-even strategy, of course. But now the $99 bidder stands to lose $99. This player will likely decide that losing $1 is better than losing $99, so the player will bid $101 for the right to purchase a one-hundred dollar bill. Now the other player must bid $102, and so on, throwing good money after bad. Game theory researchers call this the *invested equity syndrome*. During informal experiments among unsuspecting individuals, $10 bills have been sold for as much as $30 and belligerent shouting matches have spoiled otherwise amicable gatherings. Could the situation have been avoided by better reasoning?

Reasoning-based simulation

Reasoning-based simulation is based on software algorithms that mimic human thinking processes. As you've already learned, reasoning is founded on different forms of logic, including Boolean logic, Bayesian logic, and heuristic logic, as well as different forms of cognitive computing such as fuzzy logic, connectionism, and genetic programming.

Boolean logic uses if/then predicate calculus. Bayesian logic uses the permutations and combinations of probability calculus. Heuristic logic uses best-guess reasoning. Fuzzy logic uses best-fit reasoning. Connectionism uses connection-based algorithms such as neural networks Genetic programming uses selection and mutation based upon evolution.

The set of logic symbols is shown in FIG. 15-4. Examples of logic calculus are shown in FIGS. 15-5 and 15-6. The types of cognitive computing techniques are shown in FIG. 15-7.

Logic symbols

$\rightarrow$	implies
$\neg$	not
$\vee$	or
$\wedge$	and
$\forall$	for all
$\exists$	there exists

15-4 Logic symbols.

Propositional logic

Normal-language statement	Logic calculus
It is stormy.	STORMY
It is sunny.	SUNNY
If it is stormy, then it is not sunny.	STORMY $\rightarrow$ $\neg$ SUNNY
Propositional logic can represent facts from the real world as logical propositions written as wffs (well-formed formulas).	

15-5 Fundamentals of propositional logic.

Predicate logic

Normal-language statement	Logic calculus
The knight is a chess piece.	ChessPiece(knight)
The knight belongs to the white side.	WhiteSide(knight)
The white pieces are in play on the chess board.	$\forall x$: WhiteSide(x)$\rightarrow$InPlay(x)
Alekhine is a chess player.	ChessPlayer(Alekhine)
All chess pieces are controlled by either Alekhine or by his opponent.	$\forall x$: InPlay(x)$\rightarrow$ ControlledBy(x,Alekhine) $\vee$ NotControlledBy(x,Alekhine)
A chess piece is controlled by someone.	$\forall x$: $\exists y$: ControlledBy(x,y)
Predicate logic can represent facts from the real world as statements written as wffs (well-formed formulas).	

15-6 Fundamentals of predicate logic.

Reasoning

If logic provides the formal foundation for reasoning, then reasoning is the thinking process that makes inferences. Reasoning is problem-solving. The three categories of reasoning are:

- deductive
- inductive
- abductive

COGNITIVE COMPUTING		
TYPE	**PURPOSE**	**ALGORITHM**
Neural	Prediction, classification, and pattern recognition	Uses recognition, learning, and planning processes based on the behavior of the brain.
Fuzzy	Process control	Uses heuristic reasoning processes based on the behavior of the mind. Provides rule-of-thumb and best-guess approximations.
Genetic	Selection, mutation, and innovation	Uses processes based on the principles of natural selection.
Cognitive computing techniques cannot be proven or validated using the traditional analytic proofs. They rely instead on empirical evidence and field observations.		

15-7 Programming paradigms for cognitive computing.

Deductive reasoning *Deductive reasoning* can infer an effect from observed causes by relying on lessons learned from previous experience. Using deductive reasoning, you would conclude the following: *given* that squirrels are quicker than cats, *if* you observe a cat chasing a squirrel, *then* the squirrel is likely to escape. In other words, *given* your previous experience, *if* a known cause is observed, *then* a specific effect is expected.

Inductive reasoning *Inductive reasoning* uses empirical observations to learn lessons from experience. Suppose you're new to the area and you repeatedly observe the neighbor's cat chasing a squirrel who always escapes. You're likely to use inductive reasoning to generalize from these observations. You infer that squirrels are generally quicker than cats. You add to your mind's database the lesson that squirrels are usually quicker than cats.

Abductive reasoning *Abductive reasoning* infers a probable cause from observed effects. Abductive reasoning is the reverse of deductive reasoning. Here's how abductive reasoning works. Suppose you observe a squirrel scrambling up a tree. That's an effect, not a cause. Using abductive reasoning, you might infer that a possible or probable cause for the squirrel's behavior is the neighbor's cat. In the absence of contradictory information it's reasonable for you to draw that conclusion. But it's only a probability. You might attach a *truth factor* by saying you're 90% certain that the cat was involved.

Abductive reasoning is useful even if you've never seen a cat chasing a squirrel. You might observe the squirrel's behavior and infer it was being pursued by another animal of unknown type. If you've seen dogs, cats, skunks, porcupines, and raccoons in the neighborhood, you might be less certain that a cat was involved, perhaps only 25% certain.

The truth factor is the degree of confidence that you have in the inference produced by abductive reasoning. Software functions often use truth maintenance systems to store and revise the truth factors for various inferences. If you later observe, for example, that skunks, porcupines, and raccoons never seem to pursue squirrels, then you might become more confident in your inference, concluding with 50% certainty that a cat was involved. When you go back and revise your certainty factor you're using backward reasoning. When you use that knowledge in your deductive reasoning, you're using *forward reasoning.* In other words, you reason forward from what is known (deductive reasoning), and you reason backward to revise what is known (inductive reasoning and abductive reasoning). This chain of thinking is called *diagnostic reasoning.*

Diagnostic reasoning

Diagnostic reasoning using deductive, inductive, and abductive reasoning, as shown in FIG. 15-8. Diagnostic software uses mathematical set-theory to build a set of logical connections between disorders and their manifestations. (Disorders are also called *causes* or *antecedents.* Manifestations are called *effects* or *consequents.*)

The connections between antecedents and consequents are called AND/OR logic connections, as FIG. 15-8 illustrates. Diagnostic software is usually based on so-called *parsimonious covering theory.* The software seeks the simplest solution that fully explains the problem. There might be, after all, more than one solution but only one best solution. *Parsimony* means frugality, thriftiness, and economy of explanation. *Covering* means completeness.

Diagnostic software uses all three forms of reasoning that you've learned about—deductive, inductive, and abductive. It relies on fuzzy logic and probabilistic calculus to explain its findings. For example, the software performance implicit in FIG. 15-8 will not diagnose a general power supply failure if other appliances in the office are operating. This is because the AND/OR logic connection between A1 and C1 specifies that a manifestation of C1 must be present before a disorder of A1 can be inferred. But the software might make a diagnosis of power conditioner failure (30% certainty) and/or general power failure (70% certainty).

Probability

Probability is a branch of mathematics concerned with the likelihood of events happening. Probability calculations use permutations, combinations, and binomial coefficients. The probability of an event occurring is calculated by dividing the number of favorable events by the number of possible results:

$$P(event) = \frac{results^{favorable}}{results^{possible}}$$

Diagnostic software reasoning		
Antecedents The set of all known possible disorders	**Logic** The set of all known possible connections	**Consequents** The set of all known possible manifestations
Power supply failure	A1 ——————— C1	Other appliances in the office are not operating.
Power conditioner failure	A2 ———————— C2	Computer, display, and keyboard not operating.
Computer malfunction	A3 ———————— C3	Computer fan not running.
Display malfunction	A4 ———————— C4	Computer status light is off.
Keyboard malfunction	A5 ———————— C5	Display not operating.
	C6	Snow appears on the display.
	C7	Boot error message appears on the display.
	C8	Keyboard status light is off.

This table illustrates the AND/OR logic connections for software-controlled troubleshooting of a computer power-up failure using cognitive simulation.
Deductive reasoning -- For example, GIVEN A4 THEN C5, C6, C7.
Abductive reasoning -- For example, GIVEN C5 THEN A4, A2, A1.
Inductive reasoning -- Use statistical analysis of previous diagnoses to add new elements to the sets of antecedents, consequents and logic connections.

Mathematical set-theory for programmers

$A = \{A1, A2, A3, A4, A5\}$ The set of all possible disorders.

$B = \{C1, C2, C3, C4, C5, C6, C7, C8\}$ The set of all possible manifestations.

$D = \{C2, C3, C4, C5, C8\}$ The set of observed manifestations.

Active sets

$connections(A1) = \{C1, C2, C3, C4, C5, C8\}$

$connections(A2) = \{C2, C3, C4, C5, C8\}$

$connections(A3) = \{C3, C4, C7, C8\}$

$connections(A4) = \{C5, C6, C7\}$

$connections(A5) = \{C7, C8\}$

15-8 Fundamentals of diagnostic software reasoning.

Using this method, the probability of drawing the deuce of spades from a deck of 52 randomly shuffled cards is calculated as:

$$P(deuce) = \frac{1}{52} = .0192307$$

The probability of throwing two matching dice is:

$$P(matching) = \frac{6}{6 \times 6} = \frac{6}{36} = \frac{1}{6} = .166668$$

A *complementary event* is an opposite event. The probability of a complementary event is expressed as:

$$P(A) = 1 - P(\overline{A})$$

where $\overline{A}$ is the opposite of event A. The probability of throwing different numbers with two dice is:

$$P(different) = 1 - P(matching) = 1 - \left(\frac{6}{6 \times 6}\right) = 1 - \frac{1}{6} = \frac{5}{6} = .83333$$

Permutations *Permutations* are lineups of members selected from a general population. Here's an example. The total number of lineups of 4 members chosen from a population of 10 items is 5,040. The permutation calculation is $10 \times 9 \times 8 \times 7 = 5,040$. It is the order of the members in the lineup that matters, not the content. That's why the number 5,040 seems so high. When you're using permutations, you consider a lineup of *a-b-c-d* to be different from a lineup of *d-c-b-a*, even though the same four members are involved.

Combinations *Combinations* are committees of members chosen from a general population. The total number of committees that can be made up from a given population is determined by calculating the *binomial coefficient*. The formula for the binomial coefficient is:

$$\text{Binomial coefficient} = \binom{P}{M} = \frac{P!}{M!(P-M)!}$$

For example, the total number of committees of 4 members chosen from a population of 10 items is 210. The binomial calculations that produce this result are shown here:

$$\frac{10!}{4!6!} = \frac{10\times9\times8\times7\times6\times5\times4\times3\times2\times1}{4\times3\times2\times1\times6\times5\times4\times3\times2\times1} = \frac{10\times9\times8\times7}{4\times3\times2\times1} = \frac{5,040}{24} = 210$$

where P is the population and M is the number of different committees that can be chosen from the population. Note that it is the content of the committee that matters, not the order of the members. When you're using combinations, you consider a committee of *a-b-c-d* to be the same as a committee of *d-c-b-a* because the same four members are involved, only in different sequence.

Two types of lineups and committees are used in probability calculations. They are *sampling with replacement* and *sampling without replacement*. For example, the total number of three-character words that can be formed from the alphabet is $26 \times 26 \times 26 = 17,576$ words, because each character in a word can be any one of 26 available characters. This is sampling with replacement. After a character has been selected it is immediately returned to the population where it is available for the next draw. On the other hand, the total number of three-character words that can be formed from a physical alphabet comprised of 26 different Scrabble™ tiles is $26 \times 25 \times 24 = 15,600$ words. The first character in a word can be selected from 26 different tiles, but the second character can be chosen from only the remaining 25 tiles, and so on. This is sampling without replacement.

Conditional probability Conditional probability can be used to calculate the likelihood of an event occurring after a prerequisite event has occurred. The probability of event B occurring if event A has already occurred is expressed as:

$$P(B \,|\, A)$$

For example, if two cards are drawn from a randomly shuffled deck of cards, the probability of drawing a spade on the second draw after a spade was drawn on the first draw is:

$$P\left(spade^{second\_draw} \,\middle|\, spade^{first\_draw}\right) = \frac{12^{spades\_remaining}}{51^{cards\_remaining}} = .2353$$

To arrive at this figure, the number of spades remaining after the first draw is divided by the number of cards remaining after the first draw. However, if a heart was drawn on the first draw, the probability of drawing a spade on the second draw is:

$$P\left(spade^{second\_draw} \,\middle|\, heart^{first\_draw}\right) = \frac{13^{spaces\_remaining}}{51^{cards\_remaining}} = .2549$$

Sample space and probability space

When discussing probabilities, sample space contains all possible results. Probability space contains a set of probable results.

Fair probability space Each card in a deck of 52 playing cards has an equal chance of being drawn. The probability of a face card being drawn is:

$$P(facecard) = \frac{16}{52} = .3076923$$

Taking into account that each face card has a $\frac{1}{52}$ probability of being drawn, the preceding formula can also be expressed as:

$$P(facecard) = 16 \times \frac{1}{52} = \frac{16}{52} = .3076923$$

Biased probability space Suppose the face cards have been doctored by a professional magician to make them more likely to be selected by an unwitting volunteer from the audience. If each face card now has $\frac{1}{32}$ probability instead of $\frac{1}{52}$, then each number card now has $\frac{1}{72}$ probability because the sum of all probabilities must equal 100%, expressed as:

$$\left(16 \times \frac{1}{32}\right) + \left(36 \times \frac{1}{72}\right) = .5 + .5 = 1$$

The probability that a doctored face card will be drawn from this biased deck of playing cards is:

$$P(facecard) = 16 \times \frac{1}{32} = .5$$

The probability that a card valued ten or higher will be drawn from this biased deck is:

$$P(card) = \left(16 \times \frac{1}{32}\right) + \left(4 \times \frac{1}{72}\right) = .5 + .0555 = .5555$$

Binomial coefficients and probability space

A poker hand is a combination of 5 members chosen from a population of 52 items. This is expressed as *52 choose 5*, or;

$$\binom{52}{5}$$

Here is how to calculate the probability of receiving the ace of spades in a poker hand. A favorable result is a hand that contains the ace of spades and four other cards. So a favorable hand is just a committee of 4 members (the rest of the hand) drawn from a population of 51 items (the rest of the deck). The number of favorable hands is 51 choose 4, and the formula for calculating the probability is:

$$\therefore P(acespades) = \frac{\binom{51}{4}}{\binom{52}{5}} = \frac{\frac{51!}{4!47!}}{\frac{52!}{5!47!}} = \frac{51!}{4!47!} \times \frac{5!47!}{52!} = \frac{5}{52} = .0961538$$

Probability and game theory

When game theory and probability theory are combined, speculative scenarios can be analyzed. These analyses are also called *what-if scenarios.* The competitive situation described in FIG. 15-9, for example, shows how probability estimates can be integrated with a typical decision-table. The user can investigate various strategies and situations by adjusting the values of the variables in the equations.

Consider, for example, a situation where player X and player Y are in direct competition for a specific objective. Each player can adopt either a bold strategy or a cautious strategy, although both strategies begin with a period of posturing and bluffing intended to intimidate the opponent. A player using a bold strategy is called a *hawk.* A player using a cautious strategy is called a *dove.* A dove will retreat at the first indication of physical danger, but a hawk is willing to escalate the confrontation into violence. It is important to keep in mind that even for the player who wins the game, there will be a cost involved. In a best-case scenario this cost might only be stress. In a worst-case scenario the cost of winning might be physical injury.

If both players are evenly matched, then player X's probability of winning is 1 in 2 (or .5) and player Y's probability of winning is also .5, expressed as:

$$P(Xwins) = \frac{1}{2} = .5 \quad \text{denotes Player X's probability of winning, and}$$

$$P(Ywins) = \frac{1}{2} = .5 \quad \text{denotes Player Y's probability of winning.}$$

Game-theory and probability-theory

	Player X HAWK	Player X DOVE
Player Y **HAWK**	$\dfrac{V-C}{2}, \dfrac{V-C}{2}$ Moderate LOSS for X Moderate LOSS for Y	θ, V Maximum LOSS for X Maximum GAIN for Y
Player Y **DOVE**	V, θ Maximum GAIN for X Maximum LOSS for Y	$\dfrac{V}{2}, \dfrac{V}{2}$ Moderate GAIN for X Moderate GAIN for Y

where V is the value of the GAIN and $-C$ is the cost of taking part in a physical confrontation.

15-9 Assignment of probabilities in a game-theory analysis.

But suppose player X were larger, more experienced, or more skilled. You might give player X a .6 probability of winning and you might reduce player Y's probability of winning to .4.

If you inspect the decision-table in FIG. 15-9, you can see how the probability factors affect the size of the payoff to each player if both adopt a cautious strategy. In the event both adopt a bold strategy, the cost of winning is also affected by the probability calculations. In the next set of formulas, the reward for winning is represented by V; the reward for losing is represented by -C. Given that both players adopt a hawk strategy and are evenly matched, the reward that player X can realistically expect is:

$$= (V \times P(Xwins)) + ((-C) \times P(Ywins))$$
$$= \left(V \times \frac{1}{2}\right) + \left((-C) \times \frac{1}{2}\right) = \frac{V-C}{2} - C$$

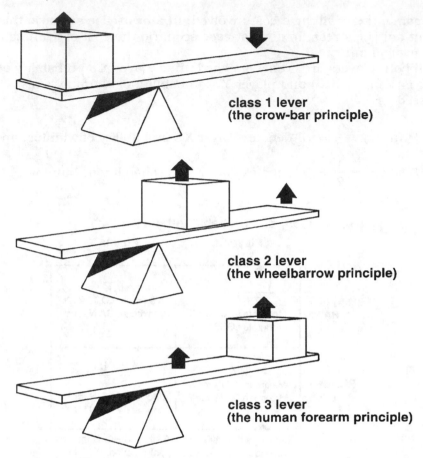

15-10 Typical principles of physics, which can be modeled by knowledge-based simulation software.

Physics-based simulation

Physics-based simulation software uses principles of physics. The software considers factors such as velocity, speed, displacement, acceleration, deceleration, mass, density, linear momentum, and kinetic energy. Figure 15-10 shows some typical principals of physics that can be modeled by knowledge-based simulation software. Figure 15-11 summarizes the fundamentals of physics that are useful in simulation programming.

Velocity *Velocity* is the rate of change of displacement over time. It is speed in a specified direction. It is a vector quantity.

Speed *Speed* is displacement over time. It is a scalar quantity, such as 65 mph or 100 kph. No direction is indicated.

Displacement *Displacement* is distance measured from a fixed reference point. It is a vector quantity that uses a specified direction.

Physics primer for programmers	
Term	**Description**
Velocity	Velocity is the rate of change of displacement over time, or speed in a specified direction. It is a vector quanity such as 15 inches per second in a northwest direction..
Speed	Speed is displacement over time. It is a scalar quantity, such as km/hr or mph.
Displacement	Displacement is distance measured from a fixed reference point. It is a vector quantity that uses a specified direction.
Acceleration	Acceleration is the rate of increase of velocity over time. It is a vector quantity, such as 2 meters per second squared.
Deceleration	Deceleration is the rate of decrease of velocity over time. It is a vector quantity.
Mass	Mass is the quantity of matter in a body. Mass is an indication of the body's inertia.
Density	Density is mass per unit of volume, or how much matter is present per unit of volume.

15-11 Fundamentals of physics useful for programmers developing knowledge-based simulation software.

Acceleration and deceleration *Acceleration* is the rate of increase of velocity over time. It is a vector quantity, such as 12 meters per second per second. *Deceleration* is the rate of decrease of velocity over time.

Mass and linear momentum *Mass* is the quantity of matter in an entity. It is an indication of the entity's inertia. *Density* is mass per unit of volume. It reflects how much matter is present per unit of volume. *Linear momentum* is the product of mass and velocity.

Kinetic energy *Kinetic energy* is the energy possessed by an entity because of its motion. It is the potential to do work.

Collisions

Collision detection and response are important components of physics-based simulations. Bounding-boxes are often used to help simplify the collision-detection process. Principles of kinematics and dynamics, which you'll investigate in the next chapter, are used to determine a collision response to either elastic collisions or inelastic collisions. Figure 15-12 presents a summary of the fundamental collision principles that are commonly used in simulation programming.

Elastic collisions In an *elastic collision*, linear momentum and kinetic energy are conserved, as shown in FIG. 15-12. The solid entities involved in an elastic collision are flexible (elastic), thereby avoiding any damage or any loss of energy. Simply stated, they bounce.

Collision simulation	
Term	**Description and sample formula**
Linear momentum	Linear momentum is the product of mass and velocity. Mass is the quantity of matter in a body, an indication of intertia. Velocity is the speed and direction of the body. Linear momentum is measured in kg m/sec. $LinearMomentum= Mass \times Velocity$
Kinetic energy	Kinetic energy is the energy possessed by a body because of its motion. Kinetic energy is measured in joules. $KineticEnergy = \frac{1}{2}Mass \times Velocity^2$
Inelastic collision	In an inelastic collision, linear momentum is conserved but kinetic energy is not conserved, because some energy is lost as heat or work done or physical damage. $FinalVelocity = \dfrac{Mass1 \times Velocity1}{Mass1 + Mass2}$
Elastic collision	Linear momentum and kinetic energy are conserved. $FinalVelocity1 = \dfrac{(M1 \times V1) - (M2 \times FV2)}{M1}$

The activity in an inelastic collision can be described by

$Mass1 \times Velocity1 = (Mass1 + Mass2) \times FinalVelocity$

The activity in an elastic collision can be described by

$Mass1 \times Velocity1 = (Mass1 \times FinalVel1) + (Mass2 \times FinalVel2)$

15-12 Fundamentals of collisions useful for programmers developing knowledge-based simulation software.

Inelastic collisions   In an *inelastic collision*, linear momentum is conserved but kinetic energy is not. Some kinetic energy is lost as heat, as work done, or as physical damage. The entities involved in an inelastic collision are rigid. Simply stated, they do not bounce—they break.

Physically based animation

Physically based animation is a subset of physics-based simulation. It is 3D animation that uses constraints to manage an entity's motion. Physically based animation is also called constraint-based animation. Constraints are forces, loads, and matter. A constraint affects the motion of an entity in a physically based animation sequence. Physically based animation can be implemented as forward kinematics, forward dynamics, inverse kinematics, and inverse dynamics.

Forward kinematics calculates what happens when velocity or acceleration is applied to an entity. *Forward dynamics* calculates what happens when force, loads, and other constraints are applied to an entity. *Inverse kinematics* calculates the amount of velocity or acceleration required to move an entity from one location to another location during a specified period of time. *Inverse dynamics* calculates the forces, loads, or other constraints required to move an entity from one location to another location during a specified period of time.

Where do you go from here?

Now that you've familiarized yourself with some of the fundamentals of implementing knowledge-based simulation on personal computers running Windows, you're ready to delve into more advanced discussions. The next chapter investigates kinematics and dynamics. You'll learn how your applications can automatically manage the motion of 3D entities by considering their velocity, starting location, and other attributes.

16
Getting started with kinematics and dynamics

This chapter teaches you about kinematics and dynamics. It describes how these paradigms can be used to automatically manage the movement and motion of 3D entities in animated scenes. Concepts such as forward kinematics, inverse dynamics, constraints, collision detection, and the simulation-modeling pipeline are all discussed and how they can be used to manage the movement and motion of 3D entities in an animated sequence.

You'll see how the dynamics engine and the kinematics engine provide the staring point for the simulation-modeling pipeline and how they provide input for the animation engine and its underpinnings, the 3D toolkit. You'll also find out about multiple constraints and collision detection. Finally, you'll acquire knowledge to prepare you for the hands-on tutorial presented in the next chapter.

Constraint-based animation

As you've learned in previous chapters, *physics-based simulation* uses principles of physics to manage the events being modeled and simulated. The software considers factors such as velocity, speed, displacement, acceleration, deceleration, mass, density, linear momentum, kinetic energy, inelastic collisions, elastic collisions, and others. The output of a physics-based simulation is displayed as *physically based animation*. Because the motion in the resulting animation sequence is affected by so-called constraints, physically based animation is also called *constraint-based animation*.

Constraint-based animation uses three modeling components. These three components are:

- primitives
- constraints
- external applied-forces

Primitives *Primitives* are 3D entities such as boxes, spheres, cylinders, cones, wedges, and complex 3D hierarchical solids. You've already learned about these in chapter 8 and experimented with a hands-on tutorial in chapter 9. Each 3D primitive is assigned attributes such as density, dimension, velocity, rotational inertia, and other attributes depending on the nature of the simulation.

Constraints *Constraints* are limiting factors that regulate the behavior of a primitive. Constraints can include forces, loads, matter, and design attributes that affect the primitive's movement, motion, deformation, evolution. For example, gravity constrains the motion of a tennis ball. The net is a constraint that affects the tennis ball's potential trajectory. The clay surface of the court is yet another constraint. The resilience and elasticity of the tennis ball itself constrain the magnitude and the direction of the ball's bounce. The roughness and coarseness of the ball's covering acts as a constraint on its propensity to spin during flight, because those attributes affect wind resistance. You've already tentatively explored constraints in chapter 13, when you investigated source code that animated a complex 3D solid with a moving part rotating around a joint.

External applied-forces *External applied-forces* are used to initiate and to motivate the simulation. For example, a brisk cross-wind over the tennis court is an external applied-force influencing the path of the tennis ball. The stroke of the racket on the tennis ball is also an external applied-force.

Methods of control

As you've already learned, physically based animation can be implemented as forward kinematics, forward dynamics, inverse kinematics, and inverse dynamics. *Forward kinematics* concerns what happens when velocity or acceleration is applied to an entity. *Forward dynamics* concerns what happens when force, loads, and other constraints are applied to an entity. *Inverse kinematics* calculates the velocity or acceleration that is required to move an entity from one location to another location during a specified period of time. *Inverse dynamics* calculates the forces, loads, or other constraints required to move an entity from one location to another location during a specified period of time.

Implementation of constraints Before any kinematics or dynamics simulation is started, the programmer must select and apply constraints that will affect the entity's behavior. Typical examples of constraints include:

- point-to-nail
- point-on-line
- point-to-point
- point-to-path
- point-on-skin

Point constraints *Point-to-nail constraints* are used to attach a point located on an entity to a point located in 3D-space. The entity can rotate and swivel about the point. *Point-on-line constraints* are used to attach a point located on an entity to a line in 3D-space. The entity can rotate and swivel about the point, which can slide along the line. *Point-to-point constraints* attach a point located on one entity to a point located on another entity. *Point-to-path constraints* are used to attach a point located on an entity to a path in 3D-space. The path can be arbitrarily curved, bent, or jointed, or it can be the result of a trajectory calculation. The entity can rotate and swivel about the point, which can slide along the path. *Point-on-skin constraints* are used to attach a point located on an entity to a point located on the surface of another entity. The first entity can rotate and swivel about the point, while the point can slide anywhere over the surface of the second entity. Other, more advanced, forms of constraints include:

- point-in-volume
- volume-in-volume
- point-outside-volume
- volume-outside-volume

Volume constraints *Point-in-volume constraints* are used to limit a point located on an entity to the interior of a specified volume located in 3D-space. The entity can rotate and swivel about the point, which itself cannot leave the volume. *Volume-in-volume constraints* are used to limit a volume (usually an entity) to the interior of another specified volume in 3D-space. This limitation can affect either the location and orientation of the constrained entity, or its dimensions, or both. *Point-outside-volume constraints* are used to limit a point located on an entity to the exterior of a specified volume located in 3D-space. *Volume-outside-volume constraints* are used to restrict a volume (usually an entity) to the exterior of another volume (usually another entity). Consider, for example, the tennis ball and the clay court mentioned previously. A volume-outside-volume constraint is used to prevent the tennis ball from passing through the surface of the clay court. Volume-outside-volume constraints are based upon collision detection.

Collision detection

Two issues are involved in collision detection. First, the simulation software must be able to detect the occurrence of a collision between two entities. Second, an appropriate post-collision response must be simulated.

Detecting a collision The most efficient algorithms for collision detection are based on 3D entities constructed from three-sided facets or four-sided facets. Suppose, for example, that two solid cubes have collided during an animated simulation. This means that one of the cubes has penetrated the other cube. Stated more precisely, one or more vertices of the striking cube is now located behind one or more facets of the struck cube.

As you've already learned, b-rep programmers always describe the vertices of a facet in counterclockwise direction as viewed from outside the solid on whose surface the facet is located. This convention means that the equation for a plane can be used to determine whether the viewpoint is located on the outside or inside of the facet in question. If the viewpoint is located inside (behind) the facet, it means the facet faces away from the viewpoint. Because it is a backward-facing facet, it cannot be seen. On the other hand, if the viewpoint is located outside the facet, it can be seen. By using the same formulas and substituting the XYZ coordinates of the suspect vertex for the XYZ coordinates of the viewpoint, your application can use the standard equation for a plane to test the vertex of the penetrating cube against the penetrated facet. Thus your application can determine whether the vertex is located inside or outside the plane of the facet in question. If the vertex is located inside (behind) all of the visible facets, then you know that the vertex is either behind or inside the struck cube. If the vertex is also located inside all of the backward-facing facets, then you can safely infer that the vertex is inside the struck cube. The equation for a plane can also detect if the vertex is located on the surface of the facet (which is, of course, the moment of collision).

Bounding-boxes *Parallelepipeds* are six-sided, right-angled primitives. A *cube* is simply a parallelepiped with equal dimensions of width, height, and depth. These types of primitives provide the most straightforward cases for collision detection. Many kinematics applications temporarily build a box around a complex 3D hierarchical solid that is being tested for collision. This parallelepiped box is called a *bounding-box,* and it is used in order to simplify the collision detection calculations. It does so by reducing the number of vertices and facets that require testing. If the offending vertex does not penetrate the bounding-box, then no collision has occurred and no further calculations are necessary. However, if the offending vertex has penetrated the bounding-box, then the software can conclude that there might have been a collision between the two entities. It is important to realize, though, that a collision might not have occurred. This is because the complex 3D entity does not completely fill the volume of the bounding-box, and the offending vertex might be located in an unoccupied portion of the bounding-box. The vertex must now be tested against most (and perhaps all) of the facets of the complex 3D entity. Some software builds a bounding-box around each primitive in the complex 3D assembly in order to further optimize the search for a collision. You can think of it as searching through a relational database of 3D primitives and points.

Responding to a collision   After a collision has been detected, a kinematics application must provide a response. The nature of the response depends on whether the collision is elastic or inelastic. In an elastic collision, linear momentum and kinetic energy are conserved. The solid entities involved in an elastic collision are flexible (elastic), thereby avoiding any damage or any loss of energy. Simply stated, they bounce, rebound, and ricochet. The application must recalculate the velocities of each entity involved in the collision. However, in an inelastic collision, linear momentum is conserved but kinetic energy is not. Some kinetic energy is lost as heat, as work done, or as physical damage. The entities involved in an inelastic collision are rigid. They do not simply bounce, rebound, or ricochet, but instead they break. The application must calculate the deformation and destruction of each entity, recalculate the kinetic energy of the deformed participants, and then recalculate the velocities of each entity involved in the collision. You can refer back to FIG. 15-12 in the previous chapter for examples of formulas for linear momentum, kinetic energy, and final velocity in elastic and inelastic collisions. Consider again the example of the clay tennis court. The tennis ball striking the clay court is an elastic collision. There is a rebound. A beanbag striking the clay is an inelastic collision. There is no rebound.

The collision plane   In a constraint-based animation, whenever an elastic collision is detected, the software temporarily inserts a stiff spring constraint between the colliding points. The standard engineering equations for spring performance can then be used to regulate the motion of the colliding entities. This approach to collision response depends on using only a single point of collision on a so-called *collision plane.* The point of collision is usually at the location of the offending vertex. The collision plane is the plane containing the penetrated facet. The collision plane determines the angle of incidence and all subsequently calculated post-collision paths and trajectories.

The simulation-modeling pipeline

The chain of calculations that an application uses to manage a physics-based simulation is called the *simulation-modeling pipeline.* If both dynamics and kinematics are being calculated, the sequence is called the *dynamics-kinematics pipeline.*

The dynamics-kinematics pipeline

Kinematics means the positions and velocities of 3D entities. *Dynamics* means laws of physics such as force, mass, momentum, and others that govern those positions and velocities.

Forward kinematics   *Forward kinematics* is the process of calculating what happens when velocity or acceleration is applied to an entity. Forward kinematics does not concern itself with forces or mass. It considers only the motion itself. Your application can use forward kinematics to check if two entities collide during an animation sequence. Kinematics can be inverted, in which case the paradigm is called inverse kinematics.

Inverse kinematics   *Inverse kinematics* is the process of calculating the velocity or acceleration required to move an entity from one location to another location during a specified period of time. Inverse kinematics uses a user-supplied target location and calculates the amount of velocity or acceleration required to move the entity to that location.

Forward dynamics   *Forward dynamics* is the process of calculating what happens when force, loads, or other constraints are applied to an entity. In general, dynamics concerns itself with the laws of physics that govern kinematics. Your application can use dynamics to calculate the motion (the kinematics) of an entity that results from forces acting on the entity. You can also use dynamics to calculate forces resulting from the motion of the entity. Forward dynamics can calculate the forces resulting from the impact of a collision. Dynamics can be inverted, in which case the paradigm is called inverse dynamics.

Inverse dynamics   *Inverse dynamics* is the process of calculating the forces or constraints required to move an entity of specified mass from one location to another location during a specified period of time. Inverse dynamics uses a user-supplied target location and calculates the forces required to move the entity to that location.

The pipeline components

The dynamics-kinematics pipeline consists of a dynamics engine, kinematics engine, animation engine, 3D engine, and a resulting display image. You'll recall how each entity must pass through the 3D transformation sequence before being displayed. Likewise, each entity in a physics-based simulation must pass through the dynamics-kinematics pipeline before being displayed.

Dynamics engine   The *dynamics engine* calculates the velocity or acceleration that results from forces being applied to an entity. These results are passed to the kinematics engine. If a simulator does not contain a dynamics engine, then the programmer provides the velocity or acceleration values.

Kinematics engine   The *kinematics engine* calculates the displacement that results from the application of velocity or acceleration to the entity. These results are passed to the animation engine.

Animation engine   The *animation engine* processes and implements the motion dynamics, update dynamics, and viewing dynamics that are used in physically-based animation. You'll want to take care to note that these three forms of animation dynamics have a meaning different from forward dynamics and inverse dynamics. As you already learned in chapter 11, animation is movement across space over time. An animated 3D entity is a display of 4D space-time using XYZT coordinates. In order to manage 4D space-time, your application must monitor and update three sets of animation dynamics at run-time. These dynamics are motion dynamics, update dynamics, and viewing dynamics. Taken together, these attributes describe an animation sequence. *Motion dynamics* refers to the location, orientation, and juxtaposition of individual entities. *Update dynamics* is concerned with changes in shape, color, and texture. During a bouncing ball sequence, for example, update dynamics ensures that the ball is suitably deformed whenever it strikes the floor. *Viewing dynamics* is concerned with changes in lighting, camera, and viewpoint.

The animation engine acts as an interface between the time-based calculations of the simulation and the frame-based calculations of the animation implementation, as shown in FIG. 16-1. The results produced by the animation engine are passed to the 3D engine, which models and renders a 3D scene for each frame in the animation sequence.

Animation Timing	
Frame Number	Elapsed time
1	.0555
2	.1111
3	.1667
4	.2222
5	.2778
6	.3333
7	.3889
8	.4444
9	.5000
10	.5555
11	.6111
12	.6667
13	.7222
14	.7778
15	.8333
16	.8889
17	.9444
18	1.0000

16-1 Correlation between frame count and elapsed time useful for animated kinematics simulation software.

Where do you go from here?

Now that you've familiarized yourself with some of the fundamentals of kinematics and dynamics, you're ready for a hands-on tutorial. The sample application in the next chapter is an interactive kinematics editor. You'll be invited to explore the capabilities of the demo program. You'll do this by loading scripts and using the scripts to build, store, and play kinematics animation sequences. The first script rotates a set of 3D entities.

The second script simulates two satellites orbiting a planet. The third script provides a moving camshaft simulation. Finally, you'll be taken on a personal guided tour through the source code so you'll acquire the knowledge you need to use kinematics functions in your own project development.

17
Tutorial:
kinematics programming

This chapter provides a hands-on tutorial that demonstrates some of the kinematics fundamentals learned in chapter 16. A User's Guide shows you how to run the sample application, and a Programmer's Guide provides explanations of how the kinematics module is integrated with the animation engine. This chapter explores how the animation engine uses functions in the kinematics module in order to build each frame in the animation sequence.

You'll learn how kinematics functions to automate the production of an animation sequence and how to use kinematics in your own animated graphics applications. The kinematics module must be fed the initial attributes of a 3D entity. You'll learn how to do this and use velocity and acceleration parameters to tell the kinematics module all it needs to know in order to plot the movement of the 3D entity.

Finally, you'll see how to use animation preview functions so you can validate the first and final frame of an animation sequence before beginning a time-consuming build. You'll find out how to use scripts to store the instructions for a kinematics animation sequence.

A user's guide to the sample application

In this section you'll learn how to use the sample application named kinematx. Before you can run kinematx you must build the executable. The program listings for the sample application are presented as FIG. C-5 in Appendix C. Source listings for toolkits that must be linked in to build the finished executable are presented in Appendix B. All source files are also provided on the companion disk. See Appendix A for tips on compiling the program.

Starting the sample application

There are two ways you can start the sample application. You can start it directly from Visual Basic or you can launch it from Windows' Program Manager.

Startup from Visual Basic You can run the sample application directly from the Visual Basic editor if you've loaded the kinematx.mak project file.

Startup from Windows' Program Manager From the Windows desktop, pull down the File menu and select Run. When the dialog box appears, type the full pathname of the program, such as

c:*directory**subdirectory*\kinematx.exe

You'll want to take care to use directory names that reflect your own system, of course. When you select the OK button of the dialog box the sample application starts.

Using the sample application

When the sample application starts up, the sign-on notice appears. Choose OK to continue.

Four menu names are displayed on the menu bar. They are File, Edit, Run, and Using. You can use the File menu to quit the program. You can use the Run menu, shown in FIG. 17-1, to load a script file from disk, to preview the first and final frames, to build the animation sequence and save it to disk, to load an animation sequence or script from disk, and to play an animation sequence.

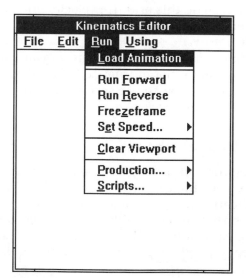

17-1 The Run menu from the sample application kinematx.frm.

You can use a mouse or the keyboard to operate this sample application. To use your mouse, just point and click. To use your keyboard, press Alt to move the focus to the menu bar, then press the appropriate mnemonic keys to pull down a menu and select an item from the menu.

The Run menu The Run menu controls the kinematics module and the animation engine. To build the default kinematics simulation, select Build Animation from the Production menu item in the Run menu, as shown in FIG. 17-2. Be sure to select wire-frame mode before starting the build process for the first time. The software will build the default kinematics animation and save it to disk.

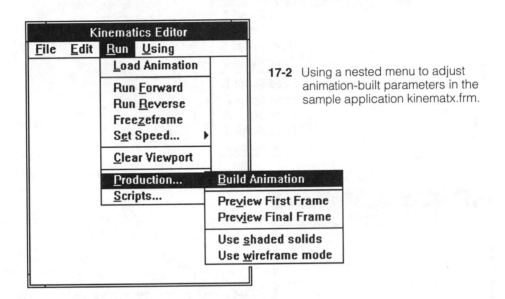

17-2 Using a nested menu to adjust animation-built parameters in the sample application kinematx.frm.

Selecting a different script If you're using the companion disk, three prewritten script files are already provided. If you're working with just the book, you'll find instructions later in this chapter covering how to prepare these scripts. To load in a script, choose Scripts from the Run menu, as shown in FIG. 17-3. The default script is Script 1, which manages the independent rotation of three primitives, as shown in FIG. 17-4. This default script is hard-coded into the demo at startup. Sample frames from the resulting animation sequence are shown in FIG. 17-5. The software overwrites this hard-coded block of data whenever you load in a script from disk. Script 2 manages a simulation of two satellites orbiting a planet. Script 3 is a simulation of a moving camshaft.

Whenever you load in a script, you must build the animation, save it to disk, and then load it in from disk before you can run it.

You can also save scripts. Whenever you select Save Script from the Run menu, the software saves to disk the current script under whichever name you've selected.

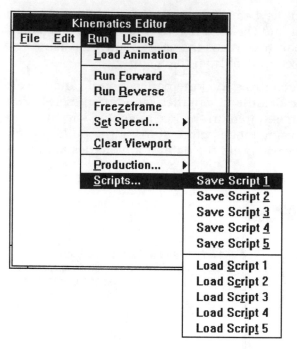

17-3 Using a nested menu to save or load a kinematics script when using the sample application kinematx.frm.

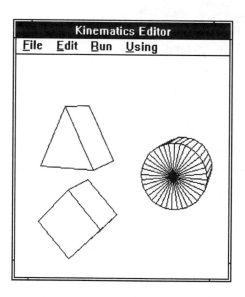

17-4 A sample image from the default script used by the sample application kinematx.frm. Shown here is wire-frame mode. The demo also supports shaded entities.

Loading an animation To load an animation sequence from disk, select Load Animation from the Run menu. The animation engine loads all 36 frames into memory. Remember, loading an animation is not the same as loading a script. An animation consists of bitmap images. A script is a set of instructions describing the motion of 3D entities.

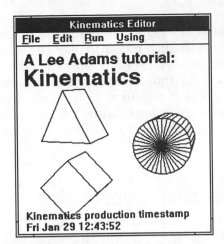
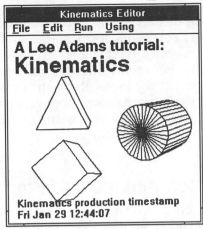

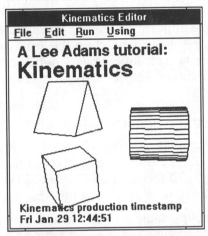
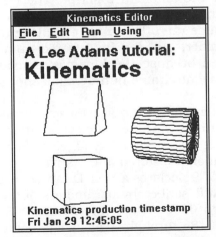
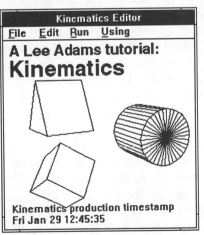

17-5 Sample frames from the kinematics animation sequence produced by the sample application kinematx.frm using script01.scr. You can use the menu system to toggle to shaded mode if desired.

Running an animation To start an animation sequence that you've loaded in from disk, select Run Forward from the Run menu. The animation begins to play. You can select Run Reverse from the Run menu to play the animation sequence backwards. To use single-step control, select Freezeframe from the Run menu while the animation is running. The keyboard controls become active. Press the right arrow key to advance to the next frame. Press the left arrow key to back up to the previous frame. Press and hold the right arrow key to play the animation sequence at the fastest rate possible on your hardware.

A programmer's guide to the sample application

This section describes how the source code works. The source listings for the sample application are presented as FIG. C-5 in Appendix C. Source listings for the linked-in toolkits are provided in Appendix B. For tips on building the sample application, see Appendix A. The source files for the sample application are also provided on the companion disk as kiglobal.bas, kimain.bas, kinematx.frm, kiplay.bas, engine3d.bas, shapes3d.bas, deform3d.bas, assemb3d.bas, lights3d.bas, and knmatx3d.bas.

How the global module works

The kiglobal.bas global module is a clone of previous listings in the book. You should pay careful attention, however, to the kinematics script at lines 0120 through 0215. Visual Basic's Type keyword is used to create a structure that describes the kinematics state of a body in 3D space.

The script database You want to note the code at lines 0124 through 0151, which declares data types for the kinematics script. The Header struct at lines 0124 through 0128 contains parameters governing the entire script, such as the animation frame rate, the number of 3D entities being animated, the first frame number, and the final frame number. Specifying the frame rate is required because the kinematics module must be able to translate elapsed time into frame numbers (as shown in FIG. 16-1 in chapter 16).

You'll also want to pay careful attention to the ActorParams struct at lines 0152 through 0180. Each 3D entity in the kinematics simulation will be described by a variable of the ActorParams struct type. Note how attributes such as velocity and acceleration are stored in the struct.

The code at lines 0181 through 0189 declares a ScriptDatabase struct. This is a database of 25 entities, each described by parameters of the ActorParams struct at lines 0152 through 0180. The members of the ScriptDatabase struct are declared at lines 0183 through 0188. They include a header, startup camera specifications, camera movement specifications, startup light-source specifications, light-source movement specifications, and 25 entities (at line 0188).

How the startup module works

The kimain.bas startup module is also a clone of earlier listings. Note lines 0061 through 0096, which initialize the filenames for the FrameFiles() array. You'll also want to pay particular attention to lines 0097 through 0101, where the filenames for the script files are initialized for the Script Files() array.

How the form module works

You'll want to understand how the kinematics functions are called by this code so you can add kinematics to your own applications. The discussion in this chapter limits itself to the use of kinematics in 3D animation sequences. You'll find chapter 12 helpful if you need a more detailed analysis of sections that are not discussed here.

Building the animation frames The animation-build process adheres to the format established by the prototype applications discussed in chapters 12 and 13. You should note, however, how line 0786 in zSaveAnimation() calls a function named zInitializeModel() to initialize the kinematics parameters. The zDrawCel() function at lines 1045 through 1075 has also been slightly modified. Take care to note how the code uses dot notation to access variables in the script database that describe the motion of the camera and the light-source. The call to kmRenderScene() at line 1074 instructs the kinematics module, knmatx3d.c, to draw the current configuration of the 3D scene.

Initializing the kinematics The zInitializeModel() function at lines 1080 through 1226 initializes (or reinitializes) the kinematics parameters for the simulation. Because the variable named Script is a structure, dot notation is used to address members in the database. After first initializing the camera and the light-source, the code specifies a set of parameters for three entities. This is where the linear velocity, rotational velocity, and acceleration are defined for each entity in the 3D scene. Finally, the code at lines 1210 through 1225 calls functions in the kinematics module in order to reset the kinematics engine. The For...Next block at line 1211 loops once for each 3D entity in the database. You can see how the arguments passed to each called function are fetched from the database by using dot notation.

Previewing the frames The zPreviewFirstFrame() function at line 0705 resets the 3D environment and draws the first frame in the animation sequence. This function makes it possible for you to view a single frame without going to the time and trouble of building the entire animation sequence. The zPreviewFinalFrame() function at line 0675 draws the final frame. Note how the code calls the zSelectPreviewFrame() function located at line 1321 to help it set up for the preview. A call to zDrawCel() passes the desired frame number to the toolkit modules.

Using script files

The zSaveScript() function at lines 1290 through 1316 saves a script database to disk. Most of this code is concerned with trapping errors and reporting progress to the user. The Open, Put, and Close statements perform the low-level work. The zLoadScript() function at lines 1259 through 1285 loads a script database from disk, overwriting the data buffer.

Rotating subobjects   The file named script01.scr describes the motion for a set of rotating primitives. A typical image produced during the animation-build process is shown in FIG. 17-4. A sampling of frames from the animation sequence in wire-frame mode is shown in FIG. 17-5. This script is hard-coded into the sample application at lines 1083 through 1208.

Orbit simulations   The file named script02.scr describes the motion for two satellites orbiting a planet. A typical image produced during the animation-build process is shown in FIG. 17-6. A sampling of frames from the animation sequence in wire-frame mode is shown in FIG. 17-7. A sampling of frames in fully-shaded mode is shown in FIG. 17-8.

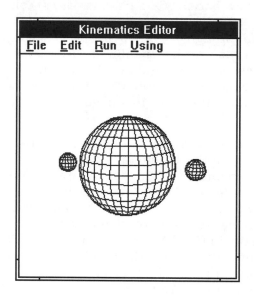

17-6   A typical image from the sample application kinematx.frm.

Camshaft simulation   The file named script03.scr describes the motion of a moving camshaft. A typical image produced during the animation-build process is shown in FIG. 17-9. A sampling of frames from the animation sequence in wire-frame mode is shown in FIG. 17-10.

Creating the scripts   The kinematics attribute settings for the orbiting sphere simulation are shown in FIG. 17-11. The kinematics attribute settings for the camshaft simulation are shown in FIG. 17-12. Simply substitute the values shown in FIG. 17-11 or FIG. 17-12 for the default values at lines 1122 through 1208 if you want to tinker with the settings for these

17-7 Sample frames from the kinematics animation sequence produced by the sample application kinematx.frm using script02.scr. See 17-8 for shaded version.

17-8 Sample frames from the kinematics animation sequence produced by the sample application kinematx.frm using script02.scr. See 17-7 for wire-frame version.

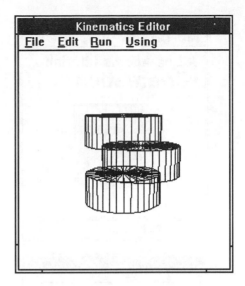

17-9 A typical image from the sample application kinematx.frm.

two simulations. After you've created your own customized simulation, you can save the script as Script 4 or Script 5 by using the Save Script menu shown in FIG. 17-3.

How the kinematics module works

The knmatx3d.c kinematics module is presented in FIG. B-7 in Appendix B. This program listing provides functions that implement a set of kinematics controls that manage the motion of entities in a 3D scene. The module calls functions in the 3D toolkit in order to draw the 3D entities whose location and orientation it has calculated from the velocities and accelerations provided by the main module. After the animation begins, the kinematics module recalculates a new location and orientation for each entity for each subsequent frame in the animation sequence.

Kinematics state The struct declared at lines 0062 through 0108 holds attributes that describe the kinematics state for each entity in the 3D scene. The code at line 0112 declares a variable of this new data type. The module supports up to 25 entities in any one simulation. You should note line 0211, which declares an index that points into the array of structs. This pointer is used to address the currently selected entity during calculations.

Initialization The kmInitializeKinematics() callable function at line 0119 initializes the kinematics environment. You'll want to note the TimeSlice variable at line 0160, which is derived from the animation frame rate. As you'll recall, this concept was illustrated by FIG. 16-1 in chapter 16. The code at lines 0162 through 0165 is smart enough to initialize only the required number of entities. It calls a function named kmInitBody() to initialize each entity's parameters.

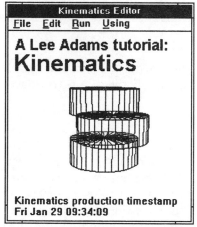

17-10 Sample frames from the kinematics animation sequence produced by the sample application kinematx.frm using script03.scr. Shaded images are also supported by the demo.

Orbiting spheres			
Attribute	**Entity 1**	**Entity 2**	**Entity 3**
Solid	zSPHERE	zSPHERE	zSPHERE
Dimensions	50,50,50	10,10,10	10,10,10
Location	0,0,0	70,0,0	-70,0,0
Velocity heading	zWEST	zSOUTH	zNORTH
Velocity pitch	zHORIZONTAL	zHORIZONTAL	zHORIZONTAL
Velocity speed	0	220	220
Heading change/sec	0	180	180
Duration (seconds)	0	2	2

17-11 Kinematics parameters for script02.scr.

Camshaft simulation			
Attribute	**Entity 1**	**Entity 2**	**Entity 3**
Solid	zCYLINDER	zCYLINDER	zCYLINDER
Dimensions	40,40,15	40,40,15	40,40,15
Location	0,-30,0	20,0,0	0,30,0
Orientation pitch	90	90	90
Velocity heading		zSOUTH	
Velocity pitch		zHORIZONTAL	
Velocity speed		62.832	
Heading change/sec		180	
Duration (seconds)		2	

17-12 Kinematics parameters for script03.scr.

Reset The kmReset() callable function at line 0173 resets the kinematics environment. It does this by setting the current frame number to 1 and by resetting the current time to 0.0.

Preview The kmSelectPreviewFrame() callable function at line 0184 adjusts the kinematics parameters for a particular preview frame. The For...Next loop at line 0190 simply steps the kinematics engine up to the desired frame. The For...Next loop at line 0194 ensures that each entity is updated.

Setting the kinematics attributes The callable functions at lines 0214 through 0417 can be called by the main module in order to set the linear acceleration, rotational acceleration, heading change rate, pitch change rate, location, orientation, dimensions, linear velocity, rotational velocity, primitive type, color, and mass of any entity in the 3D scene. Note how each function calls kmSelectBody() to reset the pointer to the database of entities.

Rendering the scene The callable kmRenderScene() function at line 0422 draws the 3D scene in its current configuration. The For...Next loop at line 0430 ensures that each entity is rendered.

Internal functions The kmInitBody() function at line 0459 uses dot notation to initialize an entity in the kinematics database with default values. The kmSelectBody() function at line 0501 adjusts the BPtr index to address the selected entity in the database. The kmRenderBody() at line 0511 uses the 3D toolkit to render a 3D entity at a particular location and orientation. Note how the BArray(BPtr).Solid dot notation is used at line 0541 to determine which type of primitive to draw.

The kinematics pipeline The seven functions that make up the kinematics modeling pipeline are located at lines 0566 through 0670. They are:

1. Get the new linear speed.
2. Get the new rotational speed.
3. Get the new velocity heading.
4. Get the new velocity pitch.
5. Calculate the new location.
6. Calculate the new orientation.
7. Calculate the new dimensions.

Note how the TimeSlice variable is used to increment these attributes by an amount appropriate to one frame change. All of these functions are internal functions which can be called only by the kinematics module itself.

Where do you go from here?

Now that you've practiced using kinematics in 3D animation sequences, you're ready to explore some advanced techniques for virtual reality. The next chapter, "Getting started with virtual reality," gives you the background information you need to grasp the virtual reality sampler presented later in the book.

18

Getting started with virtual reality

This chapter describes how virtual reality's human-computer interface can be used to animate 3D environments and the entities they contain. Concepts such as sensors, universes, degrees-of-freedom, and storage requirements are covered. The difference between interactive animation and interactive virtual reality is discussed and the practical details of implementing a virtual reality session on a personal computer running Windows, as well as reality programming.

You'll see how interactive access to a three-dimensional database of prebuilt images can be used to manage the user's view during a virtual reality session. You'll also learn about storage requirements and acquire the background information you'll need to prepare you for the hands-on tutorial presented in chapter 19.

What is virtual reality?

Virtual reality is a simulation of 4D space-time. It is viewpoint animation that is displayed in an interactive, real-time context. Virtual reality provides a way for the participant to interact with a simulated 3D environment. It is a human/computer interface, providing controls for the user to manipulate and interact with a database. The database is the 4D space-time, including the artificial reality (virtual space) and the entities (virtual objects) it contains.

A *universe* is a particular virtual reality configuration. The universe includes the virtual environment, the entities it contains, and a script for managing the simulation. Loading different universes from disk can provide different virtual experiences. Each experience is called a *virtual reality session*.

Universes contain sensors and entities. *Entities* are actors, props, and scenery elements. *Sensors* are triggers in the virtual environment that can cause entities to interact with the user. Sensors respond to the actions or to the location of the user. A programmer sees a sensor in a somewhat different context. Programmers consider sensors to be sections of code that poll the computer's input devices in order to determine if the user has done something to trigger an event. Sensors are an important component of the virtual reality's simulation manager.

The *simulation manager* is an animation engine modified to run in single-step mode for use in a virtual reality session. It performs run-time functions such as updating, enforcing, sensing, and moving. This means that the simulation manager:

- Updates the display image.
- Enforces the VR rules.
- Senses interactivity.
- Moves entities.

The simulation manager updates the display image whenever the viewpoint location or the viewing direction changes. It enforces the *VR rules*, which are programmer-defined laws that govern and regulate the behavior of the virtual reality system during a session. VR rules also regulate what actions the user can undertake. The simulation manager's sensors detect when entities in the virtual environment should respond to the user's actions. The simulation manager implements the motion of entities that have been scripted to move about in the virtual environment.

Types of virtual reality

Your application can deliver a virtual reality session in three different forms:

- passive
- exploratory
- interactive

Passive virtual reality A *passive virtual reality* session provides a hands-off, automated tour for the user through the 3D environment. The route and the views are explicitly and exclusively controlled by the software. The user has no control, except perhaps to exit the session.

Exploratory virtual reality An *exploratory virtual reality* session provides a user-directed tour through the 3D environment. The participant can select the route and the views, but cannot otherwise interact with entities contained in the 3D scene. The hands-on tutorial that you'll encounter in the next chapter is an example of exploratory virtual reality.

Interactive virtual reality An *interactive virtual reality* session provides a user-directed tour through the 3D environment. In addition, the virtual entities in the 3D environment respond and react to the participant's actions. For example, if the user moves the viewpoint towards a door, the door might appear to open and allow the participant to pass through. The simulation manager's sensors detect when the viewpoint node moves inside a specified volume of 3D-space. The simulation manager then calls a function to animate the door's opening in cyberspace.

Cyberspace vs. virtual reality *Cyberspace* is the simulated 4D space-time that is managed by the virtual reality interface. Cyberspace exists only within the computer, if it can be said to exist anywhere. Cyberspace is imaginary space. Virtual reality, on the other hand, is the human/computer interface that allows the user to experience cyberspace. You might find it convenient to think of cyberspace as the computer's imagination.

Input devices

One of the significant attributes that differentiates virtual reality from other human/computer interfaces is the variety of input devices and their capabilities. The versatility and usefulness of an input device is usually measured by degrees-of-freedom.

Degrees-of-freedom *Degrees-of-freedom* refers to the number of axes of rotation and translation provided by an input device. PC-based virtual reality sessions often use a mouse, a bat, or a bird as an input device. Joysticks, bodysuits, and facial sensors are also used for specialized input requirements.

A *mouse* provides two degrees-of-freedom. It can move on one plane along an X-axis and a Y-axis. The software nominally interprets these measurements as two members of the XYZ triplet in 3D space.

A *bat* is a floating, mouselike input device that provides three degrees-of-freedom. It can move along the X-axis, the Y-axis, and the Z-axis simultaneously. The user can usually select from XYZ translation or yaw-roll-pitch rotation, but cannot use both triples at the same time. A bat is usually handheld.

A *bird* is a floating, mouselike input device that provides six degrees-of-freedom. The user can simultaneously select from XYZ translation and yaw-roll-pitch rotation. A bird can be hand-held, but a more common configuration is a group of birds attached to the joints of a human subject.

Implementing a virtual reality environment

You can implement a virtual reality session on a Windows-based personal computer if you take special steps to overcome the extreme demands that virtual reality imposes on the processor. Virtual reality sessions are image-intensive. Each time the participant moves the viewpoint node or changes the direction of view, the processor must generate and display a fresh image. This can cause an annoying delay, especially if the imagery consists of fully shaded scenes prepared with Z-buffer hidden-surface removal. However, your application can provide instant displays if the images have been prepared in advance. There are, after all, only a finite number of viewpoint positions and viewing angles in any one particular 3D environment, especially if the exploratory form of virtual reality is being implemented.

Using columns, rows, and grids for frame storage

Suppose, for example, that the user can move about in the virtual environment, which might be a maze of dividers in a closed room. The viewpoint nodes available to the user can be stored as a two-dimensional array of views (handles to bitmap images).

At each viewpoint node, however, the user can theoretically gaze in any direction. If the programmer nominally restricts the number of available viewing directions to 36, for example, then the number of images that will be required at run-time is finite, and hence predictable. If four viewing directions (north, south, east, west) are supported at each viewpoint node, then the three-dimensional array of views shown in FIG. 18-1 is all that's required.

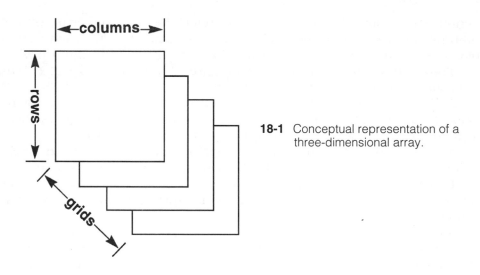

18-1 Conceptual representation of a three-dimensional array.

The first array might contain handles to bitmaps for every viewpoint node in the maze when the user is gazing north. The next two-dimensional array might hold handles for images for every possible viewpoint node in the maze when the user is gazing west. The third array provides southward gazes. The fourth array provides eastward gazes.

Managing a three-dimensional array Managing this three-dimensional array of handles to bitmap images is not unduly complicated at run-time. As FIG. 18-2 illustrates, whenever the user moves the viewpoint node, the software

**How the three-dimensional arrays
control the virtual reality environment**

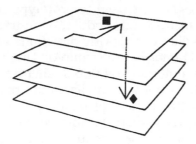

■ **selecting a different viewpoint**

◆ **selecting a different viewing direction**

18-2 Adapting a three-dimensional array to support frame-based interactive animation for virtual reality applications.

simply selects a neighboring index in the current two-dimensional array. If the user changes the viewing angle, the software simply moves up or down to a neighboring section of handles.

The hands-on virtual reality sampler that is provided in the next chapter uses this approach to simulate a 3D maze. The sample application supports 16 different viewpoint locations inside a virtual room that is partitioned by dividers. At each viewpoint, 4 different viewing directions are located. This means that each viewing direction is organized into a four-by-four array of viewpoints. The entire virtual reality cyberspace can be stored in 4 of these 4×4 arrays, as shown in FIG. 18-2.

From a programmer's context, the entire simulation is managed by manipulating an index into these arrays of views. If the animation engine you've already experimented with is running in single-step mode, then the keyboard's direction keys can be used to control movement and viewing direction. Whenever the virtual reality participant selects a new viewing direction the virtual reality engine selects a different 4×4 array of views, but it carefully retains the current index into the array of views. Whenever the VR participant selects a new viewpoint, the virtual reality engine selects a different index into the current array. In other words, when the participant changes the viewpoint location, the software changes the index, but retains the array. When the participant changes the viewing direction, the software changes the array, but retains the index.

Calculating of storage requirements Calculating the disk storage requirements is also straightforward. If the virtual reality session is running in the VGA's standard $640 \times 480 \times 16$-color mode, then each 256×255 viewport image requires 32,640 bytes of storage on disk. You've already learned that each sample application in this book uses a standard-size window whose viewport dimensions are 256 × 255 pixels.

If a virtual reality environment similar to FIG. 18-3 is planned, then 25 different viewpoint nodes can be used to prototype the application. You'll want more nodes in your finished product, of course. A sample layout is shown in FIG. 18-4. If 4 different viewing directions are supported at each node, then 25 × 4 = 100 images are required. This means 100 images at 32,640 bytes each, resulting in 3,264,000 or slightly more than 3MB of required disk space. This is not an unreasonable requirement. On a personal computer with 4MB or more of memory, the entire virtual reality image-set will fit into memory, ready for instant display. Even larger image databases can be used, of course, because the animation engine you experimented with in chapter 12 can load frames from disk on-the-fly. So the size of your virtual reality environment is limited only by the availability of disk space. This means that the virtual reality sampler provided in the next chapter will run on any personal computer that can run Windows.

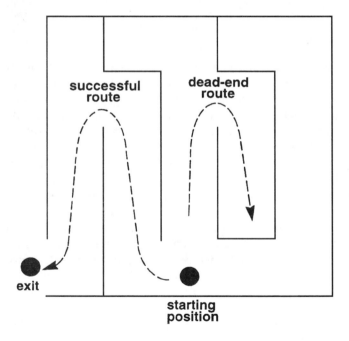

18-3 The maze design used in the virtual reality sample application presented in the next chapter.

Where do you go from here?

Now that you've familiarized yourself with some of the fundamentals of virtual reality, you're ready for a hands-on tutorial. The sample application in the next chapter is a virtual reality sampler. You'll explore the capabilities

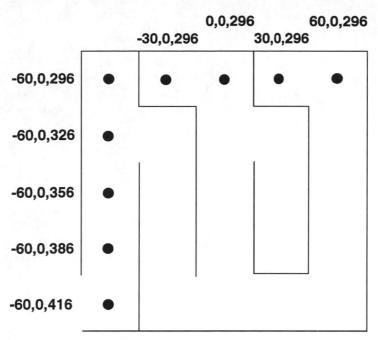

18-4 Assignment of 3D coordinates to the viewpoint nodes used in the virtual reality application presented in the next chapter.

of the demo program during your own virtual reality session as you investigate the twists and turns of a 3D maze with only one exit. You'll also delve into the source code, so you'll acquire the skills you need to use virtual reality techniques in your own applications.

19
Tutorial:
virtual reality
programming

This chapter provides a hands-on tutorial that demonstrates some of the principles of virtual reality you learned in chapter 18. A User's Guide shows you how to run the sample application, and a Programmer's Guide provides explanations of how the virtual reality session is implemented by a specially modified animation engine.

You'll discover how the animation engine uses an array of handles to bitmaps and filenames in order to build an image for each view in the 3D environment. You'll also learn how the software maps the keyboard direction keys to the array of views in order to display the proper bitmap image at run-time.

A virtual reality session can be delivered by an application running under Windows and you'll find out how to build and store all the required images in advance. You'll learn how to manipulate an index into an array of views in order to select the next appropriate image for the virtual reality user. Finally, you'll discover how to modify the animation engine to run in single-frame mode and how to use sensors to prevent the VR participant from penetrating the walls of the maze.

A user's guide to the sample application

In this section you'll learn how to use the sample application named maze. Before you can run this virtual reality sampler you must build the executable. The program listings for the sample application are presented as FIG. C-6 in Appendix C. Source listings for toolkits that must be linked in to build the finished executable are presented in Appendix B. All source files are also provided on the companion disk. See Appendix A for tips on compiling the program.

Starting the sample application

There are two ways you can start the sample application. You can start it directly from the Visual Basic editor or you can launch it from Windows' Program Manager.

Startup from Visual Basic You can run the sample application directly from Visual Basic if you've loaded the maze.mak project file.

Startup from Windows' Program Manager From the Windows desktop, pull down the File menu and select Run. When the dialog box appears, type the full pathname of the program, such as:

c:*directory**subdirectory*\maze.exe

You will, of course, use directory names that reflect your own system. When you select the OK button of the dialog box the sample application starts.

Using the sample application

Four menu names are displayed on the menu bar. They are File, Edit, VR, and Using. You can use the File menu to quit the program. You can use the VR menu, shown in FIG. 19-1, to load a universe from disk, to preview the starting position and the goal position of the maze, to build the universe and save it to disk, and to run a universe.

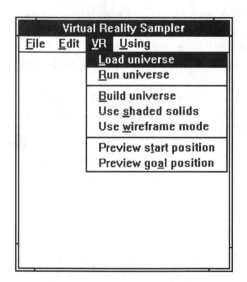

19-1 The VR menu from the virtual reality sample application maze.frm.

You can use a mouse or the keyboard to operate the menu system of this sample application. To use your mouse, just point and click. To use your keyboard, press Alt to move the focus to the menu bar, then press the appropriate mnemonic keys to pull down a menu and select an item from the menu. As you'll soon discover, you also use the direction keys of the keyboard to operate the virtual reality engine.

The VR menu The VR menu provides control over the virtual reality engine. To experience a virtual reality session you must first build a universe and save it to disk. The universe is the collection of viewpoint images that will be available when you wander through the 3D maze. After you've built a universe, you can load it from disk and run it.

Building a universe To build a universe and save its images to disk, choose Build Universe from the VR menu, as shown in FIG. 19-1. For your first session, you might consider choosing wire-frame mode from the VR menu. This reduces the amount of time required to build the 100 images.

Previewing a universe You can preview the participant's starting position and goal position before you build the universe. This is a quick way to see the universe before you go to the time and trouble of building it. The images in FIG. 19-2 show both the wire-frame and fully shaded versions of

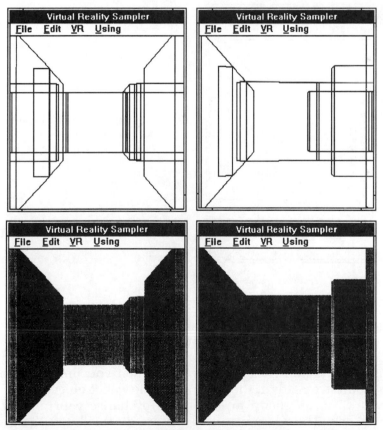

19-2 Sample images from the virtual reality sample application maze.frm. Shown above wire-frame views looking north and west from the starting position. Shown below are shaded views looking north and east from the starting point.

these preview images. The image at lower left shows the participant's startup position, gazing north. You can see an open aisle partway down the right side of the pathway, as well as another open aisle on the left near the far wall of the maze. You can compare this image with the scene directly above it in FIG. 19-2 in order to get a feeling for the difference between wire-frame and fully shaded rendering.

Loading a universe To load a universe from disk, select Load Universe from the VR menu. The virtual reality engine loads all 100 bitmap images into memory if enough space is available. Otherwise, the engine loads each image as required while the virtual reality session is in progress.

Running a universe To start the universe that you've loaded from disk, select Run Universe from the VR menu. The virtual reality session begins, and your starting position is displayed as shown in FIG. 19-3 (depicted here in wire-frame mode).

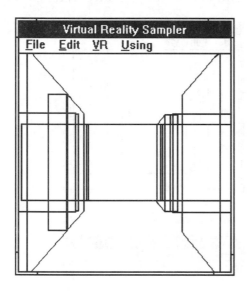

19-3 Looking north from the startup position. The doorway along the right wall of the hallway is visible.

Exploring the maze To move ahead, press the up arrow key. To move back, press the down arrow key. The left arrow and right arrow keys send you left and right, respectively. You'll want to remember that the simulation manager prevents you from moving back when you first start, because your viewpoint is already at the maze's outside wall. You can verify this by gazing westward, as shown in FIG. 19-4. To change your angle of gaze, press NumLock. The movement controls are disabled and the gaze controls become active. Press the left arrow key to gaze westward. Press the right arrow key to look eastward. Press the down arrow key to gaze southward. Pressing the up arrow key shifts your gaze northward again.

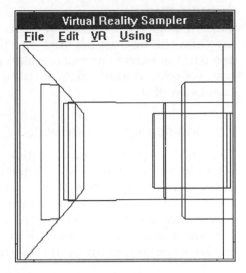

19-4 Looking west from the startup position. When the virtual reality sample application maze.frm is running in wire-frame mode, the exit position can be seen through the barrier wall. The virtual reality simulation manager does not permit the user to penetrate the wall, however.

Simply stated, here's how the numeric keypad controls work. When NumLock is off, the direction keys control your movement inside the maze. When NumLock is toggled on, the direction keys control the direction of your gaze.

If you attempt to move through one of the maze's partitions, the simulation manager issues an audio warning. The VR sensors prevent any penetration, except at the exit point, which is located at the southwestern corner of the maze. Refer back to FIG. 18-4 in the previous chapter for a reminder of how the maze is designed.

Leaving the maze If you move to the maze's exit, you'll be congratulated by a special message box. At any time during the virtual reality session, you can quit the application by selecting from the File menu.

A programmer's guide to the sample application

This section describes how the source code works. The source listings for the sample application are presented as FIG. C-6 in Appendix C. Source listings for the linked-in toolkits are provided in Appendix B. For tips on building the sample application, see Appendix A. You'll need to make a few simple changes to the engine3d.bas 3D toolkit, so check the discussion near the end of this chapter. The source files for the sample application are provided on the companion disk as maglobal.bas, mamain.bas, maze.frm, maplay.bas, engine3d.bas, shapes3d.bas, deform3d.bas, assemb3d.bas, and lights3d.bas.

How the global module works

You should pay careful attention to the virtual reality extensions in the maglobal.bas global module. The code at lines 0107 through 0133 declares variables that are unique to the virtual reality engine. The constants at lines 0108 through 0126 are simply a convenient way to keep track of various arrays and the indexes pointing into them. The array of handles declared at line 0104 is used to access the bitmap images in memory. The array of filenames declared at line 0105 is used to access the filenames of the bitmap images on disk.

How the startup module works

You need to pay careful attention to the initialization of the viewpoint nodes in the mamain.bas startup module. The code at lines 0060 through 0162 initializes the array of filenames. This array is carefully organized to represent four levels of images, as described in FIG. 18-1 and FIG. 18-2 in the previous chapter. By studying the organization of the filenames, you can see how it is possible to manage the image-display process by manipulating an index that points into this array.

How the form module works

This code is a subset of the animation engine presented in chapter 12. It emphasizes single-step displays. It does not support full forward or full reverse playback. The most important block of code is the Sub function located at lines 0210 through 0258. This function detects incoming keystrokes that control the virtual reality session. You should note how the code resets the vrMove or vrView variables before calling a function named vrWalkthrough() to select and display the next image.

Building the universe frames The animation-build process adheres to the format established by the prototype applications discussed in chapters 12 and 13. You should note, however, the code at lines 1016 through 1235 in the zDrawCel() function. This Select Case block contains the XYZ coordinates for all 100 viewpoint nodes for north-, east-, south-, and west-facing gazes. Note how these XYZ coordinates correspond to the layout in FIG. 18-2 in the previous chapter.

Drawing the maze The code that draws the maze and its partitions is located at lines 1242 through 1337 in zDrawCel(). The camera's fixed-target mode is disabled by line 1240. Rather than always pointing at the center of the 3D world, the camera can now be reoriented to point in any direction.

The virtual reality engine The vrWalkthrough() function at line 0708 is the foundation of this sample application. This function is actually a dedicated animation engine that supports only single-step playback. Most of the code in this function is concerned with ensuring that the correct bitmap image is selected for display. By using if/then deductive reasoning, the code first verifies (or updates) the direction of gaze and then marries it to the movement direction. This careful reasoning is needed because, as the switch() block at lines 0726 through 0735 illustrates, the up arrow key means move north only if the gaze is northward. If the gaze is westward, the meaning of the key changes and the up arrow key means move west. From the user's context, the up arrow key always means move ahead. From the programmer's context, the paradigm is somewhat more complex, of course.

Implementing the sensors The code that implements the sensors is located at lines 0761 through 0868. The software uses If...End If reasoning to make a decision based on the current location of the participant. At some locations, for example, a move northward is permitted. At other locations, it is prohibited because it would mean penetrating one of the maze's partitions or walls. The nested If...End If statements at lines 0870 through 0876 detect when the participant has successfully reached the maze's exit. The first statement confirms that the participant is attempting to move west, and the nested If...End If statement confirms that the participant is located at the node adjacent to the maze's exit.

Adapting the 3D toolkit Because this virtual reality sample application allows you to move the viewpoint very close to a 3D entity, the near clipping-plane functions in the engine3d.bas 3D toolkit must be disabled. Otherwise the near clipping-plane prevents many of the maze's partitions and walls from being displayed. Before you build the application, be sure to read the tips in Appendix A. In particular, you want to ensure that you've changed every occurrence of And to Or in line 1044 in engine3d.bas. And you want to be certain you've used remark tokens to disable lines 1057 through 1061, as well as lines 1343 and 1347 in engine3d.bas.

Where do you go from here?

Now that you've delved into virtual reality, you can add this skill to your Windows programming toolset, which already includes 3D modeling, animation, knowledge-based simulation, and kinematics. Where you go from here is up to you. Many of the functions in the sample applications and in the toolkits are ready to paste into your own prototypes. You'll want to remind yourself, however, that the source code in the book is optimized for clarity and for teaching, not for speed or size. It is not production-quality code. Whether you're designing your own applications for the freeware, shareware, or in-house corporate markets—or perhaps for the domestic and international retail software marketplaces—you'll want to thoroughly retest the code for stability and robustness before you release your product.

In the Appendices to the book, you can find the program listings for all the sample applications and toolkits modules there, in addition to helpful tips on building the demos. You'll also want to skim the math primer in Appendix D.

Your hands-on, guided tour through the warrens and niches of applied animation programming has reached its destination. You're ready now. Ready to begin the fun part, the challenging part, as you design, prototype, test, and build your own Windows applications using the knowledge you've gained in the book.

Like the early North American pioneers who broke the first trails through the vast wilderness, you're ready to push ahead. Your provisions are loaded, you've checked your bearings, and you've got a taste for discovery that only the restless know. Like all programmers, you'll be doing your best work mostly alone, but always among friends.

Finding your way around the appendices

This section of the book contains the program listings for the sample applications and the toolkits. Appendix A provides instructions on compiling the programs, describes hardware and software requirements, and offers troubleshooting tips. Appendix B contains the source listings for the toolkits, including engine3d.bas, shapes3d.bas, lights3d.bas, deform3d.bas, assemb3d.bas, and knmatx3d.bas. Appendix C contains the source listings for the sample applications, including startup.frm, objects.frm, animate.frm, assembly.frm, kinematx.frm, and maze.frm. Appendix D provides a math primer for graphics programmers.

A
Compiling the
sample programs

This appendix provides instructions on building the sample applications. You'll also find a discussion of software and hardware requirements, as well as a troubleshooting table.

Where do you start?

As you likely already realize, the sample applications and toolkits in this book are advanced prototype code. They've been designed to be easy to understand, easy to use, and easy to build. However, as every Windows programmer knows, there is no free launch (no free lunch either). This is especially true if you're compiling projects that use multiple source files. The fastest way to make a good compile go bad is to neglect the fundamentals. What are the fundamentals? Pretesting your development platform. It's as simple as that.

Testing your system with startup.frm

Before you try to build any of the advanced applications, you should verify your Visual Basic configuration by building the sample application that was presented first in the book, startup.frm. The source code for this application is discussed in chapter 4. The program listings are provided as FIG. C-1 in Appendix C. The source files are provided on the companion disk as startup.mak, stglobal.bas, stmain.bas, and startup.frm. After you've successfully built and run this sample application, you can proceed with confidence to the other apps in the book. You'll know that any idiosyncracies that might arise will be unique to the application being built, rather than a consequence of your version of Visual Basic or your directory structures.

What you will need

To build and run the sample applications in the book you'll need a personal computer running Windows version 3.0 in standard mode or enhanced mode; or a personal computer running Windows version 3.1 or newer in standard mode or enhanced mode. You'll also need a VGA display adapter and compatible monitor, or better.

Can you use your favorite version of Visual Basic?

Your favorite version of Visual Basic can successfully build the sample applications. At the time this is being written, this includes versions 1.0, 2.0, and 3.0 of Microsoft Visual Basic Development System for Windows, Standard Edition, and versions 1.0, 2.0, and 3.0 of Microsoft Visual Basic Development System for Windows, Professional Edition. If you're using version 1.0, you'll need to adjust the global module of the sample applications by declaring the following:

```
Global Const True = –1
Global Const False = 0
Global Const Null = 0
```

As a version 1.0 user, you'll also be required to use the Visual Basic menu design window to build the application's menu system by carefully reading the header of the .frm listing in the book. You may also need to use the Visual Basic IDE to specify your own project file.

What graphics card you need

For all practical purposes, the sample applications in the book require a VGA display adapter and compatible monitor. At the time this is being written, more than 92 percent of personal computers running Windows are equipped with VGA display adapters. You can also use SVGA display adapters, accelerator-based display adapters, and coprocessor-based display adapters, provided that they explicitly support Windows.

What computer the demos require

You'll need a personal computer running Windows version 3.0, or Windows version 3.1 or newer, in standard mode or enhanced mode. This usually means a 386 or higher.

How much memory you'll need

As long as your computer can run Windows and Visual Basic, you've got all the memory you need. Even the memory-intensive animation applications in the book are smart enough to load each frame from disk if not enough memory is available to store the entire animation sequence. However, 4MB of memory is recommended, and 8MB is even better. More memory usually means better performance.

Do you need a numeric coprocessor?

You don't require a numeric coprocessor to build and run the sample applications, but the 3D functions will run significantly faster if you have a math coprocessor because the functions use floating-point math. The Z-buffer depth-sort routines benefit some, but not much, from a numeric coprocessor because the routines use integer values, not floating-point values. Animation playback is not affected at all because the animation engine uses the computer's timer chip, not the numeric coprocessor.

How have the demo programs been tested?

The demo programs have been rigorously pretested on a variety of hardware platforms and run-time modes. Each application has been built using Microsoft Visual Basic Development System for Windows, Standard Edition, as well as Microsoft Visual Basic Development System for Windows, Professional Edition.

Display modes The demo programs have been tested at 640 × 480, 800 × 600, and 1024 × 768 resolution. The sample applications have been tested in 2-color, 16-color, and 256-color modes. As the hucksters say, however, your mileage may vary.

What type of performance can you expect on your system?

The performance that you can expect on your system from the sample applications depends on your processor speed, the display mode you're using, and the amount of memory installed.

Microprocessor speed You'll need a processor running at 25 MHz or faster using the VGA's 640 × 480 × 16-color mode in order to play animations at 18 frames per second. Keep in mind, however, that the animation sequences can be played on slower machines, but they won't run as quickly.

Display resolution and color depth The higher the display resolution the more processor power is needed to move images onto the display. The more colors the more data required to store the images, and that means more processor power is needed to move the images onto the display. The 640 × 480 × 16-color mode offers good performance with a reasonable number of colors.

Numeric coprocessor availability If a numeric coprocessor is available, the 3D functions will run 8 times faster.

Amount of memory If you've got 4MB of memory or more, each animation demo in the book will play directly from memory. All 36 frames will be loaded into RAM by the animation engine. On some systems, the 100 images of the virtual reality demo will load into 4 MB, but usually an 8 MB system is required for memory-based playback. Remember, however, that the virtual reality engine is smart enough to load each image directly from disk if memory is insufficient.

README TXT	1099	09-30-93	1:00p
LICENSE TXT	6454	09-30-93	1:00p
WELCOME TXT	3375	09-30-93	1:00p
CONTENTS TXT	4575	09-30-93	1:00p
ENGINE3D BAS	55066	09-30-93	1:00p
SHAPES3D BAS	49339	09-30-93	1:00p
DEFORM3D BAS	22762	09-30-93	1:00p
LIGHTS3D BAS	3025	09-30-93	1:00p
ASSEMB3D BAS	11821	09-30-93	1:00p
KNMATX3D BAS	25506	09-30-93	1:00p
VIRT3D BAS	55073	09-30-93	1:00p
STARTUP FRM	30058	09-30-93	1:00p
STARTUP MAK	82	09-30-93	1:00p
STGLOBAL BAS	13085	09-30-93	1:00p
STMAIN BAS	6629	09-30-93	1:00p
OBMAIN BAS	6226	09-30-93	1:00p
OBGLOBAL BAS	14045	09-30-93	1:00p
OBJECTS FRM	83718	09-30-93	1:00p
OBJECTS MAK	152	09-30-93	1:00p
ANGLOBAL BAS	16209	09-30-93	1:00p
ANMAIN BAS	7837	09-30-93	1:00p
ANIMATE FRM	42226	09-30-93	1:00p
ANPLAY BAS	6764	09-30-93	1:00p
ANIMATE MAK	164	09-30-93	1:00p
ASSEMBLY MAK	165	09-30-93	1:00p
ASSEMBLY FRM	51724	09-30-93	1:00p
ASMAIN BAS	7802	09-30-93	1:00p
ASPLAY BAS	6764	09-30-93	1:00p
ASGLOBAL BAS	18483	09-30-93	1:00p
KINEMATX FRM	58250	09-30-93	1:00p
KIMAIN BAS	8061	09-30-93	1:00p
KIGLOBAL BAS	19273	09-30-93	1:00p
KIPLAY BAS	6764	09-30-93	1:00p
KINEMATX MAK	179	09-30-93	1:00p
MAMAIN BAS	10750	09-30-93	1:00p
MAPLAY BAS	4411	09-30-93	1:00p
MAZE MAK	159	09-30-93	1:00p
MAZE FRM	52669	09-30-93	1:00p
MAGLOBAL BAS	15086	09-30-93	1:00p

A-1 The files on the companion disk.

How to use the companion disk

You get every file you need on the companion disk. Nothing is missing. The directory listing shown in FIG. A-1 is taken directly from the author's copies of the companion disk.

Installation Simply copy the contents of the companion disk to the directory on your hard disk where you normally store your source files for Visual Basic. You can use either DOS or Windows' File Manager to perform this chore.

Building Simply load the appropriate .mak project file into Visual Basic and you're ready to build and run the sample application. (Remember, if you're still using version 1.0 of Visual Basic, you'll need to use the Visual Basic IDE to create your own menu system. You may also be required to create your own project file. As a serious Visual Basic programmer, you'll probably want to give serious thought to upgrading to a newer version in order to take advantage of improved menuing and make file capabilities.)

Troubleshooting

If you encounter difficulties compiling or running the sample applications, you might find a solution in the troubleshooting table provided in FIG. A-2. As you'd expect, in order to be helpful to you, the troubleshooting table needs to be candid, direct, and occasionally blunt. It doesn't pull any punches. If you're looking for tactful guidance, don't look in FIG. A-2. But if you want results, you've come to the right place. As every programmer knows, sometimes the bug is to be found in the wetware, not in the software or the hardware.

Warning messages you might encounter Different development platforms sometimes produce different warnings during a build. If the virtual reality sampler exhibits erratic behavior, be sure you've made the changes to the engine3d.bas toolkit module as described in the header of the maze.frm listing. You can almost always avoid any warning messages whatsoever by using the project files provided on the companion disk.

If you encounter erratic behavior after loading a script file into the kinematics editor, you should check to ensure that all five script files are available on disk. If Visual Basic tries to read a script file and cannot find it on disk, it creates a new file of length zero. The companion disk ships with five script files, the last two being dummy copies of script01.scr.

Software tips from the author

The sample applications in the book have been tested with Microsoft Visual Basic 2.0. The resulting executables have been run in a variety of Windows display modes and run-time memory modes. If you experience difficulty, here's what the author suggests you do next...

Your situation...	Don't do this...	Do this...
Your Visual Basic compiler is up and running, but you can't get the samples to compile.	Don't assume the problem is in the listing. All code has been rigorously tested.	Do review the instructions in Appendix A. Use the supplied project files.
You believe you have found a minor bug in the run-time performance of a demo app.	Don't contact the publisher. Remember, the book's editors are not programmers.	Do track down the bug and fine-tune the source code to meet your own requirements.
You have an idea for a new software concept and you want to use the source code in your product development.	Don't assume that the book's editors can override the provisions of the License.	Do go ahead and use the source code, but be sure to read the License first.
Your compiler issues an error message that advises you to consult the book.	Don't contact the publisher. Remember, the books' editors are not thoroughly familiar with the source code.	Do remember that you must prepare the toolkit modules before compiling. Review Appendix A.
You're looking for a contract programmer to build a Windows app for your company.	Don't have unrealistic expectations about the service the author provides.	Do select and recruit a contract programmer through normal business channels.
You're looking for private tutoring in graphics.	Don't have unrealistic expectations of unlimited free consulting services.	Do join a special-interest group through electronic mail or investigate college courses.
You're wondering where to find more specialized books about graphics programming.	Don't have unrealistic expectations of unlimited free research or advice.	Do request the publisher's catalog. Other sources are trade journals, book clubs, and bookstores.
You've followed all the instructions in the book, but a sample application just won't compile without errors.	Don't assume the problem is with the code. Compiler configuration or subdirectory layout is often the culprit.	Do ensure that you're using clean source files from the companion disk. Review the instructions in Appendix A.
You see unintelligible characters when you view the source files with the Visual Basic text-editor.	Don't assume the worst until you check the companion disk files using a different Windows-based text-editor.	Do request a replacement copy of the companion disk from the publisher.
You tinkered with the source code and now it won't compile.	Don't contact the publisher. Remember, the book's editors are not programmers.	Do remember that you must be prepared to debug your own work.
You're using a non-standard computer system and you're having trouble with the demos.	Don't expect the publisher's staff to be hardware consultants.	Do consult your dealer or contact the manufacturer of the computer hardware.

A-2 Troubleshooting guide for the sample applications.

B
Source listings for the toolkit modules

This appendix contains the listings for the toolkit modules that must be linked in with the sample applications in order to build the executables. The 3D engine, engine3d.bas, is presented in FIG. B-1. The 3D shapes toolkit, shapes3d.bas, is provided in FIG. B-2. The 3D light-source toolkit, lights3d.bas, appears in FIG. B-3. The 3D deformation toolkit, deform3d.bas, is found in FIG. B-4. The 3D hierarchical modeling toolkit, assemb3d.bas, is presented in FIG. B-5. The 3D kinematics toolkit, knmatx3d.bas, appears in FIG. B-6.

Source listings

B-1 Source listings for the 3D modeling and shading toolkit, engine3d.bas. See Appendix C for applications that use this toolkit. See Appendix A for instructions on building the demos.

```
0001  '-----------------------------------------------------------------
0002  '         Module of 3D functions for Windows applications
0003  '-----------------------------------------------------------------
0004  'Source file:  ENGINE3D.BAS
0005  'Release version:  2.10                    Programmer:  Lee Adams
0006  'Type:  Visual Basic source file for Windows multimodule
0007  '   applications.
0008  'Output and features:  Provides control over camera pitch,
0009  '   camera heading, and camera-to-subject distance in both
0010  '   target-dependent 3D modeling mode and in target-independent
0011  '   virtual reality mode.  Provides precise control over the size,
0012  '   location, attitude, and color of each 3D object being drawn.
0013  '   Provides automatic backface culling.  Provides constant
0014  '   shading of each facet according to its illumination level
0015  '   resulting from a point light-source located above, behind, and
0016  '   to the left of the camera position.  Implements a 256-by-255
```

B-1 Continued.

```
0017  '   z-buffer ofSubvalues in far heap.  Math division
0018  '   errors are trapped.  Supports 2-color, 16-color, and 256-color
0019  '   graphics displays.
0020  'Publication: Contains material from Windcrest/McGraw-Hill book
0021  '   4225 published by TAB BOOKS Division of McGraw-Hill Inc.
0022  'License:  As purchaser of the book you are granted a royalty-
0023  '   free license to distribute executable files generated using
0024  '   this code provided you accept the conditions of the License
0025  '   Agreement and Limited Warranty described in the book and on
0026  '   the companion disk.  Government users:  This software and
0027  '   documentation are subject to restrictions set forth in The
0028  '   Rights in Technical Data and Computer Software clause at
0029  '   252.227-7013 and elsewhere.
0030  '----------------------------------------------------------------
0031  '   (c) Copyright 1992-1993 Lee Adams.  All rights reserved.
0032  '        Lee Adams(tm) is a trademark of Lee Adams.
0033  '----------------------------------------------------------------
0034      'Note:  Any variables marked as Global are also visible and
0035      'used by the functions in SHAPES3D.BAS, DEFORM3D.BAS,
0036      'LIGHTS3D.BAS, AND ASSEMB3D.BAS.  Any variables marked as
0037      'Dim are visible throughout only this ENGINE3D.BAS module.
0038
0039  Option Explicit                  'generate error if variable not declared
0040  Const zRED = 1                              'shading colors...
0041  Const zGREEN = 2
0042  Const zBROWN = 3
0043  Const zBLUE = 4
0044  Const zMAGENTA = 5
0045  Const zCYAN = 6
0046  Const zGRAY = 7
0047  Const zMAX_HEADING = 360                     'max camera heading
0048  Const zMIN_HEADING = 0                       'min camera heading
0049  Const zMAX_PITCH = 360                        'max camera pitch
0050  Const zMIN_PITCH = 270                        'min camera pitch
0051  Const zMAX_DISTANCE = 700              'max camera-to-target distance
0052  Const zMIN_DISTANCE = 0                'min camera-to-target distance
0053  Const zMAX_EXTRUDE = 50                      'max size of 3D solid
0054  Const zMIN_EXTRUDE = 2                       'min size of 3D solid
0055  Const zMAX_SHADES = 64               'num shades in logical palette
0056  Const zVIEWPOINT = 0                       'z-buffer minimum depth
0057  Const zINFINITY = 255                      'z-buffer maximum depth
0058  Const zFAR_CLIP = 200                 'virtual far clipping plane
0059  Const zNEAR_CLIP = 78                 'virtual near clipping plane
0060  Const zHIGHLIGHT16 = 255             'maximum illum for 16-color mode
0061  Const zAMBIENT16 = 47               'minimum illum for 16-color mode
0062  Const zHIGHLIGHT256 = 63            'maximum illum for 256-color mode
0063  Const zAMBIENT256 = 25             'minimum illum for 256-color mode
0064  Const COMPILING = 1
0065  '----------------------------------------------------------------
0066  '            Declaration of variables: 3D modeling
0067  '----------------------------------------------------------------
0068  Dim far_clip_plane_dist As Double
0069  Dim near_clip_plane_dist As Double
0070  Global x As Double, y As Double, z As Double
0071  Global xc1 As Double, xc2 As Double
0072  Global xc3 As Double, xc4 As Double
0073  Dim xc5 As Double, xc6 As Double, xc7 As Double
```

```
0074    Global yc1 As Double, yc2 As Double
0075    Global yc3 As Double, yc4 As Double
0076    Dim yc5 As Double, yc6 As Double, yc7 As Double
0077    Global zc1 As Double, zc2 As Double
0078    Global zc3 As Double, zc4 As Double
0079    Dim zc5 As Double, zc6 As Double, zc7 As Double
0080    Global xw1 As Double, xw2 As Double, xw3 As Double
0081    Global yw1 As Double, yw2 As Double, yw3 As Double
0082    Global zw1 As Double, zw2 As Double, zw3 As Double
0083    Global cursorx As Double
0084    Global cursory As Double, cursorz As Double
0085    Dim xa As Double, ya As Double, za As Double
0086    Dim ObjYaw As Double
0087    Dim ObjRoll As Double, ObjPitch As Double
0088    Dim sOYaw As Double, cOYaw As Double
0089    Dim sORoll As Double, cORoll As Double
0090    Dim sOPitch As Double, cOPitch As Double
0091    Dim xObj As Double, yObj As Double, zObj As Double
0092    Dim CamYaw As Double, CamRoll As Double, CamPitch As Double
0093    Dim sCYaw As Double, sCRoll As Double, sCPitch As Double
0094    Dim cCYaw As Double, cCRoll As Double, cCPitch As Double
0095    Dim xCam As Double, yCam As Double, zCam As Double
0096    Dim hcenter As Double, vcenter As Double
0097    Dim viewheight As Double
0098    Dim dist As Double
0099    Dim yawdist As Double
0100    Dim cameralens As Integer
0101    Dim pitchheading As Integer, yawheading As Integer
0102    Dim yawdelta As Double, pitchdelta As Double
0103    Dim signmx As Double, signmy As Double, signmz As Double
0104    Global cubeObj(7, 2) As Double
0105    Global cubeWorld(7, 2) As Double
0106    Global camcoords(7, 2) As Double
0107    Global bAssembly As Integer
0108    Global bUsePalette As Integer
0109    Dim bTarget As Integer
0110    Dim bUseWireframe As Integer
0111    '----------------------------------------------------------------
0112    '    Declaration of variables: rendering & backplane removal
0113    '----------------------------------------------------------------
0114    Global visible As Double
0115    Dim sp1 As Double, sp2 As Double, sp3 As Double
0116    Global xLight As Double, yLight As Double, zLight As Double
0117    Dim illum_range As Double
0118    Dim normalized_illum As Double
0119    Dim xu As Double, yu As Double, zu As Double
0120    Dim xv As Double, yv As Double, zv As Double
0121    Dim x_surf_normal As Double
0122    Dim y_surf_normal As Double
0123    Dim z_surf_normal As Double
0124    Dim v1 As Double, v2 As Double, v3 As Double
0125    Dim x_unit_vector As Double
0126    Dim y_unit_vector As Double
0127    Dim z_unit_vector As Double
0128    Dim zDeviceIllum As Integer
0129    Dim zShadingColor As Integer
0130    '----------------------------------------------------------------
0131    '        Declaration of variables: pixel-based operations
0132    '----------------------------------------------------------------
```

B-1 Continued.

```
0133  Global bInitialized As Integer
0134  Dim clipx1 As Integer, clipy1 As Integer
0135  Dim clipx2 As Integer, clipy2 As Integer
0136  Dim ViewportWidth As Integer
0137  Dim ViewportDepth As Integer
0138  Dim Shade As Integer
0139  '-------------------------------------------------------------------
0140  '   Declaration of variables: view volume and raster viewport
0141  '-------------------------------------------------------------------
0142  Dim xPersp As Double, yPersp As Double, zPersp As Double
0143  Dim xNorm As Double, yNorm As Double, zNorm As Double
0144  Dim xRect As Double, yRect As Double, zRect As Double
0145  Dim xRast As Double, yRast As Double, zRast As Double
0146  Dim Znear As Double, Zfar As Double
0147  Global Discard As Integer
0148  Global Clipped As Integer
0149  Global TestOnly As Integer
0150  Dim NumEdges As Integer
0151  Dim TempVariable As Double                      'temporary variable
0152  '-------------------------------------------------------------------
0153  '         Declaration of variables: z-buffer operations
0154  '-------------------------------------------------------------------
0155  Global ZBuffer() As String * 1          '256x255 = 65280 bytes
0156  Dim ZBufferReady As Integer        'will indicate if z-buffer ready
0157  Type ZBUFFERCOORDS1        'structure of 2D polygon-drawing coords
0158    x As Integer
0159    y As Integer
0160  End Type
0161  Dim Points(0 To 3) As ZBUFFERCOORDS1             'array of 4 xy sets
0162  Type ZBUFFERCOORDS2          'structure of 3D z-buffer coords
0163    x As Integer
0164    y As Integer
0165    z As Integer
0166  End Type
0167  Dim Raster(0 To 3) As ZBUFFERCOORDS2          'array of 4 xyz sets
0168  Type ZBUFFERCOORDS3            'structure of 3D clip-ready coords
0169    x As Double
0170    y As Double
0171    z As Double
0172  End Type
0173  Dim ViewVolume(0 To 3) As ZBUFFERCOORDS3      'array of 4 xyz sets
0174  Dim FirstY As Integer
0175  Dim FirstVertex As Integer
0176  Dim SecondVertex As Integer
0177  Dim ThirdVertex As Integer
0178  Dim FourthVertex As Integer
0179  Dim FarClip As Integer
0180  Dim NearClip As Integer
0181  '-------------------------------------------------------------------
0182  '          Declaration of variables: hidden-page workspace
0183  '-------------------------------------------------------------------
0184  Dim hPageDC As Integer
0185  Dim hPage As Integer
0186  Dim hPrevPage As Integer
0187  Dim PageReady As Integer
```

```
0188
0189   '----------------------------------------------------------------
0190   '                    3D initialization functions
0191   '----------------------------------------------------------------
0192   '                    Initialize the 3D environment
0193   '----------------------------------------------------------------
0194   Sub aazInitialize3D ()
0195   If bInitialized = True Then              'If already initialized...
0196     Exit Sub                          'then cancel this initialization
0197   End If
0198   clipx1 = 0
0199   clipy1 = 0
0200   clipx2 = zFRAMEWIDE - 1
0201   clipy2 = zFRAMEHIGH - 1
0202   '----------------------- startup notice ------------------------
0203   Form1.CurrentX = 10
0204   Form1.CurrentY = 225
0205   Form1.Print "3D toolkit tutorial version 2.10"
0206   Form1.CurrentX = 10
0207   Form1.Print "Copyright© 1993-1994 Lee Adams"
0208   '----------------------- viewport -------------------------
0209   ViewportWidth = (clipx2 - clipx1) + 1         'width of viewport
0210   ViewportDepth = (clipy2 - clipy1) + 1         'depth of viewport
0211   hcenter = ViewportWidth / 2    'calculate horiz center of viewport
0212   vcenter = ViewportDepth / 2     'calculate vert center of viewport
0213   If ViewportWidth <> 256 Then           'trap client area dimensions
0214     MsgBox "Viewport width not 256 pixels in aazInitialize3D( )
             function.", MB_OK, "3D toolkit error"
0215     ViewportWidth = 256            'force virtual width to 256 pixels
0216   End If
0217   If ViewportDepth <> 255 Then           'If font distorts the height
0218     MsgBox "Viewport height not 255 pixels in aazInitialize3D( )
             function.", MB_OK, "3D toolkit error"
0219     ViewportDepth = 255           'force virtual height to 255 pixels
0220   End If
0221   '----------------------- illumination -------------------------
0222   xLight = -.21131                              'light source...
0223   yLight = .86603
0224   zLight = .45315
0225   illum_range = 255                  'surface brightness 0 to 255
0226   zShadingColor = 4
0227   '----------------------- camera -------------------------
0228   far_clip_plane_dist = 512#        'distance to far clipping plane
0229   near_clip_plane_dist = 200#        'distance to near clipping plane
0230   viewheight = 0       '0 for camera, else set to 5 or 6 for android
0231   dist = 360                             'camera-to-target distance
0232   yawdist = 360#
0233   cameralens = 55                     'focal length of camera lens
0234   CamYaw = 0#                              'camera orientation...
0235   CamRoll = 0#
0236   CamPitch = 6.28319
0237   pitchheading = 360
0238   yawheading = 0
0239   yawdelta = 0
0240   pitchdelta = 0
0241   fczSetCamAngle
0242   xCam = 0#                                  'camera location...
```

B-1 Continued.

```
0243  yCam = 0#
0244  zCam = -360#
0245  bTarget = True                        'using fixed target for camera
0246  '------------------------- objects -----------------------------
0247  NumEdges = 4
0248  ObjYaw = 0#                                   'object orientation...
0249  ObjRoll = 0#
0250  ObjPitch = 0#
0251  fbzSetObjAngle
0252  xObj = 0#                                        'object location...
0253  yObj = 0#
0254  zObj = 0#
0255  cursorx = 15                                         'object size...
0256  cursory = 15
0257  cursorz = 15
0258  signmx = 1                           'coordinate-system tweaking...
0259  signmy = -1
0260  signmz = -1
0261  '------------- set default coords for parallelepiped--------------
0262  cubeObj(0, 0) = 10: cubeObj(0, 1) = -10: cubeObj(0, 2) = 10
0263  cubeObj(1, 0) = 10: cubeObj(1, 1) = 10: cubeObj(1, 2) = 10
0264  cubeObj(2, 0) = -10: cubeObj(2, 1) = 10: cubeObj(2, 2) = 10
0265  cubeObj(3, 0) = -10: cubeObj(3, 1) = -10: cubeObj(3, 2) = 10
0266  cubeObj(4, 0) = 10: cubeObj(4, 1) = 10: cubeObj(4, 2) = -10
0267  cubeObj(5, 0) = -10: cubeObj(5, 1) = 10: cubeObj(5, 2) = -10
0268  cubeObj(6, 0) = -10: cubeObj(6, 1) = -10: cubeObj(6, 2) = -10
0269  cubeObj(7, 0) = -10: cubeObj(7, 1) = -10: cubeObj(7, 2) = -10
0270  '----------------- view volume transformations -----------------
0271  Zfar = -1            'depth value of normalized far clipping plane
0272  If far_clip_plane_dist = 0 Then
0273    MsgBox "Attempted division by 0 in aazInitialize3D( )
          function.", MB_OK, "3D toolkit error"
0274  End If
0275  Znear = (-1) * (near_clip_plane_dist / far_clip_plane_dist) 'near
0276  Discard = False
0277  Clipped = False
0278  TestOnly = False
0279  '----------------- initialize the hidden page -----------------
0280  jazCreateHidden3DPage
0281  If PageReady = False Then
0282    bInitialized = False
0283    Exit Sub
0284  End If
0285  '----------------- initialize the z-buffer --------------------
0286  ReDim ZBuffer(256, 255) As String * 1    '256x255 = 65280 bytes
0287  ZBufferReady = True                          'z-buffer is ready
0288  '----------------- initialize other variables -----------------
0289  FarClip = zFAR_CLIP                      'far clipping plane depth
0290  NearClip = zNEAR_CLIP                   'near clipping plane depth
0291  bAssembly = False            'do not use hierarchical modeling
0292  bUsePalette = False                  'do not use custom-palette
0293  bInitialized = True                 '3D toolkit is initialized
0294  bUseWireframe = False                'use fully-shaded mode
0295  bTarget = True                       'use fixed-target mode
0296  End Sub
```

```
0297
0298    '----------------------------------------------------------------
0299    '                 Select shading or wireframe rendering
0300    '----------------------------------------------------------------
0301    Sub abzUseWireframeMode (ByVal TheMode As Integer)
0302    If TheMode = True Then
0303      bUseWireframe = True
0304    End If
0305    If TheMode = False Then
0306      bUseWireframe = False
0307    End If
0308    End Sub
0309
0310    '----------------------------------------------------------------
0311    '                    Fixed-target camera functions
0312    '----------------------------------------------------------------
0313    '              Set the fixed-target camera heading.
0314    '----------------------------------------------------------------
0315    Sub bazSetCameraHeading (ByVal Heading As Integer)
0316                            'call with Heading in degrees range 0 to 360
0317    If bInitialized = False Then
0318      fazShowMessage
0319      Exit Sub
0320    End If
0321    If bTarget = False Then                'if not using fixed target
0322      Exit Sub
0323    End If
0324    If Heading > zMAX_HEADING Then
0325      Exit Sub
0326    End If
0327    If Heading < zMIN_HEADING Then
0328      Exit Sub
0329    End If
0330    yawheading = Heading
0331    CamYaw = yawheading * .0175433
0332    If yawheading = 360 Then
0333      CamYaw = 6.28319
0334    End If
0335    If yawheading = 0 Then
0336      CamYaw = 0#
0337    End If
0338    fczSetCamAngle
0339    If CamYaw >= 4.71239 And CamYaw <= 6.28319 Then
0340      signmx = -1
0341      signmz = -1
0342      yawdelta = 6.28319 - CamYaw
0343      GoTo calccamyaw1
0344    End If
0345    If CamYaw >= 0 And CamYaw < 1.57079 Then
0346      signmx = 1
0347      signmz = -1
0348      yawdelta = CamYaw
0349      GoTo calccamyaw1
0350    End If
0351    If CamYaw >= 1.57079 And CamYaw < 3.14159 Then
0352      signmx = 1
0353      signmz = 1
```

```
0354    yawdelta = 3.14159 - CamYaw
0355    GoTo calccamyaw1
0356  End If
0357  If CamYaw >= 3.14159 And CamYaw < 4.71239 Then
0358    signmx = -1
0359    signmz = 1
0360    yawdelta = CamYaw - 3.14159
0361    GoTo calccamyaw1
0362  End If
0363  calccamyaw1:
0364  xCam = Sin(yawdelta) * yawdist * signmx
0365  zCam = Cos(yawdelta) * yawdist * signmz
0366  End Sub
0367
0368  '----------------------------------------------------------------
0369  '                 Set the fixed-target camera pitch.
0370  '----------------------------------------------------------------
0371  Sub bbzSetCameraPitch (ByVal Pitch As Integer)
0372                  'call with Pitch in range 270 to 360 (horizontal)
0373  If bInitialized = False Then
0374    fazShowMessage
0375    Exit Sub
0376  End If
0377  If bTarget = False Then
0378    Exit Sub                              'if not using fixed target
0379  End If
0380  If Pitch > zMAX_PITCH Then
0381    Exit Sub                           'do not penetrate groundplane
0382  End If
0383  If Pitch < zMIN_PITCH Then
0384    Exit Sub                              'do not exceed vertical
0385  End If
0386  pitchheading = Pitch
0387  CamPitch = pitchheading * .0174533         'convert to radians
0388  If pitchheading = 360 Then
0389    CamPitch = 6.28319
0390  End If
0391  If pitchheading = 0 Then
0392    CamPitch = 0#
0393  End If
0394  fczSetCamAngle
0395  pitchdelta = 6.28319 - CamPitch    'change in pitch from start-up
0396  yCam = Sin(pitchdelta) * dist * signmy        'new y translation
0397  yawdist = Sqr((dist * dist) - (yCam * yCam))         'hypotenuse
0398  xCam = Sin(yawdelta) * yawdist * signmx        'new x translation
0399  zCam = Sqr((yawdist * yawdist) - (xCam * xCam)) * signmz        'z
0400  End Sub
0401
0402  '----------------------------------------------------------------
0403  '                 Set the camera-to-target distance.
0404  '----------------------------------------------------------------
0405  Sub bczSetCameraDistance (ByVal Range As Integer)
0406  If bInitialized = False Then
0407    fazShowMessage
0408    Exit Sub
0409  End If
0410  If bTarget = False Then
```

```
0411   Exit Sub                               'if not using fixed target
0412 End If
0413 If Range < zMIN_DISTANCE Then
0414   Range = zMIN_DISTANCE
0415   MsgBox "Resetting camera-to-target distance to zMIN_DISTANCE.",
          MB_OK, "3D toolkit error"
0416 End If
0417 If Range > zMAX_DISTANCE Then
0418   Range = zMAX_DISTANCE
0419   MsgBox "Resetting camera-to-target distance to zMAX_DISTANCE.",
          MB_OK, "3D toolkit error"
0420 End If
0421 dist = Range
0422 yCam = Sin(pitchdelta) * dist * signmy           'new y translation
0423 yawdist = Sqr((dist * dist) - (yCam * yCam))          'hypotenuse
0424 xCam = Sin(yawdelta) * yawdist * signmx          'new x translation
0425 zCam = Sqr((yawdist * yawdist) - (xCam * xCam)) * signmz        'z
0426 End Sub
0427
0428 '-----------------------------------------------------------------
0429 '                 Set the camera lens focal length
0430 '-----------------------------------------------------------------
0431 Sub bdzSetCameraLens (ByVal iFocLength As Integer)
0432 If bInitialized = False Then
0433   fazShowMessage
0434   Exit Sub
0435 End If
0436 If iFocLength <> 55 And iFocLength <> 135 And iFocLength <> 200 Then
0437   Exit Sub
0438 End If
0439 cameralens = iFocLength
0440 End Sub
0441
0442 '-----------------------------------------------------------------
0443 '                 Virtual reality camera functions
0444 '-----------------------------------------------------------------
0445 '                 Toggle the camera target off.
0446 '-----------------------------------------------------------------
0447 Sub cazDisableTarget ()
0448       'unlocks camera from target, permits virtual reality touring
0449 If bInitialized = False Then
0450   fazShowMessage
0451   Exit Sub
0452 End If
0453 bTarget = False
0454 End Sub
0455
0456 '-----------------------------------------------------------------
0457 '                 Toggle the camera target on.
0458 '-----------------------------------------------------------------
0459 Sub cbzEnableTarget ()
0460       'locks camera to a fixed target point in the 3D environment
0461 If bInitialized = False Then
0462   fazShowMessage
0463   Exit Sub
0464 End If
0465 If bTarget = True Then
0466   Exit Sub                        'if already in fixed-target mode
0467 End If
```

```
0468   bTarget = True                                    'reset the token
0469   dist = 360                           'restore camera-to-target distance
0470   cameralens = 55                      'restore focal length of camera lens
0471   CamYaw = 0#                                'restore camera direction...
0472   CamRoll = 0#
0473   CamPitch = 6.28319
0474   pitchheading = 360
0475   yawheading = 0
0476   yawdelta = 0
0477   pitchdelta = 0
0478   fczSetCamAngle
0479   xCam = 0#                                   'restore camera location...
0480   yCam = 0#
0481   zCam = -360#
0482   End Sub
0483
0484   '----------------------------------------------------------------
0485   '              Set the target-independent camera heading.
0486   '----------------------------------------------------------------
0487   Sub cczSetVRCameraHeading (ByVal Heading As Integer)
0488                           'call with Heading in degrees range 0 to 360
0489   If bInitialized = False Then
0490     fazShowMessage
0491     Exit Sub
0492   End If
0493   If bTarget = True Then
0494     Exit Sub                           'cancel if using fixed target
0495   End If
0496   If Heading > zMAX_HEADING Then
0497     Exit Sub
0498   End If
0499   If Heading < zMIN_HEADING Then
0500     Exit Sub
0501   End If
0502   yawheading = Heading
0503   CamYaw = yawheading * .0175433
0504   If yawheading = 360 Then
0505     CamYaw = 6.28319
0506   End If
0507   If yawheading = 0 Then
0508     CamYaw = 0#
0509   End If
0510   fczSetCamAngle
0511   End Sub
0512
0513   '----------------------------------------------------------------
0514   '              Set the target-independent camera pitch.
0515   '----------------------------------------------------------------
0516   Sub cdzSetVRCameraPitch (ByVal Pitch As Integer)
0517                   ' call with Pitch in range 270 to 360 (horizontal)
0518   If bInitialized = False Then
0519     fazShowMessage
0520     Exit Sub
0521   End If
0522   If bTarget = True Then
0523     Exit Sub
```

```
0524    End If
0525    If Pitch > zMAX_PITCH Then              'do not penetrate groundplane
0526       Exit Sub
0527    End If
0528    If Pitch < zMIN_PITCH Then              'do not exceed vertical
0529       Exit Sub
0530    End If
0531    pitchheading = Pitch
0532    CamPitch = pitchheading * .0174533          'convert to radians
0533    If pitchheading = 360 Then
0534       CamPitch = 6.28319
0535    End If
0536    If pitchheading = 0 Then
0537       CamPitch = 0#
0538    End If
0539    fczSetCamAngle
0540    End Sub
0541
0542    '----------------------------------------------------------------
0543    '            Set the target-independent camera location.
0544    '----------------------------------------------------------------
0545    Sub cezSetVRCameraLocation (ByVal xPos As Integer, ByVal yPos As
            Integer, ByVal zPos As Integer)
0546                                            'call with xyz location
0547    If bInitialized = False Then
0548       fazShowMessage
0549       Exit Sub
0550    End If
0551    If bTarget = True Then
0552       Exit Sub                            'cancel if using fixed target
0553    End If
0554    xCam = (-1) * xPos
0555    yCam = (-1) * yPos
0556    zCam = (-1) * zPos
0557    End Sub
0558
0559    '----------------------------------------------------------------
0560    '                Subobject instancing functions
0561    '----------------------------------------------------------------
0562    '                Set the location of the object.
0563    '----------------------------------------------------------------
0564    Sub dazSetSubjectLocation (ByVal SSLx As Integer, ByVal SSLy As
            Integer, ByVal SSLz As Integer)
0565    If bInitialized = False Then
0566       fazShowMessage
0567       Exit Sub
0568    End If
0569    xObj = SSLx
0570    yObj = SSLy
0571    zObj = SSLz
0572    End Sub
0573
0574    '----------------------------------------------------------------
0575    '                Set the attitude of the object.
0576    '----------------------------------------------------------------
0577    Sub dbzSetSubjectAttitude (ByVal Yaw As Integer, ByVal Roll As
            Integer, ByVal Pitch As Integer)
0578    If bInitialized = False Then
```

```
0579    fazShowMessage
0580      Exit Sub
0581    End If
0582    If Yaw < 0 Then
0583      Exit Sub
0584    End If
0585    If Yaw > 360 Then
0586      Exit Sub
0587    End If
0588    If Roll < 0 Then
0589      Exit Sub
0590    End If
0591    If Roll > 360 Then
0592      Exit Sub
0593    End If
0594    If Pitch < 0 Then
0595      Exit Sub
0596    End If
0597    If Pitch > 360 Then
0598      Exit Sub
0599    End If
0600    ObjYaw = Yaw * .0175433                    'convert to radians...
0601    ObjRoll = Roll * .0175433
0602    ObjPitch = Pitch * .0175433
0603    If Yaw = 360 Then                          'tidy up boundary values...
0604      ObjYaw = 6.28319
0605    End If
0606    If Yaw = 0 Then
0607      ObjYaw = 0#
0608    End If
0609    If Roll = 360 Then
0610      ObjRoll = 6.28319
0611    End If
0612    If Roll = 0 Then
0613      ObjRoll = 0#
0614    End If
0615    If Pitch = 360 Then
0616      ObjPitch = 6.28319
0617    End If
0618    If Pitch = 0 Then
0619      ObjPitch = 0#
0620    End If
0621    fbzSetObjAngle                            'set sine and cosine factors
0622    End Sub
0623
0624    '----------------------------------------------------------------
0625    '                    Set the extrusion of the object.
0626    '----------------------------------------------------------------
0627    Sub dczSetSubjectSize (ByVal iWidth As Integer, ByVal iHeight As
            Integer, ByVal iDepth As Integer)
0628    If bInitialized = False Then
0629      fazShowMessage
0630      Exit Sub
0631    End If
0632    If iWidth < zMIN_EXTRUDE Then
0633      iWidth = zMIN_EXTRUDE
0634    End If
```

```
0635  If iWidth > zMAX_EXTRUDE Then
0636    iWidth = zMAX_EXTRUDE
0637  End If
0638  If iHeight < zMIN_EXTRUDE Then
0639    iHeight = zMIN_EXTRUDE
0640  End If
0641  If iHeight > zMAX_EXTRUDE Then
0642    iHeight = zMAX_EXTRUDE
0643  End If
0644  If iDepth < zMIN_EXTRUDE Then
0645    iDepth = zMIN_EXTRUDE
0646  End If
0647  If iDepth > zMAX_EXTRUDE Then
0648    iDepth = zMAX_EXTRUDE
0649  End If
0650  cursorx = iWidth                      'set the extrusion factors...
0651  cursory = iHeight
0652  cursorz = iDepth
0653  End Sub
0654
0655  '----------------------------------------------------------------
0656  '                    Set the current shading color
0657  '----------------------------------------------------------------
0658  Sub ddzSetShadingColor (ByVal iHue As Integer)
0659  If bInitialized = False Then
0660    fazShowMessage
0661    Exit Sub
0662  End If
0663  If iHue < 1 Then
0664    Exit Sub
0665  End If
0666  If iHue > 7 Then
0667    Exit Sub
0668  End If
0669  zShadingColor = iHue
0670  End Sub
0671
0672  '----------------------------------------------------------------
0673  '                    Clipping-plane functions
0674  '----------------------------------------------------------------
0675  '                    Set the near clipping-plane.
0676  '----------------------------------------------------------------
0677  Sub eazSetNearClippingPlane (ByVal NearDist As Integer)
0678  If bInitialized = False Then
0679    fazShowMessage
0680    Exit Sub
0681  End If
0682  If NearDist < zVIEWPOINT Then
0683    Exit Sub                            'must be between viewpoint...
0684  End If
0685  If NearDist >= FarClip Then
0686    Exit Sub                            '...and far clipping plane
0687  End If
0688  NearClip = NearDist
0689  End Sub
0690
0691  '----------------------------------------------------------------
0692  '                    Set the far clipping-plane.
0693  '----------------------------------------------------------------
```

```
0694  Sub ebzSetFarClippingPlane (ByVal FarDist As Integer)
0695  If bInitialized = False Then
0696    fazShowMessage
0697    Exit Sub
0698  End If
0699  If FarDist > zINFINITY Then
0700    Exit Sub                              'must be between infinity...
0701  End If
0702  If FarDist <= NearClip Then
0703    Exit Sub                              '...and near clipping plane
0704  End If
0705  FarClip = FarDist
0706  End Sub
0707
0708  '-------------------------------------------------------------------
0709  '                      3D system functions
0710  '-------------------------------------------------------------------
0711  '    Display a debugging message If 3D system not initialized.
0712  '-------------------------------------------------------------------
0713  Sub fazShowMessage ()
0714                    'called by 3D functions if module not initialized
0715  MsgBox "The 3D module is not initialized.", MB_OK, "3D toolkit error"
0716  End Sub
0717
0718  '-------------------------------------------------------------------
0719  '        Calculate object sine and cosine rotation factors
0720  '-------------------------------------------------------------------
0721  Sub fbzSetObjAngle ()
0722          'called by aazInitialize3D() and dbzSetSubjectAttitude()
0723        'Enter with ObjYaw,ObjRoll,ObjPitch object rotation angles.
0724                'Exit with sine, cosine object rotation factors.
0725  sOYaw = Sin(ObjYaw)
0726  cOYaw = Cos(ObjYaw)
0727  sORoll = Sin(ObjRoll)
0728  cORoll = Cos(ObjRoll)
0729  sOPitch = Sin(ObjPitch)
0730  cOPitch = Cos(ObjPitch)
0731  End Sub
0732
0733  '-------------------------------------------------------------------
0734  '        Calculate camera sine and cosine rotation factors
0735  '-------------------------------------------------------------------
0736  Sub fczSetCamAngle ()
0737              'called by aazInitialize3D() and bbzSetCameraPitch()
0738                'Enter with Yaw,Roll,Pitch world rotation angles.
0739                'Exit with sine, cosine world rotation factors.
0740  sCYaw = Sin(CamYaw)
0741  sCRoll = Sin(CamRoll)
0742  sCPitch = Sin(CamPitch)
0743  cCYaw = Cos(CamYaw)
0744  cCRoll = Cos(CamRoll)
0745  cCPitch = Cos(CamPitch)
0746  End Sub
0747
0748  '-------------------------------------------------------------------
0749  '        Calculate world coordinates from object coordinates
```

```
0750  '-----------------------------------------------------------------
0751  Sub fdzGetWorldCoords ()
0752                            'this function is called by SHAPES3D.BAS.
0753                      'Enter with xyz unclipped 3D object coordinates.
0754                      'Exit with unclipped xyz 3D world coordinates.
0755  xa = cORoll * x + sORoll * y                      'roll rotate
0756  ya = cORoll * y - sORoll * x                      'roll rotate
0757  x = cOYaw * xa - sOYaw * z                        'yaw rotate
0758  za = sOYaw * xa + cOYaw * z                       'yaw rotate
0759  z = cOPitch * za - sOPitch * ya              'pitch rotate
0760  y = sOPitch * za + cOPitch * ya              'pitch rotate
0761  x = x + xObj                              'lateral movement
0762  y = y + yObj                              'lateral movement
0763  z = z + zObj                              'lateral movement
0764  End Sub
0765
0766  '-----------------------------------------------------------------
0767  '        Calculate camera coordinates from world coordinates
0768  '-----------------------------------------------------------------
0769  Sub fezGetCameraCoords ()
0770                            'this function is called by SHAPES3D.BAS.
0771                      'Enter with unclipped xyz 3D world coordinates.
0772                      'Exit with unclipped xyz 3D camera coordinates.
0773  x = (-1) * x            'adjust for cartesian coords of 2D screen
0774  y = y - viewheight      'adjust world coords to height of viewer
0775  x = x - xCam                              'lateral movement...
0776  y = y + yCam
0777  z = z + zCam
0778  xa = cCYaw * x - sCYaw * z                        'yaw rotate
0779  za = sCYaw * x + cCYaw * z                        'yaw rotate
0780  z = cCPitch * za - sCPitch * y               'pitch rotate
0781  ya = sCPitch * za + cCPitch * y              'pitch rotate
0782  x = cCRoll * xa + sCRoll * ya                     'roll rotate
0783  y = cCRoll * ya - sCRoll * xa                     'roll rotate
0784  End Sub
0785
0786  '-----------------------------------------------------------------
0787  '     Scale perspective view volume to normalized view volume
0788  '-----------------------------------------------------------------
0789  Sub ffzNormalizeView ()                 'called by gazDrawFacet()
0790        'Enter with xPersp, yPersp, zPersp camera coordinates for
0791       '3D perspective view volume.  Exit with xNorm, yNorm, zNorm
0792        'camera coordinates normalized 3D perspective view volume.
0793  If far_clip_plane_dist = 0 Then
0794    MsgBox "Attempted division by 0 in ffzNormalizeView( )
          function.", MB_OK, "3D toolkit error"
0795  End If
0796  xNorm = xPersp / far_clip_plane_dist
0797  yNorm = yPersp / far_clip_plane_dist
0798  zNorm = zPersp / far_clip_plane_dist
0799  End Sub
0800
0801  '-----------------------------------------------------------------
0802  '     Scale normalized view volume to rectangular view volume
0803  '-----------------------------------------------------------------
0804  Sub fgzRectangularView ()               'called by gazDrawFacet()
0805            'Enter with xNorm, yNorm, zNorm camera coordinates for
0806         '3D normalized view volume.  Exit with xRect, yRect, zRect
```

```
0807          'camera coordinates for rectangular normalized view volume.
0808    TempVariable = zNorm * (-Znear / (1 + Znear))
0809    If TempVariable = 0 Then
0810      MsgBox "Attempted division by 0 in fgzRectangularView( )
               function.", MB_OK, "3D toolkit error"
0811    End If
0812    xRect = xNorm / TempVariable
0813    yRect = yNorm / TempVariable
0814    zRect = zNorm
0815    End Sub
0816
0817    '-----------------------------------------------------------------
0818    '           Scale rectangular view volume to raster viewport
0819    '-----------------------------------------------------------------
0820    Sub fhzScaleToRaster ()                  'called by gazDrawFacet()
0821              'Enter with xRect, yRect, zRect camera coordinates for
0822              'rectangular view volume.  Exit with xRast, yRast, zRast
0823          'coordinates for a view volume that maps directly onto the
0824                              '256-by-255 raster viewport.
0825    xRast = xRect * ViewportWidth            'scale x coord to viewport
0826    yRast = yRect * ViewportDepth            'scale y coord to viewport
0827    If cameralens = 55 Then                          'if using 55mm lens...
0828      xRast = xRast * 1
0829      yRast = yRast * 1
0830    End If
0831    If cameralens = 135 Then          'if using 135mm telephoto lens...
0832      xRast = xRast * 2
0833      yRast = yRast * 2
0834    End If
0835    If cameralens = 200 Then          'if using 200mm telephoto lens...
0836      xRast = xRast * 3
0837      yRast = yRast * 3
0838    End If
0839    xRast = xRast + hcenter        'shift x coord to center of viewport
0840    yRast = yRast + vcenter        'shift y coord to center of viewport
0841    zRast = zRect                            'grab the depth value
0842    zRast = zRast * (-1)    'convert -1 to 0 range to positive values
0843    zRast = zRast * zFAR_CLIP        'expand to 0 to 255 unsigned char
0844    If zRast < zVIEWPOINT Then                          'if less than 0
0845      zRast = zVIEWPOINT
0846    End If
0847    If zRast > zINFINITY Then                        'if greater than 255
0848      zRast = zINFINITY
0849    End If
0850    End Sub
0851
0852    '-----------------------------------------------------------------
0853    '                   Polygon and facet functions
0854    '-----------------------------------------------------------------
0855    '                   Draw a 4-sided polygon
0856    '-----------------------------------------------------------------
0857    Sub gazDrawFacet ()        'this function is called by SHAPES3D.BAS
0858      Dim hPrevBrush As Integer, hFacetBrush As Integer
0859      Dim hPrevRegion As Integer, hFacetRegion As Integer
0860      Dim hPrevPen As Integer, hHalfEdgePen As Integer
0861    '------------------ calculate and store coords ------------------
```

```
0862   xPersp = xc1                          'grab camera coords...
0863   yPersp = yc1
0864   zPersp = zc1
0865   ffzNormalizeView           'convert to normalized 3D view volume
0866   fgzRectangularView         'convert to rectangular 3D view volume
0867   fhzScaleToRaster                     'scale to fit the 2D viewport
0868   Points(0).x = xRast          'store 2D polygon-drawing coords...
0869   Points(0).y = yRast
0870   Raster(0).x = xRast                'store 3D z-buffer coords...
0871   Raster(0).y = yRast
0872   Raster(0).z = zRast
0873   ViewVolume(0).x = xRect            'store 3D clip-ready coords...
0874   ViewVolume(0).y = yRect
0875   ViewVolume(0).z = zRect
0876                               'repeat the process for other 3 vertices...
0877   xPersp = xc2
0878   yPersp = yc2
0879   zPersp = zc2
0880   ffzNormalizeView
0881   fgzRectangularView
0882   fhzScaleToRaster
0883   Points(1).x = xRast
0884   Points(1).y = yRast
0885   Raster(1).x = xRast
0886   Raster(1).y = yRast
0887   Raster(1).z = zRast
0888   ViewVolume(1).x = xRect
0889   ViewVolume(1).y = yRect
0890   ViewVolume(1).z = zRect
0891   xPersp = xc3
0892   yPersp = yc3
0893   zPersp = zc3
0894   ffzNormalizeView
0895   fgzRectangularView
0896   fhzScaleToRaster
0897   Points(2).x = xRast
0898   Points(2).y = yRast
0899   Raster(2).x = xRast
0900   Raster(2).y = yRast
0901   Raster(2).z = zRast
0902   ViewVolume(2).x = xRect
0903   ViewVolume(2).y = yRect
0904   ViewVolume(2).z = zRect
0905   xPersp = xc4
0906   yPersp = yc4
0907   zPersp = zc4
0908   ffzNormalizeView
0909   fgzRectangularView
0910   fhzScaleToRaster
0911   Points(3).x = xRast
0912   Points(3).y = yRast
0913   Raster(3).x = xRast
0914   Raster(3).y = yRast
0915   Raster(3).z = zRast
0916   ViewVolume(3).x = xRect
0917   ViewVolume(3).y = yRect
0918   ViewVolume(3).z = zRect
0919   '-------------- sort the vertices of the polygon --------------
```

```
0920  FirstY = Points(0).y        'find the top vertex of the polygon...
0921  FirstVertex = 0
0922  If Points(1).y < FirstY Then
0923    FirstVertex = 1
0924    FirstY = Points(1).y
0925  End If
0926  If Points(2).y < FirstY Then
0927    FirstVertex = 2
0928    FirstY = Points(2).y
0929  End If
0930  If Points(3).y < FirstY Then
0931    FirstVertex = 3
0932    FirstY = Points(3).y
0933  End If
0934  Select Case FirstVertex        'assign counterclockwise ordering...
0935    Case 0
0936      FirstVertex = 0
0937      SecondVertex = 1
0938      ThirdVertex = 2
0939      FourthVertex = 3
0940    Case 1
0941      FirstVertex = 1
0942      SecondVertex = 2
0943      ThirdVertex = 3
0944      FourthVertex = 0
0945    Case 2
0946      FirstVertex = 2
0947      SecondVertex = 3
0948      ThirdVertex = 0
0949      FourthVertex = 1
0950    Case 3
0951      FirstVertex = 3
0952      SecondVertex = 0
0953      ThirdVertex = 1
0954      FourthVertex = 2
0955  End Select
0956  '--------------- clip facet to the 3D view volume ----------------
0957  hazClipToViewVolume
0958  If Discard = True Then
0959    GoTo FACET_DONE                            'jump if not visible
0960  End If
0961  If TestOnly = True Then
0962    GoTo FACET_DONE                            'jump if in testing mode
0963  End If
0964  '--------------- if using wireframe rendering ----------------
0965  If bUseWireframe = True Then
0966    Select Case zShadingColor
0967      Case zRED
0968        hHalfEdgePen = CreatePen(PS_SOLID, 1, RGB(127, 0, 0))
0969      Case zGREEN
0970        hHalfEdgePen = CreatePen(PS_SOLID, 1, RGB(0, 127, 0))
0971      Case zBROWN
0972        hHalfEdgePen = CreatePen(PS_SOLID, 1, RGB(127, 127, 0))
0973      Case zBLUE
0974        hHalfEdgePen = CreatePen(PS_SOLID, 1, RGB(0, 0, 127))
0975      Case zMAGENTA
```

```
0976        hHalfEdgePen = CreatePen(PS_SOLID, 1, RGB(127, 0, 127))
0977      Case zCYAN
0978        hHalfEdgePen = CreatePen(PS_SOLID, 1, RGB(0, 127, 127))
0979      Case zGRAY
0980        hHalfEdgePen = CreatePen(PS_SOLID, 1, RGB(0, 0, 0))
0981    End Select
0982    hPrevPen = SelectObject(Form1.hDC, hHalfEdgePen)
0983    RetLong = MoveTo(Form1.hDC, Points(0).x, Points(0).y)
0984    RetVal = LineTo(Form1.hDC, Points(1).x, Points(1).y)
0985    RetVal = LineTo(Form1.hDC, Points(2).x, Points(2).y)
0986    RetVal = LineTo(Form1.hDC, Points(3).x, Points(3).y)
0987    RetVal = LineTo(Form1.hDC, Points(0).x, Points(0).y)
0988    RetVal = SelectObject(Form1.hDC, hPrevPen)
0989    RetVal = DeleteObject(hHalfEdgePen)
0990    Exit Sub
0991 End If
0992 '------------------- set up the shading -----------------------
0993 ibzGetBrightness                  'get brightness factor of facet
0994 If bUsePalette = False Then  'if using dithering, create brush...
0995    Select Case zShadingColor
0996      Case zRED
0997        hFacetBrush = CreateSolidBrush(RGB(zDeviceIllum, 0, 0))
0998      Case zGREEN
0999        hFacetBrush = CreateSolidBrush(RGB(0, zDeviceIllum, 0))
1000      Case zBROWN
1001        hFacetBrush = CreateSolidBrush(RGB(zDeviceIllum, zDeviceIllum, 0))
1002      Case zBLUE
1003        hFacetBrush = CreateSolidBrush(RGB(0, 0, zDeviceIllum))
1004      Case zMAGENTA
1005        hFacetBrush = CreateSolidBrush(RGB(zDeviceIllum, 0, zDeviceIllum))
1006      Case zCYAN
1007        hFacetBrush = CreateSolidBrush(RGB(0, zDeviceIllum, zDeviceIllum))
1008      Case zGRAY
1009        hFacetBrush = CreateSolidBrush(RGB(zDeviceIllum, zDeviceIllum,
           zDeviceIllum))
1010      Case Else
1011        hFacetBrush = CreateSolidBrush(RGB(0, 0, zDeviceIllum))
1012    End Select
1013 End If
1014 '----------- draw facet on hidden-page workspace ----------------
1015 '    Programmer's note:  A region created with CreatePolygonRgn()
1016 '    does not need to be selected or deselected when being used
1017 '    with Visual Basic.
1018 hFacetRegion = CreatePolygonRgn(Points(0).x, NumEdges, WINDING)
1019 If bUsePalette = False Then          'if using dithered shades...
1020                                      '...draw facet on hidden 3D workspace
1021    hPrevBrush = SelectObject(hPageDC, hFacetBrush)   'select brush
1022 '  hPrevRegion = SelectObject(hPageDC, hFacetRegion)  'and region
1023    RetVal = PaintRgn(hPageDC, hFacetRegion)         'fill the region
1024    RetVal = SelectObject(hPageDC, hPrevBrush)        'deselect brush
1025 '  RetVal = SelectObject(hPageDC, hPrevRegion)   'deselect region
1026    RetVal = DeleteObject(hFacetBrush)               'destroy brush
1027 End If
1028 '------- do z-buffer tests and draw facet on viewport -----------
1029 kbzDoZBufferTest (hFacetRegion)
1030 '------------------- tidy up and return -----------------------
1031 RetVal = DeleteObject(hFacetRegion)           'destroy region
1032 FACET_DONE:
```

B-1 Continued.

```
1033  End Sub
1034
1035  '-----------------------------------------------------------------
1036  '                  View volume clipping functions
1037  '-----------------------------------------------------------------
1038  '          Clip facets to the normalized 3D view volume
1039  '-----------------------------------------------------------------
1040  Sub hazClipToViewVolume ()                 'called by gazDrawFacet()
1041  Discard = False
1042  Clipped = False
1043  '------------- discard if facet behind viewpoint ----------------
1044  If ViewVolume(FirstVertex).z > 0 And ViewVolume(SecondVertex).z >
            0 And ViewVolume(ThirdVertex).z > 0 And
            ViewVolume(FourthVertex).z > 0 Then
1045    Discard = True
1046    Exit Sub
1047  End If
1048  '--------------- test the far clipping plane -------------------
1049  If ViewVolume(FirstVertex).z < Zfar And ViewVolume(SecondVertex).z
            < Zfar And ViewVolume(ThirdVertex).z < Zfar And
            ViewVolume(FourthVertex).z < Zfar Then
1050    Discard = True          'discard if fully beyond clipping plane
1051    Exit Sub
1052  End If
1053  If ViewVolume(FirstVertex).z < Zfar Or ViewVolume(SecondVertex).z
            < Zfar Or ViewVolume(ThirdVertex).z < Zfar Or
            ViewVolume(FourthVertex).z < Zfar Then
1054    'Clipped = True    'discard if facet penetrates clipping plane
1055    Exit Sub
1056  End If
1057  '--------------- test the near clipping plane -------------------
1058  If ViewVolume(FirstVertex).z > Znear And
            ViewVolume(SecondVertex).z > Znear And
            ViewVolume(ThirdVertex).z > Znear And
            ViewVolume(FourthVertex).z > Znear Then
1059    Discard = True
1060    Exit Sub
1061  End If
1062  '------- discard if facet outside left clipping plane -----------
1063  If ViewVolume(FirstVertex).x < -1 And ViewVolume(SecondVertex).x <
            -1 And ViewVolume(ThirdVertex).x < -1 And
            ViewVolume(FourthVertex).x < -1 Then
1064    Discard = True
1065    Exit Sub
1066  End If
1067  '------- discard if facet outside right clipping plane ----------
1068  If ViewVolume(FirstVertex).x > 1 And ViewVolume(SecondVertex).x >
            1 And ViewVolume(ThirdVertex).x > 1 And
            ViewVolume(FourthVertex).x > 1 Then
1069    Discard = True
1070    Exit Sub
1071  End If
1072  '-------- discard if facet outside bottom clipping plane --------
1073  If ViewVolume(FirstVertex).y < -1 And ViewVolume(SecondVertex).y <
            -1 And ViewVolume(ThirdVertex).y < -1 And
            ViewVolume(FourthVertex).y < -1 Then
```

```
1074    Discard = True
1075    Exit Sub
1076  End If
1077  '-------- discard if facet outside top clipping plane -----------
1078  If ViewVolume(FirstVertex).y > 1 And ViewVolume(SecondVertex).y >
          1 And ViewVolume(ThirdVertex).y > 1 And
          ViewVolume(FourthVertex).y > 1 Then
1079    Discard = True
1080    Exit Sub
1081  End If
1082  End Sub
1083
1084  '-----------------------------------------------------------------
1085  '                Facet visibility and shading functions
1086  '-----------------------------------------------------------------
1087  '             Perform the backplane visibility test
1088  '-----------------------------------------------------------------
1089  Sub iazVisibilityTest () 'this function is called by SHAPES3D.BAS
1090    'Enter with 3 vertices cam coords.  Exit with visibility token.
1091  sp1 = xc1 * (yc2 * zc3 - yc3 * zc2)
1092  sp1 = (-1) * sp1
1093  sp2 = xc2 * (yc3 * zc1 - yc1 * zc3)
1094  sp3 = xc3 * (yc1 * zc2 - yc2 * zc1)
1095  visible = sp1 - sp2 - sp3
1096  End Sub
1097
1098  '-----------------------------------------------------------------
1099  '             Calculate the brightness level of a facet
1100  '-----------------------------------------------------------------
1101  Sub ibzGetBrightness ()              'is called by gazDrawFacet()
1102      'Enter with facet world coordinates.  Exit with illum level.
1103    Dim Factor As Integer, TempIllum As Integer
1104  xu = xw2 - xw1                'vector vertex 1 to vertex 2...
1105  yu = yw2 - yw1
1106  zu = zw2 - zw1
1107  xv = xw3 - xw1                'vector vertex 1 to vertex 3...
1108  yv = yw3 - yw1
1109  zv = zw3 - zw1
1110  x_surf_normal = (yu * zv) - (zu * yv)
1111  y_surf_normal = (zu * xv) - (xu * zv)
1112  z_surf_normal = (xu * yv) - (yu * xv)
1113  y_surf_normal = y_surf_normal * (-1)      'to cartesian system...
1114  z_surf_normal = z_surf_normal * (-1)
1115  v1 = (x_surf_normal * x_surf_normal) + (y_surf_normal *
          y_surf_normal) + (z_surf_normal * z_surf_normal)
1116  v2 = Sqr(v1)           'magnitude of surface perpendicular vector
1117  If v2 = 0 Then
1118    MsgBox "Attempted division by 0 in ibzGetBrightness( )
          function.", MB_OK, "3D toolkit error"
1119  End If
1120  v3 = 1 / v2            'ratio of magnitude to length of unit vector
1121  x_unit_vector = v3 * x_surf_normal      'surf perp unit vector...
1122  y_unit_vector = v3 * y_surf_normal
1123  z_unit_vector = v3 * z_surf_normal
1124  normalized_illum = (x_unit_vector * xLight) + (y_unit_vector *
          yLight) + (z_unit_vector * zLight)          'illumination
          factor 0 to 1
1125  normalized_illum = normalized_illum * illum_range'expand 0 to 255
```

B-1 Continued.

```
1126  zDeviceIllum = normalized_illum                'cast to integer
1127  If zDeviceIllum < zAMBIENT16 Then
1128    zDeviceIllum = zAMBIENT16
1129  End If
1130  If zDeviceIllum > zHIGHLIGHT16 Then
1131    zDeviceIllum = zHIGHLIGHT16
1132  End If
1133  If bUsePalette = True Then  'if 256-color mode calculate color...
1134    Factor = zMAX_SHADES / illum_range
1135    TempIllum = normalized_illum * Factor
1136    Shade = TempIllum - 1
1137    If Shade < zAMBIENT256 Then
1138      Shade = zAMBIENT256
1139    End If
1140    If Shade > zHIGHLIGHT256 Then
1141      Shade = zHIGHLIGHT256
1142    End If
1143  End If
1144  End Sub
1145
1146  '----------------------------------------------------------------
1147  '                  Hidden 3D workspace functions
1148  '----------------------------------------------------------------
1149  '              Create a hidden-page for 3D workspace
1150  '----------------------------------------------------------------
1151  Sub jazCreateHidden3DPage ()         'called by aazInitialize3D()
1152    Dim hDisplayDC As Integer
1153  RetLong = GlobalCompact(-1&)              'maximize contiguous memory
1154  hDisplayDC = GetDC(Form1.hWnd)
1155  hPageDC = CreateCompatibleDC(hDisplayDC)          'create page...
1156  hPage = CreateCompatibleBitmap(hDisplayDC, ViewportWidth, ViewportDepth)
1157  If hPage = 0 Then            'if unable to create hidden-page...
1158    MsgBox "jazCreateHidden3DPage( ) unable to create hidden-page.",
        MB_OK, "3D toolkit error"
1159    RetVal = DeleteDC(hPageDC)
1160    RetVal = ReleaseDC(Form1.hWnd, hDisplayDC)
1161    PageReady = False
1162    Exit Sub
1163  End If
1164  hPrevPage = SelectObject(hPageDC, hPage)      'select the bitmap
1165  RetVal = PatBlt(hPageDC, 0, 0, ViewportWidth, ViewportDepth, WHITENESS)
1166  RetVal = ReleaseDC(Form1.hWnd, hDisplayDC)
1167  PageReady = True
1168  End Sub
1169
1170  '----------------------------------------------------------------
1171  '                  Clear the hidden-page
1172  '----------------------------------------------------------------
1173  Sub jbzClearHidden3DPage ()     'called by interactive main module
1174  If PageReady = False Then
1175    Exit Sub
1176  End If
1177  RetVal = PatBlt(hPageDC, 0, 0, ViewportWidth, ViewportDepth, WHITENESS)
1178  End Sub
1179
1180  '----------------------------------------------------------------
1181  '                  Discard the hidden-page
```

```
1182 '------------------------------------------------------------------
1183 Sub jczClose3d ()                'called by interactive main module
1184 If PageReady = True Then           'if a hidden-page was created...
1185   RetVal = SelectObject(hPageDC, hPrevPage)
1186   RetVal = DeleteObject(hPage)                    '...discard it
1187   RetVal = DeleteDC(hPageDC)
1188 End If
1189 End Sub
1190
1191 '------------------------------------------------------------------
1192 '    Copy a pixel from the hidden 3D page to the viewport
1193 '------------------------------------------------------------------
1194 Sub jdzCopyPixelToViewPort (ByVal xCoord As Integer, ByVal yCoord
        As Integer)
1195                     'this function is called by kbzDoZBufferTest()
1196   Dim PixelColor As Long
1197   Dim PrevPalette As Integer
1198 If PageReady = False Then
1199   Exit Sub
1200 End If
1201 If xCoord < 0 Or xCoord > (ViewportWidth - 1) Then
1202   Exit Sub
1203 End If
1204 If yCoord < 0 Or yCoord > (ViewportDepth - 1) Then
1205   Exit Sub
1206 End If
1207 If bUsePalette = False Then           'if using dithered shades...
1208   PixelColor = GetPixel(hPageDC, xCoord, yCoord)   'get pixel clr
1209   RetLong = SetPixel(Form1.hDC, xCoord, yCoord, PixelColor)  'set
1210 End If
1211 End Sub
1212
1213 '------------------------------------------------------------------
1214 '                    Z-buffer functions
1215 '------------------------------------------------------------------
1216 '      Find the depth of a specified pixel in a 3D polygon
1217 '------------------------------------------------------------------
1218 Function kazFindDepth (ByVal Xpoint As Integer, ByVal Ypoint As
        Integer) As Integer
1219                     'this function is called by kbzDoZBufferTest()
1220   Dim Zpoint As Integer
1221   Dim TempZpoint As Double
1222   Dim ZleftScan As Double, ZrightScan As Double
1223   Dim XleftScan As Double, XrightScan As Double
1224   Dim YleftScan As Double, YrightScan As Double
1225   Dim Zleft1 As Double, Zleft2 As Double
1226   Dim Zright1 As Double, Zright2 As Double
1227   Dim Yleft1 As Double, Yleft2 As Double
1228   Dim Yright1 As Double, Yright2 As Double
1229   Dim Xleft1 As Double, Xleft2 As Double
1230   Dim Xright1 As Double, Xright2 As Double
1231   Dim Index1 As Integer, Index2 As Integer
1232 If Xpoint = Raster(FirstVertex).x And Ypoint =
        Raster(FirstVertex).y Then
1233   Zpoint = Raster(FirstVertex).z
1234   kazFindDepth = Zpoint
1235 End If
1236 If Xpoint = Raster(SecondVertex).x And Ypoint =
        Raster(SecondVertex).y Then
```

```
1237    Zpoint = Raster(SecondVertex).z
1238    kazFindDepth = Zpoint
1239  End If
1240  If Xpoint = Raster(ThirdVertex).x And Ypoint =
            Raster(ThirdVertex).y Then
1241    Zpoint = Raster(ThirdVertex).z
1242    kazFindDepth = Zpoint
1243  End If
1244  If Xpoint = Raster(FourthVertex).x And Ypoint =
            Raster(FourthVertex).y Then
1245    Zpoint = Raster(FourthVertex).z
1246    kazFindDepth = Zpoint
1247  End If
1248  '------- determine appropriate line segments to be used ---------
1249  If Ypoint <= Raster(SecondVertex).y Then   'which left-side lines?
1250    Index1 = FirstVertex
1251    Index2 = SecondVertex
1252  ElseIf Ypoint <= Raster(ThirdVertex).y Then
1253    Index1 = SecondVertex
1254    Index2 = ThirdVertex
1255  Else
1256    Index1 = ThirdVertex
1257    Index2 = FourthVertex
1258  End If
1259  Zleft1 = Raster(Index1).z
1260  Yleft1 = Raster(Index1).y
1261  Xleft1 = Raster(Index1).x
1262  Zleft2 = Raster(Index2).z
1263  Yleft2 = Raster(Index2).y
1264  Xleft2 = Raster(Index2).x
1265  If Ypoint <= Raster(FourthVertex).y Then 'which right-side lines?
1266    Index1 = FirstVertex
1267    Index2 = FourthVertex
1268  ElseIf Ypoint <= Raster(ThirdVertex).y Then
1269    Index1 = FourthVertex
1270    Index2 = ThirdVertex
1271  Else
1272    Index1 = ThirdVertex
1273    Index2 = SecondVertex
1274  End If
1275  Zright1 = Raster(Index1).z
1276  Yright1 = Raster(Index1).y
1277  Xright1 = Raster(Index1).x
1278  Zright2 = Raster(Index2).z
1279  Yright2 = Raster(Index2).y
1280  Xright2 = Raster(Index2).x
1281  YleftScan = Ypoint
1282  YrightScan = Ypoint
1283      'use facet edges to interpolate the depth of the target point
1284              'STEP ONE:  calculate scan-line end-point y values
1285  If Yleft1 - Yleft2 = 0 Then
1286    ZleftScan = Zleft2
1287  Else
1288    ZleftScan = Zleft1 - (Zleft1 - Zleft2) * ((Yleft1 - YleftScan) /
          (Yleft1 - Yleft2))
1289  End If
```

```
1290  If Yright1 - Yright2 = 0 Then
1291    ZrightScan = Zright2
1292  Else
1293    ZrightScan = Zright1 - (Zright1 - Zright2) * ((Yright1 -
            YrightScan) / (Yright1 - Yright2))
1294  End If
1295                   'STEP TWO:  calculate scan-line end-point x values
1296  If Yleft1 - Yleft2 = 0 Then
1297    XleftScan = Xleft2
1298  Else
1299    XleftScan = Xleft1 - (Xleft1 - Xleft2) * ((Yleft1 - YleftScan) /
            (Yleft1 - Yleft2))
1300  End If
1301  If Yright1 - Yright2 = 0 Then
1302    XrightScan = Xright2
1303  Else
1304    XrightScan = Xright1 - (Xright1 - Xright2) * ((Yright1 -
            YrightScan) / (Yright1 - Yright2))
1305  End If
1306     'STEP THREE:  use scan line to calculate depth of target point
1307  If XrightScan - XleftScan = 0 Then
1308    TempZpoint = ZrightScan
1309  Else
1310    TempZpoint = ZrightScan - (ZrightScan - ZleftScan) *
            ((XrightScan - Xpoint) / (XrightScan - XleftScan))
1311  End If
1312  If TempZpoint < 0 Then     'floating-point math idiosyncracies...
1313                 '...can cause values to slip outside the 0 to 255...
1314    TempZpoint = 0                    '...range when a facet...
1315  End If              '...is displayed at an oblique angle so...
1316  If TempZpoint > 255 Then   '...the facet's edge is towards the...
1317                   '...viewpoint and only a few pixels are seen
1318    TempZpoint = 255                    'this behavior is...
1319  End If   '...present whether or not a numeric coprocessor is used
1320  Zpoint = TempZpoint
1321  kazFindDepth = Zpoint
1322  End Function
1323
1324  '-------------------------------------------------------------
1325  '        Process a 3D facet using the z-buffer algorithm
1326  '-------------------------------------------------------------
1327  Sub kbzDoZBufferTest (ByVal hPolyRegion As Integer)
1328                   'this function is called by gazDrawFacet()
1329    Dim bValidPt As Integer              'point inside region?
1330    Dim zPrevDepth As Integer         'existing depth in z-buffer
1331    Dim zDepth As Integer             'depth of pt being tested
1332    Dim iCurrentX As Integer, iCurrentY As Integer 'pt being tested
1333  bValidPt = False
1334  For iCurrentY = 0 To (ViewportDepth - 1) Step 1    'for each y...
1335    bValidPt = False
1336    For iCurrentX = 0 To (ViewportWidth - 1) Step 1 'for each x...
1337      bValidPt = PtInRegion(hPolyRegion, iCurrentX, iCurrentY)
1338      If bValidPt <> False Then 'if point is inside the polygon...
1339        zDepth = kazFindDepth(iCurrentX, iCurrentY)    'check depth
1340        zPrevDepth = kdzReadZBuffer(iCurrentX, iCurrentY) 'z-buffer
1341        If zDepth < zPrevDepth Then         'compare the two depths
1342                       'if depth is nearer than z-buffer value...
1343          If zDepth <= FarClip And zDepth >= NearClip Then
```

B-1 Continued.

```
1344                      '...and it is between the clipping planes...
1345          kczWriteZBuffer iCurrentX, iCurrentY, zDepth  'store it
1346          jdzCopyPixelToViewPort iCurrentX, iCurrentY    'write it
1347      End If              'end of clipping plane IfThen block
1348    End If              'end of depth comparison IfThen block
1349   End If              'logical end of bValidPt IfThen block
1350  Next iCurrentX       'logical end of iCurrentX ForNext loop
1351 Next iCurrentY        'logical end of iCurrentY ForNext loop
1352 End Sub
1353
1354 '----------------------------------------------------------------
1355 '              Write a depth value to the z-buffer
1356 '----------------------------------------------------------------
1357 Sub kczWriteZBuffer (ByVal xCoord As Integer, ByVal yCoord As
          Integer, ByVal zDepth1 As Integer)
1358                      'this function is called by kbzDoZBufferTest()
1359 If xCoord < 0 Or xCoord > (ViewportWidth - 1) Then
1360   Exit Sub
1361 End If
1362 If yCoord < 0 Or yCoord > (ViewportDepth - 1) Then
1363   Exit Sub
1364 End If
1365 If ZBufferReady = False Then
1366   Exit Sub
1367 End If
1368 ZBuffer(xCoord, yCoord) = Chr$(zDepth1)         'write to z-buffer
1369 End Sub
1370
1371 '----------------------------------------------------------------
1372 '              Read a depth value from the z-buffer
1373 '----------------------------------------------------------------
1374 Function kdzReadZBuffer (ByVal xCoord As Integer, ByVal yCoord As
          Integer) As Integer
1375                      'this function is called by kbzDoZBufferTest()
1376   Dim zDepth1 As Integer
1377 If xCoord < 0 Or xCoord > (ViewportWidth - 1) Then
1378   kdzReadZBuffer = 255
1379   Exit Function
1380 End If
1381 If yCoord < 0 Or yCoord > (ViewportDepth - 1) Then
1382   kdzReadZBuffer = 255
1383   Exit Function
1384 End If
1385 If ZBufferReady = False Then
1386   kdzReadZBuffer = 255
1387   Exit Function
1388 End If
1389 zDepth1 = Asc(ZBuffer(xCoord, yCoord))     'read from memory block
1390 kdzReadZBuffer = zDepth1               'return the value to the caller
1391 End Function
1392
1393 '----------------------------------------------------------------
1394 '                      Reset the z-buffer
1395 '----------------------------------------------------------------
1396 Sub kezResetZBuffer ()
1397              'this function is called by interactive main module
```

```
1398    Dim xCoord As Integer, yCoord As Integer
1399  If ZBufferReady = False Then
1400    Exit Sub
1401  End If
1402  If bUseWireframe = True Then              'if using wire-frame mode...
1403    Exit Sub   'then z-buffer not required for wire-frame rendering
1404  End If
1405  For yCoord = 0 To ViewportDepth - 1 Step 1 'for each scan line...
1406    For xCoord = 0 To ViewportWidth - 1 Step 1        'for each x...
1407      ZBuffer(xCoord, yCoord) = Chr$(255)           'reset the depth
1408    Next xCoord                            'loop back to do next x
1409  Next yCoord                        'loop back to do next scan line
1410  End Sub
1411
```

B-2 Source listings for the 3D shapes toolkit, shapes3d.bas. See Appendix C for applications that use this toolkit. See Appendix A for instructions on building the demos.

```
0001  '-----------------------------------------------------------------
0002  '      Module of 3D shape drivers for Windows applications
0003  '-----------------------------------------------------------------
0004  'Source file  SHAPES3D.C
0005  'Release version  1.00                      Programmer  Lee Adams
0006  'Type  Visual Basic source file for Windows applications.
0007  'Dependencies  ENGINE3D.BAS 3D functions.
0008  'Output and features  Provides drivers for the ENGINE3D.C
0009  '  3D routines in order to render spheres, boxes, cylinders,
0010  '  curved surfaces, cones, wedges, etc.
0011  'Publication Contains material from Windcrest/McGraw-Hill book
0012  '  4225 published by TAB BOOKS Division of McGraw-Hill Inc.
0013  'License  As purchaser of the book you are granted a royalty-
0014  '  free license to distribute executable files generated using
0015  '  this code provided you accept the conditions of the License
0016  '  Agreement and Limited Warranty described in the book and on
0017  '  the companion disk.  Government users  This software and
0018  '  documentation are subject to restrictions set forth in The
0019  '  Rights in Technical Data and Computer Software clause at
0020  '  252.227-7013 and elsewhere.
0021  '-----------------------------------------------------------------
0022  '    (c) Copyright 1988-1993 Lee Adams.  All rights reserved.
0023  '          Lee Adams(tm) is a trademark of Lee Adams.
0024  '-----------------------------------------------------------------
0025     'Note:  This module relies upon some Global variables
0026     'declared in ENGINE3D.BAS.  This module also calls a
0027     'function defined in ASSEMB3D.BAS.
0028
0029  Option Explicit           'generate error if variable not declared
0030  Const z00_DEGREES - 0#                        'radian angles...
0031  Const z05_DEGREES = .08727
0032  Const z10_DEGREES = .17453
0033  Const z20_DEGREES = .34907
0034  Const z90_DEGREES = 1.57079
0035  Const zMIN_RADIUS = 10                          'minimum radius
0036  Const zMIN_DIMENSION = 10          'min curved surface extrusion
0037  '-----------------------------------------------------------------
0038  '  Declaration of variables visible throughout only this module
0039  '-----------------------------------------------------------------
0040  Dim SphereX As Double                   'sphere object coords...
```

```
0041   Dim SphereY As Double, SphereZ As Double
0042   Dim SphereRadius As Double                         'radius of sphere
0043   Dim VertAngle As Double, HorizAngle As Double      'describe angle
0044   Dim PrevVert As Double, PrevHoriz As Double        'scratchpad values
0045   Dim TempX As Double                                'scratchpad value
0046   Dim SinVert As Double, CosVert As Double           'sin, cos factors...
0047   Dim SinHoriz As Double, CosHoriz As Double
0048   Dim NumStrips As Integer                           'number of strips
0049   Dim NumFacets As Integer                           'number of facets
0050   Dim Strip As Integer                               'strip loop counter
0051   Dim Facet As Integer                               'facet loop counter
0052   Dim StripHeight As Double                          'angular height
0053   Dim FacetWidth As Double                           'angular width
0054   Dim CapHeight As Double                            'angular height of cap
0055   Dim CylinderX As Double                            'cylinder object coords...
0056   Dim CylinderY As Double, CylinderZ As Double
0057   Dim CylinderRadius As Double                       'cylinder dimensions...
0058   Dim CylinderExtrude As Double
0059   Dim FacetDimension As Double                       'angular dimension of facet
0060   Dim t As Double, T2 As Double, T3 As Double        'for curve
0061   Dim PrevT As Double                                'for scratchpad
0062   Dim Pull1 As Double, Pull2 As Double               'effect of curve points...
0063   Dim Pull3 As Double, Pull4 As Double
0064   Dim CurveX1 As Double, CurveY1 As Double           'curve startpoint
0065   Dim CurveX4 As Double, CurveY4 As Double           'curve endpoint
0066   Dim CurveX2 As Double, CurveY2 As Double           'first control
0067   Dim CurveX3 As Double, CurveY3 As Double           'second control
0068   Dim SurfaceX As Double, SurfaceY As Double         'curve object coords
0069   Dim SurfaceEdge1 As Double                         'extruded edges...
0070   Dim SurfaceEdge2 As Double
0071   Dim ParamChange As Double                          'parameters...
0072   Dim ParamMax As Double, ParamMin As Double
0073   Dim ControlStrength As Double                      'effect of control points
0074   Dim SwapStorage As Double                          'scratchpad for swaps
0075   Dim ConeRadius As Double                           'cone dimensions...
0076   Dim ConeExtrude As Double
0077   Dim ConeX As Double                                'cone object coords
0078   Dim ConeY As Double, ConeZ As Double
0079
0080   '----------------------------------------------------------------
0081   '                    3D solids drivers
0082   '----------------------------------------------------------------
0083   '                 Draw a solid parallelepiped
0084   '----------------------------------------------------------------
0085   Sub azDrawCube ()                  'called by interactive main module
0086   If bInitialized = False Then
0087     MsgBox "azDrawCube( ) reports that the 3D library is not
             initialized.", MB_OK, "SHAPES3D.BAS error"
0088     Exit Sub
0089   End If
0090   bzGetCubeCoords                    'get camera coords and display coords
0091   TestOnly = True                    'reset token for first pass
0092   SECOND_PASS:                       'will loop back to here for second pass
0093   surface0:        'assign the camera coords for the first facet...
0094     xc1 = camcoords(7, 0)
0095     yc1 = camcoords(7, 1)
```

```
0096   zc1 = camcoords(7, 2)
0097   xc2 = camcoords(0, 0)
0098   yc2 = camcoords(0, 1)
0099   zc2 = camcoords(0, 2)
0100   xc3 = camcoords(3, 0)
0101   yc3 = camcoords(3, 1)
0102   zc3 = camcoords(3, 2)
0103   xc4 = camcoords(6, 0)
0104   yc4 = camcoords(6, 1)
0105   zc4 = camcoords(6, 2)
0106   iazVisibilityTest              'check for back-plane culling...
0107   If visible > 0 Then                  'if hidden, then...
0108     GoTo surface1                   'move to next surface
0109   End If
0110   xw3 = cubeWorld(7, 0)           'otherwise, assign world coords...
0111   yw3 = cubeWorld(7, 1)
0112   zw3 = cubeWorld(7, 2)
0113   xw2 = cubeWorld(0, 0)
0114   yw2 = cubeWorld(0, 1)
0115   zw2 = cubeWorld(0, 2)
0116   xw1 = cubeWorld(3, 0)
0117   yw1 = cubeWorld(3, 1)
0118   zw1 = cubeWorld(3, 2)
0119   gazDrawFacet                           '...and draw the facet
0120   If Discard = True Or Clipped = True Then   'if clipped in 3D...
0121     GoTo DISCARD_SOLID                  '...then discard entire solid
0122   End If
0123   surface1:              'repeat the same process for the next facet
0124   xc1 = camcoords(6, 0)
0125   yc1 = camcoords(6, 1)
0126   zc1 = camcoords(6, 2)
0127   xc2 = camcoords(5, 0)
0128   yc2 = camcoords(5, 1)
0129   zc2 = camcoords(5, 2)
0130   xc3 = camcoords(4, 0)
0131   yc3 = camcoords(4, 1)
0132   zc3 = camcoords(4, 2)
0133   xc4 = camcoords(7, 0)
0134   yc4 = camcoords(7, 1)
0135   zc4 = camcoords(7, 2)
0136   iazVisibilityTest
0137   If visible > 0 Then
0138     GoTo surface2
0139   End If
0140   xw3 = cubeWorld(6, 0)
0141   yw3 = cubeWorld(6, 1)
0142   zw3 = cubeWorld(6, 2)
0143   xw2 = cubeWorld(5, 0)
0144   yw2 = cubeWorld(5, 1)
0145   zw2 = cubeWorld(5, 2)
0146   xw1 = cubeWorld(4, 0)
0147   yw1 = cubeWorld(4, 1)
0148   zw1 = cubeWorld(4, 2)
0149   gazDrawFacet
0150   If Discard = True Or Clipped = True Then
0151     GoTo DISCARD_SOLID
0152   End If
0153   surface2:
```

B-2 Continued.

```
0154    xc1 = camcoords(3, 0)
0155    yc1 = camcoords(3, 1)
0156    zc1 = camcoords(3, 2)
0157    xc2 = camcoords(2, 0)
0158    yc2 = camcoords(2, 1)
0159    zc2 = camcoords(2, 2)
0160    xc3 = camcoords(5, 0)
0161    yc3 = camcoords(5, 1)
0162    zc3 = camcoords(5, 2)
0163    xc4 = camcoords(6, 0)
0164    yc4 = camcoords(6, 1)
0165    zc4 = camcoords(6, 2)
0166    iazVisibilityTest
0167    If visible > 0 Then
0168      GoTo surface3
0169    End If
0170    xw3 = cubeWorld(3, 0)
0171    yw3 = cubeWorld(3, 1)
0172    zw3 = cubeWorld(3, 2)
0173    xw2 = cubeWorld(2, 0)
0174    yw2 = cubeWorld(2, 1)
0175    zw2 = cubeWorld(2, 2)
0176    xw1 = cubeWorld(5, 0)
0177    yw1 = cubeWorld(5, 1)
0178    zw1 = cubeWorld(5, 2)
0179    gazDrawFacet
0180    If Discard = True Or Clipped = True Then
0181      GoTo DISCARD_SOLID
0182    End If
0183  surface3:
0184    xc1 = camcoords(0, 0)
0185    yc1 = camcoords(0, 1)
0186    zc1 = camcoords(0, 2)
0187    xc2 = camcoords(1, 0)
0188    yc2 = camcoords(1, 1)
0189    zc2 = camcoords(1, 2)
0190    xc3 = camcoords(2, 0)
0191    yc3 = camcoords(2, 1)
0192    zc3 = camcoords(2, 2)
0193    xc4 = camcoords(3, 0)
0194    yc4 = camcoords(3, 1)
0195    zc4 = camcoords(3, 2)
0196    iazVisibilityTest
0197    If visible > 0 Then
0198      GoTo surface4
0199    End If
0200    xw3 = cubeWorld(0, 0)
0201    yw3 = cubeWorld(0, 1)
0202    zw3 = cubeWorld(0, 2)
0203    xw2 = cubeWorld(1, 0)
0204    yw2 = cubeWorld(1, 1)
0205    zw2 = cubeWorld(1, 2)
0206    xw1 = cubeWorld(2, 0)
0207    yw1 = cubeWorld(2, 1)
0208    zw1 = cubeWorld(2, 2)
0209    gazDrawFacet
```

```
0210    If Discard = True Or Clipped = True Then
0211      GoTo DISCARD_SOLID
0212    End If
0213  surface4:
0214    xc1 = camcoords(7, 0)
0215    yc1 = camcoords(7, 1)
0216    zc1 = camcoords(7, 2)
0217    xc2 = camcoords(4, 0)
0218    yc2 = camcoords(4, 1)
0219    zc2 = camcoords(4, 2)
0220    xc3 = camcoords(1, 0)
0221    yc3 = camcoords(1, 1)
0222    zc3 = camcoords(1, 2)
0223    xc4 = camcoords(0, 0)
0224    yc4 = camcoords(0, 1)
0225    zc4 = camcoords(0, 2)
0226    iazVisibilityTest
0227    If visible > 0 Then
0228      GoTo surface5
0229    End If
0230    xw3 = cubeWorld(7, 0)
0231    yw3 = cubeWorld(7, 1)
0232    zw3 = cubeWorld(7, 2)
0233    xw2 = cubeWorld(4, 0)
0234    yw2 = cubeWorld(4, 1)
0235    zw2 = cubeWorld(4, 2)
0236    xw1 = cubeWorld(1, 0)
0237    yw1 = cubeWorld(1, 1)
0238    zw1 = cubeWorld(1, 2)
0239    gazDrawFacet
0240    If Discard = True Or Clipped = True Then
0241      GoTo DISCARD_SOLID
0242    End If
0243  surface5:
0244    xc1 = camcoords(1, 0)
0245    yc1 = camcoords(1, 1)
0246    zc1 = camcoords(1, 2)
0247    xc2 = camcoords(4, 0)
0248    yc2 = camcoords(4, 1)
0249    zc2 = camcoords(4, 2)
0250    xc3 = camcoords(5, 0)
0251    yc3 = camcoords(5, 1)
0252    zc3 = camcoords(5, 2)
0253    xc4 = camcoords(2, 0)
0254    yc4 = camcoords(2, 1)
0255    zc4 = camcoords(2, 2)
0256    iazVisibilityTest
0257    If visible > 0 Then
0258      GoTo surfaces_done
0259    End If
0260    xw3 = cubeWorld(1, 0)
0261    yw3 = cubeWorld(1, 1)
0262    zw3 = cubeWorld(1, 2)
0263    xw2 = cubeWorld(4, 0)
0264    yw2 = cubeWorld(4, 1)
0265    zw2 = cubeWorld(4, 2)
0266    xw1 = cubeWorld(5, 0)
0267    yw1 = cubeWorld(5, 1)
```

B-2 Continued.

```
0268    zw1 = cubeWorld(5, 2)
0269    gazDrawFacet
0270    If Discard = True Or Clipped = True Then
0271      GoTo DISCARD_SOLID
0272    End If
0273  surfaces_done:
0274  If TestOnly = True Then              'if just finished first pass...
0275    TestOnly = False                      'reset token and...
0276    GoTo SECOND_PASS                   'loop back for second pass
0277  End If
0278  DISCARD_SOLID:        'jump to here if facet discarded on first pass
0279  End Sub                   'fall through to here after second pass
0280
0281  '----------------------------------------------------------------
0282  '              Calculate coords for parallelepiped
0283  '----------------------------------------------------------------
0284  Sub bzGetCubeCoords ()    'this function is called by azDrawCube()
0285    Dim t As Integer
0286    Dim negx As Double, negy As Double, negz As Double
0287  negx = (-1) * cursorx      'create the negative extrusion values...
0288  negy = (-1) * cursory
0289  negz = (-1) * cursorz
0290  cubeObj(0, 0) = cursorx           'store the 8 vertices of the box...
0291  cubeObj(0, 1) = negy
0292  cubeObj(0, 2) = cursorz
0293  cubeObj(1, 0) = cursorx
0294  cubeObj(1, 1) = cursory
0295  cubeObj(1, 2) = cursorz
0296  cubeObj(2, 0) = negx
0297  cubeObj(2, 1) = cursory
0298  cubeObj(2, 2) = cursorz
0299  cubeObj(3, 0) = negx
0300  cubeObj(3, 1) = negy
0301  cubeObj(3, 2) = cursorz
0302  cubeObj(4, 0) = cursorx
0303  cubeObj(4, 1) = cursory
0304  cubeObj(4, 2) = negz
0305  cubeObj(5, 0) = negx
0306  cubeObj(5, 1) = cursory
0307  cubeObj(5, 2) = negz
0308  cubeObj(6, 0) = negx
0309  cubeObj(6, 1) = negy
0310  cubeObj(6, 2) = negz
0311  cubeObj(7, 0) = cursorx
0312  cubeObj(7, 1) = negy
0313  cubeObj(7, 2) = negz
0314  For t = 0 To 7 Step 1               'for each vertex in the box...
0315    x = cubeObj(t, 0)                     'grab object coords...
0316    y = cubeObj(t, 1)                      '...and store them...
0317    z = cubeObj(t, 2)
0318    If bAssembly = True Then        'if using hierarchical modeling...
0319      azGetAssemblyCoords           '...calculate assembly coords
0320    End If
0321    fdzGetWorldCoords                  'calculate world coords...
0322    cubeWorld(t, 0) = x                 '...and store them...
0323    cubeWorld(t, 1) = y
```

```
0324    cubeWorld(t, 2) = z
0325    fezGetCameraCoords                      'calculate camera coords...
0326    camcoords(t, 0) = x                        '...and store them...
0327    camcoords(t, 1) = y
0328    camcoords(t, 2) = z
0329  Next t                  'loop back and do the next vertex of the box
0330  End Sub
0331
0332  '-----------------------------------------------------------
0333  '                      Draw a 3D sphere
0334  '-----------------------------------------------------------
0335  Sub czDrawSphere ()        'uses global cursorx as radius of sphere
0336  If bInitialized = False Then
0337    MsgBox "czDrawSphere( ) reports that the 3D library is not
0338        initialized.", MB_OK, "SHAPES3D.BAS error"
0338    Exit Sub
0339  End If
0340  TestOnly = False                     'do not discard entire solid
0341  SphereRadius = cursorx                      'grab radius of sphere
0342  If SphereRadius < zMIN_RADIUS Then
0343    Exit Sub                                   'if radius too small
0344  End If
0345  CapHeight = z10_DEGREES            'set height of facets for cap
0346  If SphereRadius >= 25 Then    'if large radius, use smaller facets
0347    NumStrips = 16                              'num of strips
0348    NumFacets = 36                          'num of facets per strip
0349    FacetWidth = z10_DEGREES                     'width of facets
0350    StripHeight = z10_DEGREES                   'height of facets
0351    If bUsePalette = True Then          'if using 256-color mode...
0352      NumStrips = 32         'increase resolution of the rendering...
0353      NumFacets = 36
0354      FacetWidth = z10_DEGREES
0355      StripHeight = z05_DEGREES
0356    End If
0357  ElseIf SphereRadius < 25 Then    'smaller radius, larger facets...
0358    NumStrips = 8                               'num of strips
0359    NumFacets = 18                          'num of facets per strip
0360    FacetWidth = z20_DEGREES                     'width of facets
0361    StripHeight = z20_DEGREES                   'height of facets
0362  End If
0363  '----------------- draw north cap of sphere --------------------
0364  VertAngle = z00_DEGREES                     'set vertical angle
0365  HorizAngle = z00_DEGREES                    'set horiz angle
0366  For Facet = 1 To NumFacets Step 1        'for each cap facet...
0367  ' ---------------- calculate first vertex ---------------------
0368    dzGetSphereShape                        'calculate obj coords
0369    x = SphereX                              'grab obj coords...
0370    y = SphereY
0371    z = SphereZ
0372    If bAssembly = True Then
0373      azGetAssemblyCoords
0374    End If
0375    fdzGetWorldCoords                       'calculate world coords
0376    fezGetCameraCoords                      'calculate camera coords
0377    xc1 = x                                 'grab camera coords...
0378    yc1 = y
0379    zc1 = z
0380  ' ---------------- calculate second vertex ----------------------
```

```
0381    PrevHoriz = HorizAngle
0382    HorizAngle = HorizAngle + FacetWidth
0383    dzGetSphereShape
0384    x = SphereX
0385    y = SphereY
0386    z = SphereZ
0387    If bAssembly = True Then
0388      azGetAssemblyCoords
0389    End If
0390    fdzGetWorldCoords
0391    xw3 = x
0392    yw3 = y
0393    zw3 = z
0394    fezGetCameraCoords
0395    xc2 = x
0396    yc2 = y
0397    zc2 = z
0398    ' ---------------- calculate third vertex ----------------------
0399    PrevVert = VertAngle
0400    VertAngle = VertAngle + CapHeight
0401    dzGetSphereShape
0402    x = SphereX
0403    y = SphereY
0404    z = SphereZ
0405    If bAssembly = True Then
0406      azGetAssemblyCoords
0407    End If
0408    fdzGetWorldCoords
0409    xw2 = x
0410    yw2 = y
0411    zw2 = z
0412    fezGetCameraCoords
0413    xc3 = x
0414    yc3 = y
0415    zc3 = z
0416    ' ---------------- calculate fourth vertex ------------------------
0417    HorizAngle = PrevHoriz
0418    dzGetSphereShape
0419    x = SphereX
0420    y = SphereY
0421    z = SphereZ
0422    If bAssembly = True Then
0423      azGetAssemblyCoords
0424    End If
0425    fdzGetWorldCoords
0426    xw1 = x
0427    yw1 = y
0428    zw1 = z
0429    fezGetCameraCoords
0430    xc4 = x
0431    yc4 = y
0432    zc4 = z
0433    ' ----------- test visibility and render the facet --------------
0434    iazVisibilityTest                       'backface culling test
0435    If visible <= 0 Then                     'if visible, then...
0436      gazDrawFacet                          'render z-buffered facet
```

```
0437    End If
0438  ' -------------- reset to start of next facet ------------------
0439    HorizAngle = HorizAngle + FacetWidth
0440    VertAngle = PrevVert
0441  Next Facet                                'loop back to do next facet
0442  '------------------- draw body of sphere -------------------------
0443  VertAngle = z10_DEGREES                           'reset vertical angle
0444  HorizAngle = z00_DEGREES                          'reset horiz angle
0445  For Strip = 1 To NumStrips Step 1                 'for each strip...
0446    For Facet = 1 To NumFacets Step 1               'for each facet...
0447  '    --------------- calculate first vertex ------------------------
0448       dzGetSphereShape
0449       x = SphereX
0450       y = SphereY
0451       z = SphereZ
0452       If bAssembly = True Then
0453         azGetAssemblyCoords
0454       End If
0455       fdzGetWorldCoords
0456       xw3 = x
0457       yw3 = y
0458       zw3 = z
0459       fezGetCameraCoords
0460       xc1 = x
0461       yc1 = y
0462       zc1 = z
0463  '    --------------- calculate second vertex --------------------
0464       PrevHoriz = HorizAngle
0465       HorizAngle = HorizAngle + FacetWidth
0466       dzGetSphereShape
0467       x = SphereX
0468       y = SphereY
0469       z = SphereZ
0470       If bAssembly = True Then
0471         azGetAssemblyCoords
0472       End If
0473       fdzGetWorldCoords
0474       xw2 = x
0475       yw2 = y
0476       zw2 = z
0477       fezGetCameraCoords
0478       xc2 = x
0479       yc2 = y
0480       zc2 = z
0481  '    --------------- calculate third vertex ------------------------
0482       PrevVert = VertAngle
0483       VertAngle = VertAngle + StripHeight
0484       dzGetSphereShape
0485       x = SphereX
0486       y = SphereY
0487       z = SphereZ
0488       If bAssembly = True Then
0489         azGetAssemblyCoords
0490       End If
0491       fdzGetWorldCoords
0492       xw1 = x
0493       yw1 = y
0494       zw1 = z
```

```
0495        fezGetCameraCoords
0496        xc3 = x
0497        yc3 = y
0498        zc3 = z
0499   ' --------------- calculate fourth vertex ---------------------
0500        HorizAngle = PrevHoriz
0501        dzGetSphereShape
0502        x = SphereX
0503        y = SphereY
0504        z = SphereZ
0505        If bAssembly = True Then
0506          azGetAssemblyCoords
0507        End If
0508        fdzGetWorldCoords
0509        fezGetCameraCoords
0510        xc4 = x
0511        yc4 = y
0512        zc4 = z
0513   ' ---------- test visibility and render the facet -------------
0514        iazVisibilityTest
0515        If visible <= 0 Then
0516          gazDrawFacet
0517        End If
0518   ' -------------- reset to start of next facet -----------------
0519        HorizAngle = HorizAngle + FacetWidth
0520        VertAngle = PrevVert
0521      Next Facet                          'loop back to do next facet
0522      VertAngle = VertAngle + StripHeight        'select next strip
0523      HorizAngle = z00_DEGREES                'reset to first facet
0524    Next Strip                          'loop back to do next strip
0525   '----------------- draw south cap of sphere --------------------
0526   HorizAngle = z00_DEGREES                     'reset horiz angle
0527   For Facet = 1 To NumFacets Step 1          'for each cap facet...
0528   ' --------------- calculate first vertex ---------------------
0529     dzGetSphereShape
0530     x = SphereX
0531     y = SphereY
0532     z = SphereZ
0533     If bAssembly = True Then
0534       azGetAssemblyCoords
0535     End If
0536     fdzGetWorldCoords
0537     xw3 = x
0538     yw3 = y
0539     zw3 = z
0540     fezGetCameraCoords
0541     xc1 = x
0542     yc1 = y
0543     zc1 = z
0544   ' ----------------- calculate second vertex -----------------------
0545     PrevHoriz = HorizAngle
0546     HorizAngle = HorizAngle + FacetWidth
0547     dzGetSphereShape
0548     x = SphereX
0549     y = SphereY
0550     z = SphereZ
```

```
0551    If bAssembly = True Then
0552      azGetAssemblyCoords
0553    End If
0554    fdzGetWorldCoords
0555    xw2 = x
0556    yw2 = y
0557    zw2 = z
0558    fezGetCameraCoords
0559    xc2 = x
0560    yc2 = y
0561    zc2 = z
0562  ' ---------------- calculate third vertex ----------------------
0563    PrevVert = VertAngle
0564    VertAngle = VertAngle + CapHeight
0565    dzGetSphereShape
0566    x = SphereX
0567    y = SphereY
0568    z = SphereZ
0569    If bAssembly = True Then
0570      azGetAssemblyCoords
0571    End If
0572    fdzGetWorldCoords
0573    xw1 = x
0574    yw1 = y
0575    zw1 = z
0576    fezGetCameraCoords
0577    xc3 = x
0578    yc3 = y
0579    zc3 = z
0580  ' ---------------- calculate fourth vertex --------------------
0581    HorizAngle = PrevHoriz
0582    dzGetSphereShape
0583    x = SphereX
0584    y = SphereY
0585    z = SphereZ
0586    If bAssembly = True Then
0587      azGetAssemblyCoords
0588    End If
0589    fdzGetWorldCoords
0590    fezGetCameraCoords
0591    xc4 = x
0592    yc4 = y
0593    zc4 = z
0594  ' ----------- test visibility and render the facet -------------
0595    iazVisibilityTest
0596    If visible <= 0 Then
0597      gazDrawFacet
0598    End If
0599  ' --------------- reset to start of next facet -----------------
0600    HorizAngle = HorizAngle + FacetWidth
0601    VertAngle = PrevVert
0602  Next Facet
0603  End Sub
0604
0605  '----------------------------------------------------------------
0606  '        Calculate obj coords for pt on surface of sphere
0607  '----------------------------------------------------------------
0608  Sub dzGetSphereShape () 'uses VertAngle, HorizAngle, SphereRadius
```

```
0609  SinHoriz = Sin(HorizAngle)
0610  CosHoriz = Cos(HorizAngle)
0611  SinVert = Sin(VertAngle)
0612  CosVert = Cos(VertAngle)
0613  TempX = SinVert * SphereRadius
0614  SphereY = CosVert * SphereRadius
0615  SphereX = CosHoriz * TempX
0616  SphereZ = SinHoriz * TempX
0617  End Sub
0618
0619  '----------------------------------------------------------------
0620  '                        Draw a 3D cylinder
0621  '----------------------------------------------------------------
0622  Sub ezDrawCylinder () 'uses cursorx, cursorz to configure cylinder
0623  If bInitialized = False Then
0624    MsgBox "ezDrawCylinder( ) reports that the 3D library is not
            initialized.", MB_OK, "SHAPES3D.BAS error"
0625    Exit Sub
0626  End If
0627  TestOnly = False                       'do not discard entire solid
0628  CylinderRadius = cursorx                          'grab radius
0629  CylinderExtrude = cursorz                         'grab extrusion
0630  If CylinderRadius < zMIN_RADIUS Then
0631    Exit Sub                                 'if radius too small
0632  End If
0633  VertAngle = z00_DEGREES                           'vertical angle
0634  HorizAngle = z00_DEGREES                          'horiz angle
0635  If CylinderRadius >= 25 Then     'large radius, use smaller facets
0636    NumFacets = 36                              'number of facets
0637    FacetDimension = z10_DEGREES                  'width of facets
0638  ElseIf CylinderRadius < 25 Then    'smaller radius, larger facets
0639    NumFacets = 18
0640    FacetDimension = z20_DEGREES
0641  End If
0642  '-------------------- draw body of cylinder ------------------------
0643  For Facet = 1 To NumFacets Step 1            'for each facet...
0644  ' ------------------ calculate first vertex ----------------------
0645    fzGetCylindershape
0646    x = CylinderX
0647    y = CylinderY
0648    z = CylinderZ
0649    If bAssembly = True Then
0650      azGetAssemblyCoords
0651    End If
0652    fdzGetWorldCoords
0653    xw3 = x
0654    yw3 = y
0655    zw3 = z
0656    fezGetCameraCoords
0657    xc1 = x
0658    yc1 = y
0659    zc1 = z
0660  ' ------------------ calculate second vertex --------------------
0661    PrevVert = VertAngle
0662    VertAngle = VertAngle + FacetDimension
0663    fzGetCylindershape
```

```
0664    x = CylinderX
0665    y = CylinderY
0666    z = CylinderZ
0667    If bAssembly = True Then
0668      azGetAssemblyCoords
0669    End If
0670    fdzGetWorldCoords
0671    xw2 = x
0672    yw2 = y
0673    zw2 = z
0674    fezGetCameraCoords
0675    xc2 = x
0676    yc2 = y
0677    zc2 = z
0678    ' ----------------- calculate third vertex ------------------------
0679    fzGetCylindershape
0680    x = CylinderX
0681    y = CylinderY
0682    z = -CylinderZ
0683    If bAssembly = True Then
0684      azGetAssemblyCoords
0685    End If
0686    fdzGetWorldCoords
0687    xw1 = x
0688    yw1 = y
0689    zw1 = z
0690    fezGetCameraCoords
0691    xc3 = x
0692    yc3 = y
0693    zc3 = z
0694    ' ----------------- calculate fourth vertex --------------------
0695    VertAngle = PrevVert
0696    fzGetCylindershape
0697    x = CylinderX
0698    y = CylinderY
0699    z = -CylinderZ
0700    If bAssembly = True Then
0701      azGetAssemblyCoords
0702    End If
0703    fdzGetWorldCoords
0704    fezGetCameraCoords
0705    xc4 = x
0706    yc4 = y
0707    zc4 = z
0708    ' ----------- test visibility and render the facet -------------
0709    iazVisibilityTest
0710    If visible <= 0 Then
0711      gazDrawFacet
0712    End If
0713    VertAngle = VertAngle + FacetDimension
0714  Next Facet
0715  '------------------- draw ends of cylinder ---------------------
0716  VertAngle = z00_DEGREES                     'reset vertical angle
0717  For Facet = 1 To NumFacets Step 1      'for each near-end facet...
0718    ' ----------------- calculate first vertex ------------------------
0719    x = 0
0720    y = 0
0721    z = CylinderZ
```

```
0722    If bAssembly = True Then
0723      azGetAssemblyCoords
0724    End If
0725    fdzGetWorldCoords
0726    xw3 = x
0727    yw3 = y
0728    zw3 = z
0729    fezGetCameraCoords
0730    xc1 = x
0731    yc1 = y
0732    zc1 = z
0733    ' ----------------- calculate second vertex --------------------
0734    PrevVert = VertAngle
0735    VertAngle = VertAngle + FacetDimension
0736    fzGetCylindershape
0737    x = CylinderX
0738    y = CylinderY
0739    z = CylinderZ
0740    If bAssembly = True Then
0741      azGetAssemblyCoords
0742    End If
0743    fdzGetWorldCoords
0744    xw2 = x
0745    yw2 = y
0746    zw2 = z
0747    fezGetCameraCoords
0748    xc2 = x
0749    yc2 = y
0750    zc2 = z
0751    ' ----------------- calculate third vertex ------------------------
0752    VertAngle = PrevVert
0753    fzGetCylindershape
0754    x = CylinderX
0755    y = CylinderY
0756    z = CylinderZ
0757    If bAssembly = True Then
0758      azGetAssemblyCoords
0759    End If
0760    fdzGetWorldCoords
0761    xw1 = x
0762    yw1 = y
0763    zw1 = z
0764    fezGetCameraCoords
0765    xc3 = x
0766    yc3 = y
0767    zc3 = z
0768    ' ----------------- calculate fourth vertex ------------------------
0769    x = 0
0770    y = 0
0771    z = CylinderZ
0772    If bAssembly = True Then
0773      azGetAssemblyCoords
0774    End If
0775    fdzGetWorldCoords
0776    fezGetCameraCoords
0777    xc4 = x
```

```
0778    yc4 = y
0779    zc4 = z
0780 ' ----------- test visibility and render the facet --------------
0781    iazVisibilityTest
0782    If visible <= 0 Then
0783      gazDrawFacet
0784    End If
0785    VertAngle = VertAngle + FacetDimension
0786 Next Facet
0787 VertAngle = z00_DEGREES                    'reset vertical angle
0788 For Facet = 1 To NumFacets Step 1      'for each far-end facet...
0789 ' ----------------- calculate first vertex ------------------------
0790    x = 0
0791    y = 0
0792    z = -CylinderZ
0793    If bAssembly = True Then
0794      azGetAssemblyCoords
0795    End If
0796    fdzGetWorldCoords
0797    xw3 = x
0798    yw3 = y
0799    zw3 = z
0800    fezGetCameraCoords
0801    xc1 = x
0802    yc1 = y
0803    zc1 = z
0804 ' ----------------- calculate second vertex --------------------
0805    fzGetCylindershape
0806    x = CylinderX
0807    y = CylinderY
0808    z = -CylinderZ
0809    If bAssembly = True Then
0810      azGetAssemblyCoords
0811    End If
0812    fdzGetWorldCoords
0813    xw2 = x
0814    yw2 = y
0815    zw2 = z
0816    fezGetCameraCoords
0817    xc2 = x
0818    yc2 = y
0819    zc2 = z
0820 ' ----------------- calculate third vertex ------------------------
0821    VertAngle = VertAngle + FacetDimension
0822    fzGetCylindershape
0823    x = CylinderX
0824    y = CylinderY
0825    z = -CylinderZ
0826    If bAssembly = True Then
0827      azGetAssemblyCoords
0828    End If
0829    fdzGetWorldCoords
0830    xw1 = x
0831    yw1 = y
0832    zw1 = z
0833    fezGetCameraCoords
0834    xc3 = x
0835    yc3 = y
```

```
0836    zc3 = z
0837  ' ---------------- calculate fourth vertex ------------------------
0838    x = 0
0839    y = 0
0840    z = -CylinderZ
0841    If bAssembly = True Then
0842      azGetAssemblyCoords
0843    End If
0844    fdzGetWorldCoords
0845    fezGetCameraCoords
0846    xc4 = x
0847    yc4 = y
0848    zc4 = z
0849  ' ----------- test visibility and render the facet --------------
0850    iazVisibilityTest
0851    If visible <= 0 Then
0852      gazDrawFacet
0853    End If
0854  Next Facet
0855  End Sub
0856
0857  '------------------------------------------------------------------
0858  '      Calculate obj coords for pt on surface of cylinder
0859  '------------------------------------------------------------------
0860  Sub fzGetCylindershape ()
0861        'uses VertAngle, HorizAngle, CylinderRadius, CylinderExtrude
0862  SinHoriz = Sin(HorizAngle)
0863  CosHoriz = Cos(HorizAngle)
0864  SinVert = Sin(VertAngle)
0865  CosVert = Cos(VertAngle)
0866  TempX = SinVert * CylinderRadius
0867  CylinderY = CosVert * CylinderRadius
0868  CylinderX = CosHoriz * TempX
0869  CylinderZ = CylinderExtrude
0870  End Sub
0871
0872  '------------------------------------------------------------------
0873  '                      Draw a 3D curved surface
0874  '------------------------------------------------------------------
0875  Sub gzDrawCurve ()              'uses cursorx, cursory, and cursorz
0876  If bInitialized = False Then
0877    MsgBox "gzDrawCurve( ) reports that the 3D library is not
              initialized.", MB_OK, "SHAPES3D.BAS error"
0878    Exit Sub
0879  End If
0880  ParamChange = .05                          'parametric increment
0881  ParamMax = 1#                          'maximum parametric value
0882  ParamMin = 0#                          'minimum parametric value
0883  ControlStrength = .5              'influence of control points
0884  If bUsePalette = True Then            'if using 256-color mode...
0885    ParamChange = .025        'increase resolution of the rendering
0886  End If
0887  '----------- configure the curved edge of the surface -----------
0888  CurveX1 = (-1) * cursorx
0889  CurveX4 = cursorx
0890  CurveY1 = 0#
```

```
0891   CurveY4 = 0#
0892   '-------------- configure the width of the surface --------------
0893   SurfaceEdge1 = (-1) * cursorz
0894   SurfaceEdge2 = cursorz
0895   '------------ configure the magnitude of the curve --------------
0896   CurveY2 = cursory
0897   CurveY3 = (-1) * cursory
0898   CurveX2 = ControlStrength * CurveX1
0899   CurveX3 = ControlStrength * CurveX4
0900   '-------------------- render the curved surface --------------------
0901   For t = ParamMin To ParamMax Step ParamChange 'for each lamina...
0902     T2 = t * t
0903     T3 = t * t * t
0904   ' ------------------- calculate first vertex --------------------
0905     hzGetCurveShape
0906     x = SurfaceX
0907     y = SurfaceY
0908     z = SurfaceEdge1
0909     If bAssembly = True Then
0910       azGetAssemblyCoords
0911     End If
0912     fdzGetWorldCoords
0913     xw3 = x
0914     yw3 = y
0915     zw3 = z
0916     fezGetCameraCoords
0917     xc1 = x
0918     yc1 = y
0919     zc1 = z
0920   ' ------------------- calculate second vertex -------------------
0921     x = SurfaceX
0922     y = SurfaceY
0923     z = SurfaceEdge2
0924     If bAssembly = True Then
0925       azGetAssemblyCoords
0926     End If
0927     fdzGetWorldCoords
0928     xw2 = x
0929     yw2 = y
0930     zw2 = z
0931     fezGetCameraCoords
0932     xc2 = x
0933     yc2 = y
0934     zc2 = z
0935   ' ------------------- calculate third vertex --------------------
0936     PrevT = t                              'remember position on curve
0937     t = t + ParamChange          'move to next position on curve...
0938     T2 = t * t
0939     T3 = t * t * t
0940     hzGetCurveShape
0941     x = SurfaceX
0942     y = SurfaceY
0943     z = SurfaceEdge2
0944     If bAssembly = True Then
0945       azGetAssemblyCoords
0946     End If
0947     fdzGetWorldCoords
0948     xw1 = x
```

```
0949    yw1 = y
0950    zw1 = z
0951    fezGetCameraCoords
0952    xc3 = x
0953    yc3 = y
0954    zc3 = z
0955 ' ----------------- calculate fourth vertex -------------------
0956    x = SurfaceX
0957    y = SurfaceY
0958    z = SurfaceEdge1
0959    If bAssembly = True Then
0960      azGetAssemblyCoords
0961    End If
0962    fdzGetWorldCoords
0963    fezGetCameraCoords
0964    xc4 = x
0965    yc4 = y
0966    zc4 = z
0967 ' ----------- test visibility and render the lamina ------------
0968    iazVisibilityTest
0969    If visible <= 0 Then
0970      gazDrawFacet                          'if visible, draw lamina
0971    Else                          'else draw obverse side of lamina...
0972      SwapStorage = xw1
0973      xw1 = xw3
0974      xw3 = SwapStorage
0975      SwapStorage = yw1
0976      yw1 = yw3
0977      yw3 = SwapStorage
0978      SwapStorage = zw1
0979      zw1 = zw3
0980      zw3 = SwapStorage
0981      SwapStorage = xc1
0982      xc1 = xc3
0983      xc3 = SwapStorage
0984      SwapStorage = yc1
0985      yc1 = yc3
0986      yc3 = SwapStorage
0987      SwapStorage = zc1
0988      zc1 = zc3
0989      zc3 = SwapStorage
0990      gazDrawFacet
0991    End If
0992    t = PrevT                      'restore current position on curve
0993 Next t                           'loop back and render next facet
0994 End Sub
0995
0996 '----------------------------------------------------------------
0997 '      Calculate object coords for point on curved surface
0998 '----------------------------------------------------------------
0999 Sub hzGetCurveShape ()
1000 Pull1 = CurveX1 * (-T3 + 3 * T2 - 3 * t + 1)
1001 Pull2 = CurveX2 * (3 * T3 - 6 * T2 + 3 * t)
1002 Pull3 = CurveX3 * (-3 * T3 + 3 * T2)
1003 Pull4 = CurveX4 * T3
1004 SurfaceX = Pull1 + Pull2 + Pull3 + Pull4
```

```
1005  Pull1 = CurveY1 * (-T3 + 3 * T2 - 3 * t + 1)
1006  Pull2 = CurveY2 * (3 * T3 - 6 * T2 + 3 * t)
1007  Pull3 = CurveY3 * (-3 * T3 + 3 * T2)
1008  Pull4 = CurveY4 * T3
1009  SurfaceY = Pull1 + Pull2 + Pull3 + Pull4
1010  End Sub
1011
1012  '----------------------------------------------------------------
1013  '                       Draw a 3D cone
1014  '----------------------------------------------------------------
1015  Sub izDrawCone ()          'uses cursorx, cursorz to configure cone
1016  If bInitialized = False Then
1017    MsgBox "izDrawCone( ) reports that the 3D library is not
            initialized.", MB_OK, "SHAPES3D.BAS error"
1018    Exit Sub
1019  End If
1020  TestOnly = False                        'do not discard entire solid
1021  ConeRadius = cursorx                             'grab radius
1022  ConeExtrude = cursorz                            'grab extrusion
1023  If ConeRadius < zMIN_RADIUS Then
1024    Exit Sub                                   'if radius too small
1025  End If
1026  VertAngle = z00_DEGREES                          'vertical angle
1027  HorizAngle = z00_DEGREES                            'horiz angle
1028  ConeZ = ConeExtrude                      'grab 3D extrusion point
1029  If ConeRadius >= 25 Then        'large radius, use smaller facets
1030    NumFacets = 36                             'number of facets
1031    FacetDimension = z10_DEGREES                 'width of facets
1032  ElseIf ConeRadius < 25 Then     'smaller radius, use larger facets
1033    NumFacets = 18
1034    FacetDimension = z20_DEGREES
1035  End If
1036  '------------------- draw end of cone -----------------------
1037  VertAngle = z00_DEGREES                     'reset vertical angle
1038  For Facet = 1 To NumFacets Step 1          'for each facet...
1039  ' ----------------- calculate first vertex ------------------------
1040    x = 0
1041    y = 0
1042    z = ConeZ
1043    If bAssembly = True Then
1044      azGetAssemblyCoords
1045    End If
1046    fdzGetWorldCoords
1047    xw3 = x
1048    yw3 = y
1049    zw3 = z
1050    fezGetCameraCoords
1051    xc1 = x
1052    yc1 = y
1053    zc1 = z
1054  ' ----------------- calculate second vertex --------------------
1055    PrevVert = VertAngle
1056    VertAngle = VertAngle + FacetDimension
1057    jzGetConeShape
1058    x = ConeX
1059    y = ConeY
1060    z = ConeZ
1061    If bAssembly = True Then
```

```
1062        azGetAssemblyCoords
1063     End If
1064     fdzGetWorldCoords
1065     xw2 = x
1066     yw2 = y
1067     zw2 = z
1068     fezGetCameraCoords
1069     xc2 = x
1070     yc2 = y
1071     zc2 = z
1072  ' ----------------- calculate third vertex ------------------------
1073     VertAngle = PrevVert
1074     jzGetConeShape
1075     x = ConeX
1076     y = ConeY
1077     z = ConeZ
1078     If bAssembly = True Then
1079        azGetAssemblyCoords
1080     End If
1081     fdzGetWorldCoords
1082     xw1 = x
1083     yw1 = y
1084     zw1 = z
1085     fezGetCameraCoords
1086     xc3 = x
1087     yc3 = y
1088     zc3 = z
1089  ' ---------------- calculate fourth vertex ------------------------
1090     x = 0
1091     y = 0
1092     z = ConeZ
1093     If bAssembly = True Then
1094        azGetAssemblyCoords
1095     End If
1096     fdzGetWorldCoords
1097     fezGetCameraCoords
1098     xc4 = x
1099     yc4 = y
1100     zc4 = z
1101  ' ----------- test visibility and render the facet --------------
1102     iazVisibilityTest
1103     If visible <= 0 Then
1104        gazDrawFacet
1105     End If
1106     VertAngle = VertAngle + FacetDimension
1107  Next Facet
1108  '------------------------ draw body of cone -----------------------
1109  VertAngle = z00_DEGREES                  'reset vertical angle
1110  For Facet = 1 To NumFacets Step 1          'for each facet...
1111  ' ----------------- calculate first vertex ------------------------
1112     x = 0
1113     y = 0
1114     z = -ConeZ
1115     If bAssembly = True Then
1116        azGetAssemblyCoords
1117     End If
```

```
1118    fdzGetWorldCoords
1119    xw3 = x
1120    yw3 = y
1121    zw3 = z
1122    fezGetCameraCoords
1123    xc1 = x
1124    yc1 = y
1125    zc1 = z
1126  ' ----------------- calculate second vertex --------------------
1127    jzGetConeShape
1128    x = ConeX
1129    y = ConeY
1130    z = ConeZ
1131    If bAssembly = True Then
1132      azGetAssemblyCoords
1133    End If
1134    fdzGetWorldCoords
1135    xw2 = x
1136    yw2 = y
1137    zw2 = z
1138    fezGetCameraCoords
1139    xc2 = x
1140    yc2 = y
1141    zc2 = z
1142  ' ----------------- calculate third vertex ------------------------
1143    PrevVert = VertAngle
1144    VertAngle = VertAngle + FacetDimension
1145    jzGetConeShape
1146    x = ConeX
1147    y = ConeY
1148    z = ConeZ
1149    If bAssembly = True Then
1150      azGetAssemblyCoords
1151    End If
1152    fdzGetWorldCoords
1153    xw1 = x
1154    yw1 = y
1155    zw1 = z
1156    fezGetCameraCoords
1157    xc3 = x
1158    yc3 = y
1159    zc3 = z
1160  ' ----------------- calculate fourth vertex ------------------------
1161    VertAngle = PrevVert
1162    x = 0
1163    y = 0
1164    z = -ConeZ
1165    If bAssembly = True Then
1166      azGetAssemblyCoords
1167    End If
1168    fdzGetWorldCoords
1169    fezGetCameraCoords
1170    xc4 = x
1171    yc4 = y
1172    zc4 = z
1173  ' ----------- test visibility and render the facet --------------
1174    iazVisibilityTest
1175    If visible <= 0 Then
```

```
1176      gazDrawFacet
1177    End If
1178    VertAngle = VertAngle + FacetDimension
1179 Next Facet
1180 End Sub
1181
1182 '----------------------------------------------------------------
1183 '          Calculate obj coords for pt on surface of cone
1184 '----------------------------------------------------------------
1185 Sub jzGetConeShape ()
1186 SinHoriz = Sin(HorizAngle)
1187 CosHoriz = Cos(HorizAngle)
1188 SinVert = Sin(VertAngle)
1189 CosVert = Cos(VertAngle)
1190 TempX = SinVert * ConeRadius
1191 ConeY = CosVert * ConeRadius
1192 ConeX = CosHoriz * TempX
1193 End Sub
1194
1195 '----------------------------------------------------------------
1196 '                      Draw a 3D wedge
1197 '----------------------------------------------------------------
1198 Sub kzDrawWedge ()
1199 If bInitialized = False Then
1200   MsgBox "kzDrawWedge( ) reports that the 3D library is not
          initialized.", MB_OK, "SHAPES3D.BAS error"
1201   Exit Sub
1202 End If
1203 lzGetWedgeCoords                 'get camera coords and display coords
1204 TestOnly = True                          'reset token for first pass
1205 WEDGE_SECOND_PASS:               'will loop back to here for second pass
1206 wedge_surface0:
1207   xc1 = camcoords(5, 0)
1208   yc1 = camcoords(5, 1)
1209   zc1 = camcoords(5, 2)
1210   xc2 = camcoords(0, 0)
1211   yc2 = camcoords(0, 1)
1212   zc2 = camcoords(0, 2)
1213   xc3 = camcoords(2, 0)
1214   yc3 = camcoords(2, 1)
1215   zc3 = camcoords(2, 2)
1216   xc4 = camcoords(4, 0)
1217   yc4 = camcoords(4, 1)
1218   zc4 = camcoords(4, 2)
1219   iazVisibilityTest
1220   If visible > 0 Then
1221     GoTo wedge_surface1
1222   End If
1223   xw3 = cubeWorld(5, 0)
1224   yw3 = cubeWorld(5, 1)
1225   zw3 = cubeWorld(5, 2)
1226   xw2 = cubeWorld(0, 0)
1227   yw2 = cubeWorld(0, 1)
1228   zw2 = cubeWorld(0, 2)
1229   xw1 = cubeWorld(2, 0)
1230   yw1 = cubeWorld(2, 1)
```

```
1231    zw1 = cubeWorld(2, 2)
1232    gazDrawFacet
1233    If Discard = True Or Clipped = True Then
1234      GoTo WDISCARD_SOLID
1235    End If
1236  wedge_surface1:
1237    xc1 = camcoords(3, 0)
1238    yc1 = camcoords(3, 1)
1239    zc1 = camcoords(3, 2)
1240    xc2 = camcoords(5, 0)
1241    yc2 = camcoords(5, 1)
1242    zc2 = camcoords(5, 2)
1243    xc3 = camcoords(4, 0)
1244    yc3 = camcoords(4, 1)
1245    zc3 = camcoords(4, 2)
1246    xc4 = camcoords(3, 0)
1247    yc4 = camcoords(3, 1)
1248    zc4 = camcoords(3, 2)
1249    iazVisibilityTest
1250    If visible > 0 Then
1251      GoTo wedge_surface2
1252    End If
1253    xw3 = cubeWorld(3, 0)
1254    yw3 = cubeWorld(3, 1)
1255    zw3 = cubeWorld(3, 2)
1256    xw2 = cubeWorld(5, 0)
1257    yw2 = cubeWorld(5, 1)
1258    zw2 = cubeWorld(5, 2)
1259    xw1 = cubeWorld(4, 0)
1260    yw1 = cubeWorld(4, 1)
1261    zw1 = cubeWorld(4, 2)
1262    gazDrawFacet
1263    If Discard = True Or Clipped = True Then
1264      GoTo WDISCARD_SOLID
1265    End If
1266  wedge_surface2:
1267    xc1 = camcoords(1, 0)
1268    yc1 = camcoords(1, 1)
1269    zc1 = camcoords(1, 2)
1270    xc2 = camcoords(3, 0)
1271    yc2 = camcoords(3, 1)
1272    zc2 = camcoords(3, 2)
1273    xc3 = camcoords(4, 0)
1274    yc3 = camcoords(4, 1)
1275    zc3 = camcoords(4, 2)
1276    xc4 = camcoords(2, 0)
1277    yc4 = camcoords(2, 1)
1278    zc4 = camcoords(2, 2)
1279    iazVisibilityTest
1280    If visible > 0 Then
1281      GoTo wedge_surface3
1282    End If
1283    xw3 = cubeWorld(1, 0)
1284    yw3 = cubeWorld(1, 1)
1285    zw3 = cubeWorld(1, 2)
1286    xw2 = cubeWorld(3, 0)
1287    yw2 = cubeWorld(3, 1)
1288    zw2 = cubeWorld(3, 2)
```

```
1289    xw1 = cubeWorld(4, 0)
1290    yw1 = cubeWorld(4, 1)
1291    zw1 = cubeWorld(4, 2)
1292    gazDrawFacet
1293    If Discard = True Or Clipped = True Then
1294      GoTo WDISCARD_SOLID
1295    End If
1296  wedge_surface3:
1297    xc1 = camcoords(1, 0)
1298    yc1 = camcoords(1, 1)
1299    zc1 = camcoords(1, 2)
1300    xc2 = camcoords(2, 0)
1301    yc2 = camcoords(2, 1)
1302    zc2 = camcoords(2, 2)
1303    xc3 = camcoords(0, 0)
1304    yc3 = camcoords(0, 1)
1305    zc3 = camcoords(0, 2)
1306    xc4 = camcoords(1, 0)
1307    yc4 = camcoords(1, 1)
1308    zc4 = camcoords(1, 2)
1309    iazVisibilityTest
1310    If visible > 0 Then
1311      GoTo wedge_surface4
1312    End If
1313    xw3 = cubeWorld(1, 0)
1314    yw3 = cubeWorld(1, 1)
1315    zw3 = cubeWorld(1, 2)
1316    xw2 = cubeWorld(2, 0)
1317    yw2 = cubeWorld(2, 1)
1318    zw2 = cubeWorld(2, 2)
1319    xw1 = cubeWorld(0, 0)
1320    yw1 = cubeWorld(0, 1)
1321    zw1 = cubeWorld(0, 2)
1322    gazDrawFacet
1323    If Discard = True Or Clipped = True Then
1324      GoTo WDISCARD_SOLID
1325    End If
1326  wedge_surface4:
1327    xc1 = camcoords(3, 0)
1328    yc1 = camcoords(3, 1)
1329    zc1 = camcoords(3, 2)
1330    xc2 = camcoords(1, 0)
1331    yc2 = camcoords(1, 1)
1332    zc2 = camcoords(1, 2)
1333    xc3 = camcoords(0, 0)
1334    yc3 = camcoords(0, 1)
1335    zc3 = camcoords(0, 2)
1336    xc4 = camcoords(5, 0)
1337    yc4 = camcoords(5, 1)
1338    zc4 = camcoords(5, 2)
1339    iazVisibilityTest
1340    If visible > 0 Then
1341      GoTo wedge_surfaces_done
1342    End If
1343    xw3 = cubeWorld(3, 0)
1344    yw3 = cubeWorld(3, 1)
```

```
1345    zw3 = cubeWorld(3, 2)
1346    xw2 = cubeWorld(1, 0)
1347    yw2 = cubeWorld(1, 1)
1348    zw2 = cubeWorld(1, 2)
1349    xw1 = cubeWorld(0, 0)
1350    yw1 = cubeWorld(0, 1)
1351    zw1 = cubeWorld(0, 2)
1352    gazDrawFacet
1353    If Discard = True Or Clipped = True Then
1354      GoTo WDISCARD_SOLID
1355    End If
1356  wedge_surfaces_done:
1357  If TestOnly = True Then            'if just finished first pass...
1358    TestOnly = False                        'reset token and...
1359    GoTo WEDGE_SECOND_PASS               'loop back for second pass
1360  End If
1361  WDISCARD_SOLID:    'jump to here If facet discarded on first pass
1362  End Sub                      'fall through to here after second pass
1363
1364  '----------------------------------------------------------------
1365  '                  Calculate coords for wedge
1366  '----------------------------------------------------------------
1367  Sub lzGetWedgeCoords ()                   'called by kzDrawWedge()
1368    Dim t As Integer
1369    Dim negx As Double, negy As Double, negz As Double
1370  negx = (-1) * cursorx
1371  negy = (-1) * cursory
1372  negz = (-1) * cursorz
1373  cubeObj(0, 0) = cursorx
1374  cubeObj(0, 1) = negy
1375  cubeObj(0, 2) = cursorz
1376  cubeObj(1, 0) = 0
1377  cubeObj(1, 1) = cursory
1378  cubeObj(1, 2) = cursorz
1379  cubeObj(2, 0) = negx
1380  cubeObj(2, 1) = negy
1381  cubeObj(2, 2) = cursorz
1382  cubeObj(3, 0) = 0
1383  cubeObj(3, 1) = cursory
1384  cubeObj(3, 2) = negz
1385  cubeObj(4, 0) = negx
1386  cubeObj(4, 1) = negy
1387  cubeObj(4, 2) = negz
1388  cubeObj(5, 0) = cursorx
1389  cubeObj(5, 1) = negy
1390  cubeObj(5, 2) = negz
1391  For t = 0 To 5 Step 1
1392    x = cubeObj(t, 0)
1393    y = cubeObj(t, 1)
1394    z = cubeObj(t, 2)
1395    If bAssembly = True Then
1396      azGetAssemblyCoords
1397    End If
1398    fdzGetWorldCoords
1399    cubeWorld(t, 0) = x
1400    cubeWorld(t, 1) = y
1401    cubeWorld(t, 2) = z
1402    fezGetCameraCoords
```

```
1403    camcoords(t, 0) = x
1404    camcoords(t, 1) = y
1405    camcoords(t, 2) = z
1406  Next t
1407  End Sub
1408
1409  '----------------------------------------------------------------
1410  '                    Draw a 3D hemisphere
1411  '----------------------------------------------------------------
1412  Sub mzDrawHemisphere ()           'uses cursorx as radius of sphere
1413  If bInitialized = False Then
1414    MsgBox "mzDrawHemisphere( ) reports that the 3D library is not
              initialized.", MB_OK, "SHAPES3D.BAS error"
1415    Exit Sub
1416  End If
1417  TestOnly = False                      'do not discard entire solid
1418  SphereRadius = cursorx                    'grab radius of sphere
1419  If SphereRadius < zMIN_RADIUS Then
1420    Exit Sub                               'if radius too small
1421  End If
1422  CapHeight = z10_DEGREES               'set height of facets for cap
1423  If SphereRadius >= 25 Then    'if large radius, use smaller facets
1424    NumStrips = 8                             'num of strips
1425    NumFacets = 36                       'num of facets per strip
1426    FacetWidth = z10_DEGREES                 'width of facets
1427    StripHeight = z10_DEGREES               'height of facets
1428    If bUsePalette = True Then           'if using 256-color mode...
1429      NumStrips = 16            'increase resolution of the rendering
1430      NumFacets = 36
1431      FacetWidth = z10_DEGREES
1432      StripHeight = z05_DEGREES
1433    End If
1434  ElseIf SphereRadius < 25 Then    'smaller radius, larger facets
1435    NumStrips = 4                             'num of strips
1436    NumFacets = 18                       'num of facets per strip
1437    FacetWidth = z20_DEGREES                  'width of facets
1438    StripHeight = z20_DEGREES                'height of facets
1439  End If
1440  '--------------- draw flat cap of hemisphere -----------------
1441  VertAngle = z90_DEGREES                'set vertical angle
1442  HorizAngle = z00_DEGREES               'set horiz angle
1443  For Facet = 1 To NumFacets Step 1         'for each facet...
1444  ' ---------------- calculate first vertex ---------------------
1445    x = 0
1446    y = 0
1447    z = 0
1448    If bAssembly = True Then
1449      azGetAssemblyCoords
1450    End If
1451    fdzGetWorldCoords
1452    fezGetCameraCoords
1453    xc1 = x
1454    yc1 = y
1455    zc1 = z
1456  ' ---------------- calculate second vertex ----------------------
1457    PrevHoriz = HorizAngle
```

```
1458    HorizAngle = HorizAngle + FacetWidth
1459    dzGetSphereShape
1460    x = SphereX
1461    y = SphereY
1462    z = SphereZ
1463    If bAssembly = True Then
1464      azGetAssemblyCoords
1465    End If
1466    fdzGetWorldCoords
1467    xw3 = x
1468    yw3 = y
1469    zw3 = z
1470    fezGetCameraCoords
1471    xc2 = x
1472    yc2 = y
1473    zc2 = z
1474 ' ---------------- calculate third vertex ----------------------
1475    HorizAngle = PrevHoriz
1476    dzGetSphereShape
1477    x = SphereX
1478    y = SphereY
1479    z = SphereZ
1480    If bAssembly = True Then
1481      azGetAssemblyCoords
1482    End If
1483    fdzGetWorldCoords
1484    xw2 = x
1485    yw2 = y
1486    zw2 = z
1487    fezGetCameraCoords
1488    xc3 = x
1489    yc3 = y
1490    zc3 = z
1491 ' ---------------- calculate fourth vertex ------------------------
1492    x = 0
1493    y = 0
1494    z = 0
1495    If bAssembly = True Then
1496      azGetAssemblyCoords
1497    End If
1498    fdzGetWorldCoords
1499    xw1 = x
1500    yw1 = y
1501    zw1 = z
1502    fezGetCameraCoords
1503    xc4 = x
1504    yc4 = y
1505    zc4 = z
1506 ' ----------- test visibility and render the facet --------------
1507    iazVisibilityTest
1508    If visible <= 0 Then
1509      gazDrawFacet
1510    End If
1511 ' --------------- reset to start of next facet ------------------
1512    HorizAngle = HorizAngle + FacetWidth
1513 Next Facet                              'loop back to do next facet
1514 '------------------ draw body of hemisphere ----------------------
1515 VertAngle = z90_DEGREES                      'reset vertical angle
```

B-2 Continued.

```
1516  HorizAngle = z00_DEGREES                    'reset horiz angle
1517  For Strip = 1 To NumStrips Step 1           'for each strip...
1518    For Facet = 1 To NumFacets Step 1         'for each facet...
1519  '   --------------- calculate first vertex ------------------------
1520      dzGetSphereShape
1521      x = SphereX
1522      y = SphereY
1523      z = SphereZ
1524      If bAssembly = True Then
1525        azGetAssemblyCoords
1526      End If
1527      fdzGetWorldCoords
1528      xw3 = x
1529      yw3 = y
1530      zw3 = z
1531      fezGetCameraCoords
1532      xc1 = x
1533      yc1 = y
1534      zc1 = z
1535  '   --------------- calculate second vertex --------------------
1536      PrevHoriz = HorizAngle
1537      HorizAngle = HorizAngle + FacetWidth
1538      dzGetSphereShape
1539      x = SphereX
1540      y = SphereY
1541      z = SphereZ
1542      If bAssembly = True Then
1543        azGetAssemblyCoords
1544      End If
1545      fdzGetWorldCoords
1546      xw2 = x
1547      yw2 = y
1548      zw2 = z
1549      fezGetCameraCoords
1550      xc2 = x
1551      yc2 = y
1552      zc2 = z
1553  '   --------------- calculate third vertex ------------------------
1554      PrevVert = VertAngle
1555      VertAngle = VertAngle + StripHeight
1556      dzGetSphereShape
1557      x = SphereX
1558      y = SphereY
1559      z = SphereZ
1560      If bAssembly = True Then
1561        azGetAssemblyCoords
1562      End If
1563      fdzGetWorldCoords
1564      xw1 = x
1565      yw1 = y
1566      zw1 = z
1567      fezGetCameraCoords
1568      xc3 = x
1569      yc3 = y
1570      zc3 = z
1571  '   --------------- calculate fourth vertex --------------------
```

```
1572       HorizAngle = PrevHoriz
1573       dzGetSphereShape
1574       x = SphereX
1575       y = SphereY
1576       z = SphereZ
1577       If bAssembly = True Then
1578         azGetAssemblyCoords
1579       End If
1580       fdzGetWorldCoords
1581       fezGetCameraCoords
1582       xc4 = x
1583       yc4 = y
1584       zc4 = z
1585  '    ---------- test visibility and render the facet -------------
1586       iazVisibilityTest
1587       If visible <= 0 Then
1588         gazDrawFacet
1589       End If
1590  '    -------------- reset to start of next facet -----------------
1591       HorizAngle = HorizAngle + FacetWidth
1592       VertAngle = PrevVert
1593     Next Facet                          'loop back to do next facet
1594     VertAngle = VertAngle + StripHeight        'select next strip
1595     HorizAngle = z00_DEGREES                 'reset to first facet
1596   Next Strip                              'loop back to do next strip
1597  '--------------- draw south cap of hemisphere ------------------
1598   HorizAngle = z00_DEGREES                      'reset horiz angle
1599   For Facet = 1 To NumFacets Step 1          'for each cap facet...
1600  ' --------------- calculate first vertex ----------------------
1601     dzGetSphereShape
1602     x = SphereX
1603     y = SphereY
1604     z = SphereZ
1605     If bAssembly = True Then
1606       azGetAssemblyCoords
1607     End If
1608     fdzGetWorldCoords
1609     xw3 = x
1610     yw3 = y
1611     zw3 = z
1612     fezGetCameraCoords
1613     xc1 = x
1614     yc1 = y
1615     zc1 = z
1616  ' --------------- calculate second vertex ------------------------
1617     PrevHoriz = HorizAngle
1618     HorizAngle = HorizAngle + FacetWidth
1619     dzGetSphereShape
1620     x = SphereX
1621     y = SphereY
1622     z = SphereZ
1623     If bAssembly = True Then
1624       azGetAssemblyCoords
1625     End If
1626     fdzGetWorldCoords
1627     xw2 = x
1628     yw2 = y
1629     zw2 = z
```

B-2 Continued.

```
1630    fezGetCameraCoords
1631    xc2 = x
1632    yc2 = y
1633    zc2 = z
1634 ' ---------------- calculate third vertex ----------------------
1635    PrevVert = VertAngle
1636    VertAngle = VertAngle + CapHeight
1637    dzGetSphereShape
1638    x = SphereX
1639    y = SphereY
1640    z = SphereZ
1641    If bAssembly = True Then
1642      azGetAssemblyCoords
1643    End If
1644    fdzGetWorldCoords
1645    xw1 = x
1646    yw1 = y
1647    zw1 = z
1648    fezGetCameraCoords
1649    xc3 = x
1650    yc3 = y
1651    zc3 = z
1652 ' ---------------- calculate fourth vertex ------------------------
1653    HorizAngle = PrevHoriz
1654    dzGetSphereShape
1655    x = SphereX
1656    y = SphereY
1657    z = SphereZ
1658    If bAssembly = True Then
1659      azGetAssemblyCoords
1660    End If
1661    fdzGetWorldCoords
1662    fezGetCameraCoords
1663    xc4 = x
1664    yc4 = y
1665    zc4 = z
1666 ' ----------- test visibility and render the facet --------------
1667    iazVisibilityTest
1668    If visible <= 0 Then
1669      gazDrawFacet
1670    End If
1671 ' --------------- reset to start of next facet ------------------
1672    HorizAngle = HorizAngle + FacetWidth
1673    VertAngle = PrevVert
1674 Next Facet
1675 End Sub
1676
```

B-3 Source listings for the 3D light-source toolkit, lights3d.bas. See Appendix C for applications that use this toolkit. See Appendix A for instructions on building the demos.

```
0001 '------------------------------------------------------------------
0002 '   Module of 3D deformation drivers for Windows applications
0003 '------------------------------------------------------------------
0004 'Source file:  DEFORM3D.BAS
```

```
0005  'Release version:  1.00                          Programmer:  Lee Adams
0006  'Type:  Visual Basic source file for Windows applications.
0007  'Dependencies:  ENGINE3D.BAS 3D functions.
0008  'Output and features:  Provides drivers for the ENGINE3D.BAS
0009  '  3D routines in order to render half-cylinders, deformed
0010  '  parallelepipeds, etc.
0011  'Publication: Contains material from Windcrest/McGraw-Hill book
0012  '  4225 published by TAB BOOKS Division of McGraw-Hill Inc.
0013  'License:  As purchaser of the book you are granted a royalty-
0014  '  free license to distribute executable files generated using
0015  '  this code provided you accept the conditions of the License
0016  '  Agreement and Limited Warranty described in the book and on
0017  '  the companion disk.  Government users:  This software and
0018  '  documentation are subject to restrictions set forth in The
0019  '  Rights in Technical Data and Computer Software clause at
0020  '  252.227-7013 and elsewhere.
0021  '----------------------------------------------------------------
0022  '     (c) Copyright 1988-1994 Lee Adams.  All rights reserved.
0023  '          Lee Adams(tm) is a trademark of Lee Adams.
0024  '----------------------------------------------------------------
0025  '   Declaration of variables visible throughout only this file
0026  '----------------------------------------------------------------
0027      'Note:  This module relies upon some Global variables
0028      'declared in ENGINE3D.BAS.
0029
0030  Option Explicit            'generate error if variable not declared
0031  Const z00_DEGREES = 0#                        'radian angles...
0032  Const z10_DEGREES = .17453
0033  Const z20_DEGREES = .34907
0034  Const z180_DEGREES = 3.14159
0035  Const zMIN_RADIUS = 10                        'minimum radius
0036  Const zMIN_DEFORM = 2                     'min deformed thickness
0037  Dim xExtrudeRight As Integer, xExtrudeLeft As Integer      'box...
0038  Dim yExtrudeUp As Integer, yExtrudeDown As Integer
0039  Dim VertAngle As Double, HorizAngle As Double              'angles
0040  Dim PrevVert As Double                        'scratchpad values
0041  Dim TempX As Double                           'scratchpad value
0042  Dim SinVert As Double, CosVert As Double      'sin, cos factors...
0043  Dim SinHoriz As Double, CosHoriz As Double
0044  Dim NumFacets As Integer                       'num of facets
0045  Dim Facet As Integer                          'facet loop counter
0046  Dim CylinderX As Double                'cylinder object coords...
0047  Dim CylinderY As Double, CylinderZ As Double
0048  Dim CylinderRadius As Double                  'cylinder dimensions...
0049  Dim CylinderExtrude As Double
0050  Dim FacetDimension As Double            'angular dimension of facet
0051  Dim T As Double, T2 As Double, T3 As Double 'once, squared, cubed
0052  Dim PrevT As Double                            'scratchpad
0053  Dim Pull1 As Double, Pull2 As Double    'effect of curve points...
0054  Dim Pull3 As Double, Pull4 As Double
0055  Dim CurveX1 As Double, CurveY1 As Double       'curve startpoint
0056  Dim CurveX4 As Double, CurveY4 As Double       'curve endpoint
0057  Dim CurveX2 As Double, CurveY2 As Double        'first control
0058  Dim CurveX3 As Double, CurveY3 As Double       'second control
0059  Dim SurfaceX As Double, SurfaceY As Double      'obj coords
0060  Dim SurfaceEdge1 As Double, SurfaceEdge2 As Double      'extruded
0061  Dim ParamChange As Double                      'paremeters...
0062  Dim ParamMax As Double, ParamMin As Double
```

B-3 Continued.

```
0063  Dim ControlStrength As Double           'effect of control points
0064  Dim SwapStorage As Double                   'scratchpad for swaps
0065
0066  '----------------------------------------------------------------------
0067  '                      3D deformation drivers
0068  '----------------------------------------------------------------------
0069  '              Draw a deformed parallelepiped
0070  '----------------------------------------------------------------------
0071  Sub azDrawDeformBox (ByVal xRight As Integer, ByVal xLeft As
          Integer, ByVal yUp As Integer, ByVal yDown As Integer)
0072                  'deforms the south-facing facet of a parallelepiped
0073  If bInitialized = False Then
0074    MsgBox "azDrawDeformBox( ) reports 3D library is not
          initialized.", MB_OK, "DEFORM3D.BAS error"
0075    Exit Sub
0076  End If
0077  If xRight > cursorx Then                       'inhibit ranges...
0078    Exit Sub
0079  End If
0080  If xLeft < ((-1) * cursorx) Then
0081    Exit Sub
0082  End If
0083  If xRight < (xLeft + zMIN_DEFORM) Then
0084    Exit Sub
0085  End If
0086  If yUp > cursory Then
0087    Exit Sub
0088  End If
0089  If yDown < ((-1) * cursory) Then
0090    Exit Sub
0091  End If
0092  If yUp < (yDown + zMIN_DEFORM) Then
0093    Exit Sub
0094  End If
0095  xExtrudeRight = xRight               'grab deformation parameters...
0096  xExtrudeLeft = xLeft
0097  yExtrudeUp = yUp
0098  yExtrudeDown = yDown
0099  bzGetDeformBoxCoords             'get camera coords and display coords
0100  TestOnly = True                       'reset token for first pass
0101  SECOND_PASS:                   'will loop back to here for second pass
0102  surface0:
0103    xc1 = camcoords(7, 0)
0104    yc1 = camcoords(7, 1)
0105    zc1 = camcoords(7, 2)
0106    xc2 = camcoords(0, 0)
0107    yc2 = camcoords(0, 1)
0108    zc2 = camcoords(0, 2)
0109    xc3 = camcoords(3, 0)
0110    yc3 = camcoords(3, 1)
0111    zc3 = camcoords(3, 2)
0112    xc4 = camcoords(6, 0)
0113    yc4 = camcoords(6, 1)
0114    zc4 = camcoords(6, 2)
0115    iazVisibilityTest
0116    If visible > 0 Then
```

```
0117      GoTo surface1
0118    End If
0119    xw3 = cubeWorld(7, 0)
0120    yw3 = cubeWorld(7, 1)
0121    zw3 = cubeWorld(7, 2)
0122    xw2 = cubeWorld(0, 0)
0123    yw2 = cubeWorld(0, 1)
0124    zw2 = cubeWorld(0, 2)
0125    xw1 = cubeWorld(3, 0)
0126    yw1 = cubeWorld(3, 1)
0127    zw1 = cubeWorld(3, 2)
0128    gazDrawFacet
0129    If Discard = True Or Clipped = True Then
0130      GoTo DISCARD_SOLID
0131    End If
0132  surface1:
0133    xc1 = camcoords(6, 0)
0134    yc1 = camcoords(6, 1)
0135    zc1 = camcoords(6, 2)
0136    xc2 = camcoords(5, 0)
0137    yc2 = camcoords(5, 1)
0138    zc2 = camcoords(5, 2)
0139    xc3 = camcoords(4, 0)
0140    yc3 = camcoords(4, 1)
0141    zc3 = camcoords(4, 2)
0142    xc4 = camcoords(7, 0)
0143    yc4 = camcoords(7, 1)
0144    zc4 = camcoords(7, 2)
0145    iazVisibilityTest
0146    If visible > 0 Then
0147      GoTo surface2
0148    End If
0149    xw3 = cubeWorld(6, 0)
0150    yw3 = cubeWorld(6, 1)
0151    zw3 = cubeWorld(6, 2)
0152    xw2 = cubeWorld(5, 0)
0153    yw2 = cubeWorld(5, 1)
0154    zw2 = cubeWorld(5, 2)
0155    xw1 = cubeWorld(4, 0)
0156    yw1 = cubeWorld(4, 1)
0157    zw1 = cubeWorld(4, 2)
0158    gazDrawFacet
0159    If Discard = True Or Clipped = True Then
0160      GoTo DISCARD_SOLID
0161    End If
0162  surface2:
0163    xc1 = camcoords(3, 0)
0164    yc1 = camcoords(3, 1)
0165    zc1 = camcoords(3, 2)
0166    xc2 = camcoords(2, 0)
0167    yc2 = camcoords(2, 1)
0168    zc2 = camcoords(2, 2)
0169    xc3 = camcoords(5, 0)
0170    yc3 = camcoords(5, 1)
0171    zc3 = camcoords(5, 2)
0172    xc4 = camcoords(6, 0)
0173    yc4 = camcoords(6, 1)
0174    zc4 = camcoords(6, 2)
```

```
0175    iazVisibilityTest
0176    If visible > 0 Then
0177      GoTo surface3
0178    End If
0179    xw3 = cubeWorld(3, 0)
0180    yw3 = cubeWorld(3, 1)
0181    zw3 = cubeWorld(3, 2)
0182    xw2 = cubeWorld(2, 0)
0183    yw2 = cubeWorld(2, 1)
0184    zw2 = cubeWorld(2, 2)
0185    xw1 = cubeWorld(5, 0)
0186    yw1 = cubeWorld(5, 1)
0187    zw1 = cubeWorld(5, 2)
0188    gazDrawFacet
0189    If Discard = True Or Clipped = True Then
0190      GoTo DISCARD_SOLID
0191    End If
0192  surface3:
0193    xc1 = camcoords(0, 0)
0194    yc1 = camcoords(0, 1)
0195    zc1 = camcoords(0, 2)
0196    xc2 = camcoords(1, 0)
0197    yc2 = camcoords(1, 1)
0198    zc2 = camcoords(1, 2)
0199    xc3 = camcoords(2, 0)
0200    yc3 = camcoords(2, 1)
0201    zc3 = camcoords(2, 2)
0202    xc4 = camcoords(3, 0)
0203    yc4 = camcoords(3, 1)
0204    zc4 = camcoords(3, 2)
0205    iazVisibilityTest
0206    If visible > 0 Then
0207      GoTo surface4
0208    End If
0209    xw3 = cubeWorld(0, 0)
0210    yw3 = cubeWorld(0, 1)
0211    zw3 = cubeWorld(0, 2)
0212    xw2 = cubeWorld(1, 0)
0213    yw2 = cubeWorld(1, 1)
0214    zw2 = cubeWorld(1, 2)
0215    xw1 = cubeWorld(2, 0)
0216    yw1 = cubeWorld(2, 1)
0217    zw1 = cubeWorld(2, 2)
0218    gazDrawFacet
0219    If Discard = True Or Clipped = True Then
0220      GoTo DISCARD_SOLID
0221    End If
0222  surface4:
0223    xc1 = camcoords(7, 0)
0224    yc1 = camcoords(7, 1)
0225    zc1 = camcoords(7, 2)
0226    xc2 = camcoords(4, 0)
0227    yc2 = camcoords(4, 1)
0228    zc2 = camcoords(4, 2)
0229    xc3 = camcoords(1, 0)
0230    yc3 = camcoords(1, 1)
```

```
0231    zc3 = camcoords(1, 2)
0232    xc4 = camcoords(0, 0)
0233    yc4 = camcoords(0, 1)
0234    zc4 = camcoords(0, 2)
0235    iazVisibilityTest
0236    If visible > 0 Then
0237       GoTo surface5
0238    End If
0239    xw3 = cubeWorld(7, 0)
0240    yw3 = cubeWorld(7, 1)
0241    zw3 = cubeWorld(7, 2)
0242    xw2 = cubeWorld(4, 0)
0243    yw2 = cubeWorld(4, 1)
0244    zw2 = cubeWorld(4, 2)
0245    xw1 = cubeWorld(1, 0)
0246    yw1 = cubeWorld(1, 1)
0247    zw1 = cubeWorld(1, 2)
0248    gazDrawFacet
0249    If Discard = True Or Clipped = True Then
0250       GoTo DISCARD_SOLID
0251    End If
0252  surface5:
0253    xc1 = camcoords(1, 0)
0254    yc1 = camcoords(1, 1)
0255    zc1 = camcoords(1, 2)
0256    xc2 = camcoords(4, 0)
0257    yc2 = camcoords(4, 1)
0258    zc2 = camcoords(4, 2)
0259    xc3 = camcoords(5, 0)
0260    yc3 = camcoords(5, 1)
0261    zc3 = camcoords(5, 2)
0262    xc4 = camcoords(2, 0)
0263    yc4 = camcoords(2, 1)
0264    zc4 = camcoords(2, 2)
0265    iazVisibilityTest
0266    If visible > 0 Then
0267       GoTo surfaces_done
0268    End If
0269    xw3 = cubeWorld(1, 0)
0270    yw3 = cubeWorld(1, 1)
0271    zw3 = cubeWorld(1, 2)
0272    xw2 = cubeWorld(4, 0)
0273    yw2 = cubeWorld(4, 1)
0274    zw2 = cubeWorld(4, 2)
0275    xw1 = cubeWorld(5, 0)
0276    yw1 = cubeWorld(5, 1)
0277    zw1 = cubeWorld(5, 2)
0278    gazDrawFacet
0279    If Discard = True Or Clipped = True Then
0280       GoTo DISCARD_SOLID
0281    End If
0282  surfaces_done:
0283  If TestOnly = True Then          'if just finished first pass...
0284     TestOnly = False                       'reset token and...
0285     GoTo SECOND_PASS                 'loop back for second pass
0286  End If
0287  DISCARD_SOLID:        'jump to here if facet discarded on first pass
0288  End Sub                      'fall through to here after second pass
```

```
0289
0290  '-----------------------------------------------------------------
0291  '            Calculate coords for deformed parallelepiped
0292  '-----------------------------------------------------------------
0293  Sub bzGetDeformBoxCoords ()              'called by azDrawDeformBox()
0294    Dim T As Integer
0295    Dim negx As Double, negy As Double, negz As Double
0296  negx = (-1) * cursorx
0297  negy = (-1) * cursory
0298  negz = (-1) * cursorz
0299  cubeObj(0, 0) = xExtrudeRight
0300  cubeObj(0, 1) = yExtrudeDown
0301  cubeObj(0, 2) = cursorz
0302  cubeObj(1, 0) = xExtrudeRight
0303  cubeObj(1, 1) = yExtrudeUp
0304  cubeObj(1, 2) = cursorz
0305  cubeObj(2, 0) = xExtrudeLeft
0306  cubeObj(2, 1) = yExtrudeUp
0307  cubeObj(2, 2) = cursorz
0308  cubeObj(3, 0) = xExtrudeLeft
0309  cubeObj(3, 1) = yExtrudeDown
0310  cubeObj(3, 2) = cursorz
0311  cubeObj(4, 0) = cursorx
0312  cubeObj(4, 1) = cursory
0313  cubeObj(4, 2) = negz
0314  cubeObj(5, 0) = negx
0315  cubeObj(5, 1) = cursory
0316  cubeObj(5, 2) = negz
0317  cubeObj(6, 0) = negx
0318  cubeObj(6, 1) = negy
0319  cubeObj(6, 2) = negz
0320  cubeObj(7, 0) = cursorx
0321  cubeObj(7, 1) = negy
0322  cubeObj(7, 2) = negz
0323  For T = 0 To 7 Step 1
0324    x = cubeObj(T, 0)
0325    y = cubeObj(T, 1)
0326    z = cubeObj(T, 2)
0327    If bAssembly = True Then
0328      azGetAssemblyCoords
0329    End If
0330    fdzGetWorldCoords
0331    cubeWorld(T, 0) = x
0332    cubeWorld(T, 1) = y
0333    cubeWorld(T, 2) = z
0334    fezGetCameraCoords
0335    camcoords(T, 0) = x
0336    camcoords(T, 1) = y
0337    camcoords(T, 2) = z
0338  Next T
0339  End Sub
0340
0341  '-----------------------------------------------------------------
0342  '                    Draw a 3D half-cylinder
0343  '-----------------------------------------------------------------
0344  Sub czDrawHalfCylinder ()                    'uses cursorx, cursorz
```

```
0345  If bInitialized = False Then
0346    MsgBox "czDrawHalfCylinder( ) reports 3D library is not
           initialized.", MB_OK, "DEFORM3D.BAS error"
0347    Exit Sub
0348  End If
0349  TestOnly = False                        'do not discard entire solid
0350  CylinderRadius = cursorx                          'grab radius
0351  CylinderExtrude = cursorz                         'grab extrusion
0352  If CylinderRadius < zMIN_RADIUS Then        'if radius too small
0353    Exit Sub
0354  End If
0355  VertAngle = z00_DEGREES                          'vertical angle
0356  HorizAngle = z00_DEGREES                            'horiz angle
0357  If CylinderRadius >= 25 Then   'large radius, use smaller facets...
0358    NumFacets = 18                              'num of facets
0359    FacetDimension = z10_DEGREES                'width of facets
0360  ElseIf (CylinderRadius < 25) Then  'smaller radius, larger facets
0361    NumFacets = 9
0362    FacetDimension = z20_DEGREES
0363  End If
0364  '--------------- draw body of half-cylinder -------------------
0365  For Facet = 1 To NumFacets Step 1                 'for each facet...
0366    '------------ calculate first vertex ---------
0367    dzGetHalfCylShape
0368    x = CylinderX
0369    y = CylinderY
0370    z = CylinderZ
0371    If bAssembly = True Then
0372      azGetAssemblyCoords
0373    End If
0374    fdzGetWorldCoords
0375    xw3 = x
0376    yw3 = y
0377    zw3 = z
0378    fezGetCameraCoords
0379    xc1 = x
0380    yc1 = y
0381    zc1 = z
0382    '---------------- calculate second vertex -------------------
0383    PrevVert = VertAngle
0384    VertAngle = VertAngle + FacetDimension
0385    dzGetHalfCylShape
0386    x = CylinderX
0387    y = CylinderY
0388    z = CylinderZ
0389    If bAssembly = True Then
0390      azGetAssemblyCoords
0391    End If
0392    fdzGetWorldCoords
0393    xw2 = x
0394    yw2 = y
0395    zw2 = z
0396    fezGetCameraCoords
0397    xc2 = x
0398    yc2 = y
0399    zc2 = z
0400    '------------------ calculate third vertex -------------------
0401    dzGetHalfCylShape
```

```
0402    x = CylinderX
0403    y = CylinderY
0404    z = -CylinderZ
0405    If bAssembly = True Then
0406      azGetAssemblyCoords
0407    End If
0408    fdzGetWorldCoords
0409    xw1 = x
0410    yw1 = y
0411    zw1 = z
0412    fezGetCameraCoords
0413    xc3 = x
0414    yc3 = y
0415    zc3 = z
0416    '----------------calculate fourth vertex --------------------
0417    VertAngle = PrevVert
0418    dzGetHalfCylShape
0419    x = CylinderX
0420    y = CylinderY
0421    z = -CylinderZ
0422    If bAssembly = True Then
0423      azGetAssemblyCoords
0424    End If
0425    fdzGetWorldCoords
0426    fezGetCameraCoords
0427    xc4 = x
0428    yc4 = y
0429    zc4 = z
0430    '----------------test visibility and render the facet ---------
0431    iazVisibilityTest
0432    If visible <= 0 Then
0433      gazDrawFacet
0434    End If
0435    VertAngle = VertAngle + FacetDimension
0436  Next Facet
0437  '------------------ draw ends of half-cylinder -------------------
0438  VertAngle = z00_DEGREES                      'reset vertical angle
0439  For Facet = 1 To NumFacets Step 1     'for each facet of near end...
0440    '-------------------- calculate first vertex -------------------
0441    x = 0
0442    y = 0
0443    z = CylinderZ
0444    If bAssembly = True Then
0445      azGetAssemblyCoords
0446    End If
0447    fdzGetWorldCoords
0448    xw3 = x
0449    yw3 = y
0450    zw3 = z
0451    fezGetCameraCoords
0452    xc1 = x
0453    yc1 = y
0454    zc1 = z
0455    '-------------------- calculate second vertex -----------------
0456    PrevVert = VertAngle
0457    VertAngle = VertAngle + FacetDimension
```

```
0458      dzGetHalfCylShape
0459      x = CylinderX
0460      y = CylinderY
0461      z = CylinderZ
0462      If bAssembly = True Then
0463        azGetAssemblyCoords
0464      End If
0465      fdzGetWorldCoords
0466      xw2 = x
0467      yw2 = y
0468      zw2 = z
0469      fezGetCameraCoords
0470      xc2 = x
0471      yc2 = y
0472      zc2 = z
0473      '--------------------- calculate third vertex -----------------
0474      VertAngle = PrevVert
0475      dzGetHalfCylShape
0476      x = CylinderX
0477      y = CylinderY
0478      z = CylinderZ
0479      If bAssembly = True Then
0480        azGetAssemblyCoords
0481      End If
0482      fdzGetWorldCoords
0483      xw1 = x
0484      yw1 = y
0485      zw1 = z
0486      fezGetCameraCoords
0487      xc3 = x
0488      yc3 = y
0489      zc3 = z
0490      '--------------------- calculate fourth vertex ---------------
0491      x = 0
0492      y = 0
0493      z = CylinderZ
0494      If bAssembly = True Then
0495        azGetAssemblyCoords
0496      End If
0497      fdzGetWorldCoords
0498      fezGetCameraCoords
0499      xc4 = x
0500      yc4 = y
0501      zc4 = z
0502      '------------- test visibility and render the facet -----------
0503      iazVisibilityTest
0504      If visible <= 0 Then
0505        gazDrawFacet
0506      End If
0507      VertAngle = VertAngle + FacetDimension
0508    Next Facet
0509    VertAngle = z00_DEGREES                      'reset vertical angle
0510    For Facet = 1 To NumFacets Step 1    'for each facet of far end...
0511      '--------------------- calculate first vertex -----------------
0512      x = 0
0513      y = 0
0514      z = -CylinderZ
0515      If bAssembly = True Then
```

```
0516        azGetAssemblyCoords
0517     End If
0518     fdzGetWorldCoords
0519     xw3 = x
0520     yw3 = y
0521     zw3 = z
0522     fezGetCameraCoords
0523     xc1 = x
0524     yc1 = y
0525     zc1 = z
0526     '---------------- calculate second vertex -------------
0527     dzGetHalfCylShape
0528     x = CylinderX
0529     y = CylinderY
0530     z = -CylinderZ
0531     If bAssembly = True Then
0532        azGetAssemblyCoords
0533     End If
0534     fdzGetWorldCoords
0535     xw2 = x
0536     yw2 = y
0537     zw2 = z
0538     fezGetCameraCoords
0539     xc2 = x
0540     yc2 = y
0541     zc2 = z
0542     '---------------- calculate third vertex --------------
0543     VertAngle = VertAngle + FacetDimension
0544     dzGetHalfCylShape
0545     x = CylinderX
0546     y = CylinderY
0547     z = -CylinderZ
0548     If bAssembly = True Then
0549        azGetAssemblyCoords
0550     End If
0551     fdzGetWorldCoords
0552     xw1 = x
0553     yw1 = y
0554     zw1 = z
0555     fezGetCameraCoords
0556     xc3 = x
0557     yc3 = y
0558     zc3 = z
0559     '---------------- calculate fourth vertex -------------
0560     x = 0
0561     y = 0
0562     z = -CylinderZ
0563     If bAssembly = True Then
0564        azGetAssemblyCoords
0565     End If
0566     fdzGetWorldCoords
0567     fezGetCameraCoords
0568     xc4 = x
0569     yc4 = y
0570     zc4 = z
0571     '--------- test visibility and render the facet -------
```

```
0572    iazVisibilityTest
0573    If visible <= 0 Then
0574      gazDrawFacet
0575    End If
0576  Next Facet
0577  '----------------- draw flat side of half-cylinder --------------
0578  VertAngle = z00_DEGREES                              'reset angle
0579  '-------------------- calculate first vertex -------------------
0580  dzGetHalfCylShape
0581  x = CylinderX
0582  y = CylinderY
0583  z = CylinderZ
0584  If bAssembly = True Then
0585    azGetAssemblyCoords
0586  End If
0587  fdzGetWorldCoords
0588  xw3 = x
0589  yw3 = y
0590  zw3 = z
0591  fezGetCameraCoords
0592  xc1 = x
0593  yc1 = y
0594  zc1 = z
0595  '-------------------- calculate second vertex -----------------
0596  x = CylinderX
0597  y = CylinderY
0598  z = -CylinderZ
0599  If bAssembly = True Then
0600    azGetAssemblyCoords
0601  End If
0602  fdzGetWorldCoords
0603  xw2 = x
0604  yw2 = y
0605  zw2 = z
0606  fezGetCameraCoords
0607  xc2 = x
0608  yc2 = y
0609  zc2 = z
0610  '-------------------- calculate third vertex ------------------
0611  VertAngle = z180_DEGREES                             'reset angle
0612  dzGetHalfCylShape
0613  x = CylinderX
0614  y = CylinderY
0615  z = -CylinderZ
0616  If bAssembly = True Then
0617    azGetAssemblyCoords
0618  End If
0619  fdzGetWorldCoords
0620  xw1 = x
0621  yw1 = y
0622  zw1 = z
0623  fezGetCameraCoords
0624  xc3 = x
0625  yc3 = y
0626  zc3 = z
0627  '-------------------- calculate fourth vertex -----------------
0628  x = CylinderX
0629  y = CylinderY
```

B-3 Continued.

```
0630  z = CylinderZ
0631  If bAssembly = True Then
0632    azGetAssemblyCoords
0633  End If
0634  fdzGetWorldCoords
0635  fezGetCameraCoords
0636  xc4 = x
0637  yc4 = y
0638  zc4 = z
0639  '-------------- test visibility and render the facet -----------
0640  iazVisibilityTest
0641  If visible <= 0 Then
0642    gazDrawFacet
0643  End If
0644  End Sub
0645
0646  '----------------------------------------------------------------
0647  '   Calculate obj coords for pt on surface of half-cylinder
0648  '----------------------------------------------------------------
0649  Sub dzGetHalfCylShape ()          'called by czDrawHalfCylinder()
0650  SinHoriz = Sin(HorizAngle)
0651  CosHoriz = Cos(HorizAngle)
0652  SinVert = Sin(VertAngle)
0653  CosVert = Cos(VertAngle)
0654  TempX = SinVert * CylinderRadius
0655  CylinderY = CosVert * CylinderRadius
0656  CylinderX = CosHoriz * TempX
0657  CylinderZ = CylinderExtrude
0658  End Sub
0659
0660  '----------------------------------------------------------------
0661  '                    Draw a 3D bulged surface
0662  '----------------------------------------------------------------
0663  Sub ezDrawBulge ()              'cursorx, cursory, and cursorz
0664  If bInitialized = False Then
0665    MsgBox "ezDrawBulge( ) reports 3D library is not initialized.",
           MB_OK, "DEFORM3D.BAS error"
0666    Exit Sub
0667  End If
0668  ParamChange = .05                        'parametric increment
0669  ParamMax = 1#                       'maximum parametric value
0670  ParamMin = 0#                       'minimum parametric value
0671  ControlStrength = .5             'influence of control points
0672  If bUsePalette = True Then           'if using 256-color mode...
0673    ParamChange = .025         'increase resolution of the rendering
0674  End If
0675  '------------- configure the curved edge of the surface ---------
0676  CurveX1 = (-1) * cursorx
0677  CurveX4 = cursorx
0678  CurveY1 = 0#
0679  CurveY4 = 0#
0680  '-------------- configure the width of the surface -------------
0681  SurfaceEdge1 = (-1) * cursorz
0682  SurfaceEdge2 = cursorz
0683  '------------- configure the magnitude of the curve ------------
0684  CurveY2 = cursory
```

```
0685  CurveY3 = cursory
0686  CurveX2 = ControlStrength * CurveX1
0687  CurveX3 = ControlStrength * CurveX4
0688  '------------------ render the curved surface -----------------
0689  For T = ParamMin To ParamMax Step ParamChange
0690    T2 = T * T
0691    T3 = T * T * T
0692    '-------------------- calculate first vertex -----------------
0693    fzGetBulgeShape
0694    x = SurfaceX
0695    y = SurfaceY
0696    z = SurfaceEdge1
0697    If bAssembly = True Then
0698      azGetAssemblyCoords
0699    End If
0700    fdzGetWorldCoords
0701    xw3 = x
0702    yw3 = y
0703    zw3 = z
0704    fezGetCameraCoords
0705    xc1 = x
0706    yc1 = y
0707    zc1 = z
0708    '-------------------- calculate second vertex ---------------
0709    x = SurfaceX
0710    y = SurfaceY
0711    z = SurfaceEdge2
0712    If bAssembly = True Then
0713      azGetAssemblyCoords
0714    End If
0715    fdzGetWorldCoords
0716    xw2 = x
0717    yw2 = y
0718    zw2 = z
0719    fezGetCameraCoords
0720    xc2 = x
0721    yc2 = y
0722    zc2 = z
0723    '-------------------- calculate third vertex -----------------
0724    PrevT = T                          'remember position on curve
0725    T = T + ParamChange               'move to next position on curve...
0726    T2 = T * T
0727    T3 = T * T * T
0728    fzGetBulgeShape
0729    x = SurfaceX
0730    y = SurfaceY
0731    z = SurfaceEdge2
0732    If bAssembly = True Then
0733      azGetAssemblyCoords
0734    End If
0735    fdzGetWorldCoords
0736    xw1 = x
0737    yw1 = y
0738    zw1 = z
0739    fezGetCameraCoords
0740    xc3 = x
0741    yc3 = y
0742    zc3 = z
```

```
0743    '------------------- calculate fourth vertex ---------------
0744    x = SurfaceX
0745    y = SurfaceY
0746    z = SurfaceEdge1
0747    If bAssembly = True Then
0748      azGetAssemblyCoords
0749    End If
0750    fdzGetWorldCoords
0751    fezGetCameraCoords
0752    xc4 = x
0753    yc4 = y
0754    zc4 = z
0755    '-------------- test visibility and render the lamina -------
0756    iazVisibilityTest
0757    If visible <= 0 Then
0758      gazDrawFacet
0759    Else
0760      SwapStorage = xw1
0761      xw1 = xw3
0762      xw3 = SwapStorage
0763      SwapStorage = yw1
0764      yw1 = yw3
0765      yw3 = SwapStorage
0766      SwapStorage = zw1
0767      zw1 = zw3
0768      zw3 = SwapStorage
0769      SwapStorage = xc1
0770      xc1 = xc3
0771      xc3 = SwapStorage
0772      SwapStorage = yc1
0773      yc1 = yc3
0774      yc3 = SwapStorage
0775      SwapStorage = zc1
0776      zc1 = zc3
0777      zc3 = SwapStorage
0778      gazDrawFacet
0779    End If
0780    T = PrevT
0781  Next T                         'loop back and render next facet
0782  End Sub
0783
0784  '---------------------------------------------------------------
0785  '        Calculate obj coords for pt on bulged surface
0786  '---------------------------------------------------------------
0787  Sub fzGetBulgeShape ()                  'called by ezDrawBulge()
0788  Pull1 = CurveX1 * (-T3 + 3 * T2 - 3 * T + 1)
0789  Pull2 = CurveX2 * (3 * T3 - 6 * T2 + 3 * T)
0790  Pull3 = CurveX3 * (-3 * T3 + 3 * T2)
0791  Pull4 = CurveX4 * T3
0792  SurfaceX = Pull1 + Pull2 + Pull3 + Pull4
0793  Pull1 = CurveY1 * (-T3 + 3 * T2 - 3 * T + 1)
0794  Pull2 = CurveY2 * (3 * T3 - 6 * T2 + 3 * T)
0795  Pull3 = CurveY3 * (-3 * T3 + 3 * T2)
0796  Pull4 = CurveY4 * T3
0797  SurfaceY = Pull1 + Pull2 + Pull3 + Pull4
0798  End Sub
0799
```

B-4 Source listings for the 3D deformation toolkit, deform3d.bas. See Appendix C for applications that use this toolkit. See Appendix A for instructions on building the demos.

```
0001  '-----------------------------------------------------------------
0002  '    Module of 3D lighting drivers for Windows applications
0003  '-----------------------------------------------------------------
0004  'Source file:  LIGHTS3D.BAS
0005  'Release version:  1.00                     Programmer:  Lee Adams
0006  'Type:  Visual Basic source file for Windows applications.
0007  'Dependencies:  ENGINE3D.BAS functions.
0008  'Output and features:  Provides drivers for the ENGINE3D.BAS
0009  '  and SHAPES3D.BAS routines reposition the light-source.
0010  'Publication: Contains material from Windcrest/McGraw-Hill book
0011  '  4225 published by TAB BOOKS Division of McGraw-Hill Inc.
0012  'License:  As purchaser of the book you are granted a royalty-
0013  '  free license to distribute executable files generated using
0014  '  this code provided you accept the conditions of the License
0015  '  Agreement and Limited Warranty described in the book and on
0016  '  the companion disk.  Government users:  This software and
0017  '  documentation are subject to restrictions set forth in The
0018  '  Rights in Technical Data and Computer Software clause at
0019  '  252.227-7013 and elsewhere.
0020  '-----------------------------------------------------------------
0021  '    (c) Copyright 1991-1993 Lee Adams.  All rights reserved.
0022  '          Lee Adams(tm) is a trademark of Lee Adams.
0023  '-----------------------------------------------------------------
0024     'Note:  This module relies upon some Global variables
0025     'declared in ENGINE3D.BAS.
0026
0027  Option Explicit            'generate error if variable not declared
0028  Const zRADIAN = .017453                  'converts degrees to radians
0029
0030  '-----------------------------------------------------------------
0031  '                     3D lighting drivers
0032  '-----------------------------------------------------------------
0033  '                  Reposition the light-source
0034  '-----------------------------------------------------------------
0035  Sub zSetLightPosition (ByVal Elevation As Integer, ByVal Heading
         As Integer)
0036                  'this function is called by interactive main module
0037    Dim ElevationRads As Double, HeadingRads As Double
0038    Dim MaxRemainder As Double
0039
0040  '-------------- ensure the 3D library is initialized -----------
0041  If bInitialized = False Then
0042    MsgBox "zSetLightPosition( ) reports 3D library is not
           initialized.", MB_OK, "LIGHTS3D.BAS error"
00043    Exit Sub
0044  End If
0045  '-------------- trap illegal light-source parameters -----------
0046  If Elevation > 90 Or Elevation < 0 Then
0047    Exit Sub
0048  End If
0049  If Heading > 360 Or Heading < 0 Then
0050    Exit Sub
0051  End If
0052  '------------- calculate new components of unit vector ---------
0053  ' NOTE: This algorithm is from my Visualization Graphics in C,
```

B-3 Continued.

```
0054 ' (Windcrest/McGraw-Hill book #3487) page 236, published in 1991,
0055 ' ISBN 0-8306-3487-8.                        - L.A.
0056 ElevationRads = Elevation * zRADIAN
0057 -HeadingRads = Heading * zRADIAN
0058 yLight = Sin(ElevationRads)
0059 MaxRemainder = Sqr(1 - (yLight * yLight))
0060 xLight = (Sin(HeadingRads)) * MaxRemainder * (-1)
0061 zLight = (Cos(HeadingRads)) * MaxRemainder * (-1)
0062 End Sub
0063
```

B-5 Source listings for the 3D hierarchical modeling toolkit, assemb3d.bas. See Appendix C for applications that use this toolkit. See Appendix A for instructions on building the demos.

```
0001 '-------------------------------------------------------------------
0002 '    Module of 3D hierarchy drivers for Windows applications
0003 '-------------------------------------------------------------------
0004 'Source file:  ASSEMB3D.BAS
0005 'Release version:  1.00                    Programmer:  Lee Adams
0006 'Type:  Visual Basic source file for Windows applications.
0007 'Dependencies:  ENGINE3D.BAS 3D functions.
0008 'Output and features:  Provides drivers for the ENGINE3D.BAS
0009 '   3D routines in order to render complex assemblies built
0010 '   from 3D subobjects like cylinders, parallelepipeds, etc.
0011 'Publication: Contains material from Windcrest/McGraw-Hill book
0012 '   4225 published by TAB BOOKS Division of McGraw-Hill Inc.
0013 'License:  As purchaser of the book you are granted a royalty-
0014 '   free license to distribute executable files generated using
0015 '   this code provided you accept the conditions of the License
0016 '   Agreement and Limited Warranty described in the book and on
0017 '   the companion disk.  Government users:  This software and
0018 '   documentation are subject to restrictions set forth in The
0019 '   Rights in Technical Data and Computer Software clause at
0020 '   252.227-7013 and elsewhere.
0021 '-------------------------------------------------------------------
0022 '       (c) Copyright 1993 Lee Adams.  All rights reserved.
0023 '           Lee Adams(tm) is a trademark of Lee Adams.
0024 '-------------------------------------------------------------------
0025    'Note:  This module relies upon some Global variables
0026    'declared in ENGINE3D.BAS.
0027
0028 Option Explicit          'generate error if variable not declared
0029 '-------------------------------------------------------------------
0030 '  Declaration of variables visible throughout only this module
0031 '-------------------------------------------------------------------
0032 Dim xAssy As Double, yAssy As Double, zAssy As Double
0033 Dim sAYaw As Double, cAYaw As Double, sARoll As Double
0034 Dim cARoll As Double, sAPitch As Double, cAPitch As Double
0035 Dim AssyYaw As Double, AssyRoll As Double, AssyPitch As Double
0036 Dim xaa As Double, yaa As Double, zaa As Double
0037 Dim bAssembInit As Integer
0038 '------------------ variables for subassemblies ---------------
0039 Const zLEVEL1 = 1            'level of subobject in hierarchy...
0040 Const zLEVEL2 = 2
```

```
0041   Const zLEVEL3 = 3
0042   Dim HierarchyLevel As Integer
0043   Dim xSubAssy As Double                        'subassembly position...
0044   Dim ySubAssy As Double, zSubAssy As Double
0045   Dim SubAssyYaw As Double                      'subassembly orientation...
0046   Dim SubAssyRoll As Double, SubAssyPitch As Double
0047   Dim sAAYaw As Double        'subassembly sine and cosine factors...
0048   Dim cAAYaw As Double
0049   Dim sAARoll As Double, cAARoll As Double
0050   Dim sAAPitch As Double, cAAPitch As Double
0051   Dim xSubAssyPivot As Double                   'subassembly pivot-point...
0052   Dim ySubAssyPivot As Double, zSubAssyPivot As Double
0053
0054   '---------------------------------------------------------------
0055   '                   3D hierarchy drivers
0056   '---------------------------------------------------------------
0057   '            Calculate assembly-space coords
0058   '---------------------------------------------------------------
0059   Sub azGetAssemblyCoords ()               'called by other 3D modules
0060                  'Enter with unclipped xyz 3D subobject coordinates.
0061                     'Exit with unclipped xyz 3D assembly coordinates.
0062   If bInitialized = False Then
0063     MsgBox "azGetAssemblyCoords( ) reports 3D library is not
             initialized.", MB_OK, "ASSEMB3D.BAS internal error"
0064     Exit Sub
0065   End If
0066   If bAssembInit = False Then
0067     MsgBox "azGetAssemblyCoords( ) reports 3D hierarchy not
             initialized.", MB_OK, "ASSEMB3D.BAS error"
0068     Exit Sub
0069   End If
0070   xaa = cARoll * x + sARoll * y                    ' roll rotation...
0071   yaa = cARoll * y - sARoll * x
0072   x = cAYaw * xaa - sAYaw * z                       ' yaw rotation...
0073   zaa = sAYaw * xaa + cAYaw * z
0074   z = cAPitch * zaa - sAPitch * yaa         ' pitch rotation...
0075   y = sAPitch * zaa + cAPitch * yaa
0076   x = x + xAssy       ' reposition subobject in 3D assembly-space...
0077   y = y + yAssy
0078   z = z + zAssy
0079   If HierarchyLevel = zLEVEL2 Then          ' if a subassembly...
0080     kzGetSubAssyCoords
0081   End If
0082   End Sub
0083
0084   '---------------------------------------------------------------
0085   '                 Toggle the hierarchy mode.
0086   '---------------------------------------------------------------
0087   Sub bzSetHierarchyMode (ByVal Mode As Integer)
0088                           'called by the interactive main module
0089   If bInitialized = False Then
0090     MsgBox "azGetAssemblyCoords( ) reports 3D library is not
             initialized.", MB_OK, "ASSEMB3D.BAS internal error"
0091     Exit Sub
0092   End If
0093   If Mode = True Then   'initialize variables and set run-time token
0094     bAssembly = True
0095     xAssy = 0#
```

B-5 Continued.

```
0096    yAssy = 0#
0097    zAssy = 0#
0098    AssyYaw = 0#
0099    AssyRoll = 0#
0100    AssyPitch = 0#
0101    HierarchyLevel = 1                         'remembers the level
0102    xSubAssy = 0#                        'subassembly position...
0103    ySubAssy = 0#
0104    zSubAssy = 0#
0105    SubAssyYaw = 0#                      'subassembly orientation...
0106    SubAssyRoll = 0#
0107    SubAssyPitch = 0#
0108    xSubAssyPivot = 0#                   'subassembly pivot-point...
0109    ySubAssyPivot = 0#
0110    zSubAssyPivot = 0#
0111    End If
0112    If Mode = False Then
0113      bAssembly = False
0114    End If
0115    End Sub
0116
0117    '-----------------------------------------------------------------
0118    '                   Set the hierarchy level.
0119    '-----------------------------------------------------------------
0120    Sub czSetHierarchyLevel (ByVal WhichLevel As Integer)
0121                            'is called by the interactive main module
0122    If WhichLevel = zLEVEL1 Then
0123      HierarchyLevel = zLEVEL1
0124      Exit Sub
0125    End If
0126    If WhichLevel = zLEVEL2 Then
0127      HierarchyLevel = zLEVEL2
0128      Exit Sub
0129    End If
0130    If WhichLevel = zLEVEL3 Then
0131      HierarchyLevel = zLEVEL3
0132      Exit Sub
0133    End If
0134    End Sub
0135
0136    '-----------------------------------------------------------------
0137    '                   Assembly functions
0138    '-----------------------------------------------------------------
0139    '     Calculate subobject sine and cosine rotation factors
0140    '-----------------------------------------------------------------
0141    Sub dzSetSubobjectAngle ()
0142            'this function is called by ezSetSubobjectAttitude()
0143    'Enter with AssyYaw,AssyRoll,AssyPitch subobject rotation angles.
0144      'Exit with sine, cosine object rotation factors for subobject.
0145    sAYaw = Sin(AssyYaw)
0146    cAYaw = Cos(AssyYaw)
0147    sARoll = Sin(AssyRoll)
0148    cARoll = Cos(AssyRoll)
0149    sAPitch = Sin(AssyPitch)
0150    cAPitch = Cos(AssyPitch)
0151    bAssembInit = True                          ' set runtime token
```

```
0152    End Sub
0153
0154    '-----------------------------------------------------------------
0155    '              Set the attitude of the subobject.
0156    '-----------------------------------------------------------------
0157    Sub ezSetSubobjectAttitude (ByVal Yaw As Integer, ByVal Roll As
            Integer, ByVal Pitch As Integer)
0158            ' this function is called by the interactive main module
0159    If Yaw < 0 Then
0160       Exit Sub
0161    End If
0162    If Yaw > 360 Then
0163       Exit Sub
0164    End If
0165    If Roll < 0 Then
0166       Exit Sub
0167    End If
0168    If Roll > 360 Then
0169       Exit Sub
0170    End If
0171    If Pitch < 0 Then
0172       Exit Sub
0173    End If
0174    If Pitch > 360 Then
0175       Exit Sub
0176    End If
0177    AssyYaw = Yaw * .0175433                    ' convert to radians...
0178    AssyRoll = Roll * .0175433
0179    AssyPitch = Pitch * .0175433
0180    If Yaw = 360 Then                     'tidy up boundary values...
0181       AssyYaw = 6.28319
0182    End If
0183    If Yaw = 0 Then
0184       AssyYaw = 0#
0185    End If
0186    If Roll = 360 Then
0187       AssyRoll = 6.28319
0188    End If
0189    If Roll = 0 Then
0190       AssyRoll = 0#
0191    End If
0192    If Pitch = 360 Then
0193       AssyPitch = 6.28319
0194    End If
0195    If Pitch = 0 Then
0196       AssyPitch = 0#
0197    End If
0198    dzSetSubobjectAngle                   ' set sine and cosine factors
0199    End Sub
0200
0201    '-----------------------------------------------------------------
0202    '         Reposition the subobject in 3D assembly-space.
0203    '-----------------------------------------------------------------
0204    Sub fzSetSubobjectLocation (ByVal ReposX As Integer, ByVal ReposY
            As Integer, ByVal ReposZ As Integer)
0205            'this function is called by the interactive main module
0206    xAssy = ReposX
0207    yAssy = ReposY
```

```
0208   zAssy = ReposZ
0209   End Sub
0210
0211   '-----------------------------------------------------------------
0212   '                    Subassembly functions
0213   '-----------------------------------------------------------------
0214   '     Calculate subobject sine and cosine rotation factors
0215   '-----------------------------------------------------------------
0216   Sub gzSetSubAssyAngle ()
0217                    'this function is called by hzSetSubAssyRotation()
0218           'Enter with SubAssyYaw,SubAssyRoll,SubAssyPitch subassembly
0219           'rotation angles.  Exit with sine, cosine object rotation
0220           'factors for subassembly.
0221   sAAYaw = Sin(SubAssyYaw)
0222   cAAYaw = Cos(SubAssyYaw)
0223   sAARoll = Sin(SubAssyRoll)
0224   cAARoll = Cos(SubAssyRoll)
0225   sAAPitch = Sin(SubAssyPitch)
0226   cAAPitch = Cos(SubAssyPitch)
0227   End Sub
0228
0229   '-----------------------------------------------------------------
0230   '           Set the orientation of the subassembly.
0231   '-----------------------------------------------------------------
0232   Sub hzSetSubAssyRotation (ByVal Yaw As Integer, ByVal Roll As
           Inte ger, ByVal Pitch As Integer)
0233           'this function is called by the interactive main module
0234   If Yaw < 0 Then                         'trap illegal values...
0235     Exit Sub
0236   End If
0237   If Yaw > 360 Then
0238     Exit Sub
0239   End If
0240   If Roll < 0 Then
0241     Exit Sub
0242   End If
0243   If Roll > 360 Then
0244     Exit Sub
0245   End If
0246   If Pitch < 0 Then
0247     Exit Sub
0248   End If
0249   If Pitch > 360 Then
0250     Exit Sub
0251   End If
0252   SubAssyYaw = Yaw * .0175433              'convert to radians...
0253   SubAssyRoll = Roll * .0175433
0254   SubAssyPitch = Pitch * .0175433
0255   If Yaw = 360 Then                        'tidy up boundary values...
0256     SubAssyYaw = 6.28319
0257   End If
0258   If Yaw = 0 Then
0259     SubAssyYaw = 0#
0260   End If
0261   If Roll = 360 Then
0262     SubAssyRoll = 6.28319
```

```
0263  End If
0264  If Roll = 0 Then
0265    SubAssyRoll = 0#
0266  End If
0267  If Pitch = 360 Then
0268    SubAssyPitch = 6.28319
0269  End If
0270  If Pitch = 0 Then
0271    SubAssyPitch = 0#
0272  End If
0273  gzSetSubAssyAngle                 ' set sine and cosine factors
0274  End Sub
0275
0276  '------------------------------------------------------------------
0277  '          Reposition the subassembly in 3D assembly-space.
0278  '------------------------------------------------------------------
0279  Sub izSetSubAssyPosition (ByVal ReposX As Integer, ByVal ReposY
          As Integer, ByVal ReposZ As Integer)
0280            'this function is called by the interactive main module
0281  xSubAssy = ReposX
0282  ySubAssy = ReposY
0283  zSubAssy = ReposZ
0284  End Sub
0285
0286  '------------------------------------------------------------------
0287  '          Reposition the subassembly pivot-point.
0288  '------------------------------------------------------------------
0289  Sub jzSetSubAssyPivot (ByVal ReposX As Integer, ByVal ReposY As
          Integer, ByVal ReposZ As Integer)
0290            'this function is called by the interactive main module
0291  xSubAssyPivot = ReposX
0292  ySubAssyPivot = ReposY
0293  zSubAssyPivot = ReposZ
0294  End Sub
0295
0296  '------------------------------------------------------------------
0297  '          Calculate subassembly coords in assembly-space.
0298  '------------------------------------------------------------------
0299  Sub kzGetSubAssyCoords ()
0300                    'this function is called azGetAssemblyCoords()
0301              'Enter with unclipped xyz 3D subobject coordinates.
0302              'Exit with unclipped xyz 3D subassembly coordinates.
0303  x = x + xSubAssyPivot     ' reposition subassembly pivot-point...
0304  y = y + ySubAssyPivot
0305  z = z + zSubAssyPivot
0306  xaa = cAARoll * x + sAARoll * y           ' roll rotation...
0307  yaa = cAARoll * y - sAARoll * x
0308  x = cAAYaw * xaa - sAAYaw * z             ' yaw rotation...
0309  zaa = sAAYaw * xaa + cAAYaw * z
0310  z = cAAPitch * zaa - sAAPitch * yaa       ' pitch rotation...
0311  y = sAAPitch * zaa + cAAPitch * yaa
0312  x = x + xSubAssy     ' reposition subassembly in assembly-space...
0313  y = y + ySubAssy
0314  z = z + zSubAssy
0315  End Sub
0316
```

B-6 Source listings for the 3D kinematics toolkit, knmatx3d.bas. See Appendix C for applications that use this toolkit. See Appendix A for instructions on building the demos.

```
0001 '---------------------------------------------------------------------
0002 '   Module of 3D kinematics drivers for Windows applications
0003 '---------------------------------------------------------------------
0004 'Source file:  KNMATX3D.BAS
0005 'Release version:  1.00                     Programmer:  Lee Adams
0006 'Type:  Visual Basic source file for Windows applications.
0007 'Dependencies:  ENGINE3D.BAS, SHAPES3D.BAS, DEFORM3D.BAS, and
0008 '   ASSEMB3D.BAS functions.
0009 'Output and features:  Provides kinematics drivers for the
0010 '   ENGINE3D.BAS 3D routines in order to use acceleration,
0011 '   deceleration, linear velocity, angular velocity,
0012 '   solids deformation, and collision detection to control
0013 '   movement of 3D bodies in animation sequences.
0014 'Publication: Contains material from Windcrest/McGraw-Hill book
0015 '   4225 published by TAB BOOKS Division of McGraw-Hill Inc.
0016 'License:  As purchaser of the book you are granted a royalty-
0017 '   free license to distribute executable files generated using
0018 '   this code provided you accept the conditions of the License
0019 '   Agreement and Limited Warranty described in the book and on
0020 '   the companion disk.  Government users:  This software and
0021 '   documentation are subject to restrictions set forth in The
0022 '   Rights in Technical Data and Computer Software clause at
0023 '   252.227-7013 and elsewhere.
0024 '---------------------------------------------------------------------
0025 '   (c) Copyright 1993-1994 Lee Adams.  All rights reserved.
0026 '          Lee Adams(tm) is a trademark of Lee Adams.
0027 '---------------------------------------------------------------------
0028
0029 Const zMAX_BODIES = 25         'max available number of 3D bodies
0030 Const zMAX_FPS = 18.2             'max supported animation rate
0031 Const zBOX = 1                    'available solid subobjects...
0032 Const zSPHERE = 2
0033 Const zCYLINDER = 3
0034 Const zCONE = 4
0035 Const zWEDGE = 5
0036 Const zCURVE = 6
0037 Const zHEMISPHERE = 7
0038 Const zDEFORMBOX = 8
0039 Const zHALFCYL = 9
0040 Const zBULGE = 10
0041 Const zNULL = 11
0042 Const zRED = 1                           'available shading hues...
0043 Const zGREEN = 2
0044 Const zBROWN = 3
0045 Const zBLUE = 4
0046 Const zMAGENTA = 5
0047 Const zCYAN = 6
0048 Const zGRAY = 7
0049
0050 '---------------------------------------------------------------------
0051 '   Declaration of variables visible throughout only this file
0052 '---------------------------------------------------------------------
0053 Dim KinematicsReady As Integer               'True if initialized
0054 Dim fps As Double                             'animation rate
0055 Dim TimeSlice As Double                       'time resolution
```

```
0056   Dim FinalFrame As Integer                 'final frame of sequence
0057   Dim CurrentFrame As Integer                      'current frame
0058   Dim CurrentTime As Double                         'current time
0059   Dim ActiveBodies As Integer         'number of active 3D bodies
0060
0061   '--------- declare structure for kinematic state of a body ------
0062   Type KinematicState
0063       '------------------------- attributes ----------------------
0064       Solid As Integer                     'box, sphere, cone, etc.
0065       Color As Integer                              'shading color
0066       '---------------------- location -----------------------
0067       LocationX As Double             'current translation in units...
0068       LocationY As Double
0069       LocationZ As Double
0070       '----------------------- orientation --------------------
0071       Yaw As Double                 'current rotation in degrees 0 to 360...
0072       Roll As Double
0073       Pitch As Double
0074       '----------------------- size ----------------------------
0075       DimensionX As Double               'current extrusion in units...
0076       DimensionY As Double
0077       DimensionZ As Double
0078       '---------------------- linear velocity ---------------------
0079       LinearHeading As Double       'current heading in degrees 0 to 360
0080       LinearPitch As Double         'current pitch in degrees 0 to 360
0081       LinearSpeed As Double         'current speed in units per second
0082       '------------------ rotational velocity --------------------
0083       YawSpeed As Double             'yaw rotation in degrees per second
0084       RollSpeed As Double           'roll rotation in degrees per second
0085       PitchSpeed As Double          'pitch rotation in degrees per second
0086       '------------------ acceleration factors --------------------
0087       LinearAcceleration As Double           'units per second squared
0088       LinearAccelerationDuration As Double       'duration in seconds
0089       YawAcceleration As Double             'degrees per second squared
0090       RollAcceleration As Double            'degrees per second squared
0091       PitchAcceleration As Double           'degrees per second squared
0092       RotationAccelerationDuration As Double     'duration in seconds
0093       '------------------ redirection factors --------------------
0094       HeadingChange As Double                     'degrees per second
0095       HeadingChangeDuration As Double                      'seconds
0096       PitchChange As Double                       'degrees per second
0097       PitchChangeDuration As Double                        'seconds
0098       '---------------------- forward dynamics --------------------
0099       Mass As Double                             'measured in kg or g
0100       Volume As Double                       'measured in units cubed
0101       Density As Double                           ' = mass/volume
0102       Elasticity As Double          'range 0 inelastic to 1 elastic
0103       LinearMomentum As Double           ' = mass * linear velocity
0104       AngularMomentum As Double     ' = moment of inertia * rot velocity
0105       MomentOfInertia As Double      'a function of mass, size, shape
0106       LinearEnergy As Double         ' = .5 * mass * velocity * velocity
0107       RotationEnergy As Double       ' = .5 * moment * rotvel * rotvel
0108   End Type
0109
0110   '-------------------- declare some 3D bodies ------------------
0111   Dim BPtr As Integer                           'index into an...
0112   Dim BArray(1 To 25) As KinematicState         '...array of bodies
0113
```

B-6 Continued.

```
0114  '----------------------------------------------------------------
0115  '                Callable 3D kinematics functions
0116  '----------------------------------------------------------------
0117  '                Initialize the kinematics module
0118  '----------------------------------------------------------------
0119  Sub akmInitializeKinematics (FramesPerSec As Double, NumBodies As
            Integer, StartFrame As Integer, EndFrame As Integer)
0120    Dim iInitCount                                 'loop counter
0121  If KinematicsReady = True Then
0122    Exit Sub     'if kinematics module has already been initialized
0123  End If
0124  If NumBodies < 1 Or NumBodies > zMAX_BODIES Then
0125    KinematicsReady = False
0126    Exit Sub                     'if number of bodies is out of bounds
0127  End If
0128  If FramesPerSec < 3# Or FramesPerSec > zMAX_FPS Then
0129    KinematicsReady = False
0130    Exit Sub                     'if frame rate is out of bounds
0131  End If
0132  BPtr = 1          'initialize index into array of 3D bodies
0133  ActiveBodies = NumBodies     'remember number of active 3D bodies
0134  FinalFrame = EndFrame               'remember length of animation
0135  CurrentFrame = 1                     'initialize current frame
0136  CurrentTime = 0#                     'initialize current time
0137  '------------------ remember the animation rate ---------------
0138  If FramesPerSec < 3.6 Then
0139    fps = 3#
0140    GoTo DONE_FPS
0141  End If
0142  If FramesPerSec < 4.5 Then
0143    fps = 3.6
0144    GoTo DONE_FPS
0145  End If
0146  If FramesPerSec < 6.1 Then
0147    fps = 4.5
0148    GoTo DONE_FPS
0149  End If
0150  If FramesPerSec < 9.1 Then
0151    fps = 6.1
0152    GoTo DONE_FPS
0153  End If
0154  If FramesPerSec < 18.2 Then
0155    fps = 9.1
0156    GoTo DONE_FPS
0157  End If
0158  fps = 18.2
0159  DONE_FPS:
0160  TimeSlice = 1 / fps               'calculate the timing resolution
0161  '------------------ initialize the 3D bodies -------------------
0162  For iInitCount = 1 To ActiveBodies Step 1        'for each body...
0163    BPtr = iInitCount                   'set the pointer to the body
0164    rkmInitBody                         'initialize the 3D body
0165  Next iInitCount
0166  BPtr = 1                          'restore pointer to default body
0167  KinematicsReady = True                   'set the status token
0168  End Sub
```

```
0169
0170  '------------------------------------------------------------------
0171  '              Re-initialize the kinematics module
0172  '------------------------------------------------------------------
0173  Sub bkmReset ()
0174  If KinematicsReady <> True Then
0175     Exit Sub
0176  End If
0177  CurrentFrame = 1
0178  CurrentTime = 0#
0179  End Sub
0180
0181  '------------------------------------------------------------------
0182  '  Adjust kinematic parameters for a particular preview frame
0183  '------------------------------------------------------------------
0184  Sub ckmSelectPreviewFrame (WhichFrame As Integer)
0185    Dim PreviewCount As Integer
0186    Dim BodyCount As Integer
0187  If KinematicsReady <> True Then
0188     Exit Sub
0189  End If
0190  For PreviewCount = 1 To (WhichFrame - 1) Step 1
0191                        'for each frame preceding the preview frame...
0192    CurrentFrame = PreviewCount            'update the frame ID
0193    CurrentTime = CurrentTime + TimeSlice        'update the time
0194    For BodyCount = 1 To ActiveBodies Step 1     'for each body...
0195      BPtr = BodyCount                    'select the body...
0196      If CurrentFrame > 1 Then    '...and update body's kinematics
0197         ukmGetNewLinearSpeed
0198         vkmGetNewRotationalSpeed
0199         wkmGetNewHeading
0200         xkmGetNewPitch
0201         ykmGetNewLocation
0202         zkmGetNewOrientation
0203         zzkmGetNewSize
0204      End If
0205    Next BodyCount                    'do next body in the scene
0206  Next PreviewCount                      'do next preview frame
0207  CurrentFrame = CurrentFrame + 1          'set to preview frame
0208  CurrentTime = CurrentTime + TimeSlice        'set to preview frame
0209  End Sub
0210
0211  '------------------------------------------------------------------
0212  '              Set new linear acceleration
0213  '------------------------------------------------------------------
0214  Sub dkmSetLinearAcceleration (Body As Integer, UnitsPerSecSqd As
          Double, Seconds As Double)
0215  If KinematicsReady <> True Then
0216     Exit Sub
0217  End If
0218  If Body < 1 Or Body > ActiveBodies Then
0219     Exit Sub
0220  End If
0221  BPtr = Body
0222  BArray(BPtr).LinearAcceleration = UnitsPerSecSqd
0223  BArray(BPtr).LinearAccelerationDuration = Seconds
0224  End Sub
0225
```

B-6 Continued.

```
0226 '-------------------------------------------------------------------
0227 '                  Set new rotational acceleration
0228 '-------------------------------------------------------------------
0229 Sub ekmSetRotationalAcceleration (Body As Integer, AYaw As Double,
         ARoll As Double, APitch As Double, Seconds As Double)
0230 If KinematicsReady <> True Then
0231   Exit Sub
0232 End If
0233 If Body < 1 Or Body > ActiveBodies Then
0234   Exit Sub
0235 End If
0236 BPtr = Body
0237 BArray(BPtr).YawAcceleration = AYaw
0238 BArray(BPtr).RollAcceleration = ARoll
0239 BArray(BPtr).PitchAcceleration = APitch
0240 BArray(BPtr).RotationAccelerationDuration = Seconds
0241 End Sub
0242
0243 '-------------------------------------------------------------------
0244 '                  Set new heading change rate
0245 '-------------------------------------------------------------------
0246 Sub fkmSetHeadingChange (Body As Integer, DegreesPerSec As Double,
         Seconds As Double)
0247 If KinematicsReady <> True Then
0248   Exit Sub
0249 End If
0250 If Body < 1 Or Body > ActiveBodies Then
0251   Exit Sub
0252 End If
0253 BPtr = Body
0254 BArray(BPtr).HeadingChange = DegreesPerSec
0255 BArray(BPtr).HeadingChangeDuration = Seconds
0256 End Sub
0257
0258 '-------------------------------------------------------------------
0259 '                  Set new pitch change rate
0260 '-------------------------------------------------------------------
0261 Sub gkmSetPitchChange (Body As Integer, DegreesPerSec As Double,
         Seconds As Double)
0262 If KinematicsReady <> True Then
0263   Exit Sub
0264 End If
0265 If Body < 1 Or Body > ActiveBodies Then
0266   Exit Sub
0267 End If
0268 BPtr = Body
0269 BArray(BPtr).PitchChange = DegreesPerSec
0270 BArray(BPtr).PitchChangeDuration = Seconds
0271 End Sub
0272
0273 '-------------------------------------------------------------------
0274 '                  Reset the location
0275 '-------------------------------------------------------------------
0276 Sub hkmSetLocation (Body As Integer, X As Double, Y As Double, Z
         As Double)
0277 If KinematicsReady <> True Then
```

```
0278    Exit Sub
0279  End If
0280  If Body < 1 Or Body > ActiveBodies Then
0281    Exit Sub
0282  End If
0283  BPtr = Body
0284  BArray(BPtr).LocationX = X
0285  BArray(BPtr).LocationY = Y
0286  BArray(BPtr).LocationZ = Z
0287  End Sub
0288
0289  '------------------------------------------------------------------
0290  '                    Reset the orientation
0291  '------------------------------------------------------------------
0292  Sub ikmSetOrientation (Body As Integer, dYaw As Double, dRoll As
          Double, dPitch As Double)
0293  If KinematicsReady <> True Then
0294    Exit Sub
0295  End If
0296  If Body < 1 Or Body > ActiveBodies Then
0297    Exit Sub
0298  End If
0299  If dYaw < 0 Then
0300    dYaw = dYaw + 360
0301  End If
0302  If dYaw > 360 Then
0303    dYaw = dYaw - 360
0304  End If
0305  If dRoll < 0 Then
0306    dRoll = dRoll + 360
0307  End If
0308  If dRoll > 360 Then
0309    dRoll = dRoll - 360
0310  End If
0311  If dPitch < 0 Then
0312    dPitch = dPitch + 360
0313  End If
0314  If dPitch > 360 Then
0315    dPitch = dPitch - 360
0316  End If
0317  BPtr = Body
0318  BArray(BPtr).Yaw = dYaw
0319  BArray(BPtr).Roll = dRoll
0320  BArray(BPtr).Pitch = dPitch
0321  End Sub
0322
0323  '------------------------------------------------------------------
0324  '                    Reset the dimensions
0325  '------------------------------------------------------------------
0326  Sub jkmSetDimensions (Body As Integer, X As Double, Y As Double, Z
          As Double)
0327  If KinematicsReady <> True Then
0328    Exit Sub
0329  End If
0330  If Body < 1 Or Body > ActiveBodies Then
0331    Exit Sub
0332  End If
0333  BPtr = Body
```

B-6 Continued.

```
0334  BArray(BPtr).DimensionX = X
0335  BArray(BPtr).DimensionY = Y
0336  BArray(BPtr).DimensionZ = Z
0337  End Sub
0338
0339  '------------------------------------------------------------
0340  '                   Reset the linear velocity
0341  '------------------------------------------------------------
0342  Sub kkmSetLinearVelocity (Body As Integer, Heading As Double,
          Pitch As Double, Speed As Double)
0343  If KinematicsReady <> True Then
0344     Exit Sub
0345  End If
0346  If Body < 1 Or Body > ActiveBodies Then
0347     Exit Sub
0348  End If
0349  BPtr = Body
0350  BArray(BPtr).LinearHeading = Heading
0351  BArray(BPtr).LinearPitch = Pitch
0352  BArray(BPtr).LinearSpeed = Speed
0353  End Sub
0354
0355  '------------------------------------------------------------
0356  '                  Reset the rotational velocity
0357  '------------------------------------------------------------
0358  Sub lkmSetRotationalVelocity (Body As Integer, RYawSpeed
          As Double, RRollSpeed As Double, RPitchSpeed As Double)
0359  If KinematicsReady <> True Then
0360     Exit Sub
0361  End If
0362  If Body < 1 Or Body > ActiveBodies Then
0363     Exit Sub
0364  End If
0365  BPtr = Body
0366  BArray(BPtr).YawSpeed = RYawSpeed
0367  BArray(BPtr).RollSpeed = RRollSpeed
0368  BArray(BPtr).PitchSpeed = RPitchSpeed
0369  End Sub
0370
0371  '------------------------------------------------------------
0372  '                   Specify the subobject type
0373  '------------------------------------------------------------
0374  Sub mkmSetSolid (Body As Integer, Subobject As Integer)
0375  If KinematicsReady <> True Then
0376     Exit Sub
0377  End If
0378  If Body < 1 Or Body > ActiveBodies Then
0379     Exit Sub
0380  End If
0381  If Subobject < zBOX Or Subobject > zNULL Then
0382     Exit Sub
0383  End If
0384  BPtr = Body
0385  BArray(BPtr).Solid = Subobject
0386  End Sub
0387
```

```
0388 '-------------------------------------------------------------------
0389 '                    Specify the subobject color
0390 '-------------------------------------------------------------------
0391 Sub nkmSetColor (Body As Integer, Hue As Integer)
0392 If KinematicsReady <> True Then
0393    Exit Sub
0394 End If
0395 If Body < 1 Or Body > ActiveBodies Then
0396    Exit Sub
0397 End If
0398 If Hue < zRED Or Hue > zGRAY Then
0399    Exit Sub
0400 End If
0401 BPtr = Body
0402 BArray(BPtr).Color = Hue
0403 End Sub
0404
0405 '-------------------------------------------------------------------
0406 '                         Set the mass
0407 '-------------------------------------------------------------------
0408 Sub okmSetMass (Body As Integer, dMass As Double)
0409 If KinematicsReady <> True Then
0410    Exit Sub
0411 End If
0412 If Body < 1 Or Body > ActiveBodies Then
0413    Exit Sub
0414 End If
0415 BPtr = Body
0416 BArray(BPtr).Mass = dMass
0417 End Sub
0418
0419 '-------------------------------------------------------------------
0420 '               Render all the bodies in the 3D scene
0421 '-------------------------------------------------------------------
0422 Sub pkmRenderScene ()
0423    Dim iCounter As Integer
0424 If KinematicsReady <> True Then
0425    Exit Sub
0426 End If
0427 If CurrentFrame > FinalFrame Then
0428    Exit Sub
0429 End If
0430 For iCounter = 1 To ActiveBodies Step 1            'for each body
0431    BPtr = iCounter                        'reset the pointer and
0432    tkmRenderBody                               'render the body
0433 Next iCounter
0434 CurrentFrame = CurrentFrame + 1        'increment the frame counter
0435 CurrentTime = CurrentTime + TimeSlice          'increment the time
0436 End Sub
0437
0438 '-------------------------------------------------------------------
0439 '               Detect a collision between two bodies
0440 '-------------------------------------------------------------------
0441 Sub qkmDetectCollision (Body1 As Integer, Body2 As Integer)
0442 If KinematicsReady <> True Then
0443    Exit Sub
0444 End If
0445 If Body1 < 1 Or Body1 > ActiveBodies Then
```

B-6 Continued.

```
0446    Exit Sub
0447   End If
0448   If Body2 < 1 Or Body2 > ActiveBodies Then
0449    Exit Sub
0450   End If
0451   '-------------- add future code here -------------------
0452   End Sub
0453
0454   '-----------------------------------------------------------
0455   '                 Internal 3D kinematics drivers
0456   '-----------------------------------------------------------
0457   '            Initialize the currently-selected body
0458   '-----------------------------------------------------------
0459   Sub rkmInitBody ()
0460   BArray(BPtr).Solid = zBOX
0461   BArray(BPtr).Color = zGREEN
0462   BArray(BPtr).LocationX = 0
0463   BArray(BPtr).LocationY = 0
0464   BArray(BPtr).LocationZ = 0
0465   BArray(BPtr).Yaw = 0
0466   BArray(BPtr).Roll = 0
0467   BArray(BPtr).Pitch = 0
0468   BArray(BPtr).DimensionX = 25
0469   BArray(BPtr).DimensionY = 25
0470   BArray(BPtr).DimensionZ = 25
0471   BArray(BPtr).LinearHeading = 0
0472   BArray(BPtr).LinearPitch = 0
0473   BArray(BPtr).LinearSpeed = 0
0474   BArray(BPtr).YawSpeed = 0
0475   BArray(BPtr).RollSpeed = 0
0476   BArray(BPtr).PitchSpeed = 0
0477   BArray(BPtr).LinearAcceleration = 0
0478   BArray(BPtr).LinearAccelerationDuration = 0
0479   BArray(BPtr).YawAcceleration = 0
0480   BArray(BPtr).RollAcceleration = 0
0481   BArray(BPtr).PitchAcceleration = 0
0482   BArray(BPtr).RotationAccelerationDuration = 0
0483   BArray(BPtr).HeadingChange = 0
0484   BArray(BPtr).HeadingChangeDuration = 0
0485   BArray(BPtr).PitchChange = 0
0486   BArray(BPtr).PitchChangeDuration = 0
0487   BArray(BPtr).Mass = 1#
0488   BArray(BPtr).Volume = 15625
0489   BArray(BPtr).Density = 1#
0490   BArray(BPtr).Elasticity = 1#
0491   BArray(BPtr).LinearMomentum = 0
0492   BArray(BPtr).AngularMomentum = 0
0493   BArray(BPtr).MomentOfInertia = 0
0494   BArray(BPtr).LinearEnergy = 0
0495   BArray(BPtr).RotationEnergy = 0
0496   End Sub
0497
0498   '-----------------------------------------------------------
0499   '                    Select the current body
0500   '-----------------------------------------------------------
0501   Sub skmSelectBody (WhichBody As Integer)
```

```
0502   If WhichBody < 1 Or WhichBody > ActiveBodies Then
0503     Exit Sub
0504   End If
0505   BPtr = WhichBody
0506   End Sub
0507
0508   '----------------------------------------------------------------
0509   '                  Render the currently-selected body
0510   '----------------------------------------------------------------
0511   Sub tkmRenderBody ()                         'uses global variable BPtr
0512               'this function is called repeatedly by pkmRenderScene()
0513     Dim Arg1 As Integer          'used to convert Doubles to Integers...
0514     Dim Arg2 As Integer
0515     Dim Arg3 As Integer
0516   '--------- Step One:  update the body's kinematic state ---------
0517   If CurrentFrame > 1 Then 'if first frame, do not move body yet...
0518     ukmGetNewLinearSpeed
0519     vkmGetNewRotationalSpeed
0520     wkmGetNewHeading
0521     xkmGetNewPitch
0522     ykmGetNewLocation
0523     zkmGetNewOrientation
0524     zzkmGetNewSize
0525   End If
0526   '------------------- Step Two:  render the body ----------------
0527   Call bzSetHierarchyMode(False)               'specify hierarchy mode
0528   Call ddzSetShadingColor(BArray(BPtr).Color)     'set shading color
0529   Arg1 = BArray(BPtr).DimensionX       'load Doubles into Integers...
0530   Arg2 = BArray(BPtr).DimensionY
0531   Arg3 = BArray(BPtr).DimensionZ
0532   Call dczSetSubjectSize(Arg1, Arg2, Arg3)         'set the extrusion
0533   Arg1 = BArray(BPtr).Yaw
0534   Arg2 = BArray(BPtr).Roll
0535   Arg3 = BArray(BPtr).Pitch
0536   Call dbzSetSubjectAttitude(Arg1, Arg2, Arg3) 'set the orientation
0537   Arg1 = BArray(BPtr).LocationX
0538   Arg2 = BArray(BPtr).LocationY
0539   Arg3 = BArray(BPtr).LocationZ
0540   Call dazSetSubjectLocation(Arg1, Arg2, Arg3)     'set the location
0541   Select Case BArray(BPtr).Solid               'render the subobject...
0542     Case zBOX
0543       azDrawCube
0544     Case zSPHERE
0545       czDrawSphere
0546     Case zCYLINDER
0547       ezDrawCylinder
0548     Case zCONE
0549       izDrawCone
0550     Case zWEDGE
0551       kzDrawWedge
0552     Case zCURVE
0553       gzDrawCurve
0554     Case zHEMISPHERE
0555       mzDrawHemisphere
0556     Case zDEFORMBOX
0557       azDrawCube                                 '(for prototyping only)
0558     Case zHALFCYL
0559       czDrawHalfCylinder
```

B-6 Continued.

```
0560    Case zBULGE
0561       ezDrawBulge
0562  End Select
0563  Call bzSetHierarchyMode(False)      'restore default hierarchy mode
0564  End Sub
0565
0566  '------------------------------------------------------------------
0567  '          The seven-step kinematics animation pipeline
0568  '------------------------------------------------------------------
0569  'Step 1               Get new linear speed
0570  '------------------------------------------------------------------
0571  Sub ukmGetNewLinearSpeed ()
0572  BArray(BPtr).LinearSpeed = BArray(BPtr).LinearSpeed +
          (BArray(BPtr).LinearAcceleration * TimeSlice)
0573  End Sub
0574
0575  '------------------------------------------------------------------
0576  'Step2                Get new rotational speed
0577  '------------------------------------------------------------------
0578  Sub vkmGetNewRotationalSpeed ()
0579  BArray(BPtr).YawSpeed = BArray(BPtr).YawSpeed +
          (BArray(BPtr).YawAcceleration * TimeSlice)
0580  BArray(BPtr).RollSpeed = BArray(BPtr).RollSpeed +
          (BArray(BPtr).RollAcceleration * TimeSlice)
0581  BArray(BPtr).PitchSpeed = BArray(BPtr).PitchSpeed +
          (BArray(BPtr).PitchAcceleration * TimeSlice)
0582  End Sub
0583
0584  '------------------------------------------------------------------
0585  'Step 3               Get new velocity heading
0586  '------------------------------------------------------------------
0587  Sub wkmGetNewHeading ()
0588  BArray(BPtr).LinearHeading = BArray(BPtr).LinearHeading +
          (BArray(BPtr).HeadingChange * TimeSlice)
0589  If BArray(BPtr).LinearHeading < 0 Then
0590    BArray(BPtr).LinearHeading = BArray(BPtr).LinearHeading + 360
0591  End If
0592  If BArray(BPtr).LinearHeading > 360 Then
0593    BArray(BPtr).LinearHeading = BArray(BPtr).LinearHeading - 360
0594  End If
0595  End Sub
0596
0597  '------------------------------------------------------------------
0598  'Step 4               Get new velocity pitch
0599  '------------------------------------------------------------------
0600  Sub xkmGetNewPitch ()
0601  BArray(BPtr).LinearPitch = BArray(BPtr).LinearPitch +
          (BArray(BPtr).PitchChange * TimeSlice)
0602  If BArray(BPtr).LinearPitch < 0 Then
0603    BArray(BPtr).LinearPitch = BArray(BPtr).LinearPitch + 360
0604  End If
0605  If BArray(BPtr).LinearPitch > 360 Then
0606    BArray(BPtr).LinearPitch = BArray(BPtr).LinearPitch - 360
0607  End If
0608  End Sub
0609
```

```
0610  '----------------------------------------------------------------
0611  'Step 5                Calculate new location
0612  '----------------------------------------------------------------
0613  Sub ykmGetNewLocation ()
0614    Dim xFactor As Double                            'unit vector...
0615    Dim yFactor As Double
0616    Dim zFactor As Double
0617    Dim PitchRads As Double                          'radian angles...
0618    Dim HeadingRads As Double
0619    Dim MaxRemainder As Double                       'temporary variable
0620  '------------ Step One:  convert degrees to radians ------------
0621  PitchRads = BArray(BPtr).LinearPitch * .017453
0622  HeadingRads = BArray(BPtr).LinearHeading * .017453
0623  '--------- Step Two:  calculate components of unit vector --------
0624  yFactor = Cos(PitchRads)        '1 at 0 degrees, -1 at 180 degrees
0625  MaxRemainder = Sqr(1 - (yFactor * yFactor))
0626  xFactor = (Sin(HeadingRads)) * MaxRemainder
0627  zFactor = (Cos(HeadingRads)) * MaxRemainder * (-1)
0628  '--------- Step Three:  calculate the time-sliced vector ---------
0629  xFactor = xFactor * TimeSlice
0630  yFactor = yFactor * TimeSlice
0631  zFactor = zFactor * TimeSlice
0632  '----------- Step Four:  calculate the new translation -----------
0633  BArray(BPtr).LocationX = BArray(BPtr).LocationX + (xFactor *
          BArray(BPtr).LinearSpeed)
0634  BArray(BPtr).LocationY = BArray(BPtr).LocationY + (yFactor *
          BArray(BPtr).LinearSpeed)
0635  BArray(BPtr).LocationZ = BArray(BPtr).LocationZ + (zFactor *
          BArray(BPtr).LinearSpeed)
0636  End Sub
0637
0638  '----------------------------------------------------------------
0639  'Step 6                Calculate new orientation
0640  '----------------------------------------------------------------
0641  Sub zkmGetNewOrientation ()
0642  BArray(BPtr).Yaw = BArray(BPtr).Yaw + (BArray(BPtr).YawSpeed *
          TimeSlice)
0643  BArray(BPtr).Roll = BArray(BPtr).Roll + (BArray(BPtr).RollSpeed *
          TimeSlice)
0644  BArray(BPtr).Pitch = BArray(BPtr).Pitch + (BArray(BPtr).PitchSpeed
          * TimeSlice)
0645  If BArray(BPtr).Yaw < 0 Then
0646    BArray(BPtr).Yaw = BArray(BPtr).Yaw + 360
0647  End If
0648  If BArray(BPtr).Yaw > 360 Then
0649    BArray(BPtr).Yaw = BArray(BPtr).Yaw - 360
0650  End If
0651  If BArray(BPtr).Roll < 0 Then
0652    BArray(BPtr).Roll = BArray(BPtr).Roll + 360
0653  End If
0654  If BArray(BPtr).Roll > 360 Then
0655    BArray(BPtr).Roll = BArray(BPtr).Roll - 360
0656  End If
0657  If BArray(BPtr).Pitch < 0 Then
0658    BArray(BPtr).Pitch = BArray(BPtr).Pitch + 360
0659  End If
0660  If BArray(BPtr).Pitch > 360 Then
0661    BArray(BPtr).Pitch = BArray(BPtr).Pitch - 360
```

B-6 Continued.

```
0662  End If
0663  End Sub
0664
0665  '----------------------------------------------------------------
0666  'Step 7                    Calculate new size
0667  '----------------------------------------------------------------
0668  Sub zzkmGetNewSize ()
0669                          'This is a stub routine not yet implemented
0670  End Sub
0671
```

C
Source listings for the sample applications

This appendix contains the listings for the sample applications. These listings must be used with the toolkit modules presented in Appendix B in order to build the executables. Read Appendix A for tips on building the application.

The template for graphics application development, startup.frm, is presented in FIG. C-1. The 3D geometry sampler, objects.frm, is provided in FIG. C-2. The template for interactive 3D animation, animate.frm, appears in FIG. C-3. The hierarchical modeling animation sampler, assembly.frm, is found in FIG. C-4. The animated forward kinematics editor, kinematx.frm, is presented in FIG. C-5. The interactive, animated, virtual reality sampler, maze.frm, appears in FIG. C-6.

Source listings

C-1 Source listings for the sample application, startup. See Appendix B for the toolkits which must be used to build this application. See Appendix A for instructions on building the demo.

```
0001   STGLOBAL.BAS
0002   STMAIN.BAS
0003   STARTUP.FRM
0004   ProjWinSize=80,444,196,336
0005   ProjWinShow=2


0001   '-----------------------------------------------------------------
0002   '  Reusable global module for Visual Basic graphics applications
0003   '              that call Windows API functions.
0004   '-----------------------------------------------------------------
0005   '  Source file:  STGLOBAL.BAS
0006   '  Release version:  1.00              Programmer:  Lee Adams
```

C-1 Continued.

```
0007  '  Type:  Visual Basic global module for Windows applications.
0008  '  Compiler:  Microsoft Visual Basic 2.00
0009  '  Dependencies:  STARTUP.FRM primary module
0010  '                 STMAIN.BAS module containing Main()
0011  '  Output and features:  Provides declarations for Windows API
0012  '     (Application Programming Interface) functions callable by
0013  '     Visual Basic applications at runtime, including routines
0014  '     from Windows' GDI, USER, and KERNEL DLLs (dynamic link
0015  '     libraries).  Also provides declarations of various variables
0016  '     and constants.  Functions, variables, and constants declared
0017  '     in this global module are visible throughout the project.
0018  '  Publication:  Contains material from Windcrest/McGraw-Hill
0019  '     book 4225 published by TAB BOOKS Div. of McGraw-Hill Inc.
0020  '  License:  As purchaser of the book you are granted a
0021  '     royalty-free license to distribute executable files
0022  '     generated using this code provided that you accept the
0023  '     conditions of the License Agreement and Limited Warranty
0024  '     described in the book and on the companion disk.  Government
0025  '     users:  This software and documentation are subject to
0026  '     restrictions set forth in The Rights in Technical Data and
0027  '     Computer Software clause at 252.227-7013 and elsewhere.
0028  '-----------------------------------------------------------------
0029  '       (c) Copyright 1993 Lee Adams.  All rights reserved.
0030  '          Lee Adams(tm) is a trademark of Lee Adams.
0031  '-----------------------------------------------------------------
0032
0033  '-----------------------------------------------------------------
0034  '                General constants and variables
0035  '-----------------------------------------------------------------
0036  Global Const MB_OK = 0                  'OK button for message box
0037  Global Const MB_OKCANCEL = 1   'OK Cancel buttons for message box
0038  Global Const MB_YESNO = 4          'Yes No buttons for message box
0039  Global Const IDOK = 1                       'OK button selected
0040  Global Const IDCANCEL = 2               'Cancel button selected
0041  Global Const IDYES = 6                     'Yes button selected
0042  Global Const IDNO = 7                       'No button selected
0043  Global UserWants As Integer        'value returned by message box
0044  Global Const PIXELS = 3                    'pixel coordinates
0045  Global StartUp As Integer               'tracks the startup code
0046  Global IgnoreRefresh As Integer        'tracks refresh activity
0047
0048  '-----------------------------------------------------------------
0049  '                    Window specifications
0050  '-----------------------------------------------------------------
0051  Global Const zWINDOW_WIDTH = 264              'width of window
0052  Global Const zWINDOW_HEIGHT = 301            'height of window
0053  Global Const zFRAMEWIDE = 256            'width of client area
0054  Global Const zFRAMEHIGH = 255           'height of client area
0055  Global HorizTwipsPixel As Single     'twips-per-pixel (horizontal)
0056  Global VertTwipsPixel As Single       'twips-per-pixel (vertical)
0057  Global Window_Width As Single           'runtime width of window
0058  Global Window_Height As Single         'runtime height of window
0059
0060  '-----------------------------------------------------------------
0061  '                      Runtime conditions
0062  '-----------------------------------------------------------------
```

```
0063   Global hDesktopWnd As Integer                        'handle to desktop
0064   Global hDCcaps As Integer                      'display-context for desktop
0065   Global DisplayWidth As Integer                'horizontal screen resolution
0066   Global DisplayHeight As Integer                 'vertical screen resolution
0067   Global DisplayBits As Integer                    'number of bits-per-pixel
0068   Global DisplayPlanes As Integer                     'number of bitplanes
0069   Global MemoryMode As Long                         'runtime memory mode
0070   Global RetVal As Integer                     'will receive GDI return value
0071   Global RetLong As Long                       'will receive GDI return value
0072   Global MousePresent As Integer                          'mouse active?
0073   Global WindowsVersion As Long                        'version of Windows
0074
0075   '----------------------------------------------------------------
0076   '                   Hidden frame operations
0077   '----------------------------------------------------------------
0078   Global hFrameDC As Integer              'display-context for hidden-frame
0079   Global hFrame As Integer                   'handle to hidden-frame bitmap
0080   Global hPrevFrame As Integer                'default bitmap for hFrameDC
0081   Global FrameReady As Integer                    'hidden-frame created?
0082
0083   '----------------------------------------------------------------
0084   '                  256-color palette operations
0085   '----------------------------------------------------------------
0086   Type PALETTEENTRY                       'structure for a palette entry...
0087     Red As String * 1                       'red intensity 0 to 255
0088     Green As String * 1                     'green intensity 0 to 255
0089     Blue As String * 1                       'blue intensity 0 to 255
0090     Flags As String * 1                        'always set to 0
0091   End Type
0092   Type LOGPALETTE                     'structure for an entire palette...
0093     Version As Integer                       'nominal version number
0094     NumEntries As Integer             'number of entries in the palette
0095     Index(0 To 15)  As PALETTEENTRY           'array of entries
0096   End Type
0097   Global Palette As LOGPALETTE                     'a specific palette
0098   Global hPal As Integer                        'handle to the palette
0099   Global PaletteReady As Integer                'True if palette ready
0100
0101   '----------------------------------------------------------------
0102   '            Constants for Windows API functions
0103   '----------------------------------------------------------------
0104   Global Const SRCCOPY = &HCC0020                      'for bitblts...
0105   Global Const SRCINVERT = &H660046
0106   Global Const SRCPAINT = &HEE0086
0107   Global Const WHITENESS = &HFF0062
0108   Global Const BLACKNESS = &H42&
0109   Global Const ALTERNATE = 1                          'for filling...
0110   Global Const WINDING = 2
0111   Global Const R2_COPYPEN = 13                        'for pen mode...
0112   Global Const R2_XORPEN = 7
0113   Global Const TRANSPARENT = 1                  'for background mode...
0114   Global Const OPAQUE = 2
0115   Global Const PS_SOLID = 0                           'for solid pen
0116   Global Const PS_NULL = 5                       'for transparent pen
0117   Global Const BLACKONWHITE = 1                  'for bitblt scaling...
0118   Global Const WHITEONBLACK = 2
0119   Global Const COLORONCOLOR = 3
0120   Global Const HORZRES = 8                      'args for GetDeviceCaps()...
```

```
0121  Global Const VERTRES = 10
0122  Global Const BITSPIXEL = 12
0123  Global Const PLANES = 14
0124  Global Const SM_MOUSEPRESENT = 19          'for GetSystemMetrics()
0125  Global Const WF_ENHANCED = &H20            'for GetWinFlags()...
0126  Global Const WF_STANDARD = &H10
0127  Global Const CF_PALETTE = 9          'used for clipboard operations
0128
0129  '------------------------------------------------------------------
0130  '              GDI functions for display-contexts
0131  '------------------------------------------------------------------
0132  Declare Function GetDC Lib "USER" (ByVal hWnd As Integer) As
          Integer
0133  Declare Function ReleaseDC Lib "USER" (ByVal hWnd As Integer,
          ByVal hDC As Integer) As Integer
0134
0135  '------------------------------------------------------------------
0136  '              GDI functions for the desktop
0137  '------------------------------------------------------------------
0138  Declare Function GetDesktopWindow Lib "USER" () As Integer
0139
0140  '------------------------------------------------------------------
0141  '         GDI functions for creating drawing objects
0142  '------------------------------------------------------------------
0143  Declare Function CreatePen Lib "GDI" (ByVal PenStyle As Integer,
          ByVal Wd As Integer, ByVal Color As Long) As Integer
0144  Declare Function CreateSolidBrush Lib "GDI" (ByVal Color As Long)
          As Integer
0145
0146  '------------------------------------------------------------------
0147  '              GDI functions for selecting objects
0148  '------------------------------------------------------------------
0149  Declare Function SelectObject Lib "GDI" (ByVal hDC As Integer,
          ByVal hObject As Integer) As Integer
0150  Declare Function DeleteObject Lib "GDI" (ByVal hObject As Integer)
          As Integer
0151
0152  '------------------------------------------------------------------
0153  '              GDI functions for bitmaps and bitblts
0154  '------------------------------------------------------------------
0155  Declare Function CreateCompatibleDC Lib "GDI" (ByVal hDC As Integer) As
          Integer
0156  Declare Function CreateCompatibleBitmap Lib "GDI" (ByVal hDC As
          Integer, ByVal Wd As Integer, ByVal Ht As Integer) As Integer
0157  Declare Function PatBlt Lib "GDI" (ByVal hDC As Integer, ByVal X
          As Integer, ByVal Y As Integer, ByVal Wd As Integer, ByVal Ht
          As Integer, ByVal RasOp As Long) As Integer
0158  Declare Function BitBlt Lib "GDI" (ByVal hDestDC As Integer, ByVal
          DestX As Integer, ByVal DestY As Integer, ByVal Wd As Integer,
          ByVal Ht As Integer, ByVal hSrcDC As Integer, ByVal SrcX As
          Integer, ByVal SrcY As Integer, ByVal RastOp As Long) As
          Integer
0159  Declare Function DeleteDC Lib "GDI" (ByVal hDC As Integer) As
          Integer
0160
```

```
0161   '----------------------------------------------------------------
0162   '            GDI functions for drawing mode operations
0163   '----------------------------------------------------------------
0164   Declare Function SetROP2 Lib "GDI" (ByVal hDC As Integer, ByVal
             RasMode As Integer) As Integer
0165   Declare Function SetBkColor Lib "GDI" (ByVal hDC As Integer, ByVal
             Color As Long) As Long
0166   Declare Function SetBkMode Lib "GDI" (ByVal hDC As Integer, ByVal
             BkMode As Integer) As Integer
0167   Declare Function SetPolyFillMode Lib "GDI" (ByVal hDC As Integer,
             ByVal PolyMode As Integer) As Integer
0168   Declare Function SetStretchBltMode Lib "GDI" (ByVal hDC As
             Integer, ByVal StretchMode As Integer) As Integer
0169
0170   '----------------------------------------------------------------
0171   '            GDI functions for drawing operations
0172   '----------------------------------------------------------------
0173   Declare Function MoveTo Lib "GDI" (ByVal hDC As Integer, ByVal X
             As Integer, ByVal Y As Integer) As Long
0174   Declare Function LineTo Lib "GDI" (ByVal hDC As Integer, ByVal X
             As Integer, ByVal Y As Integer) As Integer
0175   Declare Function Polygon Lib "GDI" (ByVal hDC As Integer, FirstPt
             As Integer, ByVal Count As Integer) As Integer
0176   Declare Function Rectangle Lib "GDI" (ByVal hDC As Integer, ByVal
             X1 As Integer, ByVal Y1 As Integer, ByVal X2 As Integer, ByVal
             Y2 As Integer) As Integer
0177   Declare Function Ellipse Lib "GDI" (ByVal hDC As Integer, ByVal X1
             As Integer, ByVal Y1 As Integer, ByVal X2 As Integer, ByVal Y2
             As Integer) As Integer
0178   Declare Function FloodFill Lib "GDI" (ByVal hDC As Integer, ByVal
             X As Integer, ByVal Y As Integer, ByVal Color As Long) As
             Integer
0179   Declare Function SetPixel Lib "GDI" (ByVal hDC As Integer, ByVal X
             As Integer, ByVal Y As Integer, ByVal Color As Long) As Long
0180   Declare Function GetPixel Lib "GDI" (ByVal hDC As Integer, ByVal X
             As Integer, ByVal Y As Integer) As Long
0181
0182   '----------------------------------------------------------------
0183   '            GDI functions for regions
0184   '----------------------------------------------------------------
0185   Declare Function PaintRgn Lib "GDI" (ByVal hDC As Integer, ByVal
             hRgn As Integer) As Integer
0186   Declare Function CreatePolygonRgn Lib "GDI" (FirstPt As Integer,
             ByVal Count As Integer, ByVal PolyFillMode As Integer) As
             Integer
0187   '----------------------------------------------------------------
0188   '            GDI functions for palettes
0189   '----------------------------------------------------------------
0190   Declare Function CreatePalette Lib "GDI" (lpPal As LOGPALETTE) As
             Integer
0191
0192   '----------------------------------------------------------------
0193   '   GDI, USER, KERNEL functions for various runtime conditions
0194   '----------------------------------------------------------------
0195   Declare Function GetDeviceCaps Lib "GDI" (ByVal hDC As Integer,
             ByVal Item As Integer) As Integer
0196   Declare Function GetWinFlags Lib "KERNEL" () As Long
```

```
0197   Declare Function GetSystemMetrics Lib "USER" (ByVal Item As
            Integer) As Integer
0198   Declare Function GlobalCompact Lib "KERNEL" (ByVal NumBytes
            As Long) As Long
0199   Declare Function GetVersion Lib "KERNEL" () As Long
0200   Declare Function ExitWindows Lib "USER" (ByVal Reserved As Long,
            ByVal Item As Integer) As Integer
0201   Declare Function OpenClipboard Lib "USER" (ByVal hWnd As Integer)
            As Integer
0202   Declare Function SetClipboardData Lib "USER" (ByVal wFormat As
            Integer, ByVal hMem As Integer) As Integer
0203   Declare Function CloseClipboard Lib "USER" () As Integer
0204
0205   '----------------------------------------------------------------
0206   '                     End of global module.
0207   '----------------------------------------------------------------
0208


0001   VERSION 2.00
0002   Begin Form Form1
0003       Caption          =    "Prototype"
0004       ControlBox       =    0    'False
0005       Height           =    4515
0006       Left             =    2040
0007       LinkMode         =    1  'Source
0008       LinkTopic        =    "Form1"
0009       MaxButton        =    0    'False
0010       MinButton        =    0    'False
0011       ScaleHeight      =    3825
0012       ScaleWidth       =    3840
0013       Top              =    1485
0014       Width            =    3960
0015       Begin Menu POPUP_File
0016           Caption      =    "&File"
0017           Begin Menu IDM_New
0018               Caption      =    "&New"
0019               Enabled      =    0    'False
0020           End
0021           Begin Menu IDM_Open
0022               Caption      =    "&Open"
0023               Enabled      =    0    'False
0024           End
0025           Begin Menu IDM_Save
0026               Caption      =    "&Save"
0027               Enabled      =    0    'False
0028           End
0029           Begin Menu IDM_SaveAs
0030               Caption      =    "Save &As..."
0031               Enabled      =    0    'False
0032           End
0033           Begin Menu FileSep1
0034               Caption      =    "-"
0035           End
0036           Begin Menu IDM_Exit
0037               Caption      =    "E&xit..."
```

```
0038          End
0039          Begin Menu IDM_Restart
0040             Caption        =    "&Restart Windows..."
0041          End
0042       End
0043       Begin Menu POPUP_Edit
0044          Caption       =    "&Edit"
0045          Begin Menu IDM_Undo
0046             Caption        =    "&Undo"
0047             Enabled        =    0    'False
0048          End
0049          Begin Menu EditSep1
0050             Caption        =    "-"
0051          End
0052          Begin Menu IDM_Cut
0053             Caption        =    "Cu&t"
0054             Enabled        =    0    'False
0055          End
0056          Begin Menu IDM_Copy
0057             Caption        =    "&Copy"
0058             Enabled        =    0    'False
0059          End
0060          Begin Menu IDM_Paste
0061             Caption        =    "&Paste"
0062             Enabled        =    0    'False
0063          End
0064          Begin Menu IDM_Delete
0065             Caption        =    "&Delete"
0066             Enabled        =    0    'False
0067          End
0068       End
0069       Begin Menu POPUP_Go
0070          Caption       =    "&Go"
0071          Begin Menu POPUP_NestedMenu1
0072             Caption        =    "Nested menu &1..."
0073             Begin Menu IDM_ItemA
0074                Caption        =    "Menu item &1"
0075                Enabled        =    0    'False
0076             End
0077             Begin Menu IDM_ItemB
0078                Caption        =    "Menu item &2"
0079             End
0080             Begin Menu IDM_ItemC
0081                Caption        =    "Menu item &3"
0082             End
0083          End
0084          Begin Menu POPUP_NestedMenu2
0085             Caption        =    "Nested menu &2..."
0086             Begin Menu IDM_ItemD
0087                Caption        =    "Menu item &1"
0088             End
0089             Begin Menu IDM_ItemE
0090                Caption        =    "Menu item &2"
0091             End
0092          End
0093          Begin Menu DemoSep1
0094             Caption        =    "-"
0095          End
```

```
0096        Begin Menu IDM_ItemF
0097           Caption        =    "Font demo"
0098        End
0099        Begin Menu IDM_ItemG
0100           Caption        =    "Color demo"
0101        End
0102        Begin Menu DemoSep2
0103           Caption        =    "-"
0104        End
0105        Begin Menu IDM_Clear
0106           Caption        =    "Cle&ar viewport"
0107        End
0108     End
0109     Begin Menu POPUP_Use
0110        Caption        =    "&Use"
0111        Begin Menu IDM_About
0112           Caption        =    "&About"
0113        End
0114        Begin Menu IDM_License
0115           Caption        =    "&License"
0116        End
0117        Begin Menu HelpSep1
0118           Caption        =    "-"
0119        End
0120        Begin Menu IDM_Display
0121           Caption        =    "&Resolution of display"
0122        End
0123        Begin Menu IDM_Colors
0124           Caption        =    "Available &colors"
0125        End
0126        Begin Menu IDM_Mode
0127           Caption        =    "&Memory mode"
0128        End
0129        Begin Menu IDM_Version
0130           Caption        =    "Windows &version"
0131        End
0132        Begin Menu HelpSep2
0133           Caption        =    "-"
0134        End
0135        Begin Menu IDM_GeneralHelp
0136           Caption        =    "&How to use"
0137        End
0138     End
0139  End
0140  '----------------------------------------------------------------
0141  '     Reusable template for Visual Basic Windows applications
0142  '      that use a hidden frame, display-independent graphics,
0143  '                   and persistent images.
0144  '----------------------------------------------------------------
0145  ' Source file:  STARTUP.FRM
0146  ' Release version:  1.00                    Programmer:  Lee Adams
0147  ' Type:  Visual Basic global module for Windows applications.
0148  ' Compiler:  Microsoft Visual Basic 2.00
0149  ' Dependencies:  STGLOBAL.BAS global module
0150  '                STMAIN.BAS module containing Main()
0151  ' Output and features:  Demonstrates a display-independent
```

```
0152  '     graphics application that can run in different screen modes.
0153  '     Demonstrates persistent graphics that are automatically
0154  '     refreshed when covered by another window or cropped by the
0155  '     edge of the screen.  Demonstrates how to detect various
0156  '     runtime conditions such as screen resolution, number of
0157  '     available colors, memory mode (real, standard, enhanced).
0158  '     Demonstrates how to create and use custom-palettes in
0159  '     256-color modes.  Demonstrates dithered palettes in
0160  '     16-color modes and other modes.
0161  '  Publication:  Contains material from Windcrest/McGraw-Hill
0162  '     book 4225 published by TAB BOOKS Div. of McGraw-Hill Inc.
0163  '  License:  As purchaser of the book you are granted a
0164  '     royalty-free license to distribute executable files
0165  '     generated using this code provided that you accept the
0166  '     conditions of the License Agreement and Limited Warranty
0167  '     described in the book and on the companion disk.  Government
0168  '     users:  This software and documentation are subject to
0169  '     restrictions set forth in The Rights in Technical Data and
0170  '     Computer Software clause at 252.227-7013 and elsewhere.
0171  '----------------------------------------------------------------
0172  '      (c) Copyright 1993 Lee Adams.  All rights reserved.
0173  '          Lee Adams(tm) is a trademark of Lee Adams.
0174  '----------------------------------------------------------------
0175  '  Because this Visual Basic application uses a procedure named
0176  '  Main() at startup, you must select Set Startup Form from the
0177  '  Run menu before you run the program or build an .EXE file.
0178
0179  '----------------------------------------------------------------
0180  '              Refresh the client area if uncovered
0181  '----------------------------------------------------------------
0182  Sub Form_Paint ()   'is automatically called by Windows as needed
0183  zCopyToDisplay               'copy hidden frame to display window
0184  End Sub
0185
0186  '----------------------------------------------------------------
0187  '            Intercept any attempt to resize the window
0188  '----------------------------------------------------------------
0189  Sub Form_Resize ()          'is called twice when window is resized
0190  If StartUp = True Then  'if window being displayed for first time
0191    StartUp = False
0192    IgnoreRefresh = True
0193    Exit Sub
0194  End If
0195  Form1.WindowState = 0                         'reset normal size
0196  Form1.Width = Window_Width * HorizTwipsPixel       'reset width
0197  Form1.Height = Window_Height * VertTwipsPixel      'reset height
0198  Form1.Left = (Screen.Width - Form1.Width) / 2  'horizontal center
0199  Form1.Top = (Screen.Height - Form1.Height) / 2  'vertical center
0200  If IgnoreRefresh = False Then                     'if second call
0201    IgnoreRefresh = True          'reset token for next first call
0202    MsgBox "This demo uses a fixed-size window.", MB_OK, "Sample
         application"
0203    Exit Sub
0204  End If
0205  Form1.Refresh                            'refresh the client area
0206  IgnoreRefresh = False        'if first call, reset for second call
0207  End Sub
0208
```

```
0209  '------------------------------------------------------------------
0210  '                     Display the About message box
0211  '------------------------------------------------------------------
0212  Sub IDM_About_Click ()
0213  MsgBox "This is a demo from Windcrest McGraw-Hill book 4225.
           Copyright© 1993 Lee Adams.  All rights reserved.", MB_OK,
           "About this Visual Basic program"
0214  End Sub
0215
0216  '------------------------------------------------------------------
0217  '                 Clear the client area of the window
0218  '------------------------------------------------------------------
0219  Sub IDM_Clear_Click ()
0220  zClear                                    'clear the display window
0221  zClearHiddenFrame                         'clear the hidden frame
0222  End Sub
0223
0224  '------------------------------------------------------------------
0225  '               Determine number of available colors
0226  '------------------------------------------------------------------
0227  Sub IDM_Colors_Click ()
0228  If DisplayBits = 1 Then                   'if 1 bit-per-pixel...
0229    If DisplayPlanes = 4 Then                     'if 4 bitplanes...
0230      MsgBox "Running in 4-bit, 16-color mode.", MB_OK, "Available
              colors"
0231      Exit Sub
0232    End If
0233    If DisplayPlanes = 1 Then                     'if 1 bitplane...
0234      MsgBox "Running in 1-bit, 2-color mode.", MB_OK, "Available
              colors"
0235      Exit Sub
0236    End If
0237  End If
0238  If DisplayBits = 8 Then                   'if 8 bits-per-pixel...
0239    MsgBox "Running in 8-bit, 256-color mode.", MB_OK, "Available
            colors"
0240    Exit Sub
0241  End If
0242  If DisplayBits = 16 Then                  'if 16 bits-per-pixel...
0243    MsgBox "Running in 16-bit, 65000-color mode.", MB_OK, "Available
            colors"
0244    Exit Sub
0245  End If
0246  MsgBox "Running in a custom color mode.", MB_OK, "Available colors"
0247  End Sub
0248
0249  '------------------------------------------------------------------
0250  '                  Determine the screen resolution
0251  '------------------------------------------------------------------
0252  Sub IDM_Display_Click ()
0253  If DisplayWidth = 640 Then
0254    If DisplayHeight = 480 Then                            'VGA mode
0255      MsgBox "Running in 640x480 mode.", MB_OK, "Screen resolution"
0256      Exit Sub
0257    End If
0258    If DisplayHeight = 350 Then                            'EGA mode
```

```
0259        MsgBox "Running in 640x350 mode.", MB_OK, "Screen resolution"
0260        Exit Sub
0261      End If
0262    If DisplayHeight = 200 Then                          'CGA mode
0263        MsgBox "Running in 640x200 mode.", MB_OK, "Screen resolution"
0264        Exit Sub
0265      End If
0266    End If
0267    If DisplayWidth = 800 Then               'SuperVGA, 8514/A, XGA mode
0268      MsgBox "Running in 800x600 mode.", MB_OK, "Screen resolution"
0269      Exit Sub
0270    End If
0271    If DisplayWidth = 1024 Then                   '8514/A, XGA mode
0272      MsgBox "Running in 1024x768 mode.", MB_OK, "Screen resolution"
0273      Exit Sub
0274    End If
0275    If DisplayWidth = 720 Then                          'Hercules mode
0276      MsgBox "Running in 720x348 mode.", MB_OK, "Screen resolution"
0277      Exit Sub
0278    End If
0279    MsgBox "Running in custom mode.", MB_OK, "Screen resolution"
0280    End Sub
0281
0282    '-----------------------------------------------------------------
0283    '                    Terminate the application
0284    '-----------------------------------------------------------------
0285    Sub IDM_Exit_Click ()
0286    UserWants = MsgBox("Exit the demo and return to Windows?",
            MB_YESNO, "Please confirm")
0287    If UserWants = IDNO Then              'if user selected No button...
0288      Exit Sub                           'then cancel this operation
0289    End If            'otherwise continue to terminate the application...
0290    If FrameReady = True Then          'if a hidden frame was created
0291      RetVal = SelectObject(hFrameDC, hPrevFrame)      'deselect bitmap
0292      RetVal = DeleteObject(hFrame)                'delete the bitmap
0293      RetVal = DeleteDC(hFrameDC)            'delete the display-context
0294    End If
0295    End                                     'terminate the application
0296    End Sub
0297
0298    '-----------------------------------------------------------------
0299    '                    Display the Help message box
0300    '-----------------------------------------------------------------
0301    Sub IDM_GeneralHelp_Click ()
0302    MsgBox "Select from the Go menu to explore menuing.  Select from
            the Use menu to determine display resolution, available
            colors, runtime memory mode, and more  Also see the discussion
            in Windcrest/McGraw-Hill book 4225.", MB_OK, "How to use this
            demo"
0303    End Sub
0304
0305    '-----------------------------------------------------------------
0306    '                    Font demo
0307    '-----------------------------------------------------------------
0308    Sub IDM_ItemF_Click ()
0309      Dim PrevFontClr As Long                      'default font color
0310      Dim PrevFontSize As Integer                   'default font size
0311    zInitFrame                        'ensure hidden-frame initialized
```

```
0312   zClear                                    'clear the display window
0313   zClearHiddenFrame                         'clear the hidden frame
0314   '-------------- store current font's attributes -----------------
0315   PrevFontSize = Form1.FontSize          'remember current font size
0316   PrevFontClr = Form1.ForeColor          'remember current font color
0317   '-------------------- display the titles ----------------------
0318   Form1.FontSize = 16                              'set the size
0319   Form1.ForeColor = RGB(0, 0, 0)                   'set the color
0320   Form1.FontTransparent = True      'use transparent font backgrounds
0321   Form1.CurrentX = 10               'set the starting location...
0322   Form1.CurrentY = 6
0323   Form1.Print "A Lee Adams tutorial:"              'display text
0324   Form1.FontSize = 24                              'reset the size
0325   Form1.CurrentX = 8                        'reset the location...
0326   Form1.CurrentY = 24
0327   Form1.Print "Font captions"                      'display text
0328   '------------------ restore the default font --------------------
0329   Form1.FontSize = PrevFontSize                    'restore the size
0330   Form1.ForeColor = PrevFontClr                    'restore the color
0331   '-------------------- display the captions --------------------
0332   Form1.CurrentX = 10
0333   Form1.CurrentY = 214
0334   Form1.Print "The titles use sizes 16 and 24."
0335   Form1.CurrentX = 10
0336   Form1.CurrentY = 228
0337   Form1.Print "The captions use the default system font."
0338   zCopyToFrame                             'copy image to hidden frame
0339   End Sub
0340
0341   '-----------------------------------------------------------------
0342   '                         Color demo
0343   '-----------------------------------------------------------------
0344   Sub IDM_ItemG_Click ()
0345     Dim PrevFontClr As Long                       'default font color
0346     Dim PrevFontSize As Integer                   'default font size
0347     Dim hPrevBrush As Integer, hSwatchBrush As Integer      'brushes
0348     Dim hPrevPen As Integer, hBorderPen As Integer            'pens
0349     Dim iWidth As Integer, iDepth As Integer
0350     Dim iSwatchX As Integer, iSwatchY As Integer
0351     Dim iX1 As Integer, iY1 As Integer
0352     Dim iX2 As Integer, iY2 As Integer
0353     Dim iColor As Integer
0354     Dim iCount As Integer                            'loop counter
0355     Dim iRed As Integer                'intensities of RGB guns...
0356     Dim IGreen As Integer
0357     Dim iBlue As Integer
0358     Dim iBrighten As Integer            'amount to adjust RGB guns
0359   '-------------------- initialize variables --------------------
0360   PaletteReady = False                     'custom-palette not ready
0361   iWidth = 15                   'width and depth of each swatch...
0362   iDepth = 60
0363   iSwatchX = 8                    'starting location for swatches...
0364   iSwatchY = 70
0365   iBrighten = 17           'amount to increase intensity of an RGB gun
0366   '-------------------- initialize the viewport -------------------
0367   zInitFrame                             'ensure hidden-frame initialized
```

```
0368  zClear                                          'clear the display window
0369  zClearHiddenFrame                                'clear the hidden frame
0370  '---------- if 256-color mode, create a custom-palette ----------
0371  If DisplayBits = 8 Then                          'if 8 bits-per-pixel...
0372    iRed = 0                         'reset the color-component variables...
0373    IGreen = 0
0374    iBlue = 0
0375    iIncrement = 17     'reset the amount to adjust intensity of guns
0376    Palette.Version = &H300          'Windows palette version 3.00
0377    Palette.NumEntries = 16          '16 colors in this custom-palette
0378    For iCount = 0 To 15 Step 1      'for each entry in the palette...
0379      Palette.Index(iCount).Red = Chr$(iRed)         'set the red
0380      Palette.Index(iCount).Green = Chr$(IGreen)     'set the green
0381      Palette.Index(iCount).Blue = Chr$(iBlue)       'set the blue
0382      Palette.Index(iCount).Flags = Chr$(0)          'set the flags
0383      iRed = iRed + iBrighten               'and adjust for next loop
0384    Next iCount                    'loop back and do the next entry...
0385    hPal = CreatePalette(Palette)          'create a GDI palette
0386    If hPal = 0 Then
0387      MsgBox "Unable to create a GDI custom-palette.  Will use
              dithered swatches instead.", MB_OK, "Custom-palette report"
0388      GoTo DrawSystemPalette
0389    End If
0390    Clipboard.Clear                            'clear the clipboard
0391    RetVal = OpenClipboard(Form1.hWnd)         'open the clipboard
0392    If RetVal = 0 Then
0393      MsgBox "Unable to open clipboard for palette transfer.  Will
              use dithered swatches instead.", MB_OK, "Custom-palette report"
0394      GoTo DrawSystemPalette
0395    End If
0396    RetVal = SetClipboardData(CF_PALETTE, hPal) 'copy to clipboard
0397    RetVal = CloseClipboard()              'release the clipboard
0398    If RetVal = 0 Then
0399      MsgBox "Unable to release the clipboard after palette
              transfer.  Will use dithered swatches instead.", MB_OK,
              "Custom-palette report"
0400      GoTo DrawSystemPalette
0401    End If
0402    Form1.Picture = Clipboard.GetData(CF_PALETTE)       'grab palette
0403    zClear                                    'clear the viewport
0404    PaletteReady = True                       'set a run-time token
0405    Form1.AutoRedraw = True     'activate, clear VB's refresh page...
0406    RetVal = PatBlt(Form1.hDC, 0, 0, zFRAMEWIDE, zFRAMEHIGH, WHITENESS)
0407    Form1.AutoRedraw = False                'disable VB's refresh page
0408  End If
0409  '---------- draw swatches showing the system palette -----------
0410  DrawSystemPalette:
0411  iX1 = iSwatchX                     'initialize the upper-left coords...
0412  iY1 = iSwatchY
0413  iX2 = iX1 + iWidth                'initialize the lower-right coords...
0414  iY2 = iY1 + iDepth
0415  hBorderPen = CreatePen(PS_NULL, 1, RGB(0, 0, 0)) 'transparent pen
0416  hPrevPen = SelectObject(hDC, hBorderPen)            'select pen
0417  For iColor = 0 To 15 Step 1  'for 16 colors in default palette...
0418    hSwatchBrush = CreateSolidBrush(QBColor(iColor))  'create brush
0419    hPrevBrush = SelectObject(hDC, hSwatchBrush)       'select brush
0420    RetVal = Rectangle(hDC, iX1, iY1, iX2 + 1, iY2 + 1)  'rectangle
0421    RetVal = SelectObject(hDC, hPrevBrush)           'deselect brush
```

```
0422    RetVal = DeleteObject(hSwatchBrush)                    'delete brush
0423    iX1 = iX1 + iWidth                        'increment upper-left coord
0424    iX2 = iX1 + iWidth                       'increment lower-right coord
0425  Next iColor          'loop back and do next color in system palette
0426  RetVal = SelectObject(hDC, hPrevPen)                    'deselect pen
0427  RetVal = DeleteObject(hBorderPen)                         'delete pen
0428  iX1 = iSwatchX               'set upper-left corner for border...
0429  iY1 = iSwatchY
0430  iX2 = iX1 + (16 * iWidth)   'set lower-right corner for border...
0431  iY2 = iY1 + iDepth
0432  hBorderPen = CreatePen(PS_SOLID, 1, RGB(0, 0, 0))       'create pen
0433  hPrevPen = SelectObject(hDC, hBorderPen)                  'select pen
0434  RetLong = MoveTo(hDC, iX1, iY1)                     'draw border...
0435  RetVal = LineTo(hDC, iX2, iY1)
0436  RetVal = LineTo(hDC, iX2, iY2)
0437  RetVal = LineTo(hDC, iX1, iY2)
0438  RetVal = LineTo(hDC, iX1, iY1)
0439  RetVal = SelectObject(hDC, hPrevPen)                    'deselect pen
0440  RetVal = DeleteObject(hBorderPen)                         'delete pen
0441  '---------- if custom-palette available, draw swatches ----------
0442  If PaletteReady = True Then
0443    iSwatchY = 140                   'reset the starting vertical location
0444    iX1 = iSwatchX               'reinitialize the upper-left coords...
0445    iY1 = iSwatchY
0446    iX2 = iX1 + iWidth         'reinitialize the lower-right coords...
0447    iY2 = iY1 + iDepth
0448    hBorderPen = CreatePen(PS_NULL, 1, RGB(0, 0, 0))      'create pen
0449    hPrevPen = SelectObject(hDC, hBorderPen)               'select pen
0450    FillStyle = 0                       'set fill style to solid
0451    For iCount = 0 To 15 Step 1    'for each entry in the palette...
0452      iRed = Asc(Palette.Index(iCount).Red)                   'grab red
0453      IGreen = Asc(Palette.Index(iCount).Green)             'grab green
0454      iBlue = Asc(Palette.Index(iCount).Blue)               'grab blue
0455      FillColor = RGB(iRed, IGreen, iBlue)            'set fill color
0456      RetVal = Rectangle(hDC, iX1, iY1, iX2 + 1, iY2 + 1)       'draw
0457      iX1 = iX1 + iWidth     'adjust horizontal position of swatch...
0458      iX2 = iX1 + iWidth
0459    Next iCount                 'loop back for next entry in the palette
0460    RetVal = SelectObject(hDC, hPrevPen)                    'deselect pen
0461    RetVal = DeleteObject(hBorderPen)                         'delete pen
0462    iX1 = iSwatchX
0463    iY1 = iSwatchY
0464    iX2 = iX1 + (16 * iWidth)
0465    iY2 = iY1 + iDepth
0466    hBorderPen = CreatePen(PS_SOLID, 1, RGB(0, 0, 0))
0467    hPrevPen = SelectObject(hDC, hBorderPen)
0468    RetLong = MoveTo(hDC, iX1, iY1)
0469    RetVal = LineTo(hDC, iX2, iY1)
0470    RetVal = LineTo(hDC, iX2, iY2)
0471    RetVal = LineTo(hDC, iX1, iY2)
0472    RetVal = LineTo(hDC, iX1, iY1)
0473    RetVal = SelectObject(hDC, hPrevPen)
0474    RetVal = DeleteObject(hBorderPen)
0475    GoTo DisplayFonts
0476  End If
0477  '----- if 256-colors not available, draw dithered swatches ------
```

```
0478  MsgBox "Current graphics mode does not support custom-palettes.
              Will use dithering instead.", MB_OK, "Custom-palette report"
0479  DrawSwatches:        'jump to here if error in custom-palette code
0480  iSwatchY = 140               'reset the starting vertical location
0481  iX1 = iSwatchX              'reinitialize the upper-left coords...
0482  iY1 = iSwatchY
0483  iX2 = iX1 + iWidth        'reinitialize the lower-right coords...
0484  iY2 = iY1 + iDepth
0485  iRed = 0             'reinitialize RGB guns for custom-palette...
0486  IGreen = 0
0487  iBlue = 0
0488  hBorderPen = CreatePen(PS_NULL, 1, RGB(iRed, IGreen, iBlue))
0489  hPrevPen = SelectObject(hDC, hBorderPen)
0490  For iCount = 0 To 15 Step 1        'see remarks for previous loop
0491    hSwatchBrush = CreateSolidBrush(RGB(iRed, IGreen, iBlue))
0492    hPrevBrush = SelectObject(hDC, hSwatchBrush)
0493    RetVal = Rectangle(hDC, iX1, iY1, iX2 + 1, iY2 + 1)
0494    RetVal = SelectObject(hDC, hPrevBrush)
0495    RetVal = DeleteObject(hSwatchBrush)
0496    iX1 = iX1 + iWidth
0497    iX2 = iX1 + iWidth
0498    iRed = iRed + iBrighten              'adjust intensity of red gun
0499  Next iCount
0500  RetVal = SelectObject(hDC, hPrevPen)
0501  RetVal = DeleteObject(hBorderPen)
0502  iX1 = iSwatchX
0503  iY1 = iSwatchY
0504  iX2 = iX1 + (16 * iWidth)
0505  iY2 = iY1 + iDepth
0506  hBorderPen = CreatePen(PS_SOLID, 1, RGB(0, 0, 0))
0507  hPrevPen = SelectObject(hDC, hBorderPen)
0508  RetLong = MoveTo(hDC, iX1, iY1)
0509  RetVal = LineTo(hDC, iX2, iY1)
0510  RetVal = LineTo(hDC, iX2, iY2)
0511  RetVal = LineTo(hDC, iX1, iY2)
0512  RetVal = LineTo(hDC, iX1, iY1)
0513  RetVal = SelectObject(hDC, hPrevPen)
0514  RetVal = DeleteObject(hBorderPen)
0515  '-------------------- display the titles ----------------------
0516  DisplayFonts:                'jump to here after displaying swatches
0517  PrevFontSize = Form1.FontSize        'remember current font size
0518  PrevFontClr = Form1.ForeColor        'remember current font color
0519  Form1.FontSize = 16                           'set the size
0520  Form1.ForeColor = RGB(0, 0, 0)                'set the color
0521  Form1.FontTransparent = True   'use transparent font backgrounds
0522  Form1.CurrentX = 10                 'set the starting location...
0523  Form1.CurrentY = 6
0524  Form1.Print "A Lee Adams tutorial:"            'display text
0525  Form1.FontSize = 24                            'reset the size
0526  Form1.CurrentX = 8                    'reset the location...
0527  Form1.CurrentY = 24
0528  Form1.Print "Color palettes"                   'display text
0529  Form1.FontSize = PrevFontSize                  'restore the size
0530  Form1.ForeColor = PrevFontClr                  'restore the color
0531  Form1.CurrentX = 10
0532  Form1.CurrentY = 214
0533  Form1.Print "Top:  the default color-palette."
0534  Form1.CurrentX = 10
```

C-1 Continued.

```
0535  Form1.CurrentY = 228
0536  Form1.Print "Below:  a custom color-palette."
0537  '------------------ tidy up before returning --------------------
0538  zCopyToFrame                          'copy image to hidden frame
0539  End Sub
0540
0541  '-----------------------------------------------------------------
0542  '                 Display the License message box
0543  '-----------------------------------------------------------------
0544  Sub IDM_License_Click ()
0545  MsgBox "You can use this code as part of your own software product
            subject to the License Agreement and Limited Warranty in
            Windcrest McGraw-Hill book 4225 and on its companion disk.",
            MB_OK, "License Agreement"
0546  End Sub
0547
0548  '-----------------------------------------------------------------
0549  '                 Determine runtime memory mode
0550  '-----------------------------------------------------------------
0551  Sub IDM_Mode_Click ()
0552     Dim TempVariable As Long
0553  TempVariable = MemoryMode And WF_ENHANCED     'perform bitwise AND
0554  If TempVariable = WF_ENHANCED Then    'if result matches constant
0555     MsgBox "Running in enhanced mode.  Can allocate up to 16 MB
            extended memory (XMS) if available.  Virtual memory up to 4
            times physical memory (maximum 64 MB) is also available via
            automatic disk swapping of 4K pages.", MB_OK, "Memory mode"
0556     Exit Sub
0557  End If
0558  TempVariable = MemoryMode And WF_STANDARD
0559  If TempVariable = WF_STANDARD Then
0560     MsgBox "Running in standard mode.  Can allocate up to 16 MB
            extended physical memory (XMS) if available.", MB_OK, "Memory
            mode"
0561     Exit Sub
0562  End If
0563  MsgBox "Running in real mode.  Can allocate blocks of memory from
            the first 640K of RAM.  Can also allocate blocks from expanded
            memory (EMS) if available.", MB_OK, "Memory mode"
0564  And Sub
0565
0566  '-----------------------------------------------------------------
0567  '          Terminate the application and restart Windows
0568  '-----------------------------------------------------------------
0569  Sub IDM_Restart_Click ()
0570  UserWants = MsgBox("Exit the demo and restart Windows?", MB_YESNO,
            "Please confirm")
0571  If UserWants = IDNO Then               'if user selected No button...
0572     Exit Sub                             'then cancel this operation
0573  End If        'otherwise continue to terminate the application...
0574  If FrameReady = True Then       'if a hidden frame was created
0575     RetVal = SelectObject(hFrameDC, hPrevFrame)     'deselect bitmap
0576     RetVal = DeleteObject(hFrame)                   'delete the bitmap
0577     RetVal = DeleteDC(hFrameDC)             'delete the display-context
0578  End If
0579  RetVal = ExitWindows(&H42&, 0)      'terminate and restart Windows
```

```
0580   End                               'terminate the application
0581   End Sub
0582
0583   '----------------------------------------------------------------
0584   '                  Determine version of Windows
0585   '----------------------------------------------------------------
0586   Sub IDM_Version_Click ()
0587     Dim TempVar As Long
0588   TempVar = WindowsVersion And 7683   'test binary 00011110 00000011
0589   If TempVar = 7683 Then                          'if 30        3...
0590     MsgBox "Running under Windows version 3.3.", MB_OK, "Version
           report"
0591     Exit Sub
0592   End If
0593   TempVar = WindowsVersion And 5123   'test binary 00010100 00000011
0594   If TempVar = 5123 Then                          'if 20        3...
0595     MsgBox "Running under Windows version 3.2.", MB_OK, "Version
           report"
0596     Exit Sub
0597   End If
0598   TempVar = WindowsVersion And 2563   'test binary 00001010 00000011
0599   If TempVar = 2563 Then                          'if 10        3...
0600     MsgBox "Running under Windows version 3.1.", MB_OK, "Version
           report"
0601     Exit Sub
0602   End If
0603   TempVar = WindowsVersion And 3      'test binary 00000000 00000011
0604   If TempVar = 3 Then                             'if 00        3...
0605     MsgBox "Running under Windows version 3.0.", MB_OK, "Version
           report"
0606     Exit Sub
0607   End If
0608   TempVar = WindowsVersion And 4      'test binary 00000000 00000100
0609   If TempVar = 4 Then                             'if 00        4...
0610     MsgBox "Running under Windows version 4.0.", MB_OK, "Version
           report"
0611     Exit Sub
0612   End If
0613   MsgBox "Unable to report Windows version number.", MB_OK, "Version
           report"
0614   End Sub
0615
0616   '----------------------------------------------------------------
0617   '                  Clear the display window
0618   '----------------------------------------------------------------
0619   Sub zClear ()
0620   RetVal = PatBlt(hDC, 0, 0, zFRAMEWIDE, zFRAMEHIGH, WHITENESS)
0621   End Sub
0622
0623   '----------------------------------------------------------------
0624   '                  Clear the hidden frame
0625   '----------------------------------------------------------------
0626   Sub zClearHiddenFrame ()
0627   If FrameReady = False Then
0628     Exit Sub
0629   End If
0630   RetVal = PatBlt(hFrameDC, 0, 0, zFRAMEWIDE, zFRAMEHIGH, WHITENESS)
0631   End Sub
```

```
0632
0633  '-------------------------------------------------------------------
0634  '             Copy the hidden frame to the display window
0635  '-------------------------------------------------------------------
0636  Sub zCopyToDisplay ()
0637  If FrameReady = False Then
0638    Exit Sub
0639  End If
0640  RetVal = BitBlt(hDC, 0, 0, zFRAMEWIDE, zFRAMEHIGH, hFrameDC, 0, 0,
         SRCCOPY)
0641  End Sub
0642
0643  '-------------------------------------------------------------------
0644  '             Copy the display window to the hidden frame
0645  '-------------------------------------------------------------------
0646  Sub zCopyToFrame ()
0647  If FrameReady = False Then
0648    Exit Sub
0649  End If
0650  RetVal = BitBlt(hFrameDC, 0, 0, zFRAMEWIDE, zFRAMEHIGH, hDC, 0, 0,
         SRCCOPY)
0651  End Sub
0652
0653  '-------------------------------------------------------------------
0654  '                    Create the hidden frame
0655  '-------------------------------------------------------------------
0656  Sub zInitFrame ()
0657  If FrameReady = True Then          'if hidden frame already created
0658    Exit Sub
0659  End If
0660  RetLong = GlobalCompact(-1)             'maximize contiguous memory
0661  hFrameDC = CreateCompatibleDC(hDC)        'get a display-context
0662  hFrame = CreateCompatibleBitmap(hDC, zFRAMEWIDE, zFRAMEHIGH)
0663  If hFrame = Null Then                        'if error occurred
0664    MsgBox "Insufficient memory.  Hidden frame not created.", MB_OK,
           "Graphics system not ready"
0665    FrameReady = False
0666    Exit Sub
0667  End If
0668  hPrevFrame = SelectObject(hFrameDC, hFrame)   'select the bitmap
0669  FrameReady = True                            'set a global token
0670  zClearHiddenFrame                          'clear the hidden frame
0671  End Sub
0672


0001  '-------------------------------------------------------------------
0002  '             Reusable template for startup code for
0003  '             Visual Basic Windows graphics applications.
0004  '-------------------------------------------------------------------
0005  '  Source file:  STMAIN.BAS
0006  '  Release version:  1.00              Programmer:  Lee Adams
0007  '  Type:  Visual Basic startup module for Windows applications.
0008  '  Compiler:  Microsoft Visual Basic 2.00
0009  '  Dependencies:  STGLOBAL.BAS global module
0010  '                 STARTUP.FRM primary module
0011  '  Output and features:  Initializes the runtime environment
```

```
0012 '     for a Windows graphics application created with
0013 '     Visual Basic.  Ensures runtime image size and compatibility
0014 '     no matter which graphics mode is being used by Windows.
0015 ' Publication:  Contains material from Windcrest/McGraw-Hill
0016 '     book 4225 published by TAB BOOKS Div. of McGraw-Hill Inc.
0017 ' License:  As purchaser of the book you are granted a
0018 '     royalty-free license to distribute executable files
0019 '     generated using this code provided that you accept the
0020 '     conditions of the License Agreement and Limited Warranty
0021 '     described in the book and on the companion disk.  Government
0022 '     users:  This software and documentation are subject to
0023 '     restrictions set forth in The Rights in Technical Data and
0024 '     Computer Software clause at 252.227-7013 and elsewhere.
0025 '-----------------------------------------------------------------
0026 '     (c) Copyright 1993 Lee Adams.  All rights reserved.
0027 '         Lee Adams(tm) is a trademark of Lee Adams.
0028 '-----------------------------------------------------------------
0029
0030 '-----------------------------------------------------------------
0031 '        Initialization code for startup of application
0032 '-----------------------------------------------------------------
0033 Sub Main ()                          'is called by Windows at startup
0034   Dim PreviousColor As Long            'will remember default color
0035 StartUp = True     'set runtime tokens used by other procedures...
0036 IgnoreRefresh = True                 'ignore first refresh message
0037 FrameReady = False                        'backup page not ready
0038 PaletteReady = False                 '256-color palette not ready
0039 '--------------- examine the graphics adapter ------------------
0040 hDesktopWnd = GetDesktopWindow()             'grab handle to desktop
0041 hDCcaps = GetDC(hDesktopWnd)       'get display-context for desktop
0042 DisplayWidth = GetDeviceCaps(hDCcaps, HORZRES) 'horiz resolution
0043 DisplayHeight = GetDeviceCaps(hDCcaps, VERTRES)  'vert resolution
0044 DisplayBits = GetDeviceCaps(hDCcaps, BITSPIXEL)   'bits-per-pixel
0045 DisplayPlanes = GetDeviceCaps(hDCcaps, PLANES)  'num of bitplanes
0046 RetVal = ReleaseDC(hDesktopWnd, hDCcaps) 'release display-context
0047 '--------------- determine the runtime memory mode --------------
0048 MemoryMode = GetWinFlags()             'will inspect this value later
0049 '--------------- determine version of Windows ------------------
0050 WindowsVersion = GetVersion()        'will inspect this value later
0051 '-------------- set mode-dependent twips factors --------------
0052 HorizTwipsPixel = 15!: VertTwipsPixel = 15!        'set defaults...
0053 Window_Width = zWINDOW_WIDTH: Window_Height = zWINDOW_HEIGHT
0054 If DisplayWidth = 640 Then
0055   If DisplayHeight = 480 Then                    'VGA 640x480 mode
0056     HorizTwipsPixel = 15!             '9600x7200 twips full screen
0057     VertTwipsPixel = 15!
0058     Window_Width = zWINDOW_WIDTH
0059     Window_Height = zWINDOW_HEIGHT
0060   End If
0061   If DisplayHeight = 350 Then                    'EGA 640x350 mode
0062     HorizTwipsPixel = 15!             '9600x7000 twips full screen
0063     VertTwipsPixel = 20!
0064     Window_Width = zWINDOW_WIDTH
0065     Window_Height = 297!   'adjust for aspect ratio and font size
0066   End If
0067   If DisplayHeight = 200 Then   'nominal support CGA 640x200 mode
0068     HorizTwipsPixel = 15!
0069     VertTwipsPixel = 36!
```

```
0070      Window_Width = zWINDOW_WIDTH
0071      Window_Height = zWINDOW_HEIGHT
0072    End If
0073  End If
0074  If DisplayWidth = 800 Then       'SuperVGA, 8514/A, XGA 800x600 mode
0075    HorizTwipsPixel = 12!                   '9600x7200 twips full screen
0076    VertTwipsPixel = 12!
0077    Window_Width = zWINDOW_WIDTH
0078    Window_Height = 317!                        'compensate for font size
0079  End If
0080  If DisplayWidth = 1024 Then             '8514/A, XGA 1024x768 mode
0081    HorizTwipsPixel = 12!                  '12200x9216 twips full screen
0082    VertTwipsPixel = 12!
0083    Window_Width = zWINDOW_WIDTH
0084    Window_Height = 317!                        'compensate for font size
0085  End If
0086  If DisplayWidth = 720 Then                    'Hercules 720x348 mode
0087    HorizTwipsPixel = 12!
0088    VertTwipsPixel = 20!
0089    Window_Width = zWINDOW_WIDTH
0090    Window_Height = 297!      'adjust for aspect ratio and font size
0091  End If
0092  '-------------- display the splash sign-on banner ---------------
0093  UserWants = MsgBox("Graphics demo from Windcrest McGraw-Hill book
          4225.", MB_OKCANCEL, "Copyright© 1993 Lee Adams.")
0094  If UserWants = IDCANCEL Then    'if user selected Cancel button...
0095    End                                  'then cancel this startup
0096  End If
0097  '------------- initialize and display the window ----------------
0098  Form1.Width = Window_Width * HorizTwipsPixel          'set width
0099  Form1.Height = Window_Height * VertTwipsPixel         'set height
0100  Form1.Left = (Screen.Width - Form1.Width) / 2  'horizontal center
0101  Form1.Top = (Screen.Height - Form1.Height) / 2    'vertical center
0102  Form1.Caption = "Programmer's template"          'set the caption
0103  Form1.AutoRedraw = False              'disable automatic refresh
0104  Form1.BackColor = RGB(255, 255, 255)   'set the client area color
0105  Form1.ForeColor = RGB(0, 0, 0)                    'active color
0106  Form1.ScaleMode = PIXELS               'will use pixel coords
0107  Form1.Show                             'display the window
0108  '-------------------- display startup text ---------------------
0109  Form1.CurrentX = 10: Form1.CurrentY = 237        'set text coords
0110  PreviousColor = Form1.ForeColor             'remember current clr
0111  Form1.ForeColor = RGB(191, 191, 191)                  'set clr
0112  Form1.Print "© 1993 Lee Adams.  All rights reserved." '© Alt+0169
0113  Form1.ForeColor = PreviousColor             'restore default clr
0114  '------------------- check if mouse present --------------------
0115  MousePresent = GetSystemMetrics(SM_MOUSEPRESENT)
0116  If MousePresent = 0 Then                         'if no mouse
0117    Beep
0118    MsgBox "No mouse found.  Some features of this demo program may
          require a mouse.  The demo's menu system also responds to the
          keyboard.  Press <Enter> to continue.", MB_OK, "Graphics
          system warning"
0119  End If
0120  End Sub
0121
```

C-2 Source listings for the 3D geometry sampler, objects. See Appendix B for the toolkits which must be used to build this application. See Appendix A for instructions on building the demo.

```
0001   OGLOBAL.BAS
0002   OBMAIN.BAS
0003   ENGINE3D.BAS
0004   LIGHTS3D.BAS
0005   ASSEMB3D.BAS
0006   SHAPES3D.BAS
0007   DEFORM3D.BAS
0008   OBJECTS.FRM
0009   ProjWinSize=80,444,196,336
0010   ProjWinShow=2


0001   '-----------------------------------------------------------------
0002   '  Reusable global module for Visual Basic graphics applications
0003   '              that call Windows API functions.
0004   '-----------------------------------------------------------------
0005   '  Source file:  OBGLOBAL.BAS
0006   '  Release version:  1.00                    Programmer:  Lee Adams
0007   '  Type:  Visual Basic global module for Windows applications.
0008   '  Compiler:  Microsoft Visual Basic 2.00
0009   '  Dependencies:  OBJECTS.FRM primary module
0010   '                 OBMAIN.BAS module containing Main()
0011   '  Output and features:  Provides declarations for Windows API
0012   '    (Application Programming Interface) functions callable by
0013   '    Visual Basic applications at runtime, including routines
0014   '    from Windows' GDI, USER, and KERNEL DLLs (dynamic link
0015   '    libraries).  Also provides declarations of various variables
0016   '    and constants.  Functions, variables, and constants declared
0017   '    in this global module are visible throughout the project.
0018   '  Publication:  Contains material from Windcrest/McGraw-Hill
0019   '    book 4225 published by TAB BOOKS Div. of McGraw-Hill Inc.
0020   '  License:  As purchaser of the book you are granted a
0021   '    royalty-free license to distribute executable files
0022   '    generated using this code provided that you accept the
0023   '    conditions of the License Agreement and Limited Warranty
0024   '    described in the book and on the companion disk.  Government
0025   '    users:  This software and documentation are subject to
0026   '    restrictions set forth in The Rights in Technical Data and
0027   '    Computer Software clause at 252.227-7013 and elsewhere.
0028   '-----------------------------------------------------------------
0029   '      (c) Copyright 1993 Lee Adams.  All rights reserved.
0030   '         Lee Adams(tm) is a trademark of Lee Adams.
0031   '-----------------------------------------------------------------
0032
0033   Option Explicit            'generate error if variable not declared
0034   '-----------------------------------------------------------------
0035   '             General constants and variables
0036   '-----------------------------------------------------------------
0037   Global Const MB_OK = 0                    'OK button for message box
0038   Global Const MB_OKCANCEL = 1  'OK Cancel buttons for message box
0039   Global Const MB_YESNO = 4       'Yes No buttons for message box
0040   Global Const IDOK = 1                        'OK button selected
0041   Global Const IDCANCEL = 2                'Cancel button selected
0042   Global Const IDYES = 6                      'Yes button selected
0043   Global Const IDNO = 7                        'No button selected
```

```
0044   Global UserWants As Integer          'value returned by message box
0045   Global Const PIXELS = 3                      'pixel coordinates
0046   Global StartUp As Integer              'tracks the startup code
0047   Global IgnoreRefresh As Integer        'tracks refresh activity
0048   Global Const zRED = 1
0049   Global Const zGREEN = 2
0050   Global Const zBROWN = 3
0051   Global Const zBLUE = 4
0052   Global Const zMAGENTA = 5
0053   Global Const zCYAN = 6
0054   Global Const zGRAY = 7
0055
0056   '-------------------------------------------------------------------
0057   '                  Window specifications
0058   '-------------------------------------------------------------------
0059   Global Const zWINDOW_WIDTH = 264                    'width of window
0060   Global Const zWINDOW_HEIGHT = 301                  'height of window
0061   Global Const zFRAMEWIDE = 256                 'width of client area
0062   Global Const zFRAMEHIGH = 255                'height of client area
0063   Global HorizTwipsPixel As Single      'twips-per-pixel (horizontal)
0064   Global VertTwipsPixel As Single        'twips-per-pixel (vertical)
0065   Global Window_Width As Single          'runtime width of window
0066   Global Window_Height As Single         'runtime height of window
0067
0068   '-------------------------------------------------------------------
0069   '                  Runtime conditions
0070   '-------------------------------------------------------------------
0071   Global hDesktopWnd As Integer                    'handle to desktop
0072   Global hDCcaps As Integer              'display-context for desktop
0073   Global DisplayWidth As Integer        'horizontal screen resolution
0074   Global DisplayHeight As Integer         'vertical screen resolution
0075   Global DisplayBits As Integer           'number of bits-per-pixel
0076   Global DisplayPlanes As Integer            'number of bitplanes
0077   Global MemoryMode As Long                  'runtime memory mode
0078   Global RetVal As Integer            'will receive GDI return value
0079   Global RetLong As Long              'will receive GDI return value
0080   Global MousePresent As Integer               'mouse active?
0081   Global WindowsVersion As Long             'version of Windows
0082   Global CamLens                        '3D camera focal length
0083
0084   '-------------------------------------------------------------------
0085   '                  Hidden frame operations
0086   '-------------------------------------------------------------------
0087   Global hFrameDC As Integer       'display-context for hidden-frame
0088   Global hFrame As Integer           'handle to hidden-frame bitmap
0089   Global hPrevFrame As Integer        'default bitmap for hFrameDC
0090   Global FrameReady As Integer              'hidden-frame created?
0091
0092   '-------------------------------------------------------------------
0093   '                  Hierarchical modeling operations
0094   '-------------------------------------------------------------------
0095   Type SUBOBJECTSTRUCT        'declare a structure for a 3D subobject
0096     Solid As Integer                          'type of 3D solid
0097     Level As Integer                           'hierarchy level
0098     Color As Integer                           'rendering color
0099     SizeX As Integer                          'width of subobject
```

```
0100    SizeY As Integer                                    'height of subobject
0101    SizeZ As Integer                                    'depth of subobject
0102    PositionX As Integer                        'position in assembly-space...
0103    PositionY As Integer
0104    PositionZ As Integer
0105    Yaw As Integer                              'orientation assembly-space...
0106    Roll As Integer
0107    Pitch As Integer
0108    DeformRightX As Integer                      'extrusion of subobject...
0109    DeformLeftX As Integer
0110    DeformUpY As Integer
0111    DeformDownY As Integer
0112    PivotX As Integer                           'subassembly pivot-point...
0113    PivotY As Integer
0114    PivotZ As Integer
0115    SubAssyYaw As Integer         'subassy orientation in assy-space...
0116    SubAssyRoll As Integer
0117    SubAssyPitch As Integer
0118    SubAssyX As Integer               'subassy position in assy-space...
0119    SubAssyY As Integer
0120    SubAssyZ As Integer
0121    End Type
0122    Global RobotArm(10) As SUBOBJECTSTRUCT        'declare 9 subobjects
0123    Global Const zROBOT_START = 0    'parameters for rendering loop...
0124    Global Const zROBOT_FINISH = 9
0125    Global Const zBOX = 1                        'available solids...
0126    Global Const zSPHERE = 2
0127    Global Const zCYLINDER = 3
0128    Global Const zCONE = 4
0129    Global Const zWEDGE = 5
0130    Global Const zCURVE = 6
0131    Global Const zHEMISPHERE = 7
0132    Global Const zDEFORMBOX = 8
0133    Global Const zHALFCYL = 9
0134    Global Const zBULGE = 10
0135    Global Const zNULL = 11
0136    Global Const zLEVEL1 = 1                     'progeny in 3D hierarchy...
0137    Global Const zLEVEL2 = 2
0138    Global Const zLEVEL3 = 3
0139
0140    '----------------------------------------------------------------
0141    '              Constants for Windows API functions
0142    '----------------------------------------------------------------
0143    Global Const SRCCOPY = &HCC0020                      'for bitblts...
0144    Global Const SRCINVERT = &H660046
0145    Global Const SRCPAINT = &HEE0086
0146    Global Const WHITENESS = &HFF0062
0147    Global Const BLACKNESS = &H42&
0148    Global Const ALTERNATE = 1                           'for filling...
0149    Global Const WINDING = 2
0150    Global Const R2_COPYPEN = 13                         'for pen mode...
0151    Global Const R2_XORPEN = 7
0152    Global Const TRANSPARENT = 1                     'for background mode...
0153    Global Const OPAQUE = 2
0154    Global Const PS_SOLID = 0                            'for solid pen
0155    Global Const PS_NULL = 5                         'for transparent pen
0156    Global Const BLACKONWHITE = 1                       'for bitblt scaling...
0157    Global Const WHITEONBLACK = 2
```

```
0158  Global Const COLORONCOLOR = 3
0159  Global Const HORZRES = 8                'args for GetDeviceCaps()...
0160  Global Const VERTRES = 10
0161  Global Const BITSPIXEL = 12
0162  Global Const PLANES = 14
0163  Global Const SM_MOUSEPRESENT = 19        'for GetSystemMetrics()
0164  Global Const WF_ENHANCED = &H20          'for GetWinFlags()...
0165  Global Const WF_STANDARD = &H10
0166
0167  '-----------------------------------------------------------------
0168  '              GDI functions for display-contexts
0169  '-----------------------------------------------------------------
0170  Declare Function GetDC Lib "USER" (ByVal hWnd As Integer) As Integer
0171  Declare Function ReleaseDC Lib "USER" (ByVal hWnd As Integer,
          ByVal hDC As Integer) As Integer
0172
0173  '-----------------------------------------------------------------
0174  '              GDI functions for the desktop
0175  '-----------------------------------------------------------------
0176  Declare Function GetDesktopWindow Lib "USER" () As Integer
0177
0178  '-----------------------------------------------------------------
0179  '         GDI functions for creating drawing objects
0180  '-----------------------------------------------------------------
0181  Declare Function CreatePen Lib "GDI" (ByVal PenStyle As Integer,
          ByVal Wd As Integer, ByVal Color As Long) As Integer
0182  Declare Function CreateSolidBrush Lib "GDI" (ByVal Color As Long)
          As Integer
0183
0184  '-----------------------------------------------------------------
0185  '              GDI functions for selecting objects
0186  '-----------------------------------------------------------------
0187  Declare Function SelectObject Lib "GDI" (ByVal hDC As Integer,
          ByVal hObject As Integer) As Integer
0188  Declare Function DeleteObject Lib "GDI" (ByVal hObject As Integer)
          As Integer
0189
0190  '-----------------------------------------------------------------
0191  '              GDI functions for bitmaps and bitblts
0192  '-----------------------------------------------------------------
0193  Declare Function CreateCompatibleDC Lib "GDI" (ByVal hDC As
          Integer) As Integer
0194  Declare Function CreateCompatibleBitmap Lib "GDI" (ByVal hDC As
          Integer, ByVal Wd As Integer, ByVal Ht As Integer) As Integer
0195  Declare Function PatBlt Lib "GDI" (ByVal hDC As Integer, ByVal X
          As Integer, ByVal Y As Integer, ByVal Wd As Integer, ByVal Ht
          As Integer, ByVal RasOp As Long) As Integer
0196  Declare Function BitBlt Lib "GDI" (ByVal hDestDC As Integer, ByVal
          DestX As Integer, ByVal DestY As Integer, ByVal Wd As Integer,
          ByVal Ht As Integer, ByVal hSrcDC As Integer, ByVal SrcX As
          Integer, ByVal SrcY As Integer, ByVal RastOp As Long) As
          Integer
0197  Declare Function DeleteDC Lib "GDI" (ByVal hDC As Integer) As
          Integer
0198
```

```
0199  '------------------------------------------------------------------
0200  '          GDI functions for drawing mode operations
0201  '------------------------------------------------------------------
0202  Declare Function SetROP2 Lib "GDI" (ByVal hDC As Integer, ByVal
           RasMode As Integer) As Integer
0203  Declare Function SetBkColor Lib "GDI" (ByVal hDC As Integer, ByVal
           Color As Long) As Long
0204  Declare Function SetBkMode Lib "GDI" (ByVal hDC As Integer, ByVal
           BkMode As Integer) As Integer
0205  Declare Function SetPolyFillMode Lib "GDI" (ByVal hDC As Integer,
           ByVal PolyMode As Integer) As Integer
0206  Declare Function SetStretchBltMode Lib "GDI" (ByVal hDC As Integer,
           ByVal StretchMode As Integer) As Integer
0207
0208  '------------------------------------------------------------------
0209  '          GDI functions for drawing operations
0210  '------------------------------------------------------------------
0211  Declare Function MoveTo Lib "GDI" (ByVal hDC As Integer, ByVal X
           As Integer, ByVal Y As Integer) As Long
0212  Declare Function LineTo Lib "GDI" (ByVal hDC As Integer, ByVal X
           As Integer, ByVal Y As Integer) As Integer
0213  Declare Function Polygon Lib "GDI" (ByVal hDC As Integer, FirstPt
           As Integer, ByVal Count As Integer) As Integer
0214  Declare Function Rectangle Lib "GDI" (ByVal hDC As Integer, ByVal
           X1 As Integer, ByVal Y1 As Integer, ByVal X2 As Integer, ByVal
           Y2 As Integer) As Integer
0215  Declare Function Ellipse Lib "GDI" (ByVal hDC As Integer, ByVal X1
           As Integer, ByVal Y1 As Integer, ByVal X2 As Integer, ByVal Y2
           As Integer) As Integer
0216  Declare Function FloodFill Lib "GDI" (ByVal hDC As Integer, ByVal X
           As Integer, ByVal Y As Integer, ByVal Color As Long) As
           Integer
0217  Declare Function SetPixel Lib "GDI" (ByVal hDC As Integer, ByVal X
           As Integer, ByVal Y As Integer, ByVal Color As Long) As Long
0218  Declare Function GetPixel Lib "GDI" (ByVal hDC As Integer, ByVal X
           As Integer, ByVal Y As Integer) As Long
0219
0220  '------------------------------------------------------------------
0221  '          GDI functions for regions
0222  '------------------------------------------------------------------
0223  Declare Function PaintRgn Lib "GDI" (ByVal hDC As Integer, ByVal
           hRGN As Integer) As Integer
0224  Declare Function CreatePolygonRgn Lib "GDI" (FirstPt As Integer,
    ,      ByVal Count As Integer, ByVal PolyFillMode As Integer) As
           Integer
0225  Declare Function PtInRegion Lib "GDI" (ByVal hRGN As Integer,
           ByVal xCoord As Integer, ByVal yCoord As Integer) As Integer
0226
0227  '------------------------------------------------------------------
0228  '   GDI, USER, KERNEL functions for various runtime conditions
0229  '------------------------------------------------------------------
0230  Declare Function GetDeviceCaps Lib "GDI" (ByVal hDC As Integer,
           ByVal Item As Integer) As Integer
0231  Declare Function GetWinFlags Lib "KERNEL" () As Long
0232  Declare Function GetSystemMetrics Lib "USER" (ByVal Item As
           Integer) As Integer
```

C-2 Continued.

```
0233  Declare Function GlobalCompact Lib "KERNEL" (ByVal NumBytes As
          Long) As Long
0234  Declare Function GetVersion Lib "KERNEL" () As Long
0235  Declare Function ExitWindows Lib "USER" (ByVal Reserved As Long,
          ByVal Item As Integer) As Integer
0236  Declare Function SetCapture Lib "USER" (ByVal hWnd As Integer) As
          Integer
0237  Declare Sub ReleaseCapture Lib "USER" ()
0238
0239  '-----------------------------------------------------------------
0240  '                     End of global module.
0241  '-----------------------------------------------------------------
0242


0001  '-----------------------------------------------------------------
0002  '           Reusable template for startup code for
0003  '           Visual Basic Windows graphics applications.
0004  '-----------------------------------------------------------------
0005  ' Source file:  OBMAIN.BAS
0006  ' Release version:  1.00                    Programmer:  Lee Adams
0007  ' Type:  Visual Basic startup module for Windows applications.
0008  ' Compiler:  Microsoft Visual Basic 2.00
0009  ' Dependencies:  OBGLOBAL.BAS global module
0010  '                OBJECTS.FRM primary module
0011  ' Output and features:  Initializes the runtime environment
0012  '    for a Windows graphics application created with
0013  '    Visual Basic.  Ensures runtime image size and compatibility
0014  '    no matter which graphics mode is being used by Windows.
0015  ' Publication:  Contains material from Windcrest/McGraw-Hill
0016  '    book 4225 published by TAB BOOKS Div. of McGraw-Hill Inc.
0017  ' License:  As purchaser of the book you are granted a
0018  '    royalty-free license to distribute executable files
0019  '    generated using this code provided that you accept the
0020  '    conditions of the License Agreement and Limited Warranty
0021  '    described in the book and on the companion disk.  Government
0022  '    users:  This software and documentation are subject to
0023  '    restrictions set forth in The Rights in Technical Data and
0024  '    Computer Software clause at 252.227-7013 and elsewhere.
0025  '-----------------------------------------------------------------
0026  '       (c) Copyright 1993 Lee Adams.  All rights reserved.
0027  '          Lee Adams(tm) is a trademark of Lee Adams.
0028  '-----------------------------------------------------------------
0029
0030  Option Explicit            'generate error if variable not declared
0031
0032  '-----------------------------------------------------------------
0033  '        Initialization code for startup of application
0034  '-----------------------------------------------------------------
0035  Sub Main ()                      'is called by Windows at startup
0036    Dim PreviousColor As Long         'will remember default color
0037  StartUp = True      'set runtime tokens used by other procedures...
0038  IgnoreRefresh = True
0039  FrameReady = False
0040  '---------------- examine the graphics adapter ------------------
0041  hDesktopWnd = GetDesktopWindow()            'grab handle to desktop
0042  hDCcaps = GetDC(hDesktopWnd)       'get display-context for desktop
```

```
0043  DisplayWidth = GetDeviceCaps(hDCcaps, HORZRES)   'horiz resolution
0044  DisplayHeight = GetDeviceCaps(hDCcaps, VERTRES)  'vert resolution
0045  DisplayBits = GetDeviceCaps(hDCcaps, BITSPIXEL)  'bits-per-pixel
0046  DisplayPlanes = GetDeviceCaps(hDCcaps, PLANES)  'num of bitplanes
0047  RetVal = ReleaseDC(hDesktopWnd, hDCcaps) 'release display-context
0048  '-------------- determine the runtime memory mode --------------
0049  MemoryMode = GetWinFlags()            'will inspect this value later
0050  '--------------- determine version of Windows -----------------
0051  WindowsVersion = GetVersion()         'will inspect this value later
0052  '---- --------- set mode-dependent twips factors --------------
0053  HorizTwipsPixel = 15!: VertTwipsPixel = 15!      'set defaults...
0054  Window_Width = zWINDOW_WIDTH: Window_Height = zWINDOW_HEIGHT
0055  If DisplayWidth = 640 Then
0056    If DisplayHeight = 480 Then                    'VGA 640x480 mode
0057      HorizTwipsPixel = 15!           '9600x7200 twips full screen
0058      VertTwipsPixel = 15!
0059      Window_Width = zWINDOW_WIDTH
0060      Window_Height = zWINDOW_HEIGHT
0061    End If
0062    If DisplayHeight = 350 Then                    'EGA 640x350 mode
0063      HorizTwipsPixel = 15!           '9600x7000 twips full screen
0064      VertTwipsPixel = 20!
0065      Window_Width = zWINDOW_WIDTH
0066      Window_Height = 297!   'adjust for aspect ratio and font size
0067    End If
0068    If DisplayHeight = 200 Then   'nominal support CGA 640x200 mode
0069      HorizTwipsPixel = 15!
0070      VertTwipsPixel = 36!
0071      Window_Width = zWINDOW_WIDTH
0072      Window_Height = zWINDOW_HEIGHT
0073    End If
0074  End If
0075  If DisplayWidth = 800 Then     'SuperVGA, 8514/A, XGA 800x600 mode
0076    HorizTwipsPixel = 12!               '9600x7200 twips full screen
0077    VertTwipsPixel = 12!
0078    Window_Width = zWINDOW_WIDTH
0079    Window_Height = 317!                    'compensate for font size
0080  End If
0081  If DisplayWidth = 1024 Then        '8514/A, XGA 1024x768 mode
0082    HorizTwipsPixel = 12!               '12200x9216 twips full screen
0083    VertTwipsPixel = 12!
0084    Window_Width = zWINDOW_WIDTH
0085    Window_Height = 317!                    'compensate for font size
0086  End If
0087  If DisplayWidth = 720 Then                  'Hercules 720x348 mode
0088    HorizTwipsPixel = 12!
0089    VertTwipsPixel = 20!
0090    Window_Width - zWINDOW_WIDTH
0091    Window_Height = 297!     'adjust for aspect ratio and font size
0092  End If
0093  '-------------- display the splash sign-on banner --------------
0094  UserWants = MsgBox("Graphics demo from Windcrest McGraw-Hill book
          4225.", MB_OKCANCEL, "Copyright© 1993-1994 Lee Adams.")
0095  If UserWants = IDCANCEL Then   'if user selected Cancel button...
0096    End                                    'then cancel this startup
0097  End If
0098  '------------- initialize and display the window ---------------
0099  Form1.Width = Window_Width * HorizTwipsPixel            'set width
```

```
0100    Form1.Height = Window_Height * VertTwipsPixel          'set height
0101    Form1.Left = (Screen.Width - Form1.Width) / 2  'horizontal center
0102    Form1.Top = (Screen.Height - Form1.Height) / 2    'vertical center
0103    Form1.Caption = "3D view geometry"              'set the caption
0104    Form1.AutoRedraw = False              'disable automatic refresh
0105    Form1.BackColor = RGB(255, 255, 255)   'set the client area color
0106    Form1.ForeColor = RGB(0, 0, 0)                      'active color
0107    Form1.ScaleMode = PIXELS                    'will use pixel coords
0108    Form1.Show                               'display the window
0109    '------------------ check if mouse present --------------------
0110    MousePresent = GetSystemMetrics(SM_MOUSEPRESENT)
0111    If MousePresent = 0 Then                             'if no mouse
0112      Beep
0113      MsgBox "No mouse found.  Some features of this demo program may
              require a mouse.  The demo's menu system also responds to the
              keyboard.  Press <Enter> to continue.", MB_OK, "Graphics
              system warning"
0114    End If
0115    '----------------- initialize the 3D toolkit --------------------
0116    aazInitialize3D
0117    End Sub
0118

0001    VERSION 2.00
0002    Begin Form Form1
0003       Caption         =     "Prototype"
0004       ControlBox      =     0    'False
0005       Height          =     4515
0006       Left            =     2040
0007       LinkMode        =     1  'Source
0008       LinkTopic       =     "Form1"
0009       MaxButton       =     0    'False
0010       MinButton       =     0    'False
0011       ScaleHeight     =     3825
0012       ScaleWidth      =     3840
0013       Top             =     1485
0014       Width           =     3960
0015       Begin Menu POPUP_File
0016          Caption       =    "&File"
0017          Begin Menu IDM_New
0018             Caption      =    "&New"
0019             Enabled      =    0    'False
0020          End
0021          Begin Menu IDM_Open
0022             Caption      =    "&Open"
0023             Enabled      =    0    'False
0024          End
0025          Begin Menu IDM_Save
0026             Caption      =    "&Save"
0027             Enabled      =    0    'False
0028          End
0029          Begin Menu IDM_SaveAs
0030             Caption      =    "Save &As..."
0031             Enabled      =    0    'False
0032          End
0033          Begin Menu FileSep1
```

```
0034              Caption            =    "-"
0035          End
0036          Begin Menu IDM_Exit
0037              Caption            =    "E&xit..."
0038          End
0039          Begin Menu IDM_Restart
0040              Caption            =    "&Restart Windows..."
0041          End
0042      End
0043      Begin Menu POPUP_Edit
0044          Caption        =    "&Edit"
0045          Begin Menu IDM_Undo
0046              Caption            =    "&Undo"
0047              Enabled            =    0    'False
0048          End
0049          Begin Menu EditSep1
0050              Caption            =    "-"
0051          End
0052          Begin Menu IDM_Cut
0053              Caption            =    "Cu&t"
0054              Enabled            =    0    'False
0055          End
0056          Begin Menu IDM_Copy
0057              Caption            =    "&Copy"
0058              Enabled            =    0    'False
0059          End
0060          Begin Menu IDM_Paste
0061              Caption            =    "&Paste"
0062              Enabled            =    0    'False
0063          End
0064          Begin Menu IDM_Delete
0065              Caption            =    "&Delete"
0066              Enabled            =    0    'False
0067          End
0068      End
0069      Begin Menu POPUP_3D
0070          Caption        =    "&3D"
0071          Begin Menu POPUP_NestedMenu1
0072              Caption        =    "&Simple 3D objects..."
0073              Begin Menu IDM_DrawSphere
0074                  Caption        =    "&Sphere"
0075              End
0076              Begin Menu IDM_DrawHemisphere
0077                  Caption        =    "&Half-sphere"
0078              End
0079              Begin Menu IDM_DrawBox
0080                  Caption        =    "&Clipped boxes"
0081              End
0082              Begin Menu IDM_DrawDeformBox
0083                  Caption        =    "&Deformed boxes"
0084              End
0085              Begin Menu IDM_DrawCylinder
0086                  Caption        =    "C&ylinder"
0087              End
0088              Begin Menu IDM_DrawHalfCylinder
0089                  Caption        =    "Ha&lf-cylinder"
0090              End
0091              Begin Menu IDM_DrawCone
```

```
0092              Caption        =   "C&one"
0093          End
0094          Begin Menu IDM_DrawWedge
0095              Caption        =   "&Wedge"
0096          End
0097          Begin Menu IDM_DrawCurve
0098              Caption        =   "Cu&rved surface"
0099          End
0100          Begin Menu IDM_DrawBulge
0101              Caption        =   "B&ulged surface"
0102          End
0103      End
0104      Begin Menu POPUP_NestedMenu2
0105          Caption         =   "&Complex 3D Objects..."
0106          Begin Menu IDM_DrawRobotArm
0107              Caption        =   "&Fixed assembly"
0108          End
0109          Begin Menu IDM_BuildAssembly
0110              Caption        =   "&Hierarchical assembly"
0111          End
0112      End
0113      Begin Menu DemoSep1
0114          Caption         =   "-"
0115      End
0116      Begin Menu IDM_TestLighting
0117          Caption        =   "&Lighting demo"
0118      End
0119      Begin Menu POPUP_NestedMenu3
0120          Caption         =   "&Viewpoint demos..."
0121          Begin Menu IDM_VRtestA
0122              Caption        =   "View &A"
0123          End
0124          Begin Menu IDM_VRtestB
0125              Caption        =   "View &B"
0126          End
0127          Begin Menu IDM_VRtestC
0128              Caption        =   "View &C"
0129          End
0130          Begin Menu IDM_VRtestD
0131              Caption        =   "View &D"
0132          End
0133      End
0134      Begin Menu DemoSep2
0135          Caption         =   "-"
0136      End
0137      Begin Menu POPUP_NestedMenu4
0138          Caption        =   "Camera &Lens..."
0139          Begin Menu IDM_Lens1
0140              Caption        =   "Select &55m Lens"
0141          End
0142          Begin Menu IDM_Lens2
0143              Caption        =   "Select &135 mm Lens"
0144          End
0145          Begin Menu IDM_Lens3
0146              Caption        =   "Select &200 mm Lens"
0147          End
```

```
0148        End
0149        Begin Menu DemoSep3
0150           Caption          =    "-"
0151        End
0152        Begin Menu POPUP_NestedMenu5
0153           Caption          =    "&Rendering Mode..."
0154           Begin Menu IDM_UseShaded
0155              Caption       =    "Use &shaded solids"
0156           End
0157           Begin Menu IDM_UseWireframe
0158              Caption       =    "Use &wireframe mode"
0159           End
0160        End
0161        Begin Menu DemoSep4
0162           Caption          =    "-"
0163        End
0164        Begin Menu IDM_Clear
0165           Caption          =    "Cle&ar viewport"
0166        End
0167     End
0168     Begin Menu POPUP_Use
0169        Caption          =    "&Use"
0170        Begin Menu IDM_About
0171           Caption       =    "&About"
0172        End
0173        Begin Menu IDM_License
0174           Caption       =    "&License"
0175        End
0176        Begin Menu HelpSep1
0177           Caption       =    "-"
0178        End
0179        Begin Menu IDM_Display
0180           Caption       =    "&Resolution of display"
0181        End
0182        Begin Menu IDM_Colors
0183           Caption       =    "Available &colors"
0184        End
0185        Begin Menu IDM_Mode
0186           Caption       =    "&Memory mode"
0187        End
0188        Begin Menu IDM_Version
0189           Caption       =    "Windows &version"
0190        End
0191        Begin Menu HelpSep2
0192           Caption       =    "-"
0193        End
0194        Begin Menu IDM_GeneralHelp
0195           Caption       =    "&How to use"
0196        End
0197     End
0198  End
0199  '----------------------------------------------------------------
0200  '                    3D geometry sampler
0201  '----------------------------------------------------------------
0202  '  Source file:  OBJECTS.FRM
0203  '  Release version:  1.00                  Programmer:  Lee Adams
0204  '  Type:  Visual Basic global module for Windows applications.
0205  '  Compiler:  Microsoft Visual Basic 2.00
```

```
0206 '  Dependencies:   OBGLOBAL.BAS   global module
0207 '                  OBMAIN.BAS     module containing Main()
0208 '                  ENGINE3D.BAS   3D toolkit
0209 '                  SHAPES3D.BAS   3D shapes toolkit
0210 '                  DEFORM3D.BAS   3D deformations toolkit
0211 '                  LIGHTS3D.BAS   light-source toolkit
0212 '                  ASSEMB3D.BAS   hierarchical modeling toolkit
0213 '  Output and features:  Demonstrates a display-independent
0214 '    3D modelng and shading toolkit named engine3d that can be
0215 '    used to build scenes.  Demonstrates a 3D shapes driver named
0216 '    shapes3d that can be used to configure the functions in
0217 '    engine3d to render spheres, boxes, cylinders, curves, etc.
0218 '    Demonstrates a 3D lighting driver named lights3d that can
0219 '    be used to reposition the light-source.  Demonstrates
0220 '    functions to manipulate the near and far clipping planes.
0221 '    Demonstrates functions to reposition the camera for
0222 '    target-based 3D modeling and to reposition the viewpont for
0223 '    3D virtual reality scenes.
0224 '       Uses a 256-by-255 raster viewport.  Uses camera coords to
0225 '    perform backface culling and world coords to calculate
0226 '    shading levels.  Then transforms camera coords of the 3D view
0227 '    volume to a normalized 3D perspective view volume, then to a
0228 '    normalized rectangular view volume, scaled to fit a 256-by-255
0229 '    raster viewport.  Visible surface detection for the scene is
0230 '    implemented by a 256-by-255 z-buffer.
0231 '  Publication:  Contains material from Windcrest/McGraw-Hill
0232 '    book 4225 published by TAB BOOKS Div. of McGraw-Hill Inc.
0233 '  License:  As purchaser of the book you are granted a
0234 '    royalty-free license to distribute executable files
0235 '    generated using this code provided that you accept the
0236 '    conditions of the License Agreement and Limited Warranty
0237 '    described in the book and on the companion disk.  Government
0238 '    users:  This software and documentation are subject to
0239 '    restrictions set forth in The Rights in Technical Data and
0240 '    Computer Software clause at 252.227-7013 and elsewhere.
0241 '----------------------------------------------------------------
0242 '      (c) Copyright 1993 Lee Adams.  All rights reserved.
0243 '            Lee Adams(tm) is a trademark of Lee Adams.
0244 '----------------------------------------------------------------
0245 '  Because this Visual Basic application uses a procedure named
0246 '  Main() at startup, you must select Set Startup Form from the
0247 '  Run menu before you run the program or build an .EXE file.
0248
0249 Option Explicit           'generate error if variable not declared
0250
0251 '----------------------------------------------------------------
0252 '            Refresh the client area if uncovered
0253 '----------------------------------------------------------------
0254 Sub Form_Paint ()   'is automatically called by Windows as needed
0255 zCopyToDisplay               'copy hidden frame to display window
0256 End Sub
0257
0258 '----------------------------------------------------------------
0259 '            Intercept any attempt to resize the window
0260 '----------------------------------------------------------------
0261 Sub Form_Resize ()          'is called twice when window is resized
```

```
0262  If StartUp = True Then   'if window being displayed for first time
0263    StartUp = False
0264    IgnoreRefresh = True
0265    Exit Sub
0266  End If
0267  Form1.WindowState = 0                        'reset normal size
0268  Form1.Width = Window_Width * HorizTwipsPixel      'reset width
0269  Form1.Height = Window_Height * VertTwipsPixel     'reset height
0270  Form1.Left = (Screen.Width - Form1.Width) / 2  'horizontal center
0271  Form1.Top = (Screen.Height - Form1.Height) / 2  'vertical center
0272  If IgnoreRefresh = False Then                   'if second call
0273    IgnoreRefresh = True            'reset token for next first call
0274    MsgBox "This demo uses a fixed-size window.", MB_OK, "Sample
        application"
0275    Exit Sub
0276  End If
0277  Form1.Refresh                               'refresh the client area
0278  IgnoreRefresh = False          'if first call, reset for second call
0279  End Sub
0280
0281  '----------------------------------------------------------------
0282  '                   Display the About message box
0283  '----------------------------------------------------------------
0284  Sub IDM_About_Click ()
0285  MsgBox "This is a demo from Windcrest McGraw-Hill book 4225.  Copyright©
        1993 Lee Adams.  All rights reserved.", MB_OK, "About this Visual Basic
        program"0286   End Sub
0287
0288  '----------------------------------------------------------------
0289  '   Build a 3D assembly of subobjects:  hierarchical technique
0290  '----------------------------------------------------------------
0291  Sub IDM_BuildAssembly_Click ()
0292  RetVal = SetCapture(hWnd)         'call API to lock the mouse cursor
0293  zInitFrame                       'ensure the backup page is ready
0294  zClear                                    'clear the viewport
0295  Call jbzClearHidden3DPage         'clear the hidden 3D workspace
0296  '-------------------- reset the z-buffer ----------------------
0297  Form1.CurrentX = 10                      'display a progress report...
0298  Form1.CurrentY = 225
0299  Form1.Print "Resetting all z-buffer entries"
0300  Form1.CurrentX = 10
0301  Form1.Print "to the maximum depth-value..."
0302  Call kezResetZBuffer                         'reset the z-buffer
0303  zClear                                    'clear the viewport again
0304  '----------------- report the 3D view settings -----------------
0305  Form1.CurrentX = 10
0306  Form1.CurrentY = 10
0307  Form1.Print "Robotic arm structures"
0308  Form1.CurrentX = 10
0309  Form1.Print "built from hierarchy"
0310  '-------------------- configure the camera ---------------------
0311  Call bczSetCameraDistance(356)       'set camera-to-target distance
0312  Call bazSetCameraHeading(330)            'set the camera heading
0313  Call bbzSetCameraPitch(320)              'set the camera pitch
0314  Call zSetLightPosition(60, 180)      'reposition the light-source
0315  '-------------------- render one assembly ---------------------
0316  Call bzSetHierarchyMode(True)        'enable hierarchical modeling
0317  Call dbzSetSubjectAttitude(0, 0, 0) 'set orientation of assembly
```

```
0318   Call dazSetSubjectLocation(-35, 0, 0)    'set location of assembly
0319   Form1.CurrentX = 10                      'display a status report...
0320   Form1.CurrentY = 225
0321   Form1.Print "Working on robotic arm assemblies..."
0322   Call zbzBuildAssembly         'draw the first robotic arm assembly
0323   Call dbzSetSubjectAttitude(0, 0, 30) 'set orientation of assembly
0324   Call dazSetSubjectLocation(35, 0, 0)     'set location of assembly
0325   Call zbzBuildAssembly         'draw the second robotic arm assembly
0326   Call bzSetHierarchyMode(False)    'disable hierarchical modeling
0327   '--------------------- tidy up and exit ----------------------
0328   ReleaseCapture                'call API to release the mouse cursor
0329   Form1.CurrentX = 10           'display a task-completed report...
0330   Form1.Print "Rendering of 3D assemblies complete."
0331   zCopyToFrame                  'copy completed image to the backup page
0332   End Sub
0333
0334   '-----------------------------------------------------------------
0335   '             Clear the client area of the window
0336   '-----------------------------------------------------------------
0337   Sub IDM_Clear_Click ()
0338   zClear                                   'clear the display window
0339   zClearHiddenFrame                        'clear the hidden frame
0340   End Sub
0341
0342   '-----------------------------------------------------------------
0343   '             Determine number of available colors
0344   '-----------------------------------------------------------------
0345   Sub IDM_Colors_Click ()
0346   If DisplayBits = 1 Then                       'if 1 bit-per-pixel...
0347     If DisplayPlanes = 4 Then                     'if 4 bitplanes...
0348       MsgBox "Running in 4-bit, 16-color mode.", MB_OK, "Available colors"
0349       Exit Sub
0350     End If
0351     If DisplayPlanes = 1 Then                     'if 1 bitplane...
0352       MsgBox "Running in 1-bit, 2-color mode.", MB_OK, "Available colors"
0353       Exit Sub
0354     End If
0355   End If
0356   If DisplayBits = 8 Then                   'if 8 bits-per-pixel...
0357     MsgBox "Running in 8-bit, 256-color mode.", MB_OK, "Available colors"
0358     Exit Sub
0359   End If
0360   If DisplayBits = 16 Then                  'if 16 bits-per-pixel...
0361     MsgBox "Running in 16-bit, 65000-color mode.", MB_OK, "Available
           colors"
0362     Exit Sub
0363   End If
0364   MsgBox "Running in a custom color mode.", MB_OK, "Available colors"
0365   End Sub
0366
0367   '-----------------------------------------------------------------
0368   '             Determine the screen resolution
0369   '-----------------------------------------------------------------
0370   Sub IDM_Display_Click ()
0371   If DisplayWidth = 640 Then
0372     If DisplayHeight = 480 Then                         'VGA mode
```

```
0373      MsgBox "Running in 640x480 mode.", MB_OK, "Screen resolution"
0374        Exit Sub
0375      End If
0376      If DisplayHeight = 350 Then                          'EGA mode
0377        MsgBox "Running in 640x350 mode.", MB_OK, "Screen resolution"
0378        Exit Sub
0379      End If
0380      If DisplayHeight = 200 Then                          'CGA mode
0381        MsgBox "Running in 640x200 mode.", MB_OK, "Screen resolution"
0382        Exit Sub
0383      End If
0384    End If
0385    If DisplayWidth = 800 Then           'SuperVGA, 8514/A, XGA mode
0386      MsgBox "Running in 800x600 mode.", MB_OK, "Screen resolution"
0387      Exit Sub
0388    End If
0389    If DisplayWidth = 1024 Then                  '8514/A, XGA mode
0390      MsgBox "Running in 1024x768 mode.", MB_OK, "Screen resolution"
0391      Exit Sub
0392    End If
0393    If DisplayWidth = 720 Then                        'Hercules mode
0394      MsgBox "Running in 720x348 mode.", MB_OK, "Screen resolution"
0395      Exit Sub
0396    End If
0397    MsgBox "Running in custom mode.", MB_OK, "Screen resolution"
0398    End Sub
0399
0400    '-------------------------------------------------------------
0401    '          Render 3D boxes using near clipping-plane
0402    '-------------------------------------------------------------
0403    Sub IDM_DrawBox_Click ()
0404    RetVal = SetCapture(hWnd)       'call API to lock the mouse cursor
0405    zInitFrame                      'ensure the backup page is ready
0406    zClear                                    'clear the viewport
0407    Call jbzClearHidden3DPage         'clear the hidden 3D workspace
0408    '-------------------- reset the z-buffer ----------------------
0409    Form1.CurrentX = 10                    'display a progress report...
0410    Form1.CurrentY = 225
0411    Form1.Print "Resetting all z-buffer entries"
0412    Form1.CurrentX = 10
0413    Form1.Print "to the maximum depth-value..."
0414    Call kezResetZBuffer                       'reset the z-buffer
0415    zClear                                 'clear the viewport again
0416    '---------------- report the 3D view settings -----------------
0417    Form1.CurrentX = 10
0418    Form1.CurrentY = 10
0419    Form1.Print "Camera distance 356 ft."
0420    Form1.CurrentX = 10
0421    Form1.Print "Camera heading 360 degrees"
0422    Form1.CurrentX = 10
0423    Form1.Print "Camera pitch 360 degrees"
0424    Form1.CurrentX = 10
0425    If CamLens = 55 Then
0426      Form1.Print "Using 55mm camera lens"
0427    ElseIf CamLens = 135 Then
0428      Form1.Print "Using 135mm lens"
0429    ElseIf CamLens = 200 Then
0430      Form1.Print "Using 200mm lens"
```

```
0431   End If
0432   '-------------------- configure the camera ----------------------
0433   Call bczSetCameraDistance(356)        'set camera-to-target distance
0434   Call bazSetCameraHeading(360)              'set the camera heading
0435   Call bbzSetCameraPitch(360)                  'set the camera pitch
0436   Call zSetLightPosition(60, 180)        'reposition the light-source
0437   '------------ render 3 boxes using clipping planes --------------
0438   Call bzSetHierarchyMode(False)        'disable hierarchical modeling
0439   Call dczSetSubjectSize(25, 25, 25)             'set size of box
0440   Call dbzSetSubjectAttitude(30, 0, 30)      'set orientation of box
0441   Call dazSetSubjectLocation(-75, 0, 0)       'set location of box
0442   Call ddzSetShadingColor(zRED)                  'set color of box
0443   Form1.CurrentX = 10                       'display a status report...
0444   Form1.CurrentY = 225
0445   Form1.Print "Working on 3 boxes..."
0446   Call azDrawCube                                       'draw the box
0447   Call ddzSetShadingColor(zBROWN)             'reset color of box
0448   Call dazSetSubjectLocation(0, 0, 0)       'reset location of box
0449   Call eazSetNearClippingPlane(125)     'move the near clipping plane
0450   Call azDrawCube                               'draw the second box
0451   Call ddzSetShadingColor(zGREEN)             'reset color of box
0452   Call dazSetSubjectLocation(75, 0, 0)      'reset location of box
0453   Call eazSetNearClippingPlane(129)     'move the near clipping plane
0454   Call azDrawCube                                'draw the third box
0455   Call eazSetNearClippingPlane(78) 'restore default clipping plane
0456   '-------------------- tidy up and exit ----------------------
0457   ReleaseCapture              'call API to release the mouse cursor
0458   Form1.CurrentX = 10              'display a task-completed report...
0459   Form1.Print "Rendering of 3 boxes is complete."
0460   zCopyToFrame              'copy completed image to the backup page
0461   End Sub
0462
0463   '----------------------------------------------------------------
0464   '                    Render a 3D bulged surface
0465   '----------------------------------------------------------------
0466   Sub IDM_DrawBulge_Click ()
0467   RetVal = SetCapture(hWnd)         'call API to lock the mouse cursor
0468   zInitFrame                      'ensure the backup page is ready
0469   zClear                                     'clear the viewport
0470   Call jbzClearHidden3DPage          'clear the hidden 3D workspace
0471   '-------------------- reset the z-buffer ----------------------
0472   Form1.CurrentX = 10                     'display a progress report...
0473   Form1.CurrentY = 225
0474   Form1.Print "Resetting all z-buffer entries"
0475   Form1.CurrentX = 10
0476   Form1.Print "to the maximum depth-value..."
0477   Call kezResetZBuffer                         'reset the z-buffer
0478   zClear                                'clear the viewport again
0479   '---------------- report the 3D view settings ------------------
0480   Form1.CurrentX = 10
0481   Form1.CurrentY = 10
0482   Form1.Print "Camera distance 300 ft."
0483   Form1.CurrentX = 10
0484   Form1.Print "Camera heading 050 degrees"
0485   Form1.CurrentX = 10
0486   Form1.Print "Camera pitch 345 degrees"
```

```
0487   Form1.CurrentX = 10
0488   If CamLens = 55 Then
0489     Form1.Print "Using 55mm camera lens"
0490   ElseIf CamLens = 135 Then
0491     Form1.Print "Using 135mm lens"
0492   ElseIf CamLens = 200 Then
0493     Form1.Print "Using 200mm lens"
0494   End If
0495   '-------------------- configure the camera ----------------------
0496   Call bczSetCameraDistance(300)       'set camera-to-target distance
0497   Call bazSetCameraHeading(50)             'set the camera heading
0498   Call bbzSetCameraPitch(345)                'set the camera pitch
0499   Call zSetLightPosition(60, 180)       'reposition the light-source
0500   '----------- configure and render a bulged surface --------------
0501   Call bzSetHierarchyMode(False)       'disable hierarchical modeling
0502   Call dczSetSubjectSize(50, 40, 30)       'dimensions of surface
0503   Call dbzSetSubjectAttitude(0, 0, 0)         'set orientation
0504   Call dazSetSubjectLocation(0, 0, 0)            'set location
0505   Call ddzSetShadingColor(zMAGENTA)     'set color of curved surface
0506   Form1.CurrentX = 10                      'display a status report...
0507   Form1.CurrentY = 225
0508   Form1.Print "Working on bulged surface..."
0509   Call ezDrawBulge                           'draw bulged surface
0510   '-------------------- tidy up and exit -----------------------
0511   ReleaseCapture              'call API to release the mouse cursor
0512   Form1.CurrentX = 10              'display a task-completed report...
0513   Form1.Print "Rendering of 3D bulged surface complete."
0514   zCopyToFrame              'copy completed image to the backup page
0515   End Sub
0516
0517   '---------------------------------------------------------------
0518   '                      Render a 3D cone
0519   '---------------------------------------------------------------
0520   Sub IDM_DrawCone_Click ()
0521   RetVal = SetCapture(hWnd)       'call API to lock the mouse cursor
0522   zInitFrame                         'ensure the backup page is ready
0523   zClear                                     'clear the viewport
0524   Call jbzClearHidden3DPage          'clear the hidden 3D workspace
0525   '-------------------- reset the z-buffer ----------------------
0526   Form1.CurrentX = 10                    'display a progress report...
0527   Form1.CurrentY = 225
0528   Form1.Print "Resetting all z-buffer entries"
0529   Form1.CurrentX = 10
0530   Form1.Print "to the maximum depth-value..."
0531   Call kezResetZBuffer                          'reset the z-buffer
0532   zClear                                   'clear the viewport again
0533   '----------------- report the 3D view settings ------------------
0534   Form1.CurrentX = 10
0535   Form1.CurrentY = 10
0536   Form1.Print "Camera distance 300 ft."
0537   Form1.CurrentX = 10
0538   Form1.Print "Camera heading 360 degrees"
0539   Form1.CurrentX = 10
0540   Form1.Print "Camera pitch 360 degrees"
0541   Form1.CurrentX = 10
0542   If CamLens = 55 Then
0543     Form1.Print "Using 55mm camera lens"
0544   ElseIf CamLens = 135 Then
```

```
0545    Form1.Print "Using 135mm lens"
0546  ElseIf CamLens = 200 Then
0547    Form1.Print "Using 200mm lens"
0548  End If
0549  '-------------------- configure the camera ----------------------
0550  Call bczSetCameraDistance(300)        'set camera-to-target distance
0551  Call bazSetCameraHeading(360)             'set the camera heading
0552  Call bbzSetCameraPitch(360)                 'set the camera pitch
0553  Call zSetLightPosition(60, 180)      'reposition the light-source
0554  '---------------- configure and render one cone -----------------
0555  Call bzSetHierarchyMode(False)       'disable hierarchical modeling
0556  Call dczSetSubjectSize(40, 40, 40)            'radius and length
0557  Call dbzSetSubjectAttitude(0, 0, 285)     'set orientation of cone
0558  Call dazSetSubjectLocation(0, 0, 0)        'set location of cone
0559  Call ddzSetShadingColor(zGREEN)             'set color of cone
0560  Form1.CurrentX = 10                       'display a status report...
0561  Form1.CurrentY = 225
0562  Form1.Print "Working on cone..."
0563  Call izDrawCone                               'draw the cone
0564  '--------------------- tidy up and exit -----------------------
0565  ReleaseCapture                  'call API to release the mouse cursor
0566  Form1.CurrentX = 10          'display a task-completed report...
0567  Form1.Print "Rendering of 3D cone is complete."
0568  zCopyToFrame              'copy completed image to the backup page
0569  End Sub
0570
0571  '----------------------------------------------------------------
0572  '                    Render a 3D curved surface
0573  '----------------------------------------------------------------
0574  Sub IDM_DrawCurve_Click ()
0575  RetVal = SetCapture(hWnd)       'call API to lock the mouse cursor
0576  zInitFrame                      'ensure the backup page is ready
0577  zClear                              'clear the viewport
0578  Call jbzClearHidden3DPage        'clear the hidden 3D workspace
0579  '-------------------- reset the z-buffer ----------------------
0580  Form1.CurrentX = 10              'display a progress report...
0581  Form1.CurrentY = 225
0582  Form1.Print "Resetting all z-buffer entries"
0583  Form1.CurrentX = 10
0584  Form1.Print "to the maximum depth-value..."
0585  Call kezResetZBuffer                       'reset the z-buffer
0586  zClear                              'clear the viewport again
0587  '---------------- report the 3D view settings ------------------
0588  Form1.CurrentX = 10
0589  Form1.CurrentY = 10
0590  Form1.Print "Camera distance 300 ft."
0591  Form1.CurrentX = 10
0592  Form1.Print "Camera heading 050 degrees"
0593  Form1.CurrentX = 10
0594  Form1.Print "Camera pitch 345 degrees"
0595  Form1.CurrentX = 10
0596  If CamLens = 55 Then
0597    Form1.Print "Using 55mm camera lens"
0598  ElseIf CamLens = 135 Then
0599    Form1.Print "Using 135mm lens"
0600  ElseIf CamLens = 200 Then
```

```
0601    Form1.Print "Using 200mm lens"
0602    End If
0603    '-------------------- configure the camera ----------------------
0604    Call bczSetCameraDistance(300)      'set camera-to-target distance
0605    Call bazSetCameraHeading(50)            'set the camera heading
0606    Call bbzSetCameraPitch(345)               'set the camera pitch
0607    Call zSetLightPosition(60, 180)     'reposition the light-source
0608    '----------- configure and render a curved surface --------------
0609    Call bzSetHierarchyMode(False)     'disable hierarchical modeling
0610    Call dczSetSubjectSize(50, 50, 30)          'dimensions of surface
0611    Call dbzSetSubjectAttitude(0, 0, 0)               'set orientation
0612    Call dazSetSubjectLocation(-50, 0, 0)               'set location
0613    Call ddzSetShadingColor(zRED)       'set color of curved surface
0614    Form1.CurrentX = 10                       'display a status report...
0615    Form1.CurrentY = 225
0616    Form1.Print "Working on curved surface..."
0617    Call gzDrawCurve                  'draw first part of curved surface
0618    Call dazSetSubjectLocation(50, 0, 0)
0619    Call ddzSetShadingColor(zMAGENTA)
0620    Call gzDrawCurve                 'draw second part of curved surface
0621    '--------------------- tidy up and exit ----------------------
0622    ReleaseCapture              'call API to release the mouse cursor
0623    Form1.CurrentX = 10               'display a task-completed report...
0624    Form1.Print "Rendering of 3D curved surface complete."
0625    zCopyToFrame             'copy completed image to the backup page
0626    End Sub
0627
0628    '------------------------------------------------------------------
0629    '                    Render a 3D cylinder
0630    '------------------------------------------------------------------
0631    Sub IDM_DrawCylinder_Click ()
0632    RetVal = SetCapture(hWnd)          'call API to lock the mouse cursor
0633    zInitFrame                       'ensure the backup page is ready
0634    zClear                                 'clear the viewport
0635    Call jbzClearHidden3DPage           'clear the hidden 3D workspace
0636    '-------------------- reset the z-buffer ----------------------
0637    Form1.CurrentX = 10                     'display a progress report...
0638    Form1.CurrentY = 225
0639    Form1.Print "Resetting all z-buffer entries"
0640    Form1.CurrentX = 10
0641    Form1.Print "to the maximum depth-value..."
0642    Call kezResetZBuffer                       'reset the z-buffer
0643    zClear                                 'clear the viewport again
0644    '----------------- report the 3D view settings -----------------
0645    Form1.CurrentX = 10
0646    Form1.CurrentY = 10
0647    Form1.Print "Camera distance 300 ft."
0648    Form1.CurrentX = 10
0649    Form1.Print "Camera heading 315 degrees"
0650    Form1.CurrentX = 10
0651    Form1.Print "Camera pitch 320 degrees"
0652    Form1.CurrentX = 10
0653    If CamLens = 55 Then
0654      Form1.Print "Using 55mm camera lens"
0655    ElseIf CamLens = 135 Then
0656      Form1.Print "Using 135mm lens"
0657    ElseIf CamLens = 200 Then
0658      Form1.Print "Using 200mm lens"
```

```
0659   End If
0660   '------------------- configure the camera ---------------------
0661   Call bczSetCameraDistance(300)      'set camera-to-target distance
0662   Call bazSetCameraHeading(315)             'set the camera heading
0663   Call bbzSetCameraPitch(320)                 'set the camera pitch
0664   Call zSetLightPosition(60, 180)       'reposition the light-source
0665   '-------------- configure and render one cylinder --------------
0666   Call bzSetHierarchyMode(False)      'disable hierarchical modeling
0667   Call dczSetSubjectSize(40, 40, 40)              'radius and length
0668   Call dbzSetSubjectAttitude(0, 0, 0)  'set orientation of cylinder
0669   Call dazSetSubjectLocation(0, 0, 0)     'set location of cylinder
0670   Call ddzSetShadingColor(zCYAN)             'set color of cylinder
0671   Form1.CurrentX = 10                    'display a status report...
0672   Form1.CurrentY = 225
0673   Form1.Print "Working on cylinder..."
0674   Call ezDrawCylinder                             'draw the cylinder
0675   '--------------------- tidy up and exit -----------------------
0676   ReleaseCapture               'call API to release the mouse cursor
0677   Form1.CurrentX = 10             'display a task-completed report...
0678   Form1.Print "Rendering of 3D cylinder is complete."
0679   zCopyToFrame                'copy completed image to the backup page
0680   End Sub
0681
0682   '--------------------------------------------------------------
0683   '                   Render 3D deformed boxes
0684   '--------------------------------------------------------------
0685   Sub IDM_DrawDeformBox_Click ()
0686   RetVal = SetCapture(hWnd)         'call API to lock the mouse cursor
0687   zInitFrame                       'ensure the backup page is ready
0688   zClear                                        'clear the viewport
0689   Call jbzClearHidden3DPage          'clear the hidden 3D workspace
0690   '-------------------- reset the z-buffer ----------------------
0691   Form1.CurrentX = 10                    'display a progress report...
0692   Form1.CurrentY = 225
0693   Form1.Print "Resetting all z-buffer entries"
0694   Form1.CurrentX = 10
0695   Form1.Print "to the maximum depth-value..."
0696   Call kezResetZBuffer                            'reset the z-buffer
0697   zClear                                    'clear the viewport again
0698   '----------------- report the 3D view settings -----------------
0699   Form1.CurrentX = 10
0700   Form1.CurrentY = 10
0701   Form1.Print "Camera distance 300 ft."
0702   Form1.CurrentX = 10
0703   Form1.Print "Camera heading 315 degrees"
0704   Form1.CurrentX = 10
0705   Form1.Print "Camera pitch 340 degrees"
0706   Form1.CurrentX = 10
0707   If CamLens = 55 Then
0708     Form1.Print "Using 55mm camera lens"
0709   ElseIf CamLens = 135 Then
0710     Form1.Print "Using 135mm lens"
0711   ElseIf CamLens = 200 Then
0712     Form1.Print "Using 200mm lens"
0713   End If
0714   '-------------------- configure the camera ---------------------
```

```
0715   Call bczSetCameraDistance(300)      'set camera-to-target distance
0716   Call bazSetCameraHeading(315)            'set the camera heading
0717   Call bbzSetCameraPitch(340)                'set the camera pitch
0718   Call zSetLightPosition(60, 180)       'reposition the light-source
0719   '------------------- render 3 deformed boxes --------------------
0720   Call bzSetHierarchyMode(False)       'disable hierarchical modeling
0721   Call dczSetSubjectSize(25, 25, 25)             'set size of box
0722   Call dbzSetSubjectAttitude(0, 0, 0)      'set orientation of box
0723   Call dazSetSubjectLocation(-65, 0, 0)        'set location of box
0724   Call ddzSetShadingColor(zRED)                'set color of box
0725   Form1.CurrentX = 10                      'display a status report...
0726   Form1.CurrentY = 225
0727   Form1.Print "Working on 3 deformed boxes..."
0728   Call azDrawDeformBox(15, -15, 15, -15)     'draw the deformed box
0729   Call ddzSetShadingColor(zBROWN)            'reset color of box
0730   Call dazSetSubjectLocation(0, 0, 0)       'reset location of box
0731   Call azDrawDeformBox(10, -10, 10, -10)     'draw the second box
0732   Call ddzSetShadingColor(zGREEN)            'reset color of box
0733   Call dazSetSubjectLocation(60, 0, 0)      'reset location of box
0734   Call azDrawDeformBox(5, -5, 5, -5)         'draw the third box
0735   '-------------------- tidy up and exit ------------------------
0736   ReleaseCapture               'call API to release the mouse cursor
0737   Form1.CurrentX = 10             'display a task-completed report...
0738   Form1.Print "3 deformed boxes completed."
0739   zCopyToFrame            'copy completed image to the backup page
0740   End Sub
0741
0742   '-------------------------------------------------------------
0743   '                  Render a 3D half-cylinder
0744   '-------------------------------------------------------------
0745   Sub IDM_DrawHalfCylinder_Click ()
0746   RetVal = SetCapture(hWnd)       'call API to lock the mouse cursor
0747   zInitFrame                   'ensure the backup page is ready
0748   zClear                                    'clear the viewport
0749   Call jbzClearHidden3DPage        'clear the hidden 3D workspace
0750   '-------------------- reset the z-buffer ----------------------
0751   Form1.CurrentX = 10                'display a progress report...
0752   Form1.CurrentY = 225
0753   Form1.Print "Resetting all z-buffer entries"
0754   Form1.CurrentX = 10
0755   Form1.Print "to the maximum depth-value..."
0756   Call kezResetZBuffer                        'reset the z-buffer
0757   zClear                                'clear the viewport again
0758   '---------------- report the 3D view settings -----------------
0759   Form1.CurrentX = 10
0760   Form1.CurrentY = 10
0761   Form1.Print "Camera distance 300 ft."
0762   Form1.CurrentX = 10
0763   Form1.Print "Camera heading 045 degrees"
0764   Form1.CurrentX = 10
0765   Form1.Print "Camera pitch 320 degrees"
0766   Form1.CurrentX = 10
0767   If CamLens = 55 Then
0768     Form1.Print "Using 55mm camera lens"
0769   ElseIf CamLens = 135 Then
0770     Form1.Print "Using 135mm lens"
0771   ElseIf CamLens = 200 Then
0772     Form1.Print "Using 200mm lens"
```

```
0773   End If
0774   '------------------- configure the camera ---------------------
0775   Call bczSetCameraDistance(300)      'set camera-to-target distance
0776   Call bazSetCameraHeading(45)              'set the camera heading
0777   Call bbzSetCameraPitch(320)                 'set the camera pitch
0778   Call zSetLightPosition(60, 180)      'reposition the light-source
0779   '----------- configure and render one half-cylinder -------------
0780   Call bzSetHierarchyMode(False)      'disable hierarchical modeling
0781   Call dczSetSubjectSize(40, 40, 40)            'radius and length
0782   Call dbzSetSubjectAttitude(0, 0, 0)  'set orientation of cylinder
0783   Call dazSetSubjectLocation(0, 0, 0)    'set location of cylinder
0784   Call ddzSetShadingColor(zCYAN)            'set color of cylinder
0785   Form1.CurrentX = 10                     'display a status report...
0786   Form1.CurrentY = 225
0787   Form1.Print "Working on half-cylinder..."
0788   Call czDrawHalfCylinder                      'draw the half-cylinder
0789   '--------------------- tidy up and exit -----------------------
0790   ReleaseCapture                    'call API to release the mouse cursor
0791   Form1.CurrentX = 10              'display a task-completed report...
0792   Form1.Print "3D half-cylinder is completed."
0793   zCopyToFrame                 'copy completed image to the backup page
0794   End Sub
0795
0796   '--------------------------------------------------------------
0797   '                  Render a 3D half-sphere
0798   '--------------------------------------------------------------
0799   Sub IDM_DrawHemisphere_Click ()
0800   RetVal = SetCapture(hWnd)          'call API to lock the mouse cursor
0801   zInitFrame                         'ensure the backup page is ready
0802   zClear                                         'clear the viewport
0803   Call jbzClearHidden3DPage             'clear the hidden 3D workspace
0804   '-------------------- reset the z-buffer ----------------------
0805   Form1.CurrentX = 10                      'display a progress report...
0806   Form1.CurrentY = 225
0807   Form1.Print "Resetting all z-buffer entries"
0808   Form1.CurrentX = 10
0809   Form1.Print "to the maximum depth-value..."
0810   Call kezResetZBuffer                         'reset the z-buffer
0811   zClear                                   'clear the viewport again
0812   '---------------- report the 3D view settings ------------------
0813   Form1.CurrentX = 10
0814   Form1.CurrentY = 10
0815   Form1.Print "Camera distance 300 ft."
0816   Form1.CurrentX = 10
0817   Form1.Print "Camera heading 315 degrees"
0818   Form1.CurrentX = 10
0819   Form1.Print "Camera pitch 320 degrees"
0820   Form1.CurrentX = 10
0821   If CamLens = 55 Then
0822     Form1.Print "Using 55mm camera lens"
0823   ElseIf CamLens = 135 Then
0824     Form1.Print "Using 135mm lens"
0825   ElseIf CamLens = 200 Then
0826     Form1.Print "Using 200mm lens"
0827   End If
```

```
0828  '------------------- configure the camera ---------------------
0829  Call bczSetCameraDistance(300)    'set camera-to-target distance
0830  Call bazSetCameraHeading(315)        'set the camera heading
0831  Call bbzSetCameraPitch(320)            'set the camera pitch
0832  Call zSetLightPosition(60, 180)    'reposition the light-source
0833  '----------- configure and render one half-sphere -------------
0834  Call bzSetHierarchyMode(False)    'disable hierarchical modeling
0835  Call dczSetSubjectSize(50, 50, 50)    'set size of half-sphere
0836  Call dbzSetSubjectAttitude(0, 0, 25)  'orientation of half-sphere
0837  Call dazSetSubjectLocation(0, 0, 0)   'set location of half-sphere
0838  Call ddzSetShadingColor(zMAGENTA)     'set color of half-sphere
0839  Form1.CurrentX = 10                    'display a status report...
0840  Form1.CurrentY = 225
0841  Form1.Print "Working on half-sphere..."
0842  Call mzDrawHemisphere                     'draw the half-sphere
0843  '-------------------- tidy up and exit ----------------------
0844  ReleaseCapture            'call API to release the mouse cursor
0845  Form1.CurrentX = 10          'display a task-completed report...
0846  Form1.Print "3D half-sphere completed."
0847  zCopyToFrame             'copy completed image to the backup page
0848  End Sub
0849
0850  '-------------------------------------------------------------
0851  '    Build a 3D assembly of subobjects:  hardcoded technique
0852  '-------------------------------------------------------------
0853  Sub IDM_DrawRobotArm_Click ()
0854  RetVal = SetCapture(hWnd)     'call API to lock the mouse cursor
0855  zInitFrame                       'ensure the backup page is ready
0856  zClear                               'clear the viewport
0857  Call jbzClearHidden3DPage          'clear the hidden 3D workspace
0858  '-------------------- reset the z-buffer ----------------------
0859  Form1.CurrentX = 10                  'display a progress report...
0860  Form1.CurrentY = 225
0861  Form1.Print "Resetting all z-buffer entries"
0862  Form1.CurrentX = 10
0863  Form1.Print "to the maximum depth-value..."
0864  Call kezResetZBuffer                       'reset the z-buffer
0865  zClear                                'clear the viewport again
0866  '---------------- report the 3D view settings ----------------
0867  Form1.CurrentX = 10
0868  Form1.CurrentY = 10
0869  Form1.Print "Robotic arm assembly"
0870  Form1.CurrentX = 10
0871  Form1.Print "built from 3D subobjects"
0872  '------------------- configure the camera ---------------------
0873  Call bczSetCameraDistance(356)    'set camera-to-target distance
0874  Call bazSetCameraHeading(330)        'set the camera heading
0875  Call bbzSetCameraPitch(320)            'set the camera pitch
0876  Call zSetLightPosition(60, 180)    'reposition the light-source
0877  '-------------------- render one assembly ---------------------
0878  Call bzSetHierarchyMode(False)    'disable hierarchical modeling
0879  Form1.CurrentX = 10                    'display a status report...
0880  Form1.CurrentY = 225
0881  Form1.Print "Working on robotic arm assembly..."
0882  Call zazDrawRoboticArm                 'draw the robotic arm assembly
0883  '--------------------- tidy up and exit -----------------------
0884  ReleaseCapture            'call API to release the mouse cursor
```

```
0885  Form1.CurrentX = 10            'display a task-completed report...
0886  Form1.Print "Rendering of 3D assembly is complete."
0887  zCopyToFrame                  'copy completed image to the backup page
0888  End Sub
0889
0890  '----------------------------------------------------------------
0891  '                      Render a 3D sphere
0892  '----------------------------------------------------------------
0893  Sub IDM_DrawSphere_Click ()
0894  RetVal = SetCapture(hWnd)      'call API to lock the mouse cursor
0895  zInitFrame                     'ensure the backup page is ready
0896  zClear                                  'clear the viewport
0897  Call jbzClearHidden3DPage          'clear the hidden 3D workspace
0898  '-------------------- reset the z-buffer ----------------------
0899  Form1.CurrentX = 10                  'display a progress report...
0900  Form1.CurrentY = 225
0901  Form1.Print "Resetting all z-buffer entries"
0902  Form1.CurrentX = 10
0903  Form1.Print "to the maximum depth-value..."
0904  Call kezResetZBuffer                      'reset the z-buffer
0905  zClear                              'clear the viewport again
0906  '----------------- report the 3D view settings ------------------
0907  Form1.CurrentX = 10
0908  Form1.CurrentY = 10
0909  Form1.Print "Camera distance 300 ft."
0910  Form1.CurrentX = 10
0911  Form1.Print "Camera heading 315 degrees"
0912  Form1.CurrentX = 10
0913  Form1.Print "Camera pitch 320 degrees"
0914  Form1.CurrentX = 10
0915  If CamLens = 55 Then
0916    Form1.Print "Using 55mm camera lens"
0917  ElseIf CamLens = 135 Then
0918    Form1.Print "Using 135mm lens"
0919  ElseIf CamLens = 200 Then
0920    Form1.Print "Using 200mm lens"
0921  End If
0922  '------------------- configure the camera ---------------------
0923  Call bczSetCameraDistance(300)     'set camera-to-target distance
0924  Call bazSetCameraHeading(315)            'set the camera heading
0925  Call bbzSetCameraPitch(320)               'set the camera pitch
0926  Call zSetLightPosition(60, 180)      'reposition the light-source
0927  '--------------- configure and render one sphere ----------------
0928  Call bzSetHierarchyMode(False)     'disable hierarchical modeling
0929  Call dczSetSubjectSize(50, 50, 50)           'set size of sphere
0930  Call dbzSetSubjectAttitude(0, 0, 0)   'set orientation of sphere
0931  Call dazSetSubjectLocation(0, 0, 0)      'set location of sphere
0932  Call ddzSetShadingColor(zGREEN)           'set color of sphere
0933  Form1.CurrentX = 10                  'display a status report...
0934  Form1.CurrentY = 225
0935  Form1.Print "Working on sphere..."
0936  Call czDrawSphere                              'draw the sphere
0937  '---------------------- tidy up and exit -----------------------
0938  ReleaseCapture               'call API to release the mouse cursor
0939  Form1.CurrentX = 10          'display a task-completed report...
0940  Form1.Print "Rendering of 3D sphere is complete."
```

```
0941  zCopyToFrame              'copy completed image to the backup page
0942  End Sub
0943
0944  '----------------------------------------------------------------
0945  '                      Render a 3D wedge
0946  '----------------------------------------------------------------
0947  Sub IDM_DrawWedge_Click ()
0948  RetVal = SetCapture(hWnd)        'call API to lock the mouse cursor
0949  zInitFrame                       'ensure the backup page is ready
0950  zClear                                      'clear the viewport
0951  Call jbzClearHidden3DPage        'clear the hidden 3D workspace
0952  '-------------------- reset the z-buffer ----------------------
0953  Form1.CurrentX = 10                  'display a progress report...
0954  Form1.CurrentY = 225
0955  Form1.Print "Resetting all z-buffer entries"
0956  Form1.CurrentX = 10
0957  Form1.Print "to the maximum depth-value..."
0958  Call kezResetZBuffer                         'reset the z-buffer
0959  zClear                               'clear the viewport again
0960  '----------------- report the 3D view settings -----------------
0961  Form1.CurrentX = 10
0962  Form1.CurrentY = 10
0963  Form1.Print "Camera distance 300 ft."
0964  Form1.CurrentX = 10
0965  Form1.Print "Camera heading 315 degrees"
0966  Form1.CurrentX = 10
0967  Form1.Print "Camera pitch 340 degrees"
0968  Form1.CurrentX = 10
0969  If CamLens = 55 Then
0970    Form1.Print "Using 55mm camera lens"
0971  ElseIf CamLens = 135 Then
0972    Form1.Print "Using 135mm lens"
0973  ElseIf CamLens = 200 Then
0974    Form1.Print "Using 200mm lens"
0975  End If
0976  '-------------------- configure the camera ----------------------
0977  Call bczSetCameraDistance(300)      'set camera-to-target distance
0978  Call bazSetCameraHeading(315)             'set the camera heading
0979  Call bbzSetCameraPitch(340)                 'set the camera pitch
0980  Call zSetLightPosition(60, 180)        'reposition the light-source
0981  '--------------------- render 3 wedges ----------------------
0982  Call bzSetHierarchyMode(False)      'disable hierarchical modeling
0983  Call dczSetSubjectSize(25, 25, 25)          'set size of wedge
0984  Call dbzSetSubjectAttitude(0, 0, 0)     'set orientation of wedge
0985  Call dazSetSubjectLocation(-50, 0, 0)      'set location of wedge
0986  Call ddzSetShadingColor(zRED)                'set color of wedge
0987  Form1.CurrentX = 10                  'display a status report...
0988  Form1.CurrentY = 225
0989  Form1.Print "Working on 3 wedges..."
0990  Call kzDrawWedge                          'draw the first wedge
0991  Call ddzSetShadingColor(zBROWN)          'reset color of wedge
0992  Call dazSetSubjectLocation(0, 0, 0)     'reset location of wedge
0993  Call dbzSetSubjectAttitude(90, 0, 0)  'reset orientation of wedge
0994  Call kzDrawWedge                         'draw the second wedge
0995  Call ddzSetShadingColor(zGREEN)          'reset color of wedge
0996  Call dazSetSubjectLocation(50, 0, 0)    'reset location of wedge
0997  Call dbzSetSubjectAttitude(0, 0, 0)   'reset orientation of wedge
0998  Call kzDrawWedge                          'draw the third wedge
```

C-2 Continued.

```
0999  '-------------------- tidy up and exit ----------------------
1000  ReleaseCapture              'call API to release the mouse cursor
1001  Form1.CurrentX = 10         'display a task-completed report...
1002  Form1.Print "Rendering of 3 wedges is complete."
1003  zCopyToFrame                'copy completed image to the backup page
1004  End Sub
1005
1006  '----------------------------------------------------------------
1007  '                  Terminate the application
1008  '----------------------------------------------------------------
1009  Sub IDM_Exit_Click ()
1010  UserWants = MsgBox("Exit the demo and return to Windows?",
          MB_YESNO, "Please confirm")
1011  If UserWants = IDNO Then              'if user selected No button...
1012    Exit Sub                           'then cancel this operation
1013  End If          'otherwise continue to terminate the application...
1014  If FrameReady = True Then             'if a hidden frame was created
1015    RetVal = SelectObject(hFrameDC, hPrevFrame)    'deselect bitmap
1016    RetVal = DeleteObject(hFrame)                  'delete the bitmap
1017    RetVal = DeleteDC(hFrameDC)              'delete the display-context
1018  End If
1019  jczClose3d                            'shut down the 3D toolkit
1020  End                                   'terminate the application
1021  End Sub
1022
1023  '----------------------------------------------------------------
1024  '                  Display the Help message box
1025  '----------------------------------------------------------------
1026  Sub IDM_GeneralHelp_Click ()
1027  MsgBox "Select from the 3D menu to render various 3D solids using
          the 3D shapes engine.  See the discussion in
          Windcrest/McGraw-Hill book 4225 for further help.", MB_OK,
          "How to use this demo"
1028  End Sub
1029
1030  '----------------------------------------------------------------
1031  '                  Select 55mm camera lens
1032  '----------------------------------------------------------------
1033  Sub IDM_Lens1_Click ()
1034  bdzSetCameraLens (55)
1035  CamLens = 55
1036  MsgBox "55mm standard lens has been selected.", MB_OK, "3D camera"
1037  End Sub
1038
1039  '----------------------------------------------------------------
1040  '                  Select 135mm camera lens
1041  '----------------------------------------------------------------
1042  Sub IDM_Lens2_Click ()
1043  bdzSetCameraLens (135)
1044  CamLens = 135
1045  MsgBox "135mm standard lens has been selected.", MB_OK, "3D camera"
1046  End Sub
1047
1048  '----------------------------------------------------------------
1049  '                  Select 200mm camera lens
1050  '----------------------------------------------------------------
```

```
1051   Sub IDM_Lens3_Click ()
1052   bdzSetCameraLens (200)
1053   CamLens = 200
1054   MsgBox "200mm standard lens has been selected.", MB_OK, "3D camera"
1055   End Sub
1056
1057   '----------------------------------------------------------------
1058   '                 Display the License message box
1059   '----------------------------------------------------------------
1060   Sub IDM_License_Click ()
1061   MsgBox "You can use this code as part of your own software product
           subject to the License Agreement and Limited Warranty in
           Windcrest McGraw-Hill book 4225 and on its companion disk.",
           MB_OK, "License Agreement"
1062   End Sub
1063
1064   '----------------------------------------------------------------
1065   '                 Determine runtime memory mode
1066   '----------------------------------------------------------------
1067   Sub IDM_Mode_Click ()
1068     Dim TempVariable As Long
1069   TempVariable = MemoryMode And WF_ENHANCED    'perform bitwise AND
1070   If TempVariable = WF_ENHANCED Then     'if result matches constant
1071     MsgBox "Running in enhanced mode.  Can allocate up to 16 MB
           extended memory (XMS) if available.  Virtual memory up to 4
           times physical memory (maximum 64 MB) is also available via
           automatic disk swapping of 4K pages.", MB_OK, "Memory mode"
1072     Exit Sub
1073   End If
1074   TempVariable = MemoryMode And WF_STANDARD
1075   If TempVariable = WF_STANDARD Then
1076     MsgBox "Running in standard mode.  Can allocate up to 16 MB
           extended physical memory (XMS) if available.", MB_OK, "Memory
           mode"
1077     Exit Sub
1078   End If
1079   MsgBox "Running in real mode.  Can allocate blocks of memory from
           the first 640K of RAM.  Can also allocate blocks from expanded
           memory (EMS) if available.", MB_OK, "Memory mode"
1080   End Sub
1081
1082   '----------------------------------------------------------------
1083   '           Terminate the application and restart Windows
1084   '----------------------------------------------------------------
1085   Sub IDM_Restart_Click ()
1086   UserWants = MsgBox("Exit the demo and restart Windows?", MB_YESNO,
           "Please confirm")
1087   If UserWants = IDNO Then             'if user selected No button...
1088     Exit Sub                          'then cancel this operation
1089   End If        'otherwise continue to terminate the application...
1090   If FrameReady = True Then           'if a hidden frame was created
1091     RetVal = SelectObject(hFrameDC, hPrevFrame)     'deselect bitmap
1092     RetVal = DeleteObject(hFrame)                    'delete the bitmap
1093     RetVal = DeleteDC(hFrameDC)           'delete the display-context
1094   End If
1095   jczClose3d                               'shut down the 3D toolkit
1096   RetVal = ExitWindows(&H42&, 0)      'terminate and restart Windows
1097   End                                      'terminate the application
```

```
1098   End Sub
1099
1100   '----------------------------------------------------------------
1101   '                    Test the moveable light-source
1102   '----------------------------------------------------------------
1103   Sub IDM_TestLighting_Click ()
1104   RetVal = SetCapture(hWnd)        'call API to lock the mouse cursor
1105   zInitFrame                              'ensure the backup page is ready
1106   zClear                                        'clear the viewport
1107   Call jbzClearHidden3DPage              'clear the hidden 3D workspace
1108   '-------------------- reset the z-buffer ----------------------
1109   Form1.CurrentX = 10                       'display a progress report...
1110   Form1.CurrentY = 225
1111   Form1.Print "Resetting all z-buffer entries"
1112   Form1.CurrentX = 10
1113   Form1.Print "to the maximum depth-value..."
1114   Call kezResetZBuffer                         'reset the z-buffer
1115   zClear                                    'clear the viewport again
1116   '---------------- report the 3D view settings ------------------
1117   Form1.CurrentX = 10
1118   Form1.CurrentY = 10
1119   Form1.Print "Camera distance 300 ft."
1120   Form1.CurrentX = 10
1121   Form1.Print "Camera heading 315 degrees"
1122   Form1.CurrentX = 10
1123   Form1.Print "Camera pitch 340 degrees"
1124   Form1.CurrentX = 10
1125   If CamLens = 55 Then
1126     Form1.Print "Using 55mm camera lens"
1127   ElseIf CamLens = 135 Then
1128     Form1.Print "Using 135mm lens"
1129   ElseIf CamLens = 200 Then
1130     Form1.Print "Using 200mm lens"
1131   End If
1132   '-------------------- configure the camera ----------------------
1133   Call bczSetCameraDistance(300)       'set camera-to-target distance
1134   Call bazSetCameraHeading(315)               'set the camera heading
1135   Call bbzSetCameraPitch(340)                  'set the camera pitch
1136   Call zSetLightPosition(60, 180)       'reposition the light-source
1137   '-------------- render a series of rotated boxes ----------------
1138   Call bzSetHierarchyMode(False)       'disable hierarchical modeling
1139   Call dczSetSubjectSize(10, 10, 10)              'set size of box
1140   Call dbzSetSubjectAttitude(0, 0, 0)       'set orientation of box
1141   Call dazSetSubjectLocation(-90, 0, 0)      'set location of box
1142   Call ddzSetShadingColor(zGREEN)              'set color of box
1143   Form1.CurrentX = 10                       'display a status report...
1144   Form1.CurrentY = 225
1145   Form1.Print "Working on lighting demonstration..."
1146   Call azDrawCube                               'draw the first box
1147   Call dazSetSubjectLocation(-70, 0, 0)     'reset location of box
1148   Call dbzSetSubjectAttitude(0, 0, 350)     'reset orientation of box
1149   Call azDrawCube                                'draw the next box
1150   Call dazSetSubjectLocation(-50, 0, 0)     'reset location of box
1151   Call dbzSetSubjectAttitude(0, 0, 340)     'reset orientation of box
1152   Call azDrawCube                                'draw the next box
1153   Call dazSetSubjectLocation(-30, 0, 0)     'reset location of box
```

```
1154  Call dbzSetSubjectAttitude(0, 0, 330)    'reset orientation of box
1155  Call azDrawCube                             'draw the next box
1156  Call dazSetSubjectLocation(-10, 0, 0)     'reset location of box
1157  Call dbzSetSubjectAttitude(0, 0, 320)    'reset orientation of box
1158  Call azDrawCube                             'draw the next box
1159  Call dazSetSubjectLocation(10, 0, 0)      'reset location of box
1160  Call dbzSetSubjectAttitude(0, 0, 310)    'reset orientation of box
1161  Call azDrawCube                             'draw the next box
1162  Call dazSetSubjectLocation(30, 0, 0)      'reset location of box
1163  Call dbzSetSubjectAttitude(0, 0, 300)    'reset orientation of box
1164  Call azDrawCube                             'draw the next box
1165  Call dazSetSubjectLocation(50, 0, 0)      'reset location of box
1166  Call dbzSetSubjectAttitude(0, 0, 290)    'reset orientation of box
1167  Call azDrawCube                             'draw the next box
1168  Call dazSetSubjectLocation(70, 0, 0)      'reset location of box
1169  Call dbzSetSubjectAttitude(0, 0, 280)    'reset orientation of box
1170  Call azDrawCube                             'draw the next box
1171  Call dazSetSubjectLocation(90, 0, 0)      'reset location of box
1172  Call dbzSetSubjectAttitude(0, 0, 270)    'reset orientation of box
1173  Call azDrawCube                             'draw the next box
1174  '--------------------- tidy up and exit -----------------------
1175  ReleaseCapture              'call API to release the mouse cursor
1176  Form1.CurrentX = 10              'display a task-completed report...
1177  Form1.Print "Lighting demonstration is complete."
1178  zCopyToFrame                'copy completed image to the backup page
1179  End Sub
1180
1181  '-----------------------------------------------------------------
1182  '           Toggle to use fully-shaded 3D entities
1183  '-----------------------------------------------------------------
1184  Sub IDM_UseShaded_Click ()
1185  abzUseWireframeMode (False)         'call function in ENGINE3D.BAS
1186  MsgBox "Using shaded solids mode.", MB_OK, "3D status report"
1187  End Sub
1188
1189  '-----------------------------------------------------------------
1190  '           Toggle to use wire-frame entities
1191  '-----------------------------------------------------------------
1192  Sub IDM_UseWireframe_Click ()
1193  abzUseWireframeMode (True)          'call function in ENGINE3D.BAS
1194  MsgBox "Using wireframe modeling mode.", MB_OK, "3D status report"
1195  End Sub
1196
1197  '-----------------------------------------------------------------
1198  '           Determine version of Windows
1199  '-----------------------------------------------------------------
1200  Sub IDM_Version_Click ()
1201    Dim TempVar As Long
1202  TempVar = WindowsVersion And 7683  'test binary 00011110 00000011
1203  If TempVar = 7683 Then                    'if 30        3...
1204    MsgBox "Running under Windows version 3.3.", MB_OK, "Version
          report"
1205    Exit Sub
1206  End If
1207  TempVar = WindowsVersion And 5123  'test binary 00010100 00000011
1208  If TempVar = 5123 Then                    'if 20        3...
1209    MsgBox "Running under Windows version 3.2.", MB_OK, "Version report"
1210    Exit Sub
```

```
1211   End If
1212   TempVar = WindowsVersion And 2563   'test binary 00001010 00000011
1213   If TempVar = 2563 Then                       'if 10        3...
1214     MsgBox "Running under Windows version 3.1.", MB_OK, "Version
             report"
1215     Exit Sub
1216   End If
1217   TempVar = WindowsVersion And 3      'test binary 00000000 00000011
1218   If TempVar = 3 Then                          'if 00        3...
1219     MsgBox "Running under Windows version 3.0.", MB_OK, "Version
             report"
1220     Exit Sub
1221   End If
1222   TempVar = WindowsVersion And 4      'test binary 00000000 00000100
1223   If TempVar = 4 Then                          'if 00      4...
1224     MsgBox "Running under Windows version 4.0.", MB_OK, "Version
             report"
1225     Exit Sub
1226   End If
1227   MsgBox "Unable to report Windows version number.", MB_OK, "Version
             report"
1228   End Sub
1229
1230   '----------------------------------------------------------------
1231   '                    Test virtual reality view A
1232   '----------------------------------------------------------------
1233   Sub IDM_VRtestA_Click ()
1234   RetVal = SetCapture(hWnd)        'call API to lock the mouse cursor
1235   zInitFrame                            'ensure the backup page is ready
1236   zClear                                        'clear the viewport
1237   Call jbzClearHidden3DPage              'clear the hidden 3D workspace
1238   '-------------------- reset the z-buffer ----------------------
1239   Form1.CurrentX = 10                   'display a progress report...
1240   Form1.CurrentY = 225
1241   Form1.Print "Resetting all z-buffer entries"
1242   Form1.CurrentX = 10
1243   Form1.Print "to the maximum depth-value..."
1244   Call kezResetZBuffer                          'reset the z-buffer
1245   zClear                                'clear the viewport again
1246   '---------------- report the 3D view settings -----------------
1247   Form1.CurrentX = 10
1248   Form1.CurrentY = 10
1249   Form1.Print "Virtual reality viewpoint simulation"
1250   Form1.CurrentX = 10
1251   Form1.Print "Viewpoint: 0,0,356"
1252   Form1.CurrentX = 10
1253   Form1.Print "View angle: 360 degrees"
1254   '-------------------- configure the camera --------------------
1255   Call cazDisableTarget                    'unlock from fixed-target
1256   Call cezSetVRCameraLocation(0, 0, 356)        'set camera location
1257   Call cczSetVRCameraHeading(360)               'set viewing heading
1258   Call cdzSetVRCameraPitch(360)                 'set viewing pitch
1259   Call zSetLightPosition(60, 180)        'reposition the light-source
1260   '--------------------- render 3 boxes -------------------------
1261   Call bzSetHierarchyMode(False)        'disable hierarchical modeling
1262   Call dczSetSubjectSize(25, 25, 25)            'set size of box
```

```
1263   Call dbzSetSubjectAttitude(0, 0, 0)        'set orientation of box
1264   Call dazSetSubjectLocation(-60, 0, 0)       'set location of box
1265   Call ddzSetShadingColor(zRED)                'set color of box
1266   Form1.CurrentX = 10                   'display a status report...
1267   Form1.CurrentY = 225
1268   Form1.Print "Working on virtual reality view..."
1269   Call azDrawCube                                'draw the box
1270   Call ddzSetShadingColor(zBROWN)            'reset color of box
1271   Call dazSetSubjectLocation(0, 0, 0)       'reset location of box
1272   Call azDrawCube                          'draw the second box
1273   Call ddzSetShadingColor(zGREEN)            'reset color of box
1274   Call dazSetSubjectLocation(60, 0, 0)      'reset location of box
1275   Call azDrawCube                           'draw the third box
1276   Call cbzEnableTarget              'restore fixed-target mode
1277   '--------------------- tidy up and exit ----------------------
1278   ReleaseCapture              'call API to release the mouse cursor
1279   Form1.CurrentX = 10         'display a task-completed report...
1280   Form1.Print "Rendering of 3 virtual boxes is complete."
1281   zCopyToFrame              'copy completed image to the backup page
1282   End Sub
1283
1284   '------------------------------------------------------------------
1285   '                    Test virtual reality view B
1286   '------------------------------------------------------------------
1287   Sub IDM_VRtestB_Click ()
1288   RetVal = SetCapture(hWnd)       'call API to lock the mouse cursor
1289   zInitFrame                      'ensure the backup page is ready
1290   zClear                                  'clear the viewport
1291   Call jbzClearHidden3DPage      'clear the hidden 3D workspace
1292   '-------------------- reset the z-buffer ----------------------
1293   Form1.CurrentX = 10                  'display a progress report...
1294   Form1.CurrentY = 225
1295   Form1.Print "Resetting all z-buffer entries"
1296   Form1.CurrentX = 10
1297   Form1.Print "to the maximum depth-value..."
1298   Call kezResetZBuffer                       'reset the z-buffer
1299   zClear                               'clear the viewport again
1300   '----------------- report the 3D view settings -----------------
1301   Form1.CurrentX = 10
1302   Form1.CurrentY = 10
1303   Form1.Print "Virtual reality viewpoint simulation"
1304   Form1.CurrentX = 10
1305   Form1.Print "Viewpoint: -60,0,356"
1306   Form1.CurrentX = 10
1307   Form1.Print "View angle: 360 degrees"
1308   '-------------------- configure the camera ---------------------
1309   Call cazDisableTarget                    'unlock from fixed-target
1310   Call cezSetVRCameraLocation(-60, 0, 356)     'set camera location
1311   Call cczSetVRCameraHeading(360)            'set viewing heading
1312   Call cdzSetVRCameraPitch(360)                'set viewing pitch
1313   Call zSetLightPosition(60, 180)      'reposition the light-source
1314   '--------------------- render 3 boxes -------------------------
1315   Call bzSetHierarchyMode(False)     'disable hierarchical modeling
1316   Call dczSetSubjectSize(25, 25, 25)            'set size of box
1317   Call dbzSetSubjectAttitude(0, 0, 0)       'set orientation of box
1318   Call dazSetSubjectLocation(-60, 0, 0)       'set location of box
1319   Call ddzSetShadingColor(zRED)                'set color of box
1320   Form1.CurrentX = 10                   'display a status report...
```

```
1321  Form1.CurrentY = 225
1322  Form1.Print "Working on virtual reality view..."
1323  Call azDrawCube                              'draw the box
1324  Call ddzSetShadingColor(zBROWN)         'reset color of box
1325  Call dazSetSubjectLocation(0, 0, 0)     'reset location of box
1326  Call azDrawCube                         'draw the second box
1327  Call ddzSetShadingColor(zGREEN)         'reset color of box
1328  Call dazSetSubjectLocation(60, 0, 0)    'reset location of box
1329  Call azDrawCube                         'draw the third box
1330  Call cbzEnableTarget                'restore fixed-target mode
1331  '------------------- tidy up and exit -----------------------
1332  ReleaseCapture            'call API to release the mouse cursor
1333  Form1.CurrentX = 10            'display a task-completed report...
1334  Form1.Print "Rendering of 3 virtual boxes is complete."
1335  zCopyToFrame              'copy completed image to the backup page
1336  End Sub
1337
1338  '----------------------------------------------------------------
1339  '                    Test virtual reality view C
1340  '----------------------------------------------------------------
1341  Sub IDM_VRtestC_Click ()
1342  RetVal = SetCapture(hWnd)        'call API to lock the mouse cursor
1343  zInitFrame                     'ensure the backup page is ready
1344  zClear                               'clear the viewport
1345  Call jbzClearHidden3DPage        'clear the hidden 3D workspace
1346  '------------------- reset the z-buffer ----------------------
1347  Form1.CurrentX = 10                  'display a progress report...
1348  Form1.CurrentY = 225
1349  Form1.Print "Resetting all z-buffer entries"
1350  Form1.CurrentX = 10
1351  Form1.Print "to the maximum depth-value..."
1352  Call kezResetZBuffer                       'reset the z-buffer
1353  zClear                               'clear the viewport again
1354  '---------------- report the 3D view settings -----------------
1355  Form1.CurrentX = 10
1356  Form1.CurrentY = 10
1357  Form1.Print "Virtual reality viewpoint simulation"
1358  Form1.CurrentX = 10
1359  Form1.Print "Viewpoint: 60,0,356"
1360  Form1.CurrentX = 10
1361  Form1.Print "View angle: 360 degrees"
1362  '-------------------- configure the camera --------------------
1363  Call cazDisableTarget                'unlock from fixed-target
1364  Call cezSetVRCameraLocation(60, 0, 356)    'set camera location
1365  Call cczSetVRCameraHeading(360)         'set viewing heading
1366  Call cdzSetVRCameraPitch(360)            'set viewing pitch
1367  Call zSetLightPosition(60, 180)     'reposition the light-source
1368  '--------------------- render 3 boxes ------------------------
1369  Call bzSetHierarchyMode(False)     'disable hierarchical modeling
1370  Call dczSetSubjectSize(25, 25, 25)          'set size of box
1371  Call dbzSetSubjectAttitude(0, 0, 0)     'set orientation of box
1372  Call dazSetSubjectLocation(-60, 0, 0)     'set location of box
1373  Call ddzSetShadingColor(zRED)             'set color of box
1374  Form1.CurrentX = 10                  'display a status report...
1375  Form1.CurrentY = 225
1376  Form1.Print "Working on virtual reality view..."
```

```
1377   Call azDrawCube                                'draw the box
1378   Call ddzSetShadingColor(zBROWN)          'reset color of box
1379   Call dazSetSubjectLocation(0, 0, 0)      'reset location of box
1380   Call azDrawCube                          'draw the second box
1381   Call ddzSetShadingColor(zGREEN)          'reset color of box
1382   Call dazSetSubjectLocation(60, 0, 0)     'reset location of box
1383   Call azDrawCube                          'draw the third box
1384   Call cbzEnableTarget               'restore fixed-target mode
1385   '-------------------- tidy up and exit ----------------------
1386   ReleaseCapture              'call API to release the mouse cursor
1387   Form1.CurrentX = 10            'display a task-completed report...
1388   Form1.Print "Rendering of 3 virtual boxes is complete."
1389   zCopyToFrame             'copy completed image to the backup page
1390   End Sub
1391
1392   '-----------------------------------------------------------------
1393   '                    Test virtual reality view D
1394   '-----------------------------------------------------------------
1395   Sub IDM_VRtestD_Click ()
1396   RetVal = SetCapture(hWnd)      'call API to lock the mouse cursor
1397   zInitFrame                    'ensure the backup page is ready
1398   zClear                                  'clear the viewport
1399   Call jbzClearHidden3DPage       'clear the hidden 3D workspace
1400   '-------------------- reset the z-buffer ----------------------
1401   Form1.CurrentX = 10                'display a progress report...
1402   Form1.CurrentY = 225
1403   Form1.Print "Resetting all z-buffer entries"
1404   Form1.CurrentX = 10
1405   Form1.Print "to the maximum depth-value..."
1406   Call kezResetZBuffer                       'reset the z-buffer
1407   zClear                                  'clear the viewport again
1408   '----------------- report the 3D view settings -----------------
1409   Form1.CurrentX = 10
1410   Form1.CurrentY = 10
1411   Form1.Print "Virtual reality viewpoint simulation"
1412   Form1.CurrentX = 10
1413   Form1.Print "Viewpoint: 0,0,356"
1414   Form1.CurrentX = 10
1415   Form1.Print "View angle: 090 degrees"
1416   '-------------------- configure the camera --------------------
1417   Call cazDisableTarget                    'unlock from fixed-target
1418   Call cezSetVRCameraLocation(0, 0, 356)       'set camera location
1419   Call cczSetVRCameraHeading(90)               'set viewing heading
1420   Call cdzSetVRCameraPitch(360)                'set viewing pitch
1421   Call zSetLightPosition(60, 180)       'reposition the light-source
1422   '--------------------- render 3 boxes -------------------------
1423   Call bzSetHierarchyMode(False)     'disable hierarchical modeling
1424   Call dczSetSubjectSize(25, 25, 25)            'set size of box
1425   Call dbzSetSubjectAttitude(0, 0, 0)        'set orientation of box
1426   Call dazSetSubjectLocation(356, 0, 296)      'set location of box
1427   Call ddzSetShadingColor(zRED)                'set color of box
1428   Form1.CurrentX = 10                'display a status report...
1429   Form1.CurrentY = 225
1430   Form1.Print "Working on virtual reality view..."
1431   Call azDrawCube                              'draw the box
1432   Call ddzSetShadingColor(zGRAY)               'reset color of box
1433   Call dazSetSubjectLocation(356, 0, 356)      'reset location of box
1434   Call azDrawCube                              'draw the second box
```

```
1435  Call ddzSetShadingColor(zBLUE)              'reset color of box
1436  Call dazSetSubjectLocation(356, 0, 416)    'reset location of box
1437  Call azDrawCube                            'draw the third box
1438  Call cbzEnableTarget                       'restore fixed-target mode
1439  '--------------------- tidy up and exit ----------------------
1440  ReleaseCapture                'call API to release the mouse cursor
1441  Form1.CurrentX = 10                'display a task-completed report...
1442  Form1.Print "Rendering of 3 virtual boxes is complete."
1443  zCopyToFrame                'copy completed image to the backup page
1444  End Sub
1445
1446  '----------------------------------------------------------------
1447  '   Build a 3D assembly of subobjects:  hardcoded technique.
1448  '----------------------------------------------------------------
1449  Sub zazDrawRoboticArm ()
1450  Call ddzSetShadingColor(zGREEN)
1451  Call dczSetSubjectSize(20, 20, 30)             'arm extensor (1)...
1452  Call dbzSetSubjectAttitude(0, 0, 0)
1453  Call dazSetSubjectLocation(0, 0, -50)
1454  Call azDrawCube
1455  Call ddzSetShadingColor(zGREEN)
1456  Call dczSetSubjectSize(5, 20, 10)    'arm swivel extensors (2)...
1457  Call dbzSetSubjectAttitude(0, 0, 0)
1458  Call dazSetSubjectLocation(15, 0, -10)
1459  Call azDrawCube
1460  Call dazSetSubjectLocation(-15, 0, -10)
1461  Call azDrawCube
1462  Call ddzSetShadingColor(zGREEN)
1463  Call dczSetSubjectSize(20, 20, 5)      'arm swivel brackets (2)...
1464  Call dbzSetSubjectAttitude(90, 0, 0)
1465  Call dazSetSubjectLocation(15, 0, 0)
1466  Call czDrawHalfCylinder
1467  Call dazSetSubjectLocation(-15, 0, 0)
1468  Call czDrawHalfCylinder
1469  Call ddzSetShadingColor(zRED)
1470  Call dczSetSubjectSize(10, 10, 25)                'swivel pin (1)...
1471  Call dbzSetSubjectAttitude(90, 0, 0)
1472  Call dazSetSubjectLocation(0, 0, 0)
1473  Call ezDrawCylinder
1474  Call ddzSetShadingColor(zBROWN)
1475  Call dczSetSubjectSize(20, 20, 5)    'wrist swivel bracket (1)...
1476  Call dbzSetSubjectAttitude(270, 0, 0)
1477  Call dazSetSubjectLocation(0, 0, 0)
1478  Call czDrawHalfCylinder
1479  Call ddzSetShadingColor(zBROWN)
1480  Call dczSetSubjectSize(5, 20, 30)               'wrist extensor (1)...
1481  Call dbzSetSubjectAttitude(0, 0, 0)
1482  Call dazSetSubjectLocation(0, 0, 30)
1483  Call azDrawCube
1484  Call ddzSetShadingColor(zBROWN)
1485  Call dczSetSubjectSize(20, 20, 5)      'wrist swivel bracket (1)...
1486  Call dbzSetSubjectAttitude(90, 0, 0)
1487  Call dazSetSubjectLocation(0, 0, 60)
1488  Call czDrawHalfCylinder
1489  Call ddzSetShadingColor(zRED)
1490  Call dczSetSubjectSize(10, 10, 25)                'swivel pin (1)...
```

```
1491    Call dbzSetSubjectAttitude(90, 0, 0)
1492    Call dazSetSubjectLocation(0, 0, 60)
1493    Call ezDrawCylinder
1494    End Sub
1495
1496    '----------------------------------------------------------------
1497    '   Build a 3D assembly of subobjects:  hierarchical technique.
1498    '----------------------------------------------------------------
1499    Sub zbzBuildAssembly ()
1500      Dim PartID As Integer          'counter is used in the drawing loop
1501    '--------------- STEP ONE:  define the assembly ---------------
1502    RobotArm(0).Solid = zBOX                      'define the arm extensor
1503    RobotArm(0).Level = zLEVEL1
1504    RobotArm(0).Color = zGREEN
1505    RobotArm(0).SizeX = 20
1506    RobotArm(0).SizeY = 20
1507    RobotArm(0).SizeZ = 30
1508    RobotArm(0).Yaw = 0
1509    RobotArm(0).Roll = 0
1510    RobotArm(0).Pitch = 0
1511    RobotArm(0).PositionX = 0
1512    RobotArm(0).PositionY = 0
1513    RobotArm(0).PositionZ = -50
1514    RobotArm(0).DeformRightX = 0
1515    RobotArm(0).DeformLeftX = 0
1516    RobotArm(0).DeformUpY = 0
1517    RobotArm(0).DeformDownY = 0
1518    RobotArm(0).PivotX = 0
1519    RobotArm(0).PivotY = 0
1520    RobotArm(0).PivotZ = 0
1521    RobotArm(0).SubAssyYaw = 0
1522    RobotArm(0).SubAssyRoll = 0
1523    RobotArm(0).SubAssyPitch = 0
1524    RobotArm(0).SubAssyX = 0
1525    RobotArm(0).SubAssyY = 0
1526    RobotArm(0).SubAssyZ = 0
1527    RobotArm(1).Solid = zBOX               'arm swivel extensor (1 of 2)
1528    RobotArm(1).Level = zLEVEL1
1529    RobotArm(1).Color = zGREEN
1530    RobotArm(1).SizeX = RobotArm(0).SizeX / 4
1531    RobotArm(1).SizeY = RobotArm(0).SizeY
1532    RobotArm(1).SizeZ = 10
1533    RobotArm(1).Yaw = 0
1534    RobotArm(1).Roll = 0
1535    RobotArm(1).Pitch = 0
1536    RobotArm(1).PositionX = RobotArm(0).SizeX - RobotArm(1).SizeX
1537    RobotArm(1).PositionY = RobotArm(0).PositionY
1538    RobotArm(1).PositionZ = (RobotArm(0).PositionZ + RobotArm(0).SizeZ) +
            RobotArm(1).SizeZ
1539    RobotArm(1).DeformRightX = 0
1540    RobotArm(1).DeformLeftX = 0
1541    RobotArm(1).DeformUpY = 0
1542    RobotArm(1).DeformDownY = 0
1543    RobotArm(1).PivotX = 0
1544    RobotArm(1).PivotY = 0
1545    RobotArm(1).PivotZ = 0
1546    RobotArm(1).SubAssyYaw = 0
1547    RobotArm(1).SubAssyRoll = 0
```

```
1548  RobotArm(1).SubAssyPitch = 0
1549  RobotArm(1).SubAssyX = 0
1550  RobotArm(1).SubAssyY = 0
1551  RobotArm(1).SubAssyZ = 0
1552  RobotArm(2).Solid = zBOX              'arm swivel extensor (2 of 2)
1553  RobotArm(2).Level = zLEVEL1
1554  RobotArm(2).Color = zGREEN
1555  RobotArm(2).SizeX = RobotArm(0).SizeX / 4
1556  RobotArm(2).SizeY = RobotArm(0).SizeY
1557  RobotArm(2).SizeZ = 10
1558  RobotArm(2).Yaw = 0
1559  RobotArm(2).Roll = 0
1560  RobotArm(2).Pitch = 0
1561  RobotArm(2).PositionX = ((-1) * RobotArm(0).SizeX) +
          RobotArm(2).SizeX
1562  RobotArm(2).PositionY = RobotArm(0).PositionY
1563  RobotArm(2).PositionZ = (RobotArm(0).PositionZ +
          RobotArm(0).SizeZ) + RobotArm(2).SizeZ
1564  RobotArm(2).DeformRightX = 0
1565  RobotArm(2).DeformLeftX = 0
1566  RobotArm(2).DeformUpY = 0
1567  RobotArm(2).DeformDownY = 0
1568  RobotArm(2).PivotX = 0
1569  RobotArm(2).PivotY = 0
1570  RobotArm(2).PivotZ = 0
1571  RobotArm(2).SubAssyYaw = 0
1572  RobotArm(2).SubAssyRoll = 0
1573  RobotArm(2).SubAssyPitch = 0
1574  RobotArm(2).SubAssyX = 0
1575  RobotArm(2).SubAssyY = 0
1576  RobotArm(2).SubAssyZ = 0
1577  RobotArm(3).Solid = zHALFCYL         'arm swivel bracket (1 of 2)
1578  RobotArm(3).Level = zLEVEL1
1579  RobotArm(3).Color = zGREEN
1580  RobotArm(3).SizeX = RobotArm(0).SizeX
1581  RobotArm(3).SizeY = RobotArm(0).SizeY
1582  RobotArm(3).SizeZ = RobotArm(1).SizeX
1583  RobotArm(3).Yaw = 90
1584  RobotArm(3).Roll = 0
1585  RobotArm(3).Pitch = 0
1586  RobotArm(3).PositionX = RobotArm(1).PositionX
1587  RobotArm(3).PositionY = RobotArm(1).PositionY
1588  RobotArm(3).PositionZ = RobotArm(1).PositionZ + RobotArm(1).SizeZ
1589  RobotArm(3).DeformRightX = 0
1590  RobotArm(3).DeformLeftX = 0
1591  RobotArm(3).DeformUpY = 0
1592  RobotArm(3).DeformDownY = 0
1593  RobotArm(3).PivotX = 0
1594  RobotArm(3).PivotY = 0
1595  RobotArm(3).PivotZ = 0
1596  RobotArm(3).SubAssyYaw = 0
1597  RobotArm(3).SubAssyRoll = 0
1598  RobotArm(3).SubAssyPitch = 0
1599  RobotArm(3).SubAssyX = 0
1600  RobotArm(3).SubAssyY = 0
1601  RobotArm(3).SubAssyZ = 0
```

```
1602    RobotArm(4).Solid = zHALFCYL          'arm swivel bracket (2 of 2)
1603    RobotArm(4).Level = zLEVEL1
1604    RobotArm(4).Color = zGREEN
1605    RobotArm(4).SizeX = RobotArm(0).SizeX
1606    RobotArm(4).SizeY = RobotArm(0).SizeY
1607    RobotArm(4).SizeZ = RobotArm(2).SizeX
1608    RobotArm(4).Yaw = 90
1609    RobotArm(4).Roll = 0
1610    RobotArm(4).Pitch = 0
1611    RobotArm(4).PositionX = RobotArm(2).PositionX
1612    RobotArm(4).PositionY = RobotArm(2).PositionY
1613    RobotArm(4).PositionZ = RobotArm(2).PositionZ + RobotArm(2).SizeZ
1614    RobotArm(4).DeformRightX = 0
1615    RobotArm(4).DeformLeftX = 0
1616    RobotArm(4).DeformUpY = 0
1617    RobotArm(4).DeformDownY = 0
1618    RobotArm(4).PivotX = 0
1619    RobotArm(4).PivotY = 0
1620    RobotArm(4).PivotZ = 0
1621    RobotArm(4).SubAssyYaw = 0
1622    RobotArm(4).SubAssyRoll = 0
1623    RobotArm(4).SubAssyPitch = 0
1624    RobotArm(4).SubAssyX = 0
1625    RobotArm(4).SubAssyY = 0
1626    RobotArm(4).SubAssyZ = 0
1627    RobotArm(5).Solid = zCYLINDER                   'swivel pin (1)
1628    RobotArm(5).Level = zLEVEL1
1629    RobotArm(5).Color = zRED
1630    RobotArm(5).SizeX = 10
1631    RobotArm(5).SizeY = 10
1632    RobotArm(5).SizeZ = RobotArm(0).SizeX + 5
1633    RobotArm(5).Yaw = 90
1634    RobotArm(5).Roll = 0
1635    RobotArm(5).Pitch = 0
1636    RobotArm(5).PositionX = RobotArm(0).PositionX
1637    RobotArm(5).PositionY = RobotArm(3).PositionY
1638    RobotArm(5).PositionZ = RobotArm(3).PositionZ
1639    RobotArm(5).DeformRightX = 0
1640    RobotArm(5).DeformLeftX = 0
1641    RobotArm(5).DeformUpY = 0
1642    RobotArm(5).DeformDownY = 0
1643    RobotArm(5).PivotX = 0
1644    RobotArm(5).PivotY = 0
1645    RobotArm(5).PivotZ = 0
1646    RobotArm(5).SubAssyYaw = 0
1647    RobotArm(5).SubAssyRoll = 0
1648    RobotArm(5).SubAssyPitch = 0
1649    RobotArm(5).SubAssyX = 0
1650    RobotArm(5).SubAssyY = 0
1651    RobotArm(5).SubAssyZ = 0
1652    '-------------- STEP TWO:  define the subassembly --------------
1653          'This particular subassembly is already located at an
1654          'appropriate pivot-point, from where it will rotated
1655          '30 degrees in the pitch plane.
1656    RobotArm(6).Solid = zHALFCYL          'wrist swivel bracket (1)
1657    RobotArm(6).Level = zLEVEL2
1658    RobotArm(6).Color = zBROWN
1659    RobotArm(6).SizeX = RobotArm(4).SizeX
```

```
1660   RobotArm(6).SizeY = RobotArm(4).SizeY
1661   RobotArm(6).SizeZ = RobotArm(4).SizeZ
1662   RobotArm(6).Yaw = 270                          'reorient half-cylinder
1663   RobotArm(6).Roll = 0
1664   RobotArm(6).Pitch = 0
1665   RobotArm(6).PositionX = RobotArm(5).PositionX
1666   RobotArm(6).PositionY = RobotArm(5).PositionY
1667   RobotArm(6).PositionZ = RobotArm(5).PositionZ
1668   RobotArm(6).DeformRightX = 0
1669   RobotArm(6).DeformLeftX = 0
1670   RobotArm(6).DeformUpY = 0
1671   RobotArm(6).DeformDownY = 0
1672   RobotArm(6).PivotX = 0
1673   RobotArm(6).PivotY = 0
1674   RobotArm(6).PivotZ = 0
1675   RobotArm(6).SubAssyYaw = 0
1676   RobotArm(6).SubAssyRoll = 0
1677   RobotArm(6).SubAssyPitch = 30
1678   RobotArm(6).SubAssyX = 0
1679   RobotArm(6).SubAssyY = 0
1680   RobotArm(6).SubAssyZ = 0
1681   RobotArm(7).Solid = zBOX                    'wrist extensor (1)
1682   RobotArm(7).Level = zLEVEL2
1683   RobotArm(7).Color = zBROWN
1684   RobotArm(7).SizeX = RobotArm(6).SizeZ
1685   RobotArm(7).SizeY = RobotArm(6).SizeX
1686   RobotArm(7).SizeZ = 30
1687   RobotArm(7).Yaw = 0
1688   RobotArm(7).Roll = 0
1689   RobotArm(7).Pitch = 0
1690   RobotArm(7).PositionX = RobotArm(6).PositionX
1691   RobotArm(7).PositionY = RobotArm(6).PositionY
1692   RobotArm(7).PositionZ = RobotArm(6).PositionX + RobotArm(7).SizeZ
1693   RobotArm(7).DeformRightX = 0
1694   RobotArm(7).DeformLeftX = 0
1695   RobotArm(7).DeformUpY = 0
1696   RobotArm(7).DeformDownY = 0
1697   RobotArm(7).PivotX = 0
1698   RobotArm(7).PivotY = 0
1699   RobotArm(7).PivotZ = 0
1700   RobotArm(7).SubAssyYaw = 0
1701   RobotArm(7).SubAssyRoll = 0
1702   RobotArm(7).SubAssyPitch = 30
1703   RobotArm(7).SubAssyX = 0
1704   RobotArm(7).SubAssyY = 0
1705   RobotArm(7).SubAssyZ = 0
1706   RobotArm(8).Solid = zHALFCYL              'wrist swivel bracket (1)
1707   RobotArm(8).Level = zLEVEL2
1708   RobotArm(8).Color = zBROWN
1709   RobotArm(8).SizeX = RobotArm(6).SizeX
1710   RobotArm(8).SizeY = RobotArm(6).SizeY
1711   RobotArm(8).SizeZ = RobotArm(6).SizeZ
1712   RobotArm(8).Yaw = 90
1713   RobotArm(8).Roll = 0
1714   RobotArm(8).Pitch = 0
1715   RobotArm(8).PositionX = RobotArm(7).PositionX
```

```
1716    RobotArm(8).PositionY = RobotArm(7).PositionY
1717    RobotArm(8).PositionZ = RobotArm(7).PositionZ + RobotArm(7).SizeZ
1718    RobotArm(8).DeformRightX = 0
1719    RobotArm(8).DeformLeftX = 0
1720    RobotArm(8).DeformUpY = 0
1721    RobotArm(8).DeformDownY = 0
1722    RobotArm(8).PivotX = 0
1723    RobotArm(8).PivotY = 0
1724    RobotArm(8).PivotZ = 0
1725    RobotArm(8).SubAssyYaw = 0
1726    RobotArm(8).SubAssyRoll = 0
1727    RobotArm(8).SubAssyPitch = 30
1728    RobotArm(8).SubAssyX = 0
1729    RobotArm(8).SubAssyY = 0
1730    RobotArm(8).SubAssyZ = 0
1731    RobotArm(9).Solid = zCYLINDER                    'swivel pin (1)
1732    RobotArm(9).Level = zLEVEL2
1733    RobotArm(9).Color = zCYAN
1734    RobotArm(9).SizeX = RobotArm(5).SizeX
1735    RobotArm(9).SizeY = RobotArm(5).SizeY
1736    RobotArm(9).SizeZ = RobotArm(8).SizeZ + 15
1737    RobotArm(9).Yaw = 90
1738    RobotArm(9).Roll = 0
1739    RobotArm(9).Pitch = 0
1740    RobotArm(9).PositionX = RobotArm(8).PositionX
1741    RobotArm(9).PositionY = RobotArm(8).PositionY
1742    RobotArm(9).PositionZ = RobotArm(8).PositionZ
1743    RobotArm(9).DeformRightX = 0
1744    RobotArm(9).DeformLeftX = 0
1745    RobotArm(9).DeformUpY = 0
1746    RobotArm(9).DeformDownY = 0
1747    RobotArm(9).PivotX = 0
1748    RobotArm(9).PivotY = 0
1749    RobotArm(9).PivotZ = 0
1750    RobotArm(9).SubAssyYaw = 0
1751    RobotArm(9).SubAssyRoll = 0
1752    RobotArm(9).SubAssyPitch = 30
1753    RobotArm(9).SubAssyX = 0
1754    RobotArm(9).SubAssyY = 0
1755    RobotArm(9).SubAssyZ = 0
1756    '-------------- STEP THREE:  render the assembly --------------
1757    For PartID = zROBOT_START To zROBOT_FINISH Step 1
1758       Call ddzSetShadingColor(RobotArm(PartID).Color)
1759       Call dczSetSubjectSize(RobotArm(PartID).SizeX,
               RobotArm(PartID).SizeY, RobotArm(PartID).SizeZ)
1760       Call ezSetSubobjectAttitude(RobotArm(PartID).Yaw,
               RobotArm(PartID).Roll, RobotArm(PartID).Pitch)
1761       Call fzSetSubobjectLocation(RobotArm(PartID).PositionX,
               RobotArm(PartID).PositionY, RobotArm(PartID).PositionZ)
1762       If RobotArm(PartID).Level = zLEVEL1 Then         'if parent...
1763          Call czSetHierarchyLevel(zLEVEL1)
1764       ElseIf RobotArm(PartID).Level = zLEVEL2 Then     'if progeny...
1765          Call jzSetSubAssyPivot(RobotArm(PartID).PivotX,
               RobotArm(PartID).PivotY, RobotArm(PartID).PivotZ)
1766          Call hzSetSubAssyRotation(RobotArm(PartID).SubAssyYaw,
               RobotArm(PartID).SubAssyRoll, RobotArm(PartID).SubAssyPitch)
1767          Call izSetSubAssyPosition(RobotArm(PartID).SubAssyX,
               RobotArm(PartID).SubAssyY, RobotArm(PartID).SubAssyZ)
```

```
1768      Call czSetHierarchyLevel(zLEVEL2)
1769    End If
1770    Select Case RobotArm(PartID).Solid          'render the subobject
1771      Case zBOX
1772        Call azDrawCube
1773      Case zSPHERE
1774        Call czDrawSphere
1775      Case zCYLINDER
1776        Call ezDrawCylinder
1777      Case zCONE
1778        Call izDrawCone
1779      Case zWEDGE
1780        Call kzDrawWedge
1781      Case zCURVE
1782        Call gzDrawCurve
1783      Case zHEMISPHERE
1784        Call mzDrawHemisphere
1785      Case zDEFORMBOX
1786        Call azDrawDeformBox(RobotArm(PartID).DeformRightX,
          RobotArm(PartID).DeformLeftX, RobotArm(PartID).DeformUpY,
          RobotArm(PartID).DeformDownY)
1787      Case zHALFCYL
1788        Call czDrawHalfCylinder
1789      Case zBULGE
1790        Call ezDrawBulge
1791      Case Else
1792        Call azDrawCube
1793    End Select
1794  Next PartID
1795  End Sub
1796
1797  '----------------------------------------------------------------
1798  '                  Clear the display window
1799  '----------------------------------------------------------------
1800  Sub zClear ()
1801  RetVal = PatBlt(hDC, 0, 0, zFRAMEWIDE, zFRAMEHIGH, WHITENESS)
1802  End Sub
1803
1804  '----------------------------------------------------------------
1805  '                  Clear the hidden frame
1806  '----------------------------------------------------------------
1807  Sub zClearHiddenFrame ()
1808  If FrameReady = False Then
1809    Exit Sub
1810  End If
1811  RetVal = PatBlt(hFrameDC, 0, 0, zFRAMEWIDE, zFRAMEHIGH, WHITENESS)
1812  End Sub
1813
1814  '----------------------------------------------------------------
1815  '          Copy the hidden frame to the display window
1816  '----------------------------------------------------------------
1817  Sub zCopyToDisplay ()
1818  If FrameReady = False Then
1819    Exit Sub
1820  End If
1821  RetVal = BitBlt(hDC, 0, 0, zFRAMEWIDE, zFRAMEHIGH, hFrameDC, 0, 0,
        SRCCOPY)
```

```
1822  End Sub
1823
1824  '-----------------------------------------------------------------
1825  '           Copy the display window to the hidden frame
1826  '-----------------------------------------------------------------
1827  Sub zCopyToFrame ()
1828  If FrameReady = False Then
1829    Exit Sub
1830  End If
1831  RetVal = BitBlt(hFrameDC, 0, 0, zFRAMEWIDE, zFRAMEHIGH, hDC, 0, 0,
          SRCCOPY)
1832  End Sub
1833
1834  '-----------------------------------------------------------------
1835  '                    Create the hidden frame
1836  '-----------------------------------------------------------------
1837  Sub zInitFrame ()
1838  If FrameReady = True Then          'if hidden frame already created
1839    Exit Sub
1840  End If
1841  RetLong = GlobalCompact(-1)               'maximize contiguous memory
1842  hFrameDC = CreateCompatibleDC(hDC)           'get a display-context
1843  hFrame = CreateCompatibleBitmap(hDC, zFRAMEWIDE, zFRAMEHIGH)
1844  If hFrame = Null Then                          'if error occurred
1845    MsgBox "Insufficient memory.  Hidden frame not created.", MB_OK,
          "Graphics system not ready"
1846    FrameReady = False
1847    Exit Sub
1848  End If
1849  hPrevFrame = SelectObject(hFrameDC, hFrame)    'select the bitmap
1850  FrameReady = True                              'set a global token
1851  zClearHiddenFrame                              'clear the hidden frame
1852  End Sub
1853
```

C-3 Source listings for the interactive 3D animation template, animate. See Appendix B for the toolkits which must be used to build this application. See Appendix A for instructions on building the demo.

```
0001  ANGLOBAL.BAS
0002  ANMAIN.BAS
0003  ENGINE3D.BAS
0004  LIGHTS3D.BAS
0005  ASSEMB3D.BAS
0006  SHAPES3D.BAS
0007  DEFORM3D.BAS
0008  ANPLAY.BAS
0009  ANIMATE.FRM
0010  ProjWinSize=83,428,196,336
0011  ProjWinShow=2


0001  '-----------------------------------------------------------------
0002  '  Reusable global module for Visual Basic graphics applications
0003  '               that call Windows API functions.
0004  '-----------------------------------------------------------------
0005  '  Source file:  ANGLOBAL.BAS
0006  '  Release version:  1.00                    Programmer:  Lee Adams
0007  '  Type:  Visual Basic global module for Windows applications.
```

C-3 Continued.

```
0008  '  Compiler:  Microsoft Visual Basic 2.00
0009  '  Dependencies:  ANIMATE.FRM primary module
0010  '                 ANMAIN.BAS module containing Main()
0011  '                 ANPLAY.BAS animatin playback module
0012  '  Output and features:  Provides declarations for Windows API
0013  '     (Application Programming Interface) functions callable by
0014  '     Visual Basic applications at runtime, including routines
0015  '     from Windows' GDI, USER, and KERNEL DLLs (dynamic link
0016  '     libraries).  Also provides declarations of various variables
0017  '     and constants.  Functions, variables, and constants declared
0018  '     in this global module are visible throughout the project.
0019  '  Publication:  Contains material from Windcrest/McGraw-Hill
0020  '     book 4225 published by TAB BOOKS Div. of McGraw-Hill Inc.
0021  '  License:  As purchaser of the book you are granted a
0022  '     royalty-free license to distribute executable files
0023  '     generated using this code provided that you accept the
0024  '     conditions of the License Agreement and Limited Warranty
0025  '     described in the book and on the companion disk.  Government
0026  '     users:  This software and documentation are subject to
0027  '     restrictions set forth in The Rights in Technical Data and
0028  '     Computer Software clause at 252.227-7013 and elsewhere.
0029  '----------------------------------------------------------------
0030  '        (c) Copyright 1993 Lee Adams.  All rights reserved.
0031  '          Lee Adams(tm) is a trademark of Lee Adams.
0032  '----------------------------------------------------------------
0033
0034  Option Explicit           'generate error if variable not declared
0035  '----------------------------------------------------------------
0036  '                 General constants and variables
0037  '----------------------------------------------------------------
0038  Global Const MB_OK = 0                    'OK button for message box
0039  Global Const MB_OKCANCEL = 1   'OK Cancel buttons for message box
0040  Global Const MB_YESNO = 4          'Yes No buttons for message box
0041  Global Const IDOK = 1                        'OK button selected
0042  Global Const IDCANCEL = 2                'Cancel button selected
0043  Global Const IDYES = 6                      'Yes button selected
0044  Global Const IDNO = 7                        'No button selected
0045  Global UserWants As Integer        'value returned by message box
0046  Global Const PIXELS = 3                       'pixel coordinates
0047  Global StartUp As Integer            'tracks the startup code
0048  Global IgnoreRefresh As Integer       'tracks refresh activity
0049  Global Const zRED = 1
0050  Global Const zGREEN = 2
0051  Global Const zBROWN = 3
0052  Global Const zBLUE = 4
0053  Global Const zMAGENTA = 5
0054  Global Const zCYAN = 6
0055  Global Const zGRAY = 7
0056
0057  '----------------------------------------------------------------
0058  '                 Window specifications
0059  '----------------------------------------------------------------
0060  Global Const zWINDOW_WIDTH = 264              'width of window
0061  Global Const zWINDOW_HEIGHT = 301            'height of window
0062  Global Const zFRAMEWIDE = 256            'width of client area
0063  Global Const zFRAMEHIGH = 255           'height of client area
```

```
0064   Global HorizTwipsPixel As Single      'twips-per-pixel (horizontal)
0065   Global VertTwipsPixel As Single       'twips-per-pixel (vertical)
0066   Global Window_Width As Single          'runtime width of window
0067   Global Window_Height As Single         'runtime height of window
0068
0069   '----------------------------------------------------------------
0070   '                   Runtime conditions
0071   '----------------------------------------------------------------
0072   Global hDesktopWnd As Integer                  'handle to desktop
0073   Global hDCcaps As Integer             'display-context for desktop
0074   Global DisplayWidth As Integer        'horizontal screen resolution
0075   Global DisplayHeight As Integer       'vertical screen resolution
0076   Global DisplayBits As Integer          'number of bits-per-pixel
0077   Global DisplayPlanes As Integer          'number of bitplanes
0078   Global MemoryMode As Long                'runtime memory mode
0079   Global RetVal As Integer          'will receive GDI return value
0080   Global RetLong As Long            'will receive GDI return value
0081   Global MousePresent As Integer                 'mouse active?
0082   Global WindowsVersion As Long                'version of Windows
0083   Global LoadingFrame As Integer            'loading an image?
0084
0085   '----------------------------------------------------------------
0086   '                 Hidden frame operations
0087   '----------------------------------------------------------------
0088   Global hFrameDC As Integer        'display-context for hidden-frame
0089   Global hFrame As Integer          'handle to hidden-frame bitmap
0090   Global hPrevFrame As Integer        'default bitmap for hFrameDC
0091   Global FrameReady As Integer          'hidden-frame created?
0092
0093   '----------------------------------------------------------------
0094   '                   Timer operations
0095   '----------------------------------------------------------------
0096   Global Const zTIMER_PAUSE = 3              'for slow machines
0097   Global TimerCounter As Integer             'for slow machines
0098   Global TimerExists As Integer              'timer activated?
0099
0100   '----------------------------------------------------------------
0101   '                   Animation engine
0102   '----------------------------------------------------------------
0103   Global Pause As Integer                     'animation running?
0104   Global wFrameRate As Long            'arbitrary rate of 18.2 fps
0105   Global Const zFORWARD = 1          'indicates forward animation
0106   Global Const zREVERSE = 0          'indicates reverse animation
0107   Global FrameDirection As Integer            'forward or reverse
0108   Global FrameNum As Integer                   'current frame
0109   Global Const zFIRSTFRAME = 1        'first frame of animation
0110   Global Const zFINALFRAME = 36       'final frame of animation
0111   Global Const zNUMCELS = 36        'number of cels in animation
0112   Global LoopCount As Integer                    'loop counter
0113   Global hFDC As Integer        'memory DC for hidden playback bitmaps
0114   Global hPrevF As Integer              'handle to default bitmap
0115   Global BitmapHandles(zNUMCELS)        'array of bitmap handles
0116   Global FrameFiles(zNUMCELS) As String * 10    'array of filenames
0117   Global Redisplay As Integer              'for paused refresh
0118
0119   '----------------------------------------------------------------
0120   '                   Animation script
0121   '----------------------------------------------------------------
```

C-3 Continued.

```
0122   Type CameraPath              'camera movement during specified frames
0123      StartFrame As Integer
0124      EndFrame As Integer
0125      ChgHeading As Integer
0126      ChgPitch As Integer
0127      ChgDistance As Integer
0128   End Type
0129   Type LightPath       'light-source movement during specified frames
0130      StartFrame As Integer
0131      EndFrame As Integer
0132      ChgHeading As Integer
0133      ChgElevation As Integer
0134   End Type
0135   Type ActorPath               'actor movement during specified frames
0136      StartFrame As Integer
0137      EndFrame As Integer
0138      ChgYaw As Integer
0139      ChgRoll As Integer
0140      ChgPitch As Integer
0141      ChgPosX As Integer
0142      ChgPosY As Integer
0143      ChgPosZ As Integer
0144   End Type
0145   Type CameraDefine                       'camera startup parameters
0146      Heading As Integer
0147      Pitch As Integer
0148      Distance As Integer
0149   End Type
0150   Type LightDefine                    'light-source startup parameters
0151      Heading As Integer
0152      Elevation As Integer
0153   End Type
0154   Type ActorDefine                        'actor startup parameters
0155      PositionX As Integer
0156      PositionY As Integer
0157      PositionZ As Integer
0158      Yaw As Integer
0159      Roll As Integer
0160      Pitch As Integer
0161   End Type
0162   Global Cam1 As CameraDefine                      'the camera...
0163   Global Cam1Path1 As CameraPath                   '...and its path
0164   Global Lt1 As LightDefine                 'the light-source...
0165   Global Lt1Path1 As LightPath                     '...and its path
0166   Global Actor1 As ActorDefine                      'an actor...
0167   Global Actor1Path1 As ActorPath                  '...and its path
0168
0169   '----------------------------------------------------------------
0170   '                    Variables for disk I/O
0171   '----------------------------------------------------------------
0172   Global FileName As String                'name of binary image file
0173   Global FrameSaved As Integer              'frame saved to disk?
0174   Global FrameLoaded As Integer            'frame loaded from disk?
0175   Global AnimationSaved As Integer         'animation saved to disk?
0176   Global AnimationLoaded As Integer        'animation loaded from disk?
0177   Global AnimationReady As Integer         'animation ready for playback?
```

```
0178  Global PrevSaveAttempt As Integer     'previous save attempt made?
0179  Global PrevLoadAttempt As Integer     'previous load attempt made?
0180  Global UseDisk As Integer             'load each frame as needed?
0181  Global AnimationHalted As Integer     'disk error during animation?
0182
0183  '----------------------------------------------------------------
0184  '            Constants for Windows API functions
0185  '----------------------------------------------------------------
0186  Global Const SRCCOPY = &HCC0020                   'for bitblts...
0187  Global Const SRCINVERT = &H660046
0188  Global Const SRCPAINT = &HEE0086
0189  Global Const WHITENESS = &HFF0062
0190  Global Const BLACKNESS = &H42&
0191  Global Const ALTERNATE = 1                        'for filling...
0192  Global Const WINDING = 2
0193  Global Const R2_COPYPEN = 13                      'for pen mode...
0194  Global Const R2_XORPEN = 7
0195  Global Const TRANSPARENT = 1               'for background mode...
0196  Global Const OPAQUE = 2
0197  Global Const PS_SOLID = 0                          'for solid pen
0198  Global Const PS_NULL = 5                     'for transparent pen
0199  Global Const BLACKONWHITE = 1              'for bitblt scaling...
0200  Global Const WHITEONBLACK = 2
0201  Global Const COLORONCOLOR = 3
0202  Global Const HORZRES = 8                 'args for GetDeviceCaps()...
0203  Global Const VERTRES = 10
0204  Global Const BITSPIXEL = 12
0205  Global Const PLANES = 14
0206  Global Const SM_MOUSEPRESENT - 19        'for GetSystemMetrics()
0207  Global Const WF_ENHANCED = &H20             'for GetWinFlags()...
0208  Global Const WF_STANDARD = &H10
0209
0210  '----------------------------------------------------------------
0211  '            GDI functions for display-contexts
0212  '----------------------------------------------------------------
0213  Declare Function GetDC Lib "USER" (ByVal hWnd As Integer) As
          Integer
0214  Declare Function ReleaseDC Lib "USER" (ByVal hWnd As Integer,
          ByVal hDC As Integer) As Integer
0215
0216  '----------------------------------------------------------------
0217  '            GDI functions for the desktop
0218  '----------------------------------------------------------------
0219  Declare Function GetDesktopWindow Lib "USER" () As Integer
0220
0221  '----------------------------------------------------------------
0222  '        GDI functions for creating drawing objects
0223  '----------------------------------------------------------------
0224  Declare Function CreatePen Lib "GDI" (ByVal PenStyle As Integer,
          ByVal Wd As Integer, ByVal Color As Long) As Integer
0225  Declare Function CreateSolidBrush Lib "GDI" (ByVal Color As Long)
          As Integer
0226
0227  '----------------------------------------------------------------
0228  '            GDI functions for selecting objects
0229  '----------------------------------------------------------------
0230  Declare Function SelectObject Lib "GDI" (ByVal hDC As Integer,
          ByVal hObject As Integer) As Integer
```

```
0231   Declare Function DeleteObject Lib "GDI" (ByVal hObject As Integer)
          As Integer
0232
0233   '-----------------------------------------------------------------
0234   '            GDI functions for bitmaps and bitblts
0235   '-----------------------------------------------------------------
0236   Declare Function CreateCompatibleDC Lib "GDI" (ByVal hDC As
          Integer) As Integer
0237   Declare Function CreateCompatibleBitmap Lib "GDI" (ByVal hDC As
          Integer, ByVal Wd As Integer, ByVal Ht As Integer) As Integer
0238   Declare Function PatBlt Lib "GDI" (ByVal hDC As Integer, ByVal X
          As Integer, ByVal Y As Integer, ByVal Wd As Integer, ByVal Ht
          As Integer, ByVal RasOp As Long) As Integer
0239   Declare Function BitBlt Lib "GDI" (ByVal hDestDC As Integer, ByVal
          DestX As Integer, ByVal DestY As Integer, ByVal Wd As Integer,
          ByVal Ht As Integer, ByVal hSrcDC As Integer, ByVal SrcX As
          Integer, ByVal SrcY As Integer, ByVal RastOp As Long) As
          Integer
0240   Declare Function DeleteDC Lib "GDI" (ByVal hDC As Integer) As
          Integer
0241
0242   '-----------------------------------------------------------------
0243   '            GDI functions for drawing mode operations
0244   '-----------------------------------------------------------------
0245   Declare Function SetROP2 Lib "GDI" (ByVal hDC As Integer, ByVal
          RasMode As Integer) As Integer
0246   Declare Function SetBkColor Lib "GDI" (ByVal hDC As Integer, ByVal
          Color As Long) As Long
0247   Declare Function SetBkMode Lib "GDI" (ByVal hDC As Integer,
          ByVal BkMode As Integer) As Integer
0248   Declare Function SetPolyFillMode Lib "GDI" (ByVal hDC As Integer,
          ByVal PolyMode As Integer) As Integer
0249   Declare Function SetStretchBltMode Lib "GDI" (ByVal hDC As
          Integer, ByVal StretchMode As Integer) As Integer
0250
0251   '-----------------------------------------------------------------
0252   '            GDI functions for drawing operations
0253   '-----------------------------------------------------------------
0254   Declare Function MoveTo Lib "GDI" (ByVal hDC As Integer, ByVal X
          As Integer, ByVal Y As Integer) As Long
0255   Declare Function LineTo Lib "GDI" (ByVal hDC As Integer, ByVal X
          As Integer, ByVal Y As Integer) As Integer
0256   Declare Function Polygon Lib "GDI" (ByVal hDC As Integer, FirstPt
          As Integer, ByVal Count As Integer) As Integer
0257   Declare Function Rectangle Lib "GDI" (ByVal hDC As Integer, ByVal
          X1 As Integer, ByVal Y1 As Integer, ByVal X2 As Integer, ByVal
          Y2 As Integer) As Integer
0258   Declare Function Ellipse Lib "GDI" (ByVal hDC As Integer, ByVal X1
          As Integer, ByVal Y1 As Integer, ByVal X2 As Integer, ByVal Y2
          As Integer) As Integer
0259   Declare Function FloodFill Lib "GDI" (ByVal hDC As Integer, ByVal
          X As Integer, ByVal Y As Integer, ByVal Color As Long) As
          Integer
0260   Declare Function SetPixel Lib "GDI" (ByVal hDC As Integer, ByVal X
          As Integer, ByVal Y As Integer, ByVal Color As Long) As Long
0261   Declare Function GetPixel Lib "GDI" (ByVal hDC As Integer, ByVal X
          As Integer, ByVal Y As Integer) As Long
```

```
0262
0263  '-------------------------------------------------------------------
0264  '                 GDI functions for regions
0265  '-------------------------------------------------------------------
0266  Declare Function PaintRgn Lib "GDI" (ByVal hDC As Integer, ByVal
          hRGN As Integer) As Integer
0267  Declare Function CreatePolygonRgn Lib "GDI" (FirstPt As Integer,
          ByVal Count As Integer, ByVal PolyFillMode As Integer) As
          Integer
0268  Declare Function PtInRegion Lib "GDI" (ByVal hRGN As Integer,
          ByVal xCoord As Integer, ByVal yCoord As Integer) As Integer
0269
0270  '-------------------------------------------------------------------
0271  '   GDI, USER, KERNEL functions for various runtime conditions
0272  '-------------------------------------------------------------------
0273  Declare Function GetDeviceCaps Lib "GDI" (ByVal hDC As Integer,
          ByVal Item As Integer) As Integer
0274  Declare Function GetWinFlags Lib "KERNEL" () As Long
0275  Declare Function GetSystemMetrics Lib "USER" (ByVal Item As
          Integer) As Integer
0276  Declare Function GlobalCompact Lib "KERNEL" (ByVal NumBytes
          As Long) As Long
0277  Declare Function GetVersion Lib "KERNEL" () As Long
0278  Declare Function ExitWindows Lib "USER" (ByVal Reserved As Long,
          ByVal Item As Integer) As Integer
0279  Declare Function SetCapture Lib "USER" (ByVal hWnd As Integer)
          As Integer
0280  Declare Sub ReleaseCapture Lib "USER" ()
0281
0282  '-------------------------------------------------------------------
0283  '                 End of global module.
0284  '-------------------------------------------------------------------
0285


0001  '-------------------------------------------------------------------
0002  '           Reusable template for startup code for
0003  '           Visual Basic Windows graphics applications.
0004  '-------------------------------------------------------------------
0005  '   Source file:  ANMAIN.BAS
0006  '   Release version:  1.00              Programmer:  Lee Adams
0007  '   Type:  Visual Basic startup module for Windows applications.
0008  '   Compiler:  Microsoft Visual Basic 2.00
0009  '   Dependencies:  ANGLOBAL.BAS global module
0010  '                  ANIMATE.FRM primary module
0011  '                  ANPLAY.BAS animation playback module
0012  '   Output and features:  Initializes the runtime environment
0013  '     for a Windows graphics application created with
0014  '     Visual Basic.  Ensures runtime image size and compatibility
0015  '     no matter which graphics mode is being used by Windows.
0016  '   Publication:  Contains material from Windcrest/McGraw-Hill
0017  '     book 4225 published by TAB BOOKS Div. of McGraw-Hill Inc.
0018  '   License:  As purchaser of the book you are granted a
0019  '     royalty-free license to distribute executable files
0020  '     generated using this code provided that you accept the
0021  '     conditions of the License Agreement and Limited Warranty
0022  '     described in the book and on the companion disk.  Government
0023  '     users:  This software and documentation are subject to
0024  '     restrictions set forth in The Rights in Technical Data and
```

C-3 Continued.

```
0025  '     Computer Software clause at 252.227-7013 and elsewhere.
0026  '-----------------------------------------------------------------
0027  '        (c) Copyright 1993 Lee Adams.  All rights reserved.
0028  '             Lee Adams(tm) is a trademark of Lee Adams.
0029  '-----------------------------------------------------------------
0030
0031  Option Explicit            'generate error if variable not declared
0032
0033  '-----------------------------------------------------------------
0034  '        Initialization code for startup of application
0035  '-----------------------------------------------------------------
0036  Sub Main ()                         'is called by Windows at startup
0037    Dim PreviousColor As Long           'will remember default color
0038  StartUp = True                        'set the run-time tokens...
0039  IgnoreRefresh = True
0040  FrameReady = False
0041  FrameSaved = False
0042  FrameLoaded = False
0043  LoadingFrame = False
0044  TimerExists = False
0045  Pause = True
0046  AnimationSaved = False
0047  AnimationLoaded = False
0048  PrevSaveAttempt = False
0049  PrevLoadAttempt = False
0050  UseDisk = False
0051  AnimationHalted = False
0052  Redisplay = False
0053  '-------------------- initialize variables --------------------
0054  TimerCounter = zTIMER_PAUSE
0055  wFrameRate = 55
0056  FrameDirection = zFORWARD
0057  FrameNum = 1
0058  FrameFiles(0) = "ANIM01.BMP"    'initialize the array of filenames
0059  FrameFiles(1) = "ANIM02.BMP"
0060  FrameFiles(2) = "ANIM03.BMP"
0061  FrameFiles(3) = "ANIM04.BMP"
0062  FrameFiles(4) = "ANIM05.BMP"
0063  FrameFiles(5) = "ANIM06.BMP"
0064  FrameFiles(6) = "ANIM07.BMP"
0065  FrameFiles(7) = "ANIM08.BMP"
0066  FrameFiles(8) = "ANIM09.BMP"
0067  FrameFiles(9) = "ANIM10.BMP"
0068  FrameFiles(10) = "ANIM11.BMP"
0069  FrameFiles(11) = "ANIM12.BMP"
0070  FrameFiles(12) = "ANIM13.BMP"
0071  FrameFiles(13) = "ANIM14.BMP"
0072  FrameFiles(14) = "ANIM15.BMP"
0073  FrameFiles(15) = "ANIM16.BMP"
0074  FrameFiles(16) = "ANIM17.BMP"
0075  FrameFiles(17) = "ANIM18.BMP"
0076  FrameFiles(18) = "ANIM19.BMP"
0077  FrameFiles(19) = "ANIM20.BMP"
0078  FrameFiles(20) = "ANIM21.BMP"
0079  FrameFiles(21) = "ANIM22.BMP"
0080  FrameFiles(22) = "ANIM23.BMP"
```

```
0081   FrameFiles(23) = "ANIM24.BMP"
0082   FrameFiles(24) = "ANIM25.BMP"
0083   FrameFiles(25) = "ANIM26.BMP"
0084   FrameFiles(26) = "ANIM27.BMP"
0085   FrameFiles(27) = "ANIM28.BMP"
0086   FrameFiles(28) = "ANIM29.BMP"
0087   FrameFiles(29) = "ANIM30.BMP"
0088   FrameFiles(30) = "ANIM31.BMP"
0089   FrameFiles(31) = "ANIM32.BMP"
0090   FrameFiles(32) = "ANIM33.BMP"
0091   FrameFiles(33) = "ANIM34.BMP"
0092   FrameFiles(34) = "ANIM35.BMP"
0093   FrameFiles(35) = "ANIM36.BMP"
0094   '---------------- examine the graphics adapter ------------------
0095   hDesktopWnd = GetDesktopWindow()          'grab handle to desktop
0096   hDCcaps = GetDC(hDesktopWnd)        'get display-context for desktop
0097   DisplayWidth = GetDeviceCaps(hDCcaps, HORZRES)  'horiz resolution
0098   DisplayHeight = GetDeviceCaps(hDCcaps, VERTRES)  'vert resolution
0099   DisplayBits = GetDeviceCaps(hDCcaps, BITSPIXEL)   'bits-per-pixel
0100   DisplayPlanes = GetDeviceCaps(hDCcaps, PLANES)  'num of bitplanes
0101   RetVal = ReleaseDC(hDesktopWnd, hDCcaps) 'release display-context
0102   '--------------- determine the runtime memory mode --------------
0103   MemoryMode = GetWinFlags()          'will inspect this value later
0104   '--------------- determine version of Windows ------------------
0105   WindowsVersion = GetVersion()        'will inspect this value later
0106   '--------------- set mode-dependent twips factors ---------------
0107   HorizTwipsPixel = 15!: VertTwipsPixel = 15!      'set defaults...
0108   Window_Width = zWINDOW_WIDTH: Window_Height = zWINDOW_HEIGHT
0109   If DisplayWidth = 640 Then
0110      If DisplayHeight = 480 Then                  'VGA 640x480 mode
0111         HorizTwipsPixel = 15!           '9600x7200 twips full screen
0112         VertTwipsPixel = 15!
0113         Window_Width = zWINDOW_WIDTH
0114         Window_Height = zWINDOW_HEIGHT
0115      End If
0116      If DisplayHeight = 350 Then                  'EGA 640x350 mode
0117         HorizTwipsPixel = 15!           '9600x7000 twips full screen
0118         VertTwipsPixel = 20!
0119         Window_Width = zWINDOW_WIDTH
0120         Window_Height = 297!   'adjust for aspect ratio and font size
0121      End If
0122      If DisplayHeight = 200 Then   'nominal support CGA 640x200 mode
0123         HorizTwipsPixel = 15!
0124         VertTwipsPixel = 36!
0125         Window_Width = zWINDOW_WIDTH
0126         Window_Height = zWINDOW_HEIGHT
0127      End If
0128   End If
0129   If DisplayWidth = 800 Then   'SuperVGA, 8514/A, XGA 800x600 mode
0130      HorizTwipsPixel = 12!                '9600x7200 twips full screen
0131      VertTwipsPixel = 12!
0132      Window_Width = zWINDOW_WIDTH
0133      Window_Height = 317!                     'compensate for font size
0134   End If
0135   If DisplayWidth = 1024 Then            '8514/A, XGA 1024x768 mode
0136      HorizTwipsPixel = 12!              '12200x9216 twips full screen
0137      VertTwipsPixel = 12!
0138      Window_Width = zWINDOW_WIDTH
```

```
0139    Window_Height = 317!                       'compensate for font size
0140  End If
0141  If DisplayWidth = 720 Then                   'Hercules 720x348 mode
0142    HorizTwipsPixel = 12!
0143    VertTwipsPixel = 20!
0144    Window_Width = zWINDOW_WIDTH
0145    Window_Height = 297!      'adjust for aspect ratio and font size
0146  End If
0147  '-------------- display the splash sign-on banner ---------------
0148  UserWants = MsgBox("Graphics demo from Windcrest McGraw-Hill book
           4225.", MB_OKCANCEL, "Copyright© 1993-1994 Lee Adams.")
0149  If UserWants = IDCANCEL Then    'if user selected Cancel button...
0150      End                              'then cancel this startup
0151  End If
0152  '------------- initialize and display the window ----------------
0153  Form1.Width = Window_Width * HorizTwipsPixel          'set width
0154  Form1.Height = Window_Height * VertTwipsPixel         'set height
0155  Form1.Left = (Screen.Width - Form1.Width) / 2  'horizontal center
0156  Form1.Top = (Screen.Height - Form1.Height) / 2   'vertical center
0157  Form1.Caption = "3D Animation Template"         'set the caption
0158  Form1.AutoRedraw = False              'disable automatic refresh
0159  Form1.BackColor = RGB(255, 255, 255)   'set the client area color
0160  Form1.ForeColor = RGB(0, 0, 0)                     'active color
0161  Form1.ScaleMode = PIXELS                'will use pixel coords
0162  Form1.Show                            'display the window
0163  '------------------- check if mouse present --------------------
0164  MousePresent = GetSystemMetrics(SM_MOUSEPRESENT)
0165  If MousePresent = 0 Then                           'if no mouse
0166    Beep
0167    MsgBox "No mouse found.  Some features of this demo program may
           require a mouse.  The demo's menu system also responds to the
           keyboard.  Press <Enter> to continue.", MB_OK, "Graphics
           system warning"
0168  End If
0169  '----------------- initialize the 3D toolkit --------------------
0170  aazInitialize3D
0171  End Sub
0172


0001  VERSION 2.00
0002  Begin Form Form1
0003      Caption          =     "Prototype"
0004      ControlBox       =     0     'False
0005      Height           =     4515
0006      Left             =     2040
0007      LinkMode         =     1    'Source
0008      LinkTopic        =     "Form1"
0009      MaxButton        =     0     'False
0010      MinButton        =     0     'False
0011      ScaleHeight      =     3825
0012      ScaleWidth       =     3840
0013      Top              =     1485
0014      Width            =     3960
0015      Begin PictureBox Picture1
0016        Height           =     495
0017        Left             =     480
```

```
0018            ScaleHeight      =    465
0019            ScaleWidth       =    1185
0020            TabIndex         =    0
0021            Top              =    840
0022            Width            =    1215
0023         End
0024      Begin Timer TimerID1
0025            Left             =    1320
0026            Top              =    1680
0027      End
0028      Begin Menu POPUP_File
0029            Caption          =    "&File"
0030            Begin Menu IDM_New
0031               Caption       =    "&New"
0032               Enabled       =    0    'False
0033            End
0034            Begin Menu IDM_Open
0035               Caption       =    "&Open"
0036               Enabled       =    0    'False
0037            End
0038            Begin Menu IDM_Save
0039               Caption       =    "&Save"
0040               Enabled       =    0    'False
0041            End
0042            Begin Menu IDM_SaveAs
0043               Caption       =    "Save &As..."
0044               Enabled       =    0    'False
0045            End
0046            Begin Menu FileSep1
0047               Caption       =    "-"
0048            End
0049            Begin Menu IDM_Exit
0050               Caption       =    "E&xit..."
0051            End
0052            Begin Menu IDM_Restart
0053               Caption       =    "&Restart Windows..."
0054            End
0055      End
0056      Begin Menu POPUP_Edit
0057            Caption          =    "&Edit"
0058            Begin Menu IDM_Undo
0059               Caption       =    "&Undo"
0060               Enabled       =    0    'False
0061            End
0062            Begin Menu EditSep1
0063               Caption       =    "-"
0064            End
0065            Begin Menu IDM_Cut
0066               Caption       =    "Cu&t"
0067               Enabled       =    0    'False
0068            End
0069            Begin Menu IDM_Copy
0070               Caption       =    "&Copy"
0071               Enabled       =    0    'False
0072            End
0073            Begin Menu IDM_Paste
0074               Caption       =    "&Paste"
0075               Enabled       =    0    'False
```

```
0076        End
0077        Begin Menu IDM_Delete
0078            Caption         =   "&Delete"
0079            Enabled         =   0   'False
0080        End
0081    End
0082    Begin Menu POPUP_Run
0083        Caption         =   "&Run"
0084        Begin Menu IDM_LoadAnimation
0085            Caption         =   "&Load animation"
0086        End
0087        Begin Menu DemoSep1
0088            Caption         =   "-"
0089        End
0090        Begin Menu IDM_RunForward
0091            Caption         =   "Run &Forward"
0092        End
0093        Begin Menu POPUP_RunReverse
0094            Caption         =   "Run &Reverse"
0095        End
0096        Begin Menu IDM_StopAnimation
0097            Caption         =   "Free&zeframe"
0098        End
0099        Begin Menu POPUP_SetSpeed
0100            Caption         =   "S&et speed..."
0101            Begin Menu IDM_FPS182
0102                Caption         =   "&18 fps"
0103            End
0104            Begin Menu IDM_FPS91
0105                Caption         =   "&9 fps"
0106            End
0107            Begin Menu IDM_FPS61
0108                Caption         =   "&6 fps"
0109            End
0110            Begin Menu IDM_FPS45
0111                Caption         =   "&5 fps"
0112            End
0113            Begin Menu IDM_FPS36
0114                Caption         =   "&4 fps"
0115            End
0116            Begin Menu IDM_FPS30
0117                Caption         =   "&3 fps"
0118            End
0119        End
0120        Begin Menu DemoSep2
0121            Caption         =   "-"
0122        End
0123        Begin Menu IDM_Clear
0124            Caption         =   "&Clear Viewport"
0125        End
0126        Begin Menu DemoSep3
0127            Caption         =   "-"
0128        End
0129        Begin Menu POPUP_Production
0130            Caption         =   "&Production..."
0131            Begin Menu IDM_SaveAnimation
```

```
0132              Caption          =    "&Build Animation"
0133          End
0134       Begin Menu DemoSep4
0135          Caption          =    "-"
0136       End
0137       Begin Menu IDM_UseShaded
0138          Caption          =    "Use &shaded solids"
0139       End
0140       Begin Menu IDM_UseWireframe
0141          Caption          =    "Use &wireframe mode"
0142       End
0143     End
0144   End
0145   Begin Menu POPUP_Use
0146     Caption          =    "&Use"
0147     Begin Menu IDM_About
0148        Caption          =    "&About"
0149     End
0150     Begin Menu IDM_License
0151        Caption          =    "&License"
0152     End
0153     Begin Menu HelpSep1
0154        Caption          =    "-"
0155     End
0156     Begin Menu IDM_Display
0157        Caption          =    "&Resolution of display"
0158     End
0159     Begin Menu IDM_Colors
0160        Caption          =    "Available &colors"
0161     End
0162     Begin Menu IDM_Mode
0163        Caption          =    "&Memory mode"
0164     End
0165     Begin Menu IDM_Version
0166        Caption          =    "Windows &version"
0167     End
0168     Begin Menu HelpSep2
0169        Caption          =    "-"
0170     End
0171     Begin Menu IDM_GeneralHelp
0172        Caption          =    "&How to use"
0173     End
0174   End
0175 End
0176 '----------------------------------------------------------------
0177 '              3D interactive animation template
0178 '----------------------------------------------------------------
0179 '  Source file:  ANIMATE.FRM
0180 '  Release version:  1.2                      Programmer:  Lee Adams
0181 '  Type:  Visual Basic global module for Windows applications.
0182 '  Compiler:  Microsoft Visual Basic 2.00
0183 '  Dependencies:  ANGLOBAL.BAS     global module
0184 '                 ANMAIN.BAS       module containing Main()
0185 '                 ANPLAY.BAS       animation playback module
0186 '                 ENGINE3D.BAS     3D toolkit
0187 '                 SHAPES3D.BAS     3D shapes toolkit
0188 '                 DEFORM3D.BAS     3D deformations toolkit
0189 '                 LIGHTS3D.BAS     light-source toolkit
```

C-3 Continued.

```
0190 '             ASSEMB3D.BAS    hierarchical modeling toolkit
0191 ' Output and features:  Demonstrates 3D modeling and shading for
0192 '   animation sequences and storage of frames on disk.
0193 '   Demonstrates loading of frames from disk and interactive
0194 '   playback of animation sequence from RAM or from disk if
0195 '   insufficient memory available.  The startup code
0196 '   automatically sizes the window to yield a client area with
0197 '   dimensions of 256-by-255 pixels in any graphics mode.  You
0198 '   can use the menu system to toggle between wireframe and
0199 '   shaded modes.
0200 '    NUMBER OF FRAMES:  In its current implementation, the
0201 '   application produces an animation sequence of 36 frames.
0202 '   To create a sequence that uses fewer frames or more frames,
0203 '   you can edit the values of the zFINALFRAME and zNUMCELS
0204 '   constants defined in the ANGLOBAL.BAS global module.  You'll
0205 '   also need to add or delete filename strings to the array
0206 '   named FrameFiles() in the ANMAIN.BAS module.
0207 ' Publication:  Contains material from Windcrest/McGraw-Hill
0208 '   book 4225 published by TAB BOOKS Div. of McGraw-Hill Inc.
0209 ' License:  As purchaser of the book you are granted a
0210 '   royalty-free license to distribute executable files
0211 '   generated using this code provided that you accept the
0212 '   conditions of the License Agreement and Limited Warranty
0213 '   described in the book and on the companion disk.  Government
0214 '   users:  This software and documentation are subject to
0215 '   restrictions set forth in The Rights in Technical Data and
0216 '   Computer Software clause at 252.227-7013 and elsewhere.
0217 '----------------------------------------------------------------
0218 '     (c) Copyright 1993 Lee Adams.  All rights reserved.
0219 '         Lee Adams(tm) is a trademark of Lee Adams.
0220 '----------------------------------------------------------------
0221 '
0222 ' SELECT A STARTUP FORM:
0223 ' Because this Visual Basic application uses a procedure named
0224 ' Main() at startup, you must specify Sub Main as the startup
0225 ' form in the Project Options dialog box before you run the
0226 ' program and before you build an .exe file.
0227 '
0228 ' DOUBLE-CLICK THE TIMER TOOL:
0229 ' Because the program uses a timer to manage the animation
0230 ' playback, you must double-click on the timer tool in the
0231 ' toolbox at design-time to place a timer control on the form.
0232 ' Specify TimerID1 as the timer's CtlName.
0233 '
0234 ' DOUBLE-CLICK THE PICTURE-BOX TOOL:
0235 ' Because this demo uses a picture box when saving images to
0236 ' disk as .BMP files, you must double-click the Picture Box
0237 ' tool in the Toolbox at design-time to place a default-sized
0238 ' picture box on the form.
0239 '
0240 '----------------------------------------------------------------
0241
0242 Option Explicit           'generate error if variable not declared
0243
0244 '----------------------------------------------------------------
0245 '     Low-level keyboard handler for single-step animation
0246 '----------------------------------------------------------------
```

```
0247  Sub Form_KeyDown (KeyCode As Integer, Shift As Integer)
0248  If Pause = False Then                      'if animation is running...
0249    Exit Sub                                 'then cancel this function
0250  End If
0251  If AnimationLoaded = False Then    'if animation is not loaded...
0252    Exit Sub                                 'then cancel this function
0253  End If
0254  If FrameReady = False Then         'if hidden frame is not ready...
0255    Exit Sub                                 'then cancel this function
0256  End If
0257  If KeyCode = &H25 Then         'if left arrow key has been pressed...
0258    FrameDirection = zREVERSE              'reset direction token
0259    Pause = False                         'toggle off the Pause token
0260    zShowNextFrame                              'show next frame
0261    Pause = True                          'toggle on the Pause token
0262    Exit Sub                                          'return
0263  End If
0264  If KeyCode = &H27 Then     'if right arrow key has been pressed...
0265    FrameDirection = zFORWARD
0266    Pause = False
0267    zShowNextFrame
0268    Pause = True
0269    Exit Sub
0270  End If
0271  End Sub
0272
0273  '----------------------------------------------------------------
0274  '              Refresh the client area if uncovered
0275  '----------------------------------------------------------------
0276  Sub Form_Paint ()   'is automatically called by Windows as needed
0277  If LoadingFrame = True Then    'special case LoadPicture function
0278    Exit Sub
0279  End If
0280  If Pause = True Then               'if paused, redisplay current frame
0281    Redisplay = True
0282    zShowNextFrame
0283    Redisplay = False
0284    Exit Sub
0285  End If
0286  zShowNextFrame          '...else show the next frame in the animation
0287  End Sub
0288
0289  '----------------------------------------------------------------
0290  '           Intercept any attempt to resize the window
0291  '----------------------------------------------------------------
0292  Sub Form_Resize ()          'is called twice when window is resized
0293  If Startup = True Then   'if window being displayed for first time
0294    Startup = False
0295    IgnoreRefresh = True
0296    Exit Sub
0297  End If
0298  Form1.WindowState = 0                          'reset normal size
0299  Form1.Width = Window_Width * HorizTwipsPixel       'reset width
0300  Form1.Height = Window_Height * VertTwipsPixel      'reset height
0301  Form1.Left = (Screen.Width - Form1.Width) / 2 'horizontal center
0302  Form1.Top = (Screen.Height - Form1.Height) / 2 'vertical center
0303  If IgnoreRefresh = False Then                  'if second call
0304    IgnoreRefresh = True               'reset token for next first call
```

```
0305    MsgBox "This demo uses a fixed-size window.", MB_OK, "Sample
            application"
0306    Exit Sub
0307    End If
0308    Form1.Refresh                           'refresh the client area
0309    IgnoreRefresh = False       'if first call, reset for second call
0310    End Sub
0311
0312    '-----------------------------------------------------------------
0313    '                 Display the About message box
0314    '-----------------------------------------------------------------
0315    Sub IDM_About_Click ()
0316    MsgBox "This is a demo from Windcrest McGraw-Hill book 4225.
            Copyright© 1993 Lee Adams.  All rights reserved.", MB_OK,
            "About this Visual Basic program"
0317    End Sub
0318
0319    '-----------------------------------------------------------------
0320    '                 Clear the client area of the window
0321    '-----------------------------------------------------------------
0322    Sub IDM_Clear_Click ()
0323    zClear                                  'clear the display window
0324    zClearHiddenFrame                       'clear the hidden frame
0325    End Sub
0326
0327    '-----------------------------------------------------------------
0328    '                 Determine number of available colors
0329    '-----------------------------------------------------------------
0330    Sub IDM_Colors_Click ()
0331    If DisplayBits = 1 Then                 'if 1 bit-per-pixel...
0332      If DisplayPlanes = 4 Then                 'if 4 bitplanes...
0333        MsgBox "Running in 4-bit, 16-color mode.", MB_OK, "Available
            colors"
0334        Exit Sub
0335      End If
0336      If DisplayPlanes = 1 Then                 'if 1 bitplane...
0337        MsgBox "Running in 1-bit, 2-color mode.", MB_OK, "Available
            colors"
0338        Exit Sub
0339      End If
0340    End If
0341    If DisplayBits = 8 Then                 'if 8 bits-per-pixel...
0342      MsgBox "Running in 8-bit, 256-color mode.", MB_OK, "Available
            colors"
0343      Exit Sub
0344    End If
0345    If DisplayBits = 16 Then                'if 16 bits-per-pixel...
0346      MsgBox "Running in 16-bit, 65000-color mode.", MB_OK, "Available
            colors"
0347      Exit Sub
0348    End If
0349    MsgBox "Running in a custom color mode.", MB_OK, "Available colors"
0350    End Sub
0351
0352    '-----------------------------------------------------------------
0353    '                 Determine the screen resolution
0354    '-----------------------------------------------------------------
```

```
0355  Sub IDM_Display_Click ()
0356  If DisplayWidth = 640 Then
0357    If DisplayHeight = 480 Then                              'VGA mode
0358      MsgBox "Running in 640x480 mode.", MB_OK, "Screen resolution"
0359      Exit Sub
0360    End If
0361    If DisplayHeight = 350 Then                              'EGA mode
0362      MsgBox "Running in 640x350 mode.", MB_OK, "Screen resolution"
0363      Exit Sub
0364    End If
0365    If DisplayHeight = 200 Then                              'CGA mode
0366      MsgBox "Running in 640x200 mode.", MB_OK, "Screen resolution"
0367      Exit Sub
0368    End If
0369  End If
0370  If DisplayWidth = 800 Then             'SuperVGA, 8514/A, XGA mode
0371    MsgBox "Running in 800x600 mode.", MB_OK, "Screen resolution"
0372    Exit Sub
0373  End If
0374  If DisplayWidth = 1024 Then                        '8514/A, XGA mode
0375    MsgBox "Running in 1024x768 mode.", MB_OK, "Screen resolution"
0376    Exit Sub
0377  End If
0378  If DisplayWidth = 720 Then                             'Hercules mode
0379    MsgBox "Running in 720x348 mode.", MB_OK, "Screen resolution"
0380    Exit Sub
0381  End If
0382  MsgBox "Running in custom mode.", MB_OK, "Screen resolution"
0383  End Sub
0384
0385  '----------------------------------------------------------------
0386  '                    Terminate the application
0387  '----------------------------------------------------------------
0388  Sub IDM_Exit_Click ()
0389  UserWants = MsgBox("Exit the demo and return to Windows?",
          MB_YESNO, "Please confirm")
0390  If UserWants = IDNO Then            'if user selected No button...
0391    Exit Sub                          'then cancel this operation
0392  End If          'otherwise continue to terminate the application...
0393  If AnimationLoaded = True Then            'if animation loaded...
0394    RetVal = SelectObject(hFDC, hPrevF)      'select default handle
0395    For LoopCount = 1 To zNUMCELS Step 1       'for each handle...
0396      RetVal = DeleteObject(BitmapHandles(LoopCount - 1))   'delete
0397    Next LoopCount
0398    RetVal = DeleteDC(hFDC)     '...then delete memory display-context
0399  End If
0400  TimerID1.Enabled = False                          'release the timer
0401  If FrameReady = True Then          'if a hidden frame was created
0402    RetVal = SelectObject(hFrameDC, hPrevFrame)      'deselect bitmap
0403    RetVal = DeleteObject(hFrame)                     'delete the bitmap
0404    RetVal = DeleteDC(hFrameDC)            'delete the display-context
0405  End If
0406  jczClose3d                                'shut down the 3D toolkit
0407  End                                       'terminate the application
0408  End Sub
0409
0410  '----------------------------------------------------------------
0411  '                    Adjust the frame rate
0412  '----------------------------------------------------------------
```

```
0413  Sub IDM_FPS182_Click ()
0414  If TimerExists = False Then
0415    MsgBox "A timer must be activated before you can reset the frame
          rate.", MB_OK, "Animation not ready"
0416  End If
0417  TimerID1.Interval = 55                    '18 frames per second
0418  End Sub
0419
0420  '-----------------------------------------------------------------
0421  '                  Adjust the frame rate
0422  '-----------------------------------------------------------------
0423  Sub IDM_FPS30_Click ()
0424  If TimerExists = False Then
0425    MsgBox "A timer must be activated before you can reset the frame
          rate.", MB_OK, "Animation not ready"
0426  End If
0427  TimerID1.Interval = 330                      '3 frames per second
0428  End Sub
0429
0430  '-----------------------------------------------------------------
0431  '                  Adjust the frame rate
0432  '-----------------------------------------------------------------
0433  Sub IDM_FPS36_Click ()
0434  If TimerExists = False Then
0435    MsgBox "A timer must be activated before you can reset the frame
          rate.", MB_OK, "Animation not ready"
0436  End If
0437  TimerID1.Interval = 275                      '4 frames per second
0438  End Sub
0439
0440  '-----------------------------------------------------------------
0441  '                  Adjust the frame rate
0442  '-----------------------------------------------------------------
0443  Sub IDM_FPS45_Click ()
0444  If TimerExists = False Then
0445    MsgBox "A timer must be activated before you can reset the frame
          rate.", MB_OK, "Animation not ready"
0446  End If
0447  TimerID1.Interval = 220                      '5 frames per second
0448  End Sub
0449
0450  '-----------------------------------------------------------------
0451  '                  Adjust the frame rate
0452  '-----------------------------------------------------------------
0453  Sub IDM_FPS61_Click ()
0454  If TimerExists = False Then
0455    MsgBox "A timer must be activated before you can reset the frame
          rate.", MB_OK, "Animation not ready"
0456  End If
0457  TimerID1.Interval = 165                      '6 frames per second
0458  End Sub
0459
0460  '-----------------------------------------------------------------
0461  '                  Adjust the frame rate
0462  '-----------------------------------------------------------------
```

```
0463  Sub IDM_FPS91_Click ()
0464  If TimerExists = False Then
0465    MsgBox "A timer must be activated before you can reset the frame
           rate.", MB_OK, "Animation not ready"
0466  End If
0467  TimerID1.Interval = 110                    '9 frames per second
0468  End Sub
0469
0470  '----------------------------------------------------------------
0471  '                   Display the Help message box
0472  '----------------------------------------------------------------
0473  Sub IDM_GeneralHelp_Click ()
0474  MsgBox "For animation playback pick Load Animation then Run
           Forward from the Run menu.  To build and save an animation,
           choose the Production submenu.  Also see the book.", MB_OK,
           "How to use this 3D animation demo"
0475  End Sub
0476
0477  '----------------------------------------------------------------
0478  '                   Display the License message box
0479  '----------------------------------------------------------------
0480  Sub IDM_License_Click ()
0481  MsgBox "You can use this code as part of your own software product
           subject to the License Agreement and Limited Warranty in
           Windcrest McGraw-Hill book 4225 and on its companion disk.",
           MB_O K,  "License Agreement"
0482  End Sub
0483
0484  '----------------------------------------------------------------
0485  '                 Load the animation sequence from disk
0486  '  If memory limitations prevent this procedure from loading the
0487  '  entire animation sequence into physical memory or virtual
0488  '  memory, the procedure sets a token to True.
0489  '  In that case the playback procedure zShowNextFrame() will load
0490  '  each frame from disk as required during animation playback,
0491  '  otherwise all frames are expected to be in RAM.
0492  '----------------------------------------------------------------
0493  Sub IDM_LoadAnimation_Click ()
0494    Dim Bitmaps As Integer
0495  zInitializeSystem                     'ensure system is initialized
0496  If AnimationLoaded = True Then        'if frames already loaded...
0497    Form_Paint                          'refresh screen if animation running
0498    Beep
0499    MsgBox "The animation sequence has already been loaded.", MB_OK,
           "Animation ready"
0500    Exit Sub
0501  End If
0502  If PrevLoadAttempt = True Then        'if previous attempt failed...
0503    Beep
0504    MsgBox "Previous attempt to load animation failed.  Cancelling
           this attempt.", MB_OK, "Animation error report"
0505    Exit Sub
0506  End If
0507  PrevLoadAttempt = True
0508  '--------------- create bitmaps to hold the frames --------------
0509  RetLong = GlobalCompact(-1)           'maximize contiguous memory
0510  hFDC = CreateCompatibleDC(Form1.hDC)          'create compatible DC
```

```
0511  For LoopCount = 1 To zNUMCELS Step 1            'for each frame...
0512    BitmapHandles(LoopCount - 1) = CreateCompatibleBitmap(Form1.hDC,
            zFRAMEWIDE, zFRAMEHIGH)
0513    If BitmapHandles(LoopCount - 1) = Null Then       'if error...
0514      GoTo BITMAPS_NOT_OK            '...jump out of loop and tidy up
0515    End If
0516  Next LoopCount
0517  GoTo BITMAPS_OK                    'if OK, jump past error-handler
0518  '-------------------- bitmap error-handler ---------------------
0519  BITMAPS_NOT_OK:
0520  For Bitmaps = LoopCount - 1 To 1 Step -1      'for each bitmap...
0521    RetVal = DeleteObject(BitmapHandles(Bitmaps - 1)) '...delete it
0522  Next Bitmaps
0523  RetVal = DeleteDC(hFDC)                 'delete the compatible DC
0524  UseDisk = True                          'reset run-time token
0525  AnimationReady = True                   'reset run-time token
0526  MsgBox "Insufficient memory to load entire animation sequence from
            disk.  Software will load each frame as needed during
            playback.", MB_OK, "Animation advisory report"
0527  Exit Sub                                '...and return to caller
0528  BITMAPS_OK:                             'jump to here if no errors
0529  '--------------- load frame files into the bitmaps --------------
0530  For LoopCount = 1 To zNUMCELS Step 1            'for each frame...
0531    FileName = FrameFiles(LoopCount - 1)     'used by zLoadFrame()
0532    zLoadFrame                               '...and load the frame
0533    If FrameLoaded = False Then            'if disk error occurred...
0534      GoTo DISK_ERROR                      'jump to error-handler
0535    End If
0536    hPrevF = SelectObject(hFDC, BitmapHandles(LoopCount - 1))
0537    RetVal = BitBlt(hFDC, 0, 0, zFRAMEWIDE, zFRAMEHIGH, Form1.hDC,
            0, 0, SRCCOPY)
0538    RetVal = SelectObject(hFDC, hPrevF)
0539  Next LoopCount
0540  GoTo DISK_OK                    'if OK, jump past the error-handler
0541  '---------------------- disk error-handler --------------------
0542  DISK_ERROR:
0543  For LoopCount = 1 To zNUMCELS Step 1    'for each bitmap handle...
0544    RetVal = DeleteObject(BitmapHandles(LoopCount - 1))  'delete it
0545  Next LoopCount
0546  RetVal = DeleteDC(hFDC)        'delete the memory display-context...
0547  Exit Sub                                '...and return to caller
0548  '-------------------- tidy up and return ----------------------
0549  DISK_OK:
0550  hPrevF = SelectObject(hFDC, BitmapHandles(0))
0551  AnimationLoaded = True
0552  AnimationReady = True
0553  AnimationSaved = True
0554  zClear
0555  zClearHiddenFrame
0556  Beep
0557  MsgBox "Animation sequence successfully loaded from disk.", MB_OK,
            "Animation ready"
0558  End Sub
0559
0560  '--------------------------------------------------------------
0561  '                  Determine runtime memory mode
0562  '--------------------------------------------------------------
```

```
0563  Sub IDM_Mode_Click ()
0564    Dim TempVariable As Long
0565  TempVariable = MemoryMode And WF_ENHANCED    'perform bitwise AND
0566  If TempVariable = WF_ENHANCED Then      'if result matches constant
0567    MsgBox "Running in enhanced mode.  Can allocate up to 16 MB
             extended memory (XMS) if available.  Virtual memory up to 4
             times physical memory (maximum 64 MB) is also available via
             automatic disk swapping of 4K pages.", MB_OK, "Memory mode"
0568    Exit Sub
0569  End If
0570  TempVariable = MemoryMode And WF_STANDARD
0571  If TempVariable = WF_STANDARD Then
0572    MsgBox "Running in standard mode.  Can allocate up to 16 MB
             extended physical memory (XMS) if available.", MB_OK, "Memory
             mode"
0573    Exit Sub
0574  End If
0575  MsgBox "Running in real mode.  Can allocate blocks of memory from
             the first 640K of RAM.  Can also allocate blocks from expanded
             memory (EMS) if available.", MB_OK, "Memory mode"
0576  End Sub
0577
0578  '----------------------------------------------------------------
0579  '          Terminate the application and restart Windows
0580  '----------------------------------------------------------------
0581  Sub IDM_Restart_Click ()
0582  UserWants = MsgBox("Exit the demo and restart Windows?", MB_YESNO,
             "Please confirm")
0583  If UserWants = IDNO Then            'if user selected No button...
0584    Exit Sub                          'then cancel this operation
0585  End If          'otherwise continue to terminate the application...
0586  If AnimationLoaded = True Then            'if animation loaded...
0587    RetVal = SelectObject(hFDC, hPrevF)       'select default handle
0588    For LoopCount = 1 To zNUMCELS Step 1        'for each handle...
0589      RetVal = DeleteObject(BitmapHandles(LoopCount - 1))  'delete
0590    Next LoopCount
0591    RetVal = DeleteDC(hFDC)  '...then delete memory display-context
0592  End If
0593  TimerID1.Enabled = False                     'release the timer
0594  If FrameReady = True Then          'if a hidden frame was created
0595    RetVal = SelectObject(hFrameDC, hPrevFrame)   'deselect bitmap
0596    RetVal = DeleteObject(hFrame)              'delete the bitmap
0597    RetVal = DeleteDC(hFrameDC)        'delete the display-context
0598  End If
0599  jczClose3d                           'shut down the 3D toolkit
0600  RetVal = ExitWindows(&H42&, 0)     'terminate and restart Windows
0601  End                                  'terminate the application
0602  End Sub
0603
0604  '----------------------------------------------------------------
0605  '          Set animation engine to forward playback
0606  '----------------------------------------------------------------
0607  Sub IDM_RunForward_Click ()
0608  If AnimationLoaded = False Then
0609    MsgBox "You must load an animation sequence before you run the
             animation.", MB_OK, "Animation not ready"
0610    Exit Sub
0611  End If
0612  Pause = False
```

```
0613   FrameDirection = zFORWARD
0614   zShowNextFrame
0615   End Sub
0616
0617   '----------------------------------------------------------------
0618   '                    Create all frames and save to disk
0619   '----------------------------------------------------------------
0620   Sub IDM_SaveAnimation_Click ()
0621   zInitializeSystem                        'ensure system is initialized
0622   If AnimationSaved = True Then            'if animation already saved
0623     Form_Paint                             'refresh screen if animation running
0624     MsgBox "The animation sequence has already been saved to disk.",
            MB_OK, "Animation report"
0625     Exit Sub
0626   End If
0627   If PrevSaveAttempt = True Then           'if previous attempt failed
0628     MsgBox "A previous attempt to save the animation sequence to
            disk has failed.  Cancelling this attempt.  Check available
            disk space.", MB_OK, "Animation error report"
0629     Exit Sub
0630   End If
0631   PrevSaveAttempt = True     'set token to prevent subsequent calls
0632   '-------------------- initialize the camera --------------------
0633   Cam1.Heading = 330
0634   Cam1.Pitch = 320
0635   Cam1.Distance = 356
0636   Call bczSetCameraDistance(Cam1.Distance)
0637   Call bbzSetCameraPitch(Cam1.Pitch)
0638   Call bazSetCameraHeading(Cam1.Heading)
0639   '-------------- specify the path of the camera -----------------
0640   Cam1Path1.StartFrame = 1
0641   Cam1Path1.EndFrame = zNUMCELS
0642   Cam1Path1.ChgHeading = 0                        'set to -2 for dolly
0643   Cam1Path1.ChgPitch = 0                          'set to 2 for crane
0644   Cam1Path1.ChgDistance = 0
0645   '---------------- initialize the light-source ------------------
0646   Lt1.Elevation = 60
0647   Lt1.Heading = 180
0648   Call zSetLightPosition(Lt1.Elevation, Lt1.Heading)
0649   '------------ specify the path of the light-source -------------
0650   Lt1Path1.StartFrame = 1
0651   Lt1Path1.EndFrame = zNUMCELS
0652   Lt1Path1.ChgHeading = 0
0653   Lt1Path1.ChgElevation = 0
0654   '-------------------- initialize the actor --------------------
0655   Actor1.PositionX = 0            'position of actor in 3D world...
0656   Actor1.PositionY = 0
0657   Actor1.PositionZ = 0
0658   Actor1.Yaw = 0                  'orientation of actor in 3D world...
0659   Actor1.Roll = 45
0660   Actor1.Pitch = 0
0661   Call dazSetSubjectLocation(Actor1.PositionX, Actor1.PositionY
            Actor1.PositionZ)
0662   Call dbzSetSubjectAttitude(Actor1.Yaw, Actor1.Roll, Actor1.Pitch)
0663   '-------------- specify the path of the actor ------------------
0664   Actor1Path1.StartFrame = 1
```

```
0665  Actor1Path1.EndFrame = zNUMCELS              'for frames 1 to 36...
0666  Actor1Path1.ChgYaw = 0
0667  Actor1Path1.ChgRoll = 0
0668  Actor1Path1.ChgPitch = 5        'rotate entity 5 degrees each frame
0669  Actor1Path1.ChgPosX = 0
0670  Actor1Path1.ChgPosY = 0
0671  Actor1Path1.ChgPosZ = 0
0672  '----------------- build and save the cels ---------------------
0673  For LoopCount = 1 To zNUMCELS Step 1            'for each frame...
0674    FrameNum = LoopCount          'set a variable used by zDrawCel()
0675    FileName = FrameFiles(LoopCount - 1)      'set for zSaveFrame()
0676    zBuildFrame                                'build the frame
0677    If FrameSaved = False Then   'check variable set by zSaveFrame()
0678      Form1.Caption = "3D Animation Template"   'restore caption...
0679      MsgBox "The animation build process has failed because an
             image could not be saved to disk.  Please check for
             insufficient disk space.", MB_OK, "Animation production report"
0680      Exit Sub                  '...and cancel loop if error occurred
0681    End If
0682  Next LoopCount
0683  '-------------------- set tokens and tidy up --------------------
0684  Form1.Caption = "3D Animation Template"         'restore caption
0685  FrameNum = 1
0686  AnimationSaved = True
0687  PrevLoadAttempt = False
0688  zClear
0689  zClearHiddenFrame
0690  '-------------------- display advisory notice ------------------
0691  Beep
0692  MsgBox "Animation sequence successfully saved to disk.", MB_OK,
          "Animation ready"
0693  End Sub
0694
0695  '---------------------------------------------------------------
0696  '                 Pause the animation playback
0697  '---------------------------------------------------------------
0698  Sub IDM_StopAnimation_Click ()
0699  If AnimationLoaded = False Then
0700    MsgBox "You must load an animation sequence before you pause the
          animation.", MB_OK, "Animation not ready"
0701    Exit Sub
0702  End If
0703  If Pause = True Then
0704    Exit Sub
0705  End If
0706  zShowNextFrame          'cover the rect left by the menu's removal
0707  Pause = True
0708  zCopyToFrame            'copy to hidden-frame for refresh procedure
0709  End Sub
0710
0711  '---------------------------------------------------------------
0712  '             Toggle to use fully-shaded 3D entities
0713  '---------------------------------------------------------------
0714  Sub IDM_UseShaded_Click ()
0715  abzUseWireframeMode (False)        'call function in ENGINE3D.BAS
0716  MsgBox "Using shaded solids mode.", MB_OK, "Animation status
          report"
0717  End Sub
```

```
0718
0719   '-----------------------------------------------------------------
0720   '                  Toggle to use wire-frame entities
0721   '-----------------------------------------------------------------
0722   Sub IDM_UseWireframe_Click ()
0723   abzUseWireframeMode (True)            'call function in ENGINE3D.BAS
0724   MsgBox "Using wireframe modeling mode.", MB_OK, "Animation status
          report"
0725   End Sub
0726
0727   '-----------------------------------------------------------------
0728   '                    Determine version of Windows
0729   '-----------------------------------------------------------------
0730   Sub IDM_Version_Click ()
0731     Dim TempVar As Long
0732   TempVar = WindowsVersion And 7683   'test binary 00011110 00000011
0733   If TempVar = 7683 Then                            'if 30        3...
0734     MsgBox "Running under Windows version 3.3.", MB_OK, "Version
            report"
0735     Exit Sub
0736   End If
0737   TempVar = WindowsVersion And 5123   'test binary 00010100 00000011
0738   If TempVar = 5123 Then                            'if 20        3...
0739     MsgBox "Running under Windows version 3.2.", MB_OK, "Version
            report"
0740     Exit Sub
0741   End If
0742   TempVar = WindowsVersion And 2563   'test binary 00001010 00000011
0743   If TempVar = 2563 Then                            'if 10        3...
0744     MsgBox "Running under Windows version 3.1.", MB_OK, "Version
            report"
0745     Exit Sub
0746   End If
0747   TempVar = WindowsVersion And 3      'test binary 00000000 00000011
0748   If TempVar = 3 Then                               'if 00        3...
0749     MsgBox "Running under Windows version 3.0.", MB_OK, "Version
            report"
0750     Exit Sub
0751   End If
0752   TempVar = WindowsVersion And 4      'test binary 00000000 00000100
0753   If TempVar = 4 Then                          'if 00        4...
0754     MsgBox "Running under Windows version 4.0.", MB_OK, "Version
            report"
0755     Exit Sub
0756   End If
0757   MsgBox "Unable to report Windows version number.", MB_OK, "Version
          report"
0758   End Sub
0759
0760   '-----------------------------------------------------------------
0761   '        Pause to allow menu to pop up on slower machines
0762   '-----------------------------------------------------------------
0763   Sub POPUP_Edit_Click ()
0764   TimerCounter = zTIMER_PAUSE
0765   End Sub
0766
```

```
0767  '-------------------------------------------------------------------
0768  '         Pause to allow menu to pop up on slower machines
0769  '-------------------------------------------------------------------
0770  Sub POPUP_File_Click ()
0771  TimerCounter = zTIMER_PAUSE
0772  End Sub
0773
0774  '-------------------------------------------------------------------
0775  '         Pause to allow menu to pop up on slower machines
0776  '-------------------------------------------------------------------
0777  Sub POPUP_Run_Click ()
0778  TimerCounter = zTIMER_PAUSE
0779  End Sub
0780
0781  '-------------------------------------------------------------------
0782  '              Set animation engine to reverse playback
0783  '-------------------------------------------------------------------
0784  Sub POPUP_RunReverse_Click ()
0785  If AnimationLoaded = False Then
0786    MsgBox "You must load an animation sequence before you run the
           animation.", MB_OK, "Animation not ready"
0787    Exit Sub
0788  End If
0789  Pause = False
0790  FrameDirection = zREVERSE
0791  zShowNextFrame
0792  End Sub
0793
0794  '-------------------------------------------------------------------
0795  '         Pause to allow menu to pop up on slower machines
0796  '-------------------------------------------------------------------
0797  Sub POPUP_Timer_Click ()
0798  TimerCounter = zTIMER_PAUSE
0799  End Sub
0800
0801  '-------------------------------------------------------------------
0802  '         Pause to allow menu to pop up on slower machines
0803  '-------------------------------------------------------------------
0804  Sub POPUP_Using_Click ()
0805  TimerCounter = zTIMER_PAUSE
0806  End Sub
0807
0808  '-------------------------------------------------------------------
0809  '                   Manage incoming timer events
0810  '-------------------------------------------------------------------
0811  Sub TimerID1_Timer ()
0812  If Pause = True Then Exit Sub
0813  TimerCounter = TimerCounter - 1                      'decrement counter
0814  If TimerCounter > 0 Then   'if pausing to allow menu to pop up...
0815    Exit Sub                           '...then exit this procedure
0816  End If
0817  TimerCounter = 0                       'otherwise, restore counter...
0818  zShowNextFrame                         '...and show the next frame
0819  End Sub
0820
0821  '-------------------------------------------------------------------
0822  '                  Build one frame and save to disk
0823  '-------------------------------------------------------------------
```

```
0824   Sub zBuildFrame ()
0825     Dim PrevFontClr As Long
0826     Dim PrevFontSize As Integer
0827   zClear                                'clear the display window
0828   Form1.Caption = "Building frame " & FrameNum & "..." 'caption bar
0829   zDrawCel                                        'draw one frame
0830   '-------------- display the titles and captions ------------------
0831   PrevFontSize = Form1.FontSize          'remember current font size
0832   PrevFontClr = Form1.ForeColor          'remember current font color
0833   Form1.FontSize = 16                              'set the size
0834   Form1.ForeColor = RGB(0, 0, 0)                   'set the color
0835   Form1.FontTransparent = True     'use transparent font backgrounds
0836   Form1.CurrentX = 10                   'set the starting location...
0837   Form1.CurrentY = 6
0838   Form1.Print "A Lee Adams tutorial:"                'display text
0839   Form1.FontSize = 24                               'reset the size
0840   Form1.CurrentX = 8                            'reset the location...
0841   Form1.CurrentY = 24
0842   Form1.Print "3D animation"                         'display text
0843   Form1.FontSize = PrevFontSize                  'restore the size
0844   Form1.ForeColor = PrevFontClr                  'restore the color
0845   Form1.CurrentX = 10
0846   Form1.CurrentY = 214
0847   Form1.Print "Animation production timestamp"
0848   Form1.CurrentX = 10
0849   Form1.CurrentY = 228
0850   Form1.Print "Time:" & Time$ & " Date:" & Date$
0851   '-------------------- save frame to disk ----------------------
0852   zSaveFrame                                    'save frame to disk
0853   End Sub
0854
0855   '----------------------------------------------------------------
0856   '                    Clear the display window
0857   '----------------------------------------------------------------
0858   Sub zClear ()
0859   RetVal = PatBlt(hDC, 0, 0, zFRAMEWIDE, zFRAMEHIGH, WHITENESS)
0860   End Sub
0861
0862   '----------------------------------------------------------------
0863   '                    Clear the hidden frame
0864   '----------------------------------------------------------------
0865   Sub zClearHiddenFrame ()
0866   If FrameReady = False Then
0867     Exit Sub
0868   End If
0869   RetVal = PatBlt(hFrameDC, 0, 0, zFRAMEWIDE, zFRAMEHIGH, WHITENESS)
0870   End Sub
0871
0872   '----------------------------------------------------------------
0873   '          Copy the hidden frame to the display window
0874   '----------------------------------------------------------------
0875   Sub zCopyToDisplay ()
0876   If FrameReady = False Then
0877     Exit Sub
0878   End If
0879   RetVal = BitBlt(hDC, 0, 0, zFRAMEWIDE, zFRAMEHIGH, hFrameDC, 0, 0,
           SRCCOPY)
```

```
0880   End Sub
0881
0882   '----------------------------------------------------------------
0883   '            Copy the display window to the hidden frame
0884   '----------------------------------------------------------------
0885   Sub zCopyToFrame ()
0886   If FrameReady = False Then
0887     Exit Sub
0888   End If
0889   RetVal = BitBlt(hFrameDC, 0, 0, zFRAMEWIDE, zFRAMEHIGH, hDC, 0, 0,
           SRCCOPY)
0890   End Sub
0891
0892   '----------------------------------------------------------------
0893   '                Draw one 3D cel and place on frame
0894   '----------------------------------------------------------------
0895   Sub zDrawCel ()                        'uses global variable FrameNum
0896     Dim PartID As Integer        'counter is used in the drawing loop
0897   '---------------------- update the camera ----------------------
0898   If FrameNum > Cam1Path1.StartFrame And FrameNum <=
           Cam1Path1.EndFrame Then
0899           'if bounding frame numbers are specified in the script...
0900     Cam1.Distance = Cam1.Distance + Cam1Path1.ChgDistance
0901     Cam1.Heading = Cam1.Heading + Cam1Path1.ChgHeading
0902     Cam1.Pitch = Cam1.Pitch + Cam1Path1.ChgPitch
0903   End If
0904   If Cam1.Heading < 0 Then
0905     Cam1.Heading = Cam1.Heading + 360
0906   End If
0907   If Cam1.Heading > 360 Then
0908     Cam1.Heading = Cam1.Heading - 360
0909   End If
0910   If Cam1.Pitch < 0 Then
0911     Cam1.Pitch = Cam1.Pitch + 360
0912   End If
0913   If Cam1.Pitch > 360 Then
0914     Cam1.Pitch = Cam1.Pitch - 360
0915   End If
0916   Call bczSetCameraDistance(Cam1.Distance)
0917   Call bbzSetCameraPitch(Cam1.Pitch)
0918   Call bazSetCameraHeading(Cam1.Heading)
0919   '------------------- update the light-source --------------------
0920   If FrameNum > Lt1Path1.StartFrame And FrameNum <=
           Lt1Path1.EndFrame Then
0921           'if boundingframe numbers are specified in the script...
0922     Lt1.Heading = Lt1.Heading + Lt1Path1.ChgHeading
0923     Lt1.Elevation = Lt1.Elevation + Lt1Path1.ChgElevation
0924   End If
0925   If Lt1.Elevation > 90 Then
0926     Lt1.Elevation = 90
0927   End If
0928   If Lt1.Elevation < 0 Then
0929     Lt1.Elevation = 0
0930   End If
0931   If Lt1.Heading > 360 Then
0932     Lt1.Heading = Lt1.Heading - 360
0933   End If
0934   If Lt1.Heading < 0 Then
0935     Lt1.Heading = Lt1.Heading + 360
```

```
0936   End If
0937   Call zSetLightPosition(Lt1.Elevation, Lt1.Heading)
0938   '---------------------- update the actor ----------------------
0939   If FrameNum > Actor1Path1.StartFrame And FrameNum <=
           Actor1Path1.EndFrame Then
0940                     'if frame numbers are specified in the script...
0941     Actor1.PositionX = Actor1.PositionX + Actor1Path1.ChgPosX
0942     Actor1.PositionY = Actor1.PositionY + Actor1Path1.ChgPosY
0943     Actor1.PositionZ = Actor1.PositionZ + Actor1Path1.ChgPosZ
0944     Actor1.Yaw = Actor1.Yaw + Actor1Path1.ChgYaw
0945     Actor1.Roll = Actor1.Roll + Actor1Path1.ChgRoll
0946     Actor1.Pitch = Actor1.Pitch + Actor1Path1.ChgPitch
0947   End If
0948   If Actor1.Yaw < 0 Then
0949     Actor1.Yaw = Actor1.Yaw + 360
0950   End If
0951   If Actor1.Yaw > 360 Then
0952     Actor1.Yaw = Actor1.Yaw - 360
0953   End If
0954   If Actor1.Roll < 0 Then
0955     Actor1.Roll = Actor1.Roll + 360
0956   End If
0957   If Actor1.Roll > 360 Then
0958     Actor1.Roll = Actor1.Roll - 360
0959   End If
0960   If Actor1.Pitch < 0 Then
0961     Actor1.Pitch = Actor1.Pitch + 360
0962   End If
0963   If Actor1.Pitch > 360 Then
0964     Actor1.Pitch = Actor1.Pitch - 360
0965   End If
0966   Call dazSetSubjectLocation(Actor1.PositionX, Actor1.PositionY,
           Actor1.PositionZ)
0967   Call dbzSetSubjectAttitude(Actor1.Yaw, Actor1.Roll, Actor1.Pitch)
0968   '---- render actor (could also put these params in struct) ---
0969   Call dczSetSubjectSize(25, 25, 25)   'dimensions 50-by-50-by-50
0970   Call ddzSetShadingColor(zRED)                    'entity's color
0971   Call azDrawCube                                  'draw the entity
0972   End Sub
0973
0974   '--------------------------------------------------------------
0975   '                  Initialize the animation system
0976   '--------------------------------------------------------------
0977   Sub zInitializeSystem ()
0978   If FrameReady = True Then         'if hidden frame already created
0979     Form_Paint                  'refresh screen if animation running
0980     Exit Sub
0981   End If
0982   Picture1.Visible = False                     'hide the picture box
0983   Picture1.Top = 0: Picture1.Left = 0                    'reposition
0984   Picture1.Width = 402: Picture1.Height = 302                'resize
0985   RetLong = GlobalCompact(-1)          'maximize contiguous memory
0986   hFrameDC = CreateCompatibleDC(hDC)         'get a display-context
0987   hFrame = CreateCompatibleBitmap(hDC, zFRAMEWIDE, zFRAMEHIGH)
0988   If hFrame = Null Then                        'if error occurred
0989     MsgBox "Insufficient memory.  Hidden frame not created.  Close
```

```
            other Windows applications to free up more RAM.", MB_OK,
            "Animation fatal error"
0990    FrameReady = False
0991    Exit Sub
0992  End If
0993  hPrevFrame = SelectObject(hFrameDC, hFrame)      'select the bitmap
0994  FrameReady = True                              'set a global token
0995  zCopyToFrame
0996  TimerID1.Interval = wFrameRate                 'set the timer interval
0997  TimerID1.Enabled = True                        'activate the timer
0998  TimerExists = True                             'set a token
0999  Pause = True
1000  End Sub
1001

0001  '------------------------------------------------------------------
0002  '      Frame animation routines for Visual Basic applications
0003  '------------------------------------------------------------------
0004  ' Source file:  ANPLAY.BAS
0005  ' Release version:  2.00                        Programmer:  Lee Adams
0006  ' Type:  Visual Basic module for Windows applications
0007  ' Output and features:  Provides routines to manage the authoring
0008  '    process and playback engine for interactive frame animation.
0009  ' Publication:  Contains material from Windcrest/McGraw-Hill
0010  '    book 4225 published by TAB BOOKS Div. of McGraw-Hill Inc.
0011  ' License:  As purchaser of the book you are granted a
0012  '    royalty-free license to distribute executable files
0013  '    generated uSing this code provided that you accept the
0014  '    conditions of the License Agreement and Limited Warranty
0015  '    described in the book and on the companion disk.  Government
0016  '    users:  This software and documentation are subject to
0017  '    restrictions set forth in The Rights in Technical Data and
0018  '    Computer Software clause at 252.227-7013 and elsewhere.
0019  '------------------------------------------------------------------
0020  '    (c) Copyright 1992-1993 Lee Adams.  All rights reserved.
0021  '           Lee Adams(tm) is a trademark of Lee Adams.
0022  '------------------------------------------------------------------
0023  '
0024  Option Explicit            'generate error if variable not declared
0025
0026  '------------------------------------------------------------------
0027  '                     Load a frame from disk
0028  '------------------------------------------------------------------
0029  Sub zLoadFrame ()                    'uses global variable FileName
0030  If FrameReady = False Then
0031    MsgBox "Hidden frame not ready.", MB_OK, "Animation error report"
0032    Exit Sub
0033  End If
0034  LoadingFrame = True                     'disable refresh procedure
0035  On Error GoTo LoadError:                     'enable error trapping
0036  Form1.Picture = LoadPicture(FileName)            'load .BMP image
0037  On Error GoTo 0                          'disable error trapping
0038  LoadingFrame = False                    'enable refresh procedure
0039  FrameLoaded = True
0040  '-------- select persistent bitmap, clear it, deselect it -------
0041  Form1.AutoRedraw = True
0042  RetVal = PatBlt(Form1.hDC, 0, 0, zFRAMEWIDE, zFRAMEHIGH, WHITENESS)
0043  Form1.AutoRedraw = False
```

```
0044   Exit Sub
0045   '------------------------ error-handler ----------------------
0046   LoadError:
0047     On Error GoTo 0
0048     LoadingFrame = False
0049     FrameLoaded = False
0050     Beep
0051     MsgBox "Unable to load the .BMP file.  Is system initialized?]
           Does file exist on disk?", MB_OK, "Animation error report"
0052     Exit Sub
0053   End Sub
0054
0055   '-------------------------------------------------------------
0056   '                    Save a frame to disk
0057   '-------------------------------------------------------------
0058   Sub zSaveFrame ()                    'uses global variable FileName
0059     Dim ErrorOccurred As Integer
0060   ErrorOccurred = False                    'set default tokens...
0061   FrameSaved = False
0062   If FrameReady = False Then
0063     MsgBox "Hidden frame not ready.", MB_OK, "Animation error report"
0064     Exit Sub
0065   End If
0066   '-------------- copy display window to picture box --------------
0067   RetVal = BitBlt(hFrameDC, 0, 0, zFRAMEWIDE, zFRAMEHIGH, Form1.hDC,
           0, 0, SRCCOPY)
0068   Form1.Picture1.Visible = True               'show the picture box
0069   Form1.Picture1.AutoRedraw = True       'activate persistent bitmap
0070   RetVal = BitBlt(Form1.Picture1.hDC, 0, 0, zFRAMEWIDE, zFRAMEHIGH,
           hFrameDC, 0, 0, SRCCOPY)
0071   Form1.Picture1.Picture = Form1.Picture1.Image      'copy to screen
0072   Form1.Picture1.AutoRedraw = False   'disable the persistent bitmap
0073   '---------------- save picture box image to disk ----------------
0074   On Error GoTo SaveError                    'enable error trapping
0075   SavePicture Form1.Picture1.Image, FileName    'save bitmap to disk
0076   On Error GoTo 0                           'disable error trapping
0077   Form1.Picture1.Visible = False             'hide the picture box
0078   RetVal = BitBlt(Form1.hDC, 0, 0, zFRAMEWIDE, zFRAMEHIGH, hFrameDC,
           0, 0, SRCCOPY)
0079   If ErrorOccurred = True Then               'if disk error, exit
0080     Beep
0081     MsgBox "Unable to save the frame to disk as a .BMP file.
           Sufficient disk space?", MB_OK, "Animation error report"
0082     Exit Sub
0083   End If
0084   FrameSaved = True
0085   Exit Sub
0086   SaveError:                              'jump to here if disk error
0087     ErrorOccurred = True
0088   Resume
0089   End Sub
0090
0091   '-------------------------------------------------------------
0092   '                    Display the next frame
0093   '-------------------------------------------------------------
0094   Sub zShowNextFrame ()                'uses global variable FrameNum
```

```
0095  If UseDisk = True Then                 'animate using memory or disk?
0096    GoTo DISK_PLAYBACK
0097  End If
0098  '------------- manage memory-based frame animation --------------
0099  MEMORY_PLAYBACK:
0100  If AnimationReady = False Then
0101    Exit Sub
0102  End If
0103  If AnimationLoaded = False Then
0104    Exit Sub
0105  End If
0106  If Redisplay = True Then
0107    GoTo DISPLAY_FRAME
0108  End If
0109  If Pause = True Then
0110    Exit Sub
0111  End If
0112  If FrameDirection = zFORWARD Then            'if a forward loop...
0113    FrameNum = FrameNum + 1              'increment the frame number
0114    If FrameNum > zFINALFRAME Then             'if at end of loop...
0115      FrameNum = zFIRSTFRAME                        '...wraparound
0116    End If
0117  End If
0118  If FrameDirection = zREVERSE Then            'if a reverse loop...
0119    FrameNum = FrameNum - 1             'decrement the frame number
0120    If FrameNum < zFIRSTFRAME Then         'but if at end of loop...
0121      FrameNum = zFINALFRAME                        '...wraparound
0122    End If
0123  End If
0124  DISPLAY_FRAME:          'select handle and copy frame to display...
0125  RetVal = SelectObject(hFDC, BitmapHandles(FrameNum - 1))
0126  RetVal = BitBlt(Form1.hDC, 0, 0, zFRAMEWIDE, zFRAMEHIGH, hFDC, 0,
           0, SRCCOPY)
0127  Exit Sub
0128  '------------- manage disk-based frame animation ---------------
0129  DISK_PLAYBACK:
0130  If AnimationHalted = True Then
0131    Exit Sub
0132  End If
0133  If Redisplay = True Then
0134    GoTo SAME_FRAME
0135  End If
0136  If Pause = True Then
0137    Exit Sub
0138  End If
0139  If FrameDirection = zFORWARD Then            'if a forward loop...
0140    FrameNum = FrameNum + 1
0141    If FrameNum > zFINALFRAME Then
0142      FrameNum = zFIRSTFRAME
0143    End If
0144  End If
0145  If FrameDirection = zREVERSE Then            'if a reverse loop...
0146    FrameNum = FrameNum - 1
0147    If FrameNum < zFIRSTFRAME Then
0148      FrameNum = zFINALFRAME
0149    End If
0150  End If
0151  SAME_FRAME:
```

```
0152  FileName = FrameFiles(FrameNum - 1)
0153  zLoadFrame
0154  If FrameLoaded = False Then                'if an error occurred...
0155    AnimationHalted = True
0156    Beep
0157    MsgBox "Unable to load next frame from disk.  Animation
         halted.", MB_OK, "Animation error report"
0158    Exit Sub
0159  End If
0160  RetVal = BitBlt(Form1.hDC, 0, 0, zFRAMEWIDE, zFRAMEHIGH, hFrameDC,
         0, 0, SRCCOPY)
0161  End Sub
0162
```

C-4 Source listings for the interactive, animated 3D hierarchical model application, assembly. See Appendix B for the toolkits which must be used to build this application. See Appendix A for instructions on building the demo.

```
0001  ASGLOBAL.BAS
0002  ASMAIN.BAS
0003  ENGINE3D.BAS
0004  LIGHTS3D.BAS
0005  ASSEMB3D.BAS
0006  SHAPES3D.BAS
0007  DEFORM3D.BAS
0008  ASPLAY.BAS
0009  ASSEMBLY.FRM
0010  ProjWinSize=83,428,196,336
0011  ProjWinShow=2
```

```
0001  '----------------------------------------------------------------
0002  '  Reusable global module for Visual Basic graphics applications
0003  '            that call Windows API functions.
0004  '----------------------------------------------------------------
0005  '  Source file:  ASGLOBAL.BAS
0006  '  Release version:  1.00                    Programmer:  Lee Adams
0007  '  Type:  Visual Basic global module for Windows applications.
0008  '  Compiler:  Microsoft Visual Basic 2.00
0009  '  Dependencies:  ASSEMBLY.FRM primary module
0010  '                 ASMAIN.BAS module containing Main()
0011  '                 ASPLAY.BAS animatin playback module
0012  '  Output and features:  Provides declarations for Windows API
0013  '    (Application Programming Interface) functions callable by
0014  '    Visual Basic applications at runtime, including routines
0015  '    from Windows' GDI, USER, and KERNEL DLLs (dynamic link
0016  '    libraries).  Also provides declarations of various variables
0017  '    and constants.  Functions, variables, and constants declared
0018  '    in this global module are visible throughout the project.
0019  '  Publication:  Contains material from Windcrest/McGraw-Hill
0020  '    book 4225 published by TAB BOOKS Div. of McGraw-Hill Inc.
0021  '  License:  As purchaser of the book you are granted a
0022  '    royalty-free license to distribute executable files
0023  '    generated using this code provided that you accept the
0024  '    conditions of the License Agreement and Limited Warranty
0025  '    described in the book and on the companion disk.  Government
```

```
0026  '    users: This software and documentation are subject to
0027  '    restrictions set forth in The Rights in Technical Data and
0028  '    Computer Software clause at 252.227-7013 and elsewhere.
0029  '-----------------------------------------------------------------
0030  '      (c) Copyright 1993 Lee Adams.  All rights reserved.
0031  '        Lee Adams(tm) is a trademark of Lee Adams.
0032  '-----------------------------------------------------------------
0033
0034  Option Explicit          'generate error if variable not declared
0035  '-----------------------------------------------------------------
0036  '              General constants and variables
0037  '-----------------------------------------------------------------
0038  Global Const MB_OK = 0              'OK button for message box
0039  Global Const MB_OKCANCEL = 1   'OK Cancel buttons for message box
0040  Global Const MB_YESNO = 4       'Yes No buttons for message box
0041  Global Const IDOK = 1                  'OK button selected
0042  Global Const IDCANCEL = 2          'Cancel button selected
0043  Global Const IDYES = 6               'Yes button selected
0044  Global Const IDNO = 7                 'No button selected
0045  Global UserWants As Integer      'value returned by message box
0046  Global Const PIXELS = 3                'pixel coordinates
0047  Global StartUp As Integer            'tracks the startup code
0048  Global IgnoreRefresh As Integer      'tracks refresh activity
0049  Global Const zRED = 1
0050  Global Const zGREEN = 2
0051  Global Const zBROWN = 3
0052  Global Const zBLUE = 4
0053  Global Const zMAGENTA = 5
0054  Global Const zCYAN = 6
0055  Global Const zGRAY = 7
0056
0057  '-----------------------------------------------------------------
0058  '                  Window specifications
0059  '-----------------------------------------------------------------
0060  Global Const zWINDOW_WIDTH = 264             'width of window
0061  Global Const zWINDOW_HEIGHT = 301           'height of window
0062  Global Const zFRAMEWIDE = 256            'width of client area
0063  Global Const zFRAMEHIGH = 255           'height of client area
0064  Global HorizTwipsPixel As Single     'twips-per-pixel (horizontal)
0065  Global VertTwipsPixel As Single       'twips-per-pixel (vertical)
0066  Global Window_Width As Single          'runtime width of window
0067  Global Window_Height As Single         'runtime height of window
0068
0069  '-----------------------------------------------------------------
0070  '                  Runtime conditions
0071  '-----------------------------------------------------------------
0072  Global hDesktopWnd As Integer                'handle to desktop
0073  Global hDCcaps As Integer             'display-context for desktop
0074  Global DisplayWidth As Integer       'horizontal screen resolution
0075  Global DisplayHeight As Integer      'vertical screen resolution
0076  Global DisplayBits As Integer          'number of bits-per-pixel
0077  Global DisplayPlanes As Integer          'number of bitplanes
0078  Global MemoryMode As Long              'runtime memory mode
0079  Global RetVal As Integer            'will receive GDI return value
0080  Global RetLong As Long              'will receive GDI return value
0081  Global MousePresent As Integer              'mouse active?
0082  Global WindowsVersion As Long             'version of Windows
0083  Global LoadingFrame As Integer             'loading an image?
```

C-4 Continued.

```
0084
0085 '------------------------------------------------------------------
0086 '                    Hidden frame operations
0087 '------------------------------------------------------------------
0088 Global hFrameDC As Integer        'display-context for hidden-frame
0089 Global hFrame As Integer          'handle to hidden-frame bitmap
0090 Global hPrevFrame As Integer      'default bitmap for hFrameDC
0091 Global FrameReady As Integer          'hidden-frame created?
0092
0093 '------------------------------------------------------------------
0094 '                      Timer operations
0095 '------------------------------------------------------------------
0096 Global Const zTIMER_PAUSE = 3              'for slow machines
0097 Global TimerCounter As Integer            'for slow machines
0098 Global TimerExists As Integer             'timer activated?
0099
0100 '------------------------------------------------------------------
0101 '                      Animation engine
0102 '------------------------------------------------------------------
0103 Global Pause As Integer                   'animation running?
0104 Global wFrameRate As Long            'arbitrary rate of 18.2 fps
0105 Global Const zFORWARD = 1          'indicates forward animation
0106 Global Const zREVERSE = 0          'indicates reverse animation
0107 Global FrameDirection As Integer          'forward or reverse
0108 Global FrameNum As Integer                    'current frame
0109 Global Const zFIRSTFRAME = 1          'first frame of animation
0110 Global Const zFINALFRAME = 36         'final frame of animation
0111 Global Const zNUMCELS = 36        'number of cels in animation
0112 Global LoopCount As Integer               'loop counter
0113 Global hFDC As Integer        'memory DC for hidden playback bitmaps
0114 Global hPrevF As Integer              'handle to default bitmap
0115 Global BitmapHandles(zNUMCELS)        'array of bitmap handles
0116 Global FrameFiles(zNUMCELS) As String * 9    'array of filenames
0117 Global Redisplay As Integer               'for paused refresh
0118
0119 '------------------------------------------------------------------
0120 '                      Animation script
0121 '------------------------------------------------------------------
0122 '----------- declare data types for animation script -----------
0123 Type CameraPath          'camera movement during specified frames
0124    StartFrame As Integer
0125    EndFrame As Integer
0126    ChgHeading As Integer
0127    ChgPitch As Integer
0128    ChgDistance As Integer
0129 End Type
0130 Type LightPath      'light-source movement during specified frames
0131    StartFrame As Integer
0132    EndFrame As Integer
0133    ChgHeading As Integer
0134    ChgElevation As Integer
0135 End Type
0136 Type ActorPath           'actor movement during specified frames
0137    StartFrame As Integer
0138    EndFrame As Integer
0139    ChgYaw As Integer
```

```
0140      ChgRoll As Integer
0141      ChgPitch As Integer
0142      ChgPosX As Integer
0143      ChgPosY As Integer
0144      ChgPosZ As Integer
0145    End Type
0146    Type SubAssyPath      'subassembly movement during specified frames
0147      StartFrame As Integer
0148      EndFrame As Integer
0149      ChgYaw As Integer
0150      ChgRoll As Integer
0151      ChgPitch As Integer
0152    End Type
0153    Type CameraDefine                      'camera startup parameters
0154      Heading As Integer
0155      Pitch As Integer
0156      Distance As Integer
0157    End Type
0158    Type LightDefine                'light-source startup parameters
0159      Heading As Integer
0160      Elevation As Integer
0161    End Type
0162    Type ActorDefine                        'actor startup parameters
0163      PositionX As Integer        'position of actor in 3D world...
0164      PositionY As Integer
0165      PositionZ As Integer
0166      Yaw As Integer            'orientation of actor in 3D world...
0167      Roll As Integer
0168      Pitch As Integer
0169    End Type
0170    Type AssemblyDefine                  'assembly startup parameters
0171      Solid As Integer                        'type of 3D solid
0172      Level As Integer                        'hierarchy level
0173      Color As Integer                        'rendering color
0174      SizeX As Integer                        'width of subobject
0175      SizeY As Integer                       'height of subobject
0176      SizeZ As Integer                        'depth of subobject
0177      PositionX As Integer          'position in assembly-space...
0178      PositionY As Integer
0179      PositionZ As Integer
0180      Yaw As Integer                 'orientation in assembly-space...
0181      Roll As Integer
0182      Pitch As Integer
0183      DeformRightX As Integer            'extrusion of subobject...
0184      DeformLeftX As Integer
0185      DeformUpY As Integer
0186      DeformDownY As Integer
0187      PivotX As Integer                  'subassembly pivot-point...
0188      PivotY As Integer
0189      PivotZ As Integer
0190      SubAssyYaw As Integer 'subassy orientation in assembly-space...
0191      SubAssyRoll As Integer
0192      SubAssyPitch As Integer
0193      SubAssyX As Integer   'subassembly position in assembly-space...
0194      SubAssyY As Integer
0195      SubAssyZ As Integer
0196    End Type
0197    '---------- camera, light, actor, subassembly structs ----------
```

```
0198   Global Cam1 As CameraDefine                          'camera
0199   Global Cam1Path1 As CameraPath                   'camera path
0200   Global Lt1 As LightDefine                       'light-source
0201   Global Lt1Path1 As LightPath                'light-source path
0202   Global Actor1 As ActorDefine                       'an actor
0203   Global Actor1Path1 As ActorPath               'and its path
0204   Global Assembly1(10) As AssemblyDefine         'a subassembly
0205   Global Assembly1Path1 As SubAssyPath           'and its path
0206   '------------ parameters for the rendering loop ----------------
0207   Global Const zROBOT_START = 0
0208   Global Const zROBOT_FINISH = 9
0209   Global Const zBOX = 1
0210   Global Const zSPHERE = 2
0211   Global Const zCYLINDER = 3
0212   Global Const zCONE = 4
0213   Global Const zWEDGE = 5
0214   Global Const zCURVE = 6
0215   Global Const zHEMISPHERE = 7
0216   Global Const zDEFORMBOX = 8
0217   Global Const zHALFCYL = 9
0218   Global Const zBULGE = 10
0219   Global Const zNULL = 11
0220   Global Const zLEVEL1 = 1              'progeny in 3D hierarchy...
0221   Global Const zLEVEL2 = 2
0222   Global Const zLEVEL3 = 3
0223
0224   '----------------------------------------------------------------
0225   '               Variables for disk I/O
0226   '----------------------------------------------------------------
0227   Global FileName As String           'name of binary image file
0228   Global FrameSaved As Integer             'frame saved to disk?
0229   Global FrameLoaded As Integer          'frame loaded from disk?
0230   Global AnimationSaved As Integer       'animation saved to disk?
0231   Global AnimationLoaded As Integer    'animation loaded from disk?
0232   Global AnimationReady As Integer    'animation ready for playback?
0233   Global PrevSaveAttempt As Integer     'previous save attempt made?
0234   Global PrevLoadAttempt As Integer     'previous load attempt made?
0235   Global UseDisk As Integer               'load each frame as needed?
0236   Global AnimationHalted As Integer    'disk error during animation?
0237
0238   '----------------------------------------------------------------
0239   '           Constants for Windows API functions
0240   '----------------------------------------------------------------
0241   Global Const SRCCOPY = &HCC0020                  'for bitblts...
0242   Global Const SRCINVERT = &H660046
0243   Global Const SRCPAINT = &HEE0086
0244   Global Const WHITENESS = &HFF0062
0245   Global Const BLACKNESS = &H42&
0246   Global Const ALTERNATE = 1                        'for filling...
0247   Global Const WINDING = 2
0248   Global Const R2_COPYPEN = 13                     'for pen mode...
0249   Global Const R2_XORPEN = 7
0250   Global Const TRANSPARENT = 1              'for background mode...
0251   Global Const OPAQUE = 2
0252   Global Const PS_SOLID = 0                      'for solid pen
0253   Global Const PS_NULL = 5                 'for transparent pen
0254   Global Const BLACKONWHITE = 1            'for bitblt scaling...
```

```
0255  Global Const WHITEONBLACK = 2
0256  Global Const COLORONCOLOR = 3
0257  Global Const HORZRES = 8            'args for GetDeviceCaps()...
0258  Global Const VERTRES = 10
0259  Global Const BITSPIXEL = 12
0260  Global Const PLANES = 14
0261  Global Const SM_MOUSEPRESENT = 19       'for GetSystemMetrics()
0262  Global Const WF_ENHANCED = &H20          'for GetWinFlags()...
0263  Global Const WF_STANDARD = &H10
0264
0265  '----------------------------------------------------------------
0266  '              GDI functions for display-contexts
0267  '----------------------------------------------------------------
0268  Declare Function GetDC Lib "USER" (ByVal hWnd As Integer) As
          Integer
0269  Declare Function ReleaseDC Lib "USER" (ByVal hWnd As Integer,
          ByVal hDC As Integer) As Integer
0270
0271  '----------------------------------------------------------------
0272  '              GDI functions for the desktop
0273  '----------------------------------------------------------------
0274  Declare Function GetDesktopWindow Lib "USER" () As Integer
0275
0276  '----------------------------------------------------------------
0277  '         GDI functions for creating drawing objects
0278  '----------------------------------------------------------------
0279  Declare Function CreatePen Lib "GDI" (ByVal PenStyle As Integer,
          ByVal Wd As Integer, ByVal Color As Long) As Integer
0280  Declare Function CreateSolidBrush Lib "GDI" (ByVal Color As Long)
          As Integer
0281
0282  '----------------------------------------------------------------
0283  '         GDI functions for selecting objects
0284  '----------------------------------------------------------------
0285  Declare Function SelectObject Lib "GDI" (ByVal hDC As Integer,
          ByVal hObject As Integer) As Integer
0286  Declare Function DeleteObject Lib "GDI" (ByVal hObject As Integer)
          As Integer
0287
0288  '----------------------------------------------------------------
0289  '         GDI functions for bitmaps and bitblts
0290  '----------------------------------------------------------------
0291  Declare Function CreateCompatibleDC Lib "GDI" (ByVal hDC As
          Integer) As Integer
0292  Declare Function CreateCompatibleBitmap Lib "GDI" (ByVal hDC As
          Integer, ByVal Wd As Integer, ByVal Ht As Integer) As Integer
0293  Declare Function PatBlt Lib "GDI" (ByVal hDC As Integer, ByVal X
          As Integer, ByVal Y As Integer, ByVal Wd As Integer, ByVal Ht
          As Integer, ByVal RasOp As Long) As Integer
0294  Declare Function BitBlt Lib "GDI" (ByVal hDestDC As Integer, ByVal
          DestX As Integer, ByVal DestY As Integer, ByVal Wd As Integer,
          ByVal Ht As Integer, ByVal hSrcDC As Integer, ByVal SrcX As
          Integer, ByVal SrcY As Integer, ByVal RastOp As Long) As Integer
0295  Declare Function DeleteDC Lib "GDI" (ByVal hDC As Integer) As
          Integer
0296
0297  '----------------------------------------------------------------
0298  '         GDI functions for drawing mode operations
0299  '----------------------------------------------------------------
```

```
0300  Declare Function SetROP2 Lib "GDI" (ByVal hDC As Integer, ByVal
          RasMode As Integer) As Integer
0301  Declare Function SetBkColor Lib "GDI" (ByVal hDC As Integer, ByVal
          Color As Long) As Long
0302  Declare Function SetBkMode Lib "GDI" (ByVal hDC As Integer, ByVal
          BkMode As Integer) As Integer
0303  Declare Function SetPolyFillMode Lib "GDI" (ByVal hDC As Integer,
          ByVal PolyMode As Integer) As Integer
0304  Declare Function SetStretchBltMode Lib "GDI" (ByVal hDC As
          Integer, ByVal StretchMode As Integer) As Integer
0305
0306  '------------------------------------------------------------------
0307  '          GDI functions for drawing operations
0308  '------------------------------------------------------------------
0309  Declare Function MoveTo Lib "GDI" (ByVal hDC As Integer, ByVal X
          As Integer, ByVal Y As Integer) As Long
0310  Declare Function LineTo Lib "GDI" (ByVal hDC As Integer, ByVal X
          As Integer, ByVal Y As Integer) As Integer
0311  Declare Function Polygon Lib "GDI" (ByVal hDC As Integer, FirstPt
          As Integer, ByVal Count As Integer) As Integer
0312  Declare Function Rectangle Lib "GDI" (ByVal hDC As Integer, ByVal
          X1 As Integer, ByVal Y1 As Integer, ByVal X2 As Integer, ByVal
          Y2 As Integer) As Integer
0313  Declare Function Ellipse Lib "GDI" (ByVal hDC As Integer, ByVal X1
          As Integer, ByVal Y1 As Integer, ByVal X2 As Integer, ByVal Y2
          As Integer) As Integer
0314  Declare Function FloodFill Lib "GDI" (ByVal hDC As Integer, ByVal
          X As Integer, ByVal Y As Integer, ByVal Color As Long) As
          Integer
0315  Declare Function SetPixel Lib "GDI" (ByVal hDC As Integer, ByVal X
          As Integer, ByVal Y As Integer, ByVal Color As Long) As Long
0316  Declare Function GetPixel Lib "GDI" (ByVal hDC As Integer, ByVal X
          As Integer, ByVal Y As Integer) As Long
0317
0318  '------------------------------------------------------------------
0319  '              GDI functions for regions
0320  '------------------------------------------------------------------
0321  Declare Function PaintRgn Lib "GDI" (ByVal hDC As Integer, ByVal
          hRGN As Integer) As Integer
0322  Declare Function CreatePolygonRgn Lib "GDI" (FirstPt As Integer,
          ByVal Count As Integer, ByVal PolyFillMode As Integer) As
          Integer
0323  Declare Function PtInRegion Lib "GDI" (ByVal hRGN As Integer,
          ByVal xCoord As Integer, ByVal yCoord As Integer) As Integer
0324
0325  '------------------------------------------------------------------
0326  '  GDI, USER, KERNEL functions for various runtime conditions
0327  '------------------------------------------------------------------
0328  Declare Function GetDeviceCaps Lib "GDI" (ByVal hDC As Integer,
          ByVal Item As Integer) As Integer
0329  Declare Function GetWinFlags Lib "KERNEL" () As Long
0330  Declare Function GetSystemMetrics Lib "USER" (ByVal Item As
          Integer) As Integer
0331  Declare Function GlobalCompact Lib "KERNEL" (ByVal NumBytes As
          Long) As Long
0332  Declare Function GetVersion Lib "KERNEL" () As Long
```

```
0333   Declare Function ExitWindows Lib "USER" (ByVal Reserved As Long,
          ByVal Item As Integer) As Integer
0334   Declare Function SetCapture Lib "USER" (ByVal hWnd As Integer) As
          Integer
0335   Declare Sub ReleaseCapture Lib "USER" ()
0336
0337   '----------------------------------------------------------------
0338   '                       End of global module.
0339   '----------------------------------------------------------------
0340

0001   '----------------------------------------------------------------
0002   '              Reusable template for startup code for
0003   '              Visual Basic Windows graphics applications.
0004   '----------------------------------------------------------------
0005   '  Source file:  ASMAIN.BAS
0006   '  Release version:  1.00                    Programmer:  Lee Adams
0007   '  Type:  Visual Basic startup module for Windows applications.
0008   '  Compiler:  Microsoft Visual Basic 2.00
0009   '  Dependencies:  ASGLOBAL.BAS global module
0010   '                 ASSEMBLY.FRM primary module
0011   '                 ASPLAY.BAS animation playback module
0012   '  Output and features:  Initializes the runtime environment
0013   '    for a Windows graphics application created with
0014   '    Visual Basic.  Ensures runtime image size and compatibility
0015   '    no matter which graphics mode is being used by Windows.
0016   '  Publication:  Contains material from Windcrest/McGraw-Hill
0017   '    book 4225 published by TAB BOOKS Div. of McGraw-Hill Inc.
0018   '  License:  As purchaser of the book you are granted a
0019   '    royalty-free license to distribute executable files
0020   '    generated using this code provided that you accept the
0021   '    conditions of the License Agreement and Limited Warranty
0022   '    described in the book and on the companion disk.  Government
0023   '    users:  This software and documentation are subject to
0024   '    restrictions set forth in The Rights in Technical Data and
0025   '    Computer Software clause at 252.227-7013 and elsewhere.
0026   '----------------------------------------------------------------
0027   '      (c) Copyright 1993 Lee Adams.  All rights reserved.
0028   '          Lee Adams(tm) is a trademark of Lee Adams.
0029   '----------------------------------------------------------------
0030
0031   Option Explicit          'generate error if variable not declared
0032
0033   '----------------------------------------------------------------
0034   '        Initialization code for startup of application
0035   '----------------------------------------------------------------
0036   Sub Main ()                         'is called by Windows at startup
0037     Dim PreviousColor As Long           'will remember default color
0038   StartUp = True                        'set the run-time tokens...
0039   IgnoreRefresh = True
0040   FrameReady = False
0041   FrameSaved = False
0042   FrameLoaded = False
0043   LoadingFrame = False
0044   TimerExists = False
0045   Pause = True
0046   AnimationSaved = False
0047   AnimationLoaded = False
```

```
0048   PrevSaveAttempt = False
0049   PrevLoadAttempt = False
0050   UseDisk = False
0051   AnimationHalted = False
0052   Redisplay = False
0053   '-------------------- initialize variables --------------------
0054   TimerCounter = zTIMER_PAUSE
0055   wFrameRate = 55
0056   FrameDirection = zFORWARD
0057   FrameNum = 1
0058   FrameFiles(0) = "HRA01.BMP"      'initialize the array of filenames
0059   FrameFiles(1) = "HRA02.BMP"
0060   FrameFiles(2) = "HRA03.BMP"
0061   FrameFiles(3) = "HRA04.BMP"
0062   FrameFiles(4) = "HRA05.BMP"
0063   FrameFiles(5) = "HRA06.BMP"
0064   FrameFiles(6) = "HRA07.BMP"
0065   FrameFiles(7) = "HRA08.BMP"
0066   FrameFiles(8) = "HRA09.BMP"
0067   FrameFiles(9) = "HRA10.BMP"
0068   FrameFiles(10) = "HRA11.BMP"
0069   FrameFiles(11) = "HRA12.BMP"
0070   FrameFiles(12) = "HRA13.BMP"
0071   FrameFiles(13) = "HRA14.BMP"
0072   FrameFiles(14) = "HRA15.BMP"
0073   FrameFiles(15) = "HRA16.BMP"
0074   FrameFiles(16) = "HRA17.BMP"
0075   FrameFiles(17) = "HRA18.BMP"
0076   FrameFiles(18) = "HRA19.BMP"
0077   FrameFiles(19) = "HRA20.BMP"
0078   FrameFiles(20) = "HRA21.BMP"
0079   FrameFiles(21) = "HRA22.BMP"
0080   FrameFiles(22) = "HRA23.BMP"
0081   FrameFiles(23) = "HRA24.BMP"
0082   FrameFiles(24) = "HRA25.BMP"
0083   FrameFiles(25) = "HRA26.BMP"
0084   FrameFiles(26) = "HRA27.BMP"
0085   FrameFiles(27) = "HRA28.BMP"
0086   FrameFiles(28) = "HRA29.BMP"
0087   FrameFiles(29) = "HRA30.BMP"
0088   FrameFiles(30) = "HRA31.BMP"
0089   FrameFiles(31) = "HRA32.BMP"
0090   FrameFiles(32) = "HRA33.BMP"
0091   FrameFiles(33) = "HRA34.BMP"
0092   FrameFiles(34) = "HRA35.BMP"
0093   FrameFiles(35) = "HRA36.BMP"
0094   '--------------- examine the graphics adapter ------------------
0095   hDesktopWnd = GetDesktopWindow()           'grab handle to desktop
0096   hDCcaps = GetDC(hDesktopWnd)          'get display-context for desktop
0097   DisplayWidth = GetDeviceCaps(hDCcaps, HORZRES)   'horiz resolution
0098   DisplayHeight = GetDeviceCaps(hDCcaps, VERTRES)   'vert resolution
0099   DisplayBits = GetDeviceCaps(hDCcaps, BITSPIXEL)    'bits-per-pixel
0100   DisplayPlanes = GetDeviceCaps(hDCcaps, PLANES)   'num of bitplanes
0101   RetVal = ReleaseDC(hDesktopWnd, hDCcaps) 'release display-context
0102   '--------------- determine the runtime memory mode --------------
0103   MemoryMode = GetWinFlags()               'will inspect this value later
```

```
0104  '---------------- determine version of Windows ------------------
0105  WindowsVersion = GetVersion()          'will inspect this value later
0106  '--------------- set mode-dependent twips factors ---------------
0107  HorizTwipsPixel = 15!: VertTwipsPixel = 15!        'set defaults...
0108  Window_Width = zWINDOW_WIDTH: Window_Height = zWINDOW_HEIGHT
0109  If DisplayWidth = 640 Then
0110    If DisplayHeight = 480 Then                      'VGA 640x480 mode
0111      HorizTwipsPixel = 15!            '9600x7200 twips full screen
0112      VertTwipsPixel = 15!
0113      Window_Width = zWINDOW_WIDTH
0114      Window_Height = zWINDOW_HEIGHT
0115    End If
0116    If DisplayHeight = 350 Then                      'EGA 640x350 mode
0117      HorizTwipsPixel = 15!            '9600x7000 twips full screen
0118      VertTwipsPixel = 20!
0119      Window_Width = zWINDOW_WIDTH
0120      Window_Height = 297!   'adjust for aspect ratio and font size
0121    End If
0122    If DisplayHeight = 200 Then    'nominal support CGA 640x200 mode
0123      HorizTwipsPixel = 15!
0124      VertTwipsPixel = 36!
0125      Window_Width = zWINDOW_WIDTH
0126      Window_Height = zWINDOW_HEIGHT
0127    End If
0128  End If
0129  If DisplayWidth = 800 Then    'SuperVGA, 8514/A, XGA 800x600 mode
0130    HorizTwipsPixel = 12!              '9600x7200 twips full screen
0131    VertTwipsPixel = 12!
0132    Window_Width = zWINDOW_WIDTH
0133    Window_Height = 317!                    'compensate for font size
0134  End If
0135  If DisplayWidth = 1024 Then          '8514/A, XGA 1024x768 mode
0136    HorizTwipsPixel = 12!            '12200x9216 twips full screen
0137    VertTwipsPixel = 12!
0138    Window_Width = zWINDOW_WIDTH
0139    Window_Height = 317!                    'compensate for font size
0140  End If
0141  If DisplayWidth = 720 Then              'Hercules 720x348 mode
0142    HorizTwipsPixel = 12!
0143    VertTwipsPixel = 20!
0144    Window_Width = zWINDOW_WIDTH
0145    Window_Height = 297!       'adjust for aspect ratio and font size
0146  End If
0147  '-------------- display the splash sign-on banner ---------------
0148  UserWants = MsgBox("Graphics demo from Windcrest McGraw-Hill book
          4225.", MB_OKCANCEL, "Copyright© 1993-1994 Lee Adams.")
0149  If UserWants = IDCANCEL Then    'if user selected Cancel button...
0150    End                                  'then cancel this startup
0151  End If
0152  '------------- initialize and display the window ----------------
0153  Form1.Width = Window_Width * HorizTwipsPixel          'set width
0154  Form1.Height = Window_Height * VertTwipsPixel         'set height
0155  Form1.Left = (Screen.Width - Form1.Width) / 2 'horizontal center
0156  Form1.Top = (Screen.Height - Form1.Height) / 2  'vertical center
0157  Form1.Caption = "Animated 3D subassemblies"     'set the caption
0158  Form1.AutoRedraw = False            'disable automatic refresh
0159  Form1.BackColor = RGB(255, 255, 255)  'set the client area color
0160  Form1.ForeColor = RGB(0, 0, 0)                      'active color
```

```
0161   Form1.ScaleMode = PIXELS                        'will use pixel coords
0162   Form1.Show                                      'display the window
0163   '------------------ check if mouse present --------------------
0164   MousePresent = GetSystemMetrics(SM_MOUSEPRESENT)
0165   If MousePresent = 0 Then                                'if no mouse
0166     Beep
0167     MsgBox "No mouse found.  Some features of this demo program may
             require a mouse.  The demo's menu system also responds to the
             keyboard.  Press <Enter> to continue.", MB_OK, "Graphics
             system warning"
0168   End If
0169   '---------------- initialize the 3D toolkit --------------------
0170   aazInitialize3D
0171   End Sub
0172


0001   VERSION 2.00
0002     Begin Form Form1
0003       Caption         =    "Prototype"
0004       ControlBox      =    0    'False
0005       Height          =    4515
0006       Left            =    2040
0007       LinkMode        =    1    'Source
0008       LinkTopic       =    "Form1"
0009       MaxButton       =    0    'False
0010       MinButton       =    0    'False
0011       ScaleHeight     =    3825
0012       ScaleWidth      =    3840
0013       Top             =    1485
0014       Width           =    3960
0015       Begin PictureBox Picture1
0016         Height            =    495
0017         Left              =    480
0018         ScaleHeight       =    465
0019         ScaleWidth        =    1185
0020         TabIndex          =    0
0021         Top               =    840
0022         Width             =    1215
0023       End
0024       Begin Timer TimerID1
0025         Left              =    1320
0026         Top               =    1680
0027       End
0028       Begin Menu POPUP_File
0029         Caption         =    "&File"
0030         Begin Menu IDM_New
0031           Caption         =    "&New"
0032           Enabled         =    0    'False
0033         End
0034         Begin Menu IDM_Open
0035           Caption         =    "&Open"
0036           Enabled         =    0    'False
0037         End
0038         Begin Menu IDM_Save
0039           Caption         =    "&Save"
0040           Enabled         =    0    'False
```

```
0041          End
0042          Begin Menu IDM_SaveAs
0043              Caption        =    "Save &As..."
0044              Enabled        =    0    'False
0045          End
0046          Begin Menu FileSep1
0047              Caption        =    "-"
0048          End
0049          Begin Menu IDM_Exit
0050              Caption        =    "E&xit..."
0051          End
0052          Begin Menu IDM_Restart
0053              Caption        =    "&Restart Windows..."
0054          End
0055      End
0056      Begin Menu POPUP_Edit
0057          Caption        =    "&Edit"
0058          Begin Menu IDM_Undo
0059              Caption        =    "&Undo"
0060              Enabled        =    0    'False
0061          End
0062          Begin Menu EditSep1
0063              Caption        =    "-"
0064          End
0065          Begin Menu IDM_Cut
0066              Caption        =    "Cu&t"
0067              Enabled        =    0    'False
0068          End
0069          Begin Menu IDM_Copy
0070              Caption        =    "&Copy"
0071              Enabled        =    0    'False
0072          End
0073          Begin Menu IDM_Paste
0074              Caption        =    "&Paste"
0075              Enabled        =    0    'False
0076          End
0077          Begin Menu IDM_Delete
0078              Caption        =    "&Delete"
0079              Enabled        =    0    'False
0080          End
0081      End
0082      Begin Menu POPUP_Run
0083          Caption        =    "&Run"
0084          Begin Menu IDM_LoadAnimation
0085              Caption        =    "&Load animation"
0086          End
0087          Begin Menu DemoSep1
0088              Caption        =    "-"
0089          End
0090          Begin Menu IDM_RunForward
0091              Caption        =    "Run &Forward"
0092          End
0093          Begin Menu POPUP_RunReverse
0094              Caption        =    "Run &Reverse"
0095          End
0096          Begin Menu IDM_StopAnimation
0097              Caption        =    "Free&zeframe"
0098          End
```

```
0099          Begin Menu POPUP_SetSpeed
0100              Caption        =    "S&et speed..."
0101              Begin Menu IDM_FPS182
0102                  Caption        =    "&18 fps"
0103              End
0104              Begin Menu IDM_FPS91
0105                  Caption        =    "&9 fps"
0106              End
0107              Begin Menu IDM_FPS61
0108                  Caption        =    "&6 fps"
0109              End
0110              Begin Menu IDM_FPS45
0111                  Caption        =    "&5 fps"
0112              End
0113              Begin Menu IDM_FPS36
0114                  Caption        =    "&4 fps"
0115              End
0116              Begin Menu IDM_FPS30
0117                  Caption        =    "&3 fps"
0118              End
0119          End
0120          Begin Menu DemoSep2
0121              Caption        =    "-"
0122          End
0123          Begin Menu IDM_Clear
0124              Caption        =    "&Clear Viewport"
0125          End
0126          Begin Menu DemoSep3
0127              Caption        =    "-"
0128          End
0129          Begin Menu POPUP_Production
0130              Caption        =    "&Production..."
0131              Begin Menu IDM_SaveAnimation
0132                  Caption        =    "&Build Animation"
0133              End
0134              Begin Menu DemoSep4
0135                  Caption        =    "-"
0136              End
0137              Begin Menu IDM_UseShaded
0138                  Caption        =    "Use &shaded solids"
0139              End
0140              Begin Menu IDM_UseWireframe
0141                  Caption        =    "Use &wireframe mode"
0142              End
0143          End
0144      End
0145      Begin Menu POPUP_Use
0146          Caption        =    "&Use"
0147          Begin Menu IDM_About
0148              Caption        =    "&About"
0149          End
0150          Begin Menu IDM_License
0151              Caption        =    "&License"
0152          End
0153          Begin Menu HelpSep1
0154              Caption        =    "-"
```

```
0155          End
0156          Begin Menu IDM_Display
0157            Caption        =    "&Resolution of display"
0158          End
0159          Begin Menu IDM_Colors
0160            Caption        =    "Available &colors"
0161          End
0162          Begin Menu IDM_Mode
0163            Caption        =    "&Memory mode"
0164          End
0165          Begin Menu IDM_Version
0166            Caption        =    "Windows &version"
0167          End
0168          Begin Menu HelpSep2
0169            Caption        =    "-"
0170          End
0171          Begin Menu IDM_GeneralHelp
0172            Caption        =    "&How to use"
0173          End
0174      End
0175  End
0176  '----------------------------------------------------------------
0177  '              3D hierarchical modeling for animation
0178  '----------------------------------------------------------------
0179  '  Source file: ASSEMBLY.FRM
0180  '  Release version: 1.0                    Programmer:  Lee Adams
0181  '  Type:  Visual Basic global module for Windows applications.
0182  '  Compiler:  Microsoft Visual Basic 2.00
0183  '  Dependencies:  ASGLOBAL.BAS    global module
0184  '                 ASMAIN.BAS      module containing Main()
0185  '                 ASPLAY.BAS      animation playback module
0186  '                 ENGINE3D.BAS    3D toolkit
0187  '                 SHAPES3D.BAS    3D shapes toolkit
0188  '                 DEFORM3D.BAS    3D deformations toolkit
0189  '                 LIGHTS3D.BAS    light-source toolkit
0190  '                 ASSEMB3D.BAS    hierarchical modeling toolkit
0191  '  Output and features:  Demonstrates 3D hierarchical modeling
0192  '    for animation sequences and storage of frames on disk.
0193  '    Demonstrates loading of frames from disk and interactive
0194  '    playback of animation sequence from RAM or from disk if
0195  '    insufficient memory available.  The startup code
0196  '    automatically sizes the window to yield a client area with
0197  '    dimensions of 256-by-255 pixels in any graphics mode.  You
0198  '    can use the menu system to toggle between wireframe and
0199  '    shaded modes.
0200  '      NUMBER OF FRAMES:  In its current implementation, the
0201  '    application produces an animation sequence of 36 frames.
0202  '    To create a sequence that uses fewer frames or more frames,
0203  '    you can edit the values of the zFINALFRAME and zNUMCELS
0204  '    constants defined in the ANGLOBAL.BAS global module.  You'll
0205  '    also need to add or delete filename strings to the array
0206  '    named FrameFiles() in the ANMAIN.BAS module.
0207  '  Publication:  Contains material from Windcrest/McGraw-Hill
0208  '    book 4225 published by TAB BOOKS Div. of McGraw-Hill Inc.
0209  '  License:  As purchaser of the book you are granted a
0210  '    royalty-free license to distribute executable files
0211  '    generated using this code provided that you accept the
0212  '    conditions of the License Agreement and Limited Warranty
```

C-4 Continued.

```
0213   '     described in the book and on the companion disk.  Government
0214   '     users:  This software and documentation are subject to
0215   '     restrictions set forth in The Rights in Technical Data and
0216   '     Computer Software clause at 252.227-7013 and elsewhere.
0217   '-----------------------------------------------------------------
0218   '       (c) Copyright 1993 Lee Adams.  All rights reserved.
0219   '          Lee Adams(tm) is a trademark of Lee Adams.
0220   '-----------------------------------------------------------------
0221   '
0222   '   SELECT A STARTUP FORM:
0223   '   Because this Visual Basic application uses a procedure named
0224   '   Main() at startup, you must specify Sub Main as the startup
0225   '   form in the Project Options dialog box before you run the
0226   '   program and before you build an .exe file.
0227   '
0228   '   DOUBLE-CLICK THE TIMER TOOL:
0229   '   Because the program uses a timer to manage the animation
0230   '   playback, you must double-click on the timer tool in the
0231   '   toolbox at design-time to place a timer control on the form.
0232   '   Specify TimerID1 as the timer's CtlName.
0233   '
0234   '   DOUBLE-CLICK THE PICTURE-BOX TOOL:
0235   '   Because this demo uses a picture box when saving images to
0236   '   disk as .BMP files, you must double-click the Picture Box
0237   '   tool in the Toolbox at design-time to place a default-sized
0238   '   picture box on the form.
0239   '
0240   '-----------------------------------------------------------------
0241
0242   Option Explicit             'generate error if variable not declared
0243
0244   '-----------------------------------------------------------------
0245   '       Low-level keyboard handler for single-step animation
0246   '-----------------------------------------------------------------
0247   Sub Form_KeyDown (KeyCode As Integer, Shift As Integer)
0248   If Pause = False Then                'if animation is running...
0249     Exit Sub                          'then cancel this function
0250   End If
0251   If AnimationLoaded = False Then      'if animation is not loaded...
0252     Exit Sub                          'then cancel this function
0253   End If
0254   If FrameReady = False Then           'if hidden frame is not ready...
0255     Exit Sub                          'then cancel this function
0256   End If
0257   If KeyCode = &H25 Then     'if left arrow key has been pressed...
0258     FrameDirection = zREVERSE                'reset direction token
0259     Pause = False                     'toggle off the Pause token
0260     zShowNextFrame                              'show next frame
0261     Pause = True                       'toggle on the Pause token
0262     Exit Sub                                         'return
0263   End If
0264   If KeyCode = &H27 Then     'if right arrow key has been pressed...
0265     FrameDirection = zFORWARD
0266     Pause = False
0267     zShowNextFrame
0268     Pause = True
```

```
0269    Exit Sub
0270  End If
0271  End Sub
0272
0273  '----------------------------------------------------------------
0274  '              Refresh the client area if uncovered
0275  '----------------------------------------------------------------
0276  Sub Form_Paint ()    'is automatically called by Windows as needed
0277  If LoadingFrame = True Then    'special case LoadPicture function
0278    Exit Sub
0279  End If
0280  If Pause = True Then          'if paused, redisplay current frame
0281    Redisplay = True
0282    zShowNextFrame
0283    Redisplay = False
0284    Exit Sub
0285  End If
0286  zShowNextFrame        '...else show the next frame in the animation
0287  End Sub
0288
0289  '----------------------------------------------------------------
0290  '              Intercept any attempt to resize the window
0291  '----------------------------------------------------------------
0292  Sub Form_Resize ()          'is called twice when window is resized
0293  If Startup = True Then    'if window being displayed for first time
0294    Startup = False
0295    IgnoreRefresh = True
0296    Exit Sub
0297  End If
0298  Form1.WindowState = 0                         'reset normal size
0299  Form1.Width = Window_Width * HorizTwipsPixel          'reset width
0300  Form1.Height = Window_Height * VertTwipsPixel         'reset height
0301  Form1.Left = (Screen.Width - Form1.Width) / 2 'horizontal center
0302  Form1.Top = (Screen.Height - Form1.Height) / 2   'vertical center
0303  If IgnoreRefresh = False Then                      'if second call
0304    IgnoreRefresh = True            'reset token for next first call
0305    MsgBox "This demo uses a fixed-size window.", MB_OK, "Sample
          application"
0306    Exait Sub
0307  End If
0308  Form1.Refresh                              'refresh the client area
0309  IgnoreRefresh = False        'if first call, reset for second call
0310  End Sub
0311
0312  '----------------------------------------------------------------
0313  '                  Display the About message box
0314  '----------------------------------------------------------------
0315  Sub IDM_About_Click ()
0316  MsgBox "This is a demo from Windcrest McGraw-Hill book 4225.
          Copyright© 1993 Lee Adams.  All rights reserved.", MB_OK,
          "About this Visual Basic program"
0317  End Sub
0318
0319  '----------------------------------------------------------------
0320  '              Clear the client area of the window
0321  '----------------------------------------------------------------
0322  Sub IDM_Clear_Click ()
0323  zClear                              'clear the display window
```

```
0324   zClearHiddenFrame                              'clear the hidden frame
0325   End Sub
0326
0327   '-----------------------------------------------------------------
0328   '              Determine number of available colors
0329   '-----------------------------------------------------------------
0330   Sub IDM_Colors_Click ()
0331   If DisplayBits = 1 Then                    'if 1 bit-per-pixel...
0332     If DisplayPlanes = 4 Then                      'if 4 bitplanes...
0333       MsgBox "Running in 4-bit, 16-color mode.", MB_OK, "Available
             colors"
0334       Exit Sub
0335     End If
0336     If DisplayPlanes = 1 Then                       'if 1 bitplane...
0337       MsgBox "Running in 1-bit, 2-color mode.", MB_OK, "Available
             colors"
0338       Exit Sub
0339     End If
0340   End If
0341   If DisplayBits = 8 Then                    'if 8 bits-per-pixel...
0342     MsgBox "Running in 8-bit, 256-color mode.", MB_OK, "Available
           colors"
0343     Exit Sub
0344   End If
0345   If DisplayBits = 16 Then                  'if 16 bits-per-pixel...
0346     MsgBox "Running in 16-bit, 65000-color mode.", MB_OK, "Available
           colors"
0347     Exit Sub
0348   End If
0349   MsgBox "Running in a custom color mode.", MB_OK, "Available colors"
0350   End Sub
0351
0352   '-----------------------------------------------------------------
0353   '              Determine the screen resolution
0354   '-----------------------------------------------------------------
0355   Sub IDM_Display_Click ()
0356   If DisplayWidth = 640 Then
0357     If DisplayHeight = 480 Then                          'VGA mode
0358       MsgBox "Running in 640x480 mode.", MB_OK, "Screen resolution"
0359       Exit Sub
0360     End If
0361     If DisplayHeight = 350 Then                          'EGA mode
0362       MsgBox "Running in 640x350 mode.", MB_OK, "Screen resolution"
0363       Exit Sub
0364     End If
0365     If DisplayHeight = 200 Then                          'CGA mode
0366       MsgBox "Running in 640x200 mode.", MB_OK, "Screen resolution"
0367       Exit Sub
0368     End If
0369   End If
0370   If DisplayWidth = 800 Then              'SuperVGA, 8514/A, XGA mode
0371     MsgBox "Running in 800x600 mode.", MB_OK, "Screen resolution"
0372     Exit Sub
0373   End If
0374   If DisplayWidth = 1024 Then                   '8514/A, XGA mode
0375     MsgBox "Running in 1024x768 mode.", MB_OK, "Screen resolution"
0376     Exit Sub
```

```
0377   End If
0378   If DisplayWidth = 720 Then                            'Hercules mode
0379     MsgBox "Running in 720x348 mode.", MB_OK, "Screen resolution"
0380     Exit Sub
0381   End If
0382   MsgBox "Running in custom mode.", MB_OK, "Screen resolution"
0383   End Sub
0384
0385   '-----------------------------------------------------------------
0386   '                   Terminate the application
0387   '-----------------------------------------------------------------
0388   Sub IDM_Exit_Click ()
0389   UserWants = MsgBox("Exit the demo and return to Windows?",
           MB_YESNO, "Please confirm")
0390   If UserWants = IDNO Then                  'if user selected No button...
0391     Exit Sub                                 'then cancel this operation
0392   End If           'otherwise continue to terminate the application...
0393   If AnimationLoaded = True Then              'if animation loaded...
0394     RetVal = SelectObject(hFDC, hPrevF)       'select default handle
0395     For LoopCount = 1 To zNUMCELS Step 1        'for each handle...
0396       RetVal = DeleteObject(BitmapHandles(LoopCount - 1))   'delete
0397     Next LoopCount
0398     RetVal = DeleteDC(hFDC)   '...then delete memory display-context
0399   End If
0400   TimerID1.Enabled = False                        'release the timer
0401   If FrameReady = True Then         'if a hidden frame was created
0402     RetVal = SelectObject(hFrameDC, hPrevFrame)    'deselect bitmap
0403     RetVal = DeleteObject(hFrame)                 'delete the bitmap
0404     RetVal = DeleteDC(hFrameDC)          'delete the display-context
0405   End If
0406   jczClose3d                            'shut down the 3D toolkit
0407   End                                   'terminate the application
0408   End Sub
0409
0410   '-----------------------------------------------------------------
0411   '                   Adjust the frame rate
0412   '-----------------------------------------------------------------
0413   Sub IDM_FPS182_Click ()
0414   If TimerExists = False Then
0415     MsgBox "A timer must be activated before you can reset the frame
             rate.", MB_OK, "Animation not ready"
0416   End If
0417   TimerID1.Interval = 55                        '18 frames per second
0418   End Sub
0419
0420   '-----------------------------------------------------------------
0421   '                   Adjust the frame rate
0422   '-----------------------------------------------------------------
0423   Sub IDM_FPS30_Click ()
0424   If TimerExists = False Then
0425     MsgBox "A timer must be activated before you can reset the frame
             rate.", MB_OK, "Animation not ready"
0426   End If
0427   TimerID1.Interval = 330                        '3 frames per second
0428   End Sub
0429
0430   '-----------------------------------------------------------------
0431   '                   Adjust the frame rate
0432   '-----------------------------------------------------------------
```

```
0433  Sub IDM_FPS36_Click ()
0434  If TimerExists = False Then
0435    MsgBox "A timer must be activated before you can reset the frame
            rate.", MB_OK, "Animation not ready"
0436  End If
0437  TimerID1.Interval = 275                    '4 frames per second
0438  End Sub
0439
0440  '-------------------------------------------------------------------
0441  '                    Adjust the frame rate
0442  '-------------------------------------------------------------------
0443  Sub IDM_FPS45_Click ()
0444  If TimerExists = False Then
0445    MsgBox "A timer must be activated before you can reset the frame
            rate.", MB_OK, "Animation not ready"
0446  End If
0447  TimerID1.Interval = 220                    '5 frames per second
0448  End Sub
0449
0450  '-------------------------------------------------------------------
0451  '                    Adjust the frame rate
0452  '-------------------------------------------------------------------
0453  Sub IDM_FPS61_Click ()
0454  If TimerExists = False Then
0455    MsgBox "A timer must be activated before you can reset the frame
            rate.", MB_OK, "Animation not ready"
0456  End If
0457  TimerID1.Interval = 165                    '6 frames per second
0458  End Sub
0459
0460  '-------------------------------------------------------------------
0461  '                    Adjust the frame rate
0462  '-------------------------------------------------------------------
0463  Sub IDM_FPS91_Click ()
0464  If TimerExists = False Then
0465    MsgBox "A timer must be activated before you can reset the frame
            rate.", MB_OK, "Animation not ready"
0466  End If
0467  TimerID1.Interval = 110                    '9 frames per second
0468  End Sub
0469
0470  '-------------------------------------------------------------------
0471  '                    Display the Help message box
0472  '-------------------------------------------------------------------
0473  Sub IDM_GeneralHelp_Click ()
0474  MsgBox "For animation playback pick Load Animation then Run
            Forward from the Run menu.  To build and save an animation,
            choose the Production submenu.  Also see the book.", MB_OK,
            "How to  use this 3D animation demo"
0475  End Sub
0476
0477  '-------------------------------------------------------------------
0478  '                    Display the License message box
0479  '-------------------------------------------------------------------
0480  Sub IDM_License_Click ()
0481  MsgBox "You can use this code as part of your own software product
```

```
                subject to the License Agreement and Limited Warranty in
                Windcrest McGraw-Hill book 4225 and on its companion disk.",
                MB_OK, "License Agreement"
0482    End Sub
0483
0484    '----------------------------------------------------------------
0485    '                  Load the animation sequence from disk
0486    '  If memory limitations prevent this procedure from loading the
0487    '  entire animation sequence into physical memory or virtual
0488    '  memory, the procedure sets a token to True.
0489    '  In that case the playback procedure zShowNextFrame() will load
0490    '  each frame from disk as required during animation playback,
0491    '  otherwise all frames are expected to be in RAM.
0492    '----------------------------------------------------------------
0493    Sub IDM_LoadAnimation_Click ()
0494      Dim Bitmaps As Integer
0495    zInitializeSystem                    'ensure system is initialized
0496    If AnimationLoaded = True Then        'if frames already loaded...
0497      Form_Paint                    'refresh screen if animation running
0498      Beep
0499      MsgBox "The animation sequence has already been loaded.", MB_OK,
                "Animation ready"
0500      Exit Sub
0501    End If
0502    If PrevLoadAttempt = True Then        'if previous attempt failed...
0503      Beep
0504      MsgBox "Previous attempt to load animation failed.  Cancelling
                this attempt.", MB_OK, "Animation error report"
0505      Exit Sub
0506    End If
0507    PrevLoadAttempt = True
0508    '--------------- create bitmaps to hold the frames --------------
0509    RetLong = GlobalCompact(-1)          'maximize contiguous memory
0510    hFDC = CreateCompatibleDC(Form1.hDC)        'create compatible DC
0511    For LoopCount = 1 To zNUMCELS Step 1          'for each frame...
0512      BitmapHandles(LoopCount - 1) = CreateCompatibleBitmap(Form1.hDC,
                zFRAMEWIDE, zFRAMEHIGH)
0513      If BitmapHandles(LoopCount - 1) = Null Then        'if error...
0514        GoTo BITMAPS_NOT_OK              '...jump out of loop and tidy up
0515      End If
0516    Next LoopCount
0517    GoTo BITMAPS_OK                    'if OK, jump past error-handler
0518    '-------------------- bitmap error-handler --------------------
0519    BITMAPS_NOT_OK:
0520    For Bitmaps = LoopCount - 1 To 1 Step -1      'for each bitmap...
0521      RetVal = DeleteObject(BitmapHandles(Bitmaps - 1)) '...delete it
0522    Next Bitmaps
0523    RetVal = DeleteDC(hFDC)                  'delete the compatible DC
0524    UseDisk = True                          'reset run-time token
0525    AnimationReady = True                    'reset run-time token
0526    MsgBox "Insufficient memory to load entire animation sequence from
                disk.  Software will load each frame as needed during
                playback.", MB_OK, "Animation advisory report"
0527    Exit Sub                              '...and return to caller
0528    BITMAPS_OK:                          'jump to here if no errors
0529    '--------------- load frame files into the bitmaps --------------
0530    For LoopCount = 1 To zNUMCELS Step 1          'for each frame...
0531      FileName = FrameFiles(LoopCount - 1)      'used by zLoadFrame()
```

C-4 Continued.

```
0532     zLoadFrame                          '...and load the frame
0533     If FrameLoaded = False Then         'if disk error occurred...
0534       GoTo DISK_ERROR                   'jump to error-handler
0535     End If
0536     hPrevF = SelectObject(hFDC, BitmapHandles(LoopCount - 1))
0537     RetVal = BitBlt(hFDC, 0, 0, zFRAMEWIDE, zFRAMEHIGH, Form1.hDC,
           0, 0, SRCCOPY)
0538     RetVal = SelectObject(hFDC, hPrevF)
0539 Next LoopCount
0540 GoTo DISK_OK                            'if OK, jump past the error-handler
0541 '--------------------- disk error-handler ----------------------
0542 DISK_ERROR:
0543 For LoopCount = 1 To zNUMCELS Step 1    'for each bitmap handle...
0544   RetVal = DeleteObject(BitmapHandles(LoopCount - 1))  'delete it
0545 Next LoopCount
0546 RetVal = DeleteDC(hFDC)       'delete the memory display-context...
0547 Exit Sub                                '...and return to caller
0548 '-------------------- tidy up and return ----------------------
0549 DISK_OK:
0550 hPrevF = SelectObject(hFDC, BitmapHandles(0))
0551 AnimationLoaded = True
0552 AnimationReady = True
0553 AnimationSaved = True
0554 zClear
0555 zClearHiddenFrame
0556 Beep
0557 MsgBox "Animation sequence successfully loaded from disk.", MB_OK,
         "Animation ready"
0558 End Sub
0559
0560 '-----------------------------------------------------------------
0561 '                  Determine runtime memory mode
0562 '-----------------------------------------------------------------
0563 Sub IDM_Mode_Click ()
0564   Dim TempVariable As Long
0565 TempVariable = MemoryMode And WF_ENHANCED     'perform bitwise AND
0566 If TempVariable = WF_ENHANCED Then    'if result matches constant
0567   MsgBox "Running in enhanced mode.  Can allocate up to 16 MB
           extended memory (XMS) if available.  Virtual memory up to 4
           times physical memory (maximum 64 MB) is also available via
           automatic disk swapping of 4K pages.", MB_OK, "Memory mode"
0568   Exit Sub
0569 End If
0570 TempVariable = MemoryMode And WF_STANDARD
0571 If TempVariable = WF_STANDARD Then
0572   MsgBox "Running in standard mode.  Can allocate up to 16 MB
           extended physical memory (XMS) if available.", MB_OK, "Memory
           mode"
0573   Exit Sub
0574 End If
0575 MsgBox "Running in real mode.  Can allocate blocks of memory from
         the first 640K of RAM.  Can also allocate blocks from expanded
         memory (EMS) if available.", MB_OK, "Memory mode"
0576 End Sub
0577
0578 '-----------------------------------------------------------------
0579 '          Terminate the application and restart Windows
```

```
0580 '----------------------------------------------------------------
0581 Sub IDM_Restart_Click ()
0582 UserWants = MsgBox("Exit the demo and restart Windows?", MB_YESNO,
          "Please confirm")
0583 If UserWants = IDNO Then            'if user selected No button...
0584   Exit Sub                          'then cancel this operation
0585 End If        'otherwise continue to terminate the application...
0586 If AnimationLoaded = True Then            'if animation loaded...
0587   RetVal = SelectObject(hFDC, hPrevF)       'select default handle
0588   For LoopCount = 1 To zNUMCELS Step 1        'for each handle...
0589     RetVal = DeleteObject(BitmapHandles(LoopCount - 1))  'delete
0590   Next LoopCount
0591   RetVal = DeleteDC(hFDC)  '...then delete memory display-context
0592 End If
0593 TimerID1.Enabled = False                      'release the timer
0594 If FrameReady = True Then        'if a hidden frame was created
0595   RetVal = SelectObject(hFrameDC, hPrevFrame)    'deselect bitmap
0596   RetVal = DeleteObject(hFrame)                 'delete the bitmap
0597   RetVal = DeleteDC(hFrameDC)          'delete the display-context
0598 End If
0599 jczClose3d                            'shut down the 3D toolkit
0600 RetVal = ExitWindows(&H42&, 0)    'terminate and restart Windows
0601 End                                  'terminate the application
0602 End Sub
0603
0604 '----------------------------------------------------------------
0605 '           Set animation engine to forward playback
0606 '----------------------------------------------------------------
0607 Sub IDM_RunForward_Click ()
0608 If AnimationLoaded = False Then
0609   MsgBox "You must load an animation sequence before you run the
          animation.", MB_OK, "Animation not ready"
0610   Exit Sub
0611 End If
0612 Pause = False
0613 FrameDirection = zFORWARD
0614 zShowNextFrame
0615 End Sub
0616
0617 '----------------------------------------------------------------
0618 '              Create all frames and save to disk
0619 '----------------------------------------------------------------
0620 Sub IDM_SaveAnimation_Click ()
0621 zInitializeSystem                'ensure system is initialized
0622 If AnimationSaved = True Then          'if animation already saved
0623   Form_Paint                  'refresh screen if animation running
0624   MsgBox "The animation sequence has already been saved to disk.",
          MB_OK, "Animation report"
0625   Exit Sub
0626 End If
0627 If PrevSaveAttempt = True Then          'if previous attempt failed
0628   MsgBox "A previous attempt to save the animation sequence to
          disk has failed.  Cancelling this attempt.  Check available
          disk  space.", MB_OK, "Animation error report"
0629   Exit Sub
0630 End If
0631 PrevSaveAttempt = True       'set token to prevent subsequent calls
0632 '-------------------- initialize the camera --------------------
```

C-4 Continued.

```
0633  Cam1.Heading = 330
0634  Cam1.Pitch = 320
0635  Cam1.Distance = 356
0636  Call bczSetCameraDistance(Cam1.Distance)
0637  Call bbzSetCameraPitch(Cam1.Pitch)
0638  Call bazSetCameraHeading(Cam1.Heading)
0639  '---------------- specify the path of the camera ----------------
0640  Cam1Path1.StartFrame = 1
0641  Cam1Path1.EndFrame = 18
0642  Cam1Path1.ChgHeading = 0                      'set to -2 for dolly
0643  Cam1Path1.ChgPitch = 0                        'set to -2 for crane
0644  Cam1Path1.ChgDistance = 0
0645  '----------------- initialize the light-source -----------------
0646  Lt1.Elevation = 60
0647  Lt1.Heading = 180
0648  Call zSetLightPosition(Lt1.Elevation, Lt1.Heading)
0649  '-------------- specify the path of the light-source ------------
0650  Lt1Path1.StartFrame = 1
0651  Lt1Path1.EndFrame = 18
0652  Lt1Path1.ChgHeading = 0
0653  Lt1Path1.ChgElevation = 0
0654  '--------------------- initialize the actor -------------------
0655  Actor1.PositionX = 0              'position of actor in 3D world...
0656  Actor1.PositionY = 0
0657  Actor1.PositionZ = 0
0658  Actor1.Yaw = 360              'orientation of actor in 3D world...
0659  Actor1.Roll = 360
0660  Actor1.Pitch = 360
0661  Call dazSetSubjectLocation(Actor1.PositionX, Actor1.PositionY,
          Actor1.PositionZ)
0662  Call dbzSetSubjectAttitude(Actor1.Yaw, Actor1.Roll, Actor1.Pitch)
0663  '---------------- specify the path of the actor ----------------
0664  Actor1Path1.StartFrame = 1
0665  Actor1Path1.EndFrame = 18
0666  Actor1Path1.ChgYaw = 0
0667  Actor1Path1.ChgRoll = 0
0668  Actor1Path1.ChgPitch = 0
0669  Actor1Path1.ChgPosX = 0
0670  Actor1Path1.ChgPosY = 0
0671  Actor1Path1.ChgPosZ = 0
0672  '------ initialize the 3D assembly that comprises the actor -----
0673  Assembly1(0).Solid = zBOX                   'arm extensor (1 of 1)
0674  Assembly1(0).Level = zLEVEL1
0675  Assembly1(0).Color = zGREEN
0676  Assembly1(0).SizeX = 20
0677  Assembly1(0).SizeY = 20
0678  Assembly1(0).SizeZ = 30
0679  Assembly1(0).Yaw = 0
0680  Assembly1(0).Roll = 0
0681  Assembly1(0).Pitch = 0
0682  Assembly1(0).PositionX = 0
0683  Assembly1(0).PositionY = 0
0684  Assembly1(0).PositionZ = -50
0685  Assembly1(0).DeformRightX = 0
0686  Assembly1(0).DeformLeftX = 0
0687  Assembly1(0).DeformUpY = 0
```

```
0688   Assembly1(0).DeformDownY = 0
0689   Assembly1(0).PivotX = 0
0690   Assembly1(0).PivotY = 0
0691   Assembly1(0).PivotZ = 0
0692   Assembly1(0).SubAssyYaw = 0
0693   Assembly1(0).SubAssyRoll = 0
0694   Assembly1(0).SubAssyPitch = 0
0695   Assembly1(0).SubAssyX = 0
0696   Assembly1(0).SubAssyY = 0
0697   Assembly1(0).SubAssyZ = 0
0698   Assembly1(1).Solid = zBOX              'arm swivel extensor (1 of 2)
0699   Assembly1(1).Level = zLEVEL1
0700   Assembly1(1).Color = zGREEN
0701   Assembly1(1).SizeX = Assembly1(0).SizeX / 4
0702   Assembly1(1).SizeY = Assembly1(0).SizeY
0703   Assembly1(1).SizeZ = 10
0704   Assembly1(1).Yaw = 0
0705   Assembly1(1).Roll = 0
0706   Assembly1(1).Pitch = 0
0707   Assembly1(1).PositionX = Assembly1(0).SizeX - Assembly1(1).SizeX
0708   Assembly1(1).PositionY = Assembly1(0).PositionY
0709   Assembly1(1).PositionZ = (Assembly1(0).PositionZ + Assembly1(0).SizeZ) +
          Assembly1(1).SizeZ
0710   Assembly1(1).DeformRightX = 0
0711   Assembly1(1).DeformLeftX = 0
0712   Assembly1(1).DeformUpY = 0
0713   Assembly1(1).DeformDownY = 0
0714   Assembly1(1).PivotX = 0
0715   Assembly1(1).PivotY = 0
0716   Assembly1(1).PivotZ = 0
0717   Assembly1(1).SubAssyYaw = 0
0718   Assembly1(1).SubAssyRoll = 0
0719   Assembly1(1).SubAssyPitch = 0
0720   Assembly1(1).SubAssyX = 0
0721   Assembly1(1).SubAssyY = 0
0722   Assembly1(1).SubAssyZ = 0
0723   Assembly1(2).Solid = zBOX              'arm swivel extensor (2 of 2)
0724   Assembly1(2).Level = zLEVEL1
0725   Assembly1(2).Color = zGREEN
0726   Assembly1(2).SizeX = Assembly1(0).SizeX / 4
0727   Assembly1(2).SizeY = Assembly1(0).SizeY
0728   Assembly1(2).SizeZ = 10
0729   Assembly1(2).Yaw = 0
0730   Assembly1(2).Roll = 0
0731   Assembly1(2).Pitch = 0
0732   Assembly1(2).PositionX = ((-1) * Assembly1(0).SizeX) +
          Assembly1(2).SizeX
0733   Assembly1(2).PositionY = Assembly1(0).PositionY
0734   Assembly1(2).PositionZ = (Assembly1(0).PositionZ +
          Assembly1(0).SizeZ) + Assembly1(2).SizeZ
0735   Assembly1(2).DeformRightX = 0
0736   Assembly1(2).DeformLeftX = 0
0737   Assembly1(2).DeformUpY = 0
0738   Assembly1(2).DeformDownY = 0
0739   Assembly1(2).PivotX = 0
0740   Assembly1(2).PivotY = 0
0741   Assembly1(2).PivotZ = 0
0742   Assembly1(2).SubAssyYaw = 0
```

```
0743   Assembly1(2).SubAssyRoll = 0
0744   Assembly1(2).SubAssyPitch = 0
0745   Assembly1(2).SubAssyX = 0
0746   Assembly1(2).SubAssyY = 0
0747   Assembly1(2).SubAssyZ = 0
0748   Assembly1(3).Solid = zHALFCYL        'arm swivel bracket (1 of 2)
0749   Assembly1(3).Level = zLEVEL1
0750   Assembly1(3).Color = zGREEN
0751   Assembly1(3).SizeX = Assembly1(0).SizeX
0752   Assembly1(3).SizeY = Assembly1(0).SizeY
0753   Assembly1(3).SizeZ = Assembly1(1).SizeX
0754   Assembly1(3).Yaw = 90
0755   Assembly1(3).Roll = 0
0756   Assembly1(3).Pitch = 0
0757   Assembly1(3).PositionX = Assembly1(1).PositionX
0758   Assembly1(3).PositionY = Assembly1(1).PositionY
0759   Assembly1(3).PositionZ = Assembly1(1).PositionZ +
           Assembly1(1).SizeZ
0760   Assembly1(3).DeformRightX = 0
0761   Assembly1(3).DeformLeftX = 0
0762   Assembly1(3).DeformUpY = 0
0763   Assembly1(3).DeformDownY = 0
0764   Assembly1(3).PivotX = 0
0765   Assembly1(3).PivotY = 0
0766   Assembly1(3).PivotZ = 0
0767   Assembly1(3).SubAssyYaw = 0
0768   Assembly1(3).SubAssyRoll = 0
0769   Assembly1(3).SubAssyPitch = 0
0770   Assembly1(3).SubAssyX = 0
0771   Assembly1(3).SubAssyY = 0
0772   Assembly1(3).SubAssyZ = 0
0773   Assembly1(4).Solid = zHALFCYL        'arm swivel bracket (2 of 2)
0774   Assembly1(4).Level = zLEVEL1
0775   Assembly1(4).Color = zGREEN
0776   Assembly1(4).SizeX = Assembly1(0).SizeX
0777   Assembly1(4).SizeY = Assembly1(0).SizeY
0778   Assembly1(4).SizeZ = Assembly1(2).SizeX
0779   Assembly1(4).Yaw = 90
0780   Assembly1(4).Roll = 0
0781   Assembly1(4).Pitch = 0
0782   Assembly1(4).PositionX = Assembly1(2).PositionX
0783   Assembly1(4).PositionY = Assembly1(2).PositionY
0784   Assembly1(4).PositionZ = Assembly1(2).PositionZ +
           Assembly1(2).SizeZ
0785   Assembly1(4).DeformRightX = 0
0786   Assembly1(4).DeformLeftX = 0
0787   Assembly1(4).DeformUpY = 0
0788   Assembly1(4).DeformDownY = 0
0789   Assembly1(4).PivotX = 0
0790   Assembly1(4).PivotY = 0
0791   Assembly1(4).PivotZ = 0
0792   Assembly1(4).SubAssyYaw = 0
0793   Assembly1(4).SubAssyRoll = 0
0794   Assembly1(4).SubAssyPitch = 0
0795   Assembly1(4).SubAssyX = 0
0796   Assembly1(4).SubAssyY = 0
```

```
0797    Assembly1(4).SubAssyZ = 0
0798    Assembly1(5).Solid = zCYLINDER                          'swivel pin (1)
0799    Assembly1(5).Level = zLEVEL1
0800    Assembly1(5).Color = zRED
0801    Assembly1(5).SizeX = 10
0802    Assembly1(5).SizeY = 10
0803    Assembly1(5).SizeZ = Assembly1(0).SizeX + 5
0804    Assembly1(5).Yaw = 90
0805    Assembly1(5).Roll = 0
0806    Assembly1(5).Pitch = 0
0807    Assembly1(5).PositionX = Assembly1(0).PositionX
0808    Assembly1(5).PositionY = Assembly1(3).PositionY
0809    Assembly1(5).PositionZ = Assembly1(3).PositionZ
0810    Assembly1(5).DeformRightX = 0
0811    Assembly1(5).DeformLeftX = 0
0812    Assembly1(5).DeformUpY = 0
0813    Assembly1(5).DeformDownY = 0
0814    Assembly1(5).PivotX = 0
0815    Assembly1(5).PivotY = 0
0816    Assembly1(5).PivotZ = 0
0817    Assembly1(5).SubAssyYaw = 0
0818    Assembly1(5).SubAssyRoll = 0
0819    Assembly1(5).SubAssyPitch = 0
0820    Assembly1(5).SubAssyX = 0
0821    Assembly1(5).SubAssyY = 0
0822    Assembly1(5).SubAssyZ = 0
0823    Assembly1(6).Solid = zHALFCYL              'wrist swivel bracket (1)
0824    Assembly1(6).Level = zLEVEL2
0825    Assembly1(6).Color = zBROWN
0826    Assembly1(6).SizeX = Assembly1(4).SizeX
0827    Assembly1(6).SizeY = Assembly1(4).SizeY
0828    Assembly1(6).SizeZ = Assembly1(4).SizeZ
0829    Assembly1(6).Yaw = 270                    'reorient half-cylinder
0830    Assembly1(6).Roll = 0
0831    Assembly1(6).Pitch = 0
0832    Assembly1(6).PositionX = Assembly1(5).PositionX
0833    Assembly1(6).PositionY = Assembly1(5).PositionY
0834    Assembly1(6).PositionZ = Assembly1(5).PositionZ
0835    Assembly1(6).DeformRightX = 0
0836    Assembly1(6).DeformLeftX = 0
0837    Assembly1(6).DeformUpY = 0
0838    Assembly1(6).DeformDownY = 0
0839    Assembly1(6).PivotX = 0
0840    Assembly1(6).PivotY = 0
0841    Assembly1(6).PivotZ = 0
0842    Assembly1(6).SubAssyYaw = 0
0843    Assembly1(6).SubAssyRoll = 0
0844    Assembly1(6).SubAssyPitch = 0
0845    Assembly1(6).SubAssyX = 0
0846    Assembly1(6).SubAssyY = 0
0847    Assembly1(6).SubAssyZ = 0
0848    Assembly1(7).Solid = zBOX                      'wrist extensor (1)
0849    Assembly1(7).Level = zLEVEL2
0850    Assembly1(7).Color = zBROWN
0851    Assembly1(7).SizeX = Assembly1(6).SizeZ
0852    Assembly1(7).SizeY = Assembly1(6).SizeX
0853    Assembly1(7).SizeZ = 30
0854    Assembly1(7).Yaw = 0
```

```
0855  Assembly1(7).Roll = 0
0856  Assembly1(7).Pitch = 0
0857  Assembly1(7).PositionX = Assembly1(6).PositionX
0858  Assembly1(7).PositionY = Assembly1(6).PositionY
0859  Assembly1(7).PositionZ = Assembly1(6).PositionX +
          Assembly1(7).SizeZ
0860  Assembly1(7).DeformRightX = 0
0861  Assembly1(7).DeformLeftX = 0
0862  Assembly1(7).DeformUpY = 0
0863  Assembly1(7).DeformDownY = 0
0864  Assembly1(7).PivotX = 0
0865  Assembly1(7).PivotY = 0
0866  Assembly1(7).PivotZ = 0
0867  Assembly1(7).SubAssyYaw = 0
0868  Assembly1(7).SubAssyRoll = 0
0869  Assembly1(7).SubAssyPitch = 0
0870  Assembly1(7).SubAssyX = 0
0871  Assembly1(7).SubAssyY = 0
0872  Assembly1(7).SubAssyZ = 0
0873  Assembly1(8).Solid = zHALFCYL            'wrist swivel bracket (1)
0874  Assembly1(8).Level = zLEVEL2
0875  Assembly1(8).Color = zBROWN
0876  Assembly1(8).SizeX = Assembly1(6).SizeX
0877  Assembly1(8).SizeY = Assembly1(6).SizeY
0878  Assembly1(8).SizeZ = Assembly1(6).SizeZ
0879  Assembly1(8).Yaw = 90
0880  Assembly1(8).Roll = 0
0881  Assembly1(8).Pitch = 0
0882  Assembly1(8).PositionX = Assembly1(7).PositionX
0883  Assembly1(8).PositionY = Assembly1(7).PositionY
0884  Assembly1(8).PositionZ = Assembly1(7).PositionZ
          + Assembly1(7).SizeZ
0885  Assembly1(8).DeformRightX = 0
0886  Assembly1(8).DeformLeftX = 0
0887  Assembly1(8).DeformUpY = 0
0888  Assembly1(8).DeformDownY = 0
0889  Assembly1(8).PivotX = 0
0890  Assembly1(8).PivotY = 0
0891  Assembly1(8).PivotZ = 0
0892  Assembly1(8).SubAssyYaw = 0
0893  Assembly1(8).SubAssyRoll = 0
0894  Assembly1(8).SubAssyPitch = 0
0895  Assembly1(8).SubAssyX = 0
0896  Assembly1(8).SubAssyY = 0
0897  Assembly1(8).SubAssyZ = 0
0898  Assembly1(9).Solid = zCYLINDER            'swivel pin (1)
0899  Assembly1(9).Level = zLEVEL2
0900  Assembly1(9).Color = zCYAN
0901  Assembly1(9).SizeX = Assembly1(5).SizeX
0902  Assembly1(9).SizeY = Assembly1(5).SizeY
0903  Assembly1(9).SizeZ = Assembly1(8).SizeZ + 15
0904  Assembly1(9).Yaw = 90
0905  Assembly1(9).Roll = 0
0906  Assembly1(9).Pitch = 0
0907  Assembly1(9).PositionX = Assembly1(8).PositionX
0908  Assembly1(9).PositionY = Assembly1(8).PositionY
```

```
0909  Assembly1(9).PositionZ = Assembly1(8).PositionZ
0910  Assembly1(9).DeformRightX = 0
0911  Assembly1(9).DeformLeftX = 0
0912  Assembly1(9).DeformUpY = 0
0913  Assembly1(9).DeformDownY = 0
0914  Assembly1(9).PivotX = 0
0915  Assembly1(9).PivotY = 0
0916  Assembly1(9).PivotZ = 0
0917  Assembly1(9).SubAssyYaw = 0
0918  Assembly1(9).SubAssyRoll = 0
0919  Assembly1(9).SubAssyPitch = 0
0920  Assembly1(9).SubAssyX = 0
0921  Assembly1(9).SubAssyY = 0
0922  Assembly1(9).SubAssyZ = 0
0923  '-------------- specify the path of the subassembly -------------
0924  Assembly1Path1.StartFrame = 1                'from frame 1 to...
0925  Assembly1Path1.EndFrame = 18                 '...frame 18...
0926  Assembly1Path1.ChgYaw = 0
0927  Assembly1Path1.ChgRoll = 0
0928  Assembly1Path1.ChgPitch = 3          '...raise subassembly 3 degrees
0929  '------------------ build and save the cels --------------------
0930  For LoopCount = 1 To zNUMCELS Step 1            'for each frame...
0931     FrameNum = LoopCount          'set a variable used by zDrawCel()
0932     FileName = FrameFiles(LoopCount - 1)      'set for zSaveFrame()
0933     zBuildFrame                               'build the frame
0934     If FrameSaved = False Then    'check variable set by zSaveFrame()
0935        Form1.Caption = "Animated 3D subassemblies" 'restore caption
0936        MsgBox "The animation build process has failed because an
              image could not be saved to disk.  Please check for
              insufficient disk space.", MB_OK, "Animation production report"
0937        Exit Sub               '...and cancel loop if error occurred
0938     End If
0939  Next LoopCount
0940  '-------------------- set tokens and tidy up --------------------
0941  Form1.Caption = "Animated 3D subassemblies"       'restore caption
0942  FrameNum = 1
0943  AnimationSaved = True
0944  PrevLoadAttempt = False
0945  zClear
0946  zClearHiddenFrame
0947  '-------------------- display advisory notice ------------------
0948  Beep
0949  MsgBox "Animation sequence successfully saved to disk.", MB_OK,
          "Animation ready"
0950  End Sub
0951
0952  '---------------------------------------------------------------
0953  '                 Pause the animation playback
0954  '---------------------------------------------------------------
0955  Sub IDM_StopAnimation_Click ()
0956  If AnimationLoaded = False Then
0957     MsgBox "You must load an animation sequence before you pause the
          animation.", MB_OK, "Animation not ready"
0958     Exit Sub
0959  End If
0960  If Pause = True Then
0961     Exit Sub
0962  End If
```

```
0963  zShowNextFrame            'cover the rect left by the menu's removal
0964  Pause = True
0965  zCopyToFrame              'copy to hidden-frame for refresh procedure
0966  End Sub
0967
0968  '-----------------------------------------------------------------
0969  '              Toggle to use fully-shaded 3D entities
0970  '-----------------------------------------------------------------
0971  Sub IDM_UseShaded_Click ()
0972  abzUseWireframeMode (False)         'call function in ENGINE3D.BAS
0973  MsgBox "Using shaded solids mode.", MB_OK, "Animation status
          report"
0974  End Sub
0975
0976  '-----------------------------------------------------------------
0977  '              Toggle to use wire-frame entities
0978  '-----------------------------------------------------------------
0979  Sub IDM_UseWireframe_Click ()
0980  abzUseWireframeMode (True)          'call function in ENGINE3D.BAS
0981  MsgBox "Using wireframe modeling mode.", MB_OK, "Animation status
          report"
0982  End Sub
0983
0984  '-----------------------------------------------------------------
0985  '              Determine version of Windows
0986  '-----------------------------------------------------------------
0987  Sub IDM_Version_Click ()
0988    Dim TempVar As Long
0989  TempVar = WindowsVersion And 7683  'test binary 00011110 00000011
0990  If TempVar = 7683 Then                        'if 30        3...
0991    MsgBox "Running under Windows version 3.3.", MB_OK, "Version
          report"
0992    Exit Sub
0993  End If
0994  TempVar = WindowsVersion And 5123  'test binary 00010100 00000011
0995  If TempVar = 5123 Then                        'if 20        3...
0996    MsgBox "Running under Windows version 3.2.", MB_OK, "Version
          report"
0997    Exit Sub
0998  End If
0999  TempVar = WindowsVersion And 2563  'test binary 00001010 00000011
1000  If TempVar = 2563 Then                        'if 10        3...
1001    MsgBox "Running under Windows version 3.1.", MB_OK, "Version
          report"
1002    Exit Sub
1003  End If
1004  TempVar = WindowsVersion And 3     'test binary 00000000 00000011
1005  If TempVar = 3 Then                           'if 00        3...
1006    MsgBox "Running under Windows version 3.0.", MB_OK, "Version
          report"
1007    Exit Sub
1008  End If
1009  TempVar = WindowsVersion And 4     'test binary 00000000 00000100
1010  If TempVar = 4 Then                           'if 00        4...
1011    MsgBox "Running under Windows version 4.0.", MB_OK, "Version
          report"
```

```
1012    Exit Sub
1013  End If
1014  MsgBox "Unable to report Windows version number.", MB_OK, "Version
          report"
1015  End Sub
1016
1017  '-----------------------------------------------------------------
1018  '          Pause to allow menu to pop up on slower machines
1019  '-----------------------------------------------------------------
1020  Sub POPUP_Edit_Click ()
1021  TimerCounter = zTIMER_PAUSE
1022  End Sub
1023
1024  '-----------------------------------------------------------------
1025  '          Pause to allow menu to pop up on slower machines
1026  '-----------------------------------------------------------------
1027  Sub POPUP_File_Click ()
1028  TimerCounter = zTIMER_PAUSE
1029  End Sub
1030
1031  '-----------------------------------------------------------------
1032  '          Pause to allow menu to pop up on slower machines
1033  '-----------------------------------------------------------------
1034  Sub POPUP_Run_Click ()
1035  TimerCounter = zTIMER_PAUSE
1036  End Sub
1037
1038  '-------------------------------------------------------------
1039  '              Set animation engine to reverse playback
1040  '-----------------------------------------------------------------
1041  Sub POPUP_RunReverse_Click ()
1042  If AnimationLoaded = False Then
1043    MsgBox "You must load an animation sequence before you run the
          animation.", MB_OK, "Animation not ready"
1044    Exit Sub
1045  End If
1046  Pause = False
1047  FrameDirection = zREVERSE
1048  zShowNextFrame
1049  End Sub
1050
1051  '-----------------------------------------------------------------
1052  '          Pause to allow menu to pop up on slower machines
1053  '-----------------------------------------------------------------
1054  Sub POPUP_Timer_Click ()
1055  TimerCounter = zTIMER_PAUSE
1056  End Sub
1057
1058  '-----------------------------------------------------------------
1059  '          Pause to allow menu to pop up on slower machines
1060  '-----------------------------------------------------------------
1061  Sub POPUP_Using_Click ()
1062  TimerCounter = zTIMER_PAUSE
1063  End Sub
1064
1065  '-----------------------------------------------------------------
1066  '                    Manage incoming timer events
1067  '-----------------------------------------------------------------
```

```
1068  Sub TimerID1_Timer ()
1069  If Pause = True Then Exit Sub
1070  TimerCounter = TimerCounter - 1                'decrement counter
1071  If TimerCounter > 0 Then   'if pausing to allow menu to pop up...
1072    Exit Sub                            '...then exit this procedure
1073  End If
1074  TimerCounter = 0                    'otherwise, restore counter...
1075  zShowNextFrame                          '...and show the next frame
1076  End Sub
1077
1078  '----------------------------------------------------------------
1079  '                  Build one frame and save to disk
1080  '----------------------------------------------------------------
1081  Sub zBuildFrame ()
1082    Dim PrevFontClr As Long
1083    Dim PrevFontSize As Integer
1084  zClear                                  'clear the display window
1085  Form1.Caption = "Building frame " & FrameNum & "..." 'caption bar
1086  zDrawCel                                        'draw one frame
1087  '-------------- display the titles and captions -----------------
1088  PrevFontSize = Form1.FontSize           'remember current font size
1089  PrevFontClr = Form1.ForeColor         'remember current font color
1090  Form1.FontSize = 16                             'set the size
1091  Form1.ForeColor = RGB(0, 0, 0)                  'set the color
1092  Form1.FontTransparent = True     'use transparent font backgrounds
1093  Form1.CurrentX = 10                     'set the starting location...
1094  Form1.CurrentY = 6
1095  Form1.Print "A Lee Adams tutorial:"             'display text
1096  Form1.FontSize = 24                             'reset the size
1097  Form1.CurrentX = 8                      'reset the location...
1098  Form1.CurrentY = 24
1099  Form1.Print "3D subassembly"                    'display text
1100  Form1.FontSize = PrevFontSize                   'restore the size
1101  Form1.ForeColor = PrevFontClr                   'restore the color
1102  Form1.CurrentX = 10
1103  Form1.CurrentY = 214
1104  Form1.Print "Animation production timestamp"
1105  Form1.CurrentX = 10
1106  Form1.CurrentY = 228
1107  Form1.Print "Time:" & Time$ & " Date:" & Date$
1108  '-------------------- save frame to disk ----------------------
1109  zSaveFrame                              'save frame to disk
1110  End Sub
1111
1112  '----------------------------------------------------------------
1113  '                    Clear the display window
1114  '----------------------------------------------------------------
1115  Sub zClear ()
1116  RetVal = PatBlt(hDC, 0, 0, zFRAMEWIDE, zFRAMEHIGH, WHITENESS)
1117  End Sub
1118
1119  '----------------------------------------------------------------
1120  '                    Clear the hidden frame
1121  '----------------------------------------------------------------
1122  Sub zClearHiddenFrame ()
1123  If FrameReady = False Then
1124    Exit Sub
```

```
1125   End If
1126   RetVal = PatBlt(hFrameDC, 0, 0, zFRAMEWIDE, zFRAMEHIGH, WHITENESS)
1127   End Sub
1128
1129   '----------------------------------------------------------------
1130   '          Copy the hidden frame to the display window
1131   '----------------------------------------------------------------
1132   Sub zCopyToDisplay ()
1133   If FrameReady = False Then
1134     Exit Sub
1135   End If
1136   RetVal = BitBlt(hDC, 0, 0, zFRAMEWIDE, zFRAMEHIGH, hFrameDC, 0, 0,
          SRCCOPY)
1137   End Sub
1138
1139   '----------------------------------------------------------------
1140   '          Copy the display window to the hidden frame
1141   '----------------------------------------------------------------
1142   Sub zCopyToFrame ()
1143   If FrameReady = False Then
1144     Exit Sub
1145   End If
1146   RetVal = BitBlt(hFrameDC, 0, 0, zFRAMEWIDE, zFRAMEHIGH, hDC, 0, 0,
          SRCCOPY)
1147   End Sub
1148
1149   '----------------------------------------------------------------
1150   '               Draw one 3D cel and place on frame
1151   '----------------------------------------------------------------
1152   Sub zDrawCel ()                      'uses global variable FrameNum
1153     Dim PartID As Integer       'counter is used in the drawing loop
1154   Call bzSetHierarchyMode(True)         'enable hierarchy modeling
1155   '----------------------- update the actor ----------------------
1156   If FrameNum > Actor1Path1.StartFrame And FrameNum <=
          Actor1Path1.EndFrame Then
1157                     'if a frame num specified in the path struct...
1158     Actor1.PositionX = Actor1.PositionX + Actor1Path1.ChgPosX
1159     Actor1.PositionY = Actor1.PositionY + Actor1Path1.ChgPosY
1160     Actor1.PositionZ = Actor1.PositionZ + Actor1Path1.ChgPosZ
1161     Actor1.Yaw = Actor1.Yaw + Actor1Path1.ChgYaw
1162     Actor1.Roll = Actor1.Roll + Actor1Path1.ChgRoll
1163     Actor1.Pitch = Actor1.Pitch + Actor1Path1.ChgPitch
1164   End If
1165   Call dazSetSubjectLocation(Actor1.PositionX, Actor1.PositionY,
          Actor1.PositionZ)
1166   Call dbzSetSubjectAttitude(Actor1.Yaw, Actor1.Roll, Actor1.Pitch)
1167   '--------------- build actor, update subassembly ----------------
1168   For PartID = zROBOT_START To zROBOT_FINISH Step 1
1169                        'for each subobject in the assembly...
1170     Call ddzSetShadingColor(Assembly1(PartID).Color)     'set color
1171     Call dczSetSubjectSize(Assembly1(PartID).SizeX,
          Assembly1(PartID).SizeY, Assembly1(PartID).SizeZ)
1172     Call ezSetSubobjectAttitude(Assembly1(PartID).Yaw,
          Assembly1(PartID).Roll, Assembly1(PartID).Pitch)
1173     Call fzSetSubobjectLocation(Assembly1(PartID).PositionX,
          Assembly1(PartID).PositionY, Assembly1(PartID).PositionZ)
1174     If Assembly1(PartID).Level = zLEVEL1 Then          'if parent...
1175       Call czSetHierarchyLevel(zLEVEL1)
1176     ElseIf Assembly1(PartID).Level = zLEVEL2 Then     'if progeny...
```

```
1177    If FrameNum > Assembly1Path1.StartFrame And FrameNum <=
        Assembly1Path1.EndFrame Then
1178                                    '...raise the subassembly
1179      Assembly1(PartID).SubAssyYaw = Assembly1(PartID).SubAssyYaw
        + Assembly1Path1.ChgYaw
1180      Assembly1(PartID).SubAssyRoll =
        Assembly1(PartID).SubAssyRoll + Assembly1Path1.ChgRoll
1181      Assembly1(PartID).SubAssyPitch =
        Assembly1(PartID).SubAssyPitch + Assembly1Path1.ChgPitch
1182    ElseIf FrameNum > Assembly1Path1.EndFrame Then
1183                                    '...else lower the subassembly
1184      Assembly1(PartID).SubAssyYaw = Assembly1(PartID).SubAssyYaw
        - Assembly1Path1.ChgYaw
1185      Assembly1(PartID).SubAssyRoll =
        Assembly1(PartID).SubAssyRoll - Assembly1Path1.ChgRoll
1186      Assembly1(PartID).SubAssyPitch =
        Assembly1(PartID).SubAssyPitch - Assembly1Path1.ChgPitch
1187    End If
1188    Call jzSetSubAssyPivot(Assembly1(PartID).PivotX,
        Assembly1(PartID).PivotY, Assembly1(PartID).PivotZ)
1189    Call hzSetSubAssyRotation(Assembly1(PartID).SubAssyYaw,
        Assembly1(PartID).SubAssyRoll, Assembly1(PartID).SubAssyPitch)
1190    Call izSetSubAssyPosition(Assembly1(PartID).SubAssyX,
        Assembly1(PartID).SubAssyY, Assembly1(PartID).SubAssyZ)
1191    Call czSetHierarchyLevel(zLEVEL2)
1192  End If
1193  Select Case Assembly1(PartID).Solid          'render the subobject
1194    Case zBOX
1195      Call azDrawCube
1196    Case zSPHERE
1197      Call czDrawSphere
1198    Case zCYLINDER
1199      Call ezDrawCylinder
1200    Case zCONE
1201      Call izDrawCone
1202    Case zWEDGE
1203      Call kzDrawWedge
1204    Case zCURVE
1205      Call gzDrawCurve
1206    Case zHEMISPHERE
1207      Call mzDrawHemisphere
1208    Case zDEFORMBOX
1209      Call azDrawDeformBox(Assembly1(PartID).DeformRightX,
        Assembly1(PartID).DeformLeftX, Assembly1(PartID).DeformUpY,
        Assembly1(PartID).DeformDownY)
1210    Case zHALFCYL
1211      Call czDrawHalfCylinder
1212    Case zBULGE
1213      Call ezDrawBulge
1214    Case Else
1215      Call azDrawCube
1216  End Select
1217 Next PartID                      'end of subassembly rendering loop
1218 Call bzSetHierarchyMode(False)         'disable hierarchy modeling
1219 End Sub
```

```
1220
1221   '----------------------------------------------------------------
1222   '                  Initialize the animation system
1223   '----------------------------------------------------------------
1224   Sub zInitializeSystem ()
1225   If FrameReady = True Then              'if hidden frame already created
1226     Form_Paint                          'refresh screen if animation running
1227     Exit Sub
1228   End If
1229   Picture1.Visible = False                        'hide the picture box
1230   Picture1.Top = 0: Picture1.Left = 0                        'reposition
1231   Picture1.Width = 402: Picture1.Height = 302                    'resize
1232   RetLong = GlobalCompact(-1)           'maximize contiguous memory
1233   hFrameDC = CreateCompatibleDC(hDC)            'get a display-context
1234   hFrame = CreateCompatibleBitmap(hDC, zFRAMEWIDE, zFRAMEHIGH)
1235   If hFrame = Null Then                        'if error occurred
1236     MsgBox "Insufficient memory.  Hidden frame not created.  Close
            other Windows applications to free up more RAM.", MB_OK,
            "Animation fatal error"
1237     FrameReady = False
1238     Exit Sub
1239   End If
1240   hPrevFrame = SelectObject(hFrameDC, hFrame)    'select the bitmap
1241   FrameReady = True                            'set a global token
1242   zCopyToFrame
1243   TimerID1.Interval = wFrameRate            'set the timer interval
1244   TimerID1.Enabled = True                      'activate the timer
1245   TimerExists = True                            'set a token
1246   Pause = True
1247   End Sub
1248
```

```
0001   '----------------------------------------------------------------
0002   '     Frame animation routines for Visual Basic applications
0003   '----------------------------------------------------------------
0004   ' Source file:  ASPLAY.BAS
0005   ' Release version:  2.00                    Programmer:  Lee Adams
0006   ' Type:  Visual Basic module for Windows applications
0007   ' Output and features:  Provides routines to manage the authoring
0008   '   process and playback engine for interactive frame animation.
0009   ' Publication:  Contains material from Windcrest/McGraw-Hill
0010   '   book 4225 published by TAB BOOKS Div. of McGraw-Hill Inc.
0011   ' License:  As purchaser of the book you are granted a
0012   '   royalty-free license to distribute executable files
0013   '   generated uSing this code provided that you accept the
0014   '   conditions of the License Agreement and Limited Warranty
0015   '   described in the book and on the companion disk.  Government
0016   '   users:  This software and documentation are subject to
0017   '   restrictions set forth in The Rights in Technical Data and
0018   '   Computer Software clause at 252.227-7013 and elsewhere.
0019   '----------------------------------------------------------------
0020   '   (c) Copyright 1992-1993 Lee Adams.  All rights reserved.
0021   '         Lee Adams(tm) is a trademark of Lee Adams.
0022   '----------------------------------------------------------------
0023   '
0024   Option Explicit            'generate error if variable not declared
```

```
0025
0026  '----------------------------------------------------------------
0027  '                        Load a frame from disk
0028  '----------------------------------------------------------------
0029  Sub zLoadFrame ()                     'uses global variable FileName
0030  If FrameReady = False Then
0031    MsgBox "Hidden frame not ready.", MB_OK, "Animation error report"
0032    Exit Sub
0033  End If
0034  LoadingFrame = True                   'disable refresh procedure
0035  On Error GoTo LoadError:                  'enable error trapping
0036  Form1.Picture = LoadPicture(FileName)        'load .BMP image
0037  On Error GoTo 0                      'disable error trapping
0038  LoadingFrame = False                 'enable refresh procedure
0039  FrameLoaded = True
0040  '-------- select persistent bitmap, clear it, deselect it -------
0041  Form1.AutoRedraw = True
0042  RetVal = PatBlt(Form1.hDC, 0, 0, zFRAMEWIDE, zFRAMEHIGH, WHITENESS)
0043  Form1.AutoRedraw = False
0044  Exit Sub
0045  '------------------------ error-handler ----------------------
0046  LoadError:
0047    On Error GoTo 0
0048    LoadingFrame = False
0049    FrameLoaded = False
0050    Beep
0051    MsgBox "Unable to load the .BMP file.  Is system initialized?
            Does file exist on disk?", MB_OK, "Animation error report"
0052    Exit Sub
0053  End Sub
0054
0055  '----------------------------------------------------------------
0056  '                        Save a frame to disk
0057  '----------------------------------------------------------------
0058  Sub zSaveFrame ()                     'uses global variable FileName
0059    Dim ErrorOccurred As Integer
0060  ErrorOccurred = False                      'set default tokens...
0061  FrameSaved = False
0062  If FrameReady = False Then
0063    MsgBox "Hidden frame not ready.", MB_OK, "Animation error report"
0064    Exit Sub
0065  End If
0066  '------------- copy display window to picture box -------------
0067  RetVal = BitBlt(hFrameDC, 0, 0, zFRAMEWIDE, zFRAMEHIGH, Form1.hDC,
            0, 0, SRCCOPY)
0068  Form1.Picture1.Visible = True                'show the picture box
0069  Form1.Picture1.AutoRedraw = True       'activate persistent bitmap
0070  RetVal = BitBlt(Form1.Picture1.hDC, 0, 0, zFRAMEWIDE, zFRAMEHIGH,
            hFrameDC, 0, 0, SRCCOPY)
0071  Form1.Picture1.Picture = Form1.Picture1.Image     'copy to screen
0072  Form1.Picture1.AutoRedraw = False 'disable the persistent bitmap
0073  '--------------- save picture box image to disk ---------------
0074  On Error GoTo SaveError                    'enable error trapping
0075  SavePicture Form1.Picture1.Image, FileName  'save bitmap to disk
0076  On Error GoTo 0                       'disable error trapping
0077  Form1.Picture1.Visible = False              'hide the picture box
```

```
0078  RetVal = BitBlt(Form1.hDC, 0, 0, zFRAMEWIDE, zFRAMEHIGH, hFrameDC,
          0, 0, SRCCOPY)
0079  If ErrorOccurred = True Then                    'if disk error, exit
0080    Beep
0081    MsgBox "Unable to save the frame to disk as a .BMP file.
          Sufficient disk space?", MB_OK, "Animation error report"
0082    Exit Sub
0083  End If
0084  FrameSaved = True
0085  Exit Sub
0086  SaveError:                                'jump to here if disk error
0087    ErrorOccurred = True
0088  Resume
0089  End Sub
0090
0091  '-------------------------------------------------------------
0092  '                     Display the next frame
0093  '-------------------------------------------------------------
0094  Sub zShowNextFrame ()               'uses global variable FrameNum
0095  If UseDisk = True Then              'animate using memory or disk?
0096    GoTo DISK_PLAYBACK
0097  End If
0098  '------------- manage memory-based frame animation --------------
0099  MEMORY_PLAYBACK:
0100  If AnimationReady = False Then
0101    Exit Sub
0102  End If
0103  If AnimationLoaded = False Then
0104    Exit Sub
0105  End If
0106  If Redisplay = True Then
0107    GoTo DISPLAY_FRAME
0108  End If
0109  If Pause = True Then
0110    Exit Sub
0111  End If
0112  If FrameDirection = zFORWARD Then              'if a forward loop...
0113    FrameNum = FrameNum + 1              'increment the frame number
0114    If FrameNum > zFINALFRAME Then             'if at end of loop...
0115      FrameNum = zFIRSTFRAME                        '...wraparound
0116    End If
0117  End If
0118  If FrameDirection = zREVERSE Then              'if a reverse loop...
0119    FrameNum = FrameNum - 1              'decrement the frame number
0120    If FrameNum < zFIRSTFRAME Then             'but if at end of loop...
0121      FrameNum = zFINALFRAME                        '...wraparound
0122    End If
0123  End If
0124  DISPLAY_FRAME:          'select handle and copy frame to display...
0125  RetVal = SelectObject(hFDC, BitmapHandles(FrameNum - 1))
0126  RetVal = BitBlt(Form1.hDC, 0, 0, zFRAMEWIDE, zFRAMEHIGH, hFDC, 0,
          0, SRCCOPY)
0127  Exit Sub
0128  '------------- manage disk-based frame animation ---------------
0129  DISK_PLAYBACK:
0130  If AnimationHalted = True Then
0131    Exit Sub
0132  End If
```

```
0133  If Redisplay = True Then
0134    GoTo SAME_FRAME
0135  End If
0136  If Pause = True Then
0137    Exit Sub
0138  End If
0139  If FrameDirection = zFORWARD Then          'if a forward loop...
0140    FrameNum = FrameNum + 1
0141    If FrameNum > zFINALFRAME Then
0142      FrameNum = zFIRSTFRAME
0143    End If
0144  End If
0145  If FrameDirection = zREVERSE Then          'if a reverse loop...
0146    FrameNum = FrameNum - 1
0147    If FrameNum < zFIRSTFRAME Then
0148      FrameNum = zFINALFRAME
0149    End If
0150  End If
0151  SAME_FRAME:
0152  FileName = FrameFiles(FrameNum - 1)
0153  zLoadFrame
0154  If FrameLoaded = False Then                'if an error occurred...
0155    AnimationHalted = True
0156    Beep
0157    MsgBox "Unable to load next frame from disk.  Animation
         halted.", MB_OK, "Animation error report"
0158    Exit Sub
0159  End If
0160  RetVal = BitBlt(Form1.hDC, 0, 0, zFRAMEWIDE, zFRAMEHIGH, hFrameDC,
         0, 0, SRCCOPY)
0161  End Sub
0162
```

C-5 Source listings for the interactive, animated forward kinematics editor, kinematx. See Appendix B for the toolkits which must be used to build this application. See Appendix A for instructions on building the demo.

```
0001  KIGLOBAL.BAS
0002  KIMAIN.BAS
0003  ENGINE3D.BAS
0004  LIGHTS3D.BAS
0005  ASSEMB3D.BAS
0006  SHAPES3D.BAS
0007  DEFORM3D.BAS
0008  KIPLAY.BAS
0009  KNMATX3D.BAS
0010  KINEMATX.FRM
0011  ProjWinSize=83,428,196,336
0012  ProjWinShow=2
```

```
0001  '-----------------------------------------------------------------
0002  '  Reusable global module for Visual Basic graphics applications
0003  '               that call Windows API functions.
0004  '-----------------------------------------------------------------
0005  '  Source file:  KIGLOBAL.BAS
```

```
0006   ' Release version:  1.00                    Programmer:  Lee Adams
0007   ' Type:  Visual Basic global module for Windows applications.
0008   ' Compiler:  Microsoft Visual Basic 2.00
0009   ' Dependencies:  KINEMATX.FRM primary module
0010   '                KIMAIN.BAS module containing Main()
0011   '                KIPLAY.BAS animatin playback module
0012   ' Output and features:  Provides declarations for Windows API
0013   '    (Application Programming Interface) functions callable by
0014   '    Visual Basic applications at runtime, including routines
0015   '    from Windows' GDI, USER, and KERNEL DLLs (dynamic link
0016   '    libraries).  Also provides declarations of various variables
0017   '    and constants.  Functions, variables, and constants declared
0018   '    in this global module are visible throughout the project.
0019   ' Publication:  Contains material from Windcrest/McGraw-Hill
0020   '    book 4225 published by TAB BOOKS Div. of McGraw-Hill Inc.
0021   ' License:  As purchaser of the book you are granted a
0022   '    royalty-free license to distribute executable files
0023   '    generated using this code provided that you accept the
0024   '    conditions of the License Agreement and Limited Warranty
0025   '    described in the book and on the companion disk.  Government
0026   '    users:  This software and documentation are subject to
0027   '    restrictions set forth in The Rights in Technical Data and
0028   '    Computer Software clause at 252.227-7013 and elsewhere.
0029   '-----------------------------------------------------------------
0030   '       (c) Copyright 1993 Lee Adams.  All rights reserved.
0031   '          Lee Adams(tm) is a trademark of Lee Adams.
0032   '-----------------------------------------------------------------
0033
0034   Option Explicit          'generate error if variable not declared
0035   '-----------------------------------------------------------------
0036   '            General constants and variables
0037   '-----------------------------------------------------------------
0038   Global Const MB_OK = 0                   'OK button for message box
0039   Global Const MB_OKCANCEL = 1   'OK Cancel buttons for message box
0040   Global Const MB_YESNO = 4        'Yes No buttons for message box
0041   Global Const IDOK = 1                       'OK button selected
0042   Global Const IDCANCEL = 2               'Cancel button selected
0043   Global Const IDYES = 6                     'Yes button selected
0044   Global Const IDNO = 7                       'No button selected
0045   Global UserWants As Integer      'value returned by message box
0046   Global Const PIXELS = 3                      'pixel coordinates
0047   Global StartUp As Integer               'tracks the startup code
0048   Global IgnoreRefresh As Integer        'tracks refresh activity
0049   Global Const zRED = 1
0050   Global Const zGREEN = 2
0051   Global Const zBROWN = 3
0052   Global Const zBLUE = 4
0053   Global Const zMAGENTA = 5
0054   Global Const zCYAN = 6
0055   Global Const zGRAY = 7
0056
0057   '-----------------------------------------------------------------
0058   '                  Window specifications
0059   '-----------------------------------------------------------------
0060   Global Const zWINDOW_WIDTH = 264                  'width of window
0061   Global Const zWINDOW_HEIGHT = 301                'height of window
0062   Global Const zFRAMEWIDE = 256               'width of client area
0063   Global Const zFRAMEHIGH = 255              'height of client area
```

C-5 Continued.

```
0064  Global HorizTwipsPixel As Single     'twips-per-pixel (horizontal)
0065  Global VertTwipsPixel As Single      'twips-per-pixel (vertical)
0066  Global Window_Width As Single        'runtime width of window
0067  Global Window_Height As Single       'runtime height of window
0068
0069  '-----------------------------------------------------------------
0070  '                    Runtime conditions
0071  '-----------------------------------------------------------------
0072  Global hDesktopWnd As Integer                    'handle to desktop
0073  Global hDCcaps As Integer             'display-context for desktop
0074  Global DisplayWidth As Integer       'horizontal screen resolution
0075  Global DisplayHeight As Integer        'vertical screen resolution
0076  Global DisplayBits As Integer          'number of bits-per-pixel
0077  Global DisplayPlanes As Integer           'number of bitplanes
0078  Global MemoryMode As Long                 'runtime memory mode
0079  Global RetVal As Integer           'will receive GDI return value
0080  Global RetLong As Long             'will receive GDI return value
0081  Global MousePresent As Integer                   'mouse active?
0082  Global WindowsVersion As Long           'version of Windows
0083  Global LoadingFrame As Integer             'loading an image?
0084  Global Preview As Integer           'displaying a preview image?
0085
0086  '-----------------------------------------------------------------
0087  '                    Hidden frame operations
0088  '-----------------------------------------------------------------
0089  Global hFrameDC As Integer         'display-context for hidden-frame
0090  Global hFrame As Integer              'handle to hidden-frame bitmap
0091  Global hPrevFrame As Integer          'default bitmap for hFrameDC
0092  Global FrameReady As Integer              'hidden-frame created?
0093
0094  '-----------------------------------------------------------------
0095  '                    Timer operations
0096  '-----------------------------------------------------------------
0097  Global Const zTIMER_PAUSE = 3                    'for slow machines
0098  Global TimerCounter As Integer             'for slow machines
0099  Global TimerExists As Integer              'timer activated?
0100
0101  '-----------------------------------------------------------------
0102  '                    Animation engine
0103  '-----------------------------------------------------------------
0104  Global Pause As Integer                       'animation running?
0105  Global wFrameRate As Long            'arbitrary rate of 18.2 fps
0106  Global Const zFORWARD = 1            'indicates forward animation
0107  Global Const zREVERSE = 0            'indicates reverse animation
0108  Global FrameDirection As Integer              'forward or reverse
0109  Global FrameNum As Integer                     'current frame
0110  Global Const zFIRSTFRAME = 1         'first frame of animation
0111  Global Const zFINALFRAME = 36        'final frame of animation
0112  Global Const zNUMCELS = 36           'number of cels in animation
0113  Global LoopCount As Integer                     'loop counter
0114  Global hFDC As Integer     'memory DC for hidden playback bitmaps
0115  Global hPrevF As Integer                'handle to default bitmap
0116  Global BitmapHandles(zNUMCELS)             'array of bitmap handles
0117  Global FrameFiles(zNUMCELS) As String * 9   'array of filenames
0118  Global Redisplay As Integer                'for paused refresh
0119
```

```
0120  '-------------------------------------------------------------------
0121  '                    Kinematics script
0122  '-------------------------------------------------------------------
0123  Global Const zNUM_ACTORS = 25   'max number of objects in database
0124  Type Header                              'data type for database header
0125    FPS As Double                                 'frames per second
0126    NumBodies As Integer                   'number of active objects
0127    FirstFrame As Integer                            'first frame
0128    FinalFrame As Integer                            'final frame
0129  End Type
0130  Type CameraDefine                        'data type for camera specs
0131    Heading As Integer                         'camera heading
0132    Pitch As Integer                             'camera pitch
0133    Distance As Integer              'distance from camera to target
0134  End Type
0135  Type CameraPath                          'data type for camera script
0136    StartFrame As Integer                          'start cue
0137    EndFrame As Integer                             'stop cue
0138    ChgHeading As Integer         'camera heading change per frame
0139    ChgPitch As Integer             'camera pitch change per frame
0140    ChgDistance As Integer      'camera-to-target dist chge per frame
0141  End Type
0142  Type LightDefine                         'data type for light-source specs
0143    Heading As Integer                        'light-source heading
0144    Elevation As Integer                       'light-source pitch
0145  End Type
0146  Type LightPath                           'data type for light-source script
0147    StartFrame As Integer                           'start cue
0148    EndFrame As Integer                             'stop cue
0149    ChgHeading As Integer     'light-source heading change per frame
0150    ChgElevation As Integer    'light-source pitch change per frame
0151  End Type
0152  Type ActorParams                    'data type for object specifications
0153    TypeOfSubobject As Integer     'box, cylinder, sphere, other...
0154    Color As Integer                              'shading color
0155    DimensionX As Double                          'dimensions...
0156    DimensionY As Double
0157    DimensionZ As Double
0158    LocationX As Double                             'location...
0159    LocationY As Double
0160    LocationZ As Double
0161    OrientationYaw As Double                     'orientation...
0162    OrientationRoll As Double
0163    OrientationPitch As Double
0164    LinearVelocityDirection As Double        'linear velocity...
0165    LinearVelocityPitch As Double
0166    LinearVelocitySpeed As Double
0167    RotationalVelocityYawSpeed As Double     'rotational velocity...
0168    RotationalVelocityRollSpeed As Double
0169    RotationalVelocityPitchSpeed As Double
0170    LinearAccelUnitsPerSecSqd As Double      'linear acceleration...
0171    LinearAccelSeconds As Double
0172    RotationalAccelYaw As Double          'rotational acceleration...
0173    RotationalAccelRoll As Double
0174    RotationalAccelPitch As Double
0175    RotationalAccelSeconds As Double
0176    HeadingChangeDegreesPerSec As Double     'velocity direction...
0177    HeadingChangeSeconds As Double
```

```
0178     PitchChangeDegreesPerSec As Double
0179     PitchChangeSeconds As Double
0180  End Type
0181  Type ScriptDatabase                    'data type for script database
0182                   'database of 25 bodies requires 5142 bytes storage
0183     Kinematics As Header                            '14-byte header
0184     Cam1 As CameraDefine              '6-byte camera specifications
0185     Cam1Path1 As CameraPath                    '10-byte camera path
0186     Lt1 As LightDefine         '4-byte light-source specifications
0187     Lt1Path1 As LightPath              '8-byte light-source path
0188     Actor(zNUM_ACTORS)  As ActorParams        '25 204-byte bodies
0189  End Type
0190  Global Script As ScriptDatabase               'a particular script
0191  Global ScriptFiles(5) As String * 12   'array of script filenames
0192  Global ScriptLoaded As Integer              'script file loaded?
0193  Global ScriptSaved As Integer                'script file saved?
0194  Global Const zBOX = 1                     'useful entity IDs...
0195  Global Const zSPHERE = 2
0196  Global Const zCYLINDER = 3
0197  Global Const zCONE = 4
0198  Global Const zWEDGE = 5
0199  Global Const zCURVE = 6
0200  Global Const zHEMISPHERE = 7
0201  Global Const zDEFORMBOX = 8
0202  Global Const zHALFCYL = 9
0203  Global Const zBULGE = 10
0204  Global Const zNULL = 11
0205  Global Const zVERTICAL = 0                  'useful pitch values...
0206  Global Const zHORIZONTAL = 90
0207  Global Const zNORTH = 0                   'useful heading values...
0208  Global Const zEAST = 90
0209  Global Const zSOUTH = 180
0210  Global Const zWEST = 270
0211  Global Const zBODY1 = 1                       'useful body IDs...
0212  Global Const zBODY2 = 2
0213  Global Const zBODY3 = 3
0214  Global Const zBODY4 = 4
0215  Global Const zBODY5 = 5
0216
0217  '----------------------------------------------------------------
0218  '                    Variables for disk I/O
0219  '----------------------------------------------------------------
0220  Global FileName As String              'name of binary image file
0221  Global FrameSaved As Integer               'frame saved to disk?
0222  Global FrameLoaded As Integer            'frame loaded from disk?
0223  Global AnimationSaved As Integer        'animation saved to disk?
0224  Global AnimationLoaded As Integer      'animation loaded from disk?
0225  Global AnimationReady As Integer     'animation ready for playback?
0226  Global PrevSaveAttempt As Integer      'previous save attempt made?
0227  Global PrevLoadAttempt As Integer      'previous load attempt made?
0228  Global UseDisk As Integer               'load each frame as needed?
0229  Global AnimationHalted As Integer    'disk error during animation?
0230
0231  '----------------------------------------------------------------
0232  '           Constants for Windows API functions
0233  '----------------------------------------------------------------
0234  Global Const SRCCOPY = &HCC0020                   'for bitblts...
```

```
0235  Global Const SRCINVERT = &H660046
0236  Global Const SRCPAINT = &HEE0086
0237  Global Const WHITENESS = &HFF0062
0238  Global Const BLACKNESS = &H42&
0239  Global Const ALTERNATE = 1                      'for filling...
0240  Global Const WINDING = 2
0241  Global Const R2_COPYPEN = 13                   'for pen mode...
0242  Global Const R2_XORPEN = 7
0243  Global Const TRANSPARENT = 1                'for background mode...
0244  Global Const OPAQUE = 2
0245  Global Const PS_SOLID = 0                       'for solid pen
0246  Global Const PS_NULL = 5                     'for transparent pen
0247  Global Const BLACKONWHITE = 1                'for bitblt scaling...
0248  Global Const WHITEONBLACK = 2
0249  Global Const COLORONCOLOR = 3
0250  Global Const HORZRES = 8                 'args for GetDeviceCaps()...
0251  Global Const VERTRES = 10
0252  Global Const BITSPIXEL = 12
0253  Global Const PLANES = 14
0254  Global Const SM_MOUSEPRESENT = 19            'for GetSystemMetrics()
0255  Global Const WF_ENHANCED = &H20               'for GetWinFlags()...
0256  Global Const WF_STANDARD = &H10
0257
0258  '----------------------------------------------------------------
0259  '            GDI functions for display-contexts
0260  '----------------------------------------------------------------
0261  Declare Function GetDC Lib "USER" (ByVal hWnd As Integer) As
          Integer
0262  Declare Function ReleaseDC Lib "USER" (ByVal hWnd As Integer,
          ByVal hDC As Integer) As Integer
0263
0264  '----------------------------------------------------------------
0265  '            GDI functions for the desktop
0266  '----------------------------------------------------------------
0267  Declare Function GetDesktopWindow Lib "USER" () As Integer
0268
0269  '----------------------------------------------------------------
0270  '        GDI functions for creating drawing objects
0271  '----------------------------------------------------------------
0272  Declare Function CreatePen Lib "GDI" (ByVal PenStyle As Integer,
          ByVal Wd As Integer, ByVal Color As Long) As Integer
0273  Declare Function CreateSolidBrush Lib "GDI" (ByVal Color As Long)
          As Integer
0274
0275  '----------------------------------------------------------------
0276  '            GDI functions for selecting objects
0277  '----------------------------------------------------------------
0278  Declare Function SelectObject Lib "GDI" (ByVal hDC As Integer,
          ByVal hObject As Integer) As Integer
0279  Declare Function DeleteObject Lib "GDI" (ByVal hObject As Integer)
          As Integer
0280
0281  '----------------------------------------------------------------
0282  '        GDI functions for bitmaps and bitblts
0283  '----------------------------------------------------------------
0284  Declare Function CreateCompatibleDC Lib "GDI" (ByVal hDC
          As Integer) As Integer
0285  Declare Function CreateCompatibleBitmap Lib "GDI" (ByVal hDC As
          Integer, ByVal Wd As Integer, ByVal Ht As Integer) As Integer
```

```
0286  Declare Function PatBlt Lib "GDI" (ByVal hDC As Integer, ByVal X
          As Integer, ByVal Y As Integer, ByVal Wd As Integer, ByVal Ht
          As Integer, ByVal RasOp As Long) As Integer
0287  Declare Function BitBlt Lib "GDI" (ByVal hDestDC As Integer, ByVal
          DestX As Integer, ByVal DestY As Integer, ByVal Wd As Integer,
          ByVal Ht As Integer, ByVal hSrcDC As Integer, ByVal SrcX As
          Integer, ByVal SrcY As Integer, ByVal RastOp As Long) As
          Integer
0288  Declare Function DeleteDC Lib "GDI" (ByVal hDC As Integer)
          As Integer
0289
0290  '------------------------------------------------------------------
0291  '         GDI functions for drawing mode operations
0292  '------------------------------------------------------------------
0293  Declare Function SetROP2 Lib "GDI" (ByVal hDC As Integer, ByVal
          RasMode As Integer) As Integer
0294  Declare Function SetBkColor Lib "GDI" (ByVal hDC As Integer, ByVal
          Color As Long) As Long
0295  Declare Function SetBkMode Lib "GDI" (ByVal hDC As Integer, ByVal
          BkMode As Integer) As Integer
0296  Declare Function SetPolyFillMode Lib "GDI" (ByVal hDC As Integer,
          ByVal PolyMode As Integer) As Integer
0297  Declare Function SetStretchBltMode Lib "GDI" (ByVal hDC As
          Integer, ByVal StretchMode As Integer) As Integer
0298
0299  '------------------------------------------------------------------
0300  '         GDI functions for drawing operations
0301  '------------------------------------------------------------------
0302  Declare Function MoveTo Lib "GDI" (ByVal hDC As Integer, ByVal X
          As Integer, ByVal Y As Integer) As Long
0303  Declare Function LineTo Lib "GDI" (ByVal hDC As Integer, ByVal X
          As Integer, ByVal Y As Integer) As Integer
0304  Declare Function Polygon Lib "GDI" (ByVal hDC As Integer, FirstPt
          As Integer, ByVal Count As Integer) As Integer
0305  Declare Function Rectangle Lib "GDI" (ByVal hDC As Integer, ByVal
          X1 As Integer, ByVal Y1 As Integer, ByVal X2 As Integer, ByVal
          Y2 As Integer) As Integer
0306  Declare Function Ellipse Lib "GDI" (ByVal hDC As Integer, ByVal X1
          As Integer, ByVal Y1 As Integer, ByVal X2 As Integer, ByVal Y2
          As Integer) As Integer
0307  Declare Function FloodFill Lib "GDI" (ByVal hDC As Integer, ByVal
          X As Integer, ByVal Y As Integer, ByVal Color As Long) As
          Integer
0308  Declare Function SetPixel Lib "GDI" (ByVal hDC As Integer, ByVal X
          As Integer, ByVal Y As Integer, ByVal Color As Long) As Long
0309  Declare Function GetPixel Lib "GDI" (ByVal hDC As Integer, ByVal X
          As Integer, ByVal Y As Integer) As Long
0310
0311  '------------------------------------------------------------------
0312  '         GDI functions for regions
0313  '------------------------------------------------------------------
0314  Declare Function PaintRgn Lib "GDI" (ByVal hDC As Integer, ByVal
          hRGN As Integer) As Integer
0315  Declare Function CreatePolygonRgn Lib "GDI" (FirstPt As Integer,
          ByVal Count As Integer, ByVal PolyFillMode As Integer) As
          Integer
```

```
0316   Declare Function PtInRegion Lib "GDI" (ByVal hRGN As Integer,
          ByVal xCoord As Integer, ByVal yCoord As Integer) As Integer
0317
0318   '----------------------------------------------------------------
0319   '   GDI, USER, KERNEL functions for various runtime conditions
0320   '----------------------------------------------------------------
0321   Declare Function GetDeviceCaps Lib "GDI" (ByVal hDC As Integer,
          ByVal Item As Integer) As Integer
0322   Declare Function GetWinFlags Lib "KERNEL" () As Long
0323   Declare Function GetSystemMetrics Lib "USER" (ByVal Item As
          Integer) As Integer
0324   Declare Function GlobalCompact Lib "KERNEL" (ByVal NumBytes As
          Long) As Long
0325   Declare Function GetVersion Lib "KERNEL" () As Long
0326   Declare Function ExitWindows Lib "USER" (ByVal Reserved As Long,
          ByVal Item As Integer) As Integer
0327   Declare Function SetCapture Lib "USER" (ByVal hWnd As Integer) As
          Integer
0328   Declare Sub ReleaseCapture Lib "USER" ()
0329
0330   '----------------------------------------------------------------
0331   '                    End of global module.
0332   '----------------------------------------------------------------
0333


0001   '----------------------------------------------------------------
0002   '              Reusable template for startup code for
0003   '              Visual Basic Windows graphics applications.
0004   '----------------------------------------------------------------
0005   '  Source file:  KIMAIN.BAS
0006   '  Release version:  1.00                 Programmer:  Lee Adams
0007   '  Type:  Visual Basic startup module for Windows applications.
0008   '  Compiler:  Microsoft Visual Basic 2.00
0009   '  Dependencies:  KIGLOBAL.BAS global module
0010   '                 KINEMATX.FRM primary module
0011   '                 KIPLAY.BAS animation playback module
0012   '  Output and features:  Initializes the runtime environment
0013   '    for a Windows graphics application created with
0014   '    Visual Basic.  Ensures runtime image size and compatibility
0015   '    no matter which graphics mode is being used by Windows.
0016   '  Publication:  Contains material from Windcrest/McGraw-Hill
0017   '    book 4225 published by TAB BOOKS Div. of McGraw-Hill Inc.
0018   '  License:  As purchaser of the book you are granted a
0019   '    royalty-free license to distribute executable files
0020   '    generated using this code provided that you accept the
0021   '    conditions of the License Agreement and Limited Warranty
0022   '    described in the book and on the companion disk.  Government
0023   '    users:  This software and documentation are subject to
0024   '    restrictions set forth in The Rights in Technical Data and
0025   '    Computer Software clause at 252.227-7013 and elsewhere.
0026   '----------------------------------------------------------------
0027   '      (c) Copyright 1993 Lee Adams.  All rights reserved.
0028   '         Lee Adams(tm) is a trademark of Lee Adams.
0029   '----------------------------------------------------------------
0030
0031   Option Explicit          'generate error if variable not declared
0032
```

```
0033   '------------------------------------------------------------------
0034   '        Initialization code for startup of application
0035   '------------------------------------------------------------------
0036   Sub Main ()                        'is called by Windows at startup
0037     Dim PreviousColor As Long          'will remember default color
0038   StartUp = True                       'set the run-time tokens...
0039   IgnoreRefresh = True
0040   FrameReady = False
0041   FrameSaved = False
0042   FrameLoaded = False
0043   LoadingFrame = False
0044   TimerExists = False
0045   Pause = True
0046   AnimationSaved = False
0047   AnimationLoaded = False
0048   PrevSaveAttempt = False
0049   PrevLoadAttempt = False
0050   UseDisk = False
0051   AnimationHalted = False
0052   Redisplay = False
0053   ScriptLoaded = False
0054   ScriptSaved = False
0055   Preview = False
0056   '-------------------- initialize variables --------------------
0057   TimerCounter = zTIMER_PAUSE
0058   wFrameRate = 55
0059   FrameDirection = zFORWARD
0060   FrameNum = 1
0061   FrameFiles(0) = "KTX01.BMP"      'initialize the array of filenames
0062   FrameFiles(1) = "KTX02.BMP"
0063   FrameFiles(2) = "KTX03.BMP"
0064   FrameFiles(3) = "KTX04.BMP"
0065   FrameFiles(4) = "KTX05.BMP"
0066   FrameFiles(5) = "KTX06.BMP"
0067   FrameFiles(6) = "KTX07.BMP"
0068   FrameFiles(7) = "KTX08.BMP"
0069   FrameFiles(8) = "KTX09.BMP"
0070   FrameFiles(9) = "KTX10.BMP"
0071   FrameFiles(10) = "KTX11.BMP"
0072   FrameFiles(11) = "KTX12.BMP"
0073   FrameFiles(12) = "KTX13.BMP"
0074   FrameFiles(13) = "KTX14.BMP"
0075   FrameFiles(14) = "KTX15.BMP"
0076   FrameFiles(15) = "KTX16.BMP"
0077   FrameFiles(16) = "KTX17.BMP"
0078   FrameFiles(17) = "KTX18.BMP"
0079   FrameFiles(18) = "KTX19.BMP"
0080   FrameFiles(19) = "KTX20.BMP"
0081   FrameFiles(20) = "KTX21.BMP"
0082   FrameFiles(21) = "KTX22.BMP"
0083   FrameFiles(22) = "KTX23.BMP"
0084   FrameFiles(23) = "KTX24.BMP"
0085   FrameFiles(24) = "KTX25.BMP"
0086   FrameFiles(25) = "KTX26.BMP"
0087   FrameFiles(26) = "KTX27.BMP"
0088   FrameFiles(27) = "KTX28.BMP"
```

```
0089   FrameFiles(28) = "KTX29.BMP"
0090   FrameFiles(29) = "KTX30.BMP"
0091   FrameFiles(30) = "KTX31.BMP"
0092   FrameFiles(31) = "KTX32.BMP"
0093   FrameFiles(32) = "KTX33.BMP"
0094   FrameFiles(33) = "KTX34.BMP"
0095   FrameFiles(34) = "KTX35.BMP"
0096   FrameFiles(35) = "KTX36.BMP"
0097   ScriptFiles(0) = "SCRIPT01.SCR"        'initialize script filenames
0098   ScriptFiles(1) = "SCRIPT02.SCR"
0099   ScriptFiles(2) = "SCRIPT03.SCR"
0100   ScriptFiles(3) = "SCRIPT04.SCR"
0101   ScriptFiles(4) = "SCRIPT05.SCR"
0102   '--------------- examine the graphics adapter ------------------
0103   hDesktopWnd = GetDesktopWindow()            'grab handle to desktop
0104   hDCcaps = GetDC(hDesktopWnd)        'get display-context for desktop
0105   DisplayWidth = GetDeviceCaps(hDCcaps, HORZRES)  'horiz resolution
0106   DisplayHeight = GetDeviceCaps(hDCcaps, VERTRES)  'vert resolution
0107   DisplayBits = GetDeviceCaps(hDCcaps, BITSPIXEL)  'bits-per-pixel
0108   DisplayPlanes = GetDeviceCaps(hDCcaps, PLANES)   'num of bitplanes
0109   RetVal = ReleaseDC(hDesktopWnd, hDCcaps) 'release display-context
0110   '--------------- determine the runtime memory mode --------------
0111   MemoryMode = GetWinFlags()           'will inspect this value later
0112   '--------------- determine version of Windows ------------------
0113   WindowsVersion = GetVersion()        'will inspect this value later
0114   '--------------- set mode-dependent twips factors --------------
0115   HorizTwipsPixel = 15!: VertTwipsPixel = 15!      'set defaults...
0116   Window_Width = zWINDOW_WIDTH: Window_Height = zWINDOW_HEIGHT
0117   If DisplayWidth = 640 Then
0118     If DisplayHeight = 480 Then               'VGA 640x480 mode
0119       HorizTwipsPixel = 15!               '9600x7200 twips full screen
0120       VertTwipsPixel = 15!
0121       Window_Width = zWINDOW_WIDTH
0122       Window_Height = zWINDOW_HEIGHT
0123     End If
0124     If DisplayHeight = 350 Then               'EGA 640x350 mode
0125       HorizTwipsPixel = 15!               '9600x7000 twips full screen
0126       VertTwipsPixel = 20!
0127       Window_Width = zWINDOW_WIDTH
0128       Window_Height = 297!   'adjust for aspect ratio and font size
0129     End If
0130     If DisplayHeight = 200 Then    'nominal support CGA 640x200 mode
0131       HorizTwipsPixel = 15!
0132       VertTwipsPixel = 36!
0133       Window_Width = zWINDOW_WIDTH
0134       Window_Height = zWINDOW_HEIGHT
0135     End If
0136   End If
0137   If DisplayWidth = 800 Then    'SuperVGA, 8514/A, XGA 800x600 mode
0138     HorizTwipsPixel = 12!               '9600x7200 twips full screen
0139     VertTwipsPixel = 12!
0140     Window_Width = zWINDOW_WIDTH
0141     Window_Height = 317!                     'compensate for font size
0142   End If
0143   If DisplayWidth = 1024 Then          '8514/A, XGA 1024x768 mode
0144     HorizTwipsPixel = 12!               '12200x9216 twips full screen
0145     VertTwipsPixel = 12!
0146     Window_Width = zWINDOW_WIDTH
```

```
0147      Window_Height = 317!                    'compensate for font size
0148    End If
0149    If DisplayWidth = 720 Then                'Hercules 720x348 mode
0150      HorizTwipsPixel = 12!
0151      VertTwipsPixel = 20!
0152      Window_Width = zWINDOW_WIDTH
0153      Window_Height = 297!      'adjust for aspect ratio and font size
0154    End If
0155    '------------- display the splash sign-on banner ---------------
0156    UserWants = MsgBox("Graphics demo from Windcrest McGraw-Hill book
            4225.", MB_OKCANCEL, "Copyright© 1993-1994 Lee Adams.")
0157    If UserWants = IDCANCEL Then    'if user selected Cancel button...
0158      End                                    'then cancel this startup
0159    End If
0160    '------------- initialize and display the window ----------------
0161    Form1.Width = Window_Width * HorizTwipsPixel          'set width
0162    Form1.Height = Window_Height * VertTwipsPixel         'set height
0163    Form1.Left = (Screen.Width - Form1.Width) / 2  'horizontal center
0164    Form1.Top = (Screen.Height - Form1.Height) / 2   'vertical center
0165    Form1.Caption = "Kinematics Editor"              'set the caption
0166    Form1.AutoRedraw = False                  'disable automatic refresh
0167    Form1.BackColor = RGB(255, 255, 255)    'set the client area color
0168    Form1.ForeColor = RGB(0, 0, 0)                   'active color
0169    Form1.ScaleMode = PIXELS                 'will use pixel coords
0170    Form1.Show                               'display the window
0171    '------------------ check if mouse present --------------------
0172    MousePresent = GetSystemMetrics(SM_MOUSEPRESENT)
0173    If MousePresent = 0 Then                          'if no mouse
0174      Beep
0175      MsgBox "No mouse found.  Some features of this demo program may
            require a mouse.  The demo's menu system also responds to the
            keyboard.  Press <Enter> to continue.", MB_OK, "Graphics
            system  warning"
0176    End If
0177    '----------------- initialize the 3D toolkit --------------------
0178    aazInitialize3D
0179    End Sub
0180

0001    VERSION 2.00
0002      Begin Form Form1
0003      Caption         =     "Prototype"
0004      ControlBox      =     0    'False
0005      Height          =     4515
0006      Left            =     2040
0007      LinkMode        =     1   'Source
0008      LinkTopic       =     "Form1"
0009      MaxButton       =     0    'False
0010      MinButton       =     0    'False
0011      ScaleHeight     =     3825
0012      ScaleWidth      =     3840
0013      Top             =     1485
0014      Width           =     3960
0015      Begin PictureBox Picture1
0016        Height          =     495
0017        Left            =     480
```

```
0018          ScaleHeight      =    465
0019          ScaleWidth       =    1185
0020          TabIndex         =    0
0021          Top              =    840
0022          Width            =    1215
0023     End
0024     Begin Timer TimerID1
0025          Left             =    1320
0026          Top              =    1680
0027     End
0028     Begin Menu POPUP_File
0029          Caption          =    "&File"
0030          Begin Menu IDM_New
0031               Caption          =    "&New"
0032               Enabled          =    0    'False
0033          End
0034          Begin Menu IDM_Open
0035               Caption          =    "&Open"
0036               Enabled          =    0    'False
0037          End
0038          Begin Menu IDM_Save
0039               Caption          =    "&Save"
0040               Enabled          =    0    'False
0041          End
0042          Begin Menu IDM_SaveAs
0043               Caption          =    "Save &As..."
0044               Enabled          =    0    'False
0045          End
0046          Begin Menu FileSep1
0047               Caption          =    "-"
0048          End
0049          Begin Menu IDM_Exit
0050               Caption          =    "E&xit..."
0051          End
0052          Begin Menu IDM_Restart
0053               Caption          =    "&Restart Windows..."
0054          End
0055     End
0056     Begin Menu POPUP_Edit
0057          Caption          =    "&Edit"
0058          Begin Menu IDM_Undo
0059               Caption          =    "&Undo"
0060               Enabled          =    0    'False
0061          End
0062          Begin Menu EditSep1
0063               Caption          =    "-"
0064          End
0065          Begin Menu IDM_Cut
0066               Caption          =    "Cu&t"
0067               Enabled          =    0    'False
0068          End
0069          Begin Menu IDM_Copy
0070               Caption          =    "&Copy"
0071               Enabled          =    0    'False
0072          End
0073          Begin Menu IDM_Paste
0074               Caption          =    "&Paste"
0075               Enabled          =    0    'False
```

```
0076        End
0077        Begin Menu IDM_Delete
0078            Caption       =   "&Delete"
0079            Enabled       =   0    'False
0080        End
0081    End
0082    Begin Menu POPUP_Run
0083        Caption        =   "&Run"
0084        Begin Menu IDM_LoadAnimation
0085            Caption       =   "&Load animation"
0086        End
0087        Begin Menu DemoSep1
0088            Caption       =   "-"
0089        End
0090        Begin Menu IDM_RunForward
0091            Caption       =   "Run &Forward"
0092        End
0093        Begin Menu POPUP_RunReverse
0094            Caption       =   "Run &Reverse"
0095        End
0096        Begin Menu IDM_StopAnimation
0097            Caption       =   "Free&zeframe"
0098        End
0099        Begin Menu POPUP_SetSpeed
0100            Caption       =   "S&et speed..."
0101            Begin Menu IDM_FPS182
0102                Caption      =   "&18 fps"
0103            End
0104            Begin Menu IDM_FPS91
0105                Caption      =   "&9 fps"
0106            End
0107            Begin Menu IDM_FPS61
0108                Caption      =   "&6 fps"
0109            End
0110            Begin Menu IDM_FPS45
0111                Caption      =   "&5 fps"
0112            End
0113            Begin Menu IDM_FPS36
0114                Caption      =   "&4 fps"
0115            End
0116            Begin Menu IDM_FPS30
0117                Caption      =   "&3 fps"
0118            End
0119        End
0120        Begin Menu DemoSep2
0121            Caption       =   "-"
0122        End
0123        Begin Menu IDM_Clear
0124            Caption       =   "&Clear Viewport"
0125        End
0126        Begin Menu DemoSep3
0127            Caption       =   "-"
0128        End
0129        Begin Menu POPUP_Production
0130            Caption       =   "&Production..."
0131            Begin Menu IDM_SaveAnimation
```

```
0132                    Caption          =   "&Build Animation"
0133            End
0134            Begin Menu DemoSep4
0135                    Caption          =   "-"
0136            End
0137            Begin Menu IDM_PreviewFirst
0138                    Caption          =   "Pre&view First Frame"
0139            End
0140            Begin Menu IDM_PreviewFinal
0141                    Caption          =   "Prev&iew Final Frame"
0142            End
0143            Begin Menu DemoSep5
0144                    Caption          =   "-"
0145            End
0146            Begin Menu IDM_UseShaded
0147                    Caption          =   "Use &shaded solids"
0148            End
0149            Begin Menu IDM_UseWireframe
0150                    Caption          =   "Use &wireframe mode"
0151            End
0152        End
0153        Begin Menu POPUP_Scripts
0154            Caption          =   "&Scripts..."
0155            Begin Menu IDM_SaveScript1
0156                    Caption          =   "Save Script &1"
0157            End
0158            Begin Menu IDM_SaveScript2
0159                    Caption          =   "Save Script &2"
0160            End
0161            Begin Menu IDM_SaveScript3
0162                    Caption          =   "Save Script &3"
0163            End
0164            Begin Menu IDM_SaveScript4
0165                    Caption          =   "Save Script &4"
0166            End
0167            Begin Menu IDM_SaveScript5
0168                    Caption          =   "Save Script &5"
0169            End
0170            Begin Menu DemoSep6
0171                    Caption          =   "-"
0172            End
0173            Begin Menu IDM_LoadScript1
0174                    Caption          =   "Load &Script 1"
0175            End
0176            Begin Menu IDM_LoadScript2
0177                    Caption          =   "Load S&cript 2"
0178            End
0179            Begin Menu IDM_LoadScript3
0180                    Caption          =   "Load Sc&ript 3"
0181            End
0182            Begin Menu IDM_LoadScript4
0183                    Caption          =   "Load Scr&ipt 4"
0184            End
0185            Begin Menu IDM_LoadScript5
0186                    Caption          =   "Load Scrip&t 5"
0187            End
0188        End
0189    End
```

C-5 Continued.

```
0190     Begin Menu POPUP_Use
0191        Caption          =   "&Use"
0192        Begin Menu IDM_About
0193           Caption        =   "&About"
0194        End
0195        Begin Menu IDM_License
0196           Caption        =   "&License"
0197        End
0198        Begin Menu HelpSep1
0199           Caption        =   "-"
0200        End
0201        Begin Menu IDM_Display
0202           Caption        =   "&Resolution of display"
0203        End
0204        Begin Menu IDM_Colors
0205           Caption        =   "Available &colors"
0206        End
0207        Begin Menu IDM_Mode
0208           Caption        =   "&Memory mode"
0209        End
0210        Begin Menu IDM_Version
0211           Caption        =   "Windows &version"
0212        End
0213        Begin Menu HelpSep2
0214           Caption        =   "-"
0215        End
0216        Begin Menu IDM_GeneralHelp
0217           Caption        =   "&How to use"
0218        End
0219     End
0220  End
0221  '----------------------------------------------------------------
0222  '                   3D kinematics animation editor
0223  '----------------------------------------------------------------
0224  '   Source file:  KINEMATX.FRM
0225  '   Release version:  1.0                     Programmer:  Lee Adams
0226  '   Type:  Visual Basic global module for Windows applications.
0227  '   Compiler:  Microsoft Visual Basic 2.00
0228  '   Dependencies:  KIGLOBAL.BAS    global module
0229  '                  KIMAIN.BAS      module containing Main()
0230  '                  KIPLAY.BAS      animation playback module
0231  '                  ENGINE3D.BAS    3D toolkit
0232  '                  SHAPES3D.BAS    3D shapes toolkit
0233  '                  DEFORM3D.BAS    3D deformations toolkit
0234  '                  LIGHTS3D.BAS    light-source toolkit
0235  '                  ASSEMB3D.BAS    hierarchical modeling toolkit
0236  '                  KNMATX3D.BAS    kinematics toolkit
0237  '   Output and features:  Demonstrates kinematics-based control of
0238  '      for animation sequences and storage of frames on disk.
0239  '      Demonstrates loading of frames from disk and interactive
0240  '      playback of animation sequence from RAM or from disk if
0241  '      insufficient memory available.  The startup code
0242  '      automatically sizes the window to yield a client area with
0243  '      dimensions of 256-by-255 pixels in any graphics mode.  The
0244  '      menu system provides a preview mode for the first frame and
0245  '      final frame of the kinematics simulation sequence.  You can
```

```
0246  '     toggle between wireframe and shaded modes.
0247  '        NUMBER OF FRAMES:  In its current implementation, the
0248  '     application produces an animation sequence of 36 frames.
0249  '     To create a sequence that uses fewer frames or more frames,
0250  '     you can edit the values of the zFINALFRAME and zNUMCELS
0251  '     constants defined in the ANGLOBAL.BAS global module.  You'll
0252  '     also need to add or delete filename strings to the array
0253  '     named FrameFiles() in the ANMAIN.BAS module.
0254  '        KINEMATICS EDITING:  To experiment with kinematics by
0255  '     manipulating camera position, light-source, and 3D bodies,
0256  '     edit the kinematics description in zInitializeModel().  Then
0257  '     compile and run the program so you can choose Save Script
0258  '     from the Script... submenu of the Run menu to save your
0259  '     script to disk.  See the book for further guidance.
0260  '  Publication:  Contains material from Windcrest/McGraw-Hill
0261  '     book 4225 published by TAB BOOKS Div. of McGraw-Hill Inc.
0262  '  License:  As purchaser of the book you are granted a
0263  '     royalty-free license to distribute executable files
0264  '     generated using this code provided that you accept the
0265  '     conditions of the License Agreement and Limited Warranty
0266  '     described in the book and on the companion disk.  Government
0267  '     users:  This software and documentation are subject to
0268  '     restrictions set forth in The Rights in Technical Data and
0269  '     Computer Software clause at 252.227-7013 and elsewhere.
0270  '-------------------------------------------------------------
0271  '      (c) Copyright 1993 Lee Adams.  All rights reserved.
0272  '          Lee Adams(tm) is a trademark of Lee Adams.
0273  '- -----------------------------------------------------------
0274  '
0275  '  SELECT A STARTUP FORM:
0276  '  Because this Visual Basic application uses a procedure named
0277  '  Main() at startup, you must specify Sub Main as the startup
0278  '  form in the Project Options dialog box before you run the
0279  '  program and before you build an .exe file.
0280  '
0281  '  DOUBLE-CLICK THE TIMER TOOL:
0282  '  Because the program uses a timer to manage the animation
0283  '  playback, you must double-click on the timer tool in the
0284  '  toolbox at design-time to place a timer control on the form.
0285  '  Specify TimerID1 as the timer's CtlName.
0286  '
0287  '  DOUBLE-CLICK THE PICTURE-BOX TOOL:
0288  '  Because this demo uses a picture box when saving images to
0289  '  disk as .BMP files, you must double-click the Picture Box
0290  '  tool in the Toolbox at design-time to place a default-sized
0291  '  picture box on the form.
0292  '
0293  '-----------------=-    -------------------------------------
0294
0295  Option Explicit           'generate error if variable not declared
0296
0297  '-------------------------------------------------------------
0298  '      Low-level keyboard handler for single-step animation
0299  '-------------------------------------------------------------
0300  Sub Form_KeyDown (KeyCode As Integer, Shift As Integer)
0301  If Pause = False Then                  'if animation is running...
0302    Exit Sub                             'then cancel this function
0303  End If
```

```
0304   If AnimationLoaded = False Then     'if animation is not loaded...
0305     Exit Sub                            'then cancel this function
0306   End If
0307   If FrameReady = False Then        'if hidden frame is not ready...
0308     Exit Sub                            'then cancel this function
0309   End If
0310   If KeyCode = &H25 Then    'if left arrow key has been pressed...
0311     FrameDirection = zREVERSE              'reset direction token
0312     Pause = False                      'toggle off the Pause token
0313     zShowNextFrame                              'show next frame
0314     Pause = True                        'toggle on the Pause token
0315     Exit Sub                                            'return
0316   End If
0317   If KeyCode = &H27 Then    'if right arrow key has been pressed...
0318     FrameDirection = zFORWARD
0319     Pause = False
0320     zShowNextFrame
0321     Pause = True
0322     Exit Sub
0323   End If
0324   End Sub
0325
0326   '----------------------------------------------------------------
0327   '              Refresh the client area if uncovered
0328   '----------------------------------------------------------------
0329   Sub Form_Paint ()    'is automatically called by Windows as needed
0330   If LoadingFrame = True Then    'special case LoadPicture function
0331     Exit Sub
0332   End If
0333   If Preview = True Then                  'if previewing a frame...
0334     zCopyToDisplay
0335     Exit Sub
0336   End If
0337   If Pause = True Then          'if paused, redisplay current frame
0338     Redisplay = True
0339     zShowNextFrame
0340     Redisplay = False
0341     Exit Sub
0342   End If
0343   zShowNextFrame        '...else show the next frame in the animation
0344   End Sub
0345
0346   '----------------------------------------------------------------
0347   '              Intercept any attempt to resize the window
0348   '----------------------------------------------------------------
0349   Sub Form_Resize ()        'is called twice when window is resized
0350   If Startup = True Then   'if window being displayed for first time
0351     Startup = False
0352     IgnoreRefresh = True
0353     Exit Sub
0354   End If
0355   Form1.WindowState = 0                        'reset normal size
0356   Form1.Width = Window_Width * HorizTwipsPixel        'reset width
0357   Form1.Height = Window_Height * VertTwipsPixel      'reset height
0358   Form1.Left = (Screen.Width - Form1.Width) / 2 'horizontal center
0359   Form1.Top = (Screen.Height - Form1.Height) / 2  'vertical center
0360   If IgnoreRefresh = False Then                    'if second call
```

```
0361    IgnoreRefresh = True              'reset token for next first call
0362    MsgBox "This demo uses a fixed-size window.", MB_OK, "Sample
           application"
0363    Exit Sub
0364  End If
0365  Form1.Refresh                      'refresh the client area
0366  IgnoreRefresh = False       'if first call, reset for second call
0367  End Sub
0368
0369  '-------------------------------------------------------------------
0370  '               Display the About message box
0371  '-------------------------------------------------------------------
0372  Sub IDM_About_Click ()
0373  MsgBox "This is a demo from Windcrest McGraw-Hill book 4225.
           Copyright© 1993 Lee Adams.  All rights reserved.", MB_OK,
           "About this Visual Basic program"
0374  End Sub
0375
0376  '-------------------------------------------------------------------
0377  '              Clear the client area of the window
0378  '-------------------------------------------------------------------
0379  Sub IDM_Clear_Click ()
0380  Preview = False               'reset token to disable refreshing
0381  zClear                               'clear the display window
0382  zClearHiddenFrame                    'clear the hidden frame
0383  End Sub
0384
0385  '-------------------------------------------------------------------
0386  '             Determine number of available colors
0387  '-------------------------------------------------------------------
0388  Sub IDM_Colors_Click ()
0389  If DisplayBits = 1 Then                  'if 1 bit-per-pixel...
0390    If DisplayPlanes = 4 Then                'if 4 bitplanes...
0391      MsgBox "Running in 4-bit, 16-color mode.", MB_OK, "Available
             colors"
0392      Exit Sub
0393    End If
0394    If DisplayPlanes = 1 Then                'if 1 bitplane...
0395      MsgBox "Running in 1-bit, 2-color mode.", MB_OK, "Available
             colors"
0396      Exit Sub
0397    End If
0398  End If
0399  If DisplayBits = 8 Then                  'if 8 bits-per-pixel...
0400    MsgBox "Running in 8-bit, 256-color mode.", MB_OK, "Available
           colors"
0401    Exit Sub
0402  End If
0403  If DisplayBits = 16 Then                 'if 16 bits-per-pixel...
0404    MsgBox "Running in 16-bit, 65000-color mode.", MB_OK, "Available
           colors"
0405    Exit Sub
0406  End If
0407  MsgBox "Running in a custom color mode.", MB_OK, "Available colors"
0408  End Sub
0409
0410  '-------------------------------------------------------------------
0411  '              Determine the screen resolution
0412  '  -----------------------------------------------------------------
```

```
0413  Sub IDM_Display_Click ()
0414  If DisplayWidth = 640 Then
0415    If DisplayHeight = 480 Then                              'VGA mode
0416      MsgBox "Running in 640x480 mode.", MB_OK, "Screen resolution"
0417      Exit Sub
0418    End If
0419    If DisplayHeight = 350 Then                              'EGA mode
0420      MsgBox "Running in 640x350 mode.", MB_OK, "Screen resolution"
0421      Exit Sub
0422    End If
0423    If DisplayHeight = 200 Then                              'CGA mode
0424      MsgBox "Running in 640x200 mode.", MB_OK, "Screen resolution"
0425      Exit Sub
0426    End If
0427  End If
0428  If DisplayWidth = 800 Then             'SuperVGA, 8514/A, XGA mode
0429    MsgBox "Running in 800x600 mode.", MB_OK, "Screen resolution"
0430    Exit Sub
0431  End If
0432  If DisplayWidth = 1024 Then                    '8514/A, XGA mode
0433    MsgBox "Running in 1024x768 mode.", MB_OK, "Screen resolution"
0434    Exit Sub
0435  End If
0436  If DisplayWidth = 720 Then                              'Hercules mode
0437    MsgBox "Running in 720x348 mode.", MB_OK, "Screen resolution"
0438    Exit Sub
0439  End If
0440  MsgBox "Running in custom mode.", MB_OK, "Screen resolution"
0441  End Sub
0442
0443  '-----------------------------------------------------------------
0444  '                     Terminate the application
0445  '-----------------------------------------------------------------
0446  Sub IDM_Exit_Click ()
0447  UserWants = MsgBox("Exit the demo and return to Windows?",
          MB_YESNO, "Please confirm")
0448  If UserWants = IDNO Then              'if user selected No button...
0449    Exit Sub                               'then cancel this operation
0450  End If        'otherwise continue to terminate the application...
0451  If AnimationLoaded = True Then               'if animation loaded...
0452    RetVal = SelectObject(hFDC, hPrevF)        'select default handle
0453    For LoopCount = 1 To zNUMCELS Step 1        'for each handle...
0454      RetVal = DeleteObject(BitmapHandles(LoopCount - 1))   'delete
0455    Next LoopCount
0456    RetVal = DeleteDC(hFDC)   '...then delete memory display-context
0457  End If
0458  TimerID1.Enabled = False                         'release the timer
0459  If FrameReady = True Then          'if a hidden frame was created
0460    RetVal = SelectObject(hFrameDC, hPrevFrame)     'deselect bitmap
0461    RetVal = DeleteObject(hFrame)                   'delete the bitmap
0462    RetVal = DeleteDC(hFrameDC)          'delete the display-context
0463  End If
0464  jczClose3d                              'shut down the 3D toolkit
0465  End                                     'terminate the application
0466  End Sub
0467
```

```
0468 '-----------------------------------------------------------------
0469 '                      Adjust the frame rate
0470 '-----------------------------------------------------------------
0471 Sub IDM_FPS182_Click ()
0472 If TimerExists = False Then
0473   MsgBox "A timer must be activated before you can reset the frame
         rate.", MB_OK, "Animation not ready"
0474 End If
0475 TimerID1.Interval = 55                        '18 frames per second
0476 End Sub
0477
0478 '-----------------------------------------------------------------
0479 '                      Adjust the frame rate
0480 '-----------------------------------------------------------------
0481 Sub IDM_FPS30_Click ()
0482 If TimerExists = False Then
0483   MsgBox "A timer must be activated before you can reset the frame
         rate.", MB_OK, "Animation not ready"
0484 End If
0485 TimerID1.Interval = 330                       '3 frames per second
0486 End Sub
0487
0488 '-----------------------------------------------------------------
0489 '                      Adjust the frame rate
0490 '-----------------------------------------------------------------
0491 Sub IDM_FPS36_Click ()
0492 If TimerExists = False Then
0493   MsgBox "A timer must be activated before you can reset the frame
         rate.", MB_OK, "Animation not ready"
0494 End If
0495 TimerID1.Interval = 275                       '4 frames per second
0496 End Sub
0497
0498 '-----------------------------------------------------------------
0499 '                      Adjust the frame rate
0500 '-----------------------------------------------------------------
0501 Sub IDM_FPS45_Click ()
0502 If TimerExists = False Then
0503   MsgBox "A timer must be activated before you can reset the frame
         rate.", MB_OK, "Animation not ready"
0504 End If
0505 TimerID1.Interval = 220                       '5 frames per second
0506 End Sub
0507
0508 '-----------------------------------------------------------------
0509 '                      Adjust the frame rate
0510 '-----------------------------------------------------------------
0511 Sub IDM_FPS61_Click ()
0512 If TimerExists = False Then
0513   MsgBox "A timer must be activated before you can reset the frame
         rate.", MB_OK, "Animation not ready"
0514 End If
0515 TimerID1.Interval = 165                       '6 frames per second
0516 End Sub
0517
0518 '-----------------------------------------------------------------
0519 '                      Adjust the frame rate
0520 '-----------------------------------------------------------------
```

```
0521   Sub IDM_FPS91_Click ()
0522   If TimerExists = False Then
0523     MsgBox "A timer must be activated before you can reset the frame
             rate.", MB_OK, "Animation not ready"
0524   End If
0525   TimerID1.Interval = 110                    '9 frames per second
0526   End Sub
0527
0528   '----------------------------------------------------------------
0529   '                   Display the Help message box
0530   '----------------------------------------------------------------
0531   Sub IDM_GeneralHelp_Click ()
0532   MsgBox "For kinematics playback pick Load Animation then Run
             Forward from the Run menu.  To build and save an animation,
             choose the Production submenu.  To build a kinematics
             sequence, see the book.", MB_OK, "How to use this kinematics
             demo"
0533   End Sub
0534
0535   '----------------------------------------------------------------
0536   '                   Display the License message box
0537   '----------------------------------------------------------------
0538   Sub IDM_License_Click ()
0539   MsgBox "You can use this code as part of your own software product
             subject to the License Agreement and Limited Warranty in
             Windcrest McGraw-Hill book 4225 and on its companion disk.",
             MB_OK, "License Agreement"
0540   End Sub
0541
0542   '----------------------------------------------------------------
0543   '             Load the animation sequence from disk
0544   '  If memory limitations prevent this procedure from loading the
0545   '  entire animation sequence into physical memory or virtual
0546   '  memory, the procedure sets a token to True.
0547   '  In that case the playback procedure zShowNextFrame() will load
0548   '  each frame from disk as required during animation playback,
0549   '  otherwise all frames are expected to be in RAM.
0550   '----------------------------------------------------------------
0551   Sub IDM_LoadAnimation_Click ()
0552     Dim Bitmaps As Integer
0553   Preview = False                'reset token to disable refreshing
0554   zInitializeSystem              'ensure system is initialized
0555   If AnimationLoaded = True Then     'if frames already loaded...
0556     Form_Paint                   'refresh screen if animation running
0557     Beep
0558     MsgBox "The kinematics sequence has already been loaded.",
             MB_OK, "Kinematics ready"
0559     Exit Sub
0560   End If
0561   If PrevLoadAttempt = True Then     'if previous attempt failed...
0562     Beep
0563     MsgBox "Previous attempt to load kinematics sequence failed.
             Cancelling this attempt.", MB_OK, "Kinematics error report"
0564     Exit Sub
0565   End If
0566   PrevLoadAttempt = True
0567   '--------------- create bitmaps to hold the frames --------------
```

```
0568  RetLong = GlobalCompact(-1)              'maximize contiguous memory
0569  hFDC = CreateCompatibleDC(Form1.hDC)          'create compatible DC
0570  For LoopCount = 1 To zNUMCELS Step 1              'for each frame...
0571    BitmapHandles(LoopCount - 1) = CreateCompatibleBitmap(Form1.hDC,
          zFRAMEWIDE, zFRAMEHIGH)
0572    If BitmapHandles(LoopCount - 1) = Null Then          'if error...
0573      GoTo BITMAPS_NOT_OK          '...jump out of loop and tidy up
0574    End If
0575  Next LoopCount
0576  GoTo BITMAPS_OK                    'if OK, jump past error-handler
0577  '-------------------- bitmap error-handler --------------------
0578  BITMAPS_NOT_OK:
0579  For Bitmaps = LoopCount - 1 To 1 Step -1     'for each bitmap...
0580    RetVal = DeleteObject(BitmapHandles(Bitmaps - 1)) '...delete it
0581  Next Bitmaps
0582  RetVal = DeleteDC(hFDC)               'delete the compatible DC
0583  UseDisk = True                       'reset run-time token
0584  AnimationReady = True                'reset run-time token
0585  MsgBox "Insufficient memory to load entire kinematics sequence from
          disk.  Software will load each frame as needed during
          playback.", MB_OK, "Animation advisory report"
0586  Exit Sub                          '...and return to caller
0587  BITMAPS_OK:                        'jump to here if no errors
0588  '--------------- load frame files into the bitmaps --------------
0589  For LoopCount = 1 To zNUMCELS Step 1              'for each frame...
0590    FileName = FrameFiles(LoopCount - 1)      'used by zLoadFrame()
0591    zLoadFrame                              '...and load the frame
0592    If FrameLoaded = False Then          'if disk error occurred...
0593      GoTo DISK_ERROR                    'jump to error-handler
0594    End If
0595    hPrevF = SelectObject(hFDC, BitmapHandles(LoopCount - 1))
0596    RetVal = BitBlt(hFDC, 0, 0, zFRAMEWIDE, zFRAMEHIGH, Form1.hDC,
          0, 0, SRCCOPY)
0597    RetVal = SelectObject(hFDC, hPrevF)
0598  Next LoopCount
0599  GoTo DISK_OK                   'if OK, jump past the error-handler
0600  '--------------------- disk error-handler ---------------------
0601  DISK_ERROR:
0602  For LoopCount = 1 To zNUMCELS Step 1     'for each bitmap handle...
0603    RetVal = DeleteObject(BitmapHandles(LoopCount - 1)) 'delete it
0604  Next LoopCount
0605  RetVal = DeleteDC(hFDC)       'delete the memory display-context...
0606  Exit Sub                          '...and return to caller
0607  '--------------------- tidy up and return ---------------------
0608  DISK_OK:
0609  hPrevF = SelectObject(hFDC, BitmapHandles(0))
0610  AnimationLoaded = True
0611  AnimationReady = True
0612  AnimationSaved = True
0613  zClear
0614  zClearHiddenFrame
0615  Beep
0616  MsgBox "Kinematics sequence successfully loaded from disk.",
          MB_OK, "Kinematics ready"
0617  End Sub
0618
0619  '--------------------------------------------------------------
0620  '                    Load script 1 from disk
0621  '--------------------------------------------------------------
```

```
0622  Sub IDM_LoadScript1_Click ()
0623  zLoadScript (ScriptFiles(0))
0624  End Sub
0625
0626  '-----------------------------------------------------------------
0627  '                    Load script 2 from disk
0628  '-----------------------------------------------------------------
0629  Sub IDM_LoadScript2_Click ()
0630  zLoadScript (ScriptFiles(1))
0631  End Sub
0632
0633  '-----------------------------------------------------------------
0634  '                    Load script 3 from disk
0635  '-----------------------------------------------------------------
0636  Sub IDM_LoadScript3_Click ()
0637  zLoadScript (ScriptFiles(2))
0638  End Sub
0639
0640  '-----------------------------------------------------------------
0641  '                    Load script 4 from disk
0642  '-----------------------------------------------------------------
0643  Sub IDM_LoadScript4_Click ()
0644  zLoadScript (ScriptFiles(3))
0645  End Sub
0646
0647  '-----------------------------------------------------------------
0648  '                    Load script 5 from disk
0649  '-----------------------------------------------------------------
0650  Sub IDM_LoadScript5_Click ()
0651  zLoadScript (ScriptFiles(4))
0652  End Sub
0653
0654  '-----------------------------------------------------------------
0655  '                 Determine runtime memory mode
0656  '-----------------------------------------------------------------
0657  Sub IDM_Mode_Click ()
0658    Dim TempVariable As Long
0659  TempVariable = MemoryMode And WF_ENHANCED     'perform bitwise AND
0660  If TempVariable = WF_ENHANCED Then     'if result matches constant
0661    MsgBox "Running in enhanced mode.  Can allocate up to 16 MB
          extended memory (XMS) if available.  Virtual memory up to 4
          times physical memory (maximum 64 MB) is also available via
          automatic disk swapping of 4K pages.", MB_OK, "Memory mode"
0662    Exit Sub
0663  End If
0664  TempVariable = MemoryMode And WF_STANDARD
0665  If TempVariable = WF_STANDARD Then
0666    MsgBox "Running in standard mode.  Can allocate up to 16 MB
          extended physical memory (XMS) if available.", MB_OK, "Memory
          mode"
0667    Exit Sub
0668  End If
0669  MsgBox "Running in real mode.  Can allocate blocks of memory from
          the first 640K of RAM.  Can also allocate blocks from expanded
          memory (EMS) if available.", MB_OK, "Memory mode"
0670  End Sub
0671
```

```
0672 '-------------------------------------------------------------------
0673 '            Preview the final frame of the animation.
0674 '-------------------------------------------------------------------
0675 Sub IDM_PreviewFinal_Click ()
0676 zInitializeSystem
0677 zClearHiddenFrame
0678 zClear
0679 Form1.CurrentX = 10
0680 Form1.CurrentY = 214
0681 Form1.Print "Preview of final frame..."
0682 Call jbzClearHidden3DPage
0683 Call kezResetZBuffer
0684 zInitializeModel                     'reset kinematics interface...
0685 Call bkmReset
0686 FrameNum = zNUMCELS
0687 zSelectPreviewFrame (zNUMCELS)
0688 Call ckmSelectPreviewFrame(zNUMCELS)
0689 zDrawCel                                         'draw the frame
0690 Form1.CurrentX = 10
0691 Form1.CurrentY = 228
0692 Form1.Print "Completed " & Time$ & " " & Date$
0693 If FrameReady = True Then                    'copy to backup page
0694    RetVal = BitBlt(hFrameDC, 0, 0, zFRAMEWIDE, zFRAMEHIGH,
           Form1.hDC, 0, 0, SRCCOPY)
0695 End If
0696 zInitializeModel                         'tidy up and return...
0697 Call bkmReset
0698 zCopyToDisplay
0699 Preview = True                 'set a token to enable refreshing
0700 End Sub
0701
0702 '-------------------------------------------------------------------
0703 '            Preview the first frame of the animation.
0704 '-------------------------------------------------------------------
0705 Sub IDM_PreviewFirst_Click ()
0706 zInitializeSystem
0707 zClearHiddenFrame
0708 zClear
0709 Form1.CurrentX = 10
0710 Form1.CurrentY = 214
0711 Form1.Print "Preview of frame 1..."
0712 Call jbzClearHidden3DPage
0713 Call kezResetZBuffer
0714 zInitializeModel                     'reset kinematics interface...
0715 Call bkmReset
0716 FrameNum = 1
0717 zDrawCel                                         'draw the frame
0718 Form1.CurrentX = 10
0719 Form1.CurrentY - 228
0720 Form1.Print "Completed " & Time$ & " " & Date$
0721 If FrameReady = True Then                    'copy to backup page
0722    RetVal = BitBlt(hFrameDC, 0, 0, zFRAMEWIDE, zFRAMEHIGH,
           Form1.hDC, 0, 0, SRCCOPY)
0723 End If
0724 zInitializeModel                         'tidy up and return...
0725 Call bkmReset
0726 zCopyToDisplay
0727 Preview = True                 'set a token to enable refreshing
0728 End Sub
```

C-5 Continued.

```
0729
0730  '------------------------------------------------------------------
0731  '          Terminate the application and restart Windows
0732  '------------------------------------------------------------------
0733  Sub IDM_Restart_Click ()
0734  UserWants = MsgBox("Exit the demo and restart Windows?", MB_YESNO,
           "Please confirm")
0735  If UserWants = IDNO Then            'if user selected No button...
0736    Exit Sub                          'then cancel this operation
0737  End If          'otherwise continue to terminate the application...
0738  If AnimationLoaded = True Then            'if animation loaded...
0739    RetVal = SelectObject(hFDC, hPrevF)      'select default handle
0740    For LoopCount = 1 To zNUMCELS Step 1        'for each handle...
0741      RetVal = DeleteObject(BitmapHandles(LoopCount - 1))    'delete
0742    Next LoopCount
0743    RetVal = DeleteDC(hFDC)   '...then delete memory display-context
0744  End If
0745  TimerID1.Enabled = False                    'release the timer
0746  If FrameReady = True Then          'if a hidden frame was created
0747    RetVal = SelectObject(hFrameDC, hPrevFrame)      'deselect bitmap
0748    RetVal = DeleteObject(hFrame)                   'delete the bitmap
0749    RetVal = DeleteDC(hFrameDC)          'delete the display-context
0750  End If
0751  jczClose3d                            'shut down the 3D toolkit
0752  RetVal = ExitWindows(&H42&, 0)    'terminate and restart Windows
0753  End                                'terminate the application
0754  End Sub
0755
0756  '------------------------------------------------------------------
0757  '          Set animation engine to forward playback
0758  '------------------------------------------------------------------
0759  Sub IDM_RunForward_Click ()
0760  If AnimationLoaded = False Then
0761    MsgBox "You must load a kinematics sequence before you run the
           animation.", MB_OK, "Kinematics not ready"
0762    Exit Sub
0763  End If
0764  Pause = False
0765  FrameDirection = zFORWARD
0766  zShowNextFrame
0767  End Sub
0768
0769  '------------------------------------------------------------------
0770  '          Create all frames and save to disk
0771  '------------------------------------------------------------------
0772  Sub IDM_SaveAnimation_Click ()
0773  Preview = False                  'reset token to disable refreshing
0774  zInitializeSystem                    'ensure system is initialized
0775  If AnimationSaved = True Then          'if animation already saved
0776    Form_Paint                  'refresh screen if animation running
0777    MsgBox "The kinematics sequence has already been saved to
           disk.", MB_OK, "Kinematics status report"
0778    Exit Sub
0779  End If
0780  If PrevSaveAttempt = True Then          'if previous attempt failed
0781    MsgBox "A previous attempt to save the kinematics sequence to
```

```
              disk has failed.  Cancelling this attempt.  Check available
              disk space.", MB_OK, "Kinematics error report"
0782    Exit Sub
0783  End If
0784  PrevSaveAttempt = True       'set token to prevent subsequent calls
0785  '------ initialize the camera, light-source, and kinematics -----
0786  zInitializeModel
0787  '----------------- build and save the cels --------------------
0788  For LoopCount = 1 To zNUMCELS Step 1              'for each frame...
0789    FrameNum = LoopCount           'set a variable used by zDrawCel()
0790    FileName = FrameFiles(LoopCount - 1)        'set for zSaveFrame()
0791    zBuildFrame                                   'build the frame
0792    If FrameSaved = False Then   'check variable set by zSaveFrame()
0793      Form1.Caption = "Kinematics Editor"           'restore caption
0794      MsgBox "The kinematics build process has failed because an
              image could not be saved to disk.  Please check for
              insufficient disk space.", MB_OK, "Kinematics production
              report"
0795      Exit Sub                  '...and cancel loop if error occurred
0796    End If
0797  Next LoopCount
0798  '-------------------- set tokens and tidy up --------------------
0799  Form1.Caption = "Kinematics Editor"                'restore caption
0800  FrameNum = 1
0801  AnimationSaved = True
0802  PrevLoadAttempt = False
0803  zClear
0804  zClearHiddenFrame
0805  '-------------------- display advisory notice ------------------
0806  Beep
0807  MsgBox "Kinematics sequence successfully saved to disk.", MB_OK,
              "Kinematics ready"
0808  End Sub
0809
0810  '----------------------------------------------------------------
0811  '                      Save script 1 to disk
0812  '----------------------------------------------------------------
0813  Sub IDM_SaveScript1_Click ()
0814  zSaveScript (ScriptFiles(0))
0815  End Sub
0816
0817  '----------------------------------------------------------------
0818  '                      Save script 2 to disk
0819  '----------------------------------------------------------------
0820  Sub IDM_SaveScript2_Click ()
0821  zSaveScript (ScriptFiles(1))
0822  End Sub
0823
0824  '----------------------------------------------------------------
0825  '                      Save script 3 to disk
0826  '----------------------------------------------------------------
0827  Sub IDM_SaveScript3_Click ()
0828  zSaveScript (ScriptFiles(2))
0829  End Sub
0830
0831  '----------------------------------------------------------------
0832  '                      Save script 4 to disk
0833  '----------------------------------------------------------------
```

```
0834    Sub IDM_SaveScript4_Click ()
0835    zSaveScript (ScriptFiles(3))
0836    End Sub
0837
0838    '-----------------------------------------------------------------
0839    '                     Save script 5 to disk
0840    '-----------------------------------------------------------------
0841    Sub IDM_SaveScript5_Click ()
0842    zSaveScript (ScriptFiles(4))
0843    End Sub
0844
0845    '-----------------------------------------------------------------
0846    '                  Pause the animation playback
0847    '-----------------------------------------------------------------
0848    Sub IDM_StopAnimation_Click ()
0849    If AnimationLoaded = False Then
0850      MsgBox "You must load a kinematics sequence before you pause the
              animation.", MB_OK, "Kinematics not ready"
0851      Exit Sub
0852    End If
0853    If Pause = True Then
0854      Exit Sub
0855    End If
0856    zShowNextFrame          'cover the rect left by the menu's removal
0857    Pause = True
0858    zCopyToFrame            'copy to hidden-frame for refresh procedure
0859    End Sub
0860
0861    '-----------------------------------------------------------------
0862    '             Toggle to use fully-shaded 3D entities
0863    '-----------------------------------------------------------------
0864    Sub IDM_UseShaded_Click ()
0865    abzUseWireframeMode (False)        'call function in ENGINE3D.BAS
0866    MsgBox "Using shaded solids mode.", MB_OK, "Kinematics status
              report"
0867    End Sub
0868
0869    '-----------------------------------------------------------------
0870    '               Toggle to use wire-frame entities
0871    '-----------------------------------------------------------------
0872    Sub IDM_UseWireframe_Click ()
0873    abzUseWireframeMode (True)         'call function in ENGINE3D.BAS
0874    MsgBox "Using wireframe modeling mode.", MB_OK, "Kinematics status
              report"
0875    End Sub
0876
0877    '-----------------------------------------------------------------
0878    '               Determine version of Windows
0879    '-----------------------------------------------------------------
0880    Sub IDM_Version_Click ()
0881      Dim TempVar As Long
0882    TempVar = WindowsVersion And 7683  'test binary 00011110 00000011
0883    If TempVar = 7683 Then                        'if 30        3...
0884      MsgBox "Running under Windows version 3.3.", MB_OK, "Version
              report"
0885      Exit Sub
```

```
0886  End If
0887  TempVar = WindowsVersion And 5123   'test binary 00010100 00000011
0888  If TempVar = 5123 Then                            'if 20         3...
0889    MsgBox "Running under Windows version 3.2.", MB_OK, "Version
            report"
0890    Exit Sub
0891  End If
0892  TempVar = WindowsVersion And 2563   'test binary 00001010 00000011
0893  If TempVar = 2563 Then                            'if 10         3...
0894    MsgBox "Running under Windows version 3.1.", MB_OK, "Version
            report"
0895    Exit Sub
0896  End If
0897  TempVar = WindowsVersion And 3      'test binary 00000000 00000011
0898  If TempVar = 3 Then                               'if 00         3...
0899    MsgBox "Running under Windows version 3.0.", MB_OK, "Version
            report"
0900    Exit Sub
0901  End If
0902  TempVar = WindowsVersion And 4      'test binary 00000000 00000100
0903  If TempVar = 4 Then                               'if 00         4...
0904    MsgBox "Running under Windows version 4.0.", MB_OK, "Version
            report"
0905    Exit Sub
0906  End If
0907  MsgBox "Unable to report Windows version number.", MB_OK, "Version
            report"
0908  End Sub
0909
0910  '----------------------------------------------------------------
0911  '       Pause to allow menu to pop up on slower machines
0912  '----------------------------------------------------------------
0913  Sub POPUP_Edit_Click ()
0914  TimerCounter = zTIMER_PAUSE
0915  End Sub
0916
0917  '----------------------------------------------------------------
0918  '       Pause to allow menu to pop up on slower machines
0919  '----------------------------------------------------------------
0920  Sub POPUP_File_Click ()
0921  TimerCounter = zTIMER_PAUSE
0922  End Sub
0923
0924  '----------------------------------------------------------------
0925  '       Pause to allow menu to pop up on slower machines
0926  '----------------------------------------------------------------
0927  Sub POPUP_Run_Click ()
0928  TimerCounter = zTIMER_PAUSE
0929  End Sub
0930
0931  '----------------------------------------------------------------
0932  '              Set animation engine to reverse playback
0933  '----------------------------------------------------------------
0934  Sub POPUP_RunReverse_Click ()
0935  If AnimationLoaded = False Then
0936    MsgBox "You must load a kinematics sequence before you run the
            animation.", MB_OK, "Kinematics not ready"
0937    Exit Sub
```

```
0938   End If
0939   Pause = False
0940   FrameDirection = zREVERSE
0941   zShowNextFrame
0942   End Sub
0943
0944   '----------------------------------------------------------------
0945   '         Pause to allow menu to pop up on slower machines
0946   '----------------------------------------------------------------
0947   Sub POPUP_Timer_Click ()
0948   TimerCounter = zTIMER_PAUSE
0949   End Sub
0950
0951   '----------------------------------------------------------------
0952   '         Pause to allow menu to pop up on slower machines
0953   '----------------------------------------------------------------
0954   Sub POPUP_Using_Click ()
0955   TimerCounter = zTIMER_PAUSE
0956   End Sub
0957
0958   '----------------------------------------------------------------
0959   '                 Manage incoming timer events
0960   '----------------------------------------------------------------
0961   Sub TimerID1_Timer ()
0962   If Pause = True Then Exit Sub
0963   TimerCounter = TimerCounter - 1              'decrement counter
0964   If TimerCounter > 0 Then    'if pausing to allow menu to pop up...
0965     Exit Sub                          '...then exit this procedure
0966   End If
0967   TimerCounter = 0                  'otherwise, restore counter...
0968   zShowNextFrame                       '...and show the next frame
0969   End Sub
0970
0971   '----------------------------------------------------------------
0972   '                 Build one frame and save to disk
0973   '----------------------------------------------------------------
0974   Sub zBuildFrame ()
0975     Dim PrevFontClr As Long
0976     Dim PrevFontSize As Integer
0977   zClear                               'clear the display window
0978   Form1.Caption = "Building frame " & FrameNum & "..." 'caption bar
0979   zDrawCel                                         'draw one frame
0980   '-------------- display the titles and captions -----------------
0981   PrevFontSize = Form1.FontSize          'remember current font size
0982   PrevFontClr = Form1.ForeColor         'remember current font color
0983   Form1.FontSize = 16                              'set the size
0984   Form1.ForeColor = RGB(0, 0, 0)                   'set the color
0985   Form1.FontTransparent = True   'use transparent font backgrounds
0986   Form1.CurrentX = 10                'set the starting location...
0987   Form1.CurrentY = 6
0988   Form1.Print "A Lee Adams tutorial:"             'display text
0989   Form1.FontSize = 24                           'reset the size
0990   Form1.CurrentX = 8                      'reset the location...
0991   Form1.CurrentY = 24
0992   Form1.Print "Kinematics"                        'display text
0993   Form1.FontSize = PrevFontSize               'restore the size
```

```
0994   Form1.ForeColor = PrevFontClr              'restore the color
0995   Form1.CurrentX = 10
0996   Form1.CurrentY = 214
0997   Form1.Print "Kinematics production timestamp"
0998   Form1.CurrentX = 10
0999   Form1.CurrentY = 228
01000  Form1.Print "Time:" & Time$ & " Date:" & Date$
1001   '--------------------- save frame to disk -----------------------
1002   zSaveFrame                                 'save frame to disk
1003   End Sub
1004
1005   '----------------------------------------------------------------
1006   '                    Clear the display window
1007   '----------------------------------------------------------------
1008   Sub zClear ()
1009   RetVal = PatBlt(hDC, 0, 0, zFRAMEWIDE, zFRAMEHIGH, WHITENESS)
1010   End Sub
1011
1012   '----------------------------------------------------------------
1013   '                     Clear the hidden frame
1014   '----------------------------------------------------------------
1015   Sub zClearHiddenFrame ()
1016   If FrameReady = False Then
1017     Exit Sub
1018   End If
1019   RetVal = PatBlt(hFrameDC, 0, 0, zFRAMEWIDE, zFRAMEHIGH, WHITENESS)
1020   End Sub
1021
1022   '----------------------------------------------------------------
1023   '         Copy the hidden frame to the display window
1024   '----------------------------------------------------------------
1025   Sub zCopyToDisplay ()
1026   If FrameReady = False Then
1027     Exit Sub
1028   End If
1029   RetVal = BitBlt(hDC, 0, 0, zFRAMEWIDE, zFRAMEHIGH, hFrameDC, 0, 0,
         SRCCOPY)
1030   End Sub
1031
1032   '----------------------------------------------------------------
1033   '         Copy the display window to the hidden frame
1034   '----------------------------------------------------------------
1035   Sub zCopyToFrame ()
1036   If FrameReady = False Then
1037     Exit Sub
1038   End If
1039   RetVal = BitBlt(hFrameDC, 0, 0, zFRAMEWIDE, zFRAMEHIGH, hDC, 0, 0,
         SRCCOPY)
1040   End Sub
1041
1042   '----------------------------------------------------------------
1043   '             Draw one 3D cel and place on frame
1044   '----------------------------------------------------------------
1045   Sub zDrawCel ()                            'uses global variable FrameNum
1046   '--------------------- update the camera --------------------
1047   If FrameNum > Script.Cam1Path1.StartFrame And FrameNum <=
         Script.Cam1Path1.EndFrame Then
1048     Script.Cam1.Distance = Script.Cam1.Distance +
         Script.Cam1Path1.ChgDistance
```

```
1049    Script.Cam1.Heading = Script.Cam1.Heading +
          Script.Cam1Path1.ChgHeading
1050    Script.Cam1.Pitch = Script.Cam1.Pitch + Script.Cam1Path1.ChgPitch
1051  End If
1052  If Script.Cam1.Heading > 360 Then
1053    Script.Cam1.Heading = Script.Cam1.Heading - 360
1054  End If
1055  If Script.Cam1.Heading < 0 Then
1056    Script.Cam1.Heading = Script.Cam1.Heading + 360
1057  End If
1058  If Script.Cam1.Pitch > 360 Then
1059    Script.Cam1.Pitch = 360
1060  End If
1061  If Script.Cam1.Pitch < 270 Then
1062    Script.Cam1.Pitch = 270
1063  End If
1064  Call bczSetCameraDistance(Script.Cam1.Distance)
1065  Call bbzSetCameraPitch(Script.Cam1.Pitch)
1066  Call bazSetCameraHeading(Script.Cam1.Heading)
1067  '------------------- update the light-source ------------------
1068  If FrameNum > Script.Lt1Path1.StartFrame And FrameNum <=
          Script.Lt1Path1.EndFrame Then
1069    Script.Lt1.Heading = Script.Lt1.Heading +
          Script.Lt1Path1.ChgHeading
1070    Script.Lt1.Elevation = Script.Lt1.Elevation +
          Script.Lt1Path1.ChgElevation
1071  End If
1072  Call zSetLightPosition(Script.Lt1.Elevation, Script.Lt1.Heading)
1073  '---------------- update the kinematics bodies ----------------
1074  Call pkmRenderScene               'call the kinematics engine
1075  End Sub
1076
1077  '--------------------------------------------------------------
1078  '    Initialize or re-initialize the kinematics interface.
1079  '--------------------------------------------------------------
1080  Sub zInitializeModel ()
1081    Dim iLoopCount As Integer                    'loop counter
1082  '------------------- initialize the camera -------------------
1083  If ScriptLoaded = False Then    'use defaults if no script loaded
1084    Script.Cam1.Heading = 340
1085    Script.Cam1.Pitch = 350
1086    Script.Cam1.Distance = 356
1087  End If
1088  Call bczSetCameraDistance(Script.Cam1.Distance)
1089  Call bbzSetCameraPitch(Script.Cam1.Pitch)
1090  Call bazSetCameraHeading(Script.Cam1.Heading)
1091  '--------------- specify the path of the camera ---------------
1092  If ScriptLoaded = False Then
1093    Script.Cam1Path1.StartFrame = 1
1094    Script.Cam1Path1.EndFrame = zNUMCELS
1095    Script.Cam1Path1.ChgHeading = 0
1096    Script.Cam1Path1.ChgPitch = 0
1097    Script.Cam1Path1.ChgDistance = 0
1098  End If
1099  '----------------- initialize the light-source ----------------
1100  If ScriptLoaded = False Then
```

```
1101    Script.Lt1.Elevation = 60
1102    Script.Lt1.Heading = 180
1103  End If
1104  Call zSetLightPosition(Script.Lt1.Elevation, Script.Lt1.Heading)
1105  '-------------- specify the path of the light-source ------------
1106  If ScriptLoaded = False Then
1107    Script.Lt1Path1.StartFrame = 1
1108    Script.Lt1Path1.EndFrame = zNUMCELS
1109    Script.Lt1Path1.ChgHeading = 0
1110    Script.Lt1Path1.ChgElevation = 0
1111  End If
1112  '------------------- initialize the kinematics ------------------
1113  If ScriptLoaded = False Then
1114    Script.Kinematics.FPS = 18.2        '36 frames at 18 fps = 2 secs
1115    Script.Kinematics.NumBodies = 3              'number of bodies
1116    Script.Kinematics.FirstFrame = 1                'first frame
1117    Script.Kinematics.FinalFrame = zNUMCELS         'final frame
1118  End If
1119  Call akmInitializeKinematics(Script.Kinematics.FPS,
          Script.Kinematics.NumBodies, Script.Kinematics.FirstFrame,
          Script.Kinematics.FinalFrame)
1120  '-------------- specify kinematics for first body --------------
1121  If ScriptLoaded = False Then     'use defaults if no script loaded
1122    Script.Actor(0).TypeOfSubobject = zCYLINDER
1123    Script.Actor(0).Color = zRED
1124    Script.Actor(0).DimensionX = 30
1125    Script.Actor(0).DimensionY = 30
1126    Script.Actor(0).DimensionZ = 30
1127    Script.Actor(0).LocationX = 60
1128    Script.Actor(0).LocationY = 0
1129    Script.Actor(0).LocationZ = 0
1130    Script.Actor(0).OrientationYaw = 0
1131    Script.Actor(0).OrientationRoll = 0
1132    Script.Actor(0).OrientationPitch = 0
1133    Script.Actor(0).LinearVelocityDirection = zWEST
1134    Script.Actor(0).LinearVelocityPitch = zHORIZONTAL
1135    Script.Actor(0).LinearVelocitySpeed = 0
1136    Script.Actor(0).RotationalVelocityYawSpeed = 90
1137    Script.Actor(0).RotationalVelocityRollSpeed = 0
1138    Script.Actor(0).RotationalVelocityPitchSpeed = 0
1139    Script.Actor(0).LinearAccelUnitsPerSecSqd = 0
1140    Script.Actor(0).LinearAccelSeconds = 0
1141    Script.Actor(0).RotationalAccelYaw = 0
1142    Script.Actor(0).RotationalAccelRoll = 0
1143    Script.Actor(0).RotationalAccelPitch = 0
1144    Script.Actor(0).RotationalAccelSeconds = 0
1145    Script.Actor(0).HeadingChangeDegreesPerSec = 0
1146    Script.Actor(0).HeadingChangeSeconds = 0
1147    Script.Actor(0).PitchChangeDegreesPerSec = 0
1148    Script.Actor(0).PitchChangeSeconds = 0
1149  End If
1150  '-------------- specify kinematics for second body --------------
1151  If ScriptLoaded = False Then
1152    Script.Actor(1).TypeOfSubobject = zBOX
1153    Script.Actor(1).Color = zRED
1154    Script.Actor(1).DimensionX = 26
1155    Script.Actor(1).DimensionY = 26
1156    Script.Actor(1).DimensionZ = 26
```

```
1157    Script.Actor(1).LocationX = -50
1158    Script.Actor(1).LocationY = -60
1159    Script.Actor(1).LocationZ = 0
1160    Script.Actor(1).OrientationYaw = 0
1161    Script.Actor(1).OrientationRoll = 45
1162    Script.Actor(1).OrientationPitch = 0
1163    Script.Actor(1).LinearVelocityDirection = zEAST
1164    Script.Actor(1).LinearVelocityPitch = zHORIZONTAL
1165    Script.Actor(1).LinearVelocitySpeed = 0
1166    Script.Actor(1).RotationalVelocityYawSpeed = 0
1167    Script.Actor(1).RotationalVelocityRollSpeed = 0
1168    Script.Actor(1).RotationalVelocityPitchSpeed = 90
1169    Script.Actor(1).LinearAccelUnitsPerSecSqd = 0
1170    Script.Actor(1).LinearAccelSeconds = 0
1171    Script.Actor(1).RotationalAccelYaw = 0
1172    Script.Actor(1).RotationalAccelRoll = 0
1173    Script.Actor(1).RotationalAccelPitch = 0
1174    Script.Actor(1).RotationalAccelSeconds = 0
1175    Script.Actor(1).HeadingChangeDegreesPerSec = 0
1176    Script.Actor(1).HeadingChangeSeconds = 0
1177    Script.Actor(1).PitchChangeDegreesPerSec = 0
1178    Script.Actor(1).PitchChangeSeconds = 0
1179 End If
1180 '-------------- specify kinematics for third body ---------------
1181 If ScriptLoaded = False Then
1182    Script.Actor(2).TypeOfSubobject = zWEDGE
1183    Script.Actor(2).Color = zRED
1184    Script.Actor(2).DimensionX = 30
1185    Script.Actor(2).DimensionY = 30
1186    Script.Actor(2).DimensionZ = 30
1187    Script.Actor(2).LocationX = -50
1188    Script.Actor(2).LocationY = 30
1189    Script.Actor(2).LocationZ = 0
1190    Script.Actor(2).OrientationYaw = 0
1191    Script.Actor(2).OrientationRoll = 0
1192    Script.Actor(2).OrientationPitch = 0
1193    Script.Actor(2).LinearVelocityDirection = zEAST
1194    Script.Actor(2).LinearVelocityPitch = zHORIZONTAL
1195    Script.Actor(2).LinearVelocitySpeed = 0
1196    Script.Actor(2).RotationalVelocityYawSpeed = -90
1197    Script.Actor(2).RotationalVelocityRollSpeed = 0
1198    Script.Actor(2).RotationalVelocityPitchSpeed = 0
1199    Script.Actor(2).LinearAccelUnitsPerSecSqd = 0
1200    Script.Actor(2).LinearAccelSeconds = 0
1201    Script.Actor(2).RotationalAccelYaw = 0
1202    Script.Actor(2).RotationalAccelRoll = 0
1203    Script.Actor(2).RotationalAccelPitch = 0
1204    Script.Actor(2).RotationalAccelSeconds = 0
1205    Script.Actor(2).HeadingChangeDegreesPerSec = 0
1206    Script.Actor(2).HeadingChangeSeconds = 0
1207    Script.Actor(2).PitchChangeDegreesPerSec = 0
1208    Script.Actor(2).PitchChangeSeconds = 0
1209 End If
1210 '--------------- initialize the kinematics engine --------------
1211 For iLoopCount = 0 To (Script.Kinematics.NumBodies - 1) Step 1
1212                         'for each body being animated...
1213                    '...initialize it in the kinematics engine...
```

```
1214    Call mkmSetSolid(iLoopCount + 1,
            Script.Actor(iLoopCount).TypeOfSubobject)
1215    Call nkmSetColor(iLoopCount + 1, Script.Actor(iLoopCount).Color)
1216    Call jkmSetDimensions(iLoopCount + 1,
            Script.Actor(iLoopCount).DimensionX,
            Script.Actor(iLoopCount).DimensionY,
            Script.Actor(iLoopCount).DimensionZ)
1217    Call hkmSetLocation(iLoopCount + 1,
            Script.Actor(iLoopCount).LocationX,
            Script.Actor(iLoopCount).LocationY,
            Script.Actor(iLoopCount).LocationZ)
1218    Call ikmSetOrientation(iLoopCount + 1,
            Script.Actor(iLoopCount).OrientationYaw,
            Script.Actor(iLoopCount).OrientationRoll,
            Script.Actor(iLoopCount).OrientationPitch)
1219    Call kkmSetLinearVelocity(iLoopCount + 1,
            Script.Actor(iLoopCount).LinearVelocityDirection,
            Script.Actor(iLoopCount).LinearVelocityPitch,
            Script.Actor(iLoopCount).LinearVelocitySpeed)
1220    Call lkmSetRotationalVelocity(iLoopCount + 1,
            Script.Actor(iLoopCount).RotationalVelocityYawSpeed,
            Script.Actor(iLoopCount).RotationalVelocityRollSpeed,
            Script.Actor(iLoopCount).RotationalVelocityPitchSpeed)
1221    Call dkmSetLinearAcceleration(iLoopCount + 1,
            Script.Actor(iLoopCount).LinearAccelUnitsPerSecSqd,
            Script.Actor(iLoopCount).LinearAccelSeconds)
1222    Call ekmSetRotationalAcceleration(iLoopCount + 1,
            Script.Actor(iLoopCount).RotationalAccelYaw,
            Script.Actor(iLoopCount).RotationalAccelRoll,
            Script.Actor(iLoopCount).RotationalAccelPitch,
            Script.Actor(iLoopCount).RotationalAccelSeconds)
1223    Call fkmSetHeadingChange(iLoopCount + 1,
            Script.Actor(iLoopCount).HeadingChangeDegreesPerSec,
            Script.Actor(iLoopCount).HeadingChangeSeconds)
1224    Call gkmSetPitchChange(iLoopCount + 1,
            Script.Actor(iLoopCount).PitchChangeDegreesPerSec,
            Script.Actor(iLoopCount).PitchChangeSeconds)
1225    Next iLoopCount                      'loop back to do next body...
1226    End Sub
1227
1228    '-----------------------------------------------------------------
1229    '               Initialize the animation system
1230    '-----------------------------------------------------------------
1231    Sub zInitializeSystem ()
1232    If FrameReady = True Then        'if hidden frame already created
1233      Form_Paint                     'refresh screen if animation running
1234      Exit Sub
1235    End If
1236    Picture1.Visible = False                     'hide the picture box
1237    Picture1.Top = 0: Picture1.Left = 0                    'reposition
1238    Picture1.Width = 402: Picture1.Height = 302                'resize
1239    RetLong = GlobalCompact(-1)          'maximize contiguous memory
1240    hFrameDC = CreateCompatibleDC(hDC)        'get a display-context
1241    hFrame = CreateCompatibleBitmap(hDC, zFRAMEWIDE, zFRAMEHIGH)
1242    If hFrame = Null Then                        'if error occurred
1243      MsgBox "Insufficient memory.  Hidden frame not created.  Close
            other Windows applications to free up more RAM.", MB_OK,
            "Kinematics  fatal error"
1244      FrameReady = False
```

```
1245    Exit Sub
1246  End If
1247  hPrevFrame = SelectObject(hFrameDC, hFrame)    'select the bitmap
1248  FrameReady = True                              'set a global token
1249  zCopyToFrame
1250  TimerID1.Interval = wFrameRate                 'set the timer interval
1251  TimerID1.Enabled = True                        'activate the timer
1252  TimerExists = True                             'set a token
1253  Pause = True
1254  End Sub
1255
1256  '----------------------------------------------------------------
1257  '                 Load a script database from disk
1258  '----------------------------------------------------------------
1259  Sub zLoadScript (sFileName As String)
1260    Dim ErrorOccurred As Integer
1261  ErrorOccurred = False
1262  '---------------- open a disk file for writing ----------------
1263  On Error GoTo LoadError                        'activate error-trapping
1264  Open sFileName For Binary Access Read As 1
1265  '----------------- read the script from disk -------------------
1266  Get 1, , Script
1267  '------------------- close the disk file ----------------------
1268  Close 1
1269  '----------------- check results and then exit ----------------
1270  On Error GoTo 0                                'deactivate error-trapping
1271  If ErrorOccurred = True Then          'if a disk error occurred...
1272    ScriptLoaded = False
1273    Beep
1274    MsgBox "Unable to load the script from disk.  Does file exist?",
           MB_OK, "Kinematics error report"
1275    Exit Sub
1276  End If
1277  ScriptLoaded = True                           'otherwise set a token...
1278  zInitializeModel                  '...reinitialize the kinematics...
1279  MsgBox "Script loaded from disk and kinematics model
           reinitialized.", MB_OK, "Kinematics status report"
1280  Exit Sub                                       '...and exit
1281  '--------------------- error-handler -------------------------
1282  LoadError:                                'jump to here if disk error
1283    ErrorOccurred = True                        'set a token and...
1284  Resume                           '...jump back to resume execution
1285  End Sub
1286
1287  '----------------------------------------------------------------
1288  '                 Save a script database to disk
1289  '----------------------------------------------------------------
1290  Sub zSaveScript (sFileName As String)
1291    Dim ErrorOccurred As Integer
1292  ErrorOccurred = False
1293  zInitializeModel                          'reinitialize the kinematics
1294  '---------------- open a disk file for writing ----------------
1295  On Error GoTo SaveError                        'activate error-trapping
1296  Open sFileName For Binary Access Write As 1
1297  '----------------- write the script to disk -------------------
1298  Put 1, , Script
```

```
1299  '------------------- close the disk file ----------------------
1300  Close 1
1301  '----------------- check results and then exit ----------------
1302  On Error GoTo 0                        'deactivate error-trapping
1303  If ErrorOccurred = True Then           'if a disk error occurred...
1304    ScriptSaved = False
1305    Beep
1306    MsgBox "Unable to save the script to disk.  Sufficient disk
            space?", MB_OK, "Kinematics error report"
1307    Exit Sub
1308  End If
1309  ScriptSaved = True               'otherwise set a token and then exit
1310  MsgBox "Script saved to disk.", MB_OK, "Kinematics status report"
1311  Exit Sub
1312  '--------------------- error-handler --------------------------
1313  SaveError:                              'jump to here if disk error
1314    ErrorOccurred = True                  'set a token and...
1315  Resume                          '...jump back to resume execution
1316  End Sub
1317
1318  '--------------------------------------------------------------
1319  '     Adjust camera and light-source for a preview frame.
1320  '--------------------------------------------------------------
1321  Sub zSelectPreviewFrame (WhichFrame As Integer)
1322    Dim iLoopCount
1323  For iLoopCount = 1 To (WhichFrame - 1) Step 1
1324              'for each frame preceding the desired preview frame...
1325    If iLoopCount > Script.Cam1Path1.StartFrame And iLoopCount <=
          Script.Cam1Path1.EndFrame Then
1326      Script.Cam1.Distance = Script.Cam1.Distance +
            Script.Cam1Path1.ChgDistance
1327      Script.Cam1.Heading = Script.Cam1.Heading +
            Script.Cam1Path1.ChgHeading
1328      Script.Cam1.Pitch = Script.Cam1.Pitch +
            Script.Cam1Path1.ChgPitch
1329    End If
1330    If Script.Cam1.Heading > 360 Then
1331      Script.Cam1.Heading = Script.Cam1.Heading - 360
1332    End If
1333    If Script.Cam1.Heading < 0 Then
1334      Script.Cam1.Heading = Script.Cam1.Heading + 360
1335    End If
1336    If Script.Cam1.Pitch > 360 Then
1337      Script.Cam1.Pitch = 360
1338    End If
1339    If Script.Cam1.Pitch < 270 Then
1340      Script.Cam1.Pitch = 270
1341    End If
1342    If iLoopCount > Script.Lt1Path1.StartFrame And iLoopCount <=
          Script.Lt1Path1.EndFrame Then
1343      Script.Lt1.Heading = Script.Lt1.Heading +
            Script.Lt1Path1.ChgHeading
1344      Script.Lt1.Elevation = Script.Lt1.Elevation +
            Script.Lt1Path1.ChgElevation
1345    End If
1346  Next iLoopCount
1347  End Sub
1348
```

C-5 Continued.

```
0001  '-----------------------------------------------------------------
0002  '       Frame animation routines for Visual Basic applications
0003  '-----------------------------------------------------------------
0004  ' Source file:  KIPLAY.BAS
0005  ' Release version:  2.00                        Programmer:  Lee Adams
0006  ' Type:  Visual Basic module for Windows applications
0007  ' Output and features:  Provides routines to manage the authoring
0008  '   process and playback engine for interactive frame animation.
0009  ' Publication:  Contains material from Windcrest/McGraw-Hill
0010  '   book 4225 published by TAB BOOKS Div. of McGraw-Hill Inc.
0011  ' License:  As purchaser of the book you are granted a
0012  '   royalty-free license to distribute executable files
0013  '   generated uSing this code provided that you accept the
0014  '   conditions of the License Agreement and Limited Warranty
0015  '   described in the book and on the companion disk.  Government
0016  '   users:  This software and documentation are subject to
0017  '   restrictions set forth in The Rights in Technical Data and
0018  '   Computer Software clause at 252.227-7013 and elsewhere.
0019  '-----------------------------------------------------------------
0020  '   (c) Copyright 1992-1993 Lee Adams.  All rights reserved.
0021  '          Lee Adams(tm) is a trademark of Lee Adams.
0022  '-----------------------------------------------------------------
0023  '
0024  Option Explicit              'generate error if variable not declared
0025
0026  '-----------------------------------------------------------------
0027  '                     Load a frame from disk
0028  '-----------------------------------------------------------------
0029  Sub zLoadFrame ()                       'uses global variable FileName
0030  If FrameReady = False Then
0031    MsgBox "Hidden frame not ready.", MB_OK, "Animation error report"
0032    Exit Sub
0033  End If
0034  LoadingFrame = True                        'disable refresh procedure
0035  On Error GoTo LoadError:                      'enable error trapping
0036  Form1.Picture = LoadPicture(FileName)            'load .BMP image
0037  On Error GoTo 0                              'disable error trapping
0038  LoadingFrame = False                        'enable refresh procedure
0039  FrameLoaded = True
0040  '-------- select persistent bitmap, clear it, deselect it -------
0041  Form1.AutoRedraw = True
0042  RetVal = PatBlt(Form1.hDC, 0, 0, zFRAMEWIDE, zFRAMEHIGH, WHITENESS)
0043  Form1.AutoRedraw = False
0044  Exit Sub
0045  '------------------------ error-handler ----------------------
0046  LoadError:
0047    On Error GoTo 0
0048    LoadingFrame = False
0049    FrameLoaded = False
0050    Beep
0051    MsgBox "Unable to load the .BMP file.  Is system initialized?
           Does file exist on disk?", MB_OK, "Animation error report"
0052    Exit Sub
0053  End Sub
0054
0055  '-----------------------------------------------------------------
```

```
0056  '                          Save a frame to disk
0057  '----------------------------------------------------------------
0058  Sub zSaveFrame ()                        'uses global variable FileName
0059    Dim ErrorOccurred As Integer
0060  ErrorOccurred = False                        'set default tokens...
0061  FrameSaved = False
0062  If FrameReady = False Then
0063    MsgBox "Hidden frame not ready.", MB_OK, "Animation error report"
0064    Exit Sub
0065  End If
0066  '------------- copy display window to picture box --------------
0067  RetVal = BitBlt(hFrameDC, 0, 0, zFRAMEWIDE, zFRAMEHIGH, Form1.hDC,
          0, 0, SRCCOPY)
0068  Form1.Picture1.Visible = True                'show the picture box
0069  Form1.Picture1.AutoRedraw = True        'activate persistent bitmap
0070  RetVal = BitBlt(Form1.Picture1.hDC, 0, 0, zFRAMEWIDE, zFRAMEHIGH,
          hFrameDC, 0, 0, SRCCOPY)
0071  Form1.Picture1.Picture = Form1.Picture1.Image    'copy to screen
0072  Form1.Picture1.AutoRedraw = False  'disable the persistent bitmap
0073  '--------------- save picture box image to disk ---------------
0074  On Error GoTo SaveError                      'enable error trapping
0075  SavePicture Form1.Picture1.Image, FileName   'save bitmap to disk
0076  On Error GoTo 0                              'disable error trapping
0077  Form1.Picture1.Visible = False               'hide the picture box
0078  RetVal = BitBlt(Form1.hDC, 0, 0, zFRAMEWIDE, zFRAMEHIGH, hFrameDC,
          0, 0, SRCCOPY)
0079  If ErrorOccurred = True Then                 'if disk error, exit
0080    Beep
0081    MsgBox "Unable to save the frame to disk as a .BMP file.
            Sufficient disk space?", MB_OK, "Animation error report"
0082    Exit Sub
0083  End If
0084  FrameSaved = True
0085  Exit Sub
0086  SaveError:                                'jump to here if disk error
0087    ErrorOccurred = True
0088  Resume
0089  End Sub
0090
0091  '----------------------------------------------------------------
0092  '                     Display the next frame
0093  '----------------------------------------------------------------
0094  Sub zShowNextFrame ()                   'uses global variable FrameNum
0095  If UseDisk = True Then                  'animate using memory or disk?
0096    GoTo DISK_PLAYBACK
0097  End If
0098  '------------- manage memory-based frame animation --------------
0099  MEMORY_PLAYBACK:
0100  If AnimationReady = False Then
0101    Exit Sub
0102  End If
0103  If AnimationLoaded = False Then
0104    Exit Sub
0105  End If
0106  If Redisplay = True Then
0107    GoTo DISPLAY_FRAME
0108  End If
0109  If Pause = True Then
```

```
0110    Exit Sub
0111  End If
0112  If FrameDirection = zFORWARD Then              'if a forward loop...
0113    FrameNum = FrameNum + 1                 'increment the frame number
0114    If FrameNum > zFINALFRAME Then              'if at end of loop...
0115      FrameNum = zFIRSTFRAME                        '...wraparound
0116    End If
0117  End If
0118  If FrameDirection = zREVERSE Then              'if a reverse loop...
0119    FrameNum = FrameNum - 1                 'decrement the frame number
0120    If FrameNum < zFIRSTFRAME Then             'but if at end of loop...
0121      FrameNum = zFINALFRAME                        '...wraparound
0122    End If
0123  End If
0124  DISPLAY_FRAME:          'select handle and copy frame to display...
0125  RetVal = SelectObject(hFDC, BitmapHandles(FrameNum - 1))
0126  RetVal = BitBlt(Form1.hDC, 0, 0, zFRAMEWIDE, zFRAMEHIGH, hFDC, 0,
           0, SRCCOPY)
0127  Exit Sub
0128  '-------------- manage disk-based frame animation ---------------
0129  DISK_PLAYBACK:
0130  If AnimationHalted = True Then
0131    Exit Sub
0132  End If
0133  If Redisplay = True Then
0134    GoTo SAME_FRAME
0135  End If
0136  If Pause = True Then
0137    Exit Sub
0138  End If
0139  If FrameDirection = zFORWARD Then              'if a forward loop...
0140    FrameNum = FrameNum + 1
0141    If FrameNum > zFINALFRAME Then
0142      FrameNum = zFIRSTFRAME
0143    End If
0144  End If
0145  If FrameDirection = zREVERSE Then              'if a reverse loop...
0146    FrameNum = FrameNum - 1
0147    If FrameNum < zFIRSTFRAME Then
0148      FrameNum = zFINALFRAME
0149    End If
0150  End If
0151  SAME_FRAME:
0152  FileName = FrameFiles(FrameNum - 1)
0153  zLoadFrame
0154  If FrameLoaded = False Then                 'if an error occurred...
0155    AnimationHalted = True
0156    Beep
0157    MsgBox "Unable to load next frame from disk.  Animation
           halted.", MB_OK, "Animation error report"
0158    Exit Sub
0159  End If
0160  RetVal = BitBlt(Form1.hDC, 0, 0, zFRAMEWIDE, zFRAMEHIGH, hFrameDC,
           0, 0, SRCCOPY)
0161  End Sub
0162
```

C-6 Source listings for the interactive, animated virtual reality sampler, maze. See Appendix B for the toolkits which must be used to build this application. See Appendix A for instructions on building the demo.

```
0001   MAGLOBAL.BAS
0002   MAMAIN.BAS
0003   VIRT3D.BAS
0004   LIGHTS3D.BAS
0005   ASSEMB3D.BAS
0006   SHAPES3D.BAS
0007   DEFORM3D.BAS
0008   MAPLAY.BAS
0009   MAZE.FRM
0010   ProjWinSize=83,428,196,336
0011   ProjWinShow=2


0001   '------------------------------------------------------------------
0002   '  Reusable global module for Visual Basic graphics applications
0003   '             that call Windows API functions.
0004   '------------------------------------------------------------------
0005   '  Source file:  MAGLOBAL.BAS
0006   '  Release version:  1.00                     Programmer:  Lee Adams
0007   '  Type:  Visual Basic global module for Windows applications.
0008   '  Compiler:  Microsoft Visual Basic 2.00
0009   '  Dependencies:  MAZE.FRM primary module
0010   '                 MAMAIN.BAS module containing Main()
0011   '                 MAPLAY.BAS animation playback module
0012   '  Output and features:  Provides declarations for Windows API
0013   '    (Application Programming Interface) functions callable by
0014   '    Visual Basic applications at runtime, including routines
0015   '    from Windows' GDI, USER, and KERNEL DLLs (dynamic link
0016   '    libraries).  Also provides declarations of various variables
0017   '    and constants.  Functions, variables, and constants declared
0018   '    in this global module are visible throughout the project.
0019   '  Publication:  Contains material from Windcrest/McGraw-Hill
0020   '    book 4225 published by TAB BOOKS Div. of McGraw-Hill Inc.
0021   '  License:  As purchaser of the book you are granted a
0022   '    royalty-free license to distribute executable files
0023   '    generated using this code provided that you accept the
0024   '    conditions of the License Agreement and Limited Warranty
0025   '    described in the book and on the companion disk.  Government
0026   '    users:  This software and documentation are subject to
0027   '    restrictions set forth in The Rights in Technical Data and
0028   '    Computer Software clause at 252.227-7013 and elsewhere.
0029   '------------------------------------------------------------------
0030   '      (c) Copyright 1993 Lee Adams.  All rights reserved.
0031   '           Lee Adams(tm) is a trademark of Lee Adams.
0032   '------------------------------------------------------------------
0033
0034   Option Explicit            'generate error if variable not declared
0035   '------------------------------------------------------------------
0036   '              General constants and variables
0037   '------------------------------------------------------------------
0038   Global Const MB_OK = 0                'OK button for message box
0039   Global Const MB_OKCANCEL = 1    'OK Cancel buttons for message box
0040   Global Const MB_YESNO = 4         'Yes No buttons for message box
0041   Global Const IDOK = 1                  'OK button selected
0042   Global Const IDCANCEL = 2            'Cancel button selected
```

```
0043   Global Const IDYES = 6                        'Yes button selected
0044   Global Const IDNO = 7                          'No button selected
0045   Global UserWants As Integer          'value returned by message box
0046   Global Const PIXELS = 3                         'pixel coordinates
0047   Global StartUp As Integer               'tracks the startup code
0048   Global IgnoreRefresh As Integer         'tracks refresh activity
0049   Global Const zRED = 1
0050   Global Const zGREEN = 2
0051   Global Const zBROWN = 3
0052   Global Const zBLUE = 4
0053   Global Const zMAGENTA = 5
0054   Global Const zCYAN = 6
0055   Global Const zGRAY = 7
0056
0057   '-----------------------------------------------------------------
0058   '                    Window specifications
0059   '-----------------------------------------------------------------
0060   Global Const zWINDOW_WIDTH = 264                'width of window
0061   Global Const zWINDOW_HEIGHT = 301              'height of window
0062   Global Const zFRAMEWIDE = 256               'width of client area
0063   Global Const zFRAMEHIGH = 255              'height of client area
0064   Global HorizTwipsPixel As Single      'twips-per-pixel (horizontal)
0065   Global VertTwipsPixel As Single         'twips-per-pixel (vertical)
0066   Global Window_Width As Single           'runtime width of window
0067   Global Window_Height As Single         'runtime height of window
0068
0069   '-----------------------------------------------------------------
0070   '                    Runtime conditions
0071   '-----------------------------------------------------------------
0072   Global hDesktopWnd As Integer                  'handle to desktop
0073   Global hDCcaps As Integer            'display-context for desktop
0074   Global DisplayWidth As Integer       'horizontal screen resolution
0075   Global DisplayHeight As Integer       'vertical screen resolution
0076   Global DisplayBits As Integer          'number of bits-per-pixel
0077   Global DisplayPlanes As Integer           'number of bitplanes
0078   Global MemoryMode As Long                 'runtime memory mode
0079   Global RetVal As Integer            'will receive GDI return value
0080   Global RetLong As Long              'will receive GDI return value
0081   Global MousePresent As Integer                  'mouse active?
0082   Global WindowsVersion As Long              'version of Windows
0083   Global LoadingFrame As Integer             'loading an image?
0084   Global Preview As Integer           'displaying a preview image?
0085
0086   '-----------------------------------------------------------------
0087   '                    Hidden frame operations
0088   '-----------------------------------------------------------------
0089   Global hFrameDC As Integer           'display-context for hidden-frame
0090   Global hFrame As Integer             'handle to hidden-frame bitmap
0091   Global hPrevFrame As Integer          'default bitmap for hFrameDC
0092   Global FrameReady As Integer          'hidden-frame created?
0093
0094   '-----------------------------------------------------------------
0095   '                    Animation engine
0096   '-----------------------------------------------------------------
0097   Global FrameNum As Integer                     'current frame
0098   Global Const zFIRSTFRAME = 1           'first frame of animation
```

```
0099    Global Const zFINALFRAME = 100          'final frame of animation
0100    Global Const zNUMCELS = 100             'number of cels in animation
0101    Global LoopCount As Integer                      'loop counter
0102    Global hFDC As Integer      'memory DC for hidden playback bitmaps
0103    Global hPrevF As Integer              'handle to default bitmap
0104    Global BitmapHandles(zNUMCELS)              'array of bitmap handles
0105    Global FrameFiles(zNUMCELS) As String * 9    'array of filenames
0106
0107    '-------- virtual reality extensions to animation engine --------
0108    Global Const vrVIEW000 = 1                   'directions of view...
0109    Global Const vrVIEW090 = 2
0110    Global Const vrVIEW180 = 3
0111    Global Const vrVIEW270 = 4
0112    Global Const vrSTATIONARY = 5             'viewpoint movements...
0113    Global Const vrMOVE_FORWARD = 6
0114    Global Const vrMOVE_RIGHT = 7
0115    Global Const vrMOVE_BACKWARD = 8
0116    Global Const vrMOVE_LEFT = 9
0117    Global Const vrMAX_ROW = 4    'maximum, minimum viewpoint nodes...
0118    Global Const vrMAX_COLUMN = 4
0119    Global Const vrMIN_ROW = 0
0120    Global Const vrMIN_COLUMN = 0
0121    Global Const vrNUM_COLUMNS = 5   'number of columns in each array
0122    Global Const vrNUM_NODES = 25     'number of nodes in each array
0123    Global Const vrFIRST_ARRAY = 0      'indexes into viewing array...
0124    Global Const vrSECOND_ARRAY = 25
0125    Global Const vrTHIRD_ARRAY = 50
0126    Global Const vrFOURTH_ARRAY = 75
0127    Global vrMove As Integer                     'viewpoint movement
0128    Global vrView As Integer                    'direction of view
0129    Global vrRow As Integer                     'for view matrix
0130    Global vrColumn As Integer                  'for view matrix
0131    Global vrArrayOffset As Integer             'view index into array
0132    Global vrFrameID As Integer                 'node index into array
0133    Global UsingVR As Integer        'True if virtual reality running
0134
0135    '-----------------------------------------------------------------
0136    '                    Variables for disk I/O
0137    '-----------------------------------------------------------------
0138    Global FileName As String           'name of binary image file
0139    Global FrameSaved As Integer              'frame saved to disk?
0140    Global FrameLoaded As Integer            'frame loaded from disk?
0141    Global AnimationSaved As Integer       'animation saved to disk?
0142    Global AnimationLoaded As Integer     'animation loaded from disk?
0143    Global AnimationReady As Integer     'animation ready for playback?
0144    Global PrevSaveAttempt As Integer    'previous save attempt made?
0145    Global PrevLoadAttempt As Integer    'previous load attempt made?
0146    Global UseDisk As Integer            'load each frame as needed?
0147
0148    '-----------------------------------------------------------------
0149    '            Constants for Windows API functions
0150    '-----------------------------------------------------------------
0151    Global Const SRCCOPY = &HCC0020                  'for bitblts...
0152    Global Const SRCINVERT = &H660046
0153    Global Const SRCPAINT = &HEE0086
0154    Global Const WHITENESS = &HFF0062
0155    Global Const BLACKNESS = &H42&
0156    Global Const ALTERNATE = 1                        'for filling...
```

C-6 Continued.

```
0157  Global Const WINDING = 2
0158  Global Const R2_COPYPEN = 13                      'for pen mode...
0159  Global Const R2_XORPEN = 7
0160  Global Const TRANSPARENT = 1              'for background mode...
0161  Global Const OPAQUE = 2
0162  Global Const PS_SOLID = 0                             'for solid pen
0163  Global Const PS_NULL = 5                        'for transparent pen
0164  Global Const BLACKONWHITE = 1                     'for bitblt scaling...
0165  Global Const WHITEONBLACK = 2
0166  Global Const COLORONCOLOR = 3
0167  Global Const HORZRES = 8               'args for GetDeviceCaps()...
0168  Global Const VERTRES = 10
0169  Global Const BITSPIXEL = 12
0170  Global Const PLANES = 14
0171  Global Const SM_MOUSEPRESENT = 19             'for GetSystemMetrics()
0172  Global Const WF_ENHANCED = &H20                 'for GetWinFlags()...
0173  Global Const WF_STANDARD = &H10
0174
0175  '----------------------------------------------------------------
0176  '                GDI functions for display-contexts
0177  '----------------------------------------------------------------
0178  Declare Function GetDC Lib "USER" (ByVal hWnd As Integer) As
          Integer
0179  Declare Function ReleaseDC Lib "USER" (ByVal hWnd As Integer,
          ByVal hDC As Integer) As Integer
0180
0181  '----------------------------------------------------------------
0182  '                GDI functions for the desktop
0183  '----------------------------------------------------------------
0184  Declare Function GetDesktopWindow Lib "USER" () As Integer
0185
0186  '----------------------------------------------------------------
0187  '         GDI functions for creating drawing objects
0188  '----------------------------------------------------------------
0189  Declare Function CreatePen Lib "GDI" (ByVal PenStyle As Integer,
          ByVal Wd As Integer, ByVal Color As Long) As Integer
0190  Declare Function CreateSolidBrush Lib "GDI" (ByVal Color As Long)
          As Integer
0191
0192  '----------------------------------------------------------------
0193  '          GDI functions for selecting objects
0194  '----------------------------------------------------------------
0195  Declare Function SelectObject Lib "GDI" (ByVal hDC As Integer,
          ByVal hObject As Integer) As Integer
0196  Declare Function DeleteObject Lib "GDI" (ByVal hObject As Integer)
          As Integer
0197
0198  '----------------------------------------------------------------
0199  '          GDI functions for bitmaps and bitblts
0200  '----------------------------------------------------------------
0201  Declare Function CreateCompatibleDC Lib "GDI" (ByVal hDC As
          Integer) As Integer
0202  Declare Function CreateCompatibleBitmap Lib "GDI" (ByVal hDC As
          Integer, ByVal Wd As Integer, ByVal Ht As Integer) As Integer
0203  Declare Function PatBlt Lib "GDI" (ByVal hDC As Integer, ByVal X
          As Integer, ByVal Y As Integer, ByVal Wd As Integer, ByVal Ht
          As Integer, ByVal RasOp As Long) As Integer
```

```
0204   Declare Function BitBlt Lib "GDI" (ByVal hDestDC As Integer, ByVal
           DestX As Integer, ByVal DestY As Integer, ByVal Wd As Integer,
           ByVal Ht As Integer, ByVal hSrcDC As Integer, ByVal SrcX As
           Integer, ByVal SrcY As Integer, ByVal RastOp As Long) As
           Integer
0205   Declare Function DeleteDC Lib "GDI" (ByVal hDC As Integer) As
           Integer
0206
0207   '----------------------------------------------------------------
0208            GDI functions for drawing mode operations
0209   '----------------------------------------------------------------
0210   Declare Function SetROP2 Lib "GDI" (ByVal hDC As Integer, ByVal
           RasMode As Integer) As Integer
0211   Declare Function SetBkColor Lib "GDI" (ByVal hDC As Integer, ByVal
           Color As Long) As Long
0212   Declare Function SetBkMode Lib "GDI" (ByVal hDC As Integer, ByVal
           BkMode As Integer) As Integer
0213   Declare Function SetPolyFillMode Lib "GDI" (ByVal hDC As Integer,
           ByVal PolyMode As Integer) As Integer
0214   Declare Function SetStretchBltMode Lib "GDI" (ByVal hDC As
           Integer, ByVal StretchMode As Integer) As Integer
0215
0216   '----------------------------------------------------------------
0217   '            GDI functions for drawing operations
0218   '----------------------------------------------------------------
0219   Declare Function MoveTo Lib "GDI" (ByVal hDC As Integer, ByVal X
           As Integer, ByVal Y As Integer) As Long
0220   Declare Function LineTo Lib "GDI" (ByVal hDC As Integer, ByVal X
           As Integer, ByVal Y As Integer) As Integer
0221   Declare Function Polygon Lib "GDI" (ByVal hDC As Integer, FirstPt
           As Integer, ByVal Count As Integer) As Integer
0222   Declare Function Rectangle Lib "GDI" (ByVal hDC As Integer, ByVal
           X1 As Integer, ByVal Y1 As Integer, ByVal X2 As Integer, ByVal
           Y2 As Integer) As Integer
0223   Declare Function Ellipse Lib "GDI" (ByVal hDC As Integer, ByVal X1
           As Integer, ByVal Y1 As Integer, ByVal X2 As Integer, ByVal Y2
           As Integer) As Integer
0224   Declare Function FloodFill Lib "GDI" (ByVal hDC As Integer, ByVal
           X As Integer, ByVal Y As Integer, ByVal Color As Long) As
           Integer
0225   Declare Function SetPixel Lib "GDI" (ByVal hDC As Integer, ByVal X
           As Integer, ByVal Y As Integer, ByVal Color As Long) As Long
0226   Declare Function GetPixel Lib "GDI" (ByVal hDC As Integer, ByVal X
           As Integer, ByVal Y As Integer) As Long
0227
0228   '----------------------------------------------------------------
0229   '                  GDI functions for regions
0230   '----------------------------------------------------------------
0231   Declare Function PaintRgn Lib "GDI" (ByVal hDC As Integer, ByVal
           hRGN As Integer) As Integer
0232   Declare Function CreatePolygonRgn Lib "GDI" (FirstPt As Integer,
           ByVal Count As Integer, ByVal PolyFillMode As Integer) As
           Integer
0233   Declare Function PtInRegion Lib "GDI" (ByVal hRGN As Integer,
           ByVal xCoord As Integer, ByVal yCoord As Integer) As Integer
0234
0235   '----------------------------------------------------------------
0236   '   GDI, USER, KERNEL functions for various runtime conditions
0237   '----------------------------------------------------------------
```

```
0238   Declare Function GetDeviceCaps Lib "GDI" (ByVal hDC As Integer,
           ByVal Item As Integer) As Integer
0239   Declare Function GetWinFlags Lib "KERNEL" () As Long
0240   Declare Function GetSystemMetrics Lib "USER" (ByVal Item As
           Integer) As Integer
0241   Declare Function GlobalCompact Lib "KERNEL" (ByVal NumBytes As
           Long) As Long
0242   Declare Function GetVersion Lib "KERNEL" () As Long
0243   Declare Function ExitWindows Lib "USER" (ByVal Reserved As Long,
           ByVal Item As Integer) As Integer
0244   Declare Function SetCapture Lib "USER" (ByVal hWnd As Integer) As
           Integer
0245   Declare Sub ReleaseCapture Lib "USER" ()
0246
0247   '------------------------------------------------------------------
0248   '                     End of global module.
0249   '------------------------------------------------------------------
0250


0001   '------------------------------------------------------------------
0002   '             Reusable template for startup code for
0003   '             Visual Basic Windows graphics applications.
0004   '------------------------------------------------------------------
0005   '   Source file:  MAMAIN.BAS
0006   '   Release version:  1.00                 Programmer:  Lee Adams
0007   '   Type:  Visual Basic startup module for Windows applications.
0008   '   Compiler:  Microsoft Visual Basic 2.00
0009   '   Dependencies:  MAGLOBAL.BAS global module
0010   '                   MAZE.FRM primary module
0011   '                   MAPLAY.BAS animation playback module
0012   '   Output and features:  Initializes the runtime environment
0013   '     for a Windows graphics application created with
0014   '     Visual Basic.  Ensures runtime image size and compatibility
0015   '     no matter which graphics mode is being used by Windows.
0016   '   Publication:  Contains material from Windcrest/McGraw-Hill
0017   '     book 4225 published by TAB BOOKS Div. of McGraw-Hill Inc.
0018   '   License:  As purchaser of the book you are granted a
0019   '     royalty-free license to distribute executable files
0020   '     generated using this code provided that you accept the
0021   '     conditions of the License Agreement and Limited Warranty
0022   '     described in the book and on the companion disk.  Government
0023   '     users:  This software and documentation are subject to
0024   '     restrictions set forth in The Rights in Technical Data and
0025   '     Computer Software clause at 252.227-7013 and elsewhere.
0026   '------------------------------------------------------------------
0027   '       (c) Copyright 1993 Lee Adams.  All rights reserved.
0028   '           Lee Adams(tm) is a trademark of Lee Adams.
0029   '------------------------------------------------------------------
0030
0031   Option Explicit            'generate error if variable not declared
0032
0033   '------------------------------------------------------------------
0034   '       Initialization code for startup of application
0035   '------------------------------------------------------------------
0036   Sub Main ()                     'is called by Windows at startup
0037     Dim PreviousColor As Long         'will remember default color
```

```
0038   StartUp = True                        'set the run-time tokens...
0039   IgnoreRefresh = True
0040   FrameReady = False
0041   FrameSaved = False
0042   FrameLoaded = False
0043   LoadingFrame = False
0044   UsingVR = False
0045   AnimationSaved = False
0046   AnimationLoaded = False
0047   PrevSaveAttempt = False
0048   PrevLoadAttempt = False
0049   UseDisk = False
0050   Preview = False
0051   '-------------------- initialize variables --------------------
0052   FrameNum = 1
0053   vrMove = vrSTATIONARY
0054   vrView = vrVIEW000
0055   vrRow = 4                        'set row and colum for view matrix...
0056   vrColumn = 2
0057   vrArrayOffset = vrFIRST_ARRAY              'set the view index
0058   vrFrameID = 0                              'set the node index
0059   '-------------------- 000 degree view angle --------------------
0060   FrameFiles(0) = "VR01.BMP"          'column 0, rows 0 through 4...
0061   FrameFiles(1) = "VR02.BMP"
0062   FrameFiles(2) = "VR03.BMP"
0063   FrameFiles(3) = "VR04.BMP"
0064   FrameFiles(4) = "VR05.BMP"
0065   FrameFiles(5) = "VR06.BMP"          'column 1, rows 0 through 4...
0066   FrameFiles(6) = "VR07.BMP"
0067   FrameFiles(7) = "VR08.BMP"
0068   FrameFiles(8) = "VR09.BMP"
0069   FrameFiles(9) = "VR10.BMP"
0070   FrameFiles(10) = "VR11.BMP"         'column 2, rows 0 through 4...
0071   FrameFiles(11) = "VR12.BMP"
0072   FrameFiles(12) = "VR13.BMP"
0073   FrameFiles(13) = "VR14.BMP"
0074   FrameFiles(14) = "VR15.BMP"
0075   FrameFiles(15) = "VR16.BMP"         'column 3, rows 0 through 4...
0076   FrameFiles(16) = "VR17.BMP"
0077   FrameFiles(17) = "VR18.BMP"
0078   FrameFiles(18) = "VR19.BMP"
0079   FrameFiles(19) = "VR20.BMP"
0080   FrameFiles(20) = "VR21.BMP"         'column 4, rows 0 through 4...
0081   FrameFiles(21) = "VR22.BMP"
0082   FrameFiles(22) = "VR23.BMP"
0083   FrameFiles(23) = "VR24.BMP"
0084   FrameFiles(24) = "VR25.BMP"
0085   '-------------------- 090 degree view angle --------------------
0086   FrameFiles(25) = "VR26.BMP"         'column 0, rows 0 through 4...
0087   FrameFiles(26) = "VR27.BMP"
0088   FrameFiles(27) = "VR28.BMP"
0089   FrameFiles(28) = "VR29.BMP"
0090   FrameFiles(29) = "VR30.BMP"
0091   FrameFiles(30) = "VR31.BMP"         'column 1, rows 0 through 4...
0092   FrameFiles(31) = "VR32.BMP"
0093   FrameFiles(32) = "VR33.BMP"
0094   FrameFiles(33) = "VR34.BMP"
0095   FrameFiles(34) = "VR35.BMP"
```

```
0096    FrameFiles(35) = "VR36.BMP"         'column 2, rows 0 through 4...
0097    FrameFiles(36) = "VR37.BMP"
0098    FrameFiles(37) = "VR38.BMP"
0099    FrameFiles(38) = "VR39.BMP"
0100    FrameFiles(39) = "VR40.BMP"
0101    FrameFiles(40) = "VR41.BMP"         'column 3, rows 0 through 4...
0102    FrameFiles(41) = "VR42.BMP"
0103    FrameFiles(42) = "VR43.BMP"
0104    FrameFiles(43) = "VR44.BMP"
0105    FrameFiles(44) = "VR45.BMP"
0106    FrameFiles(45) = "VR46.BMP"         'column 4, rows 0 through 4...
0107    FrameFiles(46) = "VR47.BMP"
0108    FrameFiles(47) = "VR48.BMP"
0109    FrameFiles(48) = "VR49.BMP"
0110    FrameFiles(49) = "VR50.BMP"
0111    '-------------------- 180 degree view angle --------------------
0112    FrameFiles(50) = "VR51.BMP"         'column 0, rows 0 through 4...
0113    FrameFiles(51) = "VR52.BMP"
0114    FrameFiles(52) = "VR53.BMP"
0115    FrameFiles(53) = "VR54.BMP"
0116    FrameFiles(54) = "VR55.BMP"
0117    FrameFiles(55) = "VR56.BMP"         'column 1, rows 0 through 4...
0118    FrameFiles(56) = "VR57.BMP"
0119    FrameFiles(57) = "VR58.BMP"
0120    FrameFiles(58) = "VR59.BMP"
0121    FrameFiles(59) = "VR60.BMP"
0122    FrameFiles(60) = "VR61.BMP"         'column 2, rows 0 through 4...
0123    FrameFiles(61) = "VR62.BMP"
0124    FrameFiles(62) = "VR63.BMP"
0125    FrameFiles(63) = "VR64.BMP"
0126    FrameFiles(64) = "VR65.BMP"
0127    FrameFiles(65) = "VR66.BMP"         'column 3, rows 0 through 4...
0128    FrameFiles(66) = "VR67.BMP"
0129    FrameFiles(67) = "VR68.BMP"
0130    FrameFiles(68) = "VR69.BMP"
0131    FrameFiles(69) = "VR70.BMP"
0132    FrameFiles(70) = "VR71.BMP"         'column 4, rows 0 through 4...
0133    FrameFiles(71) = "VR72.BMP"
0134    FrameFiles(72) = "VR73.BMP"
0135    FrameFiles(73) = "VR74.BMP"
0136    FrameFiles(74) = "VR75.BMP"
0137    '-------------------- 270 degree view angle --------------------
0138    FrameFiles(75) = "VR76.BMP"         'column 0, rows 0 through 4...
0139    FrameFiles(76) = "VR77.BMP"
0140    FrameFiles(77) = "VR78.BMP"
0141    FrameFiles(78) = "VR79.BMP"
0142    FrameFiles(79) = "VR80.BMP"
0143    FrameFiles(80) = "VR81.BMP"         'column 1, rows 0 through 4...
0144    FrameFiles(81) = "VR82.BMP"
0145    FrameFiles(82) = "VR83.BMP"
0146    FrameFiles(83) = "VR84.BMP"
0147    FrameFiles(84) = "VR85.BMP"
0148    FrameFiles(85) = "VR86.BMP"         'column 2, rows 0 through 4...
0149    FrameFiles(86) = "VR87.BMP"
0150    FrameFiles(87) = "VR88.BMP"
0151    FrameFiles(88) = "VR89.BMP"
```

```
0152  FrameFiles(89) = "VR90.BMP"
0153  FrameFiles(90) = "VR91.BMP"              'column 3, rows 0 through 4...
0154  FrameFiles(91) = "VR92.BMP"
0155  FrameFiles(92) = "VR93.BMP"
0156  FrameFiles(93) = "VR94.BMP"
0157  FrameFiles(94) = "VR95.BMP"
0158  FrameFiles(95) = "VR96.BMP"              'column 4, rows 0 through 4...
0159  FrameFiles(96) = "VR97.BMP"
0160  FrameFiles(97) = "VR98.BMP"
0161  FrameFiles(98) = "VR99.BMP"
0162  FrameFiles(99) = "VR00.BMP"
0163  '--------------- examine the graphics adapter ------------------
0164  hDesktopWnd = GetDesktopWindow()         'grab handle to desktop
0165  hDCcaps = GetDC(hDesktopWnd)      'get display-context for desktop
0166  DisplayWidth = GetDeviceCaps(hDCcaps, HORZRES)  'horiz resolution
0167  DisplayHeight = GetDeviceCaps(hDCcaps, VERTRES)  'vert resolution
0168  DisplayBits = GetDeviceCaps(hDCcaps, BITSPIXEL)   'bits-per-pixel
0169  DisplayPlanes = GetDeviceCaps(hDCcaps, PLANES)  'num of bitplanes
0170  RetVal = ReleaseDC(hDesktopWnd, hDCcaps) 'release display-context
0171  '--------------- determine the runtime memory mode --------------
0172  MemoryMode = GetWinFlags()          'will inspect this value later
0173  '--------------- determine version of Windows ------------------
0174  WindowsVersion = GetVersion()       'will inspect this value later
0175  '--------------- set mode-dependent twips factors ---------------
0176  HorizTwipsPixel = 15!: VertTwipsPixel = 15!      'set defaults...
0177  Window_Width = zWINDOW_WIDTH: Window_Height = zWINDOW_HEIGHT
0178  If DisplayWidth = 640 Then
0179    If DisplayHeight = 480 Then               'VGA 640x480 mode
0180      HorizTwipsPixel = 15!           '9600x7200 twips full screen
0181      VertTwipsPixel = 15!
0182      Window_Width = zWINDOW_WIDTH
0183      Window_Height = zWINDOW_HEIGHT
0184    End If
0185    If DisplayHeight = 350 Then               'EGA 640x350 mode
0186      HorizTwipsPixel = 15!           '9600x7000 twips full screen
0187      VertTwipsPixel = 20!
0188      Window_Width = zWINDOW_WIDTH
0189      Window_Height = 297!   'adjust for aspect ratio and font size
0190    End If
0191    If DisplayHeight = 200 Then   'nominal support CGA 640x200 mode
0192      HorizTwipsPixel = 15!
0193      VertTwipsPixel = 36!
0194      Window_Width = zWINDOW_WIDTH
0195      Window_Height = zWINDOW_HEIGHT
0196    End If
0197  End If
0198  If DisplayWidth = 800 Then    'SuperVGA, 8514/A, XGA 800x600 mode
0199    HorizTwipsPixel = 12!              '9600x7200 twips full screen
0200    VertTwipsPixel = 12!
0201    Window_Width = zWINDOW_WIDTH
0202    Window_Height = 317!                    'compensate for font size
0203  End If
0204  If DisplayWidth = 1024 Then            '8514/A, XGA 1024x768 mode
0205    HorizTwipsPixel = 12!           '12200x9216 twips full screen
0206    VertTwipsPixel = 12!
0207    Window_Width = zWINDOW_WIDTH
0208    Window_Height = 317!                    'compensate for font size
0209  End If
```

```
0210  If DisplayWidth = 720 Then                    'Hercules 720x348 mode
0211    HorizTwipsPixel = 12!
0212    VertTwipsPixel = 20!
0213    Window_Width = zWINDOW_WIDTH
0214    Window_Height = 297!      'adjust for aspect ratio and font size
0215  End If
0216  '-------------- display the splash sign-on banner ---------------
0217  UserWants = MsgBox("Graphics demo from Windcrest McGraw-Hill book
          4225.", MB_OKCANCEL, "Copyright© 1993-1994 Lee Adams.")
0218  If UserWants = IDCANCEL Then   'if user selected Cancel button...
0219    End                                      'then cancel this startup
0220  End If
0221  '------------- initialize and display the window ----------------
0222  Form1.Width = Window_Width * HorizTwipsPixel          'set width
0223  Form1.Height = Window_Height * VertTwipsPixel         'set height
0224  Form1.Left = (Screen.Width - Form1.Width) / 2  'horizontal center
0225  Form1.Top = (Screen.Height - Form1.Height) / 2   'vertical center
0226  Form1.Caption = "Virtual Reality Sampler"         'set the caption
0227  Form1.AutoRedraw = False            'disable automatic refresh
0228  Form1.BackColor = RGB(255, 255, 255)   'set the client area color
0229  Form1.ForeColor = RGB(0, 0, 0)                      'active color
0230  Form1.ScaleMode = PIXELS                   'will use pixel coords
0231  Form1.Show                                  'display the window
0232  '------------------ check if mouse present --------------------
0233  MousePresent = GetSystemMetrics(SM_MOUSEPRESENT)
0234  If MousePresent = 0 Then                            'if no mouse
0235    Beep
0236    MsgBox "No mouse found.  Some features of this demo program may
          require a mouse.  The demo's menu system also responds to the
          keyboard.  Press <Enter> to continue.", MB_OK, "Graphics
          system  warning"
0237  End If
0238  '----------------- initialize the 3D toolkit --------------------
0239  aazInitialize3D
0240  End Sub
0241

0001  VERSION 2.00
0002  Begin Form Form1
0003      Caption          =   "Prototype"
0004      ControlBox       =   0   'False
0005      Height           =   4515
0006      Left             =   2040
0007      LinkMode         =   1 'Source
0008      LinkTopic        =   "Form1"
0009      MaxButton        =   0   'False
0010      MinButton        =   0   'False
0011      ScaleHeight      =   3825
0012      ScaleWidth       =   3840
0013      Top              =   1485
0014      Width            =   3960
0015      Begin PictureBox Picture1
0016        Height         =     495
0017        Left           =     480
0018        ScaleHeight    =     465
0019        ScaleWidth     =     1185
```

```
0020        TabIndex        =   0
0021        Top             =   840
0022        Width           =   1215
0023    End
0024    Begin Menu POPUP_File
0025        Caption         =   "&File"
0026        Begin Menu IDM_New
0027            Caption     =   "&New"
0028            Enabled     =   0    'False
0029        End
0030        Begin Menu IDM_Open
0031            Caption     =   "&Open"
0032            Enabled     =   0    'False
0033        End
0034        Begin Menu IDM_Save
0035            Caption     =   "&Save"
0036            Enabled     =   0    'False
0037        End
0038        Begin Menu IDM_SaveAs
0039            Caption     =   "Save &As..."
0040            Enabled     =   0    'False
0041        End
0042        Begin Menu FileSep1
0043            Caption     =   "-"
0044        End
0045        Begin Menu IDM_Exit
0046            Caption     =   "E&xit..."
0047        End
0048        Begin Menu IDM_Restart
0049            Caption     =   "&Restart Windows..."
0050        End
0051    End
0052    Begin Menu POPUP_Edit
0053        Caption         =   "&Edit"
0054        Begin Menu IDM_Undo
0055            Caption     =   "&Undo"
0056            Enabled     =   0    'False
0057        End
0058        Begin Menu EditSep1
0059            Caption     =   "-"
0060        End
0061        Begin Menu IDM_Cut
0062            Caption     =   "Cu&t"
0063            Enabled     =   0    'False
0064        End
0065        Begin Menu IDM_Copy
0066            Caption     =   "&Copy"
0067            Enabled     =   0    'False
0068        End
0069        Begin Menu IDM_Paste
0070            Caption     =   "&Paste"
0071            Enabled     =   0    'False
0072        End
0073        Begin Menu IDM_Delete
0074            Caption     =   "&Delete"
0075            Enabled     =   0    'False
0076        End
0077    End
```

```
0078      Begin Menu POPUP_Run
0079         Caption         =    "&VR"
0080         Begin Menu IDM_LoadAnimation
0081            Caption         =    "&Load universe"
0082         End
0083         Begin Menu IDM_VirtualReality
0084            Caption         =    "&Run universe"
0085         End
0086         Begin Menu DemoSep1
0087            Caption         =    "-"
0088         End
0089         Begin Menu IDM_SaveAnimation
0090            Caption         =    "&Build universe"
0091         End
0092         Begin Menu IDM_UseShaded
0093            Caption         =    "Use &shaded solids"
0094         End
0095         Begin Menu IDM_UseWireframe
0096            Caption         =    "Use &wireframe mode"
0097         End
0098         Begin Menu DemoSep2
0099            Caption         =    "-"
0100         End
0101         Begin Menu IDM_PreviewFirst
0102            Caption         =    "Preview s&tart position"
0103         End
0104         Begin Menu IDM_PreviewFinal
0105            Caption         =    "Preview go&al position"
0106         End
0107      End
0108      Begin Menu POPUP_Use
0109         Caption         =    "&Use"
0110         Begin Menu IDM_About
0111            Caption         =    "&About"
0112         End
0113         Begin Menu IDM_License
0114            Caption         =    "&License"
0115         End
0116         Begin Menu HelpSep1
0117            Caption         =    "-"
0118         End
0119         Begin Menu IDM_Display
0120            Caption         =    "&Resolution of display"
0121         End
0122         Begin Menu IDM_Colors
0123            Caption         =    "Available &colors"
0124         End
0125         Begin Menu IDM_Mode
0126            Caption         =    "&Memory mode"
0127         End
0128         Begin Menu IDM_Version
0129            Caption         =    "Windows &version"
0130         End
0131         Begin Menu HelpSep2
0132            Caption         =    "-"
0133         End
```

```
0134        Begin Menu IDM_GeneralHelp
0135           Caption        =    "&How to use"
0136        End
0137      End
0138    End
0139    '----------------------------------------------------------------
0140    '                   3D virtual reality sampler
0141    '----------------------------------------------------------------
0142    '  Source file: MAZE.FRM
0143    '  Release version:  1.0                    Programmer:  Lee Adams
0144    '  Type:  Visual Basic global module for Windows applications.
0145    '  Compiler:  Microsoft Visual Basic 2.00
0146    '  Dependencies:  MAGLOBAL.BAS    global module
0147    '                 MAMAIN.BAS      module containing Main()
0148    '                 MAPLAY.BAS      animation playback module
0149    '                 ENGINE3D.BAS    3D toolkit (modified)
0150    '                 SHAPES3D.BAS    3D shapes toolkit
0151    '                 DEFORM3D.BAS    3D deformations toolkit
0152    '                 LIGHTS3D.BAS    light-source toolkit
0153    '                 ASSEMB3D.BAS    hierarchical modeling toolkit
0154    '  Output and features:  Demonstrates cyberspace-based control
0155    '     of virtual reality animation sequences.  The interactive
0156    '     demo provides a maze environment which can be traversed
0157    '     by the player, who uses the arrow keys to move from node
0158    '     to node in the artificial environment.  The viewpoint
0159    '     images require 3.2 MB of storage.  If insufficient memory
0160    '     is available for RAM-based playback, then each frame will
0161    '     be loaded from disk as needed during an interactive
0162    '     virtual reality session.
0163    '  Build notes:  This project relies on the 3D functions in
0164    '     ENGINE3D.BAS.  Before building the executable, you must
0165    '     make the following changes to ENGINE3D.BAS.  First, edit
0166    '     line 1044 in the hazClipToViewVolume() function, identified
0167    '     by the remark "discard if facet behind viewpoint", by
0168    '     changing And to Or.  Second, use remark tokens to disable
0169    '     lines 1057 through 1061 in hazClipToViewVolume(),
0170    '     identified by the remark "test the near clipping plane",
0171    '     comprising an entire If...End If block of code.  Third,
0172    '     use remark tokens to disable lines 1343 and 1347 in
0173    '     hbzDoZBufferTest(), so that the two statements enclosed by
0174    '     the If...End If block will always execute (disable the
0175    '     statement If zDepth <= FarClip And zDepth >= NearClip etc).
0176    '  Publication:  Contains material from Windcrest/McGraw-Hill
0177    '     book 4225 published by TAB BOOKS Div. of McGraw-Hill Inc.
0178    '  License:  As purchaser of the book you are granted a
0179    '     royalty-free license to distribute executable files
0180    '     generated using this code provided that you accept the
0181    '     conditions of the License Agreement and Limited Warranty
0182    '     described in the book and on the companion disk.  Government
0183    '     users:  This software and documentation are subject to
0184    '     restrictions set forth in The Rights in Technical Data and
0185    '     Computer Software clause at 252.227-7013 and elsewhere.
0186    '----------------------------------------------------------------
0187    '     (c) Copyright 1993 Lee Adams.  All rights reserved.
0188    '          Lee Adams(tm) is a trademark of Lee Adams.
0189    '----------------------------------------------------------------
0190    '
0191    '  SELECT A STARTUP FORM:
```

```
0192  '  Because this Visual Basic application uses a procedure named
0193  '  Main() at startup, you must specify Sub Main as the startup
0194  '  form in the Project Options dialog box before you run the
0195  '  program and before you build an .exe file.
0196  '
0197  '  DOUBLE-CLICK THE PICTURE-BOX TOOL:
0198  '  Because this demo uses a picture box when saving images to
0199  '  disk as .BMP files, you must double-click the Picture Box
0200  '  tool in the Toolbox at design-time to place a default-sized
0201  '  picture box on the form.
0202  '
0203  '----------------------------------------------------------------
0204
0205  Option Explicit            'generate error if variable not declared
0206
0207  '----------------------------------------------------------------
0208  '       Low-level keyboard handler for single-step animation
0209  '----------------------------------------------------------------
0210  Sub Form_KeyDown (KeyCode As Integer, Shift As Integer)
0211  If AnimationLoaded = False Then    'if animation is not loaded...
0212    Exit Sub                        'then cancel this function
0213  End If
0214  If FrameReady = False Then         'if hidden frame is not ready...
0215    Exit Sub                        'then cancel this function
0216  End If
0217  If UsingVR = False Then            'if virtual reality not running...
0218    Exit Sub                        'then cancel this function
0219  End If
0220  '--------- the arrow keys manage the viewpoint movement ---------
0221  If KeyCode = &H25 Then            'VR participant wants to move left
0222    vrMove = vrMOVE_LEFT                      'set viewpoint movement
0223    Call vrWalkthrough(vrMove, vrView)                  'call VR
0224    vrMove = vrSTATIONARY                    'reset viewpoint movement
0225  End If
0226  If KeyCode = &H27 Then           'VR participant wants to move right
0227    vrMove = vrMOVE_RIGHT
0228    Call vrWalkthrough(vrMove, vrView)
0229    vrMove = vrSTATIONARY
0230  End If
0231  If KeyCode = &H26 Then         'VR participant wants to move forward
0232    vrMove = vrMOVE_FORWARD
0233    Call vrWalkthrough(vrMove, vrView)
0234    vrMove = vrSTATIONARY
0235  End If
0236  If KeyCode = &H28 Then        'VR participant wants to move backward
0237    vrMove = vrMOVE_BACKWARD
0238    Call vrWalkthrough(vrMove, vrView)
0239    vrMove = vrSTATIONARY
0240  End If
0241  '----- the numeric keypad keys manage the viewing direction -----
0242  If KeyCode = &H68 Then          'VR participant wants to look North
0243    vrView = vrVIEW000
0244    Call vrWalkthrough(vrMove, vrView)
0245  End If
0246  If KeyCode = &H66 Then          'VR participant wants to look East
0247    vrView = vrVIEW090
```

```
0248    Call vrWalkthrough(vrMove, vrView)
0249  End If
0250  If KeyCode = &H62 Then          'VR participant wants to look South
0251    vrView = vrVIEW180
0252    Call vrWalkthrough(vrMove, vrView)
0253  End If
0254  If KeyCode = &H64 Then          'VR participant wants to look West
0255    vrView = vrVIEW270
0256    Call vrWalkthrough(vrMove, vrView)
0257  End If
0258  End Sub
0259
0260  '----------------------------------------------------------------
0261  '              Refresh the client area if uncovered
0262  '----------------------------------------------------------------
0263  Sub Form_Paint ()   'is automatically called by Windows as needed
0264  If LoadingFrame = True Then    'special case LoadPicture function
0265    Exit Sub
0266  End If
0267  If Preview = True Then                    'if previewing a frame...
0268    zCopyToDisplay                        'then copy from backup page
0269    Exit Sub
0270  End If
0271  If UsingVR = True Then          'if virtual reality is running...
0272    Call vrWalkthrough(vrMove, vrView)      'then redisplay the view
0273    Exit Sub
0274  End If
0275  zCopyToDisplay                        'otherwise copy from backup page
0276  End Sub
0277
0278  '----------------------------------------------------------------
0279  '           Intercept any attempt to resize the window
0280  '----------------------------------------------------------------
0281  Sub Form_Resize ()        'is called twice when window is resized
0282  If Startup = True Then   'if window being displayed for first time
0283    Startup = False
0284    IgnoreRefresh = True
0285    Exit Sub
0286  End If
0287  Form1.WindowState = 0                          'reset normal size
0288  Form1.Width = Window_Width * HorizTwipsPixel          'reset width
0289  Form1.Height = Window_Height * VertTwipsPixel         'reset height
0290  Form1.Left = (Screen.Width - Form1.Width) / 2  'horizontal center
0291  Form1.Top = (Screen.Height - Form1.Height) / 2    'vertical center
0292  If IgnoreRefresh = False Then                     'if second call
0293    IgnoreRefresh = True               'reset token for next first call
0294    MsgBox "This demo uses a fixed-size window.", MB_OK, "Sample
           application"
0295    Exit Sub
0296  End If
0297  Form1.Refresh                              'refresh the client area
0298  IgnoreRefresh = False        'if first call, reset for second call
0299  End Sub
0300
0301  '----------------------------------------------------------------
0302  '              Display the About message box
0303  '----------------------------------------------------------------
0304  Sub IDM_About_Click ()
```

C-6 Continued.

```
0305  MsgBox "This is a demo from Windcrest McGraw-Hill book 4225.
          Copyright© 1993 Lee Adams.  All rights reserved.", MB_OK,
          "About this Visual Basic program"
0306  End Sub
0307
0308  '-------------------------------------------------------------------
0309  '               Clear the client area of the window
0310  '-------------------------------------------------------------------
0311  Sub IDM_Clear_Click ()
0312  Preview = False                       'reset token to disable refreshing
0313  zClear                                    'clear the display window
0314  zClearHiddenFrame                         'clear the hidden frame
0315  End Sub
0316
0317  '-------------------------------------------------------------------
0318  '               Determine number of available colors
0319  '-------------------------------------------------------------------
0320  Sub IDM_Colors_Click ()
0321  If DisplayBits = 1 Then                    'if 1 bit-per-pixel...
0322    If DisplayPlanes = 4 Then                'if 4 bitplanes...
0323      MsgBox "Running in 4-bit, 16-color mode.", MB_OK, "Available
          colors"
0324      Exit Sub
0325    End If
0326    If DisplayPlanes = 1 Then                'if 1 bitplane...
0327      MsgBox "Running in 1-bit, 2-color mode.", MB_OK, "Available
          colors"
0328      Exit Sub
0329    End If
0330  End If
0331  If DisplayBits = 8 Then                    'if 8 bits-per-pixel...
0332    MsgBox "Running in 8-bit, 256-color mode.", MB_OK, "Available
          colors"
0333    Exit Sub
0334  End If
0335  If DisplayBits = 16 Then                   'if 16 bits-per-pixel...
0336    MsgBox "Running in 16-bit, 65000-color mode.", MB_OK, "Available
          colors"
0337    Exit Sub
0338  End If
0339  MsgBox "Running in a custom color mode.", MB_OK, "Available colors"
0340  End Sub
0341
0342  '-------------------------------------------------------------------
0343  '               Determine the screen resolution
0344  '-------------------------------------------------------------------
0345  Sub IDM_Display_Click ()
0346  If DisplayWidth = 640 Then
0347    If DisplayHeight = 480 Then                        'VGA mode
0348      MsgBox "Running in 640x480 mode.", MB_OK, "Screen resolution"
0349      Exit Sub
0350    End If
0351    If DisplayHeight = 350 Then                        'EGA mode
0352      MsgBox "Running in 640x350 mode.", MB_OK, "Screen resolution"
0353      Exit Sub
0354    End If
0355    If DisplayHeight = 200 Then                        'CGA mode
```

```
0356      MsgBox "Running in 640x200 mode.", MB_OK, "Screen resolution"
0357      Exit Sub
0358    End If
0359  End If
0360  If DisplayWidth = 800 Then              'SuperVGA, 8514/A, XGA mode
0361    MsgBox "Running in 800x600 mode.", MB_OK, "Screen resolution"
0362    Exit Sub
0363  End If
0364  If DisplayWidth = 1024 Then                   '8514/A, XGA mode
0365    MsgBox "Running in 1024x768 mode.", MB_OK, "Screen resolution"
0366    Exit Sub
0367  End If
0368  If DisplayWidth = 720 Then                      'Hercules mode
0369    MsgBox "Running in 720x348 mode.", MB_OK, "Screen resolution"
0370    Exit Sub
0371  End If
0372  MsgBox "Running in custom mode.", MB_OK, "Screen resolution"
0373  End Sub
0374
0375  '----------------------------------------------------------------
0376  '                     Terminate the application
0377  '----------------------------------------------------------------
0378  Sub IDM_Exit_Click ()
0379  UserWants = MsgBox("Exit the virtual reality session and return to
          Windows?", MB_YESNO, "Please confirm")
0380  If UserWants = IDNO Then             'if user selected No button...
0381    Exit Sub                             'then cancel this operation
0382  End If         'otherwise continue to terminate the application...
0383  If AnimationLoaded = True Then            'if animation loaded...
0384    RetVal = SelectObject(hFDC, hPrevF)      'select default handle
0385    For LoopCount = 1 To zNUMCELS Step 1        'for each handle...
0386      RetVal = DeleteObject(BitmapHandles(LoopCount - 1))   'delete
0387    Next LoopCount
0388    RetVal = DeleteDC(hFDC)    '...then delete memory display-context
0389  End If
0390  If FrameReady = True Then          'if a hidden frame was created
0391    RetVal = SelectObject(hFrameDC, hPrevFrame)    'deselect bitmap
0392    RetVal = DeleteObject(hFrame)                 'delete the bitmap
0393    RetVal = DeleteDC(hFrameDC)          'delete the display-context
0394  End If
0395  jczClose3d                          'shut down the 3D toolkit
0396  End                                 'terminate the application
0397  End Sub
0398
0399  '----------------------------------------------------------------
0400  '                  Display the Help message box
0401  '----------------------------------------------------------------
0402  Sub IDM_GeneralHelp_Click ()
0403  MgBox "The VR menu manages the virtual reality player.  Select
          Build Universe to create viewpoint nodes and save virtual
          reality sequence to disk.  Select Load Universe, then Run
          Universe, to start a virtual reality simulation.", MB_OK, "How
          to use this 000403  virtual reality demo"
0404  End Sub
0405
0406  '----------------------------------------------------------------
0407  '                  Display the License message box
0408  '----------------------------------------------------------------
0409  Sub IDM_License_Click ()
```

C-6 Continued.

```
0410  MsgBox "You can use this code as part of your own software product
          subject to the License Agreement and Limited Warranty in
          Windcrest McGraw-Hill book 4225 and on its companion disk.",
          MB_OK, "License Agreement"
0411  End Sub
0412
0413  '-----------------------------------------------------------------
0414  '            Load the virtual reality universe from disk
0415  '-----------------------------------------------------------------
0416  Sub IDM_LoadAnimation_Click ()
0417    Dim Bitmaps As Integer
0418  Preview = False                    'reset token to disable refreshing
0419  zInitializeSystem                       'ensure system is initialized
0420  If AnimationLoaded = True Then         'if frames already loaded...
0421    Form_Paint                       'refresh screen if animation running
0422    Beep
0423    MsgBox "The universe has already been loaded.", MB_OK, "Already
          loaded"
0424    Exit Sub
0425  End If
0426  If PrevLoadAttempt = True Then       'if previous attempt failed...
0427    Beep
0428    MsgBox "Previous attempt to load universe failed.  Cancelling
          this attempt.", MB_OK, "Virtual reality error report"
0429    Exit Sub
0430  End If
0431  PrevLoadAttempt = True
0432  '--------------- create bitmaps to hold the frames --------------
0433  RetLong = GlobalCompact(-1)          'maximize contiguous memory
0434  hFDC = CreateCompatibleDC(Form1.hDC)      'create compatible DC
0435  For LoopCount = 1 To zNUMCELS Step 1             'for each frame...
0436    BitmapHandles(LoopCount - 1) = CreateCompatibleBitmap(Form1.hDC,
          zFRAMEWIDE, zFRAMEHIGH)
0437    If BitmapHandles(LoopCount - 1) = Null Then       'if error...
0438      GoTo BITMAPS_NOT_OK              '...jump out of loop and tidy up
0439    End If
0440  Next LoopCount
0441  GoTo BITMAPS_OK                       'if OK, jump past error-handler
0442  '-------------------- bitmap error-handler --------------------
0443  BITMAPS_NOT_OK:
0444  For Bitmaps = LoopCount - 1 To 1 Step -1      'for each bitmap...
0445    RetVal = DeleteObject(BitmapHandles(Bitmaps - 1)) '...delete it
0446  Next Bitmaps
0447  RetVal = DeleteDC(hFDC)                 'delete the compatible DC
0448  UseDisk = True                             'reset run-time token
0449  AnimationReady = True                      'reset run-time token
0450  MsgBox "Insufficient memory to load entire universe from disk.
          Software will load each view as needed during VR session.",
          MB_OK, "Virtual reality advisory report"
0451  Exit Sub                               '...and return to caller
0452  BITMAPS_OK:                          'jump to here if no errors
0453  '--------------- load frame files into the bitmaps --------------
0454  For LoopCount = 1 To zNUMCELS Step 1            'for each frame...
0455    FileName = FrameFiles(LoopCount - 1)     'used by zLoadFrame()
0456    zLoadFrame                             '...and load the frame
0457    If FrameLoaded = False Then        'if disk error occurred...
0458      GoTo DISK_ERROR                     'jump to error-handler
```

```
0459    End If
0460    hPrevF = SelectObject(hFDC, BitmapHandles(LoopCount - 1))
0461    RetVal = BitBlt(hFDC, 0, 0, zFRAMEWIDE, zFRAMEHIGH, Form1.hDC,
            0, 0, SRCCOPY)
0462    RetVal = SelectObject(hFDC, hPrevF)
0463    Next LoopCount
0464    GoTo DISK_OK                    'if OK, jump past the error-handler
0465    '---------------------- disk error-handler ----------------------
0466    DISK_ERROR:
0467    For LoopCount = 1 To zNUMCELS Step 1    'for each bitmap handle...
0468      RetVal = DeleteObject(BitmapHandles(LoopCount - 1))  'delete it
0469    Next LoopCount
0470    RetVal = DeleteDC(hFDC)      'delete the memory display-context...
0471    Exit Sub                            '...and return to caller
0472    '-------------------- tidy up and return ----------------------
0473    DISK_OK:
0474    hPrevF = SelectObject(hFDC, BitmapHandles(0))
0475    AnimationLoaded = True
0476    AnimationReady = True
0477    AnimationSaved = True
0478    zClear
0479    zClearHiddenFrame
0480    Beep
0481    MsgBox "Universe successfully loaded from disk.", MB_OK, "Virtual
            reality ready"
0482    End Sub
0483
0484    '----------------------------------------------------------------
0485    '                 Determine runtime memory mode
0486    '----------------------------------------------------------------
0487    Sub IDM_Mode_Click ()
0488      Dim TempVariable As Long
0489    TempVariable = MemoryMode And WF_ENHANCED    'perform bitwise AND
0490    If TempVariable = WF_ENHANCED Then    'if result matches constant
0491      MsgBox "Running in enhanced mode.  Can allocate up to 16 MB
            extended memory (XMS) if available.  Virtual memory up to 4
            times physical memory (maximum 64 MB) is also available via
            automatic disk swapping of 4K pages.", MB_OK, "Memory mode"
0492      Exit Sub
0493    End If
0494    TempVariable = MemoryMode And WF_STANDARD
0495    If TempVariable = WF_STANDARD Then
0496      MsgBox "Running in standard mode.  Can allocate up to 16 MB
            extended physical memory (XMS) if available.", MB_OK, "Memory
            mode"
0497      Exit Sub
0498    End If
0499    MsgBox "Running in real mode.  Can allocate blocks of memory from
            the first 640K of RAM.  Can also allocate blocks from expanded
            memory (EMS) if available.", MB_OK, "Memory mode"
0500    End Sub
0501
0502    '----------------------------------------------------------------
0503    '                   Preview the goal position.
0504    '----------------------------------------------------------------
0505    Sub IDM_PreviewFinal_Click ()
0506    If UsingVR = True Then
0507      MsgBox "The virtual reality universe is already running.",
            MB_OK, "Virtual reality status"
```

```
0508    Exit Sub
0509  End If
0510  zInitializeSystem
0511  zClearHiddenFrame
0512  zClear
0513  Form1.CurrentX = 10
0514  Form1.CurrentY = 214
0515  Form1.Print "Preview of maze goal position..."
0516  Call jbzClearHidden3DPage
0517  Call kezResetZBuffer
0518  FrameNum = zNUMCELS
0519  zDrawCel                                          'draw the frame
0520  Form1.CurrentX = 10
0521  Form1.CurrentY = 228
0522  Form1.Print "Completed " & Time$ & " " & Date$
0523  If FrameReady = True Then                  'copy to backup page
0524    RetVal = BitBlt(hFrameDC, 0, 0, zFRAMEWIDE, zFRAMEHIGH,
          Form1.hDC, 0, 0, SRCCOPY)
0525  End If
0526  zCopyToDisplay
0527  Preview = True                  'set a token to enable refreshing
0528  End Sub
0529
0530  '----------------------------------------------------------------
0531  '                  Preview the startup position.
0532  '----------------------------------------------------------------
0533  Sub IDM_PreviewFirst_Click ()
0534  If UsingVR = True Then
0535    MsgBox "The virtual reality universe is already running.",
          MB_OK, "Virtual reality status"
0536    Exit Sub
0537  End If
0538  zInitializeSystem
0539  zClearHiddenFrame
0540  zClear
0541  Form1.CurrentX = 10
0542  Form1.CurrentY = 214
0543  Form1.Print "Preview of maze starting position..."
0544  Call jbzClearHidden3DPage
0545  Call kezResetZBuffer
0546  FrameNum = 23
0547  zDrawCel                                          'draw the frame
0548  Form1.CurrentX = 10
0549  Form1.CurrentY = 228
0550  Form1.Print "Completed " & Time$ & " " & Date$
0551  If FrameReady = True Then                  'copy to backup page
0552    RetVal = BitBlt(hFrameDC, 0, 0, zFRAMEWIDE, zFRAMEHIGH,
          Form1.hDC, 0, 0, SRCCOPY)
0553  End If
0554  zCopyToDisplay
0555  Preview = True                  'set a token to enable refreshing
0556  End Sub
0557
0558  '----------------------------------------------------------------
0559  '          Terminate the application and restart Windows
0560  '----------------------------------------------------------------
```

```
0561   Sub IDM_Restart_Click ()
0562   UserWants = MsgBox("Exit the virtual reality session and restart
              Windows?", MB_YESNO, "Please confirm")
0563   If UserWants = IDNO Then              'if user selected No button...
0564     Exit Sub                           'then cancel this operation
0565   End If        'otherwise continue to terminate the application...
0566   If AnimationLoaded = True Then             'if animation loaded...
0567     RetVal = SelectObject(hFDC, hPrevF)     'select default handle
0568     For LoopCount = 1 To zNUMCELS Step 1        'for each handle...
0569       RetVal = DeleteObject(BitmapHandles(LoopCount - 1))    'delete
0570     Next LoopCount
0571     RetVal = DeleteDC(hFDC)   '...then delete memory display-context
0572   End If
0573   If FrameReady = True Then          'if a hidden frame was created
0574     RetVal = SelectObject(hFrameDC, hPrevFrame)     'deselect bitmap
0575     RetVal = DeleteObject(hFrame)               'delete the bitmap
0576     RetVal = DeleteDC(hFrameDC)          'delete the display-context
0577   End If
0578   jczClose3d                              'shut down the 3D toolkit
0579   RetVal = ExitWindows(&H42&, 0)       'terminate and restart Windows
0580   End                                  'terminate the application
0581   End Sub
0582
0583   '----------------------------------------------------------------
0584   '              Create all frames and save to disk
0585   '----------------------------------------------------------------
0586   Sub IDM_SaveAnimation_Click ()
0587   If UsingVR = True Then
0588     MsgBox "The virtual reality universe is already running.",
              MB_OK, "Virtual reality status"
0589     Exit Sub
0590   End If
0591   Preview = False              'reset token to disable refreshing
0592   zInitializeSystem                    'ensure system is initialized
0593   If AnimationSaved = True Then          'if animation already saved
0594     Form_Paint                   'refresh screen if animation running
0595     MsgBox "The universe has already been saved to disk.", MB_OK,
              "Virtual reality status report"
0596     Exit Sub
0597   End If
0598   If PrevSaveAttempt = True Then          'if previous attempt failed
0599     MsgBox "A previous attempt to save the universe to disk has
              failed.  Cancelling this attempt.  Check available disk
              space.", MB_OK, "Virtual reality error report"
0600     Exit Sub
0601   End If
0602   PrevSaveAttempt = True      'set token to prevent subsequent calls
0603
0604   '------------------ build and save the cels -----  --------------
0605   For LoopCount = 1 To zNUMCELS Step 1             'for each frame...
0606     FrameNum = LoopCount          'set a variable used by zDrawCel()
0607     FileName = FrameFiles(LoopCount - 1)      'set for zSaveFrame()
0608     zBuildFrame                               'build the frame
0609     If FrameSaved = False Then  'check variable set by zSaveFrame()
0610       Form1.Caption = "Virtual Reality Player"     'restore caption
0611       MsgBox "The universe build process has failed because an image
              could not be saved to disk.  Please check for insufficient
              disk space.", MB_OK, "Virtual reality production report"
```

```
0612       Exit Sub                    '...and cancel loop if error occurred
0613     End If
0614 Next LoopCount
0615 '------------------- set tokens and tidy up -------------------
0616 Form1.Caption = "Virtual Reality Player"              'restore caption
0617 FrameNum = 1
0618 AnimationSaved = True
0619 PrevLoadAttempt = False
0620 zClear
0621 zClearHiddenFrame
0622 '------------------- display advisory notice ------------------
0623 Beep
0624 MsgBox "Universe successfully saved to disk.", MB_OK, "Virtual
          reality ready"
0625 End Sub
0626
0627 '---------------------------------------------------------------
0628 '             Toggle to use fully-shaded 3D entities
0629 '---------------------------------------------------------------
0630 Sub IDM_UseShaded_Click ()
0631 If UsingVR = True Then
0632   MsgBox "The virtual reality universe is already running.",
          MB_OK, "Mode already set"
0633   Exit Sub
0634 End If
0635 abzUseWireframeMode (False)          'call function in ENGINE3D.BAS
0636 MsgBox "Using shaded solids mode.", MB_OK, "Virtual reality status
          report"
0637 End Sub
0638
0639 '---------------------------------------------------------------
0640 '             Toggle to use wire-frame entities
0641 '---------------------------------------------------------------
0642 Sub IDM_UseWireframe_Click ()
0643 If UsingVR = True Then
0644   MsgBox "The virtual reality universe is already running.",
          MB_OK, "Mode already set"
0645   Exit Sub
0646 End If
0647 abzUseWireframeMode (True)            'call function in ENGINE3D.BAS
0648 MsgBox "Using wireframe modeling mode.", MB_OK, "Virtual reality
          status report"
0649 End Sub
0650
0651 '---------------------------------------------------------------
0652 '             Determine version of Windows
0653 '---------------------------------------------------------------
0654 Sub IDM_Version_Click ()
0655   Dim TempVar As Long
0656 TempVar = WindowsVersion And 7683  'test binary 00011110 00000011
0657 If TempVar = 7683 Then                          'if 30        3...
0658   MsgBox "Running under Windows version 3.3.", MB_OK, "Version
          report"
0659   Exit Sub
0660 End If
0661 TempVar = WindowsVersion And 5123  'test binary 00010100 00000011
```

```
0662  If TempVar = 5123 Then                          'if 20          3...
0663    MsgBox "Running under Windows version 3.2.", MB_OK, "Version
          report"
0664    Exit Sub
0665  End If
0666  TempVar = WindowsVersion And 2563  'test binary 00001010 00000011
0667  If TempVar = 2563 Then                          'if 10          3...
0668    MsgBox "Running under Windows version 3.1.", MB_OK, "Version
          report"
0669    Exit Sub
0670  End If
0671  TempVar = WindowsVersion And 3     'test binary 00000000 00000011
0672  If TempVar = 3 Then                             'if 00          3...
0673    MsgBox "Running under Windows version 3.0.", MB_OK, "Version
          report"
0674    Exit Sub
0675  End If
0676  TempVar = WindowsVersion And 4     'test binary 00000000 00000100
0677  If TempVar = 4 Then                             'if 00          4...
0678    MsgBox "Running under Windows version 4.0.", MB_OK, "Version
          report"
0679    Exit Sub
0680  End If
0681  MsgBox "Unable to report Windows version number.", MB_OK, "Version
          report"
0682  End Sub
0683
0684  '----------------------------------------------------------------
0685  '                       Run universe
0686  '----------------------------------------------------------------
0687  Sub IDM_VirtualReality_Click ()
0688  If UsingVR = True Then
0689    MsgBox "The virtual reality universe is already running.",
          MB_OK, "Already running"
0690    Exit Sub
0691  End If
0692  If AnimationReady = False Then
0693    MsgBox "Universe images not ready for playback.", MB_OK,
          "Virtual reality not ready"
0694    Exit Sub
0695  End If
0696  UsingVR = True                                  'set a run-time token
0697  MsgBox "You can use the keyboard to navigate the virtual reality
          environment.  The arrow keys move you ahead, back, left,
          right.  Use the arrow keys with NumLock toggled on to look
          North, East, South, West.  Also refer to the book.", MB_OK,
          "Universe 000697   startup"
0698  vrMove = vrSTATIONARY                    'reset viewpoint movement
0699  vrView = vrVIEW000                        'reset direction of view
0700  vrRow = 4                                'reselect the view node...
0701  vrColumn = 2
0702  Call vrWalkthrough(vrMove, vrView)              'display the scene
0703  End Sub
0704
0705  '----------------------------------------------------------------
0706  '    Display next frame in interactive virtual reality mode.
0707  '----------------------------------------------------------------
0708  Sub vrWalkthrough (CameraMove As Integer, CameraAngle As Integer)
```

```
0709  '----------------- update the direction of view -----------------
0710  If CameraMove = vrSTATIONARY Then  'if viewpoint is stationary...
0711                      '...then the direction of view is being changed
0712     Select Case CameraAngle
0713       Case vrVIEW000
0714         vrArrayOffset = vrFIRST_ARRAY
0715       Case vrVIEW090
0716         vrArrayOffset = vrSECOND_ARRAY
0717       Case vrVIEW180
0718         vrArrayOffset = vrTHIRD_ARRAY
0719       Case vrVIEW270
0720         vrArrayOffset = vrFOURTH_ARRAY
0721     End Select
0722     GoTo DISPLAY_VR                  'jump past viewpoint movement code
0723  End If
0724  '----- marry the movement direction to the direction of view ----
0725  If CameraAngle = vrVIEW090 Then
0726     Select Case CameraMove
0727       Case vrMOVE_FORWARD
0728         CameraMove = vrMOVE_RIGHT
0729       Case vrMOVE_RIGHT
0730         CameraMove = vrMOVE_BACKWARD
0731       Case vrMOVE_LEFT
0732         CameraMove = vrMOVE_FORWARD
0733       Case vrMOVE_BACKWARD
0734         CameraMove = vrMOVE_LEFT
0735     End Select
0736  End If
0737  If CameraAngle = vrVIEW180 Then
0738     Select Case CameraMove
0739       Case vrMOVE_FORWARD
0740         CameraMove = vrMOVE_BACKWARD
0741       Case vrMOVE_RIGHT
0742         CameraMove = vrMOVE_LEFT
0743       Case vrMOVE_LEFT
0744         CameraMove = vrMOVE_RIGHT
0745       Case vrMOVE_BACKWARD
0746         CameraMove = vrMOVE_FORWARD
0747     End Select
0748  End If
0749  If CameraAngle = vrVIEW270 Then
0750     Select Case CameraMove
0751       Case vrMOVE_FORWARD
0752         CameraMove = vrMOVE_LEFT
0753       Case vrMOVE_RIGHT
0754         CameraMove = vrMOVE_FORWARD
0755       Case vrMOVE_LEFT
0756         CameraMove = vrMOVE_BACKWARD
0757       Case vrMOVE_BACKWARD
0758         CameraMove = vrMOVE_RIGHT
0759     End Select
0760  End If
0761  '----------- inhibit any attempt to move through a wall ---------
0762  If CameraMove = vrMOVE_FORWARD Then     'if want to move North...
0763     If vrRow = vrMIN_ROW Then
0764       GoTo PROHIBIT
```

```
0765    End If
0766    If vrRow = 1 And vrColumn = 1 Then
0767      GoTo PROHIBIT
0768    End If
0769    If vrRow = 1 And vrColumn = 3 Then
0770      GoTo PROHIBIT
0771    End If
0772    If vrRow = vrMAX_ROW And vrColumn = 3 Then
0773      GoTo PROHIBIT
0774    End If
0775  End If
0776  If CameraMove = vrMOVE_BACKWARD Then       'if want to move South...
0777    If vrRow = vrMAX_ROW Then
0778      GoTo PROHIBIT
0779    End If
0780    If vrRow = vrMIN_ROW And vrColumn = 1 Then
0781      GoTo PROHIBIT
0782    End If
0783    If vrRow = vrMIN_ROW And vrColumn = 3 Then
0784      GoTo PROHIBIT
0785    End If
0786    If vrRow = 3 And vrColumn = 3 Then
0787      GoTo PROHIBIT
0788    End If
0789  End If
0790  If CameraMove = vrMOVE_RIGHT Then          'if want to move East...
0791    If (vrColumn = vrMAX_COLUMN) Then
0792      GoTo PROHIBIT
0793    End If
0794    If vrColumn = vrMIN_COLUMN And vrRow <> 1 Then
0795      GoTo PROHIBIT
0796    End If
0797    If vrColumn = 1 And vrRow = 1 Then
0798      GoTo PROHIBIT
0799    End If
0800    If vrColumn = 1 And vrRow = 2 Then
0801      GoTo PROHIBIT
0802    End If
0803    If vrColumn = 1 And vrRow = 3 Then
0804      GoTo PROHIBIT
0805    End If
0806    If vrColumn = 2 And vrRow = 0 Then
0807      GoTo PROHIBIT
0808    End If
0809    If vrColumn = 2 And vrRow = 2 Then
0810      GoTo PROHIBIT
0811    End If
0812    If vrColumn = 2 And vrRow = 3 Then
0813      GoTo PROHIBIT
0814    End If
0815    If vrColumn = 3 And vrRow = 1 Then
0816      GoTo PROHIBIT
0817    End If
0818    If vrColumn = 3 And vrRow = 2 Then
0819      GoTo PROHIBIT
0820    End If
0821    If vrColumn = 3 And vrRow = 3 Then
0822      GoTo PROHIBIT
```

```
0823    End If
0824  End If
0825  If CameraMove = vrMOVE_LEFT Then            'if want to move West...
0826    If vrColumn = vrMIN_COLUMN And vrRow  vrMAX_ROW Then
0827      GoTo PROHIBIT
0828    End If
0829    If vrColumn = 1 And vrRow = 0 Then
0830      GoTo PROHIBIT
0831    End If
0832    If vrColumn = 1 And vrRow = 2 Then
0833      GoTo PROHIBIT
0834    End If
0835    If vrColumn = 1 And vrRow = 3 Then
0836      GoTo PROHIBIT
0837    End If
0838    If vrColumn = 1 And vrRow = 4 Then
0839      GoTo PROHIBIT
0840    End If
0841    If vrColumn = 2 And vrRow = 1 Then
0842      GoTo PROHIBIT
0843    End If
0844    If vrColumn = 2 And vrRow = 2 Then
0845      GoTo PROHIBIT
0846    End If
0847    If vrColumn = 2 And vrRow = 3 Then
0848      GoTo PROHIBIT
0849    End If
0850    If vrColumn = 3 And vrRow = 0 Then
0851      GoTo PROHIBIT
0852    End If
0853    If vrColumn = 3 And vrRow = 2 Then
0854      GoTo PROHIBIT
0855    End If
0856    If vrColumn = 3 And vrRow = 3 Then
0857      GoTo PROHIBIT
0858    End If
0859    If vrColumn = vrMAX_COLUMN And vrRow = 1 Then
0860      GoTo PROHIBIT
0861    End If
0862    If vrColumn = vrMAX_COLUMN And vrRow = 2 Then
0863      GoTo PROHIBIT
0864    End If
0865    If vrColumn = vrMAX_COLUMN And vrRow = 3 Then
0866      GoTo PROHIBIT
0867    End If
0868  End If
0869  '------------------- detect a winning position ----------------
0870  If CameraMove = vrMOVE_LEFT Then     'if want to move West and...
0871    If vrColumn = vrMIN_COLUMN And vrRow = vrMAX_ROW Then
0872      Beep                          '...if located at row 0 column 4...
0873      MsgBox "You have found the maze's exit.", MB_OK, _
             "Congratulations!"
0874      Exit Sub
0875    End If
0876  End If
0877  '---------------- update the viewpoint location ----------------
```

```
0878  Select Case CameraMove
0879    Case vrMOVE_FORWARD
0880      If vrRow > vrMIN_ROW Then
0881        vrRow = vrRow - 1
0882      End If
0883    Case vrMOVE_RIGHT
0884      If vrColumn < vrMAX_COLUMN Then
0885        vrColumn = vrColumn + 1
0886      End If
0887    Case vrMOVE_LEFT
0888      If vrColumn > vrMIN_COLUMN Then
0889        vrColumn = vrColumn - 1
0890      End If
0891    Case vrMOVE_BACKWARD
0892      If vrRow < vrMAX_ROW Then
0893        vrRow = vrRow + 1
0894      End If
0895  End Select
0896  '---- use bitmaps resident in RAM to display appropriate view ---
0897  DISPLAY_VR:
0898  vrFrameID = (vrArrayOffset + vrNUM_COLUMNS * vrRow) + vrColumn
0899  If UseDisk = True Then
0900    GoTo LOAD_FROM_DISK                        'jump if using disk
0901  End If
0902  RetVal = SelectObject(hFDC, BitmapHandles(vrFrameID))     'handle
0903  RetVal = BitBlt(Form1.hDC, 0, 0, zFRAMEWIDE, zFRAMEHIGH, hFDC, 0,
          0, SRCCOPY)
0904  GoTo DISPLAY_POSITION               'jump past disk-based code...
0905  '------- load bitmap from disk to display appropriate view ------
0906  LOAD_FROM_DISK:
0907  FileName = FrameFiles(FrameNum - 1)
0908  zLoadFrame
0909  If FrameLoaded = False Then             'if an error occurred...
0910    UsingVR = False
0911    Beep
0912    MsgBox "Unable to load next image from disk.", MB_OK,
          "Unexpected virtual reality condition"
0913    Exit Sub
0914  End If
0915  RetVal = BitBlt(Form1.hDC, 0, 0, zFRAMEWIDE, zFRAMEHIGH, hFrameDC,
          0, 0, SRCCOPY)
0916  '------------------ display the viewpoint status ----------------
0917  DISPLAY_POSITION:
0918  Select Case CameraAngle
0919    Case vrVIEW000
0920      Form1.Caption = "Looking North from node " & vrRow & " " &
          vrColumn
0921    Case vrVIEW090
0922      Form1.Caption = "Looking East from node " & vrRow & " " &
          vrColumn
0923    Case vrVIEW180
0924      Form1.Caption = "Looking South from node " & vrRow & " " &
          vrColumn
0925    Case vrVIEW270
0926      Form1.Caption = "Looking West from node " & vrRow & " " &
          vrColumn
0927  End Select
0928  Exit Sub
```

```
0929  '------------- prohibit any movement through walls --------------
0930  PROHIBIT:       'jump to here if user attempts to move through wall
0931  Beep
0932  MsgBox "Movement through walls prohibited.  Please select another
            move.", MB_OK, "Virtual reality rule"
0933  End Sub
0934
0935  '----------------------------------------------------------------
0936  '                 Build one frame and save to disk
0937  '----------------------------------------------------------------
0938  Sub zBuildFrame ()
0939    Dim PrevFontClr As Long
0940    Dim PrevFontSize As Integer
0941  zClear                                      'clear the display window
0942  Form1.Caption = "Building image " & FrameNum & "..." 'caption bar
0943  zDrawCel                                          'draw one frame
0944  '-------------- display the titles and captions -----------------
0945  PrevFontSize = Form1.FontSize          'remember current font size
0946  PrevFontClr = Form1.ForeColor          'remember current font color
0947  Form1.FontSize = 16                            'set the size
0948  Form1.ForeColor = RGB(0, 0, 0)                'set the color
0949  Form1.FontTransparent = True      'use transparent font backgrounds
0950  Form1.CurrentX = 10                     'set the starting location...
0951  Form1.CurrentY = 6
0952  Form1.Print "A Lee Adams tutorial:"            'display text
0953  Form1.FontSize = 24                            'reset the size
0954  Form1.CurrentX = 8                        'reset the location...
0955  Form1.CurrentY = 24
0956  Form1.Print "Virtual reality"              'display text
0957  Form1.FontSize = PrevFontSize              'restore the size
0958  Form1.ForeColor = PrevFontClr             'restore the color
0959  Form1.CurrentX = 10
0960  Form1.CurrentY = 214
0961  Form1.Print "Find the exit from the maze."
0962  Form1.CurrentX = 10
0963  Form1.CurrentY = 228
0964  Form1.Print "Time:" & Time$ & " Date:" & Date$
0965  '-------------------- save frame to disk ----------------------
0966  zSaveFrame                                 'save frame to disk
0967  End Sub
0968
0969  '----------------------------------------------------------------
0970  '                   Clear the display window
0971  '----------------------------------------------------------------
0972  Sub zClear ()
0973  RetVal = PatBlt(hDC, 0, 0, zFRAMEWIDE, zFRAMEHIGH, WHITENESS)
0974  End Sub
0975
0976  '----------------------------------------------------------------
0977  '                   Clear the hidden frame
0978  '----------------------------------------------------------------
0979  Sub zClearHiddenFrame ()
0980  If FrameReady = False Then
0981    Exit Sub
0982  End If
0983  RetVal = PatBlt(hFrameDC, 0, 0, zFRAMEWIDE, zFRAMEHIGH, WHITENESS)
```

```
0984   End Sub
0985
0986   '----------------------------------------------------------------
0987   '           Copy the hidden frame to the display window
0988   '----------------------------------------------------------------
0989   Sub zCopyToDisplay ()
0990   If FrameReady = False Then
0991     Exit Sub
0992   End If
0993   RetVal = BitBlt(hDC, 0, 0, zFRAMEWIDE, zFRAMEHIGH, hFrameDC, 0, 0,
            SRCCOPY)
0994   End Sub
0995
0996   '----------------------------------------------------------------
0997   '           Copy the display window to the hidden frame
0998   '----------------------------------------------------------------
0999   Sub zCopyToFrame ()
1000   If FrameReady = False Then
1001     Exit Sub
1002   End If
1003   RetVal = BitBlt(hFrameDC, 0, 0, zFRAMEWIDE, zFRAMEHIGH, hDC, 0, 0,
            SRCCOPY)
1004   End Sub
1005
1006   '----------------------------------------------------------------
1007   '              Draw one 3D cel and place on frame
1008   '----------------------------------------------------------------
1009   Sub zDrawCel ()                         'uses global variable FrameNum
1010   Call cazDisableTarget                'unlock camera from fixed target
1011   Call zSetLightPosition(60, 180)          'set light-source position
1012   Call cdzSetVRCameraPitch(360)                    'set camera pitch
1013   '------------- set node-dependent camera parameters -------------
1014   If FrameNum <= 25 Then                   'if view angle = 0 degrees...
1015     Call cczSetVRCameraHeading(360)            'set the camera heading
1016     Select Case FrameNum        'set the appropriate node location...
1017        Case 1
1018          Call cezSetVRCameraLocation(-60, 0, 296)
1019        Case 2
1020          Call cezSetVRCameraLocation(-30, 0, 296)
1021        Case 3
1022          Call cezSetVRCameraLocation(0, 0, 296)
1023        Case 4
1024          Call cezSetVRCameraLocation(30, 0, 296)
1025        Case 5
1026          Call cezSetVRCameraLocation(60, 0, 296)
1027        Case 6
1028          Call cezSetVRCameraLocation(-60, 0, 326)
1029        Case 7
1030          Call cezSetVRCameraLocation( 30, 0, 326)
1031        Case 8
1032          Call cezSetVRCameraLocation(0, 0, 326)
1033        Case 9
1034          Call cezSetVRCameraLocation(30, 0, 326)
1035        Case 10
1036          Call cezSetVRCameraLocation(60, 0, 326)
1037        Case 11
1038          Call cezSetVRCameraLocation(-60, 0, 356)
1039        Case 12
```

C-6 Continued.

```
1040          Call cezSetVRCameraLocation(-30, 0, 356)
1041       Case 13
1042          Call cezSetVRCameraLocation(0, 0, 356)
1043       Case 14
1044          Call cezSetVRCameraLocation(30, 0, 356)
1045       Case 15
1046          Call cezSetVRCameraLocation(60, 0, 356)
1047       Case 16
1048          Call cezSetVRCameraLocation(-60, 0, 386)
1049       Case 17
1050          Call cezSetVRCameraLocation(-30, 0, 386)
1051       Case 18
1052          Call cezSetVRCameraLocation(0, 0, 386)
1053       Case 19
1054          Call cezSetVRCameraLocation(30, 0, 386)
1055       Case 20
1056          Call cezSetVRCameraLocation(60, 0, 386)
1057       Case 21
1058          Call cezSetVRCameraLocation(-60, 0, 416)
1059       Case 22
1060          Call cezSetVRCameraLocation(-30, 0, 416)
1061       Case 23
1062          Call cezSetVRCameraLocation(0, 0, 416)
1063       Case 24
1064          Call cezSetVRCameraLocation(30, 0, 416)
1065       Case 25
1066          Call cezSetVRCameraLocation(60, 0, 416)
1067    End Select
1068    GoTo CAMERA_UPDATED                    'jump past other view angles
1069  End If
1070  If FrameNum <= 50 Then                   'if view angle = 90 degrees...
1071    Call cczSetVRCameraHeading(90)
1072    Select Case FrameNum
1073       Case 26
1074          Call cezSetVRCameraLocation(-60, 0, 296)
1075       Case 27
1076          Call cezSetVRCameraLocation(-30, 0, 296)
1077       Case 28
1078          Call cezSetVRCameraLocation(0, 0, 296)
1079       Case 29
1080          Call cezSetVRCameraLocation(30, 0, 296)
1081       Case 30
1082          Call cezSetVRCameraLocation(60, 0, 296)
1083       Case 31
1084          Call cezSetVRCameraLocation(-60, 0, 326)
1085       Case 32
1086          Call cezSetVRCameraLocation(-30, 0, 326)
1087       Case 33
1088          Call cezSetVRCameraLocation(0, 0, 326)
1089       Case 34
1090          Call cezSetVRCameraLocation(30, 0, 326)
1091       Case 35
1092          Call cezSetVRCameraLocation(60, 0, 326)
1093       Case 36
1094          Call cezSetVRCameraLocation(-60, 0, 356)
1095       Case 37
```

```
1096          Call cezSetVRCameraLocation(-30, 0, 356)
1097      Case 38
1098        Call cezSetVRCameraLocation(0, 0, 356)
1099      Case 39
1100        Call cezSetVRCameraLocation(30, 0, 356)
1101      Case 40
1102        Call cezSetVRCameraLocation(60, 0, 356)
1103      Case 41
1104        Call cezSetVRCameraLocation(-60, 0, 386)
1105      Case 42
1106        Call cezSetVRCameraLocation(-30, 0, 386)
1107      Case 43
1108        Call cezSetVRCameraLocation(0, 0, 386)
1109      Case 44
1110        Call cezSetVRCameraLocation(30, 0, 386)
1111      Case 45
1112        Call cezSetVRCameraLocation(60, 0, 386)
1113      Case 46
1114        Call cezSetVRCameraLocation(-60, 0, 416)
1115      Case 47
1116        Call cezSetVRCameraLocation(-30, 0, 416)
1117      Case 48
1118        Call cezSetVRCameraLocation(0, 0, 416)
1119      Case 49
1120        Call cezSetVRCameraLocation(30, 0, 416)
1121      Case 50
1122        Call cezSetVRCameraLocation(60, 0, 416)
1123    End Select
1124    GoTo CAMERA_UPDATED
1125  End If
1126  If FrameNum <= 75 Then              'if view angle = 180 degrees...
1127    Call cczSetVRCameraHeading(180)
1128    Select Case FrameNum
1129      Case 51
1130        Call cezSetVRCameraLocation(-60, 0, 296)
1131      Case 52
1132        Call cezSetVRCameraLocation(-30, 0, 296)
1133      Case 53
1134        Call cezSetVRCameraLocation(0, 0, 296)
1135      Case 54
1136        Call cezSetVRCameraLocation(30, 0, 296)
1137      Case 55
1138        Call cezSetVRCameraLocation(60, 0, 296)
1139      Case 56
1140        Call cezSetVRCameraLocation(-60, 0, 326)
1141      Case 57
1142        Call cezSetVRCameraLocation(-30, 0, 326)
1143      Case 58
1144        Call cezSetVRCameraLocation(0, 0, 326)
1145      Case 59
1146        Call cezSetVRCameraLocation(30, 0, 326)
1147      Case 60
1148        Call cezSetVRCameraLocation(60, 0, 326)
1149      Case 61
1150        Call cezSetVRCameraLocation(-60, 0, 356)
1151      Case 62
1152        Call cezSetVRCameraLocation(-30, 0, 356)
1153      Case 63
```

```
1154          Call cezSetVRCameraLocation(0, 0, 356)
1155      Case 64
1156          Call cezSetVRCameraLocation(30, 0, 356)
1157      Case 65
1158          Call cezSetVRCameraLocation(60, 0, 356)
1159      Case 66
1160          Call cezSetVRCameraLocation(-60, 0, 386)
1161      Case 67
1162          Call cezSetVRCameraLocation(-30, 0, 386)
1163      Case 68
1164          Call cezSetVRCameraLocation(0, 0, 386)
1165      Case 69
1166          Call cezSetVRCameraLocation(30, 0, 386)
1167      Case 70
1168          Call cezSetVRCameraLocation(60, 0, 386)
1169      Case 71
1170          Call cezSetVRCameraLocation(-60, 0, 416)
1171      Case 72
1172          Call cezSetVRCameraLocation(-30, 0, 416)
1173      Case 73
1174          Call cezSetVRCameraLocation(0, 0, 416)
1175      Case 74
1176          Call cezSetVRCameraLocation(30, 0, 416)
1177      Case 75
1178         Call cezSetVRCameraLocation(60, 0, 416)
1179   End Select
1180   GoTo CAMERA_UPDATED
1181 End If
1182 If FrameNum <= 100 Then              'if view angle = 270 degrees...
1183   Call cczSetVRCameraHeading(270)
1184   Select Case FrameNum
1185      Case 76
1186         Call cezSetVRCameraLocation(-60, 0, 296)
1187      Case 77
1188         Call cezSetVRCameraLocation(-30, 0, 296)
1189      Case 78
1190         Call cezSetVRCameraLocation(0, 0, 296)
1191      Case 79
1192         Call cezSetVRCameraLocation(30, 0, 296)
1193      Case 80
1194         Call cezSetVRCameraLocation(60, 0, 296)
1195      Case 81
1196         Call cezSetVRCameraLocation(-60, 0, 326)
1197      Case 82
1198         Call cezSetVRCameraLocation(-30, 0, 326)
1199      Case 83
1200         Call cezSetVRCameraLocation(0, 0, 326)
1201      Case 84
1202         Call cezSetVRCameraLocation(30, 0, 326)
1203      Case 85
1204         Call cezSetVRCameraLocation(60, 0, 326)
1205      Case 86
1206         Call cezSetVRCameraLocation(-60, 0, 356)
1207      Case 87
1208         Call cezSetVRCameraLocation(-30, 0, 356)
1209      Case 88
```

```
1210        Call cezSetVRCameraLocation(0, 0, 356)
1211      Case 89
1212        Call cezSetVRCameraLocation(30, 0, 356)
1213      Case 90
1214        Call cezSetVRCameraLocation(60, 0, 356)
1215      Case 91
1216        Call cezSetVRCameraLocation(-60, 0, 386)
1217      Case 92
1218        Call cezSetVRCameraLocation(-30, 0, 386)
1219      Case 93
1220        Call cezSetVRCameraLocation(0, 0, 386)
1221      Case 94
1222        Call cezSetVRCameraLocation(30, 0, 386)
1223      Case 95
1224        Call cezSetVRCameraLocation(60, 0, 386)
1225      Case 96
1226        Call cezSetVRCameraLocation(-60, 0, 416)
1227      Case 97
1228        Call cezSetVRCameraLocation(-30, 0, 416)
1229      Case 98
1230        Call cezSetVRCameraLocation(0, 0, 416)
1231      Case 99
1232        Call cezSetVRCameraLocation(30, 0, 416)
1233      Case 100
1234        Call cezSetVRCameraLocation(60, 0, 416)
1235    End Select
1236    GoTo CAMERA_UPDATED
1237  End If
1238  '--------------------- render the scenery ---------------------
1239  CAMERA_UPDATED:                 'jump to here after camera updated
1240  Call bzSetHierarchyMode(False)     'disable hierarchical modeling
1241  '----------------- draw the exterior walls -------------------
1242  Call dczSetSubjectSize(15, 15, 2)     'set subobject extrusion
1243  Call dbzSetSubjectAttitude(0, 0, 0) 'set subobject orientation
1244  Call ddzSetShadingColor(zRED)                     'North wall...
1245  Call dazSetSubjectLocation(-60, 0, 281)
1246  Call azDrawCube
1247  Call dazSetSubjectLocation(-30, 0, 281)
1248  Call azDrawCube
1249  Call dazSetSubjectLocation(0, 0, 281)
1250  Call azDrawCube
1251  Call dazSetSubjectLocation(30, 0, 281)
1252  Call azDrawCube
1253  Call dazSetSubjectLocation(60, 0, 281)
1254  Call azDrawCube
1255  Call ddzSetShadingColor(zRED)          'all exterior walls are red
1256  Call dbzSetSubjectAttitude(90, 0, 0)                  'East wall...
1257  Call dazSetSubjectLocation(75, 0, 296)
1258  Call azDrawCube
1259  Call dazSetSubjectLocation(75, 0, 326)
1260  Call azDrawCube
1261  Call dazSetSubjectLocation(75, 0, 356)
1262  Call azDrawCube
1263  Call dazSetSubjectLocation(75, 0, 386)
1264  Call azDrawCube
1265  Call dazSetSubjectLocation(75, 0, 416)
1266  Call azDrawCube
1267  Call ddzSetShadingColor(zRED)
```

C-6 Continued.

```
1268   Call dbzSetSubjectAttitude(0, 0, 0)                    'South wall...
1269   Call dazSetSubjectLocation(-60, 0, 431)
1270   Call azDrawCube
1271   Call dazSetSubjectLocation(-30, 0, 431)
1272   Call azDrawCube
1273   Call dazSetSubjectLocation(0, 0, 431)
1274   Call azDrawCube
1275   Call dazSetSubjectLocation(30, 0, 431)
1276   Call azDrawCube
1277   Call dazSetSubjectLocation(60, 0, 431)
1278   Call azDrawCube
1279   Call ddzSetShadingColor(zRED)
1280   Call dbzSetSubjectAttitude(90, 0, 0)                   'West wall...
1281   Call dazSetSubjectLocation(-75, 0, 296)
1282   Call azDrawCube
1283   Call dazSetSubjectLocation(-75, 0, 326)
1284   Call azDrawCube
1285   Call dazSetSubjectLocation(-75, 0, 356)
1286   Call azDrawCube
1287   Call dazSetSubjectLocation(-75, 0, 386)
1288   Call azDrawCube
1289   ' Call dazSetSubjectLocation(-75,0,416)                'the doorway...
1290   ' Call azDrawCube
1291   '-------------------- draw the interior walls --------------------
1292   Call ddzSetShadingColor(zBROWN)       'North-South walls are yellow
1293   Call dbzSetSubjectAttitude(90, 0, 0)
1294   Call dazSetSubjectLocation(-45, 0, 296)
1295   Call azDrawCube
1296   Call dazSetSubjectLocation(-45, 0, 356)
1297   Call azDrawCube
1298   Call dazSetSubjectLocation(-45, 0, 386)
1299   Call azDrawCube
1300   Call dazSetSubjectLocation(-45, 0, 416)
1301   Call azDrawCube
1302   Call ddzSetShadingColor(zGREEN)           'East-West walls are green
1303   Call dbzSetSubjectAttitude(0, 0, 0)
1304   Call dazSetSubjectLocation(-30, 0, 311)
1305   Call azDrawCube
1306   Call ddzSetShadingColor(zBROWN)
1307   Call dbzSetSubjectAttitude(90, 0, 0)
1308   Call dazSetSubjectLocation(-15, 0, 326)
1309   Call azDrawCube
1310   Call dazSetSubjectLocation(-15, 0, 356)
1311   Call azDrawCube
1312   Call dazSetSubjectLocation(-15, 0, 386)
1313   Call azDrawCube
1314   Call ddzSetShadingColor(zBROWN)
1315   Call dbzSetSubjectAttitude(90, 0, 0)
1316   Call dazSetSubjectLocation(15, 0, 296)
1317   Call azDrawCube
1318   Call dazSetSubjectLocation(15, 0, 356)
1319   Call azDrawCube
1320   Call dazSetSubjectLocation(15, 0, 386)
1321   Call azDrawCube
1322   Call ddzSetShadingColor(zGREEN)
1323   Call dbzSetSubjectAttitude(0, 0, 0)
```

```
1324  Call dazSetSubjectLocation(30, 0, 311)
1325  Call azDrawCube
1326  Call ddzSetShadingColor(zBROWN)
1327  Call dbzSetSubjectAttitude(90, 0, 0)
1328  Call dazSetSubjectLocation(45, 0, 326)
1329  Call azDrawCube
1330  Call dazSetSubjectLocation(45, 0, 356)
1331  Call azDrawCube
1332  Call dazSetSubjectLocation(45, 0, 386)
1333  Call azDrawCube
1334  Call ddzSetShadingColor(zGREEN)
1335  Call dbzSetSubjectAttitude(0, 0, 0)
1336  Call dazSetSubjectLocation(30, 0, 401)
1337  Call azDrawCube
1338  '---------------------- tidy up and return -------------------
1339  Call cbzEnableTarget          'restore fixed-target camera mode
1340  End Sub
1341
1342  '--------------------------------------------------------------
1343  '                  Initialize the animation system
1344  '--------------------------------------------------------------
1345  Sub zInitializeSystem ()
1346  If FrameReady = True Then          'if hidden frame already created
1347    Form_Paint                       'refresh screen if animation running
1348    Exit Sub
1349  End If
1350  Picture1.Visible = False                      'hide the picture box
1351  Picture1.Top = 0: Picture1.Left = 0              'reposition
1352  Picture1.Width = 402: Picture1.Height = 302        'resize
1353  RetLong = GlobalCompact(-1)          'maximize contiguous memory
1354  hFrameDC = CreateCompatibleDC(hDC)        'get a display-context
1355  hFrame = CreateCompatibleBitmap(hDC, zFRAMEWIDE, zFRAMEHIGH)
1356  If hFrame = Null Then                      'if error occurred
1357    MsgBox "Insufficient memory.  Hidden frame not created.  Close
          other Windows applications to free up more RAM.", MB_OK,
          "Virtual reality fatal error"
1358    FrameReady = False
1359    Exit Sub
1360  End If
1361  hPrevFrame = SelectObject(hFrameDC, hFrame)      'select the bitmap
1362  FrameReady = True                          'set a global token
1363  zCopyToFrame
1364  UsingVR = False
1365  End Sub
1366

0001  '--------------------------------------------------------------
0002  '     Frame animation routines for Visual Basic applications
0003  '--------------------------------------------------------------
0004  ' Source file:  MAPLAY.BAS
0005  ' Release version:  2.00                  Programmer:  Lee Adams
0006  ' Type:  Visual Basic module for Windows applications
0007  ' Output and features:  Provides routines to manage the authoring
0008  '   process and playback engine for interactive VR sessions.
0009  ' Publication:  Contains material from Windcrest/McGraw-Hill
0010  '   book 4225 published by TAB BOOKS Div. of McGraw-Hill Inc.
0011  ' License:  As purchaser of the book you are granted a
0012  '   royalty-free license to distribute executable files
```

C-6 Continued.

```
0013 '    generated uSing this code provided that you accept the
0014 '    conditions of the License Agreement and Limited Warranty
0015 '    described in the book and on the companion disk.  Government
0016 '    users:  This software and documentation are subject to
0017 '    restrictions set forth in The Rights in Technical Data and
0018 '    Computer Software clause at 252.227-7013 and elsewhere.
0019 '----------------------------------------------------------------
0020 '    (c) Copyright 1992-1993 Lee Adams.  All rights reserved.
0021 '          Lee Adams(tm) is a trademark of Lee Adams.
0022 '----------------------------------------------------------------
0023 '
0024 Option Explicit            'generate error if variable not declared
0025
0026 '----------------------------------------------------------------
0027 '                      Load a frame from disk
0028 '----------------------------------------------------------------
0029 Sub zLoadFrame ()                    'uses global variable FileName
0030 If FrameReady = False Then
0031   MsgBox "Hidden frame not ready.", MB_OK, "Virtual reality error
         report"
0032   Exit Sub
0033 End If
0034 LoadingFrame = True                      'disable refresh procedure
0035 On Error GoTo LoadError:                  'enable error trapping
0036 Form1.Picture = LoadPicture(FileName)        'load .BMP image
0037 On Error GoTo 0                        'disable error trapping
0038 LoadingFrame = False                   'enable refresh procedure
0039 FrameLoaded = True
0040 '-------- select persistent bitmap, clear it, deselect it -------
0041 Form1.AutoRedraw = True
0042 RetVal = PatBlt(Form1.hDC, 0, 0, zFRAMEWIDE, zFRAMEHIGH, WHITENESS)
0043 Form1.AutoRedraw = False
0044 Exit Sub
0045 '------------------------- error-handler ----------------------
0046 LoadError:
0047   On Error GoTo 0
0048   LoadingFrame = False
0049   FrameLoaded = False
0050   Beep
0051   MsgBox "Unable to load the .BMP file.  Is system initialized?
         Does file exist on disk?", MB_OK, "Virtual reality error
         report"
0052   Exit Sub
0053 End Sub
0054
0055 '----------------------------------------------------------------
0056 '                      Save a frame to disk
0057 '----------------------------------------------------------------
0058 Sub zSaveFrame ()                    'uses global variable FileName
0059   Dim ErrorOccurred As Integer
0060 ErrorOccurred = False                     'set default tokens...
0061 FrameSaved = False
0062 If FrameReady = False Then
0063   MsgBox "Hidden frame not ready.", MB_OK, "Virtual reality error
         report"
0064   Exit Sub
```

```
0065   End If
0066   '-------------- copy display window to picture box --------------
0067   RetVal = BitBlt(hFrameDC, 0, 0, zFRAMEWIDE, zFRAMEHIGH, Form1.hDC,
          0, 0, SRCCOPY)
0068   Form1.Picture1.Visible = True              'show the picture box
0069   Form1.Picture1.AutoRedraw = True        'activate persistent bitmap
0070   RetVal = BitBlt(Form1.Picture1.hDC, 0, 0, zFRAMEWIDE, zFRAMEHIGH,
          hFrameDC, 0, 0, SRCCOPY)
0071   Form1.Picture1.Picture = Form1.Picture1.Image      'copy to screen
0072   Form1.Picture1.AutoRedraw = False   'disable the persistent bitmap
0073   '---------------- save picture box image to disk ----------------
0074   On Error GoTo SaveError                     'enable error trapping
0075   SavePicture Form1.Picture1.Image, FileName   'save bitmap to disk
0076   On Error GoTo 0                            'disable error trapping
0077   Form1.Picture1.Visible = False             'hide the picture box
0078   RetVal = BitBlt(Form1.hDC, 0, 0, zFRAMEWIDE, zFRAMEHIGH, hFrameDC,
          0, 0, SRCCOPY)
0079   If ErrorOccurred = True Then                'if disk error, exit
0080     Beep
0081     MsgBox "Unable to save the frame to disk as a .BMP file.
          Sufficient disk space?", MB_OK, "Virtual reality error report"
0082     Exit Sub
0083   End If
0084   FrameSaved = True
0085   Exit Sub
0086   SaveError:                                  'jump to here if disk error
0087     ErrorOccurred = True
0088   Resume
0089   End Sub
0090
```

D
Math primer for graphics programming

Graphics programmers tend to use mathematics more often than other programmers, but that doesn't mean you need to be a mathematician to be a graphics programmer. Quite the opposite is true. All you usually need to help you solve a particular problem is a quick primer or thumbnail synopsis of the relevant math. That's what this appendix provides.

2D vectors

A 2D vector is a line with both magnitude and direction. A vector is defined by its offsets from the XY origin. For example, a vector described as (1,1) would have one endpoint at 0,0 and the other endpoint at 1,1. As a consequence of its attributes, a vector defined as (1,1) would possess a magnitude (length) of 1 and a direction of 45 degrees. A vector defined as (–1,1) would possess a direction of 315 degrees, of course. The length of a vector is the square root of the sum of the squares of its two components. This means a vector defined as (10,10) would be 14 units in length.

Addition and subtraction When you add or subtract 2D vectors, you perform the operations on the corresponding components of the two vectors:

$$\vec{u} = (a,b)$$
$$\vec{v} = (c,d)$$
$$\vec{u} + \vec{v} = (a + c, b + d)$$
$$\vec{u} - \vec{v} = (a - c, b - d)$$

Scalar multiplication When you multiply a 2D vector by a scalar (regular) number, you multiply each of the vector's components by the scalar value:

$$\vec{u} = (a,b)$$
$$t\vec{u} = t(a,b)$$
$$\therefore t\vec{u} = (ta,tb)$$

Dot products A *dot product* is the result of a special way of multiplying two 2D vectors in order to produce a scalar number. A dot product of two vectors is the sum of the multiplication of the vectors' individual components:

$$\vec{u} = (a,b)$$
$$\vec{v} = (c,b)$$
$$\vec{u} \bullet \vec{v} = (a,b) \bullet (c,d) = ac + bd$$

2D vector representation of lines You can use 2D vector subtraction and scalar multiplication to represent lines, as shown here:

$$\vec{u} = \vec{w} - \vec{v}$$

If $\vec{x}$ is a vector extending from (0,0) to a point on a line that contains points P and Q then $\vec{x} - \vec{v}$ will be a multiple of $\vec{u}$.

$$\vec{x} - \vec{v} = t\vec{u}$$
$$\therefore \vec{x} = \vec{v} + t\vec{u}$$

Each choice of t will result in a specific point (x,y) that lies on the line.

3D vectors

A 3D vector is a line in 3D-space with both magnitude and direction. A 3D vector is defined by its offsets from the XYZ origin. For example, a vector described as (1,1,1) would have one endpoint at 0,0,0 and the other endpoint at 1,1,1. As a consequence of its attributes, a vector defined as (1,1,1) would possess a magnitude of 1 and a yaw-right of 45 degrees and a pitch-up of 45 degrees. A vector defined as (–1,1,1) would possess a yaw direction of 315 degrees and a pitch of 45 degrees, of course. The length of a 3D vector is the square root of the sum of the squares of its three components. This means a vector defined as (10,10,10) would be 17 units in length.

Addition and subtraction When you add or subtract 3D vectors, you perform the operations on the corresponding components of the two vectors:

$$\vec{v} = (2,1,7)$$
$$\vec{w} = (3,2,-5)$$
$$\therefore \vec{v} + \vec{w} = (2,1,7) + (3,2,-5) = (5,3,2)$$
$$\therefore \vec{v} - \vec{w} = (2,1,7) - (3,2,-5) = (-1,-1,12)$$

Scalar multiplication When you multiply a 3D vector by a scalar (regular) number, you multiply each of the vector's components by the scalar value:

$$\vec{v} = (2,1,7)$$
$$4\vec{v} = 4(2,1,7) = (8,4,28)$$

Dot products A 3D dot product results from a special way of multiplying two 3D vectors in order to produce a scalar number. A dot product of two 3D vectors is the sum of the multiplication of the vectors' individual components:

$$\vec{u} = (a,b,c)$$
$$\vec{v} = (d,e,f)$$
$$\vec{u} \bullet \vec{v} = (a,b,c) \bullet (d,e,f) = ad + be + cf$$
$$length\ of\ \vec{v} = |\vec{v}| \qquad length\ of\ \vec{u} = |\vec{u}|$$
$$\vec{u} \bullet \vec{v}\ |\vec{u}||\vec{v}|\ \cos\theta \quad where\ \cos\theta\ is\ the\ angle\ between\ \vec{u}\ and\ \vec{v}$$

If the angle between the two vectors is between 0° and 90°, then the dot product is a positive value. If the angle is between 90° and 180° degrees, then the dot product is a negative value. Cosine and arc cosine can be used to calculate the angle between two vectors using their dot product:

$$\cos\theta = \frac{\vec{u} \bullet \vec{v}}{|\vec{u}||\vec{v}|}$$

The angle between the two vectors is:

$$arccos \frac{\vec{u} \bullet \vec{v}}{|\vec{u}||\vec{v}|}$$

This capability is important for 3D shading.

Cross products The cross product of two 3D vectors is a vector that is *normal* (perpendicular) to the plane in which the two 3D vectors reside, as shown here:

$$\vec{u} = (a,b,c)$$
$$\vec{v} = (d,e,f)$$
$$\vec{u} \times \vec{v} = (bf - ce, cd - af, ae, bd)$$

This is essentially how 3D shading works. First, the software calculates the surface normal by computing the cross product of two 3D vectors (two half-edges) from the facet being considered. Next, the software uses dot products (see the previous paragraph) to calculate the angle between the surface normal and the incoming light ray (a vector). The size of the angle determines how much light is striking the facet, which in turn determines how brightly the facet should be shaded by the software.

Cross products are useful for back-face culling of facets because of the opposite direction nature of some cross products. Note in the previous example that $\vec{u} \times \vec{v}$ and $\vec{v} \times \vec{u}$ have opposite directions.

3D vector representation of lines You can use 3D vector subtraction and scalar multiplication to represent lines. The line that passes through (2,1,7) and (3,2,5) can be represented as $\vec{x} = \vec{v} + t\vec{u}$ where

$$\vec{u} = \vec{w} - \vec{v} = (3,2,-5) - (2,1,7) = (1,1,-12)$$

This means that the vector form of the equation of the line is:

$$(x,y,z) = (2,1,7) + t(1,1,-12)$$
$$\text{or } (x,y,z) = (2,1,7) + t((3,2,-5) - (2,1,7))$$
$$\text{or } (x,y,z) = \vec{v} + t\vec{u} \text{ where } \vec{u} = \vec{w} - \vec{v}$$

Matrix math

A *matrix* is a mathematical array of values. A matrix with 3 rows and 4 columns is usually depicted as:

$$A = \begin{bmatrix} a_{11} & a_{12} & a_{13} & a_{14} \\ a_{21} & a_{22} & a_{23} & a_{24} \\ a_{31} & a_{32} & a_{33} & a_{34} \end{bmatrix}$$

Special notation is used to identify specific members of a matrix, similar to the way in which an index is used by software to identify members of an array. For example, the notation a_{34} signifies the element located at row 3, column 4.

Multiplying two matrices Use this template when you want to multiply two matrices:

$$\begin{bmatrix} a_{11} & a_{12} \\ a_{21} & a_{22} \end{bmatrix} \begin{bmatrix} b_{11} & b_{12} \\ b_{21} & b_{22} \end{bmatrix} = \begin{bmatrix} a_{11}b_{11} + a_{12}b_{21} & a_{11}b_{12} + a_{12}b_{22} \\ a_{21}b_{11} + a_{22}b_{21} & a_{21}b_{12} + a_{22}b_{22} \end{bmatrix}$$

You'll want to pay careful attention to the fact that matrix multiplication is not commutative ($AB \neq BA$), but rather is associative: $A(BC) = (AB)C$. In other words, the order of the matrices being multiplied is important.

Transformation matrices A *transformation matrix* can transform a point to another location, provided that the point has first been associated with its own matrix. Consider matrix A:

$$\begin{bmatrix} a & b \\ c & d \end{bmatrix}$$

Any matrix A provides a means to associate a point (x,y) with the point $(ax + cy, bx + dy)$.

$$(x,y) \begin{bmatrix} 4 & 2 \\ 8 & 9 \end{bmatrix} = (4x + 8y, 2x + 9y)$$

Point (x,y) can be transformed to point $(ax + ay, bx + dy)$ using the matrix of transformation:

$$\begin{bmatrix} a & b \\ c & d \end{bmatrix}$$

Homogeneous coordinates Homogeneous coordinates are XYZ coordinates with a nominal fourth coordinate added. This fourth axis makes it possible to use a 4×4 matrix to transform the XYZ coordinates. This transformation matrix can be designed to translate, to rotate, or to scale the XYZ coordinates. For example, this four-dimensional representation can be scaled by multiplying each coordinate by the same factor, because the XYZ formulas preserve the ratios:

$$x = \frac{x^1}{w} \quad y = \frac{y^1}{w} \quad z = \frac{z^1}{w}$$

Points located at infinity can be represented by $w = 0$.

Translation in 3D space Use the template provided here to translate 3D XYZ coordinates to a new location in 3D-space:

$$[x\,y\,z\,w]\begin{bmatrix} 1 & 0 & 0 & 0 \\ 0 & 1 & 0 & 0 \\ 0 & 0 & 1 & 0 \\ t_x & t_y & t_z & 1 \end{bmatrix} = [x + t_x w \quad y + t_y w \quad z + t_z w \quad w]$$

Rotation in 3D space Use the three templates provided here to rotate a set of XYZ coordinates around the X-axis, Y-axis, or Z-axis in 3D-space.

For rotation around the Z-axis, adjusting roll by A radians:

$$\begin{bmatrix} \cos A & \sin A & 0 & 0 \\ -\sin A & \cos A & 0 & 0 \\ 0 & 0 & 1 & 0 \\ 0 & 0 & 0 & 1 \end{bmatrix}$$

For rotation around the X-axis, adjusting pitch by A radians:

$$\begin{bmatrix} 1 & 0 & 0 & 0 \\ 0 & \cos A & \sin A & 0 \\ 0 & -\sin A & \cos A & 0 \\ 0 & 0 & 0 & 1 \end{bmatrix}$$

For rotation around the Y-axis, adjusting pitch by A radians:

$$\begin{bmatrix} \cos A & 0 & -\sin A & 0 \\ 0 & 1 & 0 & 0 \\ \sin A & 0 & \cos A & 0 \\ 0 & 0 & 0 & 1 \end{bmatrix}$$

Scaling in 3D space Use this template if you want to scale a set of XYZ coordinates in 3D-space:

$$\begin{bmatrix} S_x & 0 & 0 & 0 \\ 0 & S_y & 0 & 0 \\ 0 & 0 & S_z & 0 \\ 0 & 0 & 0 & 1 \end{bmatrix}$$

Vector math for ray tracing

3D math for ray tracing uses parametric representation of vectors to compute different points along the path of the light ray (which is a vector). The template provided here shows how to calculate a particular XYZ location along the light ray by varying the parameter variable. By inspecting the resulting XYZ location, you can determine if the light-ray (a vector) has intersected a 3D entity (a facet) in the scene.

Assume that x_0, y_0, z_0 is the location of the camera. Assume that x_1, y_1, z_1 is a point on the viewplane window that represents the center of a pixel on the raster viewport. Then each point along the vector adheres to a parametric representation where the parameter t ranges from 0 to 1. In particular, $t = 0$ at the origin (the camera location) and $t = 1$ at the surface of the viewplane window:

$$x = x_0 + t(x_1 - x_0)$$
$$y = y_0 + t(y_1 - y_0)$$
$$z = z_0 + t(z_1 - z_0)$$

Assume that

$$\Delta x = x_1 - x_0$$
$$\Delta y = y_1 - y_0$$
$$\Delta z = z_1 - z_0$$

Then

$$x = x_0 + t(\Delta x)$$
$$y = y_0 + t(\Delta y)$$
$$z = z_0 + t(\Delta z)$$

To calculate the intersection of a vector with a facet, substitute the equation for a plane

$$A_X + B_Y + C_Z + D = 0$$

into the parametric representation for the vector

$$x = x_0 + t(\Delta x)$$
$$y = y_0 + t(\Delta y)$$
$$z = z_0 + t(\Delta z)$$

which yields

$$t = -\frac{(A_{X_0} + B_{Y_0} + C_{Z_0} + D)}{(A\Delta x + B\Delta y + C\Delta z)}$$

If the denominator is 0, then the vector does not intersect the plane in which the facet lies.

Glossary

actor A movable 2D or 3D object in procedural animation and physically based animation. Also called a cast member in procedural animation.

algorithm A method for solving a problem.

alias (1) The jagged effect, or jaggies, produced by diagonal or curved lines on monitors with coarse resolution. See supersampling. (2) The awkward jumping effect present in animations where the frame display rate is too slow to smoothly simulate actors moving at speed across the image. See motion blur. See anti-aliasing. (3) One of several names which refer to the same memory location or variable. See union.

alphanumeric A set of characters containing both letters and numbers.

animate on ones Animating by displaying each frame no longer than the frame rate, usually $\frac{1}{30}$ second (TV and VTR) or $\frac{1}{24}$ second (film). On personal computers the system timer chip issues an interrupt at 55 ms intervals (about 18.2 times per second), thereby limiting computer animation to animating on twos. See animate on twos.

animate on twos Animating by display each frame for a length of time that is twice the frame rate. TV and VTR animation is usually played at 30 frames per second. If an animation sequence is animated on twos, each frame is held on display for $\frac{1}{15}$ second instead of $\frac{1}{30}$ second (66.7 ms). The system timer chip in personal computers issues an interrupt at 55 ms intervals, permitting a close approximation of animating on twos.

animation A rapid display of separate images that deceives the human eye into perceiving motion. Animation is based on an optical illusion called image retention that is characteristic of all human eyes. Rather than seeing two separate images, the first image is retained long enough by the rods and cones of the eye to blur the transition to the next image when viewing film animation, television animation, or computer animation.

animation control The process of managing the objects and events that are being animated. See also animation implementation.

animation engine A block of code or a module that loads and manages the playback of an animation sequence.

animation implementation The mechanics of creating the illusion of movement on the computer screen. See also animation control.

anti-aliasing The process of reducing the visual impact of jagged lines or jumpy animation movement. See aliasing, motion blur.

area fill To fill a specified region with a specified color or pattern. The color attribute surrounding the region to be filled is called the boundary.

area process An image-processing function that modifies an individual pixel or picture element as a result of considering the surrounding pixels (the neighborhood). See point process, neighborhood.

argument A value passed to a function by the caller. The value received by a function or method is called a parameter.

array A set of data elements of similar type grouped together under a single name, usually arranged in rows and columns. An array can be scalar (consisting of numeric or string data) or graphic (consisting of pixel attributes).

articulated motion Movement of individual parts of a complex 3D assembly.

articulated motion editor An interactive, 3D application that can be used to specify the local motion and positioning of articulated entities (progeny and parent) in an animation sequence. See also staging editor and hierarchical modeling.

artificial reality Virtual reality.

audio track The sound component of an animation sequence or multimedia presentation. Microsoft Windows provides support for audio from a wave audio sound file, a musical MIDI file, or directly from CD-ROM or videodisc.

authoring Designing, creating, and testing an animation sequence, multimedia presentation, or virtual reality application.

authoring platform The personal computer system on which an animation sequence, multimedia presentation, or virtual reality application is prototyped and tested. See delivery platform.

AVI Acronym for audio-video interleaved, a Microsoft Windows animation standard supporting a 160-by-120 pixel viewport at 15 frames-per-second in 256-color mode using 8-bit palettized color, with audio at 11,025 Hz sampling rate at 8 bits-per-sample.

backface culling Backplane removal. Also see culling.

background color The underlying color over which the graphics are drawn. The GDI sets the default background color for a new window to white.

backplane removal The elimination of backward-facing facets from convex polyhedra like cubes, spheres, and cylinders in 3D scenes. Also called backface culling.

bar sheet A written, visual representation of the sound track for an animation sequence. Used to synchronize character movement with dialog and sound effects. See lip sync.

binary file A file stored in binary format, as opposed to ASCII or ANSI format (text). Sometimes called a binary image in graphics programming.

bit array A graphic array or bitblt image.

bitblt An acronym for bit block transfer. Also called block graphics and graphic array.

bitblt animation Graphic array animation.

bitblt image A graphic array.

bit block transfer See bitblt.

bitmap An arrangement of bytes in display memory or conventional memory representing a virtual display surface upon which graphics can be drawn. A device-dependent bitmap can be displayed on a particular device (ie a graphics adapter). A device-independent bitmap contains a generalized description of its contents, enabling the application (or Windows GDI) to modify it for display on a diverse range of devices.

bitplane One of four separate buffers that are sandwiched together by VGA, EGA, Super VGA, and other graphics adapters in order to drive video output. Also called a color plane.

bit tiling Mixing pixels of different colors to create patterns or shades. Windows' built-in bit tiling is called dithering.

black box A block of code that has been previously tested and debugged and is assumed to operate correctly. The programmer is unconcerned with the algorithm or processes used by the black box code, but rather with the input and output. See white box.

black-box testing Program testing that is concerned with input and output, not with the inner functioning of code. See white-box testing.

blitting Using bitblts (graphic arrays) in a graphics program.

block graphics Same as graphic array. See bitblt.

body suit Data suit.

Boolean logic Logic calculus employing operators such as NOT, AND, OR, XOR, and others.

bounding-box (1) In 3D computer graphics, a parallelepiped (a six-sided box) that encompasses all the vertices of a 3D model or subobject; (2) In 2D computer graphics, a rectangle that surrounds the vertices of an object. Also called a stand-in.

bounding-box test Using the bounding boxes of two objects to determine if a potential conflict exists.

b-rep Boundary representation, a method of creating images of 3D models by using planes, polygons, and facets. The outer surfaces or skin are used to model the so-called boundaries of the 3D object. See CSG.

buffer An area of memory used for temporary storage of data or images.

bump mapping The intentional random displacement of surface normals to simulate a rough surface on a 3D model.

camera coordinates The XYZ coordinates that describe how a 3D model will appear to a hypothetical viewer at a given location in the 3D scene. Also called view coordinates.

camera instruction sheet See dope sheet.

canonical view-volume A 3D view-volume derived from a cube whose vertices are located within a −1 to 1 range. Also called a normalized view-volume.

caption bar The title bar of an application's main window. Usually contains the name of the application.

cast-based animation An object-oriented form of animation control whereby multiple actors are independently animated in front of a scene. Also called procedural animation.

cast member See actor.

CATA An acronym for computer-assisted traditional animation.

CD-ROM An acronym for compact disk read-only memory. A 4.7-inch diameter plastic disc that stores digital data by pits and lands (bumps) that are etched into its surface. The data is read by interpreting the plastic surface with a laser beam. A CD-ROM disk can store 600 MB of data, representing numeric, text, sound, or graphic information.

cel (1) An image painted on acetate as used in traditional film animation studios. (2) The rectangular space occupied by a single character in a particular font. (3) A bitblt or bitmap used for computer animation sequences.

cel animation Computer animation that emulates traditional methods of cel animation, where actors or scenic elements painted on transparent acetate are manipulated in front of static background art while being filmed using a single-exposure camera.

chroma-key See key color.

CGI Computer-generated image.

CGM The ANSI computer graphics metafile format for exchanging images between application programs or between computer systems.

claymation A form of pixilation animation in which clay and plasticine models are used as actors and scenery. See pixilation, stop-motion photography.

client area The interior image space of a Windows application's main window that is available for use by the application. Also called the window viewport.

clipboard A block of global memory that is managed by Windows in order to permit applications to pass data and images to other applications.

clock tick An interrupt issued at intervals of 54.925 ms (about 18.2 times each second) by the system timer chip. See INT 08H.

CMY model The cyan-magenta-yellow color model used primarily by printers and publishers using offset lithography.

clipping See line clipping.

cognitive computing Software processes that mimic human thinking by means of neural-based, fuzzy-based, or genetic-based algorithms.

collision detection Detecting the moment when a vertex or facet of one solid 3D model conflicts with the space occupied by another solid 3D model. Collision response refers to the action taken by the software after collision is detected.

color cycling A method for producing animation by swapping palette values.

color interpolation Determining the color of a pixel from its neighbors or from its distance between two pixels whose colors are known.

computer visualization Using graphics to interpret, manipulate, or create data. Specialized fields of computer visualization include scientific visualization, 3D modeling and rendering, computer animation, biomedicine, fluid dynamics, tomography, computer vision, image processing, and others.

constructive solid geometry See CSG.

conventional memory RAM up to 640K.

coordinate system The arrangement of x axis and y axis in a 2D graphics environment or the arrangement of x axis, y axis, and z axis in a 3D graphics environment.

copy To provide a handle to the Windows clipboard.

cosine The cosine of an angle in a right-angle triangle defines the relationship between the hypotenuse and the adjacent side.

CSG Constructive solid geometry, a method of creating images of 3D models by using primitives (subobjects) such as cubes, cylinders, spheres, and cones. See b-rep.

culling (1) A 3D modeling paradigm that discards an entity that would occupy only a few pixels; (2) A 3D modeling algorithm that detects and discards backward-facing facets from 3D solids. Also see backface culling.

cut To instantly change from one full-frame image to another during animation playback. See also dissolve.

cyberspace A virtual environment consisting of multiple computers, databases, and users. Sometimes used to mean artificial reality.

cycle See loop.

data suit A full-body suit used in virtual reality applications to provide input representing the positions and orientation of various parts of the user's body.

decrement To make smaller by a specified number of units.

default A condition assumed to exist unless defined otherwise by the user or developer.

deformation See squashing-and-stretching.

degrees-of-freedom The translation and rotation input values permitted by a virtual reality input device. A mouse provides two degrees-of-freedom or 2D input. A bat provides 3D input (XYZ translation or yaw-roll-pitch rotation). A bird provides 6D input (XYZ translation and yaw-roll-pitch rotation).

delivery platform The personal computer system(s) on which a finished animation sequence, multimedia presentation, or virtual reality application is intended to be played. Also called a playback platform. See authoring platform.

depth cuing The use of colors or line styles to assist the viewer in interpreting depth in a computer-generated 3D image.

depth sort Ordering (sorting) the visible facets of a 3D scene into a sequence so that the 3D modeler draws the facets in farthest-to-nearest order (the so-called painter's algorithm).

detail polygon A two-dimensional facet containing line and color detailing that is mapped to a corresponding facet on a 3D entity in order to provide enhanced visual detail.

development platform The configuration of hardware and software used to build a software product. See target platform.

digital camera A still camera that stores imagery in digital format instead of on photographic film. Dedicated software permits the image data to be exported to a personal computer via the parallel or serial port.

digital video interactive A combination of hardware and software methods for combining graphics, video, audio, titling, and other multimedia components into a computer-controlled presentation. See multimedia.

digitize To convert an analog image or signal to a corresponding series of bits and bytes.

dirty rectangle animation Refresh animation.

display context A Windows data structure that defines an output device and the various drawing attributes associated with it, such as drawing tools, colors, dimensions, and others.

display coordinates Screen coordinates. Refers primarily to the converted camera coordinates of a 3D modeling application.

display-independent Refers to algorithms, functional code, graphics, and Windows applications that perform consistently across a diverse range of different display modes and display hardware.

display schedule A script that manages the playback of an animation sequence.

dissolve To smoothly replace one image with another by fading out the first image while fading up the second image. Also called a crossfade.

dithering The bit tiling or patterning of pixels used to implement a shading or coloring scheme. Windows uses dithering to simulate colors beyond the limited selection available in the 16-color VGA mode. See bit tiling.

DLL See dynamic link library.

do-nothing routine A routine that simply returns control to the caller. Do-nothing routines are used during preliminary program development and debugging. Also called a stub.

dope sheet A camera instruction sheet for animation production.

double-buffer animation A method of animation whereby the software builds the next frame on a hidden bitmap while displaying the current frame on the application's display window. To display the next finished image the application copies the hidden bitmap to the screen. Double-buffer animation is implemented differently in applications running under DOS.

dpi Dots per inch. Often used to describe the graphics resolution of laser printers and scanners.

DVI An acronym for digital video interactive.

dynamic link library A library of routines and data that can be called or accessed by any Windows application. The Graphics Device Interface (GDI) is a dynamic link library (DLL). A DLL file might use either the dll or exe filename extension.

dynamics The study of motion as it relates to force, mass, and other constraints in animation sequences.

electronic darkroom Refers to image-processing routines that manipulate images to produce results otherwise obtained by sending negatives, transparencies, or prints to professional photography labs or retouching services.

elegant See optimize.

elision A 3D modeling paradigm that refrains from rendering entities past a specified distance in order to avoid cluttering a 3D image.

EMB Extended memory blocks.

emulation (1) Simulation of unavailable hardware by available hardware and software; (2) Simulation of a real-world situation or event by software.

EMS Expanded memory specification. Expanded memory is used to provide additional physical RAM for computers which are otherwise limited to 640K RAM. Access is through a page manager. See XMS.

enhanced mode Windows runtime memory mode requiring an 80286, 80386, 80486 or higher processor with more than 2MB RAM running in protected mode and providing virtual memory via disk swapping when physical memory is exhausted.

ensemble animation Refresh animation.

ensemble processing An image-processing function whereby the content of two images is compared. See also ensemble animation and refresh animation.

ergonomics Refers to compatibility of hardware or software with human psychology and physiology.

error-handler An algorithm or routine used to handle exceptions occurring at runtime.

error trapping Using a programmer-defined routine to detect and respond to errors caused by hardware or software exceptions at runtime.

Euler operators Logical and arithmetic operators for the manipulation of 3D solids. The standard operations are join, intersection, and subtraction.

expanded memory See EMS.

exploratory VR A virtual reality environment that allows the user to actively explore but not otherwise interact with the environment. See also passive VR and interactive VR.

expression A combination of operators acting on variables.

extended memory See XMS.

extrusion Stretching or deforming an object in a 3D scene. See rotation. See translation.

4D Four dimensional. Often used to refer to animated 3D computer graphics because the fourth dimension of time has been added to the image. Usually represented by (x,y,z,t) notation.

4D space-time A display of 3D-space over time. See 4D.

facet A polygonal plane surface used to create solid 3D models constructed by the B-rep method.

filtering A method of color interpolation useful for anti-aliasing (removal of jaggies).

fitted curve A computer-generated curve.

fixed-loop animation An animation sequence driven by a block of code that executes repeatedly for a fixed number of iterations. See idle-loop animation.

font A cohesive set of alphanumeric characters in a particular point size (i.e.,12 pt.) of a particular typeface (i.e., Arial) in a particular type style (i.e., bold).

font file A file containing the bitmap data or vector formulas required to generate and display a particular font. See font.

force constraints The forces acting upon actors in a physically based animation sequence. See geometric constraints.

forensic animation Computer-generated animation used as evidence in criminal proceedings or civil litigation, often in motor vehicle collision cases.

forward dynamics The process of calculating the result of the application of force, loads, or constraints on an object. See inverse dynamics.

forward kinematics The process of calculating the result of the application of velocity or acceleration on an object. See inverse kinematics.

fourier analysis Using rate of change as the discriminating factor to analyze image data.

fourier window A method of anti-aliasing.

fps Frames per second, used to express the display rate of animation programs. Traditional film animation uses 24 frames per second (25 fps in Europe). North American NTSC television animation uses 30 frames per second (25 fps in Europe). See NTSC.

frame (1) A single image in an animation sequence, usually intended to mean a full screen image. (2) A complete image that is being interpreted or manipulated by an image-processing function.

frame animation The rapid display of previously created graphic images (frames). Frames can be stored as metafiles or as bitmaps in convention memory, extended memory, or on hard disk. See animation engine.

frame buffer The bitmap or viewport where the color values or image of a Z-buffer-rendered 3D scene is stored. The corresponding depth-values are stored in the Z-buffer.

frame grab Capturing a graphic image from an external source and storing it in a buffer or on disk. Typical external sources include scanners, live video, videotape players, and others.

frame process An image-processing function that manipulates or combines two input images to produce a third image. Each image is called a frame.

frames per second The rate of animation, expressed as new images per second. Also called fps.

freeze-frame To display over a period of time a single frame from an animated sequence.

frequency The rate of change found by fourier analysis.

frisket (1) A paper or cellophane shield used by graphic artists and film animators to protect portions of artwork from being inadvertently colored during airbrushing; (2) A bitmap matte used to protect an existing background during a transparent put operation. See transparent put.

GDI Graphics Device Interface, the host graphics engine built into Windows as a dynamic link library (DLL) whose routines can be called by any Windows application.

gdi.exe The Windows dynamic link library that provides device independent graphics functions for Windows applications. See user.exe and kernel.exe.

geometric constraints The dimensional conditions affecting physically based animation. See also force constraints.

geometric model A mathematical definition of an object.

geometric processing Image processing functions such as move, copy, shear, stretch, and others.

geometry Mathematics concerned with points, lines, angles, shapes, solids, and surfaces.

gnomon A visual representation of the XYZ axis system in a 3D application.

Gouraud shading Smooth shading.

gradient A subtle transition between two hues. Also called a ramp.

graphics device interface See GDI.

graphic array A rectangular image that has been saved in RAM as a bit array (bitblt) for later retrieval and display. Also called a block. See bitblt.

graphic array animation Placing one or more graphic arrays (bitblts) onto the display in order to produce animation. Also called bitblt animation and block animation.

graphics driver A module of executable code designed to interact directly with the graphics hardware. The VGA graphics driver shipped with the retail version of Windows is named VGA.DRV.

gray scale Refers to images or to the palette scheme used by images displayed as a range of gray tones.

groundplane A graphic representation of the orientation of the 3D environment in modeling and shading software.

GUI Graphical user interface.

handle An identifier that is provided by Windows to an application at runtime that permits the application to use or manipulate a window, display context, bitmap, data, or other object identified by the handle.

hexadecimal The base 16 numbering system. The decimal system uses base 10. The base is also called the radix.

hidden line A line that is hidden by another graphic.

hidden surface A plane or facet that is hidden by other surfaces.

hidden surface elimination See hidden surface removal.

hidden surface removal The process of removing from a 3D scene all surfaces that should be hidden from view. Visible surface algorithms falls into two broad categories: image-space methods and object-space methods.

hierarchical modeler An interactive, 3D application that can be used to design and construct complex assemblies of subobjects (primitives). See also primitives modeler.

hierarchical modeling A 3D modeling paradigm that uses hierarchies of related subobjects to built complex assemblies and subassemblies. Also see parent. Also see progeny.

hierarchy A database of related 3D subobjects or entities (parents and progeny). See hierarchical modeling.

high memory The first 64K segment of memory in RAM physically located above 1 MB on an 80286, 80386, 80486, or newer computer. Through an addressing idiosyncrasy DOS applications can access this portion of memory and can use it as a page to access simulated EMS, which is actually located in XMS.

histogram A table describing the distribution of gray values or color in an image being manipulated by image-processing software.

HLS The hue-luminance-saturation color model.

HMA High memory area.

HMD Head-mounted display used in virtual reality.

host graphics engine The runtime graphics library being used. Windows applications use the Graphics Device Interface (GDI) as the host engine.

HSV The hue-saturation-value color model.

Hungarian notation A convention of rules for naming and capitalization of functions, variables, and constants in Windows applications source files.

HVC The hue-value-chroma color model.

icon A miniature bitmap image that represents a minimized Windows application.

idle-loop animation An animation sequence driven by a block of code that executes repeatedly, but only when there are no other demands on the Windows operating environment. See fixed-loop animation.

illumination model A paradigm that explains the process whereby a computer-generated 3D scene is lighted.

image file A binary file that contains a graphic image or the algorithm for recreating the image.

image-precision algorithms Refers to 3D hidden-surface and illumination routines that perform their calculations on pixels rather than on the 3D coordinates. Also called image-space methods. Also see object-precision algorithms.

image processing Analyzing, interpreting, and modifying a digitized image with a computer. Typical applications include photo retouching and enhancement, blur removal, edge detection, geometric processing (stretch, invert, mirror, flop), contrast adjustment, cut and paste, computer vision, morphing and tweening, pattern recognition, target-recognition, ensemble processing, and others.

image-space methods Image-precision algorithms.

include file A text file that is logically but not physically merged into the source code at compile time.

increment To make larger by a specified number of units.

ink and paint In traditional film animation, refers to the final rendering (or inking and painting) of cels derived from the pencil sketches used to prototype the animation sequence. In computer animation, refers to coloring the frames, whether by interactive paint software or by computer-controlled automatic methods.

instance (1) A single occurrence of a graphical entity in an image or scene. (2) A running copy of a Windows application.

instancing Creating a complex 2D or 3D model by multiple occurrences of the same entity at different locations in the scene.

int 08H An interrupt issued 18.2 times each second (once each 54.925 milliseconds) by the computer's system timer chip. Used by Windows' virtual timer. See clock tick.

integer A whole number with no fractional parts or decimal point.

interactive Responds to input from the user at runtime.

interactive graphics Software that creates or modifies a graphical display in timely response to user input.

interactive VR A virtual reality environment that allows the user to explore and interact with the environment. See also passive VR and exploratory VR.

interop Interoperability, the ability of software to operate on and share data across different hardware platforms.

intersection See Euler operators.

inverse dynamics The process of calculating the forces or constraints required to move an object of a certain mass from one position to another over a fixed period of time. See forward dynamics.

inverse kinematics The process of calculating the velocity or acceleration required to move an object from one position to another over a fixed period of time. See forward kinematics.

iterative See loop.

jiffy The shortest time interval between two frames during playback of an animation sequence. Conversely, frames per second refers to the number of frames displayed per second during playback. See fps.

join See Euler operators.

kernel.exe The Windows dynamic link library that provides system resources such as memory management and resource management to Windows applications at runtime. See user.exe and gdi.exe.

key color A color that will appear transparent when the image is overlaid on another image or background. Called chroma-key by the broadcast television industry.

keyframe A significant frame in an animation script, tweening session, or morphing sequence. Typically, the developer or the user provides a set of keyframes and the software provides the in-between images (tweens).

kinematics The study of motion as it relates to the positions and velocities of objects in animation sequences.

kinematic animation Computer animation that is managed by algorithms conforming more or less to the laws of physics. See procedural animation. See kinematics.

lamina A 3D plane of null thickness that can be viewed from either side.

language binding A module that calls compiler-dependent routines in a graphics library or runtime library.

lens distortion error field A bitmap schematic that indicates the areas of lens distortion in images grabbed from a live video camera attached to a computer.

lerping Linear interpolation.

library A file containing modules of object code representing functions available for use by the developer's C or C++ program.

line clipping Deletion of a line segment that exceeds the physical range of the viewport.

line styling Dotted or dashed lines.

linear interpolation An algorithm for generating in-between images from keyframes whereby the movement of a vertex is assumed to follow a straight line. Also called lerping. See spline interpolation.

lip sync Synchronization of a cartoon character's mouth movements to a sound track. See bar sheet.

local variable Same as static variable. See also global variable.

logical operators And and Or, which perform logical operations on bytes being compared. The && token is used to AND two bytes (the resulting bit will be on only if both the bits being evaluated were on). The || token is used to OR two bytes (the resulting bit will be on if either of the bits being evaluated were on).

logical palette A table of colors defined by a Windows application for its own use. Where possible the colors in a logical palette are mapped by Windows to matching hues in the system palette (hardware palette). If no match is possible, Windows uses dithering to simulate the color requested by the logical palette. See system palette.

lookup table The logical table used by the graphics adapter to match color index numbers (used by the application software) to RGB gun settings (used by the display monitor). Windows sets the values of the lookup table at startup.

loop A repeating set of frames that comprises an animation cycle, as in a run cycle. In traditional film animation, lengths of film were spliced end to end to form repeating loops. See idle loop.

LUT Lookup table.

mach band An optical illusion whereby the human eye emphasizes the subtle differences between two adjacent shaded areas.

matte A bitblt mask that is used in conjunction with GDI raster operations to permit an irregularly shaped, multicolor bitblt image to be cleanly placed onto a multicolored background. Also called a key matte. In traditional filmmaking a matte is a black mask that prevents a designated part of each frame from being exposed, thereby permitting other images to be added later. See travelling matte.

MDK Multimedia development kit.

message loop The block of statements in a Windows application that retrieves input messages from the application queue maintained by the Windows operating system.

metafile The GDI statements and the data necessary to reconstruct an image. A Windows metafile can exist in RAM, can be stored on disk for later use, and can be passed to the clipboard for use by other Windows applications.

model photography See stop-motion photography.

model sheet A set of reference design drawings showing a cartoon character in typical poses.

modeling Creating a geometric shape representing a 3D object.

module The block of C or C++ code contained in a separate source file. Can also mean a cohesive block of code that performs a specific function.

morgue A collection of reference photographs and drawings used by artists, animators, designers, and writers.

morphing A gradual transformation of a graphics object to a different object. Derived from the term metamorphosis.

motion-control model photography See stop-motion photography.

motion blur In traditional film photography, image fuzziness caused by the subject moving faster than the frame rate of the camera. Animation software often employs intentional image blurring (temporal anti-aliasing) to overcome temporal aliasing. See temporal aliasing.

motion dynamics Changes in location, orientation, and juxtaposition of objects during an animation sequence. See update dynamics and viewing dynamics.

motion test a prototype animation sequence used to test timing, pacing, and movement before producing the final images. Traditional film animators used an animation pencil-test for the same purpose.

MPC Acronym for multimedia personal computer.

multimedia A collection of hardware and software methods for combining graphics, full-motion video, audio, titling, and other components from diverse sources into a computer-controlled presentation. See digital video interactive.

multimedia personal computer A PC with multimedia-capable hardware components.

neighborhood The grouping of picture elements (pixels) that surrounds the subject picture element being analyzed. Neighborhoods are considered by image-processing software functions when manipulating an image or when detecting edges. See spatial filter.

nested loop A program loop contained within another loop.

normalized coordinates Coordinates that have been scaled to the range −1 to +(1) Normalized coordinates are considered device-independent. Also see canonical view-volume.

normalized view-volume Canonical view-volume.

NTSC A video signal that adheres to the accepted technical standards of the broadcast industry in the United States, Canada, Mexico, Central America, and Japan. NTSC is defined as 525 lines refreshed 30 frames per second. The PAL standard, used in Europe, Australia, and New Zealand, is 625 lines at 25 fps. See VTR.

nybble Half a byte, or four bits.

object A cohesive 2D or 3D graphical entity.

object-precision algorithms Refers to 3D hidden-surface and illumination routines that perform their calculations on the 3D coordinates rather than on pixels. Also called object-space methods. Also see image-precision algorithms.

object-space methods Object-precision algorithms.

objectification Representing a phenomenon as form, color, texture, motion, and time. See visualization.

onion skin A feature provided by animation software, whereby the previous three or four cels can be superimposed over the current cel. See cel animation.

operand A constant or a variable operated on by operators in an expression.

optimize To improve a program's execution speed or to reduce its memory requirements at runtime.

overlay A module of data or executable code that is loaded from disk at runtime over an existing block of code or data.

painter's algorithm A method of 3D hidden object removal. See Z-buffer method.

PAL See NTSC.

pan To move an image left or right. See scroll.

parameter A value that a function expects to receive when called. Also called an argument, but many technical writers and developers make a distinction between the two.

parent A subobject in a 3D hierarchical modeling environment that serves as a reference point for other subobjects (progeny) whose position and orientation are expressed relative to the parent. Also see progeny.

passive VR A virtual reality environment that allows the user to observe but not interactive. See also exploratory VR and interactive VR.

paste To retrieve a handle from the Windows clipboard.

pencil-test See motion test.

persistent image Refers to graphics displayed in the client area of a window that are preserved when the window is moved, clipped or unclipped by the edge of the screen, covered or uncovered by another application's window, or resized.

physically based animation An animation sequence managed according to laws of physics. See forward kinematics, inverse kinematics, forward dynamics, and inverse dynamics.

pixel Picture element. A pixel is the smallest addressable graphic on a display screen. In RGB systems, a pixel is a triad comprised of a red dot, a green dot, and a blue dot.

pixilation Animation created by single-frame exposures of inanimate models. Claymation is a form of pixilation. See stop-motion photography. See claymation.

plane equation A vector formula that describes the qualities of a plane, including the location of a given point relative to the surface of the plane. Plane equations are useful for hidden surface removal.

plane equation test Testing to determine if a given point is located on the inside or outside of a given facet in a 3D scene.

platform-independent Refers to applications able to execute on a diverse range of hardware configurations.

point process An image-processing function that modifies an individual pixel or a single picture element as a result of considering the value or location of the pixel. Neighboring pixels are not considered. See area process. See neighborhood.

polygon Usually intended to mean a plane surface used to create a 3D solid model constructed by the B-rep method. Also used to describe a multi-sided, closed geometric shape.

POV Point of view, also called viewpoint.

primitive A fundamental 3D solid such as a sphere, cylinder, cone, parallelepiped, wedge, and others. Also called a subobject.

primitives modeler An interactive, 3D application that can be used to design and construct 3D primitives (subobjects) and simple assemblies. See also hierarchical modeler.

procedural animation Object-oriented animation. See cast-based animation.

progeny A subobject in a 3D hierarchical modeling environment whose position and orientation are expressed relative to another subobject (parent). Also see parent.

prototype (1) The initial declaration of a function in a C or C++ program, usually containing the return type and argument list of the function. (2) A tentative mock-up of a program for project-planning purposes.

pruning A 3D modeling paradigm that discards an entity if it falls wholly outside the view-volume.

quadric primitive A 3D subobject.

RAD Rapid applications development, a method of efficient software development that stresses preliminary prototypes, client feedback, and clearly defined goals.

radian A length of arc based upon the relationship between elements of a unit circle (whose radius equals one unit).

radiosity An algorithm that considers the overall energy levels from different light sources in a 3D scene.

radix The base of a numbering system. The radix of the hexadecimal numbering system is 16, of the decimal system is 10.

ramp See gradient.

rapid applications development See RAD.

raster operations Boolean operators that affect bitmap operations performed by GDI functions. Some common raster operations are XOR, AND, OR, and overwrite.

ray tracing An algorithm that calculates the illumination level of a model by tracing a ray of light back from the viewer's eye to the model and eventually to the light source.

real-time animation (1) An animation sequence that is being created and displayed at runtime; (2) An animation sequence intended to correspond to or react to events occurring in the real world at runtime.

reflection mapping Mathematically projecting onto the surface of a 3D model a previously defined bitmap containing a visual reflection of other objects in the scene. The reflection bitmap is acquired by temporarily placing the viewpoint on the surface of the mirrored object.

refresh animation Computer animation that detects corrupted portions of a hidden frame and refreshes only those corresponding rectangles on the display image. Also called dirty rectangle animation and ensemble animation.

refresh buffer The display buffer. The display hardware uses the display buffer to refresh the display monitor.

regen Regeneration of a graphic entity or image. The instructions necessary to implement regen are sometimes stored in a metafile.

registration points The user-specified coordinates in keyframes that will be used to create tweens. See tweening.

rendering Adding illumination, shading, and color to a 3D scene.

reveal See wipe.

RGB model The color model used by most personal computer graphics adapters and monitors.

rotation Adjusting the yaw, roll, or pitch attitude of an object in a 3D scene. See translation. See Extrusion.

rotoscoping Deriving realistic images for use in animated sequences by tracing the shapes found in live-action films.

rubberbanding The rapid erasing and redrawing of guidelines that represent the shape and position of a graphical entity to be drawn by the software if the user's current selection were used.

run-cycle A loop of frames that can be repeated in order to produce a running actor in an animated sequence. Static run cycles are usually overlayed on a panning background. Dynamic run cycles often use bitblts to move the actor across a static background.

runtime The time when the application is executing.

scalar A mathematical quantity that has quantity but not direction. A vector has quantity and direction.

scanner A peripheral device capable of grabbing a continuous tone hardcopy image and storing it in computer memory as a digitized image.

scientific visualization The graphical representation of formulas or phenomena for the purpose of scientific research.

scripted animation The computer-assisted equivalent of traditional cel animation.

scroll To move an image upwards or downwards. See pan.

section A cross-section, cutaway view of a 3D object.

sensor Program code or virtual trigger-spot that manages how an entity responds to the user or to other entities in a virtual reality environment.

sfx Sound effects.

shading Adding the effects of illumination, shadow, and color to a 3D model. Sometimes called rendering.

shadow map A two-dimensional image of a 3D scene from the viewpoint of the light-source. Entities which are not visible to the light-source will be cloaked in shadow in the frame buffer (viewport display).

simulation An imitation of a real-world event.

simulation manager The software engine that manages a virtual reality session.

simulator A program that imitates a real-world event.

sine The sine of an angle in a right-angle triangle defines the relationship between the hypotenuse and the side opposite.

single-step To advance to and pause at the next frame of an animation sequence after receiving explicit input (usually a keystroke) from the user. See freeze frame.

6D Six-dimensional. Usually refers to virtual reality input devices offering six degrees-of-freedom (x,y,z translation and yaw, roll, pitch rotation).

slow-in/slow-out The avoidance of unnatural instant-start and instant-stop events in computer animation sequences.

solid model A 3D model with hidden surfaces removed. It can be constructed by the constructive solid geometry method (CSG) or the boundary representation method (B-rep).

spatial filter A matrix calculation used by image-processing routines to manipulate images. See neighborhood.

specular reflection A highlight on the surface of a 3D model.

spline interpolation An algorithm for generating in-between images from keyframes whereby the movement of a vertex is assumed to follow a fitted curve or freeform curve. See linear interpolation.

squashing-and-stretching Deformation of an object or actor as a result of movement, acceleration, deceleration, collision, or other events.

staging Choreographing or directing an animation sequence or an individual frame.

staging editor An interactive, 3D application that can be used to specify the movement and positioning of entities (actors) in an animation sequence. See also articulated motion editor.

stamp A field of data in the header of a Windows application file. The resource compiler stamps each application with the Windows version for which the executable file is intended. Windows will not launch any application that does not contain the appropriate stamp.

standard mode Windows runtime memory mode requiring an 80286, 80386, 80486 or higher processor with less than 2MB RAM, running in protected mode.

stand-in A bounding-box.

stereo vision Computer vision implemented with two video cameras.

stereolithography A process that uses 3D software to drive lasers that sculpt prototype solids from plastic, acrylic, wood, or light metal. Used for industrial prototyping.

stock font A font that is built into the retail versions of Windows. Stock fonts are guaranteed to be available for use by an application at runtime. See font.

stop-motion photography A method for production animation whereby inanimate models are photographed a few frames at a time and manually moved between each exposure. Also called model animation and motion-control model animation. See claymation. See pixellation.

structure A set of items grouped under a single name. The elements might be of different types. In an array, the elements must be of similar type.

stub See do-nothing routine.

subobject A fundamental 3D solid such as a sphere, cylinder, cone, parallelepiped, wedge, and others. Also called a primitive.

subtraction See Euler operators.

supersampling Creating an image at a resolution that is greater than the actual screen resolution. When the image is scaled down to fit into the display buffer, many digital artifacts like jagged lines are suppressed as a convenient by-product of the scaling mathematics.

Super VGA Graphics adapters that extend the capabilities of the standard VGA.

surface normal A line that is perpendicular to the surface of a plane in a 3D environment. The illumination level of a surface can be derived by comparing the surface normal to the angle of incidence of incoming light rays.

swish pan A rapid pan. Also called a zip pan.

system palette The current hardware palette, composed of a lookup table (LUT) that correlates a specified color index (usually an integer) with a particular triad of voltage settings for the RGB guns of the display monitor. A VGA running Windows can provide a system palette of 16 distinct and simultaneously displayable hues. A Super VGA, 8514/A, or XGA running Windows can provide a system palette of 256 hues. See logical palette.

3D Three dimensional. Refers to computer images representing objects possessing the three dimensions of width, height, and depth. See 4D.

target platform The group of personal computers and operating system configuration versions for which a software product is developed.

temporal aliasing Refers to an awkward jumping effect present in computer-animated sequences when the frame rate is too slow to smoothly simulate actors moving at speed across the image. See motion blur. See anti-aliasing.

timer A logical timing device maintained by Windows in order to send a WM_TIMER message to the application at an interval defined by the application. See the entry for animate on twos.

timer-based animation An animation sequence driven by WM_TIMER timer messages from the Windows API.

titling Adding titles, production credits, and labels to an animated sequence or multimedia presentation.

toon An actor (cartoon character) in a computer-animated cartoon sequence.

touring See walkthrough.

traceback The portion of an animation frame that is unchanged from the previous frame.

translation Repositioning of an object in a 3D scene. See rotation. See extrusion.

transparent put The graphics effect of cleanly placing a random-shaped, multicolored bitblt image over a multicolored background scene. See frisket.

travelling matte A matte whose shape changes as it accompanies a moving image. See matte.

trigonometry Mathematics concerned with the relationship of two sides opposite a specific angle in a right-angle triangle. Sine and cosine are particularly useful for 3D computer graphics.

tween An in-between image that software has interpolated from keyframes provided by the user or developer. See keyframe.

tweening Generating tweens.

UMB Upper memory blocks.

universe The collection of entities, scripts, and rules that comprise a particular virtual reality environment or session.

update dynamics Changes in shape, color, and texture during an animation sequence. See motion dynamics and viewing dynamics.

user.exe The Windows dynamic link library that provides window management functions for Windows applications at runtime. See kernel.exe and gdi.exe.

vector A mathematical value that has quantity and direction. A scalar value has only quantity.

VGA Video graphics array. Windows runs in the 640 × 480 × 16-color mode on VGA adapters.

videodisc A large-format plastic disc used to store digital or analog information. Read by laser beam. Often used to store and play full-motion video and audio. Similar in concept to CD-ROM.

view coordinates See camera coordinates.

viewing dynamics Changes in lighting, camera, and viewpoint during an animation sequence. See motion dynamics and update dynamics.

viewport A subset of the display screen.

view-volume The volume of space visible to the camera in a 3D modeling environment, generally taken to be a frustum (a decapitated pyramid). Also see canonical view-volume.

virtual reality Generally, a field of computer science concerned with real-time, interactive, 3D simulations that mimic the real world or fictional worlds by providing a virtual environment with which a user can interact. Specifically, the particular environment being modeled and simulated. Virtual reality sessions can be passive, exploratory, or interactive. See cyberspace.

visibility Describes whether or not a function or a variable can be used by other parts of a C or C++ program.

visual algorithm The graphical representation of a computer function or algorithm.

visualization Using graphics to interpret, manipulate, or create data. Specialized fields of computer visualization include scientific visualization, 3D modeling and rendering, computer animation, biomedicine, fluid dynamics, tomography, computer vision, image processing, and others. See objectification.

visualization graphics The graphics used for computer visualization. See visualization.

volume visualization Using 3D objects to represent data. See scientific visualization.

VR Acronym for virtual reality.

VR rules The specific rules and protocol that govern a particular virtual reality environment or session.

vtr Videotape recorder or videotape recording. See NTSC.

waldo A facial input device used in virtual reality applications.

walk-through Animation of a 3D architectural model, intended to simulate a walk-through by the viewer. Also called touring.

weighted sum An image-processing operation whereby the sum of values of a pixel and its neighbors are calculated in compliance with a spatial filter.

white box A block of code currently under development and whose algorithms and processes are being adjusting during testing. See black box.

white-box testing Program testing that requires access to the inner workings of a block of code. See black-box testing.

window (1) The display space used by a Windows application. (2) A viewport on the display screen. (3) The logical relationship between the display screen and the world coordinates in 3D graphics programming.

wipe Revealing the next image by selectively manipulating the image buffer. Similar in concept to opening a set of venetian blinds to reveal a scene or opening a sliding door to reveal a room. Also called a reveal.

wire-frame A 3D object modeled with edges, with no hidden surfaces removed.

world coordinates The XYZ coordinates that describe the position and orientation of an object in a 3D environment.

XGA Extended graphics adapter. As defined by IBM, an XGA adapter provides a $640 \times 480 \times 256$-color mode, $1024 \times 768 \times 256$-color mode, a $640 \times 480 \times 65,536$-color mode, and all VGA modes.

XMS Extended memory specification. XMS memory is physical memory located above 1MB which can be accessed by an 80286, 80386, 80486, or newer microprocessor. See EMS.

YIQ model The color model used by commercial television components.

z-buffer A buffer containing the depth values for each pixel in a 3D scene, allowing the software to draw only the nearest entity at any particular location. The corresponding color values for each pixel are stored in a frame buffer. Also see frame buffer.

z-buffer method A method of hidden surface removal whereby depth-values for each non-obstructed pixel are stored in a Z-buffer and the corresponding color values for each visible pixel are stored in a frame buffer. Also called the painter's algorithm. Also see Z-buffer.

zip pan See swish pan.

zoom To move the camera closer to or farther away from the objects in a 3D scene.

zoom axis The 3D axis that represents the near/far context in a 3D scene. The zoom axis is perpendicular to the image plane. The 3D routines in the demonstration programs in this book use the z axis to represent near/far.

Index

Order Form for Readers
Requiring a Single 3.5" Disk

This Windcrest/McGraw-Hill software product is also available on a 3.5"/720K disk. If you need the software in 3.5" format, simply follow these instructions:

- Complete the order form below. Be sure to include the exact title of the Windcrest/McGraw-Hill book for which you are requesting a replacement disk.

- Make check or money order made payable to *Glossbrenner's Choice*. The cost is **$5.00** (**$8.00** for shipments outside the U.S.) to cover media, postage, and handling. Pennsylvania residents, please add 6% sales tax.

- Foreign orders: please send an international money order or a check drawn on a bank with a U.S. clearing branch. We cannot accept foreign checks.

- Mail order form and payment to:

  Glossbrenner's Choice
  Attn: Windcrest/McGraw-Hill Disk Replacement
  699 River Road
  Yardley, PA 19067-1965

Your disks will be shipped via First Class Mail. Please allow one to two weeks for delivery.

✂ ···

Windcrest/McGraw-Hill
Disk Replacement

Please send me a replacement disk in 3.5"/720K format for the following Windcrest/McGraw-Hill book:

Book Title _____

Name _____

Address _____

City/State/ZIP _____

DISK WARRANTY

This software is protected by both United States copyright law and international copyright treaty provision. You must treat this software just like a book, except that you may copy it into a computer in order to be used and you may make archival copies of the software for the sole purpose of backing up our software and protecting your investment from loss.

By saying "just like a book," McGraw-Hill means, for example, that this software may be used by any number of people and may be freely moved from one computer location to another, so long as there is no possibility of its being used at one location or on one computer while it also is being used at another. Just as a book cannot be read by two different people in two different places at the same time, neither can the software be used by two different people in two different places at the same time (unless, of course, McGraw-Hill's copyright is being violated).

LIMITED WARRANTY

Windcrest/McGraw-Hill takes great care to provide you with top-quality software, thoroughly checked to prevent virus infections. McGraw-Hill warrants the physical diskette(s) contained herein to be free of defects in materials and workmanship for a period of sixty days from the purchase date. If McGraw-Hill receives written notification within the warranty period of defects in materials or workmanship, and such notification is determined by McGraw-Hill to be correct, McGraw-Hill will replace the defective diskette(s). Send requests to:

Customer Service
Windcrest/McGraw-Hill
13311 Monterey Lane
Blue Ridge Summit, PA 17294-0850

The entire and exclusive liability and remedy for breach of this Limited Warranty shall be limited to replacement of defective diskette(s) and shall not include or extend to any claim for or right to cover any other damages, including but not limited to, loss of profit, data, or use of the software, or special, incidental, or consequential damages or other similar claims, even if McGraw-Hill has been specifically advised of the possibility of such damages. In no event will McGraw-Hill's liability for any damages to you or any other person ever exceed the lower of suggested list price or actual price paid for the license to use the software, regardless of any form of the claim.

McGRAW-HILL, INC. SPECIFICALLY DISCLAIMS ALL OTHER WARRANTIES, EXPRESS OR IMPLIED, INCLUDING, BUT NOT LIMITED TO, ANY IMPLIED WARRANTY OF MERCHANTABILITY OR FITNESS FOR A PARTICULAR PURPOSE.

Specifically, McGraw-Hill makes no representation or warranty that the software is fit for any particular purpose and any implied warranty of merchantability is limited to the sixty-day duration of the Limited Warranty covering the physical diskette(s) only (and not the software) and is otherwise expressly and specifically disclaimed.

This limited warranty gives you specific legal rights; you may have others which may vary from state to state. Some states do not allow the exclusion of incidental or consequential damages, or the limitation on how long an implied warranty lasts, so some of the above may not apply to you.

If you need help
with the enclosed disk . . .

The enclosed 3½-inch diskette contains one self-extracting file named 4225DISK.EXE. Make a subdirectory on your hard drive to copy the file to:

C:\> MD *directory_name*

where *directory_name* is the name of the directory that you want to create. Next, make this new directory the current directory:

C:\> CD *directory_name*

where *directory_name* is the name of the directory that you just created. Then, copy the self-extracting file to this directory:

C:\> COPY *d*:4225DISK.EXE

where *d* is the letter of the floppy drive containing the companion diskette.

   To uncompress the files in 4225DISK.EXE, simply type the name at the DOS prompt:

C:\> 4225DISK

The file will expand to the 69 program files contained in the self-extracting file.